C0-ARR-927

The Theology of Langdon B. Gilkey
Systematic and Critical Studies

Langdon Brown Gilkey

[L]et us recall that every proposal from any of us is fragmentary, tentative, and vulnerable. Another can see these holes in our defenses more clearly than can we, and we can only be encouraged to strengthen the entire edifice if some critical but interested eye has surveyed our efforts with candor.

—Langdon Gilkey, "A Theology in Process: Schubert Ogden's Developing Theology," *Interpretation* 21 (October 1967): 458-59.

THE THEOLOGY OF LANGDON B. GILKEY
SYSTEMATIC AND CRITICAL STUDIES

edited by

Kyle A. Pasewark

and

Jeff B. Pool

MERCER UNIVERSITY PRESS
1979 · 1999
Twenty Years of Publishing Excellence

ISBN 0-86554-643-6
ISBN 0-86554-644-4

MUP/H479
MUP/P191

The Theology of Langdon B. Gilkey
Systematic and Critical Studies
Copyright ©1999
Mercer University Press, Macon, Georgia 31210-3960 USA
Printed in the United States of America

The paper used in this publication meets the minimum requirements
of American National Standard for Information Sciences—
Permanence of Paper for Printed Library Materials,
ANSI Z39.48-1984. ∞

Library of Congress Cataloging-in-Publication Data

The theology of Langdon B. Gilkey : systematic and critical studies
/ edited by Kyle A. Pasewark and Jeff B. Pool.
    p. cm.
    Includes bibliographical references (p. 525).
    ISBN 0-86554-643-6 (casebound : alk. paper) —
    ISBN 0-86554-644-4 (perfectbd. : alk. paper).
        1. Gilkey, Langdon Brown, 1919– .
    I. Pasewark, Kyle A., 1959– . II. Pool, Jeff B., 1951– .
BX4827.G55 T44 1999
230'.044'092—dc21   99-048594

Contents

Abbreviations

CCM   *Catholicism Confronts Modernity: A Protestant View.* New York: Seabury Press, A Crossroad Book, 1975.

CT   *Creationism on Trial: Evolution and God at Little Rock.* San Francisco: Harper & Row Publishers, 1985.

GOT   *Gilkey on Tillich.* New York: Crossroad Publishing Company, 1990.

HCCM   *How the Church Can Minister to the World without Losing Itself.* New York: Harper & Row Publishers, 1964.

ME   *Message and Existence: An Introduction to Christian Theology.* New York: Seabury Press, 1979.

MHE   *Maker of Heaven and Earth: The Christian Doctrine of Creation in the Light of Modern Knowledge.* Garden City, New York: Doubleday and Company, Inc., 1959; reprint, Lanham, Maryland: University Press of America, 1985.

NRS   *Nature, Reality, and the Sacred: The Nexus of Science and Religion.* Theology and the Sciences Series. Edited by Kevin J. Sharpe. Minneapolis: Fortress Press, 1993.

NW   *Naming the Whirlwind: The Renewal of God-Language.* Indianapolis and New York: The Bobbs-Merrill Company, 1969.

RSF   *Religion and the Scientific Future: Reflections on Myth, Science, and Theology.* New York: Harper & Row Publishers, 1970; London: SCM Press, 1970; reprint: ROSE–Reprints of Scholarly Excellence. Macon, Georgia: Mercer University Press, 1981.

RW   *Reaping the Whirlwind: A Christian Interpretation of History.* New York: Seabury Press, 1976.

SAS   *Society and the Sacred: Toward a Theology of Culture in Decline.* New York: Crossroad Publishing Company, 1981.

SC   *Shantung Compound: The Story of Men and Women under Pressure.* New York: Harper & Row Publishers, 1966.

TT   *Through the Tempest: Theological Voyages in a Pluralistic Culture.* Edited by Jeff B. Pool. Minneapolis: Fortress Press, 1991.

With admiration, respect, and affection, to

LANGDON BROWN GILKEY
9 February 1919 —

theologian, scholar, teacher, and friend.

Preface

Langdon Gilkey taught theology at the University of Chicago Divinity School for twenty-five years, from 1963 until his retirement from the Divinity School in 1989, at age seventy. For forty-five years, Gilkey has helped to track and shape the direction of contemporary theology in North America and throughout the world. Gilkey has influenced contemporary theological scholarship due to the tremendous scope of his thought, with a lens wide enough to encompass the seascape of both classic theological themes and the newest theological, philosophical, scientific, cultural, and historical movements. On the basis of his critical retrievals of classic Christian symbols and his equally critical assessments of the shifting contemporary cultural situation, Gilkey has developed a theological perspective that respects the plurality of both contemporary culture and religious tradition, without becoming enslaved to either one.

I. Purpose

We conceived this project several years ago. As former students of Langdon Gilkey during his final years as a professor at the University of Chicago Divinity School, we have long appreciated his scholarship and teaching. Consequently, we conceived this book as a critical exposition and appraisal of Langdon Gilkey's theology. This book is not a *Festschrift*. A *Festschrift* neither necessarily nor always examines the thought of the honored scholar's own work. This book does celebrate the life and work of Langdon Gilkey, but specifically in the context of examining the major contours of Gilkey's own theological labors. Those of us who were his students can give no higher compliment to him: Langdon Gilkey taught us to examine the thought of our forbears (including his own thought) carefully and critically, rather than simply repeating their formulations, proposals, or answers. Indeed, in his review of a book by Schubert Ogden, Gilkey has expressed this sentiment: "[i]t is through making our *own* reasonable sense in the face of *our* problems today that we honor our teachers and argue for them—not by trying to move our readers into the corral of their school."[1]

We have produced this book for two other reasons as well. First, with this book, we wanted to examine systematically and critically the thought of one major North American Christian theologian in the latter half of the twentieth century. From that perspective, this book qualifies as *historical* theology, a contribution to the assessment of a particular period—albeit one still in process—in the history of Christian thought. Second, through the studies in this book, we aimed for the contributors to engage in *constructive* theology, by interpreting and employing Gilkey's thought as a resource with which to address their own theological proposals.

Thus, we hope readers, both those already acquainted with Gilkey's work and those newly introduced to Gilkey's thought, will experience excitement as they grapple with the theology of this subtle and bold theologian through the studies that follow. Furthermore, through the book's expositions and evaluations of Langdon Gilkey's theology, we also hope the book will become a resource through which readers can engage as critically and creatively as possible the issues, problems, and tasks for theology as the next millennium begins. Rather than attempting to make disciples for Gilkey, with these studies we hope to help other students of theology to live with the theological passion, freedom, conviction, openness, sensitivity, and discernment that we have witnessed in Langdon Gilkey.

This volume of studies examines and appraises the contours of Gilkey's thought as well as some of its principal alterations across the span of his career, from his first major work to his most recent. We initiate this critical examination of Gilkey's thought with a view toward vitalizing theology for the present and the future.[2] In this light, we

---

[1]Langdon Gilkey, "A Theology in Process: Schubert Ogden's Developing Theology," review of *The Reality of God and Other Essays*, by Schubert Ogden, in *Interpretation* 21 (October 1967): 458.

[2]With some apparent differences, our objectives with this book resemble those envisioned by Paul A. Schilpp for the Library of Living Philosophers, and later imitated by Charles W. Kegley and Robert W. Bretall in the Library of Living Theology: see Paul Arthur Schilpp, "General Introduction to 'The Library of Living Philosophers,' " in *The Philosophy of John Dewey*, 2nd ed., Library of Living Philosophers series, ed. Paul Arthur Schilpp (New York: Tudor Publishing Company, 1951) ix; cf. *The Theology of Paul Tillich*, Library of Living Theology series, ed. Charles W. Kegley (New York: Macmillan and Company, 1952; 2nd rev. ed.: New York: Pilgrim Press, 1982); *Reinhold Niebuhr: His Religious, Social, and Political Thought*, Library of Living Theology series, ed.

mention several important features of the book.

First, this volume of studies systematically examines the principal or central loci of Gilkey's thought, rather than collecting a variety of essays that may hit or miss the central elements of Gilkey's thought. Second, these analyses and appraisals aim more pointedly toward an elaboration of the resources in Gilkey's thought for addressing issues in contemporary cultural and theological contexts. Third, we have included the most comprehensive bibliography available to date, in order to indicate the extent and quality of his theological labors as well as the recent history of the effects of his work.

II. Contributors

We have chosen most of the contributors to this volume of studies from two sometimes overlapping categories of scholars: Gilkey's former Ph.D. students and those scholars who have already produced studies of Gilkey's thought. We also chose both senior scholars and those representing a new generation of theologians. Although we allowed considerable latitude to the contributors in developing their interpretations of Gilkey's thought, all of them included in their studies at least the following components: (1) *exposition* of the topic under consideration in Gilkey's theology, as developed across the course of his theological career; (2) critical *evaluation* of this particular feature or component of Gilkey's thought; and (3) some *comparison* of Gilkey's position on the topic of focus with theological and/or cultural alternatives of the past and present.

Each scholar considers one area in Gilkey's thought. Although this book does not survey every field that Gilkey has tilled, these studies together constitute the most comprehensive treatment of his thought available to date. Moreover, the book generates a plurality of interpretations, some conflicting, providing resources for readers to reflect, consider, and return to Gilkey's work.

III. Structure of the Book

The structure of the book itself exhibits an outline of Gilkey's thought and method. We have divided the volume into four parts.

Part 1, "Situating Gilkey's Thought," locates Gilkey's work historically and prospectively. In chapter 1, "Making Sense of Ultimacy:

Charles W. Kegley and Robert W. Bretall (New York: Macmillan and Company, 1956).

Truths of Experience in Langdon Gilkey's Theological Development," Gary J. Dorrien introduces theological themes in Gilkey's work by situating them in the context of Gilkey's life. Whereas Dorrien focuses on the experiential sources of Gilkey's theology, Kyle A. Pasewark, in chapter 2, "Debts and Contributions: The Milieu of Langdon Gilkey's Theology," examines the major theological influences on the development of Gilkey's thought and Gilkey's contributions to theology on those bases. Through the lens of Gilkey's concept of the polarity of destiny and freedom, Pasewark examines Gilkey's theological heritage and his transformation of it. In chapter 3, "Beyond Postliberal Foundationalism: The Theological Method of Langdon Gilkey," Jeff B. Pool both traces the development of Gilkey's theological method, taking bearings from Gilkey's evolving posture toward natural theology as a marker to indicate Gilkey's specific modifications in his theological method, and analyzes Gilkey's theological method by comparing his theory of theological method with his use of it. Concluding part 1 with chapter 3 introduces the next two parts of the book, supplying the rationale for distinguishing the studies in part 2, "Gilkey's Interpretations of Culture," from those in part 3, "Gilkey's Interpretations of Christian Symbols."

Part 2 begins with chapter 4, "Becoming Langdon Gilkey: The Theological Significance of *Shantung Compound*," by Joseph Bessler-Northcutt. Bessler-Northcutt extends the methodological considerations of chapter 3, by analyzing the literary character and rhetorical strategies of Gilkey's *Shantung Compound*. He argues that *Shantung Compound* represents an early example of narrative theology and a key to understanding Gilkey as an empirical theologian. In this way, Bessler-Northcutt explores a neglected and virtually uncharted area in studies of Gilkey's theology. Four more studies focus on central features in Gilkey's interpretation of the religious dimensions of culture. In chapter 5, "History, Society, and Politics: Langdon Gilkey's Theology of Culture," Brian J. Walsh examines Gilkey's broad interpretation of late twentieth-century public life, discussing Gilkey's dialectical critique of the political and social regions of experience, particularly in light of their religious dimensions. Donald W. Musser, in chapter 6, "Sovereigns Past and Present: The Sciences and the Religious in the Theology of Langdon Gilkey," analyzes Gilkey's understanding of science, its practice, cultural functions, and religious meanings. Musser engages the categories and analyses of Process philosophies and theologies. In chapter 7, "Relative Absoluteness: Langdon Gilkey's Approach to Religious Pluralism," Mary Ann Stenger applies themes from the chapters by Pool and Walsh to the pressing issue of religious pluralism inside and outside the academy. Stenger concentrates on Gilkey's conversation with Buddhist thought, noting the mutual transformation of Buddhist and Christian conceptions encouraged by Gilkey's dialogue with Buddhism. Stenger also reiterates the significance of interpreting both religions and the religious dimension of experience in order effectively to understand cultural pluralism, further refining understanding of Gilkey's method. Charles Winquist concludes part 2 with chapter 8, "Theology, Symbolism, and Language in the Thought of Langdon Gilkey." Winquist examines a more specific feature of Gilkey's method, concentrating on the character of symbols and their religious investment. Therefore, Winquist's interpretation of Gilkey mediates the translation and confluence between cultural and religious symbolism; this mediation links part 2 with part 3, "Gilkey's Interpretations of Christian Symbols."

Part 3 examines Gilkey's interpretations of five central Christian symbols: (1) God; (2) divine providence; (3) sin, evil, and tragedy; (4) Christ and salvation; and (5) the church. The writers of chapters 9 through 13 focus upon Gilkey's interpretation of religious symbols, correlating with themes addressed especially by the chapters of part 2. In chapter 9, "Navigating in the Whirlwind: Langdon Gilkey's Doctrine of God," Eric H. Crump connects his considerations with the dialectic between polarity and freedom in chapter 2 and the place of natural theology in Gilkey's thought in chapter 3. He also discusses Gilkey's understanding of God in terms of traditional Christian trinitarian issues. Crump's chapter introduces themes and issues that Kyle A. Pasewark explores in chapter 10, "Power, Freedom, and History: The Symbol of Divine Providence in Langdon Gilkey's Theology." Pasewark concentrates on Gilkey's understanding of freedom, the political implications of Gilkey's use of providence, and the theology of history resulting from these. Pasewark argues that Gilkey's admirable focus on providence is, nonetheless, distinctly modern; in contrast, Pasewark advocates a postmodern, pluralistic theology of providence and history. Larry D. Bouchard, in chapter 11, "Contingency, Tragedy, Sin, and Ultimacy: Trajectories in Langdon Gilkey's Interpretations of History and Nature," provides the anthropological fulcrum of the volume, emphasizing Gilkey's theology of human being, which the other studies of the book all assume. Gilkey's concept of the human condition implies a corresponding notion of salvation, the subject of chapter 12, by James O. Yerkes, " 'A Sharp

Turn': Christology in a 'Time of Troubles.' " Yerkes analyzes Gilkey's interpretation of the significance of Jesus as the Christ for Christian life and theology. Yerkes locates this set of themes with special focus on its relation to religious pluralism. H. Frederick Reisz, Jr. completes part 3 with chapter 13, "Langdon Gilkey's Theology of the Servant Church." In this chapter, Reisz examines Gilkey's theology in terms of the religious community that gave birth to it, and to which his theology repeatedly returns. This concluding chapter of part 3 rejoins the discussions, this time from an ecclesiological perspective, of theological method and Christology. The practical considerations in Reisz's contribution, with his emphasis on the ecclesial character of Gilkey's theology, supplies a bridge to part 4, which emphasizes the practice of theology.

Part 4, "Gilkey's Practice of Theology," contains two chapters. In chapter 14, "From Liberalism to Postmodernism: The Role of Integrity in the Thought of Langdon Gilkey," Jennifer L. Rike hypothesizes that "integrity" is the key criterion of Gilkey's theology. Rike rejoins the themes related to the influence of Gilkey's experience on his theology (as discussed in various ways in chapters 1, 3, and 4, and specifically as narrated in his intellectual autobiography in chapter 16). Rike offers an invitation for a more personal consideration of Gilkey as a teacher, which Joseph L. Price accepts in chapter 15, "Pedagogy and Theological Method: The Praxis of Langdon Gilkey." Price reflects on Gilkey's character as a teacher and the ways in which his theological method influenced his style of teaching. The expositions of Gilkey's thought by Rike and Price focus on a special dimension of practical theology, one of interest for current controversies about theological education specifically and educational theory more generally. Thus, whereas part 1 situates Gilkey's thought systematically, part 4 does so practically, completing the book's interpretive tasks.

In part 5, "Reflections by Langdon Gilkey," we reprint Gilkey's intellectual autobiography, originally published by Meyer-Stone Books. Hence, in chapter 16, "A Retrospective Glance at My Work," Gilkey traces his own understanding of the relation between his life and his thought.

IV. Dedication

Dedications hold special significance, usually, however, a significance known primarily or only by both the one who makes the dedication and the person or persons to whom authors or editors dedicate their works.

Usually authors or editors dedicate their books to lovers, spouses, children, parents, friends, students, or colleagues. Dedications of books often document deep emotions and commitments as well, such as gratitude for help or support, appreciation for inspiration, respect and admiration for courage or example, mutual love and affection, remembrance of family members and friends lost to death, and even commemorations of births.

As we reflected on the dedication of this book, we also considered the example of our teacher. Langdon Gilkey has dedicated his books to people in all of the previous categories. Gilkey originally dedicated *Maker of Heaven and Earth* to his first wife: "To my wife Dorothy." In the acknowledgments he thanked most notably his two teachers, Reinhold Niebuhr and Paul Tillich. *How the Church Can Minister to the World without Losing Itself* Gilkey dedicated to his parents: "In Loving Appreciation / To My Parents / Geraldine Brown Gilkey / Charles Whitney Gilkey." *Shantung Compound* Gilkey addressed to his second wife: "To / my / love / Sonja." Gilkey dedicated *Naming the Whirlwind* to his sons: "For Mark Whitney Gilkey / and Amos Welcome Gilkey." With the dedication of *Religion and the Scientific Future*, Gilkey commemorated the birth of his daughter in 1969: "For / Frouwkje Tjakien Rachael Gilkey." Gilkey dedicated *Catholicism Confronts Modernity* to his sister: "For / Mary Jane." *Reaping the Whirlwind* carries an inscription to his teachers: "*In gratitude for the life and thought of* / REINHOLD NIEBUHR / *and* / PAULUS TILLICH." With his dedication of *Message and Existence*, Gilkey expresses his appreciation of close friends: "In gratitude to three friends / David Burt / Jerald Brauer / David Tracy." Through the dedication of *Society and the Sacred*, Gilkey honored his Dutch father-in-law: "For / Wilhelm Hermann Weber / of / Aalsmeer." In *Creationism on Trial*, Gilkey inscribed a memorial dedication to his sister: "Dedicated / with love / to my sister / Mary Jane Gilkey / June 1917–February 1983." Gilkey dedicated *Gilkey on Tillich* to those with, among, and for whom he had exercised his profession as a theologian at the University of Chicago: "This volume / is dedicated in affection and respect / to all my colleagues / at / The Divinity School of the University of Chicago: / the deans, the faculty, the students, / and the staff / 1963–1989." In *Through the Tempest*, Gilkey acknowledged the affectionate bonds between his own family and another family: "With affection to the / Goldstein Family / Paul, Iris, Tom, Kaylin, Alexa, and Leigh." Finally, Gilkey has dedicated his most recent book, *Nature, Reality, and the Sacred*, again to one of his sons: "Dedicated, with love

and admiration, to / Amos Welcome Gilkey / 'It isn't life that matters.
. . . / 'Tis the courage that you bring to it.' / Hugh Walpole, *Fortitude*."
    The dedications of Gilkey's books, like the foam in the crest of an
ocean wave, suggest depths of relationships and love that have undergirded and sustained his life as a theologian in the stormy tumult of
history. As Gilkey says in one published expression of gratitude to his
family, "[q]uite literally there is little of worth and excitement in life
without love and those whom we can love."[3] If one writes books, one
should live well and long enough, should have enough significant experience, should have reflected carefully enough upon that experience, even
should have gathered enough wisdom, to dedicate a book to each significant person in one's life and, in offering such dedications, to celebrate
and express such love. Gilkey has done precisely that.
    We always knew to whom we would dedicate the labors this book
represents. Although expressions of gratitude, such as dedications in
books, lack the richness of affection and gratitude actually felt, they can
at least point to the depths of the heart. We can do nothing less than
thank Langdon Gilkey for that which we have received from him, remember the satisfying time spent with him, our teacher and friend, and express
our admiration of, respect for, and affection toward him. We dedicate this
book to our teacher, Langdon Brown Gilkey.

Kyle A. Pasewark   *Jeff B. Pool*
    Yale Law School   Brite Divinity School
    New Haven, Connecticut   Fort Worth, Texas

    June 1999

---

[3]Langdon Gilkey, *Society and the Sacred: Toward a Theology of Culture in Decline*
(New York: Crossroad Publishing Company, 1981) xii.

Part 1

Situating Gilkey's Thought

Chapter 1

Making Sense of Ultimacy: Truths of Experience in Langdon Gilkey's Theological Development[1]

Gary J. Dorrien

Introduction

Throughout most of his distinguished theological career, Langdon Gilkey has been inclined to emphasize his religious doubts and relative lack of religious certainties. In the early 1960s, establishing his early reputation as a leading advocate of American-style neoorthodoxy, he issued a devastating critique of neoorthodox Biblical Theology that sharply questioned the coherence of his own theological tradition. In his major succeeding work, *Naming the Whirlwind* (1969), Gilkey spent hundreds of pages detailing the reasons why modern theologians were coping poorly with the challenges of modern science, secularism, and historical consciousness. Through all of the shifts in theological position and orientation, however, and for all of his emphasis on various critical problems that he believed modern theology had to confront, Gilkey's theological work is anchored by a cluster of certainties pertaining to human *experiences of sin, ultimacy, and grace*. These grounding religious truths, I suggest, are certainties of his own experience.

The developments and continuities of Gilkey's theology are traceable to these experienced truths; therefore, one approaches Gilkey's theological concepts and his biography in tandem, as mutually reflecting parts of a whole. The close connection between thought and existence is obvious from the beginning. Indeed, Gilkey became a theologian in the first place through his desire to comprehend the immense world-historical evils of the 1930s and 1940s. Even more important personally, he sought—under the influence of Reinhold Niebuhr and Paul Tillich—to make sense of his own experience as a prisoner of war during World War II. His perceptive attention to what he later called "dimensions of ultimacy" in this experience gave him a basis for his early attempts to carry forward the theological vision of Niebuhr and Tillich. The same reflective attention to the

---

[1]With permission from the publisher, I have adapted portions of the first and last sections of this chapter from my recent book, *The Word as True Myth: Interpreting Modern Theology* (Louisville: Westminster John Knox Press, 1997).

sacral elements of human experience gave Gilkey a basis for rethinking his approach to theology after he came to believe that his acquired neoorthodoxy was not credible. In these cases, as in all of his theological work, Gilkey emphasized critical doubt and negation; however, he retained his theological bearings by affirming religious truths that he knew as truths of experience. The demonstration of the mutual reflections of thought and life, doubt and certitude, begins with a crucial pivot in Gilkey's theological life—neoorthodoxy's detachment from the shores of certainty.

I. Neoorthodoxy Unmoored

In the mid-1960s, well after Langdon Gilkey had established a reputation as a leading advocate of American-style neoorthodox theology, he reported in the *Christian Century* that he appeared to have lost his entire structure of certainties. He had begun his career thinking that he knew what theology was about and how it should proceed. He explained, however, that in recent years the ostensibly "solid earth" of neoorthodoxy had "turned out to be shifting ice." He no longer claimed to know what theology was about or how it should carry out whatever work it presumed to pursue. He confessed that he found it "immensely embarrassing" to be asked about the direction of his religious thinking. Neither was it any comfort to him that several of his friends were going through the same crisis. While perched on the cracking ice of neoorthodoxy, he reflected: "some of us have in horror found ourselves staring down into rushing depths of dark water."[2] Gilkey later recalled that, while he was certain that his teacher, Reinhold Niebuhr, would have known during his prime how to respond to this crisis of belief, "I could find no handle with which to begin."[3]

A. Neoorthodoxy and Biblical Theology

The downfall of neoorthodoxy to which Gilkey responded was, in one significant respect, the consequence of his own pointed criticism. Gilkey's early neoorthodoxy was a patchwork of arguments that he appropriated from Emil Brunner, from various leaders of the Biblical Theology

---

[2]Langdon Gilkey, "Dissolution and Reconstruction in Theology," *Christian Century* 82 (3 February 1965): 135.

[3]Langdon Gilkey, *Gilkey on Tillich* (New York: Crossroad Publishing Co., 1990) xiii; hereafter cited as *GOT*.

movement, and especially from his teachers Reinhold Niebuhr and Paul Tillich. To Gilkey, the key to neoorthodoxy was its distinctive blend of classical (especially Reformationist) and modern elements. In his words, neoorthodox theology was "a new synthesis of two widely divergent interpretations of the Christian religion, that of the Reformation and that of nineteenth-century liberalism."[4] The neoorthodox movement recovered the classical Reformationist language of sin, redemption, transcendence, and grace, but was not a mere throwback to any premodern perspective. Neoorthodoxy made traditional-sounding appeals to biblical revelation and the authority of biblical narrative, but gave meanings to these appeals that derived from various currents of theological liberalism.

Gilkey's early writings celebrated this two-sided dialectical identity as the key to "the unusual grace of neoorthodox Christianity."[5] His first major work, *Maker of Heaven and Earth*, proposed that neoorthodoxy alone made sense of the Christian doctrine of creation. Conservative theologies invariably turned the doctrine of creation into a form of bad science or philosophy; liberal theologies averted conflicts with science by accommodating the modernist worldview, partly by relinquishing the idea of divine transcendence. Both approaches assumed that the doctrine of creation commits Christian theology to some kind of scientific or philosophical perspective on the natural world. By reconceptualizing the Christian idea of creation as a religious response to a religious question, Gilkey proposed, theological neoorthodoxy took a more fruitful tack. It recognized that the religious question is fundamentally existential. The point of a theology of creation is not to pursue unsolvable scientific or metaphysical problems, but to explore the ultimately uncontrollable mysteries of life and death. The neoorthodox approach made it possible for theology to recover the true meaning of the doctrine of creation, Gilkey asserted, which is that we are creatures of God who are ultimately dependent upon God's power and love.[6]

---

[4]Langdon B. Gilkey, "Neo-Orthodoxy," in *A Handbook of Christian Theology: Definition Essays on Concepts and Movement of Thought in Contemporary Protestantism*, ed. Marvin Halverson and Arthur A. Cohen (Cleveland: World Publishing Company, 1958) 260.

[5]Gilkey, "Neo-Orthodoxy," 259.

[6]Langdon Gilkey, *Maker of Heaven and Earth: A Study of the Christian Doctrine of Creation* (Garden City NY: Doubleday, 1959).

It was crucially important to Gilkey to affirm that neoorthodoxy constituted a third way in theology. By all outward appearances, the strength of the Biblical Theology movement seemed to confirm this claim. In the 1940s and 1950s, British and American scholars such as H. H. Rowley, Alan Richardson, G. Ernest Wright, and Bernard Anderson built a field-dominating biblical-studies movement on the basis of their contention that neoorthodox "Biblical Theology" provided the strongest foundation for biblical scholarship and theology. In the process of seeking to clarify the content of this claim, however, Gilkey began to doubt that there was such a thing as neoorthodoxy. He noted that, for all of the movement's outward success and all of its spirited polemics against theological liberalism, so-called "Biblical Theology" had no theoretical basis apart from its basis in liberal theology.

Biblical theologians sharply rejected the liberal emphasis on divine immanence, in favor of the biblical appeal to God's objective activity in special events, Gilkey explained, but took for granted the liberal assumption of a causal continuum of space-time experience. They invested no religious, historical, or apologetic significance in biblical testimonies to miracles. Like their liberal predecessors, they presupposed the existence of a causal order among phenomenal events and did not accept miracle stories either as forms of historical explanation or as apologetics. At most, they appealed (vaguely) to faith as a form of special understanding of miracle stories. Biblical Theology emphasized the biblical idea of God as the transcendent source of historical revelation, but did not share the biblical understanding of God as a miracle-making, interventionist agent. Although they emphasized the historical character of biblical religion, Biblical Theologians such as Wright and Anderson quickly dismissed the historicity of key biblical accounts.[7]

Gilkey pressed the point that these were not negligible differences. In the Bible, God created the world in six days; the fall occurred in a real

---

[7]Langdon Gilkey, "Cosmology, Ontology, and the Travail of Biblical Language," *Journal of Religion* 41 (July 1961): 194-205. On the Biblical Theology movement, see Brevard S. Childs, *Biblical Theology in Crisis* (Philadelphia: Westminster Press, 1970). For central examples of the scholarship in the Biblical Theology movement, see the following: H. H. Rowley, *The Unity of the Bible* (Philadelphia: Westminster Press, 1955); Bernard W. Anderson, *Rediscovering the Bible* (New York: Association Press, 1951); G. Ernest Wright, *God Who Acts: Biblical Theology as Recital* (London: SCM Press, 1952). Gilkey's critique of Biblical Theology focused on the writings of Anderson and Wright.

space-time Eden; and the patriarchs received audible commands from God; later, God intervened directly in history to bring about the exodus from Egypt, the gift of the Mosaic law, the conquest, and the formation of Israel. In the Bible itself, these were the "mighty acts of God" that revealed God's existence and providential care, Gilkey observed. Biblical Theology, however, assigned these events to "the never-never land of 'religious interpretation' by the Hebrew people." The upshot was that the world of the Bible no longer existed even for those who persisted in calling themselves Biblical Theologians. Not only did modern people refuse to believe that God would sanction anything so grossly immoral as the mass murder of the Amalekites, Gilkey noted. For educated modern people, all of the verbal divine commands, promises, and interventions reported in the scriptures are gone: "Whatever the Hebrews believed, *we* believe that the biblical people lived in the same causal continuum of space and time in which we live, and so one in which no divine wonders transpired and no divine voices were heard."[8]

Neoorthodoxy retained the biblical language about God as revealer and divine agent, but it did not use these words in the univocal fashion of the biblical writers. The biblical writers spoke univocally about God "acting" and "speaking" in history. For Biblical Theology, however, what the Bible actually described was the faith of Hebrew religion. In the Bible, God is the subject of the verbs; but, in Biblical Theology, Hebrew faith displaced God as the subject of the verbs. Neoorthodoxy used religious language analogously without explaining how God's "acts" were like human acts, Gilkey observed. That movement claimed to recover the theology of the Bible, while regarding key biblical narratives as parabolic illustrations of Hebrew faith. Gilkey's summary was deflating: "For us, then, the Bible is a book of acts Hebrews believed God might have done and the words he might have said had he done and said them—but of course we recognize he did not."[9]

The Biblical Theology movement blasted theological liberalism for making faith the object of religion—and then repeated the liberal approach to the Bible. Neoorthodoxy sounded like a biblical corrective to liberal theology, until one recognized that "the whole is included within gigantic parentheses marked 'human religion,' " Gilkey remarked. If the key words and categories of Scripture could not be used univocally

---

[8]Gilkey, "Cosmology, Ontology, and the Travail of Biblical Language," 196.
[9]Gilkey, "Cosmology, Ontology, and the Travail of Biblical Language," 197.

to refer to observable actions and audible voices, did they retain any intelligible content? What does it mean to assert that God "acts" or "speaks," if God does not act or speak as humans do? Gilkey replied that modern theologians had no answers to these fundamental questions. Even the "special understanding" provided by faith was never clearly explained. Since Biblical Theology was unable to give specific content to its basic analogies, he argued, the neoorthodox rhetoric of revelation and mighty acts was literally meaningless, except for the sense in which it actually contradicted the fundamental claim of neoorthodoxy.

The contradiction was that neoorthodox thinkers condemned liberal theology while practicing an inconsistent form of it. For all of its talk about the priority of revelation over experience and the "mighty acts" of God in history, Biblical Theology was based on a religious interpretation of natural phenomena. "Having castigated the liberals, who at least knew what their fundamental theological principles were, we proclaim that our real categories are orthodox." Biblical Theology played up the "uniqueness" of history-centered Hebrew faith and denigrated the more cosmopolitan Wisdom literature of Hebrew religion. It treated the Old Testament as a Christian bulwark against paganism. The movement sought to protect Christianity from external relativizing critiques that reduced theological liberalism to religious subjectivity. Neoorthodoxy, however, is not a different *kind* of theology from liberalism, Gilkey objected. Having stripped the biblical narrative of its wonders and voices, neoorthodox theologians employed a vaguely analogical language of divine agency and revelation that carried no determinate meaning.[10] Modern theology was left in desperate need of a theological ontology that reestablished the basis of its God-language. "For if there is any middle ground between the observable deed and the audible dialogue which we reject, and what the liberals used to call religious insight, then it has not yet been spelled out," Gilkey declared.[11]

This critique of neoorthodoxy carefully avoided any discussion of Christology. Did Gilkey still believe, as he affirmed in *Maker of Heaven and Earth*, that the divine self-disclosure in Christ establishes the crucial point of contact that Christian God-language requires to secure its intelligibility? In the early 1960s, his writings avoided the critical thrust

---

[10]For an additional discussion of this issue, see Eric Crump's study of Gilkey's understanding of God, later in this book.

[11]Gilkey, "Cosmology, Ontology, and the Travail of Biblical Language," 202-203.

of this question, while tacitly assuming an affirmative answer to it. Gilkey assured that "I surely know at once of my own sin and, correspondingly, that God is a holy judge and a loving father—for I experience his wrath at my sin and his forgiving mercy in Jesus Christ."[12] He continued to assert that Protestant theology must remain faithful to a Word-oriented revelationism that "enthroned" Jesus Christ and that testified to Christ's sovereign living presence. He insisted that modern Protestantism could sustain its spiritual identity and purpose on no other basis: "In the message about Jesus Christ, His life, death, and resurrection, we know in faith of God's establishment of this new humanity; we know the judgment of God on our sins; we know of His forgiving love, which accepts the repentant into new fellowship; and we know of His promise in the Spirit that in faith we may grow in Christian holiness."[13]

B. Historical Limits of Neoorthodoxy: Challenge of Secularism

Less than a year after publishing these assuring words, however, Gilkey confessed that he no longer knew what theology was about or how it should proceed. His critique of neoorthodoxy suggested that he was actually some kind of theological liberal, but he resisted this conclusion. His then most recent writings placed an increasingly heavy burden on existential claims, though he recognized the problematic character of this strategy for theology. The crucial problem with existential interpretation was that it limited the field of religious knowledge to the sphere of personal encounters. Gilkey worried that this strategic resort relinquished much of the social, moral, and spiritual meaning of Christianity. He thought that the influence of existentialism over the past generation of theologians had left modern theologians with little or no epistemological basis for making claims about a wide range of traditional Christian doctrines. The doctrine of divine providence supplied a notable example.[14]

It was chastening to Gilkey that most contemporary theologians had very little to say about providence. He recognized that this problem had several serious causes. On the one hand, the liberal notion of providence

---

[12]Langdon Gilkey, "The Concept of Providence in Contemporary Theology," *Journal of Religion* 43 (July 1963): 183.

[13]Langdon Gilkey, *How the Church Can Minister to the World without Losing Itself* (New York: Harper & Row, 1964) 75, 84.

[14]Kyle A. Pasewark supplies a concentrated discussion of the development of Gilkey's theology of providence in chap. 10 of this book.

as progressive development was no longer credible after two world wars and the Holocaust. On the other hand, modern theologians were too influenced by modern humanism, scientific rationalism, and romanticism to return to any premodern conception of divine sovereignty. For Gilkey, the modern ideal of the free, autonomous, creative individual was too deeply insinuated in modern theologies to permit any recourse to the worldview of Thomas Aquinas or John Calvin.[15] For these reasons, in addition to their tendency to emphasize existential interpretation, most contemporary theologians gave little attention to the idea of providence. The only significant exception was Karl Barth, who developed a highly paradoxical account of divine sovereignty that posited a nonontological "nothing" as the root of *real* evil in existence.[16] Gilkey kept his distance from this account, while affirming Barth's contention that a new understanding of providence was needed. He admired Barth's creative attempt to provide one. Much of Gilkey's subsequent work was marked by his deep concern to rethink the ontological groundwork of religious knowledge and the meaning of divine sovereignty.

At the critical turn in his theological career, when he gave up the claim to a third way in theology, Gilkey reasoned that it had been one thing for an earlier generation of theologians to reclaim the language of prophetic faith during the turmoil of the Great Depression and the struggle against fascism. It was another matter entirely for theologians to proclaim the same faith during a period of peace and prosperity, when the foundations of Christian belief were being subjected to closer scrutiny. What *was* the meaning of the fall if it had no point of historical origin? What *was* revelation without univocal acts or voices from God? What *were* God's "mighty acts," if the biblical miracles were eliminated as real events? What *was* providence without God's actual rule? Accordingly, Gilkey made the following observation: "Instead of the desperate wartime cry for help: 'How can we be saved in this mess? How can we find meaning in this holocaust of evil?' we now ask, 'How can we understand in the light of modern science and modern views of causality and value the salvation we thought we had experienced?' "[17]

---

[15]Gilkey, "Concept of Providence in Contemporary Theology," 171-75.

[16]See Karl Barth, *Church Dogmatics* III/3: *The Doctrine of Creation*, trans. G. W. Bromiley and R. J. Erlich (Edinburgh: T. & T. Clark, 1961) 3-288 (on divine providence), 289-368 (on God and nothingness).

[17]Gilkey, "Dissolution and Reconstruction in Theology," 135.

Neoorthodoxy had begun as a theology of crisis. Implicit in all of Gilkey's questions was the troubling suggestion that, for all of its intellectual power and eloquence, neoorthodoxy was plausible only as a reaction to the world-historical crisis of Niebuhr's generation. Gilkey's own generation faced a more daunting, elusive, and disillusioning historical situation. Beneath the various intellectual problems with which contemporary theologians struggled, a deeper and more pervasive cultural pressure threatened to delegitimize theology itself. This was the "increasingly potent mood of secularism in our age." Secularism was not an alternative philosophy, Gilkey observed, but a basic attitude toward life. It consisted essentially of an intuitive sense about the meaning of life. Modern secularism was rooted in the visceral sense that reality lies nowhere "but amidst the visible and the tangible, that all causes are physical or human causes, that all events begin and end here and all interests lie solely in this world."[18] As he later put it, the modern secular mood was a "radically this-worldly" mindset.[19]

To argue against this mood with arguments for God's existence is to misunderstand the nature of the phenomenon of secularism, Gilkey cautioned. Theology could respond meaningfully to secularism only by entering and addressing the realm of reflective experience from which it arose. More importantly, in Gilkey's view, theology could provide an alternative to the secularist sensibility, only if theology could point to positive experiences of ultimacy and transcendence on the same deep level of subjectivity from which secularism arose. This was the key to the "drastic reconstruction" of theology that he vaguely proposed.

II. Neoorthodoxy, Secularism, and Biography: Gilkey's Dialectical Response

A. Correlating Life and Theology

At the critical turn in his thinking, when he was embarrassed to be asked about his theological standpoint, Gilkey clung to the few religious truths that he knew for sure. These were truths that had become certainties to him through his personal experience and reflection. These certainties

---

[18]Gilkey, "Dissolution and Reconstruction in Theology," 135-36.

[19]Langdon Gilkey, *Naming the Whirlwind: The Renewal of God-Language* (Indianapolis: Bobbs-Merrill, 1969) 39; hereafter cited as *NW*.

would mark his thinking through all of its various twists and turns afterward. For all of his talk about dissolved certainties and rushing depths of dark water, Gilkey never doubted that Niebuhr's critique of liberal optimism and moralism was correct, or that sin is a powerful and destructive *religious* phenomenon, or that religious language is meaningful, or that the existentialist aspects of neoorthodoxy were indispensable to theology, or that the "strangely potent figure of Jesus" embodies the ideal of true religion.[20]

With careful allowance for the limitations of existential interpretation, he proposed that theology was obliged to begin with the human subject. Though he retained the neoorthodox language of existential encounter and its concern to establish nonobjectivist ways of speaking about God, he was finished with neoorthodox appeals to a revelationist starting point. "If we felt sure that the divine word in Scripture was the truth, then the Bible might be our starting point," he explained. "Or if we felt some assurance that existence as a whole was coherent, a metaphysical beginning might be possible. But in our situation these two certainties are lacking." To take secularism seriously relinquishes these starting points and begins the work of theology by explicating the human experience of relationality to an ultimate beyond the self. Put differently, theology was obliged to return to Schleiermacher's starting point. It needed to focus on the religious dimension of human existence, while emphasizing other aspects of human spirituality than the dynamics of dependency and feeling emphasized by Schleiermacher. The needed theology would explicate the religious sources of joy, hope, longing, anxiety, and terror, Gilkey proposed. It would show that secular accounts of human existence are too thin to account for humankind's most important experiences.[21]

Having judged that he needed to relinquish a position that claimed too much, Gilkey refounded his thinking on the truth of an inner sacral dimension that he knew from experience. Paul Tillich's language of ultimate concern and his correlational method were vital to Gilkey's reformulation of this perspective; much of its substance, however, derived from his reflection on personal experiences far removed from the academy. Gilkey came to theology from inheritance and conversion, as well as from a prolonged period of confinement as a prisoner of war

---

[20]Gilkey, "Dissolution and Reconstruction in Theology," 137-38.

[21]Gilkey, "Dissolution and Reconstruction in Theology," 137; see Gilkey, *NW*, 247-413.

during World War II. Much of the realism and religious insight that fill his writings derive from experiences that made him feel "infinitely old and thoroughly experienced" before he began his formal graduate studies in theology.[22]

His father, Charles W. Gilkey, was a nationally renowned pastor, chaplain, and liberal theologian; his mother, Geraldine, was a prominent feminist and national leader of the YWCA. Charles Gilkey had been pastor of Chicago's prestigious Hyde Park Baptist Church until 1928, when he became the first Dean of the Chapel at the University of Chicago. The Gilkeys were pious and socially progressive. In their liberal Protestant home, as Gilkey later recalled, to be "Christian" was to embrace the modern critical spirit and the social-gospel commitment to "social and racial justice and peace—above all, peace." In his experience, social-gospel Christianity regarded all forms of racial and religious prejudice and any kind of class or nationalistic chauvinism as anathema to genuine Christianity: "I grew up hating the anti-Semitism and the segregationist customs (not to mention the laws) still characteristic then of American society, scorning the 'economic royalists' of the 1930s, and utterly devoted to the permanent establishment of peace." His family supported Franklin Roosevelt in the 1930s and worried that the rise of fascist movements in Europe and the United States would destroy the progressive social gains of the past generation.[23]

Like many children of social-gospel liberalism, Gilkey quickly discarded his religion after entering college, while retaining the idealism and social progressivism of his parents. As a first-year Harvard student in 1936, he reasoned that philosophy offered a more credible language for his moral and intellectual concerns than the liberal Christianity in which he had been raised. He attended chapel services only when his father's friends came to Harvard to preach. Gilkey adopted George Santayana's naturalistic realism and judged, like Santayana, that Western civilization had progressed beyond the mythical religious picture of reality. Ethical humanism defined reality, while the liberal Christian faith of his parents no longer added anything to the enlightened struggle for a better world.

---

[22]Langdon Gilkey, "Introduction: A Retrospective Glance at My Work," in *The Whirlwind in Culture: Frontiers in Theology: Essays in Honor of Langdon Gilkey*, ed. Donald W. Musser and Joseph L. Price (Bloomington IN: Meyer-Stone Books, 1988) 12.

[23]Gilkey, "Retrospective Glance at My Work," 3-4.

Gilkey's secular idealism was a credible faith in the privileged academic culture of prewar Harvard University. It retained his family's liberal Christian commitment to humanistic social progress, while dispensing with the discredited theism of Christian religion. The apparent rationality of his acquired worldview made him impervious to its religious elements. He gave little thought to the religious character of his humanism, which amounted to a substitute faith; nor did he reflect upon the religious character of his idealism, which rested on the belief that a just world order is achievable through rationality and moral effort. In September 1939, however, Gilkey was in France with the Harvard tennis team when Hitler invaded Poland. The team narrowly escaped from Europe and returned to Cambridge.

Frightened by the outbreak of World War II, Gilkey's first impulse was to reassert his pacifism. His loathing of war was a deeper impulse than his contempt for the Nazi invaders. His parents' generation of progressives and liberal church leaders had vowed never to support another war; he had been raised to abhor the violence and irrationality of America's previous wars, especially the Great War. By the time Hitler's armies had devoured France and the smaller territories of Western Europe, however, Gilkey found himself caught in the wrenching contradiction between his pacifism and his commitment to freedom and justice. "I was stretched between two moral absolutes, peace and justice, and quite unable to qualify or to relinquish either one," he later explained. "Further, I found that for my humanism to survive these must remain *absolute* requirements, else all descend into cynicism."[24]

Gilkey tried to convince himself that he could support the ends of justice without relinquishing his pacifism; as Hitler's armies conquered Western Europe and prepared to attack England, however, Gilkey found himself resorting to increasingly cynical rationalizations for keeping America out of the war. He heard himself pontificating on the inevitability of European unification and the futility of resisting the march of history. The consolidation of a single European state would unfortunately require a certain amount of cruelty and violence, but why should Americans stand in the way of Europe's historical destiny? For that matter, why shouldn't Hitler be the one finally to bring about a unified Europe? Gilkey found himself ridiculing most of his moral beliefs in

---

[24]Gilkey, "Retrospective Glance at My Work," 6.

order to maintain his pacifism. His moral absolutism threatened to consume his moral sensibility. "Gone were the social ideals and the confidence in progress towards justice that heretofore—though I had not fully realized it—buoyed up and guided my spiritual existence," he later recounted. "I was left a clever cynic, directed only by the requirements of self-interest in a world going nowhere. The cold blast of historical reality had made my intellectual and moral humanism come apart at the seams; I realized I detested myself and the world I lived in."[25]

In this state of spiritual confusion and disillusionment, he heeded his father's plea, in April 1940, to "go hear Reinie preach sometime." Though Reinhold Niebuhr was already a major figure in American Christianity and national public affairs, Gilkey thought of him simply as one of his father's friends. He had little sense of Niebuhr's perspective or stature, though he dimly remembered his father's pronouncement upon reading *Moral Man and Immoral Society* that "Reinie's gone crazy!"[26] In the early 1930s, when Niebuhr began to denounce liberal Christianity for its moralistic sentimentality, Charles Gilkey still believed that, with enough education and religiously inspired moral effort, Americans could build the cooperative commonwealth that social-gospel preaching idealized. He tried to maintain this faith through the bitter years of the Great Depression and the rise of fascist mass movements in Europe and the United States. By the time the Nazis rampaged through the Continent, however, the elder Gilkey had begun to concede that it was Niebuhr who made sense. The prospect of a cataclysmic struggle for the world made Niebuhr's depiction of the demonic power of collective egotism seem prophetic. While struggling to absorb the implications of Niebuhr's dark vision for his own faith, Charles Gilkey urged his son to listen to Niebuhr. Without comprehending the irony of his father's plea, Langdon Gilkey ambled into Memorial Chapel on a Sunday when Niebuhr was a guest preacher there, completely unprepared for the power of Niebuhr's message.

The sermon stunned Gilkey. It described the ambiguous, conflictual, sinful world of Gilkey's recent experience without descending into any kind of cynicism. Niebuhr's spiritually grounded realism tore apart not

---

[25]Gilkey, "Retrospective Glance at My Work," 6.

[26]Langdon Gilkey, "Reinhold Niebuhr as Political Theologian," in *Reinhold Niebuhr and the Issues of Our Time*, ed. Richard Harries (Grand Rapids MI: Eerdmans, 1986) 182; my conversation with Langdon Gilkey, 22 October 1987.

only the illusions of liberal Christianity, but the pretensions of Gilkey's ethical humanism. "Suddenly, as the torrent of insight poured from the pulpit, my world in disarray spun completely around, steadied, and then settled into a new and quite firm and intelligible structure," he later recalled. Niebuhr's dialectical realism rescued Gilkey from his paralyzing either/or. It was a conversion experience: "I thought to myself, 'Now I am in touch with *reality* and not with the illusions of humanistic idealism.' " To Gilkey's astonishment, Niebuhr maintained that the moral perspective of *biblical* religion was grounded in an unflinching realism about the inevitability of personal and collective egotism. Unlike the make-believe yearnings of liberal Christian idealism, biblical religion invested no faith in the goodness of human nature or the socially redeeming effects of moral effort. In Niebuhr's telling, biblical faith presented a realistic account of the pervasive reality of personal and social evil, while calling Christians to bring the light of Christ—through their own weakness and fallibility—to a fallen world. Realism and a passionate moral concern were not contradictory. For Gilkey, this was the core of Niebuhr's liberating message. Its effects were profound: "The dichotomy that had wrecked my humanism—*either* believe in moral ideals and the moral capacities of human groups at the price of ignoring the sordid realities of social life *or* be realistic about those realities and therefore cynical—had dissipated into a new understanding." The reality of humankind's estrangement from the ideal made humanism an illusory faith; but the biblical myth of the fall did not imply that the ideal was erased from human nature or history: "For there is God, transcendent to the fallen, warring world and yet seeking to bring it back to its true self and all of us to our own true selves."[27]

Gilkey heard Niebuhr speak three times during his visit to Harvard and read all of his books in the following two weeks. By the time he finished *Beyond Tragedy,* Gilkey was a Niebuhrian. He had little sense of neoorthodoxy as a theological movement, having never heard of Barth or Søren Kierkegaard. Niebuhr gave to him not any particular neo-orthodox argument about Christian revelation or theological method, but the deeper, unexpected perception that biblical faith distinctively makes sense of the world as it is. Gilkey explained, "[w]hereas prior to that Sunday morning, naturalistic humanism appeared to me to represent hard-

---

[27]Gilkey, "Retrospective Glance at My Work," 7.

headed 'reality' and religious doctrines a worthy but sentimental set of 'illusions,' now naturalistic humanism—despite its claim to scientific realism—seemed to me hopelessly mired in optimistic and naïve illusions about progress and about human rational and moral goodness."[28] Gilkey thus relinquished his college humanism near the end of his college experience to embrace a form of the faith in which he had been raised, but which he barely understood. His renewed faith in the plausibility and relevance of Christianity was an unexpected discovery that was sorely tested after the United States entered the war.

In midwinter, he had signed a two-year contract to teach English at Yenching University in Peking (Beijing), an American/British university for Chinese students. Yenching University was one of ten privately owned Christian colleges in China that sought to Christianize the impact of Western civilization in the Orient. When Gilkey sailed to China in August 1940, the British were holding against Hitler and the American war with Japan was more than a year away. Thus, Gilkey felt no particular anxiety about traveling to the Orient as an American. The British, French, and Dutch empires were still intact; though China was technically a sovereign nation, it remained deeply colonized in every aspect of its political, economic, and cultural life. Treaty ports such as Shanghai and Tien Tsin remained under British control and Westerners enjoyed vast extraterritorial rights by virtue of their connection to a "superior" civilization. Though he was repulsed by the arrogance of many Westerners whom he met in Peking, Gilkey basked in the privileges that his presumed superiority brought to him. For sixteen months, he taught English-language courses on modern Western thought, presenting Niebuhr's "new religious understanding" as the needed corrective to an "irrelevant" secular humanism. Thus, Gilkey taught the Western theology of the only theologian he had ever studied to Chinese students, during what proved to be the final months of Western hegemony in China.

The Japanese occupation of eastern China was in its fourth year when Gilkey arrived in Beijing. In the succeeding months, his exposure to the brutality of the Japanese invaders purged him of his lingering pacifism. Gilkey sympathized with the Chinese victims of aggression and vowed that, if he ever had the opportunity to take up arms in a viable struggle against their oppressors, he would do so. This fantasy was swiftly

---

[28]Gilkey, "Retrospective Glance at My Work," 8.

dispelled in the aftermath of the Japanese attack on Pearl Harbor in December 1941, when the Japanese occupiers placed all "enemy nationals" in China under house arrest. Gilkey passed the time reading theology—especially the first volume of Niebuhr's *Nature and Destiny of Man*—until March 1943, when he was sent to an internment camp in Shandong province along with nearly 2,000 other civilians.

The group consisted of approximately 800 Britons, 600 Americans, 250 Netherlanders, and 250 Belgians, along with smaller groups of Russians, Palestinian Jews, and others. Nearly 400 of the internees were Protestant missionaries, ranging from social-gospel liberals to fundamentalists; another 250 were Dutch and Belgian monks; most of the rest were industrialists, merchants, engineers, educators, doctors, or other professionals associated in some way with the treaty ports or other business interests. This relatively well-educated, industrious collection of foreigners was forced to create a new civilization in the tattered remains of a walled-off Presbyterian mission station near Weihsien, North China, where Henry Luce had been born decades earlier. Though deprived of their Chinese servants and confined to a compound that was too small for their numbers and without running water or central heating, the Shandong internees were treated relatively decently by their captors. They established a division of labor and a series of institutional policies that made it possible for them to survive the stark conditions of their captivity. Gilkey was appointed to deal with the community's housing problems. Over the next two years, his experiences in this role convinced him that classical Christianity knew more about human beings than either liberal Christianity or humanism.[29]

For all of his exposure to Niebuhr's theology, he had arrived in China still believing in the basic goodness of human nature. Faced with the task of organizing a fair distribution of the compound's living space, he expected people to be reasonable and cooperative in working out fair accommodations for families, adolescents, people with special needs, and the like. What he repeatedly found, however, was that nearly everyone was much less rational and more selfish than he anticipated. They were not the nice people he was expecting; some were nothing like the nice people he thought he had known in Beijing. When asked to give up a bit

---

[29]Langdon Gilkey, *Shantung Compound: The Story of Men and Women under Pressure* (New York: Harper & Row, 1966) 2-9 (hereafter cited as *SC*); idem, "Retrospective Glance at My Work," 8-12.

of their space to make room for others who had nothing, some people slammed the door in Gilkey's face; others lectured him about the primacy of private property; others—especially the religious people—gave "moral" reasons for declining to help. Gilkey eventually decided that he preferred the straightforward selfishness of the first group to the self-interested moralizing of the missionaries. There were no guest rooms or extra provisions in the internment camp; with an absolute minimum of everything, every act of generosity was costly. With the notable exceptions of the monks and the Salvation Army missionaries, who were accustomed to scarcity, the conditions of camp life made nearly everyone, including Gilkey at times, behave with little regard for the needs of others. "In such circumstances no one feigns virtue any longer, and few aspire to it, for it hurts rather than pays to be good," Gilkey later remarked. "The camp was an excellent place in which to observe the inner secrets of our own human selves—especially when there were no extras to fall back on and when the thin polish of easy morality and of just dealing was worn off."[30]

In this situation, the persistent attempts of the community's leaders to bring about a just distribution of social goods were mostly unsuccessful. As Gilkey observed, order and justice are impossible in the midst of moral decay. Rationally and morally, it was obvious that the internees needed to share space, resources, and responsibilities to ensure their survival. Gilkey kept assuring himself that, when things got bad enough, people would recognize this necessity and begin to cooperate. What he witnessed, instead, even in himself, was that reason and morality are the servants of interest. For many of the internees in Shandong, a remarkably shortsighted understanding of interest drove them to steal food, hoard supplies, refuse to share living space, and refuse to work, even while giving lip service to the importance of cooperating with each other.

One episode epitomized the camp's moral difficulties in sustaining a minicivilization under the conditions of material scarcity and insecurity. In the winter of 1944–1945, the captors sharply cut food supplies to the camp, thus reducing everyone to a daily ration of six slices of bread, boiled water, a bowl of stew for lunch, and a cup of soup for supper. Morale in the camp sank to an all-time low; in January, though, an enormous shipment of unaddressed American Red Cross food parcels arrived unexpectedly, creating tremendous excitement among the 200

---

[30]Gilkey, *SC*, 92.

Americans who remained in the camp. Each parcel was three feet long and weighed over 50 pounds. The Americans shouted with joy as the number of packages mounted, incredibly, into the hundreds; when it became evident that more than a thousand parcels were being unloaded, however, the mood in the camp shifted uneasily. 1,550 parcels were finally counted in a camp that contained 1,450 internees. Did the American Red Cross mean to feed the non-Americans? The non-Americans exulted that the answer was surely yes, while many Americans indignantly claimed that all 1,550 parcels belonged to them.

To the Japanese authorities, the distribution issue was not complicated; they announced that each internee would receive one parcel and each American would receive an extra half parcel. Gilkey was elated by this decision and eagerly awaited his package; a group of Americans, however, officially protested that the Japanese captors had no right to feed others with their gifts. The American protest delayed any further Japanese action and sparked bitter arguments between Americans and other groups in the camp. Gilkey assured himself, however, that the protesters were only a vocal minority. To break the impasse, he and his friends polled the American community to see if they could muster a declaration of American support for sharing the food parcels. They were sharply disabused. "The American community found itself in the unenviable position of preventing the distribution of life-giving parcels to their hungry fellows. Apparently we were content to let them go hungry so long as we got our seven and one-half parcels."[31]

Some Americans told Gilkey's group that there was nothing to discuss. The packages had come from the American Red Cross and, therefore, belonged to Americans only. Others explained that the crucial issue was the primacy of private property. It was not a question of greed or lack of compassion, but a question of whether the legal principle of the right of American property would be upheld. This right was the bedrock of civilization. Others contended that a deeper moral question was at stake. As an elderly conservative missionary told Gilkey, the crucial issue was whether any moral quality would be served by the distribution of the parcels. There was no virtue whatever in being forced to share the packages, he reasoned. The only moral way to deal with the issue was to

---

[31]Gilkey, *SC*, 103.

give the Americans all of their parcels and, thus, allow them to make the morally virtuous choice of giving one or two of them to someone else.

By even the most optimistic projection, this would have meant that each of the non-Americans would get less than one-fourth of a parcel, while each American kept five or six. Gilkey asked if this would be moral sharing, when everybody was equally hungry. The missionary, however, looked at Gilkey in bewilderment, since this was not what he meant by morality. A redistributive action could only be moral if it was done freely by an individual in order to be good, he explained. If the action were carried out by any higher agency, such as the government or, in this case, the Japanese captors, there was no morality in it. The important question for him was not whether he would get to keep more than one parcel, he assured Gilkey, but whether all Americans would get their rightful opportunity to become virtuous.[32]

This episode elicited the virtue of humor in at least one group. In addition to the food parcels, a huge pile of unsorted clothing and footwear was also delivered to the camp. Sometime after the dispute over the parcels sent the entire camp into an uproar, it was discovered that the clothing pile included 200 pairs of boots from the South African Red Cross. The Americans were reminded that it was not only in the United States that Red Cross volunteers labored to comfort the afflicted. There were only two South Africans in the camp, and after the boots were discovered, they posted the following notice. "Due to the precedent that has been set, the South African community is laying claim to all 200 of the boots donated by their Red Cross. We shall wear each pair for three days to signal our right to what is our own property, and then shall be glad to lend some out when not in use to any non-South Africans who request our generous help."[33]

Early in his camp experience, Gilkey had stopped thinking about theology, after reflecting upon its seeming lack of relevance there. The engineers, carpenters, administrators, and doctors all had valuable skills to offer in creating a new social order, he observed. Their training met real needs, while his own training in philosophy and theology seemed useless. He noted that no minister tried to claim that his pastoral work counted as work; ministry did not compare to engineering or carpentry.

---

[32]Gilkey, *SC*, 96-116.

[33]Gilkey, *SC*, 113. The Japanese authorities ultimately settled the matter by giving one parcel to each prisoner and sending the remaining parcels to another camp.

Religion was a side issue, Gilkey thought; like philosophy, it had no vital work to do. It lived off the surplus of a functioning civilization, while contributing nothing that was essential to civilized life.

As Gilkey began to perceive that the worst threat to his community's survival was its own moral disfunctionality, however, he was driven back to religion. The point was not so much that people need religion to be moral; many of the missionaries were less moral than the camp's out-spoken atheists. Religion excused some of them from having any social conscience at all. Moreover, Gilkey took little interest in the religious services and activities that various clergy organized in the camp. He was not driven back to religion by an experience of loneliness or despair or any other emotional condition produced by the conditions of his im-prisonment. He was fascinated by the camp's unending conflicts over how to govern itself; they absorbed his time and attention. By contrast, religion as a phenomenon that transcended these concerns held little interest for him.

Christian theology, however, enabled him finally to make sense of the political and moral problems that constantly threatened the camp's existence. Why was it so difficult to make this collection of human beings work together for the sake of their *own* good? Why was it so diffi-cult to convince this relatively well-educated group that unyielding self-ishness was self-defeating? Was the problem simply that the inheritance of animal instincts in human nature had not been brought sufficiently under rational control? This was the answer that Gilkey's formal educa-tion had given to him; his experience in the camp, nevertheless, drove him to reject his acquired psychological picture of an inner human con-flict between instincts and mind. The pervasive selfishness that he witnessed in the camp, especially among moralistic Christians who always denied that they were motivated by self-interest, convinced him that egotism is more than a problem or phenomenon of instinct. The roots of human selfishness seemed to inhere in fears about the self's security, he observed, "which only a self-conscious and intelligent being could experience."[34] For this reason, the fierce determination to hoard food for one's self, while vulnerable and weaker neighbors starved, was more appropriately regarded as a "human" rather than an "animal" reaction.

---

[34]Gilkey, *SC*, 114.

Gilkey later reflected that, while instinctive needs can be satisfied in a moment, only the human mind looks far into the future, calculates the dangers to human existence, and moves to protect the self and its loved ones from every possible negative contingency. The character of human-kind's will to live is thus transformed by human consciousness. Because of the human agent's reflexive consciousness, the instinctive will to live is transformed into the far more aggressive, dynamic, and possessive will to power. Animals, by comparison, are innocent. Gilkey reasoned that, therefore, not so much the instinctive will to survival, but the demands of instinct accelerated by humankind's capacities of mind or spirit make human beings distinctively grasping, alienated, and destructive.

This partly articulated insight had a reorienting impact on Gilkey's fundamental outlook. It drove him to conclude that the problem of humankind's moral and political existence is much more than a matter of bringing a rebellious instinctive nature under the control of enlightened reason and disciplined will. The dualisms of faculty-psychology obscured the more complicated and perplexing interactions of a unified self. That is, beneath and within the complex interactions of mind, will, and instinct is a unified self whose totality is obscured by the schematisms of faculty-psychology. Moreover, "it is that total psychophysical organism, that total existing self in its unity, which determines whether the 'higher' powers of mind and of will are going to be used creatively or destructively," Gilkey reasoned. It followed that a person's moral condition depends primarily on the fundamental character and direction of his or her self as a whole; as Gilkey later put it, it depends on the bent "of this deepest level of his being where his spiritual unity is achieved." The human problem is that this "fundamental bent of the total self" is self-regarding; it consumes aggressive egotists and "self-denying" moralists alike.[35]

B. Theology's Return: The Religious Dimension of Experience

With this intuition of a unifying spiritual dimension in human life, Gilkey found what would later become a fundamental principle of his theology. His interest in theology revived during the last months of his captivity, as he sought to make sense of his experiences in the camp. The core of his later theology was prefigured in his insight that one cannot adequately account for ordinary "secular" experience on secular grounds. "Having found these truths about human existence enacted before my eyes, I

---

[35]Gilkey, SC, 115.

began to recall some of the theological ideas I had almost forgotten in the bustle and activity of camp life," Gilkey maintains. "Among the most relevant, it now seemed, was the old idea of original sin."[36]

In Beijing, Gilkey had participated in a theological discussion group with a liberal Protestant pastor who fervently insisted that the Christian doctrines of the fall and original sin were "so much tommyrot." The pastor denounced not only the literalistic understandings of these doctrines, but their symbolic meanings as well. To him, the notion that human beings are inherently selfish was a form of apostasy. It contradicted the heart of his faith, which was that world justice and peace are achievable through the mobilization of moral good will, aided by the inspiriting power of liberal Christianity. This faith had brought the pastor and his family to China as missionaries. They were committed to the world-transforming idealism of social-gospel religion. To Gilkey, they represented this faith at its best: "educated, liberal, kindhearted, epitomizing good will and Christian concern."[37]

After the foreigners were herded into Weihsien camp, however, this missionary couple proved to be no more generous or kindhearted, when it mattered, than their self-protecting neighbors. When Gilkey asked them to help solve the camp's housing crisis, they were eager to contribute; when they learned that "helping" would require giving up some of their living space, they resisted with fierce determination. In their case, refusing to provide shelter for homeless neighbors required a moral rationale, which they found in their duty to provide a "good Christian home" for their teenaged sons. Gilkey observed that their moralism compelled them to find a moral justification for all of their actions, but offered little challenge to their self-interest. It provided, when serious interests were at stake, an arsenal of "moral" reasons for making the most self-regarding choice.

Thus, Gilkey was drawn back to theology by the force of two interrelated convictions that his camp experience gave to him. First, human beings are fundamentally selfish, yet often confused and conflicted by the unnaturalness of their consuming self-regard. If human beings were *naturally* selfish, he reflected, they would be less conflicted about their egotism and certainly less driven to cover it up. The fact that selfishness is so pervasive in human relations, and yet so persistently

---

[36]Gilkey, *SC*, 115.
[37]Gilkey, *SC*, 85.

denied, provided the central clue, for Gilkey, to the superiority of Christian theology over humanistic and naturalistic accounts of the human condition. Like Niebuhr, Gilkey reasoned that the Christian account does not require any belief in a historical "fall" (as in fundamentalism) or in the transmission of original sin through procreation (as in the later Augustine). The truth of the Christian understanding of sin does not depend on any mechanical explanation of its origin or transmission; it is, rather, confirmed by every human interaction. Drawing directly upon Niebuhr, Gilkey concluded that injustice "is the social consequence of an inward idolatry, the worship of one's own self or group. The moral problems of selfishness, the intellectual problems of prejudice, and the social problems of dishonesty, inordinate privilege, and aggression are all together the result of the deeper religious problem of finding in some partial creature the ultimate security and meaning which only the Creator can give."[38]

The reality of the "deeper religious problem" moved Gilkey to become a theologian. His camp experience convinced him that every person's moral strivings and failures are rooted in a unifying spiritual center that is unique to each individual. This spiritual center or soul provides whatever sense of meaning, coherence, or direction that a person possesses. Tillich's theology of ultimate concern later gave him a language for this perception of an underlying spiritual locus of security and meaning. Still later, the notion would provide the groundwork for Gilkey's theology, after he rejected much of the fundamental conceptuality of neoorthodoxy. In its earliest form, however, the notion of a conflicted, unifying spiritual center made sense of Gilkey's wartime experience. When the total meaning of a person's life depends upon one's personal welfare, he perceived—or the welfare of one's group—then the subject is not free to be moral or rational *in the very moments when morality and rationality are most needed*. The pressure to forsake otherwise binding moral interests becomes intolerable whenever the security of one's ultimate concern is threatened. "When man's self is basically threatened, when *he* is involved in the crisis, a new power enters the scene, a power seemingly stronger than either the moral consciousness

---

[38]Gilkey, *SC*, 232. See Reinhold Niebuhr, *Moral Man and Immoral Society: A Study in Ethics and Politics* (New York: Charles Scribner's Sons, 1932); and idem, *An Interpretation of Christian Ethics* (New York: Harper & Brothers, 1935).

or the objective mind," Gilkey explains. "It is the embattled ego fighting with every weapon at its disposal for its own security."[39]

The crucial question for each individual is, therefore, not whether he or she possesses an ultimate concern, but whether one's ultimate concern is worthy of the ultimacy invested in it. Though Gilkey had only begun to think through the implications of this perception when the war ended in 1945, he recognized that the concern underlying his various intellectual and political interests was religious. If the religious dimension of human existence was the source of humanity's greatest evil, what kind of religion might provide the ground for a worthy ultimate concern? What kind of religion might provide the ground for a redeeming hope? Gilkey entered Union Theological Seminary with these questions in mind, already deeply influenced by Niebuhr's theology, whose work he knew line by line. At the seminary, he studied with Niebuhr and Tillich, when both theologians were at the height of their influence and creative energy. All of his subsequent writings bore the marks of their considerable influence on his thinking. Gilkey emerged from graduate school as he had entered it, religiously defined by Niebuhr's understanding of Christian history and theology. He joined Niebuhr's crusade against an expiring liberal establishment and embraced, like many American theologians of his generation, a form of neoorthodox theology that was quite free of any directly Barthian influence. Upon judging that neoorthodoxy was neither really a third way in theology nor continuous with traditional theology, he reconceptualized his position in a way that brought out the essentially liberal character of Niebuhrian and Tillichian theology.

III. Holding the Poles Together:
The Persistence of Liberalism, Neoorthodoxy,
and the Secular in Gilkey's Theology

Gilkey's teachers sought to bridge the gap between Christian faith and modern secular experience. Expanding on their bridge-building work, but with a keener sense of his relation to the various strands of modern theological thinking, Gilkey urged that theology needed to find the basis of its discourse in secular experience, if it was to become intelligible to the modern secular mind. *Naming the Whirlwind* (1969) uncovered the dimensions of ultimacy in personal experience; *Religion and the Scientific*

---

[39]Gilkey, *SC*, 232.

Future (1970) and *Nature, Reality, and the Sacred* (1993) looked for dimensions of ultimacy in cognitive experience, especially scientific inquiry; *Shantung Compound* (1966) and *Reaping the Whirlwind* (1976) found dimensions of ultimacy in social and historical existence; *Society and the Sacred* (1981) and *Through the Tempest* (1991) found sacral dimensions in various aspects of modern culture; *Catholicism Confronts Modernity* (1975) and *Message and Existence* (1979) used the method of this disclosure of ultimacy to explicate Gilkey's constructive theology. In this remarkable body of work, he has persistently sought to synthesize the myths, stories, and symbols of Christian experience with modern scientific and philosophical reason. The influence of Niebuhr and Tillich marks nearly every page of this corpus; as Gilkey developed his construc-tive theology of history in the 1970s, however, he acquired a nearly equal debt to Whitehead's process thought.[40] He also increasingly revealed the impact of his internment experience upon his thinking.

Gilkey's prolonged effort to rethink the Christian doctrine of providence was constitutive to both developments. For many years, Gilkey reflected on the religious meaning of his wartime experience; for nearly as many years, he puzzled over the fact that modern theology had so little to say about providence. *Shantung Compound* described the influence of his imprisonment on his understanding of human conscious-ness and evil. *Reaping the Whirlwind* similarly interpreted the Christian understanding of divine providence in the light of modern historical consciousness and the ambiguities of modern social existence. In an early section of this dense, symphonic work, Gilkey remarked that those who scorn the guardians of social order merely reveal that they have never been hungry or faced the prospect of anarchy. Because it is good to be, he declared, the work of politics is good work. Human life cannot flourish in the absence of stable social structures. At the same time, the anxieties that human beings rightly have about their security can easily become demonic, "and this concern for our being generates the peculiar intensity of political and economic conflict, as well as the dominance of these areas over other values of life."[41]

His major work of constructive theology, thus, focused its rethinking of divine sovereignty on the human historical struggle for survival and

---

[40]On this point, see the following chapter by Kyle A. Pasewark.

[41]Langdon Gilkey, *Reaping the Whirlwind: A Christian Interpretation of History* (New York: Seabury Press, 1976) 48; hereafter cited as *RW*.

freedom. One of the fundamental debates in modern theology centers on the following questions. Should theologians conceptualize history fundamentally in terms of its metaphysical structure or historical process? Should a Christian understanding of human existence give priority to a metaphysical account of the permanent structures of being or to a philosophy of history that emphasizes the dynamic movement of historical change? Gilkey's theology of history sought to hold together both poles of this question in a way that did not overemphasize either structure or process.

It appropriated much of Alfred North Whitehead's process dialectic of destiny and freedom, without committing Christian theology to Whitehead's metaphysical system, especially his conceptions of divine reality or providence. Whitehead taught that, because even the most creative and autonomous human actions require a universal order of possibilities, the very possibility of openness to the future requires a divine ground. In his metaphysical system, God was the ground in actuality of all possibility, or, put differently, the metaphysical reality that unites actuality and possibility.[42]

Gilkey's alternative wedded the traditional Christian understanding of God as the source of all being to Whitehead's metaphysical dialectic of destiny and freedom. He proposed that God should be understood as the source of being, but that God's being should be conceptualized in terms of the process dialectic of achieved actuality and future possibility. Whitehead conceived divine reality as distinct from the more basic reality of creativity. Gilkey argued, however, that creativity should be understood as constitutive in the power of being that is God's being. "It is God as the power of being that carries forward the total destiny of the past into the present where it is actualized by freedom," he explains. "Creativity, the flux or élan of existence out of which in process thought each new occasion arises becomes, in other words, the power of being of God, the providential creativity of God that originates and sustains our continuing existence."[43]

---

[42]See Alfred North Whitehead, *Process and Reality: An Essay in Cosmology* (New York: Macmillan Co., 1929) 27-45; idem, *Modes of Thought* (New York: Free Press, 1966).

[43]Gilkey, *RW*, 249; see idem, *Nature, Reality, and the Sacred: The Nexus of Science and Religion*, Theology and the Sciences series, ed. Kevin J. Sharpe (Minneapolis: Fortress Press, 1993) 202-204; hereafter cited as *NRS*.

As the creative power of being and source of our total existence, the divine being influences, through secondary causes, all self-actualizations of the present as well as the causal efficacy of the past upon the present. God is the power that makes the process of becoming possible. As the dynamic power that transcends contingency and temporality, God is the ground of the possibility of process and is, therefore, also the ground for the possibility of causation, order, and cognition. Christian theology should take from process thought the notion that God is in dynamic process, Gilkey urged, but must reject the Whiteheadian notion that God is subject to process: "For process, if taken seriously, means the passing out of existence of what has been."[44] If the reality of the given world is to be affirmed, there must be a divine being whose power transcends the finite temporality of destiny and freedom. If God is such a power, however, and thus the worthy object of Christian devotion, God must not be subject to passage.

This argument that God "acts" in and through the secondary causes of destiny and freedom yielded the core of Gilkey's reformulation of divine providence. As the ground of the movement from the actual into the possible, he argued, God is the limiting and ordering ground of future possibility. It followed that divine providence is "the sustaining and creating work of God within the ambiguity of historical life that leads to the divine eschatological fulfillment as the latter's presupposition and ground."[45] Put differently, Gilkey affirmed the liberal understanding of providence: God is the divine ground of all being that sustains the historical movement of being. In Gilkey's case, however, theology never simply returns to the categories of a pre-neoorthodox liberalism. Theological neo-orthodoxy made certain claims during its heyday that it could not justify, he allows; neoorthodoxy was, nonetheless, a type of theological liberalism that importantly corrected the liberal tendency to interpret history solely in terms of the movement of freedom. To the liberal tradition, freedom is always on the side of the good in opening creative new possibilities. History is a movement of freedom in confrontation with various forms of nonfreedom.

Reaping the Whirlwind countered that freedom can also become sin. The possibilities open to freedom and made possible by God can be betrayed; destiny can become fate. This was the great truth of the neoortho-

---

[44]Gilkey, *RW*, 249.
[45]Gilkey, *RW*, 253.

dox reaction, Gilkey recalled. To a generation that found the predatory powers of freedom being unleashed in displays of apocalyptic violence, only evil seemed free. Niebuhrian realism arose from this experience. Niebuhr's doctrine that evil is always constitutive in the good helped a chastened generation make sense of its experience of history as tragedy.[46] In Niebuhrian neoorthodoxy, the doctrine of original sin rightly became one of the existential certainties of faith. It is a truism not only for Niebuhr's time but ours, Gilkey cautioned, that freedom can produce not only futility and illusion, but also forms of monstrous evil.

The tragic realities of human freedom and providential possibility ensure that providence will never be enough. With all of its creative and emancipating possibilities, history remains deeply ambiguous. Niebuhr taught that, because evil is inextricably bound with every good act and intention, the possibilities of evil grow with the possibilities of good.[47] Gilkey urged that this truism stands as a judgment on all theologies that overemphasize providence. Not even a chastened liberal conception of providence is sufficient by itself, for providence needs to be supplemented by redemption and eschatology. Christianity depends as much upon the redeeming work of Christ and the kingdom hope of eschatology as upon its faith in divine providence, Gilkey argued. Augustine's chief argument against Pelagius goes to the point: Freedom cannot be the determining ground of redemption, because freedom shares in the corruption of a fallen humanity. It followed for Gilkey that the same freedom that brings about the actualization of creative divine possibilities in history, therefore, *itself* must be transformed by grace, "if the possibilities of history are to be realized."[48] Without the redeeming work of Christ, freedom remains in estrangement and the hope of a new age has no basis.

Typically for Gilkey, *Reaping the Whirlwind* devoted most of its ample argument to his reformulation of a liberal theme; yet, the book was held together by its neoorthodox motifs. It divided the field of theology into liberal, neoorthodox, and eschatological approaches. It called for a new theological synthesis that featured a liberal doctrine of providence, neoorthodox doctrines of sin and redemption, and a liberationist emphasis on the coming new age of the kingdom. In its final pages, this dialectic yielded a closing discussion of God as being, logos, and love. In each

---

[46]See Niebuhr, *Interpretation of Christian Ethics*, 58-61.
[47]Niebuhr, *Interpretation of Christian Ethics*, 60.
[48]Gilkey, *RW*, 266.

case, the middle member of the triad received the least attention while doing the most work theologically. Gilkey developed an elaborate theory of God's preserving and concurring work in history; at the crucial turn in his argument, however, having declared that God's providential activity is not enough to redeem humanity or to sustain human hope for a new age to come, he asserted that God's redemptive activity in the saving Word is necessary and real. The doctrine of providence required an extensive regrounding in neoclassical metaphysics. The affirmation that held Gilkey's position together, nevertheless, was not the outcome of a metaphysical argument.

Edward Farley suggested that perhaps Gilkey meant to imply that God's redemptive activity is analogous to God's providential reordering.[49] On this reading, Gilkey might have been expected to develop a process Christology that reconfigured Christ and redemption according to the logic of his account of providence. The fact that he never moved in this direction is surely telling, however. Against a host of contrary interpretations, Gilkey always insisted that the heart of Tillich's system was his affirmation of Christ as the new being. The fact that Tillich had less to say about this idea than he had to say about the idea of God or the meaning of culture was not significant.[50] In a similar way, Gilkey's work places the "strangely potent figure of Jesus" at the center of his theology, while remaining comparatively reticent about how Christ should be understood. Though his theology is relatively short on Christological reflection, it unfailingly places Christ at the center of its dialectics. To conceive Christ undialectically is to falsify everything else in Christian teaching, he declares: "He is the Messiah only as the weak, the vulnerable, the suffering, the disgraced, and the forsaken one; he is lord only as he who was crucified; he is savior and giver of life only as he who was not saved and who died."[51]

In Christ, the dialectic of Christian existence bursts forth concretely: "Being and nonbeing, affirmation and negation, life and death are here united, and yet differentiated, held together dialectically so that each, in

---

[49]Edward Farley, review of *Reaping the Whirlwind,* by Langdon Gilkey, in *Religious Studies Review* 4 (October 1978): 236.

[50]See Gilkey, *GOT,* 138-57.

[51]Langdon Gilkey, *Message and Existence: An Introduction to Christian Theology* (San Francisco: Harper & Row, 1979) 182-83; hereafter, cited as *ME.*

participating in the other, transcends its own limitations."[52] Through his life of free self-giving love, Jesus embodied and disclosed the pattern of authentic humanity. Christ is lord because he embodies the ideal of true religion, Gilkey affirms. "In all the mystery of existence, with its emptiness, its ambiguity and its evil, surely this is clear. We find ourselves when, as Jesus did, we can lose ourselves in love for others. In this sense he is our 'Lord,' who provides us with our ethical model or perspective."[53] On the strength of that liberal certainty and the certainty of a sacral dimension in life, Gilkey has recovered much of the inner meaning of God-language for secularized individuals who yearn, often without knowing it, for redemption and grace. In his exemplary work, Christian theology unites the sacred dimension of human life, which is universal, to the particular saving power of the figure of Christ.

On this basis—not some "perennial philosophy" or purportedly universal religious principle—Christian theologians should pursue constructive dialogues with Buddhists, Muslims, and others. Instead of pursuing these dialogues on the basis of some purportedly common essence that exists only in the minds of a handful of intellectuals, Gilkey explains, Christian theologians should engage in interreligious discussion as Christians. Genuine dialogue requires that both participants reinterpret their own traditions in light of the "parity" of religions. It cannot simply endeavor to find or validate aspects of one's own tradition in the traditions of others. True interreligious dialogue looks, in other traditions, for manifestations of grace and truth that cannot be found in one's own tradition. At the same time, Gilkey judges, a genuinely Christian-Buddhist dialogue can only take place between conversation partners who begin from explicitly Christian and Buddhist centers. Too often, what passes for interreligious "dialogue" is a comparison of academic typologies or categories that are not rooted in any religious tradition.[54]

---

[52]Gilkey, *ME*, 183.

[53]Gilkey, "Dissolution, and Reconstruction in Theology," 138.

[54]Langdon Gilkey, "Plurality and Its Theological Implications, in *The Myth of Christian Uniqueness: Toward a Pluralistic Theology of Religions*, ed. John Hick and Paul F. Knitter (Maryknoll NY: Orbis Books, 1987) 38-42; idem, "Retrospective Glance at My Work," 34-35; personal conversation with Langdon Gilkey, 22 October 1987. For more on this issue, see both Mary Ann Stenger's chapter on Gilkey's interpretation of pluralism and Kyle A. Pasewark's chapter on Gilkey's concept of providence in this book.

With a distinctively ecumenical spirit, though not without unfortunate limitations and generous blinders, Gilkey has pursued theology as an open-ended dialogical enterprise. Negatively, his Niebuhrian sense of paradox and tragedy made him too inclined to assess liberation theology as utopian; his early fixation on Jürgen Moltmann's futurism caused him to criticize Moltmann as a political utopian and pure eschatologist long after Moltmann corrected these misreadings; and his appropriation of feminist theology has been slight. These shortcomings are ironic in light of Gilkey's overall achievement, however, which features a distinctively generous and integrative approach to theology. He has identified with and reinterpreted the liberal and neoorthodox traditions, appropriated White-headian process thought and eschatological theology, without adopting those perspectives entirely, rethought the relation of theological reasoning and science in light of contemporary postmodern critiques of epistemo-logical foundationalism, and pursued the ecumenical project of interreli-gious dialogue without giving up his Christian center. The remaining essays in this volume address each of these themes in detail. To a post-modern theological generation that prizes novelty and thrives on fads, Gilkey offers theological rethinking that is always on the cutting edge of religious and intellectual concern, but that also persistently relates itself to the major traditions of modern and classical Christian thought.[55] Gilkey shows that Christian theology can and must keep its religious center while seeking truth from other religious and secular traditions. Gilkey's work is, therefore, distinctively instructive to those who seek religious truth in a world of many gods.

---

[55]See the chapters in this book by Jennifer Rike on the role of integrity in Gilkey's thought and Kyle A. Pasewark on Gilkey's concept of providence.

Chapter 2

Debts and Contributions:
The Milieu of Langdon Gilkey's Theology

Kyle A. Pasewark

I. Destiny, Freedom, Fate: A Center for Gilkey's Theology

Any attempt to outline the heritage and contributions of a thinker who
ranges as widely as Langdon Gilkey is likely to have the feel of a desperate effort to stay afloat in deep water far from land. Gilkey has produced
concentrated reflection on most Christian doctrines, extensive analyses of
mid- to late-twentieth-century culture, discussions of important philosophical thinkers, and, late in his career, perspectives on pluralism, especially
in extensive conversation with Buddhism and Sikhism. In order not to
drown in a sea of diverse forms of theological life or despair of reaching
shore, the analyst must build a craft capable of traversing the vastness
without becoming hopelessly lost in it.

I will focus on what, since 1976, Gilkey contends is the fundamental
structure of human existence, the polarity of destiny and freedom. The
selection of a core insight from which other dimensions of Gilkey's
theology radiate has its disadvantages. First, I lose a claim to be comprehensive in outlining Gilkey's theological, cultural, and philosophical
heritage. Only quick glances will hint at the importance of the cultural
tradition of American pragmatism and empiricism (sometimes reflected
for Gilkey through John Dewey), pre-twentieth-century thinkers (such as
Augustine of Hippo, John Calvin, and Søren Kierkegaard), the hermeneutical theories of Paul Ricoeur and David Tracy, the historian of religions
Mircea Eliade, and less crucial figures such as Gerhard von Rad and
Ernst Bloch.[1] Gilkey also remains indebted, despite misgivings, to nine-
teenth- and early twentieth-century theological liberalism, a debt that
places him in fundamental sympathy—but often doctrinal conflict—with
newer movements in theology, notably theologies oriented toward liberation of the oppressed.[2] Second, certain themes that are important in

---

[1]Gilkey comments that Eliade "is much closer to who I am at the present time"
(Langdon Gilkey, "Theology and Culture: Reflections on the Conference," *Criterion* 28
[Autumn 1989]: 3).

[2]Mary Ann Stenger supplies an additional instance of the importance for Gilkey of

Gilkey's thought—plurality, for example—disappear from consideration, although the remaining essays in this book, which focus on special themes and therefore allow the reader to compensate for inevitable limitations of each contribution, mitigate that disadvantage.[3]

The advantages of a single focus are more compelling. One can give sustained attention to a consuming theme of Gilkey's theology, observe its development over the course of his long career, watch as its implications radiate throughout other themes in his theology, and note the uses and transformations of the three pivotal influences on Gilkey's thought: Reinhold Niebuhr, Paul Tillich, and Alfred North Whitehead. Although the choice of the polarity of destiny and freedom, as the device by which to negotiate Gilkey's theological environment, is not necessary, neither is it arbitrary. Not only does the polarity of destiny and freedom pervade most of Gilkey's major theological works, it is also the fundamental structure of human existence and the source of its distortions. The strength with which Gilkey maintains this position allows him to knit together uniquely and transformatively the theologians and traditions that most influenced him.

In *Reaping the Whirlwind*, Gilkey began consistently to claim that freedom and destiny is the fundamental ontological polarity. It is not merely that "history . . . is structured ontologically . . . by the polarity of destiny and freedom," but that "this ontological structure in turn entails that human beings are in history."[4] With this dual claim—that human beings are historical beings and that history is constituted by the interaction of destiny and freedom—Gilkey maintains that there is nothing more basic to human life or our understanding of God than the structure of destiny and freedom. Destiny is "the given," which "set[s] the limits and pose[s] the conditions for human response."[5] Four aspects of

---

theological liberalism in her chapter in this book. Stenger's discussion of Gilkey's sympathy with liberationist movements may seem inconsistent with my perspective but is not. Whereas Stenger emphasizes the congruence of aim between Gilkey's and liberation-oriented thought, I note the difference in theological execution of that aim. In other words, Gilkey believes that much liberation-oriented theology, although correct in its objective, mitigates against that objective in some of its theological concepts.

[3]For example, Jeff B. Pool, Stenger, James O. Yerkes, and I discuss pluralism in other chapters of this book.

[4]Langdon Gilkey, *Reaping the Whirlwind: A Christian Interpretation of History* (New York: Seabury Press, 1976) 91; hereafter cited as *RW*.

[5]Gilkey, *RW*, 43.

destiny inhere in any situation: (1) the "material environment"; (2) "habitual modes of relationship and of behavior established in the social system governed by the symbolic 'social world' participated in by all the members"; (3) "slow, unintended changes (for example, the growth of industrialism or the spread of rationalization) within this interlocking system"; and (4) "the contingent (unplanned and unnecessary) coming together of a multiplicity of innumerable factors into a new constellation of conditions."[6] Destiny sets limits to freedom; "we cannot overreach the real limits. . . . It is with *this*, and with nothing else, that our own being in time begins."[7]

Although destiny limits freedom, freedom could not exist in any real sense without destiny, for destiny gives freedom all the material with which it operates and through which it acts. "Present freedom" acts on the inheritance of destiny, and "union of the two creates the 'event' in the present which then becomes 'world' and 'self,' or destiny, for the next present, for the future. Because process and freedom are basic ontologically, the primary ontological structure is for us constituted by destiny and freedom, actuality and possibility, not by world and self."[8]

Into this complex, seemingly inevitably (though not necessarily, Gilkey is careful to agree with Niebuhr and Tillich), steps fate. Fate is subjected destiny, a destiny that is "incapable of self-determination and of freedom; it can barely 'be' because it has no power, and thus is the situation unjust."[9] As destiny becomes more fateful, less controllable, freedom is lost progressively; fate is the ultimate threat to the physical existence of beings (one *is* solely at the pleasure of another) and their meaning (the capacity to participate in determining and responding to meaning diminishes).[10] Paradoxically, distorted freedom is responsible for freedom's destruction and the transmutation of destiny into fate. Fate "represents the fall of freedom in sin" and into inordinate self-concern.[11] Thus, historical actuality (as distinct from ontological structure), cannot be analyzed exclusively in terms of the polarity of destiny and freedom; the fall and its result, fate, must be included. If one applies Tillich's

---

[6]Gilkey, *RW*, 43-44.
[7]Gilkey, *RW*, 44.
[8]Gilkey, *RW*, 49.
[9]Gilkey, *RW*, 26.
[10]Gilkey, *RW*, 50.
[11]Gilkey, *RW*, 55.

language, the ontological structure of destiny and freedom is "essential," whereas its corruption by freedom and into fate characterizes "existence." This is an *empirical* claim; exclusively ontological analyses do not capture the texture of actual events.[12] Gilkey's empirical orientation is characteristically American, although his positions are conceived often in opposition to reigning American mythologies. His incessant objection to the cultural myth of progress—following Niebuhr—that held such sway on empirically-oriented American culture is that this myth is not empirically supportable, that it is clearly belied by the facts of history.[13] Whatever else theology does, it must provide a credible and empirically supportable interpretation of *actual existence*.[14]

This summary of the basic contours of destiny, freedom, and fate is somewhat ahead of the story. The substance of the polarity of freedom and destiny was assuredly present in Gilkey's earlier thought and experience. He did not always ascribe to it the privileged status, however, that he later asserted for it. The career of the categories of destiny, freedom, and fate in Gilkey's work provides a lens through which we can see the shifting influences on his thought. It is a fair hypothesis that Gilkey's early influences were principally the liberal neoorthodoxies of Niebuhr and Tillich. Indeed, throughout Gilkey's works, it is nearly impossible—and unnecessary—to differentiate the influences of Niebuhr and Tillich, partly owing to the closeness of their two theologies, partly due to Gilkey's synthetic treatment of characteristic themes in their works.

The increasing dominance of the ontological polarity of destiny and freedom owes its rise to Gilkey's growing sympathy with Whitehead's process philosophy. Gilkey's appropriation of Whitehead and enduring appreciation of Tillich provide the ground from which Gilkey rejects the claim of the eschatological theologians of the late 1960s and early 1970s: that God acts primarily from the future. Still, dialectical theologian that he is, Gilkey never became an orthodox process theologian. "White-

---

[12]Gilkey, *RW*, 256.

[13]For an extended discussion of the "myth of progress" as Gilkey's theological foil, see my later chapter in this book: Pasewark, "Power, Freedom, and History."

[14]Langdon Gilkey, *Message and Existence: An Introduction to Christian Theology* (New York: Seabury Press, 1981) 60; hereafter cited as *ME*. Gilkey's use of Tillich's method of correlation is Gilkey's methodological expression of this empirical interest. I bypass consideration of Gilkey's theological method here for two reasons: first, Gilkey maintains that method is a second-order reflection (Gilkey, "Theology and Culture," 4); and second, several other chapters in the present volume treat Gilkey's method.

headians," Gilkey said in 1989, "notice the same old opponent, then and now."[15] With respect to Whitehead, it will be important to ask two questions. First, what effect does Whitehead's growing influence have on Gilkey's thought? Second, why and with what result does Gilkey remain unwilling fully to embrace Whitehead's thought? To understand Gilkey's later dialectical synthesis of Niebuhr, Tillich, and Whitehead, however, we must first consider the significance of destiny, freedom, and fate in Gilkey's earlier thought.

II. Naming Freedom, Destiny, and Fate: 1959–1970

Gilkey had always maintained a place for the Tillichian polarity of destiny and freedom. His earliest book, *Maker of Heaven and Earth* (1959), discusses freedom and destiny along with fate's distortion of both. For example, Gilkey notes that "the complexity of human existence is such that it contains both structural and intentional elements; it is made up both of determined processes and freedom." Gilkey ties "faith in historical destiny" to the conception of religion as the "feeling of absolute dependence" of the great progenitor of theological liberalism, Friedrich Schleiermacher. "The wholeness and excellence of man come when his freedom is in unity with his creaturely dependence. . . . In such unity both man's dependence and his freedom are creative and good."[16] The unity of freedom with the given was, from Gilkey's earliest work, the *desideratum* of historical life and the aim of God's grace in the world.

Although the polarity of freedom and destiny (or its cognate) was present in his first book, it was not the core of Gilkey's theology. In his treatment of philosophy's "search for the universal structures of experience," Gilkey begins with the distinction between the "object of knowledge and the subject who knows," a species of Tillich's crucial polarity of self and world.[17] Also, the later conception of destiny is nowhere mentioned in this discussion of the central problems of philosophy; freedom, however, is. Gilkey, giving off the faint scent of Tillichian cologne, argues that philosophy's attempt rationally to comprehend the world necessarily loses its abutment with actual, empirical existence. The reason is that existence includes freedom, which philosophical rationality

---

[15]Gilkey, "Theology and Culture," 3

[16]Langdon Gilkey, *Maker of Heaven and Earth: A Study of the Christian Doctrine of Creation* (New York: Doubleday, 1959) 75, 187, 230; hereafter cited as *MHE*.

[17]Gilkey, *MHE*, 143.

cannot incorporate. "Existence . . . will not be completely reduced to any clear and precise sequence of relationships. There are depths of freedom, of creativity, and even of incoherence, within the mystery of being, which defy the attempt to organize life into simple rational patterns."[18]

The adequacy of this understanding of philosophy beyond the narrow philosophical enterprise of mid-century Anglo-American analytic philosophy is not my concern. Significantly, freedom is the cause of rationality's rupture. This explains why—even in a volume on the doctrine of creation—fate becomes an important theme. The concept of fate in *Maker of Heaven and Earth*, however, is less focused and more ambiguous than it would later become. Gilkey does say that fate is "the first guise of unmanageable [and therefore unrationalizable] evil."[19] As he explains this claim, however, fate does not seem inevitably evil; indeed, it seems no different from destiny, which *can* be evil but need not be. Although fate is "terrifying," in that there are "great social and historical forces that both defy our wisdom and good will," it is less clear why it should frighten us that "[w]e cannot control [these forces] because they form the context within which we act in history." The examples which Gilkey gives to illustrate his point include some quite desirable "fates": the end of British imperialism, the coming end of western colonialism, the *finis* of aristocracy. "Fate" means what "destiny" will later mean: that "[o]ur fundamental contingency and temporality has made union with the consequences of our past creativity *and* sin to form a historical fate for our lives that seems to move us *either* to glory or to destruction."[20]

If "fate" is a relatively neutral category, sin obviously is not. Gilkey's analyses of sin always bear an indelible Niebuhrian imprint. Sin, in *Maker of Heaven and Earth*, is the "second guise of evil" and "the most important contributor to the external fate of history."[21] Sin is, thus, the ground of unhealthy fate; Gilkey takes from Niebuhr and Augustine the paradoxical character of sin's relation to freedom. Sin is an "internal fate," a "baffling irresistible force that subtly twists each of our acts and intentions into a glorification of self, that turns the self on itself." The source of sin is fallen freedom, but freedom nonetheless. "Despite the fact that it arises from our freedom, this is also a mighty force which we

---

[18]Gilkey, *MHE*, 145.
[19]Gilkey, *MHE*, 242.
[20]Gilkey, *MHE*, 243; emphasis mine.
[21]Gilkey, *MHE*, 244.

cannot control. We cannot control it, not because it is beyond our power, but because it *is* our power. . . . a self that is diseased cannot provide its own health."[22] Here we see several themes that never abate in Gilkey's thought: (1) "original" sin or sin's universality and irresistibility; (2) the content of sin as inordinate self-concern; (3) the source of sin in the very freedom that sin destroys; and (4) the need for grace to heal inward self-corruption. All are indebted to Niebuhr and his recovery of Augustine.[23]

That Gilkey should give an analysis of sin and the perversion of freedom in a book on creation is not a surprise, for these themes were his irresistible analytic tools for understanding one of the pivotal events of his life, his internment in Shandong province toward the end of the Second World War, an experience narrated in *Shantung Compound* and published as American military involvement in another Asian war, Vietnam, was becoming inexorable. The texture of Gilkey's experience in the prison provides a vital clue to his later treatment of freedom, destiny, and fate, though it does so without much explicit reflection on these themes. It was Gilkey's destiny to be trapped in China during the Japanese occupation when war broke out between Japan and the United States. This was the given. In 1943, when the Japanese sent subjects of the Allied powers to an overcrowded camp in Shandong, the prisoners were given the task of building a civilization from scratch, with only minimal initial interference from their Japanese overseers. Here was an opportunity to test the Western vision of progress and the good of unlimited reason and freedom. Here was the opportunity to imitate, it seemed, the act of God, to create out of nothing. This was, it should be emphasized, an empirical test, and the failure to be able to look later on this creation and remark unequivocally, "it was good," demonstrated empirically the error of progressive notions of human good and perfectibility; conversely, it confirmed much of Niebuhr's theology, particularly his incessant criticism of progressivism, which also became a linchpin of Gilkey's thought.

---

[22]Gilkey, *MHE*, 244.

[23]"Irresistibility" means neither that one can never resist sin nor that one could do nothing other than sin. Gilkey's meaning resembles the perspective of Thomas Aquinas, when Thomas says that the natural person can avoid *each* mortal sin but not *every* one: Thomas Aquinas, *Aquinas on Nature and Grace*, ed. A. M. Fairweather (Philadelphia: Westminster, 1954) 150-53 (*Summa Theologiae* 12ae, Q. 109, art. 8).

The beginning of camp experience was uplifting, and caused Gilkey to question the significance of any broad philosophical or theological outlook. In a remarkable reflection, Gilkey says,

> to camp I went, replete with theological jargon, many secondhand concepts, and a conviction that mine was the only way in which to view life. For a person thus encumbered, those first months of camp raised the most urgent and devastating of questions: What's so important anyway about the way a person looks at life? . . . The real issues of life are surely material and political. . . . These matters are resolved by practical experience and by techniques, not by this or that philosophy or religious faith. . . . It was not that I thought religion wrong; I simply thought it irrelevant.[24]

Irrelevant, that is, if one thought that human beings were ingenious creatures without inevitable inward limitations; if one was convinced, as were many Enlightenment thinkers, that reason was unambiguously good and would direct freedom toward the good.

These issues—the goodness and progress of reason, as well as the possible historical beatification of humanity—were central to Niebuhr's theology. The democratized Augustinian (one might say Madisonian) rapier that Niebuhr thrust into the heart of these Western confidences was that oppression was not principally a matter of external social structures that were always malleable to technical reasons' repair. Rather, the central source of human evil was human, all too human, ingenuity turned against itself by inordinate self-interest that perverted and misused all good things. Moreover, Niebuhr recovered the Augustinian insight that desire was not rationally bound—enough was never enough—because humans had the ability to imagine the infinite, always more, that they were then prone to desire, an insight paralleled in Tillich's understanding of concupiscence. It should be noted that Niebuhr also has a tendency to narrow the Augustinian category of "pride" to "self-interest."[25]

Social arrangements, according to Niebuhr, can do no better than to control and limit inordinate and destructive desires. Importantly, they *can* exercise such control, but one must be aware of the limits of the human character if one is to build workable safeguards into social arrangements.

---

[24]Langdon Gilkey, *Shantung Compound: The Story of Men and Women under Pressure* (New York: Harper & Row Publishers, 1966) 73; hereafter cited as *SC*.

[25]See esp. Reinhold Niebuhr, *Moral Man and Immoral Society* (New York: Charles Scribner's Sons, 1933) 19.

Human societies are in a universal quandary: always they are poised between the twin dangers of anarchy and tyranny. Human societies require a structure of power in order to give the group a center and to prevent Hobbes' war of all against all, which arises from the infinity of desire. On the other hand, the very representatives of power that human beings create in order to contain corrupt desire are similarly infected with sin, and desire ever more power by which to fulfill their own unlimited desires. In this latter point, Niebuhr is closer to James Madison than to Augustine, who maintained that the church was largely exempt from this dilemma.

In *Shantung Compound*, Gilkey brings Niebuhr's weight to bear on the creation of camp civilization. Rather, the experience in Shandong seemed ample confirmation of Niebuhr's insights. The narrow self-interests of the internees frustrated at nearly every turn the attempt to create a workable, fair, and just government. Moreover, far from admitting that their self-interest motivated them, the residents covered their motives (especially to themselves) under a thick, syrupy torrent of moral justification. For example, an American attorney anxiously upheld "legal principle," but denied that he stood on *this* principle because it allowed him to hoard Red Cross rations.[26] Not secularists alone are infected with self-interest. Gilkey directed his deepest loathing against the pious who used religion to cover their selfishness: for example, the liberal missionary family who, for "religious" reasons, would not cede space, gaining the courage to refuse only after prayer.[27] Gilkey follows Niebuhr's interpretation of pride as self-interest and his analysis of the ambiguity of religion:

> I was continually reminded of Reinhold Niebuhr's remark that religion is not the place where the problem of man's egotism is automatically solved. Rather, it is there that the ultimate battle between human pride and God's grace takes place. Insofar as human pride may win that battle, religion can and does become one of the instruments of human sin. But insofar as there the self does meet God and so can surrender to something beyond his own self-interest, religion may provide the one possibility for a much needed and very rare release from our common self-concern.[28]

---

[26]Gilkey, *SC*, 108.
[27]Gilkey, *SC*, 85-87.
[28]Gilkey, *SC*, 193.

What is required, Gilkey concludes, is not simply "religion," which is present in virtually everyone's existence as their "ultimate concern" (a Tillichian definition of religion that Gilkey maintains for the rest of his career). Rather, humans require an ultimate concern that is concerned about that which really is ultimate; otherwise, religion is idolatry, the ultimate worship of a finite good that reflects self-interest:

> While all men are thus religious, by no means are all forms of religion equally creative or uncreative. The common idea that a man's religion is a purely subjective and personal matter, without relevance to his behavior or character is . . . quite false. It separates inward commitment and outward behavior, which are intimately related. It is, in fact the otherwise admirable trait of loyalty to one's family, one's group or nation which, when it becomes central, is the root of much . . . injustice, pride, and selfishness. . . . The only hope in the human situation is that the "religiousness" of men find its true center in God, and not in the many idols which appear in the course of our experience.[29]

In addition, Gilkey endorses Niebuhr's notion that human society is always threatened by the twin evils of anarchy and tyranny. There is an ingeniousness to *Shantung Compound*; if one knows only the "wartime prison" setting, one expects Japanese tyranny in the camp to be the central problem. It was not; rather, the greater difficulty was the constant threat of anarchy, a danger that required the camp government to request interventions and threats of power from the Japanese, who would have preferred to remain uninvolved in the day-to-day management of the camp.[30] The fragility of democratic arrangements for governmental power is also clear, and that threat is also not principally from the Japanese, who lacked a democratic tradition, but from the Westerners who were, one would think, irrevocably committed to democratic government. The internees, however, wanted "one powerful man in whom could be embodied the will of the camp," "a strong leader to represent our needs to the Japanese," whereas the Japanese refused, for their own reasons, to allow this structure of government.[31] Against all "enlightened" humanistic education, anarchy and tyranny alike begin as inward desires, the products of "rational" self-interest and rationalized unlimited desire.

---

[29]Gilkey, *SC*, 233-34.
[30]See Gilkey, *SC*, 79, 141-62.
[31]Gilkey, *SC*, 28.

To turn that which is purely given into creative living, to unite free-dom and destiny, is so much the background of *Shantung Compound* that it may not be surprising that Gilkey includes little explicit discussion of the polarity of destiny and freedom. Still, the terms of his presentation are not these; the polarity of destiny and freedom is a *background* issue. Moreover, Gilkey's polemical thrust is not directed principally toward the ambiguity of freedom, but in the more Niebuhrian direction of the ambi-guities of reason and ingenuity. The problem of freedom and destiny may be the presupposition for Gilkey's insights into the failed creation from nothing of Shandong; but it will take time for that presupposition to gestate into the central focus of his theology. On the other hand, the Western myth of progress, whether rational, libertarian, or both, was placed in sharp relief; Gilkey's claim that "progress" was the false idol, the diseased cultural religion of the West throughout much of the nine-teenth and twentieth centuries, gains its foothold in *Shantung Compound*.

By the close of the 1960s, in both *Naming the Whirlwind* (1969) and *Religion and the Scientific Future* (1970), Gilkey's argument against progressivism began to shift from Niebuhr's emphasis on reason to the underlying presupposition of reason's champion, freedom. In *Naming the Whirlwind*, when Gilkey moved his ontic analysis "into those more uniquely personal, moral, and communal areas of our common experience to see again where it is that the dimension of the sacred reveals itself, and how it shapes ordinary life," he turned to the question of "freedom and autonomy."[32] Gilkey did not depart from the "substantial agreement" in modern thought that "the essence of man lies in his freedom." Among others, Gilkey invoked Whitehead's claim "that each entity finally comes to realization through a self-creativity in freedom."[33] Gilkey, however, did depart from the judgments that freedom is independence and that it is entirely a matter of decision; such claims omit destiny from the ontologi-cal portrait. Gilkey argued that

> we are (fortunately) carried forward by forces far deeper than the intellectual assent to certain standards and the acts of the conscious will in accordance with those standards. In these cases, we may say that our conscious selves discover rather than create or decide upon the direction in which we are as

---

[32]Langdon Gilkey, *Naming the Whirlwind: The Renewal of God-Language* (Indianapolis: Bobbs-Merrill, 1969) 365; hereafter cited as *NW*.

[33]Gilkey, *NW*, 366.

a total self already going. There is destiny as well as conscious freedom in all that we do. Otherwise, there would be little organic unity to our being, little affect or love in our important relations, and little enthusiasm and drive (*eros*) in what we do.[34]

Destiny is not an unfortunate ontological partner of freedom; rather, it is essential and desirable if freedom is to be meaningful.

As we should expect, the category of fate soon rears its head, interrupting any idyllic picture of freedom. Gilkey somewhat more carefully distinguished the categories of destiny and fate, moreover, than he had done in *Maker of Heaven and Earth*. Fate now appears to arise from an excess of freedom that is intent on eliminating destiny: "when men attempt too eagerly to control their destiny, more often than not a more terrible form of fate threatens the very freedom and autonomy they seek." Autonomy, then, "has not conquered either the demons of sin or of fate, nor are we free from their corresponding effects of guilt, anxiety, and the threat of meaninglessness."[35]

In *Religion and the Scientific Future*, Gilkey gives sustained attention to one remarkable triumph of freedom and reason—modern science—and argues that its great accomplishments should not obscure the danger that it poses to the very rationally directed freedom that birthed it. Technology has "the character of fate" for several reasons. First, "the *fact* of the development or further expansion of technology cannot be stopped and is thus quite beyond human control. . . . [I]t is very hard to see how the word 'decision,' so often used by writers on the subject of the uses of science, applies even remotely." Second, "technology represents a modern form of fate because the *shape* or *direction* of this unstoppable expansion is also not under any measure of rational determination or control." Third, in the final act of free human creation turning upon its creators, "technology is a radical symbol for fate because the development and use of technology reveals itself to be the servant, not at all of our rational and moral wisdom, but rather of our bondage, that is, of our more sinful or greedy impulses—of the profit motive, of national pride, and of national or class paranoia."[36]

---

[34]Gilkey, *NW*, 375.

[35]Gilkey, *NW*, 258.

[36]Langdon Gilkey, *Religion and the Scientific Future: Reflections on Myth, Science, and Theology* (New York: Harper and Row Publishers, 1970; repr.: ROSE 2, Macon GA: Mercer University Press, 1981) 93-94.

Such an analysis sounds more fatalistic than it is. Fate is always a question of degrees, as Gilkey's extensive ontological analysis of destiny and freedom in *Reaping the Whirlwind* will make clear. In any event, Gilkey increasingly turns to the tripartite structure of destiny, freedom, fate in order to analyze the situation which any dialectical, correlative theology must confront.[37] That said, Gilkey has not yet committed himself to conceiving of freedom and destiny as *the* fundamental ontological polarity.

III. Freedom, Destiny, Fate: Reaping the Harvest

In *Reaping the Whirlwind*, when Gilkey centralizes his ontological analysis around the polarity of destiny and freedom, his theology stabilizes in such a way that, from the vantage point of the ontological analysis, the next two decades of Gilkey's thought can be considered as a whole. Gilkey maintains in *Reaping the Whirlwind* that the polarity of destiny and freedom is "the most fundamental ontological structure."[38] In *Through the Tempest*, he reiterates that "[h]istory is the outcome of the polarity of destiny and freedom, of situations and conditions, on the one hand, and of our responses to them, on the other."[39] Gilkey not only sustains this focus on destiny and freedom in his later effort at a theology of nature; he expands it to an analogous ontological understanding of the nonhuman natural world. In *Nature, Reality, and the Sacred*, the "five fundamental ontological characteristics of all that is in our experience—of all finite actuality, or in theological language, of all 'created reality' "— are telescoped into the polarity of destiny / givenness / actuality and freedom / possibility. These are the five structures:

> Temporality or passage: the appearance of what is, the vanishing of what is, and the further appearance of what is new.
> The definiteness and determinateness of actuality and the given: what is achieved in process is definite, a new unity in and for itself and so

---

[37]It is worth noting that *Religion and the Scientific Future* introduces the problem of the human relation to nature, which has occupied Gilkey ever more intently during his career.

[38]Langdon Gilkey, *Reaping the Whirlwind: A Christian Interpretation of History* (New York: Seabury Press, 1976) 285; hereafter cited as *RW*.

[39]Langdon Gilkey, *Through the Tempest: Theological Voyages in a Pluralistic Culture*, ed. Jeff B. Pool (Minneapolis: Fortress Press, 1991) 131; hereafter cited as *TT*.

effective beyond itself—and (as characteristic 1 makes clear) then it
vanishes.

Possibility and novelty: there are genuine, relevant possibilities that have not
been actual before. . . . One cannot understand nature as process or
human existence in history as open and intentional without the category
of possibility as a paradoxical aspect of "reality."

Order as "self-maintaining": that is, order as an aspect of the nature and the
behavior of actualities in passage. . . .

Self-determination: in actuality there is a self-constitution at each level of
being, from the spontaneity evident in inorganic existence through self-
direction in organic and social life to the self-choosing and autonomy
of human existence. On each level given conditions (destiny) inexorably
set the terms and limits for spontaneity or freedom. We are never free
to choose more than the possibilities inherent in the given, more than
the possibilities provided by our "destinies"—we can only, as Søren
Kierkegaard said, "choose ourselves."[40]

Modalities of destiny and freedom characterize all created reality—
including the nonhuman. Gilkey's question in *Reaping the Whirlwind*,
whether the " 'process' interpretation" of "historical passage" "can be
successfully applied to other areas of experience and other dimensions of
reality," is answered affirmatively, because historical passage now is itself
extended to the nonhuman natural world.[41]

The "polar" language as well as the choice of the terms "freedom"
and "destiny" to describe one polarity are Tillichian. Whereas for Tillich
the central ontological polarity was that of self / world, however, Gilkey
makes a different choice. In describing the polarity of destiny and
freedom, it is true, Gilkey employs both Tillichian language and
Niebuhr's metaphor of history as a "drama" regularly.[42] Much of his
language is Whiteheadian as well, however. For example, the "deep
ontological interaction of individual and community [Tillich]" is
"veritably a historical doctrine of internal relations [Whitehead]."[43]
Furthermore, Gilkey's persistent employment of the Whiteheadian

---

[40]Langdon Gilkey, *Nature, Reality, and the Sacred: The Nexus of Science and
Religion*, Theology and the Sciences series, ed. Kevin J. Sharpe (Minneapolis: Fortress
Press, 1993) 199-200; hereafter cited as *NRS*.

[41]Gilkey, *RW*, 300.

[42]Gilkey, *RW*, 8.

[43]Gilkey, *RW*, 38.

terminology of "order," "novelty," and "creativity" hints that something differently nuanced may be happening.[44]

In the choice of freedom / destiny rather than world / self, however, the growing influence of Whitehead is most clear. Although the language is Tillichian, the priority is more in conformity with Whitehead than Tillich—in fact, Gilkey gives priority to the very polarity that Tillich had placed third in the three ontological elements (individualization / participation, dynamics / form, freedom / destiny), all of which were subsidiary to the ontological "structure" of self / world.[45] "Process" and "change" become the central categories from which Gilkey understands all life, and God's relation to all life. Why make this move? One difficulty with the polarity of world and self is that it can be conceived without necessary reference to time. It is possible to understand—indeed, most Western philosophical and theological traditions did understand—knowledge, the subject, the aim of existence, or all of these, as atemporal. Gilkey argues that Tillich's theology was always indecisive about whether it would be conceived in the static Greek categories that understood change as incidental and / or the enemy to be conquered, or in dynamic process categories such as Whitehead's. Gilkey identifies the resulting lack of clarity in Tillich's polarity of dynamics and form, redeeming Tillich's unclarity by bringing him closer to Whitehead:

> I suspect (though I do not know) that here Tillich saw new difficulties arising, could not resolve them in terms of his older categories, and so left the matter somewhat cloudy. The first unclear matter has to do with the relation of the polarity of dynamics and form to potentiality. Tillich begins this discussion, one might say, "as Greek." . . . But clearly, Tillich is not satisfied thus merely to reproduce the Greek worldview. . . . Tillich's thought is here itself in process: if new forms arise, then potentiality, and with it relative nonbeing, infect the realm of forms as they do the dynamic principle of becoming. Hence, as Whitehead saw, the more radical ontological contrast lies between settled actuality in the past and possibility or novelty in the future than it does between changing matter and changeless form.[46]

---

[44]See Gilkey, *RW*, chap. 1, in which Gilkey structures his opening discussion of destiny and freedom around these Whiteheadian conceptions (also see Gilkey, *NRS*, 35-76).

[45]Paul Tillich, *Systematic Theology* (Chicago: University of Chicago Press, 1951) 1:168-86.

[46]Langdon Gilkey, *Gilkey on Tillich* (New York: Crossroad Publishing Company, 1990) 90-91; hereafter cited as *GOT*.

It is not that Tillich could not avoid the staticness of Greek form; Gilkey thinks that Tillich's thought moves toward Whitehead's position.[47] Whitehead's analysis clarifies Tillich's, not the reverse; in *Nature, Reality, and the Sacred*, Gilkey interweaves Tillich and Whitehead persistently, commenting that "the ontologies of Tillich and Whitehead are remarkably similar," because Gilkey's Tillich has moved in Whitehead's direction.[48] The prominence of Whitehead and the central place of the historical polarity of destiny and freedom (which allows Gilkey to evade the potentially static implications of several of Tillich's formulations) arise simultaneously.

If it is plausible that Whitehead's thought is the means by which Gilkey locks *time* into the center of his ontological analysis, it might be surprising that Gilkey never identifies himself as a member of a process school or a Whiteheadian. There are, I believe, two reasons for Gilkey's refusal. One is metaphysical. Gilkey suspects that, for Whitehead, "God is clearly not the source of all things but one of the factors among them. It was this that I disagreed with and continue to disagree with."[49] This metaphysical objection lies beyond the scope of this chapter. The second cause for Gilkey's hesitance, however, lies in the center of his treatment of freedom and destiny, namely, that Whitehead did not sufficiently appreciate the ambiguity of "creativity"; he failed to confront the category of "fate" and was, therefore, too much an ontologist and not enough an empirical philosopher of history. Put another way, Whitehead was an unrepentant "progressivist," who maintained with a host of his contemporaries that "the 'ascent' of forms in the process as a whole manifests and so requires the divine immanent purpose."[50] This unreconstructed liberal immanence, however, cannot account for fate's persistence in history, which fate requires a divine transcendence that judges and redeems historical beings. Neither does Whitehead leave a place for the "atoning death of Jesus as the Christ," in which "divine love is . . . known as *agape* as well as reuniting grace."[51]

Indeed, the empirical and metaphysical objections coalesce. Whitehead did not require a transcendent God, because history was unambigu-

---

[47]Gilkey, *GOT*, 91.
[48]Gilkey, *NRS*, 64.
[49]Gilkey, "Theology and Culture," 4; also see idem, *RW*, 306-10.
[50]Gilkey, *NRS*, 22.
[51]Gilkey, *RW*, 317.

ously progressive, extending to higher and more complex forms. Whitehead, despite "his otherwise profound interpretation of life," committed the "Pelagian" error of believing "that the underlying will of the entity, represented by the subjective aim, is a pure and uncompromised aim toward value."[52] This is not, of course, an error simply because Pelagius was declared a heretic, but because he was empirically wrong, as the facts of history testify. If fate is real, freedom perverse, and history thus in need of transcendent meaning, God cannot be *only* one element *within* historical process, but must be both within and transcendent to that process.[53] Despite the considerable value that Gilkey discovers in Whitehead's thought for the clarification of the ontological structures of existence, then, providential immanence (the focus on which is the enduring contribution of liberalism) is always trumped by redemption, Whitehead by Niebuhr and Tillich.[54] The latter are necessary because human freedom is destructive as well as creative, because fate is inevitably intertwined in history with destiny and freedom: the "misuse of freedom in which freedom is itself bound" cannot be described "in ontological terms—for ontology knows only structure and not its misuse."[55]

The dialectical synthesis of Gilkey's neoorthodox and process forbears, however, allows him to maintain many of his abiding perspectives, while simultaneously expanding the reach of his theology. A comprehensive analysis of the fruits of Gilkey's synthesis is out of the question. We can provide, though, two illustrations of the tendency in Gilkey's theology to retain its Niebuhrian and Tillichian roots only to grow new shoots because of the addition of Whiteheadian nutrients: (1) his reaction to various contemporary Christian theological movements (the eschatological theologians and liberation-oriented theologies); and (2) his development of new concentrations in his theological project, especially his theology of nature.

---

[52]Gilkey, *NW*, 385.

[53]Gilkey notes that in the case of "fallen and so . . . guilty freedom . . . the norm of justice appears not as a 'call' or as a 'lure' [Whitehead] but as a judgment" (Gilkey, *RW*, 318; idem, *NW*, 395).

[54]Gilkey, *MHE*, 11. The clearest example of this is the structure of Langdon Gilkey, "Introduction: A Retrospective Glance at My Work," in *The Whirlwind in Culture: Frontiers in Theology: Essays in Honor of Langdon Gilkey*, ed. Donald W. Musser and Joseph L. Price (Bloomington IN: Meyer-Stone Books, 1988) 1-35; also reprinted in this book.

[55]Gilkey, *RW*, 256.

With respect to his theological contemporaries, his response to liberation-oriented theologies, particularly those influenced heavily by Marxism, retains an almost exact parallel with Niebuhr's critique of liberal progressives such as the social gospel movement.[56] Here, one can detect almost none of Gilkey's increased attention to Whitehead.[57] Like Niebuhr, Gilkey can hardly be accused of social quietism, despite his objections to the standard political theologies of his day. Like Niebuhr, therefore, Gilkey wants to provide "another base for a gospel that is social."[58] There are at least two objections to the early political and liberation theologies that spanned roughly the 1960s to the 1980s, and still hold sway in some circles. The radical proclamations—following Marx—of creating a society without "power," Gilkey argues, is fictive. Here, he follows Niebuhr's and Tillich's analyses almost exactly. Power is necessary in order to center the social group; thus, "it is the radically unequal balance of power that is at fault, not the fact or presence of power. Correspondingly, it is by a redress in that balance of power, a gaining of significant power by those who lack it, not by an evacuation of power from the scene, that social justice or 'liberation' will be achieved."[59] As important, some theological radicalism failed to reckon with the polarity of destiny and freedom; it failed to recognize that the "liberators" could not create from nothing, but instead were bound by the limits of old social forms and ways of thinking.[60] Moreover, it located the *origin* of fate and oppression incorrectly in external social structures; but fate is not, "as Marx thought, the *cause* of inner estrangement. Rather it is the inexorable *consequence* of estrangement."[61] Consequently, Gilkey maintains, any effort to liberate us from *sin* in history is doomed at the

---

[56]Most of Gilkey's comments on theologies of liberation predate the collapse of Marxism in 1989, and therefore also the strenuous—and sometimes successful—efforts of liberation theologians to begin anew, without a Marxist crutch.

[57]The same could be said of Gilkey's criticism of the "secular" religion of science (in which Whitehead's progressivism is part of the problem); this criticism is sufficiently grounded in Gilkey's use of Niebuhr's concept of idolatry and Tillich's definition of religion as "ultimate concern." Donald W. Musser analyzes Gilkey's argument in detail later in this book; it needs no further comment here.

[58]Langdon Gilkey, *Society and the Sacred: Toward a Theology of Culture in Decline* (New York: Crossroad Publishing Company, 1981) 48; hereafter cited as *SAS*.

[59]Gilkey, *RW*, 26.

[60]Gilkey, *SAS*, 48-51.

[61]Gilkey, *SAS*, 51.

outset and is likely to produce even more brutal modes of oppression due to the blindness of the "liberators" to their own inward corruption. The task *is* "political liberation," but "not, let us note, a liberation from sin. . . . [I]t is a liberation from the dire consequences of sin, from the fate which sin continually creates."[62] To be sure, "objective social betterment feeds back into *relative* inner transformation," but relative inner transformation is the best that is possible historically.[63] Gilkey—with Niebuhr—believes that any social transformation is likely only if we remain continually aware of its limits. His sympathy with the aims of social liberation impels him to criticize the naïveté of some of its advocates.

If Whitehead's influence does not much impinge on Gilkey's critique of social liberation movements, it does—in concert with Tillich—affect his criticism of the "eschatological theologians." These theologians (the early Pannenberg and Moltmann, Metz, and some Latin American liberation theologians) "pivoted the basic axis of Christian thought and concern from a *vertical* axis relating time and eternity, creatureliness and transcendence, into a *horizontal* axis relating present and future, a godless world of the now with a God whose 'being is future.' "[64] Partially, the interest of these theologians was in theodicy; one could avoid the problem of attaching evil to God if one said that God's being was not exposed in the present, evil situation, but would be manifest in the future eschatological fulfillment: "as eschatological God is not the God of the present."[65] Aside from the logical problem involved, Gilkey's criticism of these theologians is located firmly in his conception of destiny.[66] History is composed of order and novelty, actuality and possibility, destiny and freedom; yet, the eschatological God operates not from possibility but creates the future "*ex nihilo* out of the future."[67] In so "negating the inheritance from the past," eschatological theology "provides no theological grounds for the creative union of destiny and of freedom which is the basis for human political action amidst the possibilities developing out of

---

[62]Gilkey, *SAS*, 51.

[63]Gilkey, *RW*, 286.

[64]Gilkey, *RW*, 229.

[65]Gilkey, *RW*, 231.

[66]"[I]f God is to master every future, has he not also mastered *all* futures, even those of the past and the present, and thus been responsible, as was any 'theistic' God, for all that has happened in history?" (Gilkey, *RW*, 235).

[67]Gilkey, *RW*, 235.

the past and so latent in the social situation of the present."[68] Gilkey's claim is that, contrary to their own intentions, the eschatological theologians, were they self-consistent, could not engage in creative political action, which presupposes precisely that the given—actuality—contains a nonarbitrary range of possibilities for transformation within it. The "ordered" character of the world, fundamental for Whitehead, is also the condition for the possibility of transformative, "novel" action.

If Gilkey's response to his theological contemporaries reflected the influence of the triumvirate of Niebuhr, Tillich, and Whitehead—although in some cases Whitehead's influence was refused—still these disputes were well within Gilkey's long-standing concern for the relation of theology to social thought and action. Perhaps the most significant effect of the influence of Whitehead, however, was to allow Gilkey to forge a path into a theology of nature. Although Gilkey's theology of nature is replete with Niebuhrian and Tillichian themes, it is difficult to see how those alone could have taken Gilkey in this direction.[69] Niebuhr, for his part, maintained a fairly sharp division between the natural and human world, and made almost no effort to cast his theological glance—to say nothing of his conclusions—in the direction of nonhuman nature.[70] Tillich was a more subtle case. Tillich's analysis—in the third volume of his *Systematic Theology*—of the homologies of being, the analogies that are both possible and inevitable between humans and nature, do provide a possible doorway through which Gilkey's theology of nature can enter. Still, Tillich's discussion of the homologies is simultaneously expansive and tentative. In finding analogies between inorganic, organic, animal, and human life everywhere, he provides no focus for future theological investigations. That focus is provided, as we have seen, when Gilkey moves Tillich nearer to Whitehead and ensconces destiny and freedom as the fundamental ontological structure. The analogy between human and nonhuman nature now has a focus, which *Nature, Reality, and the Sacred* uses as its theological basis: the common passage of all entities through history and time, the lack of absolute-other determination for any of

---

[68]Gilkey, *RW*, 236.

[69]It is true, of course, that Gilkey was for a long time involved in a dialectical criticism of science, largely on the strength of Tillich's conception of religion and the religious substance of culture. To treat the practitioners of a discipline theologically, however, is a different matter than dealing with their subject matter.

[70]Niebuhr's discussion of "vitality" is a partial exception.

them, the persistence of order and novelty throughout all ontic realities. In his theology of nature, Gilkey is indebted to each of his forbears, but to none of them more than Whitehead.

Gilkey enjoyed Lois Gehr Livezey's characterization of his theology as one of "Tillichian categories with Niebuhrian sentiments."[71] Although that description is undeniably true, the privilege that Gilkey gives to the ontological polarity of destiny and freedom belies another influence—Whitehead. Gilkey acknowledge's Whitehead's influence, of course, but with a certain tentativeness. His hesitance is unnecessary. Indeed, his addition of Whitehead to his Niebuhrian-Tillichian theological framework gives clarity to Gilkey's theological career. In Gilkey's own opinion, "[i]f you've gone to your reward, people begin to talk about the 'early stage' and the 'later stage.' Fortunately, for now, it's only 'confused.' "[72] Regarding the judgment of confusion, if we acknowledge the growing influence of Whitehead's thought, we are entitled to affectionate dissent.

---

[71]Gilkey, "Theology and Culture," 3.
[72]Gilkey, "Theology and Culture," 2.

Chapter 3

Beyond Postliberal Foundationalism:
The Theological Method of Langdon Gilkey

Jeff B. Pool

Steering a Course: The Secret of Method

In this chapter, I examine the *practice* and *theory* of Langdon Gilkey's strategy for producing relevant Christian theology.[1] In order to understand

---

[1]Regardless of Gilkey's numerous and sophisticated discussions of theological method, he has consistently warned his contemporaries against excessive preoccupation with questions of theological method (or concern primarily with *how to do* theology), thereby failing *to do* theology itself. "Theology must cease speaking entirely about itself, i.e., about method, and begin to talk about its essential object: the historical life of men and women *coram deo* and in community—for good or for ill—with one another" (Langdon Gilkey, "Theology and the Future," *Andover Newton Quarterly* 17 [March 1977]: 255). In another essay, Gilkey described the preoccupation with method as "the present temptation lying in wait for the contemporary theologian, especially one in a major university graduate school." "This is the temptation to linger so long in the preparatory enterprise of hermeneutical method, of answering the question of how to go about doing theology, that the theologian never in fact realizes, re-presents, or reexpresses a single aspect of the original message. Let us remember that a modern and contemporary method of constructive theology, however brilliant it may be, is not itself the gospel or even a modern, contemporary reinterpretation of the gospel, and that the problems that a method of theological inquiry faces in the academic community are not the same as the problems that wrack and threaten to destroy the world's existence. Thus, doing theological method is not yet doing theology, however much it may seem in academia that the two are one and the same. As with getting in shape, the concentration on method is important and necessary, but it is not the same as running the race that must be run" (Langdon Gilkey, "Theology as the Interpretation of Faith for Church and World," in *The Vocation of the Theologian*, ed. Theodore W. Jennings, Jr. [Philadelphia: Fortress Press, 1985], 96; also reprinted in Langdon Gilkey, *Through the Tempest: Theological Voyages in a Pluralistic Culture*, ed. Jeff B. Pool [Minneapolis: Fortress Press, 1991] 43; hereafter cited as *TT*). In response to papers on his thought presented during a conference commemorating his retirement in 1989 ("Theology and Culture: Engaging Langdon Gilkey's Thought," 14-15 April 1989, The University of Chicago Divinity School; conference announcement in *Criterion* 27 [Autumn 1988]: 26), Gilkey admitted that even he has fallen victim to the temptation to talk about method instead of doing theology. Gilkey added, however, "[b]ut I have tried to say nonetheless that instead you should think about what you intend to think about. Then, begin to think about how you've done this specific piece of thinking. In other words, be as careful as you can, as wise as you can, and only *then* think about what it is you've just done. Then you'll write a good piece on method. But if you *start* with method, you'll never get down to real thinking" (Langdon Gilkey, "Theology and Culture: Reflections on the Conference," *Criterion* 28 [Autumn 1989]: 4). Gilkey certainly had

the most prominent features in his mature theological method, I trace the *development* of that method, steering a course especially with repeated reference to one significant marker: Gilkey's changing perspective on natural theology. Taking bearings from Gilkey's evolving posture toward natural theology helps to identify significant shifts in the development of his theological method and, finally, serves as the key in my characterization of his method as *postliberal foundationalism*. I punctuate this study of Gilkey's theological method with critical observations as his shifting perspectives alert me to problems or questions. I aim principally, however, to discern the movement and basic character of his theological method. I offer this interpretation as a friendly critic, after having observed as carefully as possible that which Gilkey has described as the "first rule of criticism," trying to understand and describe his perspective fairly.[2]

---

followed this procedure himself in several of his books. In his first book, Gilkey reserved his fullest discussion of methodological concerns for the last chapter: *Maker of Heaven and Earth: A Study of the Christian Doctrine of Creation* (Garden City NY: Doubleday, 1959) 319-60; hereafter cited as *MHE*. In his second book, he repeated this pattern: *How the Church Can Minister to the World without Losing Itself* (New York: Harper & Row Publishers, 1964) 128-46; hereafter cited as *HCCM*. Again, even in his fifth book, he followed this same pattern of reserving methodological issues for his final chapter: *Religion and the Scientific Future: Reflections on Myth, Science, and Theology* (New York: Harper & Row Publishers, 1970; London: SCM Press, 1970; repr.: ROSE 2, Macon GA: Mercer University Press, 1981) 101-36; hereafter cited as *RSF*. Although always keenly aware of methodological issues, Gilkey's most extensive attention to method only *began to appear* in his fourth book (Langdon Gilkey, *Naming the Whirlwind: The Renewal of God-Language* [Indianapolis: Bobbs-Merrill Company, 1969]; hereafter cited as *NW*), nonetheless, still *after* his initial theological interpretations of the Christian doctrines of (1) creation (*MHE*), (2) church (*HCCM*), and (3) sin (*Shantung Compound: The Story of Men and Women under Pressure* [New York: Harper & Row Publishers, 1966]; hereafter cited as *SC*).

[2]Langdon Gilkey, "Responses to Peter Berger," *Theological Studies* 39 (September 1978): 496. Among the numerous assessments of Gilkey's theological method, see the following studies: Brian J. Walsh, *Langdon Gilkey: Theologian for a Culture in Decline* (Lanham NY: University Press of America, 1991) esp. 3-67; Thomas B. Ommen, "Verification in Theology: A Tension in Revisionist Method," *The Thomist* 43 (July 1979): 357-84; William Thompson, "Theology's Method and Linguistic Analysis in the Thought of Langdon Gilkey," *The Thomist* 36 (July 1972): 363-94; J. Wesley Robbins, "Professor Gilkey and Alternative Methods of Theological Construction," review of *Naming the Whirlwind*, in *Journal of Religion* 52 (January 1972): 84-101; Ted Peters, "The Whirlwind as Yet Unnamed," *Journal of the American Academy of Religion* 42 (December 1974): 699-709; Gordon Stanley Kane, "God-Language and Secular Experience," *International Journal for Philosophy of Religion* 2 (Summer 1971): 78-95;

I will develop the following argument about the contours and character of Gilkey's theological method on the basis of a twofold thesis. Without a doubt and as Gilkey himself has often claimed, his method has possessed a correlational character since he began writing and teaching theology. For him, this method has most generally entailed the correlation of answers in the Christian message to the questions raised by the problems and issues of human existence.[3]

(1) First, without aiming to defend the obvious validity of the previous claim about Gilkey's method, a more general thesis will guide my study of Gilkey's theological method: *Gilkey has altered key features of this correlational theological approach across the course of his career, in light of the results from his continual employment of that theological strategy of correlating the questions of human existence with the answers of the Christian message.* As Gilkey has said, "perhaps the secret of method is to make the variety of category, of symbol and of argument fit the complexity of the object of understanding."[4] The most prominent features in the present form of Gilkey's theological method have resulted from Gilkey's consistent application of that method to *itself,* in his efforts adequately to interpret the object of theological understanding. *Thus, a reflexive mechanism in Gilkey's theological method has repeatedly submitted even the method itself to critical scrutiny and revision.*[5] Further-

---

Thomas E. Hosinski, "Experience and the Sacred: A Retrospective Review of Langdon Gilkey's Theology," *Religious Studies Review* 11 (July 1985): 228-35.

[3]This claim, of course, I neither need nor intend to defend: Gilkey makes this claim about his own work. Furthermore, one may easily discern and trace some version of this correlational theological approach in all of Gilkey's work. Gilkey humbly admits, for example, that "[q]uite unintentionally, therefore, my thought has reflected a 'correlational' approach: as when a sailboat hugs a massive but variegated shoreline, its course has been determined by the twists and turns of twentieth-century events" (Langdon Gilkey, "Introduction: A Retrospective Glance at My Work," in *The Whirlwind in Culture: Frontiers in Theology: In Honor of Langdon Gilkey,* ed. Donald W. Musser and Joseph L. Price [Bloomington, Indiana: Meyer-Stone Books, 1988] 1). This characteristic of his theology, as it adjusts its course to the changes in the contemporary situation or context, serves as part of the background to my argument in this chapter.

[4]Langdon Gilkey, *Reaping the Whirlwind: A Christian Interpretation of History* (New York: Seabury Press, 1976) 128; hereafter cited as *RW*.

[5]This becomes most obvious in Gilkey's recent versions of theological method, which one might describe as the dialectical or, as David Tracy describes it, the mutually critical correlation of interpretations of both Christian message and human existence (see David Tracy, *Blessed Rage for Order: The New Pluralism in Theology* [New York: Seabury Press, 1975] 32-34, 79-81). For example, Gilkey illustrates this by comparing his method

more, the consistent operation of this reflexive mechanism defines one central aspect of the continuity in Gilkey's theological approach, despite the alterations in his theology across the course of his career due to his use of this method.[6] Although not a complex thesis, by demonstrating the

---

of correlation with the correlative theological method of David Tracy. "The difference . . . is that whereas with Tracy the two analyses are relatively independent endeavors, phenomenological on the one hand and hermeneutical on the other, the results being correlated in transcendental or in his case metaphysical analysis . . . , ours stipulates (1) that 'common human experience' is not to be understood except in abstracto until it is comprehended by means of the symbols derivative from the Christian fact, nor (2) are these symbols appropriable by modern minds until they have been reinterpreted in the light of 'common modern experience.' Thus is our 'method' relatively jumbled, our analyses more intertwined, and the 'correlation' with regard to both meaning and truth achieved—if at all—at the level not either of prolegomena nor of fundamental theology, but only at the level of constructive theology when the entire spectrum of Christian symbols is applied interpretatively to the entire width of 'common human experience' " (Gilkey, RW, 373n.1). Elsewhere, in his most recent overview of his own work, Gilkey refers to his theological method as "a symptom and not a cause of a more basic pattern of thinking, namely to ponder the character of our existence, both personal and historical, before God in the light of the historical and social situation, the massive contours of events, in which we find ourselves." He says that his "life work reflects a dialectic of message and existence" (Gilkey, "Retrospective Glance at My Work," 1). Specifically in reference to Tracy's revisionist theology, Gilkey notes that, frequently, people had asked him if he considered himself "to be a 'revisionist theologian.' " Gilkey playfully says, "On thinking carefully about this, I have realized that unquestionably I am. Every time I read something I have written before, I think to myself, 'That *really* needs revision!' " (Langdon Gilkey, *Message and Existence: An Introduction to Christian Theology* [New York: Seabury Press, 1981] 19n.2; hereafter cited as *ME*).

[6]According to Paul Tillich, "[s]ystematic theology uses the method of correlation. It has always done so, sometimes more, sometimes less, consciously, and must do so consciously and outspokenly, especially if the apologetic point of view is to prevail. The method of correlation explains the contents of the Christian faith through existential questions and theological answers in mutual interdependence" (Paul Tillich, *Systematic Theology* [Chicago: University of Chicago Press, 1951] 1:60). Walter Lowe has explored "the possibility of an alternative to the theological method of correlation," without offering, as he admits, an *actual* alternative theological method: he has addressed, therefore, a sort of transcendental question to the correlational methods of theologians like Paul Tillich, Langdon Gilkey, and David Tracy. Furthermore, he followed a very pertinent path of inquiry through this exploration. "Criticism of the method is left with only the slightest toehold, in the form of a misgiving—can this really be the *only* viable method? Can it be that correlation, which is so committed to pluralism and dialogue, does not itself have an 'other'?" Lowe has directed much of his argument "against an ideological monism which would suppress difference" (Walter Lowe, *Theology and Difference: The Wound of Reason*, Indiana Series in the Philosophy of Religion, ed. Merold Westphal [Bloomington: Indiana University Press, 1993] xii, xiii). Lowe's concerns, of course, exhibit another version of criticisms made by George Lindbeck against the perspective that he construes as the "experiential-expressivist" theory of religion (see George A.

validity of this argument, I hope also simultaneously to underscore two of the most important qualities of Gilkey's theology: its *boldness* as well as its *humility*.

Thus, I will trace the development of Gilkey's theological method, with special attention to the ways in which Gilkey has applied that method to itself, its reflexive operations, through which he has altered prominent features in his correlative strategy for doing Christian theology. Paul Tillich perceived the need for theological method to remain open to revision and, hence, to avoid "methodological imperialism," a wisdom

---

Lindbeck, *The Nature of Doctrine: Religion and Theology in a Postliberal Age* [Philadelphia: Westminster Press, 1984] esp. 46-72). Lowe's questions about correlational method, naturally, resemble William H. Willimon's caricature of liberal (correlational?) theology as "quite imperialistic" (William H. Willimon, "Answering Pilate: Truth and the Postliberal Church," *Christian Century* 104 [28 January 1987]: 82). Lowe's questions, nonetheless, rightly deserve the most serious attention. With Lowe's aim, I agree. In this chapter, however, I do not intend *either to argue* that Gilkey's correlative method fundamentally suppresses difference through an ideological monism *or explicitly to defend* Gilkey's version of correlative method against the charge that it does suppress difference. Nonetheless, were I to address such an issue, I would contend rather that, despite certain weaknesses in Gilkey's theory and practice of theological method, the character of the reflexive mechanism in his theological method supplies the key for responding to Lowe's line of inquiry. Perhaps the only evidence of correlative method's other or alternative theological method are the additional features in Gilkey's correlative method that have resulted from the transformation of that method through its reflexive application, its work upon itself in light of both the changing realities of the situation and the plurality among the Christian traditions themselves. While one might not so easily identify the methodo- logical alternative to correlation, one can discern the refusal by Gilkey's correlative method of an ideological monism that suppresses difference, in the method's application to itself or its reflexive operations. As a preliminary critical response to Lowe's line of inquiry, however, a correlative theologian might rightly wonder how Lowe's possible alternative would be something other than some form of Barthian approach, an alternative much more likely to suppress difference through ideological monism than a correlative approach. David Tracy notes that "Christian theology today is marked by a great divide," which he identifies as Christianity's "intense internal conflict over its proper response to modernity" or, more specifically, as "a conflict between two basic theological strategies on the proper Christian response to modernity": the conflict between the strategies of correlational theologies and the strategies of revelation-based theologies (David Tracy, foreword to *God Without Being: Hors-Texte*, by Jean-Luc Marion, trans. Thomas A. Carlson, Religion and Postmodernism Series, ed. Mark C. Taylor [Chicago: University of Chicago Press, 1991] ix-x). Would not Tracy's openness to such revelation-based strategies (as illustrated, for example, by his appreciative foreword to Marion's book) and even Gilkey's initial employment of a Niebuhrian version of a revelation-based strategy (as well as his retention of several basic features from that Niebuhrian neoorthodoxy, as I will later argue) indicate something about the theological strategy of correlation quite other than an ideological monism that suppresses difference and eschews an other?

that the development of Gilkey's theological method beautifully illustrates: "Whether or not a method is adequate cannot be decided *apriori*; it is continually being decided in the cognitive process itself."[7] Gilkey has claimed, on the one hand, that his own theological perspective originated as he embraced and elaborated the neoorthodox theology of Reinhold Niebuhr. On the other hand, he has also claimed in more recent years that his own theological perspective owes more to the theology of Paul Tillich than to his original Niebuhrian neoorthodoxy. Even more recently, he has described the development in his thought as "a movement from Niebuhr to Tillich to Eliade—who is much closer to who I am at the present time."[8] Nonetheless, and despite the character of his current engagement in interreligious dialogues, I will also argue that Gilkey's theology remains essentially neoorthodox or postliberal, but in a highly qualified sense. For, I will identify Gilkey's own addition of a fourth and very significant name to the previous trinity: Alfred North Whitehead. Under the influence of Whitehead's thought, Gilkey altered his postliberal theology with a foundationalism (however transformed), in a way that prepared him for the next leg of his voyage to Eliade. In this light, I will

---

[7]Tillich, *Systematic Theology* 1:60.

[8]Gilkey, "Retrospective Glance at My Work," 13; idem, "Namer and Tamer of the Whirlwind," interview by Kendig Brubaker Cully, *The New Review of Books and Religion* 2 (February 1978): 3; idem, *Gilkey on Tillich* (New York: Crossroad Pub. Co., 1990) xiv-xv; hereafter cited as *GOT*; idem, "An Appreciation of Karl Barth," in *How Karl Barth Changed My Mind*, ed. Donald K. McKim (Grand Rapids MI: Eerdmans, 1986) 150; idem, "Theology and Culture: Reflections on the Conference," 3. Despite Gilkey's insistence on the largely Niebuhrian character of his earliest theology, one sees even in his first book, *Maker of Heaven and Earth*, an oscillation between his reliance on Niebuhr's thought and his use of Tillich's categories, even though Niebuhr's influence clearly dominates (e.g., *MHE*, 317-60). See L. Harold DeWolf's discussion of this issue in his review of Gilkey's first book: L. Harold DeWolf, "Creation, as Viewed by Science, Philosophy, and Theology: A Review Article," *Religion in Life* 29 (Winter 1959–1960): 132-33. Of course, even in the preface to *Maker of Heaven and Earth*, Gilkey acknowledges his gratitude to both Niebuhr and Tillich. "First of all I wish to thank my two teachers at Union Theological Seminary, Reinhold Niebuhr and Paul Tillich, who have laid the theological foundations for so many of us who were their students and are their friends. To Dr. Niebuhr especially I owe my own first interest in theology as well as the fundamental bent of my thought. My indebtedness, both personal and intellectual, to each of these men is better revealed by these chapters than by inadequate words of preface" (*MHE*, vii). This dual influence has continued to inspire Gilkey. He dedicated *Reaping the Whirlwind* to both of his former teachers: "there is hardly a page of this volume that does not represent the insights of one or of both of these two thinkers, and thus is this volume appropriately dedicated in gratitude to the memory of both of them" (*RW*, viii).

retrace the course of Gilkey's voyage from his Niebuhrian theological orientation to that which he describes as his more recent Eliadian perspective.

(2) As the concrete support for my broader and more general guiding thesis or argument about Gilkey's theological method, this study will argue a second major, yet far more specific (and complex) thesis: *the movement in Gilkey's method between his Niebuhrian and Eliadian perspectives has occurred in five major stages, culminating in the present form of Gilkey's theological method, a postliberal foundationalism radically altered in light of the plurality of religions as parity.* As I have structured this chapter, however, the first stage in the development of Gilkey's theological method actually provides a background to Gilkey's theological development: I have referred to it as the liberal Baptist Christian social matrix of Gilkey's theological method. This stage in the development of Gilkey's theological orientation most certainly represents the port from which Gilkey embarked. In the second stage, Gilkey adopts a Niebuhrian neoorthodoxy or postliberalism. A third stage in the evolution of Gilkey's theological method represents a transitional stage: from a Niebuhrian to a Tillichian postliberalism or neoorthodoxy. Building on the previous stage, in a fourth stage, Gilkey again transforms his theological method, with grafts from Whitehead's process philosophy, into a postliberal foundationalism. As a fifth stage, Gilkey's engagement with religious plurality modifies quite strikingly Gilkey's theological method into its present form, as condensed into the emblematic phrase, the relative-absolute.

I. Liberal Baptist Christian Social Matrix

One cannot adequately account for the development of Gilkey's theological method, however, without some understanding of his religious background, the matrix for his earliest Christian experience. Langdon Gilkey proudly and gratefully remembers his heritage as the son of liberal Baptist Christian parents. Gilkey describes his mother, Geraldine Brown Gilkey, as "an early feminist." He also recounts that his father, Charles Whitney Gilkey, who served as minister of Hyde Park Baptist Church and professor in the University of Chicago Divinity School, later became the Dean of Rockefeller Chapel at the University of Chicago.[9]

---

[9]Gilkey, "Retrospective Glance at My Work," 3. Hyde Park Baptist Church in

Even Gilkey explicitly acknowledges a significant indebtedness to the liberal Christian ethos and concerns of his boyhood home: "this inheritance . . . made its permanent imprint on my conscience and has never ceased to provide the foundation for whatever has been good in my makeup." Gilkey summarizes this liberal Christian influence on himself, in the shape that it assumed during his years as a university student, as his commitment to "two moral absolutes, peace and justice."[10] One should not underestimate the influence of this liberal Christian matrix on Langdon Gilkey's thought. This background supplied resources that eventually and essentially contributed to the practical quality of Gilkey's systematic and constructive theology, with its emphasis upon experience, both personal and social. Nevertheless, I neither propose a psychosocial comparison of Langdon Gilkey's thought to the thought of his father, Charles Gilkey, nor identify his father's theology as a direct causal factor in the development of Langdon Gilkey's thought. A brief sketch of a few facets from the thought and career of Charles Gilkey, however, will illustrate my claim about the liberal matrix from which Langdon Gilkey's theological method originated.

Chicago participated in the Northern Baptist Convention (now the American Baptist Churches/U.S.A.) not in the Southern Baptist Convention. See also Gilkey's loving respect for the religion of his parents in a letter (published anonymously), through which he reflected on the meaning of the gospel during his own experience of his mother's death (Langdon Gilkey, "In Faith . . . Praise, Thanksgiving and Joy," *Christianity and Crisis* 16 [10 December 1956]: 168-69; see a reference by Gilkey to this letter in Langdon Gilkey, "Anathemas and Orthodoxy: A Reply to Avery Dulles," *Christian Century* 94 [9 November 1977]: 1027).

[10]Gilkey, "Retrospective Glance at My Work," 4, 6. Not insignificantly, Gilkey later dedicated his book on *ecclesiology* to his parents (Gilkey, *HCCM*, iv). Although more implicitly, Langdon Gilkey's work also indicates a debt to the *Baptist* Christian ethos of his family, and even to the Baptist ethos of the University of Chicago in the 1920s. In this connection, see Gilkey's brief reflection on the now long vanished Baptist presence in the faculty and administration of the University of Chicago: Langdon Gilkey, "The Christian Congregation as a Religious Community," in *American Congregations*, vol. 2, *New Perspectives in the Study of Congregations*, ed. James P. Wind and James W. Lewis (Chicago: University of Chicago Press, 1994) 131n.10. Gilkey also refers to his "Baptist ancestors in Rhode Island and Maine" (Langdon Gilkey, "Religion and Culture: A Persistent Problem," *Journal of Mormon History* 12 [1985]: 31).

A. Priority of Experience to Doctrine

First, in his sermons and reflections about Christianity, Charles Gilkey consistently emphasized the *priority of experience to doctrine*. He sounded this theme quite clearly in lectures on the person and ministry of Jesus that he delivered to students in India in 1925.

> What he [Jesus] has given men in religion is not a definition of God, an argument, or even a doctrine about him, a reasoned proof of his existence, or even (except in a secondary and derived sense) a new conception of him. What he has given us is something much rarer and more valuable than any of these. It is an experience of God so deep and constant and revealing that we might better call it a life with God. We search in vain through Jesus' teaching for what others—without ever being quite able to put the eternal question beyond a peradventure of intellectual doubt—have nevertheless given us in abundance: abstract argument, formal definition, attempted conclusive proof.[11]

Charles Gilkey's emphasis on experience reflected his keen concern that religion should have practical (not merely cognitive) significance for human life, both personally and socially. Like many others, he insisted that, "[n]ot . . . the logical consistency of its [religion's] doctrines or even the efficiency of its institutions," but "its power to lift individual lives to new levels of quality" was "the truest test of religion in every generation."[12]

Despite Langdon Gilkey's later genuine, careful concerns with theological concepts, as *both* adequate to the Christian traditions *and* conceptually coherent and consistent, his theology has consistently indicated its essential relationship to human experience, with a special sense of theology's political dimensions.[13] This becomes apparent in Langdon

---

[11]Charles Whitney Gilkey, *Jesus and Our Generation*, Barrows Lectures Series 1924–1925 (Chicago: University of Chicago Press, 1925) 64-65.

[12]Charles W. Gilkey, "The Truest Test of Religion," in *Perspectives* (New York: Harper & Brothers, 1933) 58. He published this book of sermons while he was Dean of Rockefeller Chapel at the University of Chicago.

[13]"He also claims an affinity with the theology of liberation, or eschatological theology. *Reaping the Whirlwind* was partly inspired by it and partly critical of it. 'I'd like to put the inspiration first. Since my father (a sometime chaplain of the University of Chicago) was a social gospeller, and it was Reinhold Niebuhr who got me into theology, the idea that theology is related to politics is by no means a new idea to me' " (Kendig Brubaker Cully and Gilkey, "Namer and Tamer of the Whirlwind," 3).

Gilkey's earliest theological work, dependent as it was on Reinhold Niebuhr's neoorthodox thought.

B. Baptist Christian Experience

Second, Charles Gilkey's theological emphasis on the priority of experience to doctrine did not originate *only* from his liberal Christian perspective with its focus on the social significance of the gospel. His insistence on this point derived its forcefulness equally as much from his *Baptist Christian experience* as from his theological liberalism. Evidence for this claim appears most prominently in his comments about characteristics of Baptist identity. He drew a contrast between, on the one hand, the "history of religious authoritarianism and totalitarianism" and, on the other hand, "our distinctive Baptist witness to the spiritual competence of the individual soul before God," "our Baptist protest against all binding man-made creeds," and "our Baptist appeal, against all dictatorship in church and state, to God as the sole Lord of the conscience, mind, and spirit of man." He especially affirmed the Baptist protest against binding creeds, either as criteria for membership in Baptist churches or as the basis for the unity of the many churches and denominations. Rather, as he put it, "[w]e Baptists put our faith and hope for the Christian church of the future, not in required creeds, but in the Holy Spirit as a living bond of Christian fellowship." Even earlier in his career, Charles Gilkey had drawn a similar critical contrast between organized, formulaic, institutional religion and Jesus, directing his audiences to the person of Jesus himself.[14]

---

[14]Charles W. Gilkey, "The Distinctive Baptist Witness," *The Chronicle* 8 (July 1945): 102, 105; cf. Gilkey, "Wishful Thinking in Religion," in *Perspectives*, 19; idem, *Jesus and Our Generation*, 27, 28, 53. Charles Gilkey succinctly makes this point also in another sermon: "the Christian religion . . . finds its clearest revelation of the meaning of human life, and of the character and purpose of God Himself, not in a creed or a book or an institution, but in a *person*: in the life of Jesus" (Gilkey, "Refining Religion," in *Perspectives*, 94-95). At least early in his career, Langdon Gilkey continued to identify himself with the Baptist tradition (broadly understood) as he experienced it in the Northern Baptist Convention or the American Baptist Churches/U.S.A. (also, see Gilkey, "Retrospective Glance at My Work," 15). Gilkey acknowledged this, while explicitly differentiating his heritage from that of the Southern Baptist Convention, in correspondence with several members of Mercer University's faculty and administration during the Elliott controversy at Midwestern Baptist Theological Seminary in the early 1960s: see Langdon B. Gilkey, Vanderbilt University Divinity School (Nashville, Tennessee), to Prof. Edwin D. Johnston, Mercer University (Macon, Georgia), 7 November 1962 (the files of

C. Human Freedom

Third, Charles Gilkey, remaining consistent with both the liberalism of his theological training and his Baptist heritage, gave a place of prominence to the *role of human freedom* in personal and social experience. While Gilkey wholeheartedly affirmed God's initiative in human salvation

---

Langdon B. Gilkey; Charlottesville, Virginia). Gilkey also refers to the Elliott controversy elsewhere: Langdon Gilkey, "The Authority of the Bible: The Relation of the Bible to the Church," *Encounter* 27 (Spring 1966): 120; idem, *HCCM*, 42, 42n.13. As Langdon Gilkey mentions in the letter to faculty members at Mercer University, he was even at that time still a member of Hyde Park Baptist Church in Chicago. For a brief discussion of the Elliott Controversy, see Jeff B. Pool, "Chief Article of Faith: The Preamble of *The Baptist Faith and Message (1963)*," in *Sacred Mandates of Conscience: Interpretations of The Baptist Faith and Message*, ed. Jeff B. Pool (Macon GA: Smyth & Helwys Publishing, 1997) 39. See Elliott's own account of this controversy as well: Ralph H. Elliott, *The "Genesis Controversy" and Continuity in Southern Baptist Chaos: A Eulogy for a Great Tradition* (Macon GA: Mercer University Press, 1992).

In an article on Baptists, Langdon Gilkey also notes that, due to certain historic emphases of Baptists, their history has manifested "startlingly opposite characteristics." (1) On the one hand, due to their emphasis on a literal interpretation of the Christian scriptures, a "strict puritan (or Victorian) ethic," and "the absolute necessity of personal faith and personal holiness," "most" Baptists have remained "conservative even fundamentalist, in matters of both faith and morals." The commitments of this first trajectory have produced several results among Baptists: (a) impatience with theological compromises, whether with science, philosophy, or liberal politics; (b) refusal "to join the ecumenical movement in any official way"; (c) ignoring the social gospel; and (d) retention of "a deep loyalty to the efficacy of individualistic revivalism." (2) On the other hand, due to "their emphasis on freedom of conscience and personal believing, on the importance of Christian life and works rather than on ritual, on their distaste for creeds, dogmas, and ecclesiastical authority, Baptists have *also* been leaders in theological and social liberalism." As examples of results from this second characteristic trajectory, Gilkey mentions the following items: (a) Walter Rauschenbusch as the first and most powerful theological proponent of the social gospel; (b) Morgan Park Seminary (a Baptist school originally located in Morgan Park, Illinois, a suburb of Chicago), which became the Divinity School of the University of Chicago, as "the first theological center in this country explicitly to be founded on the principles of the critical and historical study of the Bible and Church history"; (c) "many Baptist seminaries and churches" known for "their liberal theology, style of worship, and social attitudes"; and (d) Baptists as "consistently important leaders in the establishment of the ecumenical movement of the early twentieth century" (*The Academic American Encyclopedia* [Princeton NJ: Arete Pub. Co., 1979], s.v. "The Baptists," by Langdon Gilkey, 3:73-74). Insofar as he has continued to identify with Baptists at all, Langdon Gilkey has followed the second trajectory in Baptist life and thought.

and spiritual growth, he also reminded his congregations that "part of the responsibility is our own." From the teaching of Jesus, Gilkey noted "certain readjustments which we may make in our own lives, that will increase our spiritual capacity and make more sensitive our spiritual hearing": (1) "humility of spirit"; (2) "persistent eagerness of desire"; and (3) "daily determination to do the will of God."[15] Rather than construing the Christian life as obedience to divine commands or rules, however, Gilkey spoke about *God's gift of principles* to guide people in their various situations and changing circumstances, principles that people in their freedom apply to the different experiences of life. For Charles Gilkey, in this sense, Jesus most clearly stated the basis for life as a Christian, when he summarized God's aim in divine revelation as the human's complete love of God and love of neighbor as self. Thus, Gilkey referred to Jesus's teaching as "one fundamental principle with a double application," rather than as rule, law, or command. For Gilkey, a person might follow a list of rules or laws to the letter and still leave the spirit of those rules completely unfulfilled. Thus, for him, God risked giving principles to people in their freedom, in order to encourage genuine love and authentic human life from their voluntary application of those principles in their daily experiences.[16]

D. Revisionist Character of Religion

Fourth, Charles Gilkey highlighted *the "revisionist" character of religion*, rather than its conservationist tendencies. Accordingly, religion "bids men revise and revise yet again, not only their thoughts of God as these show themselves to be inadequate in the light of advancing knowledge and deepening insight, but also and no less the direction of their living, as His greater and worthier purposes are more fully made known to them." Perhaps in light of this very conviction (also very likely as much a result of his Baptist heritage as of his liberal theological education), Charles

---

[15]Gilkey, "Spiritual Understanding," in *Perspectives*, 82.

[16]Gilkey, *Jesus and Our Generation*, 44-45, 47. To illustrate this viewpoint, Charles Gilkey referred to his own then six-year-old son, Langdon. He compared, on the one hand, giving his son two rules to follow with, on the other hand, giving him a single principle, concluding his illustration with the following comments. "In every situation he has had to think for himself as to what the right thing to do is, and to summon up his strength to do it. My principle is teaching my boy to grow up into the kind of man I most want him to be" (Gilkey, *Jesus and Our Generation*, 38-40).

Gilkey suggested that God's activity did not cease with the founding events of Christian religion itself.[17]

Obviously, one might discover even more in the life and thought of Charles Gilkey that would illumine various aspects of Langdon Gilkey's thought. Furthermore, I admit reluctance to suggest any strict correlation between the theologies of father and son. The previous facets from the theology of Charles Gilkey, however, disclose a significant core of the ethos that nurtured the religious sensibility of Langdon Gilkey, as even he has often acknowledged. Although I will not trace the reappearance of these themes in the theology of Langdon Gilkey at this point, they will reappear in various ways as this study progresses.

In spite of the profound influence of his family's religion on him, as Langdon Gilkey admits, during his studies as a student at Harvard University, he came to doubt the value of religion itself, retaining only an unswerving commitment to the most concrete social values of peace and justice. Nonetheless, as Gilkey has confessed, he experienced even the collapse of his own highest moral ideals or his very world, in light of both his cynical intellectualism and the global crises that eventually led

---

[17]Gilkey, "Wishful Thinking in Religion," in *Perspectives*, 21; emphasis mine. Although Charles Gilkey does not discuss other religious traditions extensively, he states something near to this possibility in his discussion of distinctive Baptist beliefs. "We cannot believe that the working of God in history stopped at any date long ago, or in any place far away: we find too many evidences of that working in the Protestant Reformation, and in the present crisis of our own day and generation. To us it is profoundly significant that out of the birth pangs of the modern world, when at the time of the Renaissance and the Reformation the institutions of democracy as we now know them were coming to birth, our Baptist movement should also have been born, with its characteristic witness of freedom of conscience and religious liberty." Even as he spoke of Christian ecclesiology, he quoted the Johannine text, in which the Christ refers to "other sheep," "not of this fold" (John 10:16) (Gilkey, "Distinctive Baptist Witness," 101). In addition, Gilkey delivered the Barrows Lectures (1924–1925) to audiences of university students in India. Caroline E. Haskell had established that series of lectures to be given either by *"leading Christian scholars"* or by *"scholarly representatives of non-Christian faiths,"* as lectures *"in which, in a friendly, temperate, and conciliatory way, and in the fraternal spirit which pervaded the Parliament of Religions, the great questions of the truths of Christianity, its harmonies with the truths of other religions, its rightful claims, and the best methods of setting them forth, should be presented to the scholarly and thoughtful people of India"* (Caroline E. Haskell, Chicago, to President William R. Harper, Chicago, 12 October 1894, in *Jesus and Our Generation*, by Gilkey, x, xi). Charles Gilkey most certainly exerted such comparative effort, allowing that dialogical spirit to pervade his lectures that year.

the United States into World War II. Virtually recounting even the process of Langdon's own personal experience just prior to his graduation from Harvard University, Charles Gilkey made the following comments in a lecture that he delivered prior to the bombing of Pearl Harbor by the Japanese: *"My own observation has been that students do not fully appreciate either the values of religion or the functions of the church, until they get out of 'preparation for life' into the 'great essential experiences of human life,' in business or profession, in marriage and parenthood, in all human relations."*[18]

II. Postliberal Theology: Niebuhrian Neoorthodoxy

Langdon Gilkey has described himself, following the collapse of his social ideals during his university studies and just before the beginning of World War II, as a "clever cynic, directed only by the requirements of self-interest in a world going nowhere." According to Gilkey, at that point, he discovered that he "detested" himself and his "world," that he experienced a "world in disarray," a condition resulting even from the conflict between his two moral absolutes of peace and justice. In that spiritual turmoil and confusion, he attended Harvard Chapel, where he heard his father's friend, Reinhold Niebuhr, speak. Gilkey emphatically claims that Niebuhr's biblical realism immediately swept away the cynical remnants of his own shredded humanistic idealism, describing his experience as a "quick and complete" "conversion" to "[t]hat personal and theological principle (theological and yet also ethical) of a divine *transcendence* and yet a continual *relevance* and relatedness," which "has

---

[18]Charles W. Gilkey, "The Place of Religion in Higher Education," in *Religion and the Modern World: University of Pennsylvania Bicentennial Conference* (Philadelphia: University of Pennsylvania Press, 1941; repr.: Port Washington NY: Kennikat Press, 1969) 86; emphasis mine. Charles Gilkey delivered this lecture while associate dean of the Divinity School and dean of Rockefeller Chapel, University of Chicago. Among others, notable participants in that conference included Paul Tillich, Reinhold Niebuhr, Robert Calhoun, and Jacques Maritain, each of whom also contributed lectures to that volume as well. Charles Gilkey had also graduated from Harvard University (Gilkey, "Place of Religion in Higher Education," 76). For more than forty years, Langdon Gilkey has consistently underscored the significance of the collapse of liberal theology and its optimism: Langdon Gilkey, "The Christian Response to the World Crisis," *Christianity and Crisis* 15 (8 August 1955): 107-109; idem, "The Threshold of a New Common Freedom," *Criterion* 37 (Autumn 1998): 16, 18.

remained absolutely central to my life and work ever since."[19] Originating from both this collapse of his own liberal ideals and his subsequent "conversion" to the neoorthodox perspective of Reinhold Niebuhr, Gilkey's own theological perspective initially developed as a critique of the fundamental position and assumptions of theological liberalism.[20]

---

[19]Gilkey, "Retrospective Glance at My Work," 6, 7, emphasis mine; also see idem, *SC*, 71-75; idem, review of *Reinhold Niebuhr: A Biography*, by Richard Wrightman Fox, in *Journal of Religion* 68 (April 1988): 263-64. See Gilkey's brief accounts both of the confusion resulting from the conflict between the moral ideals of peace and justice, as his class graduated in 1940 from Harvard University, and of his eulogy for the dead members of that graduating class at the class's twenty-fifth reunion in 1965: Gilkey, *ME*, 255-56n.2; idem, "Dimensions of Basic Faith and the Special Traditions," *Second Opinion: Health, Faith, and Ethics* 2 (1986): 114-15; idem, "The Protestant View of Sin," in *The Human Condition in Jewish and Christian Traditions*, ed. Frederick E. Greenspahn (Hoboken NJ: KTAV Publishing House, 1986) 152-53. Gilkey does admit, however, that, although he had become a Niebuhrian, he remained "unsettled and confused, torn still between two worlds, on the boundary between my college humanism and the new intimations of divine reality that had so recently been opened up for me" (Gilkey, "Retrospective Glance at My Work," 8). In one of his earliest publications, Gilkey described the then present crisis as the collapse of modernity and liberal theology, to which neoorthodoxy had supplied a creative response: "The creative union of reason, meaning and culture has dissipated itself before our eyes, much as in late Classical Society" (Gilkey, "Christian Response to the World Crisis," 107). Gilkey's understanding of himself as torn between these two worlds may also explain Gilkey's deep and abiding appreciation for (maybe even sympathetic identification with) Augustine, as a person caught between the dissolution of Late Antiquity and the emergence of the medieval world (despite Gilkey's significant disagreements with various aspects of Augustine's theology). About Augustine, Gilkey says the following: "His breakdown amid the variety of Roman alternatives was cured by the new Christian alternative; his intellectual doubts as a late antique philosopher were resolved by Hebrew and Christian truth; his dissatisfaction with professional advancement in Rome was rechanneled into an enthusiasm for the new society of the ecclesia" (Langdon Gilkey, "Ordering the Soul: Augustine's Manifold Legacy," *Christian Century* 105 [27 April 1988]: 426). See also Gary Dorrien's interpretation of Gilkey's theology as a mediation between the modern and postmodern worlds: Gary Dorrien, *The Word as True Myth: Interpreting Modern Theology* (Louisville: Westminster/John Knox Press, 1997) 128-86.

[20]Although Gilkey has openly admitted the neoorthodox "shape" of his own theology, he has also clearly and emphatically noted that "Barth had no role in *forming* that theological point of view." He also records his own surprise at the revival of interest in the theology of Karl Barth in the mid-1980s among doctoral students at the University of Chicago Divinity School. During one academic quarter, he had planned to offer a seminar on the thought of A. N. Whitehead. When several graduate students asked him to offer a course on the theology of Karl Barth, he allowed the students of the Theology Area to

A. *Ultimate Questions of Human Existence and Answers in Divine Self-Revelation*

In Gilkey's first three books, largely using the approach of Reinhold Niebuhr, he understood theology as the correlation of the peculiarly *religious or ultimate questions of human experience* to the *Christian symbols of divine self-revelation in history as the answers* to those unique existential questions.[21] Religious or ultimate questions inquire into *the meaning* of human life and history, both about "a purpose in existence as a whole" to which one "can 'anchor' " one's own smaller purposes and about "a resource of power and of love that can overcome the tragedy, the conflict, and the guilt that darken" one's "personal and social existence." Furthermore, "precisely the ambiguities *in* the ordinary experiences of life," rather than "the pervasive coherencies and connections of existence," raise "the burning personal questions of religion." Nonetheless, because the ambiguities, tragedy, conflict, and guilt of human life generate such ultimate or religious *questions*, humans cannot unveil divine reality (that reality which transcends everything finite) as the answer to those questions by their own analyses of that "general human experience" itself.[22] At this stage in his career, as Gilkey would later note, he considered it enough for theological reflection "to relate the eidetic [or historical] meaning of the symbol to lived, existential experience in order for us to conceive it," without expressing that theological language in "modern ontological and philosophical form."[23]

---

vote on whether the seminar would study Whitehead or Barth. As he put it, "it came out two to one for Barth." As one of the graduate students who made that request, I participated in Gilkey's seminar on Barth. The seminar occurred in the spring of 1984 (as my academic transcript from the University of Chicago indicates), rather than in 1985 as Gilkey has remembered (Gilkey, "An Appreciation of Karl Barth," 151, 152).

[21]Gilkey, *MHE*, 4-7, 13-14, 19-25, 139-43, 150-55, 325, 350-51; cf. idem, *HCCM*, 134-46; idem, *SC*, 223-42.

[22]Gilkey, *MHE*, 35.

[23]Gilkey refers to his *Maker of Heaven and Earth* as an example of this approach (Langdon Gilkey, *Catholicism Confronts Modernity: A Protestant View* [New York: Seabury Press, 1975] 126, 208n.6; hereafter cited as *CCM*). This would change for Gilkey in next stage of his methodological development.

B. *Inadequacy of Natural Theology*

For that reason, then, at this stage of his career, Gilkey also followed the majority of neoorthodox theologians, in his rejection of natural theologies as human efforts or "methods of discovery" to prove the existence of God and to discern the character of God so proven through analyses of ordinary experience. Such efforts to know God, according to Gilkey, accomplish only one of two things: either (1) they reduce God "to the level of creatures whom we can understand," "to a part of the structure of the world," thus never actually proving God to unbelievers; or (2) they conceive of God "negatively as an abstract, lifeless absolute," losing God "in abstraction and negation," never disclosing a "satisfactory" God to believers. Although Gilkey acknowledged that such efforts arise from a "dim awareness of deity," he still maintained strongly the characteristic neoorthodox stance: "If, then, *natural theology* is the attempt to reach God the Creator either through man's experience of the immanent coherence of the world or through his general religious experience, it *can only uncover an idol, never the true God*." Gilkey would later admit just how strongly he opposed natural theology: "I have prided myself on being one of the leading opponents of natural theology for a good number of years; . . . And I was fully convinced, for various very good reasons, that natural theology was not only impossible, but just a little bit blasphemous—if you can be only a 'little bit' blasphemous."[24]

---

[24]Gilkey, *MHE*, 103, 156, 321, 322, emphasis mine; idem, "Theology and Culture: Reflections on the Conference," 3. Also, see Gilkey's notation of this point in his various analyses of neoorthodoxy: Langdon Gilkey, "Theology," in *The Great Ideas Today, 1967* (Chicago: Encyclopedia Britannica, Inc., 1967) 244-45; idem, "Trends in Protestant Apologetics," *Concilium* 6 (June 1969): 60-63; also in *The Development of Fundamental Theology*, ed. J. B. Metz (New York: Paulist Press, 1969) 127-57. "An academic proof of God's existence will not help a man who is overcome with futility or guilt. His problem is not ignorance or unclarity of mind, so much as it is turbulence and anxiety of spirit. What he needs, therefore, is not a demonstrated concept of deity in his mind, so much as an experienced encounter with Almighty God. For only in such an encounter, and the living relation that flows from it, can a man find the courage and conviction, the purpose and inner strength to accept and to conquer the 'mysteries' of existence" (Gilkey, *MHE*, 21-22). In spite of Gilkey's strong opposition to natural theologies in his discussion of divine immanence in *Maker of Heaven and Earth* (see Gilkey, *MHE*, 106-107), he supplies the seeds even there for his own later argument or proof for God's reality (cf. Gilkey, *RW*, 300-306; idem, *ME*, 78-81; idem, *Society and the Sacred: Toward a Theology of Culture in Decline* [New York: Crossroad Pub. Co., 1981] 31-37; hereafter

C. Sin as Barrier to Knowledge of God

Moreover, not merely the characteristics of finitude prevent the human from proving the existence of God through analyses of those creaturely realities themselves. According to Gilkey, human sin itself represents "the most serious barrier to the knowledge of God." Gilkey understood sin as the human's willful refusal to discover the "answer" to "questions about the infinite" in "self-surrender to God."[25] In this understanding of the doctrine of sin, Gilkey followed the essential contours of Reinhold Niebuhr's analysis of sin as the intentional dissolution of the "union" between the human's "dependence as a creature" and the human's "free spiritual life." Although humans know themselves as "contingent and temporal," they "experience," through the power of their minds and the freedom of their wills, their own "spiritual transcendence" over themselves and "the world" around them. Hence, their minds and freedom tempt them "to regard" themselves as "independent" in their "spirits." Falling prey to this temptation, they attempt "to become the spiritual center" of their own existence: "to establish" their "security," despite their "manifest contingency"; "to carve out the meaning" of their lives, despite their "weakness and temporality"; and "to attain," through their own thought, "to the truth," despite their "finite partiality." In other words, humans try to be their own gods, "to replace the source and center" of their own being by their own "creaturely powers." This exercise of the human's created capacities distorts and perverts human "nature," in terms of the human's relationship to God, to self, and to the remainder of creation.[26]

---

cited as SAS). Gilkey has publicly admitted his own embarrassment about this radical shift in his thought (Gilkey, "Theology and Culture: Reflections on the Conference," 3). I reserve my discussions of this significant change in Gilkey's thought, however, until later in this chapter.

[25]Gilkey, *MHE*, 99n.16, 325.

[26]Gilkey, *MHE*, 231-32; also see, idem, "Christ and the City," *Motive* 17 (April 1957): 29; cf. Reinhold Niebuhr, *The Nature and Destiny of Man*, vol. 1, *Human Nature* (New York: Charles Scribner's Sons, 1941) 180-86. Although dialogue with the sciences significantly informs Gilkey's later interpretations of the Christian doctrine of original sin, he retains the basic structure and meaning of his interpretation of that doctrine: see Gilkey, *RW*, 253-65; idem, "The Protestant View of Sin," 147-68; idem, *ME*, 111-57; idem, "Human Existence: Selfishness and Altruism," in *TT*, 195-213; idem, "Ordering the Soul: Augustine's Manifold Legacy," 429-30; idem, *Nature, Reality, and the Sacred: The Nexus of Science and Religion*, Theology and the Sciences series, ed. Kevin J. Sharpe (Minneapolis: Fortress Press, 1993) 169-73; hereafter cited as *NRS*; idem, "From Shantung

For Gilkey, this assessment arose not only from a study of the Christian scriptures themselves, but also from an *empirical* examination of personal and social human experience.[27] As for Niebuhr, the role of hamartiology (or the doctrine of sin) in Gilkey's theological method arose from an honest (*realistic*) examination of the cultural situation—the historical crises that led to the collapse of liberal theology's optimism in humanity's moral progress and development: "the main article of faith of the humanist, namely, the goodness of mankind and man's consequent capacity to be moral, is refuted by any careful study of human nature."[28]

---

to Sarajevo: Reflections after 50 Years," *Christian Century* 112 (16-23 August 1995): 782-86.

[27]On this point, I disagree with certain aspects of the argument in Joseph Bessler-Northcutt's recent and very insightful dissertation on Gilkey's thought. He develops an argument to support the following thesis: "Over against both Niebuhr and Tillich Gilkey insists on the importance of *beginning* from an empirical analysis of secular experience, not from a Niebuhrian affirmation of revelation and not with Tillich's ontological approach to reality" (Joseph Bessler-Northcutt, "Shantung Trilogy: The Rhetorical Shaping of Langdon Gilkey's Theology of Culture and History" [Ph.D. diss., University of Chicago, 1996] 3; also see esp. chap. 4, 119-47). Without a doubt, Gilkey performs "an empirical analysis of secular experience" (of one sort) even in his earliest neoorthodox books. Nonetheless, at least in his earliest work (as easily seen in *MHE*, *HCCM*, and *SC*), he accomplishes this "empirical" analysis, while simultaneously and explicitly employing "a Niebuhrian affirmation of revelation." One may also dispute, on various grounds, the implication of Bessler-Northcutt's comments to the effect that Niebuhr himself did not begin theology with an empirical analysis. Although I will not engage that issue here, one should note this point: whether or not Niebuhr began with an empirical analysis of secular experience, Gilkey at least thinks Niebuhr approached theological questions in this way. In Gilkey's otherwise scathing review of Fox's biography of Niebuhr, Gilkey agrees with Fox on this point: "He [Fox] is quite right that perhaps the main characteristic of Niebuhr's peculiar mode of social and theological thinking was his *empiricism*, his insistence on looking at what he called 'the facts of experience' as the most important ground for any sort of significant comprehension" (Langdon Gilkey, review of *Reinhold Niebuhr: A Biography*, by Richard Wrightman Fox, 265; see also, idem, "Reinhold Niebuhr's Theology of History," *Journal of Religion* 54 [October 1974]: 361, 373, 375, 377, 383; also in *The Legacy of Reinhold Niebuhr*, ed. Nathan A. Scott, Jr. [Chicago: University of Chicago Press, 1975] 36-62).

[28]Gilkey, *SC*, 230. Gilkey also considered it "irrational to defend a humanistic faith that the *evidence* so universally contradicts." According to Gilkey, his "camp *experience*" of internment by the Japanese during World War II "*demonstrated*" that "under pressure" the human "loves himself and his own more than he will ever admit" (Gilkey, *SC*, 230); emphasis mine. According to Gilkey, *Shantung Compound* "argued that liberal optimism about human rationality and goodness was a false and 'unempirical' view and that only

On this point, as Gilkey understands Niebuhr's theological method, he followed Niebuhr also. As a consequence, this *doctrine* essentially determines the shape of Gilkey's neoorthodox theological *method*.

D. The Need for Divine Self-Revelation in History

As a result of *both* human limits to discover that which transcends finitude through analyses of general experience itself *and* human "alienation from God in sin," the human's "dim awareness of deity never becomes an adequate understanding of God, until it is clarified and corrected by God's revelation of Himself in history." Thus, the human cannot find answers to its religious or ultimate questions through itself or its world; rather, God must answer those questions through divine self-revelation in history. Accordingly, Gilkey neither explicitly claims nor intends to imply "that 'religious truth' is merely a matter of human questions and human answers." Rather, for Gilkey, "[r]eligious truth is first and foremost a matter of divine revelation," a revelation "always received and understood as the answer to the specifically religious, and not the scientific or even the philosophical, questions a man asks about this life." Thus, "knowledge of God" means much more than a cognitive discovery or an intellectual security about the existence of ultimate reality and its characteristics. Only divine self-revelation discloses "the ultimate purpose of God" and reveals that to be God's "personal fellowship" with the human creature. Furthermore, "God is *most directly known*," for Gilkey, "in historical revelation, and *especially in the person of Jesus Christ*," in whom God displays this ultimate purpose. Again, following the pattern of most

---

the traditional symbol of original sin could make sense out of our ordinary individual and communal behavior" (Gilkey, "Responses to Peter Berger," 489). Similarly, later in *Naming the Whirlwind*, Gilkey directed readers to his previous book, *Shantung Compound*, as "an empirical validation of these facets [sinful expressions of self-interest] of man's life" (Gilkey, *NW*, 386n.12). On this point, Gilkey follows Reinhold Niebuhr's view that human history itself attests to the truth in the myth of the fall: see Reinhold Niebuhr, *An Interpretation of Christian Ethics* (New York: Harper & Brothers, 1935; repr.: New York: Seabury Press, 1963) 53-54; idem, *Nature and Destiny of Man*, 1:265-80; also see Dorrien, *Word as True Myth*, 124-26. In this regard, even later in *Naming the Whirlwind*, which itself claims and which Gilkey has always understood to be philosophical anthropology and not theology in any sense, he identifies in the secular experience of human autonomy the appearance of demonic potential and sin (Gilkey, *NW*, 321-22n.14, 365-413).

neoorthodox theologians, Gilkey claimed that, for Christians, Jesus Christ is "the *only* clear clue to the Father's will for us."[29]

E. Divine Self-Revelation, Scripture, Theological Language

For Gilkey, the God who can answer the ultimate or religious questions of human existence cannot be completely immanent within creation itself. Humans could use various methods to analyze general or common experience to discover an immanent god. Nevertheless, such an immanent god would only remain a being like other beings, subject to the same structures and conditions of finitude, no matter how much greater or better that god might be than all other creatures. Only the God who transcends the creation, who is unconditioned by finitude itself, can genuinely answer the human's ultimate questions. Precisely this "unconditionedness," "the transcendent element of deity," defines the holiness of God for Gilkey: God is absolutely, completely, or "wholly other" than the creation. Because the human cannot find this unconditioned God through various "methods of discovery," the human receives answers to its religious questions, or knowledge of God, only through divine self-revelation in the events of human history. For Gilkey, like neoorthodox theologians generally, God and divine self-revelation are objective realities, not reducible to the subjectivity and relativity of human experience.[30]

As a consequence, according to Gilkey, "Christian theology rightly feels that all that it can validly say about the transcendent God must be based upon and guided by God's revelation of Himself." God's self-revelation occurred in historical events, as "the mighty acts of God in history." The events of divine self-manifestation are historical events like all other events, observable and analyzable like those events. The "divine dimension and significance of these events," however, "is known only to faith" or by revelation, not by human analysis or methods.[31]

Unlike orthodoxy and conservative or fundamentalist Protestantism, however, Gilkey did not identify divine revelation with the Christian

---

[29]Gilkey, *MHE*, 6, 23-24n.5, 274, 275, 322, 325, 359; emphasis mine. About the anxieties that arise from human experiences of weakness, contingency, and mortality, Gilkey makes a similar claim regarding the uniqueness of Christianity: "To these anxieties of our finitude, the Christian faith in the creative and providential power of God provides *the only sufficient answer*" (Gilkey, *MHE*, 6; emphasis mine).

[30]Gilkey, *MHE*, 38, 91, 97-98, 103, 104.

[31]Gilkey, *MHE*, 104, 154-55.

scriptures themselves. The Bible points or witnesses to the events of divine self-revelation in history; the "words of the Bible," however, "are not themselves the revelation," but a "medium of divine revelation." For this reason, Gilkey understood the Christian Bible as a "human document," one which, like all human documents, "reflects the limited and often wrong concepts and views of its time and place"—or is "a fallible human work." Thus, Gilkey describes the Christian Bible as "a twofold reality," both "absolute" and "relative" in its authority for Christians and Christian communities: (1) on the one hand, *absolute*, as an "indispensable" witness to "God's word in this salvation history," without which "these events and the God revealed in and through them are inaccessible to us"; (2) on the other hand, *relative*, as a product and reflection of "the scientific, philosophical, social, political and historical notions" of its time, "a human response to the divine activity"—an understanding of the Bible, of course, retained by neoorthodoxy from liberal theology. The Bible, then, "can become a revelational authority only if through theological mediation the word of God in the scriptures, centered about Jesus Christ, is separated from the ancient words of the documents themselves."[32]

Because God transcends the creation ontologically, God also transcends the creation epistemologically. Since God is not completely immanent in creation and, therefore, does not exist alongside all other creatures as they exist, humans cannot describe either the divine activity "literally" or God "as an entity in our ordinary experience," without losing "the religious sense of the transcendent holiness and mystery of God" or reducing God to "a creature among creatures." Thus, all language about God and divine activity is analogical, symbolic, or mythical—including biblical language itself. Theological language, then, uses analogies from creaturely experience and reality to describe God and God's activity, which means that those ultimate or divine realities are both " 'like' some event in our more usual experience" and " 'unlike' all the events we know." More precisely, however, since humans come to know God by God's "own self-manifestation to us within the world, not by our intellectual ascent beyond the world" to God, "[t]he analogies by

---

[32]Gilkey, *MHE*, 27-28, 154, 326-29; idem, "Authority of the Bible," 115, 117-18; idem, "Christian Response to the World Crisis," 108; idem, "Neo-Orthodoxy," in *A Handbook of Christian Theology*, ed. Marvin Halverson (New York: Meridian Books, 1958) 259.

which we seek to understand God stem, therefore, from our special experience of revelation, rather than from the general experiences of our common life." Hence, all language and knowledge about the nature and activity of God remain partial, indirect, paradoxical, and imprecise descriptions of or claims about the ultimate mystery. Nonetheless, Gilkey identifies the point of contact for the most direct and least symbolic knowledge of God in "historical revelation, and especially in the person of Jesus Christ." By receiving God in faith through Jesus Christ, humans "can now experience and know with overwhelming immediacy the nature of God as holy love united with holy power."[33]

F. Relevant Transcendence

According to Gilkey, through divine self-revelation in historical events, God has answered the ultimate or religious questions that human existence has raised and continues to raise for itself. The theologian, then, works to articulate and clarify the divine answers to the basic human problems or questions. In this sense, the theologian aims to produce coherent concepts about God, the world, and human life that respond relevantly to the problems, issues, and concerns of the contemporary situation. Theology or religious thought "seeks to understand the ordinary levels of life in terms of an apprehension of its deepest meaning, discovered in some particular and irreplaceable experience." Hence, "the purpose of theological discourse is to point to, express, and so far as is possible make intelligible the appearance of the holy in our experience."[34]

Theology bases its claims about the divine dimension of experience or the transcendent God on God's self-manifesting activity in human history. Thus, necessarily, Christian theology uses the Christian Bible as

---

[33]Gilkey, *MHE*, 54, 67, 85-99, 100, 101, 325-26, 334-60. Gilkey's theory of the analogical, symbolic, and mythical character of all religious and theological language resembles and relies upon Paul Ricoeur's careful and extensive work on the nature of metaphor, symbol, and myth: cf. Paul Ricoeur, *The Symbolism of Evil*, trans. Emerson Buchanan (Boston: Beacon Press, 1967) 14-18; idem, *Interpretation Theory: Discourse and The Surplus of Meaning* (Fort Worth: Texas Christian University Press, 1976) 54-63; idem, "Biblical Hermeneutics," *Semeia* 4 (1975): 75-106; idem, *The Rule of Metaphor: Multi-Disciplinary Studies of the Creation of Meaning in Language*, trans. Robert Czerny (Toronto: University of Toronto Press, 1977) 216-313. By the time he had completed *Naming the Whirlwind*, Gilkey had incorporated many of Ricoeur's earliest insights into the nature of metaphor, symbol, and myth.

[34]Gilkey, *MHE*, 35-36, 83; idem, *HCCM*, 145-46.

a library of witnesses to the events of divine self-revelation in history, as a collection of symbols that "point or refer to the dimension of transcendence or of the holy."[35] As a result, Gilkey identifies two basic tasks for theology. First, *biblical theology*, as a subset of historical theology, seeks to discover and to state "what the biblical writers meant to say, a statement couched in the Bible's own terms, cosmological, historical, and theological." This first task, therefore, does not address questions of the truth or validity of theological claims made by the scriptures. Second, *confessional or systematic theology* seeks to state "what that Word might mean for us today, what *we* believe God actually to have done," "what *we* believe the truth about God and about what he has done to be."[36]

Gilkey aims, with theology, to identify and clarify the answers for the questions of human existence, as disclosed through divine self-revelation in the historical events to which the Christian scriptures attest. Scientific or historical evidence does not prove the validity of those answers. Rather, those answers "can only be validated by their ability to provide a meaningful context for those basic intuitions which are taken to be the ultimate certainties of our experience."[37] Thus, theology contains a practical impulse, the drive to articulate the ultimate meaning or divine dimension of human life. Whatever problems or questions about human existence theology endeavors to address, it always works with this "dialectic or tension between transcendence and relevance."[38] On this basis, then, Gilkey distinguishes apologetic theology from natural theology. Even in the earliest expressions of his theological method, he clearly understood his own theology as apologetic, while rejecting natural theology as a wasted (even idolatrous) human effort to discover God. By "apologetics," Gilkey meant "any consistently argued effort to show the relevance and the meaning (and even in some cases the validity) of the Christian view of things, an effort which for the strength of its argument appeals to some elements of general (as opposed to Christian) experience and so does not depend exhaustively or *in toto* on either revelational authority or the assent of faith." Thus, apologetic theology, in this sense, operated as "a prolegomenon or an introduction to faith," "preparatory

---

[35]Gilkey, *HCCM*, 138.

[36]Langdon Gilkey, "Cosmology, Ontology, and the Travail of Biblical Language," *Journal of Religion* 41 (July 1961): 204.

[37]Gilkey, *MHE*, 350-51.

[38]Gilkey, *HCCM*, 55; idem, "Christian Response to the World Crisis," 109.

work" that can generate neither "the symbols and doctrines of the faith" nor "belief itself." Rather, such an approach only attempted to "make the given or revealed faith seem relevant and meaningful to man's experienced situation," to show the "relevance," "value," and "illuminating power" of faith, or even to "present the viewpoint of faith as a powerful *option* or *possibility* for the man who understands himself correctly."[39]

In light of the character of this approach, then, Gilkey firmly emphasized the need for "correct theology" in his first three books.[40] A comment from his book, *Maker of Heaven and Earth*, illustrates this point well:

> Men cannot afford to be vague about what they really believe in. They must *know* that in which they put their trust. If God is a vague amorphous nothing to us, the "nothing" will be filled by more compelling gods, the concrete idols of our cultural life, such as nation, race, and personal prestige. As the Old Testament struggle against idolatry shows, only a clear and honest concept of God can drive the fertility and tribal idols from our religious life.[41]

Nevertheless, because Gilkey understood the character of theological discourse to be inexact, partial, analogical, and symbolic, he admitted the need for constant revision of theological perspectives and formulations. This he also had received from neoorthodoxy, again as part of its own inheritance from liberalism. He described this as "the unusual grace of neoorthodox Christianity at its best: namely, that it at once emphasizes the uniqueness of Christian belief and the importance of a sound theology, without at the same time being intolerant or creedal in its spirit."[42]

---

[39]Gilkey, "Trends in Protestant Apologetics," 60.

[40]Gilkey, "Retrospective Glance at My Work," 14.

[41]Gilkey, *MHE*, 82.

[42]Gilkey, "Neo-Orthodoxy," 260. During the period when Gilkey taught at Vanderbilt University Divinity School, he participated in The Christian Church (Disciples of Christ). Gilkey noticed with some apprehension both the loss of the Bible's relevance in the everyday concerns of Christian churches and the people's ignorance about that which they believe. Gilkey's concern for correct theology assumed a practical form in this case. He proposed three new emphases for noncredal, free churches: (1) training the pastor "as much as an effective teacher of Bible, theology and church history as he is as a counselor and preacher"; (2) reemploying "confessions of faith, not as criteria for membership, but as guides to teaching, study and discussion, and as a reference point when issues of belief or of other action arise for us as individuals or for the community as a whole"; and (3) instituting "more real theological and biblical education in the church" at two levels: (a) "confirmation classes" of a year in length for older teenagers and (b) "adult classes, for

G. Postliberal Theological Method

In the 1950s, Gilkey described the neoorthodox response to the collapse of liberal theology as "postliberal Christianity." By "postliberal," of course, he meant fundamentally that humans could not discover the answers for the ultimate questions or problems of the human situation from human experience itself; rather, those answers came only as revealed in human history by the God who transcends the entire creation both ontologically and epistemologically. Whereas liberal theology had emphasized the "continuity between Christianity and culture," postliberal theology emphasized the "dominant motifs" of "discontinuity and trans-cendence."[43] Consequently, Gilkey's type of postliberal theology argued apologetically, while both still depending on divine self-revelation for answers to the ultimate questions of the human situation and continuing to eschew natural theologies themselves.

A little later in Gilkey's career, he noted two predominant forms of "neo-orthodox apologetics." (1) In one form, neoorthodox or postliberal apologetic theology attempted to identify the "inadequacy" or "the error of competing points of view," such as "naturalistic, scientific, liberal-humanitarian, idealistic" perspectives. Neoorthodox theologians often explicitly and intentionally based their arguments "on historical, social,

---

those church members that are interested in thinking out their faith" (Gilkey, "Authority of the Bible," 122-23).

[43]Gilkey, "Christian Response to the World Crisis," 108; idem, "Theology," 244-47. Also, see other references by Gilkey to "postliberal" theologians and the "postliberal generation" (Gilkey, "Theology," 245; idem, HCCM, 50n.21). Even into the late 1970s, Gilkey continued to use this term, referring, for example, to "postliberal Protestantism" (Langdon Gilkey, "A Covenant with the Chinese," Dialog 17 [Summer 1978]: 182; also as "The Covenant with the Chinese," in China and Christianity: Historical and Future Encounters, ed. James D. Whitehead, Yu Ming Shaw, and N. J. Girardot [Notre Dame IN: University of Notre Dame, the Center of Pastoral and Social Ministry, 1979] 120; also published as chap. 10, "Revelation and an Ancient Civilization," in SAS, 141). Of course, Gilkey's use of this terminology certainly does not carry the full range of meaning more recently given to the phrase by George Lindbeck or William C. Placher, in their identification of the phrase with a "cultural-linguistic" theory of religion (see, e.g., Lindbeck, Nature of Doctrine, 30-45, 112-38; also see William C. Placher, Unapologetic Theology: A Christian Voice in a Pluralistic Conversation [Louisville: Westminster/John Knox Press, 1989]). Also, see Charles Allen's insightful and critical, though appreciative, review of Placher's proposal: Charles W. Allen, "Between Revisionists and Postliberals: A Review Article," Encounter 51 (Autumn 1990): 389-401.

and psychological evidence of various sorts," seeking to demonstrate both that "neither man's reason nor his virtue was as 'pure' as humanists believed them to be" and that "the hope or faith of humanism in man's goodness and his capacity autonomously to create meaning was in fact an illusion–whether in his individual life or his social-historical existence." Hence, for humans to discover meaning and hope in life, "*then* Christianity provides the only really relevant alternative." (2) In a second form, neoorthodox apologetic theology "found its common ground not in the character of the human situation but in the assumed values of our Western cultural life, values which, it was maintained, owed their existence to the biblical tradition." The second apologetic approach, then, drew two implications from this claim: (a) "the Greeks were mostly to blame for the errors in our cultural life–completely reversing the assessment of German classicism and romanticism of the Hellenic and the Hebrew spirits"; and (b) implicitly, "[t]he biblical tradition *must . . .* have revelation as its ultimate source if so much that we now recognize as true and significant comes out of that tradition." Gilkey identifies works by Reinhold Niebuhr, Emil Brunner, Alan Richardson, J. V. Langmead-Casserly, as well as his own *Maker of Heaven and Earth*, as examples of the first approach. Nonetheless, one may also detect certain elements of the second postliberal approach to apologetics in that same book by Gilkey.[44]

In light of the previous discussions, Gilkey's earliest theological method operated from an obvious neoorthodox or postliberal perspective, while also functioning nonetheless as an apologetic theology. In the earli-

---

[44]Gilkey, "Trends in Protestant Apologetics," 61, 70n.4. Gilkey's analysis of his internment by the Japanese in China employs most obviously the first form of postliberal apologetic theology: for example, through his sociological and theological study of that experience, he refutes "the main article of faith of the humanist, namely, the goodness of mankind and man's consequent capacity to be moral" (Gilkey, *SC*, 230; similarly, see Gilkey, *HCCM*, 47-55). Gilkey uses the second neoorthodox form of apologetics, for example, when he examines both the Greek inheritance of and the Christian contribution to the development of modern science. According to Gilkey, although ancient Greek culture assumed the intelligibility of the world, "only a radical change from the classical presuppositions about the character of the world's order could have produced the kind of empirical science that we enjoy." After showing the radical difference between the scientific assumptions of classical culture and those of modern culture, Gilkey makes the following apologetic claim: "Now the conception which effected this fundamental reinterpretation of the world's order, and so provided those presuppositions of modern science, was the Christian idea of creation" (Gilkey, *MHE*, 123-30).

est stages of his career, consequently, Gilkey's theology qualified as correlational without being foundational.[45] This correlational pattern appears quite clearly in Gilkey's first three books.

In *Maker of Heaven and Earth*, Gilkey exercises his neoorthodox or postliberal correlational method on the Christian doctrine of creation. As he states the correlation, "[t]he idea of creation is, therefore, the concept in theology which answers the problems of our 'creatureliness,' namely our dependence and temporality." Hence, he begins in the first chapter by examining the current situation—that is, the major objections to the Christian doctrine of creation from science, philosophy, and liberal theology. Then, in chapters 2 through 4, Gilkey describes the contours of *the Christian symbol or doctrine of creation*. After his analysis of the Christian doctrine of creation, he applies the meaning of this doctrine to contemporary life in chapters 5 through 9, as the Christian response to the human situation. He follows this correlational pattern with his final chapter on methodological concerns, as I have noted previously.[46]

In *How the Church Can Minister to the World without Losing Itself*, Gilkey follows the same pattern generally, this time, however, with attention to ecclesiology. (1) Initially, he describes the problematic situation for the contemporary North American church in his first chapter. Roughly, Gilkey condenses this problematic situation to the church's loss of the sense of holiness or transcendence in North American ecclesiastical denominationalism, a loss that eliminates the meaningfulness of the

---

[45]In this regard, Gilkey represents the sort of theologian (at least, early in his career) whom Charles Allen discerned (or, at least, hoped to find) in William Placher earlier in this present decade (Allen, "Between Revisionists and Postliberals," 394-97). On contemporary issues and discussions about foundationalism and revisionist theology, see the following: David Tracy, "Defending the Public Character of Theology," *Christian Century* 98 (1 April 1981): 350-56; William Placher, "Revisionist and Postliberal Theologies and the Public Character of Theology," *The Thomist* 49 (1985): 392-416; William Werpehowski, "Ad Hoc Apologetics," *Journal of Religion* 66 (1986): 282-301; William Placher, "Paul Ricoeur and Postliberal Theology: A Conflict of Interpretations?" *Modern Theology* 4 (October 1987): 35-52; Gary L. Comstock, "Two Types of Narrative Theology," *Journal of the American Academy of Religion* 55 (Winter 1987): 687-717; Douglas F. Ottati, "Between Foundationalism and Nonfoundationalism," *Affirmation* 4 (Fall 1991): 27-47; Richard Lints, "The Postpositivist Choice: Tracy or Lindbeck?" *Journal of the American Academy of Religion* 61 (Winter 1993): 655-77; Ronald F. Thiemann, "Piety, Narrative, and Christian Identity," *Word & World* 3 (Spring 1983): 148-59.

[46]Gilkey, *MHE*, 6, 7-14, 15-116, 117-318, 319-60.

church's theological language about itself. Gilkey discerns the cause of that situation in two major factors: (a) in the contemporary church's denominational language about itself, the church has made a "category mistake," equating its official doctrines or symbols (the ideal), which express "the *relation* of God to the life of existing churches," with "the substantial *elements*" in the actual composition of the churches, a mistake that leaves the existing contemporary church with abstract and unrealistic language about itself; and (b) the ecumenical impulse to find a "common view" of the church among the "conflicting denominational theories" produced a second level of abstraction, since ecumenists constructed their own definition of this shared perspective from the already abstract denominational theories themselves. As a corrective to this problem, and as the first step in ecclesiology, Gilkey proposed "an empirical investigation that seeks to uncover what the actual religious reality of the contemporary denominational church is." Nevertheless, Gilkey insisted that such an empirical analysis remain "theologically informed and motivated," in order to "inform the questions asked rather than to provide content for answers received." In that way, Gilkey aimed to make visible the "actual" instead of the "ideal" "religious character" of the churches.[47] (2) As a second step in ecclesiology, Gilkey called for both historical and theological analyses of the results from the empirical study. (a) The *historical phase* of this second step mediates between the empirical and theological analyses: serving as a sort of second stage in his empirical analysis of the contemporary church, insofar as the historical study seeks to discover the historical factors that produced the contemporary situation. (b) In the *theological phase* of Gilkey's second step in ecclesiology, the theologian aims to understand the contemporary church "in relation to the great symbols, both biblical and historical, that give theological structure to the church." Thus, Gilkey employed three Christian symbols of the church ("the people of God," "hearers of the Word," and "the Body of Christ") in chapters 3 through 5, as the divine response to the church's contemporary situation. These three symbols "point or refer to the dimension of transcendence or of the holy in the church's life—to the ways in which God works within the church in judgment and grace." As I noted previously, in chapter 6, he follows the previous correlation of

[47]Gilkey, *HCCM*, 1-27, 134-37.

Christian symbols to the contemporary situation with a discussion of the theological method that he had just employed.[48]

Finally, in *Shantung Compound*, Gilkey attempted a similar correlation between an analysis of his experience as a prisoner in an internment camp by the Japanese during World War II and an interpretation of the Christian doctrine of original sin. One cannot as easily identify specific chapters with the two sides in Gilkey's correlation of an analysis of the situation to an interpretation of this traditional Christian doctrine, especially due to the genre in which Gilkey communicates this theological perspective—a narrative or story of his experience, based as it was on the diaries and journals that he had kept in China during his internment. Nonetheless, as his story proceeds through the various chapters, Gilkey gradually discloses his sense of the need for a Christian interpretation of that experience of internment, insofar as that experience functions paradigmatically for all human experience. Hence, in his final chapter, he brings various strands of this growing awareness together into his final theological interpretation of the Christian message for the situation.[49]

III. Postliberal Theology in Transition:
Tillichian Neoorthodoxy and Phenomenology

As Gilkey has recounted, however, he began to detect signs of a growing crisis for neoorthodox thought in the late 1940s after his return from China.[50] This crisis of neoorthodox theology, however, only signaled a

---

[48]Gilkey, *HCCM*, 28-55, 56-127, 137-40.

[49]See Gilkey, *SC*, 87, 223-42.

[50]Gilkey notes this in a story about his participation in a conference of Baptist clergy (of the Northern Baptist Convention or American Baptist Churches/U.S.A.). During that conference, the younger Baptist theologians (of the neoorthodox variety) found themselves joining with the conservatives or evangelicals, in the conflict between conservatives and liberals that had long troubled the Northern Baptist Convention. After Gilkey spoke about history and the essential need for the traditional Christian eschatological symbols to interpret history, an older evangelical minister (enthusiastic about the younger generation's interest in this topic) asked Gilkey questions about "the second Coming." In those moments, Gilkey realized that, despite those elements that neoorthodoxy had in common with orthodoxy, it also differed vastly from orthodoxy and conservative Christianity in the U.S.A. On the one hand, neoorthodoxy as a whole (and his own neoorthodox theology with it) held basic "secular" and "unsupernaturalistic" assumptions about "the objective course of history." On the other hand, Gilkey realized "how very symbolic" was the neoorthodox "use of traditional theological concepts, such as judgment, last judgment, and

larger crisis for all theologies. This cultural crisis supplied a new situation for theology. In responding to this new situation, Gilkey deepened his theological method, primarily relying on the basic structure and character of Paul Tillich's correlational theological method.[51]

A. New Situation for Theology

Gilkey assessed theology's new situation principally in light of the juxtaposition of two major theological movements: neoorthodox theologies and the God-is-dead or radical theologies of the 1960s. In his efforts to respond both to inherent problems in the theological perspective of neoorthodox thought and to the legitimate challenges of the radical theologies, Gilkey discerned the pressing need for a modification of theological method.

1. *Inherent Problems of Neoorthodox Theology.* As one major impetus for the publication of his fourth book, *Naming the Whirlwind*, Gilkey began to discern certain internal problems in neoorthodox theology itself. Gilkey's deep discomfort with these inherent problems in the neoorthodox theological method that he had inherited, nevertheless, does not appear *significantly* in his first three books. Still, in several articles and book reviews during that same period, Gilkey did begin to register his growing awareness of the basis for the problems internal to neoorthodoxy. He discovered this problematic basis at the very core of that which characterized the neoorthodox message: its claim and attempt

---

Second Coming." As he expressed it, "[t]he problem of what we *did* mean by these theological symbols, however intelligible they seemed to be in relation to all the evidence . . . , was beginning to appear on my horizon" (Gilkey, "Retrospective Glance at My Work," 15). Despite Gilkey's growing awareness of the internal problems in neoorthodox theological method, that awareness does not appear in most of Gilkey's earliest publications: see Langdon Gilkey, "Academic Freedom and the Christian Faith," *Christianity and Crisis* 12 (22 December 1952): 171-73; idem, "Christ and the City," 2-3, 29; idem, "Darwin and Christian Thought," *Christian Century* 77 (6 January 1960): 7-11 (also later reprinted in *Science and Religion*, ed. Ian Barbour [New York: Harper & Row, 1968] 159-81); idem, "Morality and the Cross," *Christianity and Crisis* 14 (5 April 1954): 35-38. Nevertheless, in one of his earliest publications, he does register his growing awareness of the internal problems and confusion of neoorthodox thought, even if he only enumerates and analyzes some of those problems without at that time proposing any solutions: see Gilkey, "Christian Response to the World Crisis," 109-11.

[51]"In *Naming the Whirlwind* I became much more Tillichean. I've been steadily moving in a philosophical and imanentist [*sic*] direction" (Gilkey, "Namer and Tamer of the Whirlwind," 3; cf. idem, "Retrospective Glance at My Work," 13).

to offer a *relevant transcendence*. Initially, Gilkey identified the primary cause of neoorthodoxy's internal problems as a dual inheritance, or the retention of two convictions, from liberal theology. (1) According to Gilkey, neoorthodox theologians retained a fundamental "liberal conviction": that "true Christianity is and must be relevant to the cultural situation of man" as "one of the guiding norms" for the newer and revised theology (neoorthodoxy). Precisely for this reason, at least in the United States, theologians had formulated a neoorthodoxy, not because they had considered liberal theology to be "either unbiblical or unorthodox," but because they had found liberalism "to be inadequate to deal with the cultural crisis in which our society found itself"—precisely because liberal theology did not respond *relevantly* to the contemporary human situation. Thus, neoorthodox theologians dissociated Christianity from culture, as Christianity's ultimate source and norm, in favor of the Christian scriptures and tradition, "as the bases for its [Christianity's] faith and life." In its stress upon the discontinuity between Christianity and culture, neoorthodox theology accentuated the transcendent reality that could address the contemporary situation relevantly, since it did so with resources not dependent upon or derived from the situation itself. (2) Neoorthodox thought also retained a second liberal "conviction": "that all products of human religious life, whether they be 'sacred' writings, theological statements, religious codes of ethics of religious institutions, are relative to the spatio-temporal process so that they reflect in part the finitude, partiality and error of any cultural creation." On the basis of that second conviction, as a consequence, neoorthodoxy emphasized "the strict continuity of religion and culture" in its basic tenet "that no scripture, creed, law or church is directly to be identified with the divine."[52]

Gilkey acknowledged both the creativity of neoorthodoxy's response to the global crises of the 1920s, 1930s, and 1940s and that external changes in the situation had intensified the difficulties in neoorthodoxy's own ability to respond to the postwar world of the late 1940s and 1950s. Nevertheless, he also insisted that neoorthodoxy's problems resulted from "the inherent character of that theology": the dual heritage from liberalism, from which neoorthodoxy developed its own "corresponding dual emphasis on both transcendence and relevance." Gilkey condensed the basis of the initial difficulties to the following thought: "Because it [neo-

---

[52]Gilkey, "Christian Response to the World Crisis," 108-109.

orthodoxy] regards the will of God as transcendent to the relativity of all cultural life, and because it recognizes clearly the ambiguity of everything human, contemporary Christianity can never regard any specific kind of action as unqualifiedly Christian." Due to this perspective, Christianity literally cannot find "an unequivocal Christian standard for practical, actual decisions." A Christian must make decisions or responses "on the purely pragmatic basis of what seems both possible and best in this concrete situation," which means that "the form of the Christian's action is culturally determined." Hence, "the transcendent, absolute quality of the Christian ethic in society can enter" only "in the inward attitude of the Christian to his own action": with knowledge of the partiality and sinfulness of the action, with repentance for that sin, in confidence of divine mercy, and with forgiveness toward his or her enemies. Gilkey claimed, although at that point he offered no concrete proposals, that the newer situation "required" more "from the Christian faith than the inward comfort for what is outwardly a cultural decision."[53]

Gilkey continued, however, to refine his understanding of neoorthodoxy's inherent stress fractures. Accordingly, Gilkey perceived neoorthodoxy's aporias in another facet of its dual posture. On the one hand, neoorthodox theology *retained* the liberal insistence on modern scientific cosmology, "the causal continuum of space-time experience," on the basis of which assumption theology "does not expect, nor does it speak of, wondrous divine events on the surface of natural and historical life." Yet, on the other hand, neoorthodox theology *rejected* the liberal "reduction" of "revelation to subjective human insight" or to a "subjective human creation," thus affirming revelation as "objective divine activity" in human history and using biblical or orthodox language to speak theologically about those "mighty acts of God." Gilkey recognized that, while "both the biblical and the orthodox understanding of theological language was *univocal*," neoorthodox usage of the biblical and orthodox language was *analogical*. As a consequence, since neoorthodox theologians also used this language without clearly understanding either the analogy's meaning (how they used the analogy) or the analogy's referent (that to which the analogy points), Gilkey claimed that such analogical language became "empty and unintelligible," "abstract," "self-contradictory," and,

---

[53]Gilkey, "Christian Response to the World Crisis," 109-10.

thus, *"equivocal."*[54] Gilkey demonstrated the validity of his claim by analyzing two categories of neoorthodox theological language.

First, he examined *the category of God's mighty acts.* Clearly, this language refers to God's activity in human history in wondrous events or miracles. As Gilkey observed, for an event to qualify as "a mighty act of God," then that event "must in some sense be more than an ordinary run-of-the-mill event," "must be objectively or ontologically different from other events." Nevertheless, neoorthodox and biblical theologies interpreted those divine events in terms of natural phenomena, thus denying the actuality as well as the possibility of miracles. Hence, this way of interpreting the biblical language emptied the content from the language of "God's mighty acts," effectively reducing those events to the status of all other historical or natural events. Only people with faith can discern "the mighty act of God" in the historical and natural occurrences of ordinary experience.[55]

Second, Gilkey also inquired into the meaning of *the category of revelation* in "a mighty acts theology." On the one hand, as I noted previously, neoorthodox and biblical theologies asserted that "God is not known through general, natural, historical, or inward experience" (hence, neoorthodoxy's rejection of all natural theologies). On the other hand, the events of God's mighty acts are merely ordinary natural and historical phenomena, *interpreted* as God's mighty acts *by faith,* but also explainable in terms of contemporary science and history. Gilkey perceived a glaring self-contradiction in this perspective. Thus, he raised this question: since the person of faith interprets ordinary events as God's mighty acts, from where does that faith first originate, if not through the ordinary experience already denied as an avenue for the origination of faith? As a result, Gilkey identified two mortal weaknesses in this neo-

---

[54]Gilkey, "Cosmology, Ontology, and the Travail of Biblical Language," 194-96, 203; emphasis mine.

[55]Gilkey, "Cosmology, Ontology, and the Travail of Biblical Language," 200. Gilkey had begun to see this as early as 1958 in an article in which he reviewed two books: John Knox, *The Death of Christ* (Nashville: Abingdon Press, 1958); and Richard Reinhold Niebuhr, *Resurrection and Historical Reason* (New York: Charles Scribner's Sons, 1957). In his appreciative comments about Niebuhr's book, Gilkey declares the book's significance to be "in the clarity and power with which he [Niebuhr] has grasped and expressed the central issue for theology in the immediate future, the problem of 'historicity' in biblical faith" (Langdon B. Gilkey, "Biblical Theology and Historical Reality," *Encounter* 19 [Spring 1958]: 218).

orthodox perspective. (1) Since the person of faith discerns the activity of God through the various phenomena of ordinary experience, for Gilkey, this approach qualified as a sort of natural religion or theology, in spite of neoorthodoxy's rejection of this epistemological avenue for faith and theology. (2) Although biblical and neoorthodox theologians constructed their theologies on the basis of the claim that God had acted *objectively* in human history, by emphasizing the events of God's mighty acts as the interpretation of natural or historical phenomena by faith, "religious insight and imagination" or "subjective experience," they eliminated objectivity from the category of revelation and reduced the concept of revelation to "a daring human hypothesis."[56]

Through recognition of these severe internal weaknesses in the neoorthodox perspective to which he remained committed, Gilkey identified the desperate need for "a theological ontology" that would "put intelligible and credible meanings into our analogical categories of divine deeds and of divine self-manifestation through events." Gilkey called for "an ontology of events" that would specify "what God's relation to ordinary events is like, and thus what his relation to special events might be." This task, according to Gilkey, belongs to philosophical theology.[57] Before theology can proceed intelligibly and credibly—that is to say, *relevantly*—in the contemporary situation, it must address this issue adequately and without delay.

Another central impulse in Gilkey's theology, specifically his major *doctrinal concern with divine providence*, also arose from his insights about the disintegration of neoorthodox theology. Because neoorthodoxy insisted on revelation as "the saving encounter of the inward self in faith and surrender to God's word [not to be understood, of course, as identical to the words of scripture themselves] and can reveal God *only* as he appears and acts in that personal, inward relationship," neoorthodox method restricted "theological statements about God" to knowledge of God gained through that "immediate, personal encounter of faith." As Gilkey noted, then, this position implicitly placed "theological statements about God's works outside this inward relation to his people beyond the

---

[56]Gilkey, "Cosmology, Ontology, and the Travail of Biblical Language," 201, 202. Gilkey develops these criticisms more precisely later: see Gilkey, "Theology," 247-50.

[57]Gilkey, "Cosmology, Ontology, and the Travail of Biblical Language," 200, 203, 204, 205. With this assessment, of course, Gilkey prepared himself to assume just such a philosophical task in *Naming the Whirlwind*.

range of theology." This meant that theology spoke "not about God," but about human "knowing of God." This resulted in neoorthodoxy's "epistemological bias": theological discourse about God that originates outside the personal encounter with God "*must* involve an objective biblicism or an objective natural theology." This neoorthodox bias bothered Gilkey, since, as he expressed it, "some essential doctrines do concern God's actions in the world beyond his relationship with us and the covenant community in its existential encounter with him." Neoorthodox epistemology and method eliminated the ability of this theological movement to develop an adequate account of the Christian doctrine of providence, the doctrine that "concerns God's relations to ordinary events as such, events in nature and in history generally" or "speaks of the relations of God to creatures quite outside the special, revealing acts of God, and also outside the inward faith response of believing men." For Gilkey, this doctrinal deficiency in neoorthodox theology (a deficiency directly resulting from neoorthodox theological method) required a significant methodological change, in order to escape that which finally amounted to (however unintentionally) neoorthodoxy's very anthropocentric and soteriological approach. Thus, Gilkey's concern about recovering the doctrine of providence in contemporary theology yielded his aim to develop a more adequate "theological ontology," in order to specify the meaning of theology's analogical language about "the sovereignty or lordship of God," "the mighty acts of God," or "the meaning of historical existence," an aim that led him finally to reform his own theological method.[58]

---

[58]Langdon B. Gilkey, "The Concept of Providence in Contemporary Theology," *Journal of Religion* 43 (July 1963): 181-86. Thus, Gilkey's two later books, *Naming the Whirlwind* and *Reaping the Whirlwind*, would always have an essential relationship to one another and originate from these basic insights and commitments. In *NW*, Gilkey aims to establish the conditions for meaningful theological reflection, by discovering within the characteristics of secular experience itself the experience of ultimacy and sacrality: that is, Gilkey searched to find the referent of religious language and its essential character, hence establishing *the meaningfulness of that discourse*. Furthermore, in *RW*, Gilkey employs the theological method proposed in *NW* to elaborate the theological meaning of the Christian doctrine of providence. Not merely coincidentally had the meaninglessness of religious discourse appeared alongside the disappearance of the doctrine of providence from neoorthodox theology. Once Gilkey had established the meaning of religious discourse, by discerning the dimension of ultimacy in ordinary or secular experience, not only had he made possible meaningful theological reflection in general and meaningful theological reflection on the doctrine of providence in particular. Most importantly for my present point, Gilkey's discovery of this religious dimension in secular experience also

2. *Challenge of The God-Is-Dead Theologies.* In the early 1960s, the appearance of a radical theology, proclaiming the death of God and proposing a Christianity without God, closely followed the disintegration of neoorthodox thought. Gilkey even characterized this radical theology as a "rebellion against the prevailing modes of neoorthodoxy," identifying the instigators of that insurrection as "the new rebellious Titans."[59] Those

---

verified the Christian doctrine of providence itself. The doctrine of providence, which "concerns God's relations to ordinary events as such, events in nature and in history generally" or "speaks of the relations of God to creatures quite outside the special, revealing acts of God, and also outside the inward faith response of believing men," affirms precisely the actuality (and, therefore, the possibility) of that dimension of sacrality in ordinary experience, quite outside those special historical events of divine revelation affirmed by faith. As Gilkey would later note about the referentiality of religious discourse in ordinary experience, the Christian doctrine or symbol of "providence is *about*" humanity's ordinary experience of the "search for meaning," just as "the symbol of creation is *about*" humanity's "ordinary experiences of contingency" (Langdon Gilkey, "New Modes of Empirical Theology," in *Essays in Divinity*, ed. Jerald C. Brauer, vol. 7, *The Future of Empirical Theology*, ed. Bernard E. Meland [Chicago: University of Chicago Press, 1969], 361). On this point, Gilkey also said the following: "But such a divine presence in the present, grounding the possibilities of our meaningful work toward God's future, is precisely God's hidden but real activity in the present, which has been 'named' by the symbol of providence" (Gilkey, *CCM*, 146, also see 147-55). Gilkey's interpretation of the doctrine of providence implied the sacral dimension of ordinary experience that he discovered in his analysis of the characteristics of secular experience, while his analysis of secular experience presupposed precisely a doctrine of providence.

[59]Langdon Gilkey, "Is God Dead? An Examination of a Contemporary View," *The Voice: Bulletin of Crozier Theological Seminary* 57 (January 1965): 4; idem, "A Paganized Judaism," review of *After Auschwitz*, by Richard Rubenstein, in *Christian Century* 84 (10 May 1967): 628. As Gilkey noted, Rubenstein's argument for the death of God, of course, differed significantly from most arguments made by other death-of-God theologians, not depending on "an obsolete verification principle" to support his "attack on God-language," but rather upon "the most profound of bases: the mystery of terrible evil and arbitrary death" (Gilkey, "A Paganized Judaism," 628). As examples of this theology, Gilkey referred to specific works by three younger theologians: William Hamilton, *The New Essence of Christianity* (New York: Association Press, 1961); Paul M. van Buren, *The Secular Meaning of the Gospel: Based on an Analysis of Its Language* (New York: Macmillan Co., 1963); and Thomas J. J. Altizer, *Oriental Mysticism and Biblical Eschatology* (Philadelphia: Westminster Press, 1961). Although Gilkey did not agree with this new radical theology, he admits that he "had a hand in the founding of that potent if brief movement." William Hamilton and Gilkey were friends. In the fall of 1963, shortly after reading Hamilton's *New Essence of Christianity*, within a period of three weeks, Gilkey had also met first Thomas Altizer and then Paul M. van Buren, both

who espoused God-is-dead theologies perceived the inherent problems of neoorthodox thought, as most apparent in its dualism: its acceptance of both secularism's "naturalistically interpreted world" and "a biblically understood God giving meaning and coherence thereto." According to Gilkey, however, the aporias of neoorthodoxy did not produce its "sudden demise," but rather reflected the more basic problem, the "fundamental mood of secularism" with which neoorthodoxy finally could not cope. Many of the radical theologians, who themselves had experienced "secular doubt" due to a variety of factors, accepted secularism's empirical methods of verification and falsification, and perceived the inability of neoorthodox claims to withstand those tests. Since the claims of neoorthodox theology, such as its language about the mighty acts of God, could be neither verified with the empirical methods of secularism nor explained naturalistically, those claims became meaningless and unintelligible.[60]

Most importantly, Gilkey noted, for God-is-dead theologies, religious and theological discourse is meaningless and unintelligible not merely due to internal inconsistencies in one or several theological perspectives. Rather, for the radical theologies, religious and theological discourse was meaningless because God "is not there at all." Religious language does

---

of whom he subsequently introduced to one another and to Hamilton (Gilkey, "Retrospective Glance at My Work," 23-24). With his second book, Gilkey registered his initial encounters with the God-is-dead theologies, as he addressed the problems posed by secularism for the churches in the North American society of the early 1960s (e.g., Gilkey, HCCM, 20-27). Gilkey's extensive analysis and critique of the radical or death-of-God theologies forms an essential element in his argument for the meaningfulness of God-language (see Gilkey, NW, 107-78). Martin Marty noted almost two decades ago that Gilkey had admitted "that he then tailored more of his own thinking to the secular outlook than he now likes to remember," seeing since that time "a great loss of faith in science and reason and a quickening of interest again in the sacred, in the religious evidences in the world around the theologian" (Martin E. Marty, "How Their Minds Have Changed," in *Theologians in Transition: The Christian Century "How My Mind Has Changed" Series*, ed. James M. Wall [New York: Crossroad Pub. Co., 1981] 10).

[60]Langdon Gilkey, "Secularism's Impact on Contemporary Theology," *Christianity and Crisis* 25 (5 April 1965): 65, 66; idem, "Trends in Protestant Apologetics," 64-65; idem, "Is God Dead," 6; idem, "Dissolution and Reconstruction in Theology," *Christian Century* 82 (3 February 1965): 135-36. In his analysis of the problem of the contemporary North American churches, Gilkey had already identified "the disappearance of the holy" or the "religious dimension" of human experience largely as the cause of "the irrelevance and unintelligibility of theological language about the church" (Gilkey, HCCM, 145).

not refer to anything real and verifiable by secular methods, "so language and thought about him [God] are meaningless and all relations to him vacant, empty, and unreal." Thus, the very *word* "God" had died for these radical theologies. This claim, consequently, applied to every view or concept of God, not only to neoorthodoxy's concept of God.[61]

B. Shift to Anthropology in Theological Method

Because neoorthodox theology had begun to disintegrate from inherent problems in the dualism of its methodological approach to the secular world, and because that disintegration had resulted in the challenges represented so forcefully by the God-is-dead theologies, Gilkey realized that theology must take a different approach altogether to address the central contemporary problem for theology: the reality of God and, therefore, the meaningfulness of God-language itself.[62] On the one hand, Gilkey had recognized "that theology must reflect the secular consciousness of our time if it is to be relevant."[63] Hence, he knew that he must directly address this central problem for theology, in order for theology

---

[61]Langdon Gilkey, review of *The Secular Meaning of the Gospel*, by Paul M. van Buren, in *Journal of Religion* 44 (July 1964): 240; idem, "New Modes of Empirical Theology," 351; idem, "Secularism's Impact on Contemporary Theology," 64; idem, "A Theology in Process: Schubert Ogden's Developing Theology," review of *The Reality of God and Other Essays*, by Schubert Ogden, in *Interpretation* 21 (October 1967): 457; idem, *NW*, 3-145. Gilkey thoroughly disagreed with theologians (such as Schubert M. Ogden, John B. Cobb, Jr., Daniel Day Williams, and Leslie Dewart) who claimed that declarations of God's death in the radical theologies, the then-contemporary problem of God, had originated as reactions to the God of classical theism or to the traditional idea of "the Absolute God" (Gilkey, "New Modes of Empirical Theology," 351n.2; idem, "A Theology in Process: Schubert Ogden's Developing Theology," 448-50; idem, "Process Theology," *Vox Theologica* 34 (January 1973): 7-9; idem, "The Problem of God: A Programmatic Essay," in *Traces of God in a Secular Culture*, ed. George F. McClean [Staten Island NY: Alba House, 1973] 4). Gilkey rightly perceived the problem of God in the radical theologies as a far more serious situation for theology: the word "God" simply referred to nothing verifiable in secular or ordinary experience, whether the concept of God originated from ancient Greek philosophical ontology, neoorthodox revelational theology, liberal theology, process theology, or any other theological or metaphysical perspective. Gilkey several times referred to this aspect of secularism as "one of the main ingredients of the present secular mood," describing it variously as a " 'posture of metaphysical modesty,' " the " 'inferiority complex of speculative reason,' " or the "modern mood of metaphysical modesty" (Gilkey, *NW*, 223, 448).

[62]Gilkey, "Dissolution and Reconstruction in Theology," 136.

[63]Gilkey, "Secularism's Impact on Contemporary Theology," 66.

to regain its relevance for contemporary human life. On the other hand, he also perceived the fundamental need of the contemporary human situation, as so deeply experienced in its secularism, for healing and meaning from an ultimate reality that transcends the situation itself. Nonetheless, Gilkey knew that, in order for the gospel to speak meaningfully to the secularism of the contemporary situation, he must begin with a study of human experience or an anthropology, a beginning that would examine the characteristics of secularism to discern its own religious character and, therefore, its own need for a reality that transcends everything creaturely. Gilkey described this anthropological analysis as "phenomenological," an analysis of "those realms of ordinary experience that we call secular," that "will reveal dimensions for which only language about God is sufficient and thus will manifest the meaningfulness of that language."[64]

C. Stages of Revised Correlational Theological Method

Although Gilkey significantly modified his theological method, his theological method remained correlational, empirical, apologetic, and still essentially neoorthodox.[65] Gilkey, however, extended his assessment of the human problem in the contemporary situation. This shift to a philosophical anthropology as prolegomenon to theology certainly did not introduce the analysis of experience into Gilkey's correlational theology. Rather, it deepened that analysis. Nonetheless, this shift did represent Gilkey's effort to establish the meaningfulness of theological language for

---

[64]Gilkey, "Dissolution and Reconstruction in Theology," 137; idem, "If There Is No God: The Problem of God and the Study of Theology," *Criterion* 6 (Spring 1967): 6; idem, "Secularism's Impact on Contemporary Theology," 67.

[65]About this innovation in his method, Gilkey later made the following claim: "As is evident, I was seeking here to preserve what I regarded as the essential core of my earlier neoorthodoxy while giving to that core a now much needed ground or base in common experience." Gilkey also then repeated his reliance on Paul Tillich's method of correlation at this stage in the development of his own theological method (Gilkey, "Retrospective Glance at My Work," 25; also see idem, *NW*, 455n.23). Gilkey's most recent interpretation of Tillich's correlational theological method also illuminates his own approach to theological method beginning in this and continuing throughout the later periods of Gilkey's career: Gilkey, *GOT*, 56-78; idem, "Tillich: The Master of Mediation," in *The Theology of Paul Tillich*, 2nd ed., ed. Charles W. Kegley (New York: Pilgrim Press, 1982) 26-59; cf. George F. Thomas, "The Method and Structure of Tillich's Theology," in *The Theology of Paul Tillich*, 2nd ed., ed. Charles W. Kegley (New York: Pilgrim Press, 1982) 120-39.

human experience by analyzing that experience differently, prior to interpreting traditions of testimony to divine revelation in history as answers
to the questions or problems of the contemporary human situation. Here
the then-present problem in the human situation was secularism, the loss
of meaningfulness from religious discourse. About "method in theology,"
Gilkey perceived, like Tillich before him, the intimate relationship
between method and content. As Tillich expressed this point, "a method
is not an 'indifferent net' in which reality is caught, but the method is an
element of the reality itself."[66] Gilkey realized also that method is both
"a part of that wider whole which is expressed in an entire philosophical
or theological system" and, finally, "an expression, and only a partial one,
of that deeper vision of things which dominates a whole era of cultural
experience and thought."[67]

Gilkey employed a specific theory of meaning as the basis for his
theological approach. Most generally, according to that theory, "meaning
results from an interaction of experience and symbol, and thus the
meaning of religious symbols is, in the first instance, found in relation to
the experiences which they thematize and bring to expression and
clarity." Gilkey expanded his theological method into four stages or tasks,
the "union" of which "constitutes the creative effort of systematic or constructive theology."[68] First, Gilkey proposed a phenomenological hermeneutic of secular experience, through which the theologian as philosopher
discovers or unveils the problems of the human situation, the questions
arising from human experience. Second, Gilkey followed this with an
eidetic analysis of specific religious symbols, in which the theologian
interprets the symbols or language of the Christian tradition and discerns
divinely given answers to the questions or the human situation as
expressed through the Christian tradition. Third, Gilkey proposed to bring
these two analyses together in a dialectical interpretation or correlation of
both experienced secular questions and received symbolic Christian
answers in contemporary language, categories, and concepts. Fourth,
according to Gilkey, theology must finally delineate the implications of
the intrinsic political meaning of religious symbols for contemporary
moral, social, and political experience.[69]

---

[66]Tillich, *Systematic Theology* 1:60.
[67]Gilkey, *NW*, 190.
[68]Gilkey, *CCM*, 115.
[69]In *Naming the Whirlwind*, Gilkey identified and described three stages in theological

1. *Phenomenology of Secular Experience: Questions of Human Existence.* Gilkey described the first stage of his theological method as a prolegomenon to theology, a philosophy of religion, an anthropology, not as theology itself. In light of both the collapse of neoorthodox theological method and the corresponding challenge of the God-is-dead theologies, Gilkey perceived the need to establish the meaningfulness of theological discourse. He aimed to accomplish this task through a phenomenology or a phenomenological hermeneutic of secular experience. In this phenomenological hermeneutic, Gilkey sought to accomplish two goals: first, to discover the region of religious discourse or the experience of ultimacy and sacrality in ordinary or secular experience; and, second, to establish the character of religious discourse itself.

---

method in the following order: (1) phenomenological hermeneutic of secular experience; (2) eidetic analysis of religious symbols; and (3) ontological elucidation of religious symbols (in terms of other fields of contemporary human understanding, such as psychology, epistemology, ethics, sociology, politics) (Gilkey, *NW*, 454-59; also see idem, "New Modes of Empirical Theology," 366-70; idem, "Problem of God," 19-23; idem, "The Universal and Immediate Presence of God," in *The Future of Hope*, ed. Frederick Herzog [New York: Herder and Herder, 1970] 98-101). In *Catholicism Confronts Modernity*, however, Gilkey identified four stages in theological method or four tasks for theology, with a change in their order: (1) hermeneutical and historical or eidetic analysis of religious or Christian symbols; (2) "analysis of contemporary, lived experience," the "phenomenological and existential" task of theology; (3) ontological elucidation; and (4) moral and political action (Gilkey, *CCM*, 115-26, 128-55; cf. idem, *RSF*, 127-36). A look at Gilkey's criteria for relevant and adequate theological discourse as he describes them in *NW*, however, will clarify this discrepancy between the stages of theological method as proposed in *NW* and those proposed in *CCM*. In *NW*, aiming at his goal to reestablish the meaningfulness of God-language, Gilkey distinguished the meaning of religious or theological discourse from the validity of that discourse. As a result, Gilkey outlined four criteria with which he attended, on the one hand, to the meaning and, on the other hand, to the validity of theological language. Consequently, theological language became meaningful and valid (or true) as it met four conditions or exhibited four characteristics: (1) "traditional depth," fidelity to or "consistent expression of the symbolic forms of the historical community"; (2) "existential concreteness" or "relevance to contemporary existence"; (3) "width of intelligibility," "ontological elucidation," or "width of relevance" and "explanatory power"; and (4) "participation in the symbol as a vehicle of the ultimate and the sacred" or "existential involvement in both the questions that are being asked and the answers that are being received" (Gilkey, *NW*, 459-65). It appears that Gilkey developed the fourth stage in his method, as proposed in *CCM*, from elements of the fourth criterion of existential involvement as expressed in *NW*.

(a) Aiming toward his *first goal*, then, *Gilkey identified four basic characteristics of secular experience: contingency or finitude, relativity, temporality or transience, and autonomy or freedom.* Through analyses of these characteristics, he demonstrated that all aspects of secular experience point beyond themselves, manifesting both positive and negative ultimate concerns or questions of ultimacy in human experience. For example, negatively, each of these characteristics of secular experience produces a corresponding form of anxiety for humans: a sense of *fatedness* in contingency; *meaninglessness* resulting from the relativity of all human values; the *unpredictable or threatening future and the mortality* in temporality; and the *ambiguity* of autonomy or freedom as reflected in its demonic potential and sin. The human seeks to overcome each of these threats and the anxieties that correspond to them, to answer these questions about human life: searching for that which guarantees the human's ultimate *security, purpose or meaning, lasting significance*, and *salvation*. Yet, the human discovers that it can neither overcome the characteristics of experience that produce these anxieties nor project the dissolution of those anxieties themselves through finitude alone.[70]

---

[70]Gilkey, *NW*, 39-71, 315-413; idem, "Unbelief and the Secular Spirit," in *The Presence and Absence of God*, ed. C. F. Mooney (New York: Fordham University Press, 1969) 50-68; idem, "New Modes of Empirical Theology," 358-61; idem, "Problem of God," 5-15; idem, *RSF*, 35-64, 127-28; cf. idem, *CCM*, 63-83, 163, 173-74; idem, "Retrospective Glance at My Work," 24-25. Compare Gilkey's earlier interpretation of the four characteristics of secular experience with his most recent interpretation of "*five* fundamental ontological characteristics of all that is in our experience—of all of finite actuality or, in theological language, all of 'created reality.' " While Gilkey reshapes the original four characteristics, he retains those four characteristics, but identifies and adds a fifth characteristic: "Order as 'self-maintaining' " (Gilkey, *NRS*, 196-200; emphasis mine). Also, note that Gilkey's phenomenological analysis, prolegomenon to theology, or philosophical anthropology identifies in the ambiguity of human autonomy the presence of its negative or demonic potential—sin.

If Gilkey developed his initial interpretation of the Christian doctrine of creation, in *Maker of Heaven and Earth*, as the answer to the question of fatedness implied by the human experience of contingency, in *Naming the Whirlwind* he turned his attention primarily to the human experience of relativity in order to provide the basis to respond to the human anxiety over the threat of meaninglessness in that relativity. In this sense, then, despite Gilkey's claim that this prolegomenon is not theology itself, *Naming the Whirlwind* still supplied the first stage to a Christian doctrine of providence, not completed until the second stage in his *Reaping the Whirlwind*.

According to Gilkey, the questions of ultimacy that arise in relation to each of these four characteristics of secular experience constitute four general *situations* in ordinary experience to which religious discourse refers or responds or answers and in which religious discourse finds an appropriate (and inescapable or necessary) use.[71] Nonetheless, in this first stage, Gilkey quite rightly distinguishes this effort from systematic theology proper, insofar as he establishes the condition of possibility in human experience for the meaningfulness in general of religious discourse, by unveiling the ultimate questions in secular experience that religious discourse articulates and to which religious language responds. For systematic theology, the specific situations to which the Christian message responds in various ways would require further analyses and specification.

The results from Gilkey's phenomenological analysis of actual secular experience proved to vary from the claims of secularism about secular experience itself. The characteristics of secular experience (contingency, temporality, relativity, and autonomy) raise questions of ultimacy for humans that secularism itself cannot answer on its own terms. Thus,

---

[71]Gilkey, *NW*, 297. The first step of Gilkey's method follows closely the character of the first stage in Tillich's correlational method. For Tillich, systematic theology "makes an analysis of the human situation out of which the existential questions arise, and it demonstrates that the symbols used in the Christian message are the answers to these questions." Most significantly, these questions are humans themselves: "Man is the question he asks about himself, before any question has been formulated." Furthermore, "[t]he analysis of the human situation employs materials made available by man's creative self-interpretation in all realms of culture. . . . The theologian organizes these materials in relation to the answer given by the Christian message" (Tillich, *Systematic Theology* 1:62, 63). In his own effort to answer the concerns of linguistic philosophy (specifically, in reference to the work of J. L. Austin and A. J. Ayer), Gilkey generally described a situation in terms of the production of meaning. "Meaning is thus assuredly related to usage and a given communal context. But what, we may ask, is really going on when we inquire about usage? What are we doing when we describe a paradigmatic situation or context in which people appropriately use a word or a family of words? In answer we suggest that in fact we are elucidating, appealing to, or evoking a memory of that region or area of our immediate or direct, and commonly shared, experience of things—for a 'situation' is a region or element of our experience of being in the world—in which or to which the word is applicable. And this applicability to or in a given situation signifies that there the word serves an important function of clarifying and so, through the provision of thematic and symbolic forms, gives 'meaning' to the felt character of that experience or situation which the community of usage shares amongst them" (Gilkey, *NW*, 268-69).

Gilkey concluded, secular experience required *religious* discourse, a language that could thematize the human experience of ultimacy or the unconditioned, a language that secularism had already yet inconsistently declared to be meaningless on the basis of the empirical methods and questions of the secular worldview: for example, in terms of the criteria of verification and falsification as developed by positivistic linguistic philosophy. Accordingly, since secular experience manifested a religious dimension to which religious language referred and which religious language thematized, then religious language was meaningful even when tested by the empirical criteria of secularism itself. Religious discourse referred to something empirical, something in human experience itself; religious language thematized the human experience of ultimacy. While Gilkey sought to establish the *meaningfulness* of religious discourse by unveiling the religious dimension in ordinary experience to which it referred, however, he quite intentionally distinguished this task from the effort to establish the *validity or truth* of religious language. Gilkey neither pretended to prove the existence of the ultimate (the unconditioned, the sacred, or God) nor to prove the truth of Christian claims about God with his phenomenological hermeneutic of secular experience. He only hoped to prove the reality of the religious dimension of ordinary human experience, thus establishing the meaningfulness of religious language. Without a doubt, Gilkey knew that religious discourse referred to God or the ultimate, but only as experienced and encountered. Hence, although religious language referred to *the experience* of the ultimate, the presence of the religious dimension in human experience did not necessarily either prove the existence or clarify the character of the divine.[72] Nonetheless, by identifying the religious dimension of all human experience, philosophy (in this case phenomenological hermeneutics) only gives to theology " 'potentialities for meaning' through its delineation of

---

[72]Gilkey, "Dissolution and Reconstruction in Theology," 137-38; idem, *NW*, 247-304; idem, "New Modes of Empirical Theology," 356-61, 366; idem, "Problem of God," 9-13, 19; idem, *CCM*, 163. Regarding his distinction between the *meaning* and the *validity* (or *truth*) of religious language, Gilkey notes the following: "In such an investigation [a phenomenological hermeneutic of secular experience], all the religious symbols, positive and negative, plural and singular, ours and theirs, can be investigated with regard to the dimension of our experience to which these all refer, without raising the question whether this one or that, or any of them, is ontologically *true* or not" (Gilkey, *NW*, 283n.25).

the experiences which religious symbols mean and in terms of which these symbols are to be comprehended."[73]

(b) After discovering the region in human experience to which religious language referred, the region in experience of its proper use for religious language, or the religious dimension of ordinary human experience, Gilkey then pursued *the second goal* of his prolegomenon: *to describe the character of religious language, or the way in which religious language conveys meaning.* According to Gilkey, a phenomenological analysis of secular experience discloses a religious dimension that secularity cannot avoid completely yet cannot articulate without religious language. Thus, as I noted previously, most basically, religious discourse articulates, "expresses," "thematizes," or brings "to clarity" the religious dimension in ordinary or secular experience.[74] Religious language, there-

---

[73]Gilkey, "Problem of God," 19; idem, "New Modes of Empirical Theology," 366.

[74]Gilkey, "Universal and Immediate Presence of God," 98-101; idem, *NW*, 269-70, 456; idem, *RSF*, 127-28; idem, *CCM*, 163; idem, "New Modes of Empirical Theology," 366; idem, "Problem of God," 19. Even in *HCCM*, Gilkey had already begun to employ a version of this theory of religious language as he tried to address the problem of the church in a secular culture. For example, according to Gilkey, "the purpose of theological discourse is to point to, *express*, and so far as is possible make intelligible the appearance of the holy in our *experience*. If the holy seems not at all to appear, then it is natural that discourse about it should seem irrelevant, meaningless, and empty" (Gilkey, *HCCM*, 145-46). Nonetheless, in *HCCM*, Gilkey's theory of religious language remained very close to, even if a significant deepening of, his previous understanding of the nature of religious language in *MHE*, although Gilkey's earliest emphasis on divine revelation reflects a more Niebuhrian than Tillichian character. "The analogies by which we seek to understand God stem, therefore, from our special experiences of revelation, rather than from the general experiences of our common life." For Gilkey, Christian theology is "a system of concepts *drawn from* and so *expressive* of the meaning of definite historical events." The Christian symbols "are analogical, and so 'mythical,' *expressions of* the meaning that is discerned to be *the deeper dimension* of the historical fact of Jesus of Nazareth" (Gilkey, *MHE*, 325-26, 344; emphasis mine). In his *Nature of Doctrine*, Lindbeck does not refer at all to Gilkey's theological method. In Lindbeck's discussion of approaches to the study of religion and theological method, to his own preference for a "cultural-linguistic" approach (which he construes as a "postliberal" method), he contrasts an approach that he describes as the "experiential-expressive model." Lindbeck includes Paul Tillich, Bernard Lonergan, Karl Rahner, and David Tracy, among many others, in his list of proponents of an experiential-expressive approach that began with Friedrich Schleiermacher (Lindbeck, *Nature of Doctrine*, 15-45). Gilkey's theological method, in this third phase of its development (as most clearly seen in *NW*), clearly represents that theological approach which Lindbeck describes as "experiential-expressivism," although Gilkey's correlational theological method still retains its original postliberal character as well. Lindbeck's typology seems

fore, acquires its peculiar character precisely because it refers to the unconditioned, the ultimate, the transcendent, the sacred, the holy, or the divine in ordinary experience, to that which transcends and undergirds all aspects of the ordinary course of existence and life. The referentiality of religious discourse, as a consequence, differentiates its character from that of all other discourse. Relying heavily on theories of symbol and myth developed by Mircea Eliade and Paul Ricoeur (as historical and philosophical resources to deepen his essentially Tillichian understanding of religious symbol), Gilkey identified "three characteristic features" of "all religious discourse" or all religious symbolism that tend to differentiate such language or symbolism from other types of language. First, religious language possesses a multivalence or a double intentionality, with both a reference to something *finite or empirical* as the medium through and in which the ultimate manifests itself, as the symbol that points beyond itself to the transcendent, and a reference to the *infinite or unconditioned* through that finite symbol. Second, religious symbols concern "existential or ultimate issues of life, the questions that involve us because they center around the security, meanings, frustrations, and hopes of our existence both individual and social." Third, religious symbols supply or offer crucial standards, models, or norms "by which life is directed and judged, and so by which culture as a whole is itself guided and assessed."[75]

In light of these studies in his prolegomenon, therefore, Gilkey discerned four kinds of meaning in religious language or symbols. Gilkey presupposed this theory of meaning as the basis from which he would produce relevant Christian theology. The *first level of meaning* in religious language, of course, concerns its primary referentiality: "those aspects of common experience which it [religious language] thematizes, conceptualizes, and so discloses to specific awareness and communication." Theological method, therefore, requires "a phenomenological hermeneutic of experience," precisely the work Gilkey has done in this

---

simply unable to allow the empirical evidence to present a form of postliberal theological method that also carries essential elements of experiential-expressivism even as Lindbeck describes it. Perhaps, for this reason, Lindbeck does not include Gilkey's theological method in either of his contrasting alternatives.

[75]Gilkey, *NW*, 284-95, 464. On Gilkey's theory of religious language or symbol during this period, also see the following: Gilkey, "Symbols, Meaning, and the Divine Presence," *Theological Studies* 35 (June 1974): 249-67; reprinted under the same title, as chap. 4, in Gilkey, *TT*, 49-65.

first stage of his method, to discover this level of meaning in religious language. The *second level of meaning* in religious language appears as its usage "in the activities and speech of a community," the community's "ordinary or current (though possibly technical) speech" which includes that language, the proper situations in which such language finds appropriate employment, or the context that reflects "the rules and patterns of its use." Methodologically, for this second level of meaning, according to Gilkey, theology requires "a linguistic analysis of ordinary or 'stock' usage," in order to discover this sort of meaning in religious language or symbols. Gilkey refers to a *third level of meaning* in religious language as its eidetic meaning, "the interrelations" of a religious symbol "to other symbols in the same structural system," or "to the other symbols with which it forms a system of symbols." Gilkey identifies this eidetic structure as the primary sort of meaning with which most biblical, historical, and systematic theologies have usually concerned themselves. To discover this third level of meaning, Gilkey calls for an eidetic analysis, to discover "the essential structure or essence of a symbol." Gilkey describes a *fourth level of meaning* in religious language as "its ontological or philosophical meaning," how religious language means when related "systematically to all that we know of other things" or when understood "within the system of things I call the world." To discover such meaning for religious language requires both the employment of contemporary epistemology and ontology; methodologically, theology must perform an ontological analysis or a search for the "relation of symbols to the universal structures of being."[76]

2. *Eidetic Phenomenology of Religious Symbols: Answers of Divine Revelation.* Strictly speaking, systematic theology properly begins only after the theologian has completed a phenomenological (philosophical) analysis of ordinary or secular experience. The analysis of secular experience yields ultimate questions or identifies the region in experience of the unconditioned, sacred, or transcendent reality. Gilkey describes this religious dimension of all ordinary experience as "[g]eneral revelation" or "the mode in which the universal presence—or sense of absence—of the unconditioned and the sacred enters into human awareness." Nevertheless, phenomenological analysis discloses this religious dimension in the questions that human finitude generates for itself, in the

---

[76]Gilkey, *NW*, 274-75.

problem that finitude becomes for itself. Finitude alone, however, can only raise *questions* "about an ultimate, about that which it itself is not." Because the questions arise from human experience of contingency, relativity, temporality, and autonomy, the *answers to those questions* require "an essential ingredient of ultimacy or unconditionedness that no creature can possess or create." An answer, therefore, must come *"from* transcendence *to* finitude, from that which in *not* sharing in these dependencies of the creature is itself *more than* creaturely." For this reason, Gilkey's phenomenological hermeneutic of secular experience cannot supply answers to the ultimate questions that it discovers. As Gilkey expresses it, "[a] *break* must appear at this point in the course of the argument of our prolegomenon; a *new* and a *particular* assumption must be made, an assumption based on some special experience of the ultimate nature of things." Accordingly, "[t]he 'new' must enter underived from the analysis that has gone before," precisely because "the affirmation of the answer," the new and particular assumption or faith itself, "always depends on the particularity of concrete special experiences where something has *entered* the ambiguity of life to clarify, re-create, and redeem it, and not on the general character of universal experience." Thus, according to Gilkey, because the sacred always enters into human awareness through "socially and historically conditioned" experience, "through definite historical symbolic media peculiar to that community," thus resulting in "some quite definite form of an answer to these universal problems," "[g]eneral revelation is always and in each case special revelation." In the human experience of answers to the ultimate questions of finitude itself, the "new" appears, the sacred, transcendent, unconditioned, or divine reality discloses itself. The human receives "such a manifestation of the sacred" by partaking of "two different levels of apprehension which generally accompany and supplement one another, but which in special circumstances may exist apart": (1) *the existential level*, the level of feeling or mood, experienced "as a confidence in life, a sense of worthful meaning, an apprehension of and commitment to certain values, a sense of unity and reconciliation, and the courage to face death"; and (2) *the symbolic level*, in which the self and its community express, thematize, and structure "experience as a whole" through "symbolic forms." Because the human's special experiences of answers to its ultimate questions originate from that which transcends everything creaturely, Gilkey described this symbolic expression or thematization of those experiences as "positive God-language," which he identified as "revelation" itself.[77]

On this basis, Gilkey defined *theology*, in general, as "the systematic reflection on the meaning and validity of the symbolic forms of a given religious community, from the point of view of one who shares that community's faith and life and so seeks responsibly to express its religious ethos" and *Christian* theology, in particular, as "the positive explication of the faith of this [Christian] community and so of the meaning for our day of the originating and traditional symbolic forms of its life." Elsewhere, Gilkey similarly defined Christian theology as "understanding, reflection on, and comprehension of our human experience, our being in the world, in terms of the symbols of the Christian tradition; much as being a Christian is existing (as opposed to reflecting) in the light and grace of that tradition."[78] Although these definitions tend to accentuate the theologian's responsibility to interpret the symbolic answers proposed by a religious or a Christian community, even in these definitions, Gilkey emphasized interpreting the meaning of these symbols "for our day." For this reason, Gilkey stressed that, "because Bible and tradition no longer function as direct and infallible authorities for Christian thought," because "nothing with regard to scripture or tradition is presupposed as an absolute authority today," the theologian's interpretations of the community's historic testimonies "are not *sufficient* for meaningful religious or theological affirmations."[79] An analysis of the questions in ordinary or secular experience must always accompany theological interpretations of the community's religious symbols if the latter would be meaningful, just as an interpretation of a religious community's symbols must accompany an analysis of ordinary experience if the interpretation of experience would be theological.

Thus, the second stage or essential element of a systematic theology requires an interpretation of this religious language. Gilkey describes this as an "eidetic analysis" of the central symbols of the Christian tradition or an "eidetic phenomenology of historic symbols in Biblical and historical theology," borrowing from the methods of both hermeneutic phenomenology and the phenomenological method employed by the history of religions. This stage of Gilkey's method directs its attention to

---

[77]Gilkey, *NW*, 417-19, 427-28, 445, 447, 450-51.
[78]Gilkey, *NW*, 421, 454; idem, *CCM*, 115.
[79]Gilkey, *NW*, 458-59; idem, *CCM*, 162.

the historic symbols of a religious community, the symbols of the *Christian* community in Gilkey's own theological work, specifically as those symbols appear in the community's scripture and tradition.[80]

In this second stage of theological method, the theologian aims to clarify or elucidate "the eidetic, intrinsic meaning" of a Christian symbol, "the intrinsic form of the symbol in itself," or the symbol's "intrinsic character," "intentional structure," or "structural" meaning. With the term "eidetic," Gilkey refers to the symbol's essential meaning and how it functions "in the system of symbols expressive" of the faith in a particular religious tradition or community. All religious symbols (here Gilkey refers specifically to "verbal symbols") possess eidetic meaning, "an essential structure of their own, a unique gestalt, an integrity and a logic which has objective status, and which gives to that system of symbols that characterize a particular religion or point of view its 'essence' and differentiates it from other religions and points of view." As Gilkey expressed it, as the "ultimate goal" for theology, an eidetic analysis aims to discover "a unified, coherent set of meanings inherent in each major symbol."[81]

In meeting that aim, Gilkey's eidetic analysis itself contains two steps. The first step of eidetic analysis reflects an objectivity (depending more on the object of study), while the second step reflects more subjectivity (depending more on the theologian who makes the study).

(a) *Objective Step: Eidetic Abstraction.* In the first step, the theologian abstracts the historic symbols of the religious community from their meaning for contemporary experience, life, and thought. Eidetic abstraction, as largely "a work of objective historical scholarship," analyzes the Christian symbols as transmitted in the Christian scriptures and traditions. Although Gilkey considers "the biblical sources" to be primary, "as the closest and most significant witnesses to the divine activity foundational to the community and the tradition, an initiating activity expressed originally through this symbolic witness and in the terms of these symbolic interpretations," he acknowledges that "[s]cripture and tradition are two aspects of one historical source." Thus, an eidetic analysis seeks

---

[80]Gilkey, *NW*, 283n.25, 458-61; idem, *CCM*, 115-22, 162-63; idem, "New Modes of Empirical Theology," 366-67; idem, "Problem of God," 19-20; idem, "Universal and Immediate Presence of God," 98-100; idem, "Christian Theology," *Criterion* 13 (Winter 1974): 12.

[81]Gilkey, *CCM*, 115-16, 120, 173; idem, *NW*, 458, 460-61.

to discover the objective meaning of the historic symbols of a community, not the meaning of these historic symbols for contemporary experience. Gilkey perceived three ways in which objectivity characterizes an eidetic analysis. *First*, an eidetic analysis aims to discover the meaning of a religious symbol in the past of the religious community, that which the symbol *meant* for the ancient Hebrews, the early Christians, the apostle Paul, Augustine, John Calvin, Schleiermacher, and many others. In this first sense, the theologian focuses on past understandings of the symbol, on that which was true for previous participants in the community. *Second*, objectivity also characterizes eidetic analysis, inasmuch as this task involves historical inquiry about the persons, events, and actions that form the basis of the stories, histories, or narratives of the historical sources (scriptures and traditions), inquiry into the history that lies behind and around the texts of scripture and tradition. The theologian, however, cannot allow her personal faith or "the dogmatic requirements" of the tradition to determine the conclusions of such historical inquiry. *Third*, the "main object of inquiry" shapes the principal form of objectivity in an eidetic analysis. This historical task focuses upon the referent of the text, "the meaning (or *noema*) of the text, or of the symbol or symbols with which the text is concerned: *the view of self, world, history, the future, and God that the text portrays through the symbols.*"[82]

(b) *Subjective Step: Eidetic Reduction.* The second step in an eidetic analysis introduces a primarily subjective character into the inquiry. As Gilkey openly notes, "[e]ach one of these original symbols has a variety of meanings in the whole scripture, and thus they are as plural and relative, as 'historical,' as anything else among the data of theology." Moreover, the Christian community has interpreted and reinterpreted this variety of biblical meanings, thus extending the tradition. Because scripture and tradition "have interpenetrated one another" in this way, Gilkey says that "they must be interpreted together." The "variety" or the "vast plurality of meanings, characteristic even of scripture itself, with regard to every major symbol," "increases in the history of the church's interpretations of these same symbols." Thus, in order for the theologian to use the plurality of the tradition, she must "distill the essential elements of

---

[82]Gilkey, *CCM*, 118-20; idem, *NW*, 461. Gilkey's understanding of the "main object of inquiry" in this historical study resembles the notion of referentiality in Paul Ricoeur's theory of written discourse. Reference designates the thing, the issue, or the world projected by discourse: Ricoeur, *Interpretation Theory*, 89-95.

these symbols' 'meanings' from these materials" (scripture and tradition), or render "some unifying synthesis of this diversity of meanings into one coherent or eidetic meaning." Gilkey refers to this exercise as "eidetic reduction." The theologian searches for "that common core of meanings that runs through all the variety of its traditional and legitimate uses." Nonetheless, Gilkey acknowledges the risk in this step of eidetic analysis, since the theologian must create "this unified symbol" from a diversity of meanings. Furthermore, that creative task involves the use of some meanings as "central to the entire scripture," as a sort of canon within the canon, "to provide the clue for understanding the whole body of biblical materials"; and, correspondingly, this creative task also requires the rejection of other forms of the same symbols as not central or not adequate to the essential meanings of those symbols. As Gilkey claims, "such a synthetic unity ("what the symbol has meant") can hardly be accepted from the past without criticism or reformulation." As a consequence, eidetic reduction contains " 'involved,' personal, intuitive" elements. Although biblical and historical theologies function as the primary disciplines to help the theologian perform an eidetic analysis, according to Gilkey, "this act of creative synthesis requires that ultimacy does speak to the interpreter through those chosen, central symbols and in those forms." Precisely this creative synthesis or eidetic reduction represents the transition between historical theologies (in which biblical theologies form a subset) and constructive or systematic theology, the latter of which "requires personal and existential involvement."[83]

3. *Ontological Elucidation of Religious Symbols.* Gilkey describes the third stage of his theological method as the ontological elucidation of religious symbols. With this third stage as well as with the next or final stage, Gilkey introduced new elements into the method of his Niebuhrian postliberalism.[84] Gilkey explained the task of ontological elucidation as

---

[83]Gilkey, *CCM*, 101, 116, 117, 120, 121, 122; idem, *NW*, 283n.25, 458, 461. Gilkey also uses the phrase, "phenomenological reduction, the *epoche* or bracket" in a second way: to refer to his adoption (in his phenomenological hermeneutic of secular experience) of the philosophical (Husserlian) practice of bracketing or shutting out "questions of 'explanation,' of the reality and the ontological structure lying behind what appears," in order to examine "the actual character of experience" (through an ontic analysis) to discover its dimension of ultimacy (Gilkey, *NW*, 282-83).

[84]As I noted previously, during this period of his theological development, Gilkey referred to his *Maker of Heaven and Earth* as an example of the Niebuhrian approach that he had modified, a method in which he did not consider ontological elucidation necessary

the "elaboration of a 'Christian philosophy,' " a labor in which the theologian extends "the primary religious symbolism" about all aspects relating to God, humanity, and the world "into more general ontological categories capable of elucidation in relation to all other special fields." To fulfill this task, the theologian must borrow "the conceptuality of a modern ontology" from "some example of contemporary philosophy." Only in this way does the theologian extend a symbolic system's "width of relevance and its adequacy of explanatory power." Fulfilling this task expands constructive theology's "scope of cultural relevance," by general reflection on the relation of religious symbols to "the totality of our experience," to everything that humans experience and think "of space and time, of substance and causality, of terms and relations, of forms and process, of necessity and freedom." Nonetheless, Gilkey admits the difficulty of this task, inasmuch as the theologian risks proclaiming "a modern secular ontology as unequivocally Christian, and our gods be different than God," as Gilkey thought that many of the radical theologians had done. For this reason, Gilkey claimed that "[t]he Christian symbol must rule the use" made "of any modern ontology," noting that, when borrowing such modern ontologies, the theologian must transform them "to fit the symbols of our tradition." Furthermore, Gilkey openly acknowledged the lack of an "available 'method' to set secure rules for this use of metaphysics and ontology in theology." Thus, even in this stage, Gilkey noted that the theologian can only "hope that our expression of Christian truth in modern and relevant ontological form is a faithful rendition of the Christian symbols" and "pray for the help of the Spirit" in the accomplishment of that goal.[85]

4. *Moral and Political Application of Religious Symbols.* In *Naming the Whirlwind*, Gilkey distinguished between the *meaningfulness or relevance* and the *truth or validity* of religious language, demonstrating the necessity of God-language for the expression of the human experience of ultimacy. In this way, Gilkey established the meaningfulness of religious discourse. The validity or truth of religious language, and most specifically the truth of Christian symbols as one form of that language, however, Gilkey did not attempt to prove there. On this point, Gilkey's

---

to theological construction (Gilkey, *CCM*, 126, 208n.6). With the introduction of this third and the fourth stages, Gilkey significantly modified his theological method.

[85]Gilkey, *NW*, 461, 463-64; idem, *CCM*, 102-104, 123-27, 163-64, 173-74; idem, "New Modes of Empirical Theology," 368-69; idem, "Problem of God," 20-23.

understanding remained consistent with his earlier neoorthodoxy: "Religious truth is truth in which the whole existence of every man is unconditionally involved." Nevertheless, he did state the condition of or the criterion for the validity or truthfulness of religious language: "participation in the symbol as a vehicle of the ultimate and the sacred." Accordingly, "a religious symbol is 'true' if it becomes for us a medium of the sacred, and it becomes 'false' when that communicative power vanishes." Even more strongly, Gilkey claimed that "religious symbols function as religious symbols and so are known to be true *only* by those to whom they communicate a religious meaning, i.e., an awareness of an ultimate ground to life's passage and an ultimate answer to life's crises." Gilkey naturally considered this to be a more subjective criterion than the "three more objective criteria," which derive from the three previous stages of his method during this period: (1) fidelity to tradition, (2) adequacy to contemporary experience, and (3) width of intelligibility or cultural scope. Nevertheless, Gilkey designated this subjective criterion, this "involvement implied in any apprehension of sacrality" or this "existential reception of the hierophany," as the "most important" criterion for a relevant theology.[86]

---

[86]Gilkey, *NW*, 260-66, 464-65; cf. idem, "New Modes of Empirical Theology," 369-70; idem, "Problem of God," 21-22; idem, "Christian Theology," 12-13; emphasis mine. Gilkey persistently repeated this claim from his more Niebuhrian period to this Tillichian stage of his theological development. "If the 'myth' of creation is taken to be literally and simply 'true,' that is, true in the sense that a description of any objective fact is true, then it loses all its religious character. For religious truth is truth in which the whole existence of every man is unconditionally involved. . . . [Christian doctrines] can never be simply proved by 'evidence,' for they themselves involve the more basic decision as to what sort of evidence is relevant. They can only be validated by their ability to provide a meaningful context for those basic intuitions which are taken to be the ultimate certainties of our experience" (Gilkey, *MHE*, 347, 350-51). "Of course one must add at once that the *validity* of God-language is by no means demonstrated by pointing out these depths in man's nature. No analysis of man can establish the reality of God; it may well be that the ultimate which man longs and searches for exists nowhere! Only a personal awareness of the total power and meaning of life, some positive apprehension of grace in its widest extent, can validate any form of language about God and thus provide the real starting point for a positive theology. Religious language is *meaningful* when it reflects and concerns man's inherent quest for an ultimate basis for his existence, a quest that reveals itself in the most concrete of his ordinary experiences. Religious language is *valid* (that is, true with regard to the reality in and by which man exists) in so far as it reflects not just man's 'religious nature' but a positive experience of this ultimate ground, an experience of an ultimate power, meaning and love which completes, fulfills and heals

During the fullest flowering of Gilkey's insights from his work in *Naming the Whirlwind*, he obviously tended to emphasize personal or individual validation of the Christian message, much as the earlier neo-orthodox theologians had done in their own ways. In spite of his heavy focus on the validation of religious discourse in personal experience, during this same period in his *Catholicism Confronts Modernity*, Gilkey expanded his understanding of the meaning of participation or involvement in, or reception of, the sacred as manifested through religious symbols. According to Gilkey, in addition to (1) the phenomenological hermeneutic of secular experience, (2) the hermeneutical and historical or eidetic analysis of the religious tradition, and (3) the ontological elucidation of that historic language, theological understanding has a fourth task: *to elaborate the moral and political meaning of the Christian symbols*. Although Gilkey expands his understanding of the meaning of religious symbols at this point, he does so on the basis of a function of religious symbols that he had identified in *Naming the Whirlwind*: according to Gilkey, religious symbols also "provide models and norms by which our freedom, individual and cultural, can guide itself."[87]

The moral and political meaning of religious symbols, however, originates from the symbols themselves, without being imposed on the symbols. The moral, social, and political meaning of religious symbols "must be intrinsic to their eidetic meaning if they are to function genuinely as origins of creative action." As a result, Gilkey examines Christian symbols and discerns within them a dialectical quality, which he understands as "their teleological or *unstable* character" or their "essential instability": "their dual emphases on what has been and is and yet also what *should* and *will* be in the future." Gilkey understands this dialectical quality as the Christian symbol's drive to transcend itself, to move beyond itself, to point to God as transcendent, not only as source and ground of all that is in the present, but also as the goal in the future: "God is Alpha *and* Omega." Thus, from this dialectic, originate, on the

---

the fragmentariness and waywardness that beset human life" (Gilkey, "Dissolution and Reconstruction in Theology," 137-38).

[87]Gilkey, *CCM*, 115-27, 128-29; idem, *NW*, 464. Also compare this additional notion of the "ethical and political meaning" of religious symbols in *CCM* with my previous discussion of Gilkey's earlier description of four kinds of meaning in religious symbols: (1) experiential referentiality, (2) linguistic usage, (3) eidetic or historical sense, and (4) ontological relevance (Gilkey, *NW*, 274-75).

one hand, critical evaluations of the deficiencies of present ethical, social, and political realities and, on the other hand, proposals of new possibilities in the future. As a result, the Christian symbols not only thematize the experience of ultimacy in ordinary experience, but they also can "shape the structure of the present world in which we have our being and in which we must act." This dialectical quality of all Christian symbols Gilkey understands as disclosing a dialectic between God's present and future work, between divine providence and divine promise or eschatological completion. From this basic dialectic at the heart of Christian symbols, Gilkey develops three criteria for Christian political, social, and moral action, criteria correlated to characteristics of secular experience: contingency, temporality, relativity, and autonomy. (1) Based on the experiential knowledge of God as the ground and sustainer of life, "we know that we are called to act politically to eradicate whatever makes others insecure or in want, or threatens their life." Accordingly, "[b]asic material justice as a political norm has its ultimate roots in the value of our human being and our life." (2) Furthermore, because humans know that God works in the world "to bring meaning, and participation in community," social structures that either impede meaning in life for any person or any group of people or hinder any person or group from such participation in community oppose themselves to God's providential work. (3) Finally, on the basis of experiencing God as the source of healthy communities grown "with real individuals, with a measure of autonomy and freedom, with mutual respect and love," humans receive the call "politically to help fashion such communities."[88]

D. Empirical, Apologetic, but Not Natural Theology

Although the four stages of Gilkey's theological method indicate a highly empirical and apologetic approach to Christian theology, in this period of his theological development, his basic orientation remained essentially neoorthodox, even if decidedly more Tillichian than previously.[89] Consistent with that posture, during this period of his theological work, he continued to refuse to practice, and to identify his theology as, natural

---

[88]Gilkey, *CCM*, 130-55.

[89]As Gilkey later indicated, at this stage of his theological development, he sought "to preserve" that which he regarded "as the essential core" of his "earlier neoorthodoxy while giving to that core a now much needed ground or base in common experience" (Gilkey, "Retrospective Glance at My Work," 25).

theology. While Gilkey's phenomenological hermeneutic of secular experience did disclose a dimension of ultimacy in the human experiences of contingency, temporality or transience, relativity, and autonomy or freedom, ultimacy appears in secular existence *ambiguously*, "as much negatively as positively, as the hiddenness of the sacred and so as the Void, as well as the creative presence of the sacred." According to Gilkey, precisely the *ambiguity of the human experiences of ultimacy*, as disclosed through his analysis, "renders impossible a natural theology based on general experience," as an empirical basis for the validity or truth of the claim that God exists, even if it does establish the meaningfulness of religious language itself[90] Thus, for Gilkey, a prolegomenon to theology, his phenomenological hermeneutic of secular experience, cannot prove either the reality of God or the truth of God-language. Such a form of apologetics cannot assume "the form of a natural theology since the ability of reason to uncover by metaphysical inquiry the ultimate structure of the real cannot be presupposed," and that precisely due to the ambiguity in human experience itself.[91] Although Gilkey developed an extensive analysis and criticism of natural theology and proofs of the reality of God, thus maintaining his neoorthodox (and negative) posture

---

[90]Gilkey, "Universal and Immediate Presence of God," 102. Gilkey had made this point earlier: "No analysis of man can establish the reality of God; it may well be that the ultimate which man longs and searches for exists nowhere!" (Gilkey, "Dissolution and Reconstruction in Theology," 138). In the fullness of this stage of his thinking, Gilkey extended this thought: "I take it that the near demise of traditional forms of natural theology, in both Protestant and Catholic thought recently, is one reflection of just this difficulty inherent in the modern apprehension of contingency and so the modern spirit of empiricism" (Gilkey, *NW*, 46).

[91]Gilkey, "New Modes of Empirical Theology," 355; idem, "Problem of God," 8; idem, "Trends in Protestant Apologetics," 68-69. Gilkey understood natural theology "to include some form of what has traditionally been called a 'philosophical' proof of God." According to Gilkey, "[b]y such a proof of God, we mean the establishment, through some sort of philosophical inquiry based upon ordinary secular experience, of the reality of that to which the symbol of God can legitimately refer, and the consequent elucidation of intelligible forms of language about him." "Thus in any proof of God thought must ascend beyond the level of 'real creatures' or 'actual entities' to what in some sense transcends them in some sort of unique function—for example, gives to them existence or form, provides them or the whole of which they are a part with order and value, imparts direction and purpose to their passage, and so on" (Gilkey, *NW*, 205, 217). Cf. Lonnie D. Kliever, "A New Style Natural Theology," in *Philosophy of Religion and Theology: 1971*, ed. David Ray Griffin (Chambersburg PA: American Academy of Religion, 1971) 82-103.

toward this traditional form of apologetics, his basis for rejecting natural theology changes:

> It is not so much that these arguments to God are logically invalid, nor even that they are "idolatrous," though both might well in fact be true. It is that the rationalistic assumptions on which natural theology is predicated, and without which it cannot legitimately proceed, are not assumptions which the secular mind finds it either easy or natural to make.[92]

Thus, Gilkey insists repeatedly in both *Naming the Whirlwind* and *Catholicism Confronts Modernity* that his theology, though empirical and apologetic, is not a natural theology or a proof of the reality of God.[93]

For this reason, although he taught at the University of Chicago Divinity School during this period, he explicitly distinguished himself "from the 'Chicago school,' " precisely because, as he expressed it, "a study of culture, while essential to theology, reveals more of man's problems and situation than it does of the surprising answers he may hope for."[94] Even though he disagreed with the approach of the then "recent Chicago tradition of empirical theology," which tended to develop its own version of natural theology replete with proofs of the divine reality, he soon saw his own approach as *empirical*, even if not also a proof for the existence or reality of God or ultimate reality itself.[95] In this way, Gilkey

---

[92]Gilkey, *NW*, 203-28, esp. 222.

[93]Also see, e.g., Gilkey, *CCM*, 179.

[94]Gilkey, "If There Is No God," 6. Gilkey wrote this article from Rome during his first study leave from the University of Chicago in 1965, when he studied the Catholic theology behind the changes of Vatican II (Gilkey, "Retrospective Glance at My Work," 21).

[95]Gilkey, "New Modes of Empirical Theology," 347, 354-70; cf. idem, "Problem of God," 11-23. Gilkey's continued rejection of natural theology during this period resulted, of course, both in his defense of neoorthodoxy and in his criticisms of various forms of natural theology. In many of these criticisms, Gilkey indirectly identified and exposed weaknesses in the arguments of A. N. Whitehead: Langdon Gilkey, review of *A Christian Natural Theology*, by John B. Cobb, Jr., in *Theology Today* 22 (January 1966): 530-45; cf. idem, "Process Theology," 5-29. Gilkey even noted that one of Wolfhart Pannenberg's arguments for the existence of God resembles Whitehead's argument for God: Langdon Gilkey, "Pannenberg's *Basic Questions in Theology*: A Review Article," review of *Basic Questions in Theology*, vols. 1 and 2, by Wolfhart Pannenberg, in *Perspectives* 14 (Spring 1973): 41; similarly, idem, *CCM*, 207n.2. About Ogden's argument against neoorthodoxy's inability to verify its propositions directly according to the standards of linguistic positivism and Ogden's argument for his own Hartshornian metaphysical proof of the reality of God, Gilkey says the following: "[t]his entails, if the positivists be right about

later seemed to discover a way to include himself in the "Chicago school," without surrendering the essential contours of his neoorthodoxy.

Thus, even though Gilkey's neoorthodox posture against natural theology remained intact, his reasons for that perspective have changed since *Maker of Heaven and Earth*. As I will show in my analysis of the next major stage in the development of Gilkey's theological method, however, even Gilkey's neoorthodox posture toward natural theology will change there.

E. Postliberal, Revisionist Christian Theological Method in Transition

This third major period in the development of Gilkey's theological method originated as Gilkey's response to the crisis that secularism had generated for neoorthodoxy or postliberal Christian theology. For Gilkey, that also meant addressing the crisis in his own theological method. Although Gilkey deepened his correlational method through more specific empirical analyses of human experience, his correlational theological method remained neoorthodox, but now more similar to Paul Tillich's neoorthodox theological approach than to Reinhold Niebuhr's version of

---

theology, the descent of all metaphysics to the same ocean floor": Gilkey, "Theology in Process: Schubert Ogden's Developing Theology," 457. In a related matter, Gilkey chided Paul van Buren for using the verification principle of positivistic linguistic philosophy to reveal the meaninglessness of all God-language, then dismissing natural theology on the basis of Karl Barth's argument "that natural theology dishonored and distorted the God of revelation!" (Gilkey, review of *Secular Meaning of the Gospel*, 242; cf. idem, *NW*, 208-209n.17; idem, "Is God Dead," 7). Here, one should remember that Gilkey had written his Ph.D. dissertation on the Christian doctrine of *creatio ex nihilo*, responding critically to Whitehead, "not in agreement with him" (Gilkey, "Namer and Tamer of the Whirlwind," 3; idem, "Maker of Heaven and Earth: A Thesis on the Relation between Metaphysics and Christian Theology with Special Reference to the Problem of Creation as that Problem Appears in the Philosophies of F. H. Bradley and A. N. Whitehead and in the Historic Leaders of Christian Thought" (Ph.D. diss., Columbia University, 1954). See Gilkey's brief discussion of theology at the University of Chicago Divinity School as distinctively an "indigenous" North American theology: Langdon Gilkey, "Social and Intellectual Sources of Contemporary Protestant Theology in America," *Daedalus* 96 (Winter 1967): 86; cf. Bernard E. Meland, "Introduction: The Empirical Tradition in Theology at Chicago," in *Essays in Divinity*, ed. Jerald C. Brauer, vol. 7, *The Future of Empirical Theology*, ed. Bernard E. Meland (Chicago: University of Chicago Press, 1969) 1-62.

neoorthodoxy.[96] Gilkey essentially has continued to retain the broad contours of the fully developed correlational theological method from this third period of his career across even the most recent years of his work. Gilkey employed his correlational theological method, precisely in its present form, in slightly later theological interpretations of divine providence (*Reaping the Whirlwind*) and the whole system of Christian symbols (*Message and Existence*). Because of one significant alteration in his theological approach, however, I will discuss a fourth period in the development of his theological method after the present discussion.

Three of Gilkey's books, however, represent this third period in the development of Gilkey's theological method: *Naming the Whirlwind, Religion and the Scientific Future*, and *Catholicism Confronts Modernity*. None of these books represents an example of Gilkey's fully correlational theological method in practice, where one might look to find a systematic theology. As I have discussed previously, *Naming the Whirlwind* (1969) represents only one stage among the four stages in Gilkey's theological method: the phenomenological hermeneutic of secular experience, the prolegomenon, in which Gilkey seeks to disclose the ultimacy at the basis of ordinary (and mostly personal) experience. With *Religion and the Scientific Future* (1970), Gilkey inquired "into modern science, the heart of modern secular culture, to show the religious dimension latent there," again only operating as one stage in a systematic theology, a phenomenological hermeneutic of secular experience. Even *Catholicism Confronts Modernity* functions as a program in theological method for Roman Catholic theology in the contemporary world, rather than a correlational systematic theology.[97]

Nonetheless, even though remaining books marked primarily by methodological and prolegomenal concerns, a correlational pattern does emerge in both *Naming the Whirlwind* and *Catholicism Confronts Modernity*, even though this does not represent systematic theology for

---

[96]Gilkey, "Retrospective Glance at My Work," 25; idem, "Namer and Tamer of the Whirlwind," 3.

[97]Gilkey, "Retrospective Glance at My Work," 24-25. Although I have assigned both *Naming the Whirlwind* and *Catholicism Confronts Modernity* to this third period of Gilkey's developing method, to some extent, *CCM* functions as a transition in the development of Gilkey's method from this third period to the fourth period, insofar as it includes a more developed form of Gilkey's fourth methodological stage or step (the moral and political application of religious symbols), one which becomes much more prominent in *Reaping the Whirlwind*.

Gilkey. In *Naming the Whirlwind*, Gilkey describes the present situation and needs in the book's first part, "The Challenge to God-Language," then proposes his solution to that problem in the book's second part, "The Renewal of God-Language."[98] When Gilkey wrote *Catholicism Confronts Modernity*, he had entitled it as *Crisis and Promise*, a title reflecting this correlational pattern again. The publisher, however, changed Gilkey's title to its published form. In this book, Gilkey endeavored to address the then present crisis of secularism for the Roman Catholic Church, by examining the resources of Roman Catholicism in dialogue with the issues and requirements of secularism. In this regard, he applied the program that he had developed in *Naming the Whirlwind* to the situation of the Roman Catholic Church. After describing the crisis and larger situation (chaps. 1 and 2), Gilkey examined the Roman Catholic tradition in light of the various levels of meaning ingredient in religious symbols: the level of the religious dimension in ordinary experience (chap. 3); the level of eidetic or historical meaning (chap. 4); the level of moral-political meaning (chap. 5); and the level of ontological and existential meanings, with a focus on the concerns of validity and truth (chaps. 6 and 7).[99]

As I have tried to show in the previous discussion, Langdon Gilkey's theology during this period certainly remained neoorthodox. Nevertheless, his form of neoorthodox theology differed significantly from the Niebuhrian neoorthodox approach with which he began his career. Despite its revisionary character, nevertheless, Gilkey's theological method remained thoroughly postliberal, even though he had modified his analysis of human experience or the human situation quite significantly.

IV. Postliberal Theology Transformed:
Tillichian Neoorthodoxy and Process Philosophy

Although one may properly understand the previous period in the development of Gilkey's theological method as its fullest flowering, by the time that he had employed the newest version of his method in his next major work, *Reaping the Whirlwind*, he had introduced one further change into his theological approach: specifically, his new posture toward

---

[98]Part 1 includes six chapters (Gilkey, *NW*, 1-228), while part 2 contains five chapters (Gilkey, *NW*, 229-470).

[99]Gilkey, "Retrospective Glance at My Work," 22-23; idem, *CCM*, 1-83, 84-104, 105-27, 128-55, 156-99.

natural theology, through his new appreciation for elements in the process philosophy of Alfred North Whitehead.[100] Due to the significance and effects of that change for Gilkey's theological orientation and subsequent direction, I have distinguished this fourth period in the development of Gilkey's theological method from the previous periods in his career.[101]

---

[100]Since his doctoral studies, Gilkey had appreciated many aspects of Alfred North Whitehead's philosophy. Nevertheless, during his days as an "aggressive" neoorthodox student, Gilkey had vehemently opposed the basic character of Whitehead's philosophical system and several of its central ideas. Numerous elements in Whitehead's thought, including especially those that expressed and affirmed the liberal vision, drew heavy resistance from Gilkey, such as Whitehead's metaphysical dualism, his notion of the finite God that depends on the principle of creativity, his rejection of the Christian doctrine of *creatio ex nihilo*, his lack of awareness of sin, his treatment of the problem of evil, his vision of cosmic and historical progress, and even the rationalism in his empirical proof of God's existence (see Gilkey, *MHE*, 46, 89, 110, 213n.2; idem, *NW*, 75-76n.3, 186n.1, 188, 213n.20, 356-57n.33, 385-86n.11, 443-44). In spite of his vehement rejection of many elements in Whitehead's larger system, even in *Naming the Whirlwind* Gilkey employed resources from Whitehead to expose weaknesses in Moltmann's concept of a "*totally* open" future. "As Whitehead realized, a creatively open future must have a structural relation to present actuality; its possibilities must be limited by past actualities and by present decisions, if that future is to give meaning and hope to our present activities. . . . Eschatology must be tempered by Providence if either social or revolutionary action is to be meaningful" (Gilkey, *NW*, 346n.24). Gilkey's still-severe criticism of Whitehead's thought, however, appears as late as 1973, only three years prior to the publication of *Reaping the Whirlwind*: see Gilkey, "Process Theology," 5-29. Gilkey's appreciative opposition to Whitehead's process philosophy persisted until Gilkey began writing *Reaping the Whirlwind*. In that book, despite his continued criticism of Whitehead's distinction between creativity and God, as well as his continued rejection of Whitehead's liberal progressivism and its inability to comprehend adequately the demonic or the bondage of freedom, Gilkey nevertheless came even more highly to regard Whitehead's account of "the possibility of possibility" as "by far the best picture presented," an account upon which Gilkey depended for the development of his own understanding of the possibility of possibility. Furthermore, in *Catholicism Confronts Modernity*, Gilkey expressed appreciation for Whitehead's elegant argument for the necessity of God, even though Gilkey does not employ Whitehead's argument for God in that book to support his own approach methodologically: see Gilkey, *CCM*, 95-96; idem, "God: Eternal Source of Newness," in *Living with Change, Experience, Faith*, ed. Francis A. Eigo (Villanova PA: Villanova University Press, 1976) 153, 165n.11; cf. idem, *RW*, 111, 114, 431n.17; idem, "Namer and Tamer of the Whirlwind," 3; idem, "Theology and Culture: Reflections on the Conference," 4-5.

[101]In one respect especially, Gilkey's theological approach has remained consistent even since the introduction of the major modification to his method in *Reaping the Whirlwind*. I refer to Gilkey's adoption of natural theology, with his development of three

In this period of his theological development, as previously, Gilkey refused to exhaust his theological energies with methodological preoccupations. Almost reluctantly, Gilkey discusses method in several places, continuing to exhibit some disdain for the overemphasis on method in contemporary theological studies. For example, when introducing his task in *Message and Existence*, a short overview of basic Christian views, beliefs, or doctrines, he describes his goal as "more a reflective description of what is seen on the theological journey than a manual for driving," or as "a travelog and not a driver's manual."[102] He desires,

---

arguments for the existence of God as entailed by the ontological structure of finitude (the polarity of destiny and freedom or actuality and possibility). Gilkey also begins to develop his theology in dialogue with other religious traditions (most notably, Buddhism) roughly during this same period. Nevertheless, due to the differences between his major systematic theological works (*Reaping the Whirlwind* and *Message and Existence*) and his theological formulations as developed in interreligious dialogue (e.g., *Through the Tempest*), I have relegated my discussion of this latter group of issues to a final period in Gilkey's developing theological method. I emphatically note, however, that these two periods in the development of Gilkey's theological method (at least, as I have distinguished them) overlap one another enough chronologically that one could construe them as aspects of one most recent period in the evolution of Gilkey's theological method.

[102]Gilkey, *ME*, 3. In *Message and Existence*, Gilkey departs from his preference to discuss methodological issues after his theological interpretations of Christian symbols, instead introducing his summary of Christian theology with two chapters related to concerns with method: see Gilkey, *ME*, 7-65. Gilkey's departure from this preference, however, appears to originate from his efforts to follow the structure of the *Apostles Creed*, which begins with "I believe." In *Reaping the Whirlwind*, Gilkey develops two full chapters on theological method. Nonetheless, similar to previous books in which he did not begin the books with his methodological considerations, Gilkey did not begin *Reaping the Whirlwind* with chapters on method. Instead, Gilkey places his two chapters on method in the middle of the book. Gilkey considered *Reaping the Whirlwind* as only "an *illustration* of a coherent and intelligible method [as proposed in *NW*], not a book on method." As he expressed it, he suspended the argument of the book, introducing two methodological chapters into the middle of the book, in order to illuminate and clarify a significant dimension or stage of his method itself. Many of Gilkey's interpreters had misunderstood *Naming the Whirlwind*, misreading it as an example of a theology that had capitulated to secularism, rather than, as Gilkey claimed in the book itself, as a *prolegomenon* to systematic theology: see, e.g., Peter L. Berger, "Secular Theology and the Rejection of the Supernatural: Reflections on Recent Trends," *Theological Studies* 38 (March 1977): 39-56; cf. Gilkey, "Responses to Peter Berger," 486-507. For this reason, after beginning *Reaping the Whirlwind* with a phenomenological hermeneutic of the secular experience of historical passage or temporality (part 1, with four chapters, which he entitled "Prolegomenon"), Gilkey introduced his two chapters on method. In this way,

instead, to exercise his abilities on the theological topics themselves. In itself, this conviction or élan in Gilkey reflects a concern for praxis, a concern for the answers that Christian traditions have to offer to the problems and questions of contemporary persons and communities—at least when the theologian carefully interprets both the contemporary situation and the Christian traditions dialectically, mutually critically, or in light of one another.

A. Stages in Theological Method

In most ways, Gilkey's theological method did not change during this period. He continued to correlate the questions and problems of human life with the symbolic answers of the Christian traditions. He maintained his commitment to the deepening of this correlational approach through his ontic analysis or phenomenological hermeneutic of secular or ordinary human experience.[103] Gilkey produced three books during this period: *Reaping the Whirlwind* (1976), *Message and Existence* (1979), and *Society and the Sacred* (1981).[104] The formal stages of his theological method, as developed in both *Naming the Whirlwind* and *Catholicism Confronts Modernity* and as employed especially in *Reaping the Whirlwind, Message and Existence*, and *Society and the Sacred*, however, did not change drastically during this period.

Gilkey most certainly introduced minor methodological variations, elaborations, and corrections here and there, as he proceeded through this period of his theological development. Nevertheless, I will concentrate only on the major change, namely the shift in his posture toward natural theology, that appears in this period: this change has profound significance for and effect upon Gilkey's broader theological perspective.

A brief summary of the stages in Gilkey's theological method during this period, however, will supply the background for understanding the significance of this change for Gilkey's theological orientation. As in the

---

so that no one would misunderstand his move, he physically broke into the argument, at the very point where he moved from an analysis of ordinary experience to an interpretation of the Christian symbol of providence (Gilkey, *RW*, 117, 369n.2).

[103]Gilkey, *ME*, 2-3, 7-18, 53-64.

[104]This same period generally includes the remainder of Gilkey's books as well; not all of them, however, engage as directly with the problems of method, even though they do consider various aspects of methodological questions: e.g., see Langdon Gilkey, *Creationism on Trial: Evolution and God at Little Rock* (San Francisco: Harper & Row, 1985) 209-34, 257-59; hereafter cited as *CT*.

previous period of his developing method, Gilkey discerned four levels of meaning in religious symbols and, consequently, in the theology produced by reflection on those symbols: (1) eidetic or historical, (2) experiential-phenomenological, (3) ontological, and (4) ethical-political levels of meaning. These levels of meaning correlate to the different stages of theological method, as seen in the previous period of Gilkey's theological development. With these stages in his method, Gilkey endeavors especially to meet the most objective theological criteria, as well as the fourth and more subjective criterion, for a relevant theology: (1) fidelity to the religious tradition; (2) adequacy to experience; (3) intelligibility in terms of contemporary categories and concepts; and (4) existential, moral, and political involvement, still the ultimate issue of truth or validity for Gilkey.[105]

I will not discuss *all* of these stages in Gilkey's method again, even though his *use* of this method during this period does exhibit some minor differences from his *theory* of this method in *Naming the Whirlwind* and *Catholicism Confronts Modernity*. I will examine briefly, nevertheless, one stage in his method, since through this particular stage appears the significant alteration that justifies distinguishing this period from the previous period in the development of Gilkey's theological method. I refer to the prolegomenal stage in his method, that which he had described in *Naming the Whirlwind* as a phenomenological hermeneutic of secular experience.

I examine the prolegomenal stage of Gilkey's theological method, however, through his use of this method in, perhaps, his most definitive work, *Reaping the Whirlwind*, his interpretation of the Christian symbol of providence. In order to illustrate the character of the change that appears in Gilkey's employment of his phenomenological hermeneutic of

---

[105]Gilkey, *RW*, 134-46. In *Message and Existence*, although Gilkey neither discusses these levels of meaning and the four stages of theological method that correspond to them nor clearly distinguishes them from one another in his actual interpretations of Christian symbols, his qualification (in *ME*) to his discussion of these levels of meaning in *Reaping the Whirlwind* helps to clarify the differences on this issue between the two books: although he distinguishes "four different aspects of meaning ingredient in a fundamental religious symbol or system of symbols and so necessarily explicated by theological reflection," according to Gilkey, "[t]his does not mean that these four aspects must be dealt with either singly, separately or in serial order; rather it means that any full theological understanding must be inclusive of all of them and must satisfy the particular requirements that each of these four aspects imposes" (Gilkey, *RW*, 139).

secular experience in *Reaping the Whirlwind*, however, I recall briefly the central feature of that prolegomenon as proposed and operative in *Naming the Whirlwind*.

Aiming to establish the meaningfulness of religious language in human experience, Gilkey performed an ontic analysis in *Naming the Whirlwind*, an analysis of the ordinary or secular experiences of contingency, relativity, temporality or transience, and autonomy or freedom. Through his ontic analysis, he discovered a dimension of ultimacy, a dimension raising questions *un*answerable on the basis of secularism's claims alone, a dimension of experience that requires religious language for its articulation. As Gilkey has noted, in *Naming the Whirlwind*, he performed an *ontic* analysis of "predominantly *individual* experience."[106] In *Reaping the Whirlwind*, however, Gilkey enhanced or modified the prolegomenon's role at least in two ways. (1) First, because Gilkey sought to interpret the Christian symbol of divine providence, he specifically analyzed or interpreted the human experience of *social change and political experience* as the situation to which the symbol of divine providence correlates. Through both an "ethical and 'existential' analysis of the experience of social change" and a "phenomenological analysis of political experience," he discovered again "religious issues of ultimate concern" or a "religious dimension of historical existence."[107] The ethical and existential analysis conforms most to Gilkey's ontic analysis in *Naming the Whirlwind*. (2) Second, nevertheless, although the phenomenological analysis of political experience also accomplishes a goal similar to that of the ontic analysis in *Naming the Whirlwind* (in its disclosure of the religious dimension of historical experience), the second analysis does something more. In a first step, Gilkey's phenomenological analysis, *unlike* his ontic analysis in *Naming the Whirlwind*, uncovered "the ontological structure" of historical experience: the polarity of destiny and freedom; in this sense, his second analysis was *ontological not ontic*. *Like* his analysis of individual experience in *Naming the Whirlwind*, however, in a second step, Gilkey's second analysis also disclosed "the horizon within which social and political events were experienced," a

---

[106]Gilkey, *NW*, 305-13; idem, *RW*, 369-70n.5; emphasis mine.

[107]Gilkey, *RW*, 120. Gilkey's ethical and existential analysis of the experience of social change occurs in chap. 1, "Change, Politics and the Future: The Historicity of Human Being," while his phenomenological analysis of political experience occurs in chap. 2, "Ultimacy in Historical and Political Experience" (Gilkey, *RW*, 3-35, 36-69).

religious dimension, "a dimension of ultimacy . . . as the real horizon of secular communal experience." This dimension of ultimacy appears as quests for "the ultimate sovereignty that rules historical time," for "the ultimate order or logos that gives meaning" to human activities, and for "the ultimate norm that grounds" human "moral decisions," questions of ultimacy directly originating from the social or communal experiences of (1) the contingency and temporality of political existence, (2) the relativity of all values, and (3) human autonomy or freedom. Most importantly, according to Gilkey, "[t]hese three fundamental characteristics of historical existence show that the ontological structure of destiny and freedom which structures history is set within a horizon that is religious."[108]

Thus, rather than completing his prolegomenon of historical passage with an ontic analysis of secular experience (as in *Naming the Whirlwind*), Gilkey subjected the features of social change and political experience to an ontological analysis as well, in which he uncovered the ontological structures at the basis of historical experience. At one level of abstraction, Gilkey discovered the fundamental ontological structure of historical experience in the *polarity of freedom and destiny*. According to Gilkey, however, that structure "entails a further ontological polarity," a more abstract ontological structure in which even the polarity of freedom and destiny subsists: "the polarity of actuality and possibility." Of equal importance for historical experience, Gilkey's analyses had disclosed that a religious horizon (appearing in the quests for continuance and expansion of being, for a system of ultimate meaning, and for an ultimate norm) held the ontological polarities within it.[109] With the discernment

---

[108]Gilkey, *RW*, 36-46, 46-69, 118-19, 301. In one respect, Gilkey's deepening of his prolegomenon with the addition of an *ontological* analysis raises a question: How does Gilkey distinguish this step in his prolegomenon from the stage of ontological elucidation of the Christian symbols later? To an extent, this move either almost eliminates the need for, or even presupposes already, the stage of ontological elucidation in theological method.

[109]Gilkey, *RW*, 118-19. In the first two chapters of *Reaping the Whirlwind*, Gilkey performs ontic and ontological analyses of social change and historical and political experience; in those chapters, he uncovers both the ontological polarity of destiny and freedom (as well as the ontological polarity of actuality and possibility) and the religious dimension to historical and political experience. In the next two chapters, Gilkey analyzes both contemporary scientific views of history (chap. 3) and contemporary philosophical views of history (chap. 4), in both of which he discerns this religious dimension or

and elucidation of the ontological structure of temporal process, therefore, Gilkey fulfilled his vision of the need for an "ontology of events" or an ontology of historical process—finally supplying the philosophical basis to address the serious deficiency in neoorthodox thought, the virtual absence of the doctrine of providence.

B. New Appearance of Natural Theology: Divine Reality as Rational

Gilkey's ontological analysis of finitude as historical process, however, does not conclude with his disclosure of temporality's basic ontological structure: the dialectical polarities of destiny and freedom, actuality and possibility. Nevertheless, at this point, I introduce another section in my own analysis of Gilkey's method, in order to emphasize the location where Gilkey decisively modifies or changes his theological method and to clarify the essential character of that modification in both his theological method and his convictions.

Openly yet critically borrowing from Whitehead, Gilkey introduces another step, albeit somewhat tentatively, into his ontological analysis of historical process.[110] According to Gilkey, the ontological structure of fini-

---

questions of ultimacy as well.

[110]As Gilkey says, "[w]e shall refer to this argument [Whitehead's argument for the necessity of God's existence] repeatedly, and even expand it, although we do not wish . . . to base our theological interpretation of history *solely* on its cogency" (Gilkey, *RW*, 125). In *Reaping the Whirlwind*, Gilkey initially introduced Whitehead's argument for the necessity of God's reality or the divine ground within the context of his prolegomenon, at the point where he examined contemporary philosophical reflection on the nature of historical process for traces of the religious dimension in human experience (Gilkey, *RW*, 110-14). Whitehead's argument for the reality of God next appears in *Reaping the Whirlwind* as Gilkey makes a methodological break in his analysis, to emphasize formally the distinction between his prolegomenon and the next stages of systematic theology proper (Gilkey, *RW*, 122-30). Gilkey's adoption and modification of Whitehead's argument for the reality of God appears also in the final chapter of *Reaping the Whirlwind*, chap. 12, "The God of Process, of Possibility and of Hope" (Gilkey, *RW*, 300-306). Incidentally, the section in chap. 5 of *Reaping the Whirlwind*, where this natural theology appears, the first part of Gilkey's methodological "interlude," contains the three moments that Gilkey later describes as "the dialectic of Christian belief" (see Langdon Gilkey, "The Dialectic of Christian Belief: Rational, Incredible, and Credible," in *Rationality and Religious Belief*, ed. C. F. Delaney, University of Notre Dame Studies in the Philosophy of Religion 1 [Notre Dame IN: University of Notre Dame Press, 1979] 65-83; also published as chap. 3, "The Dialectic of Christian Belief," in *Society and The Sacred*, 26-41). That dialectic, of course, operates fully and extensively throughout the

tude, in the polarities of destiny and freedom or "achieved actuality and undetermined possibility," implies, "seems to call for," requires, "necessitates," or "entails" a transcendent or divine "foundation," "a kind of self-transcending infinitude," "a deeper, necessary, all-encompassing ground as the condition of its [the ontological structure of temporal process] possibility." The ontological structure of temporality requires God as its ground, foundation, or condition of possibility precisely as the guarantee for the *intelligibility* of "all three phases of temporal passage" or temporality: (1) the *past*, "the relation of past destiny to present," or "continuity"; (2) the *present*, "the self-actualization of the present out of that destiny and novel possibility," or "self-actualizing freedom"; and (3) the *future*, "the relation of future possibility to present," or "novelty." Thus, Gilkey describes this "theistic claim that there is a divine ground to historical passage," a claim that he makes on the basis of "the ontological structure of passage," as "[t]he structural *foundation* of Christian faith."[111]

With his threefold argument for the necessity of divine reality, Gilkey completes his ontological analysis of finitude. I will not repeat, however, Gilkey's argument for the necessity of God's existence here, in an effort to remain as focused as possible on the methodological concerns of this chapter.[112] The critical issue for this chapter revolves around how this theological move affects Gilkey's theological method. Gilkey makes no attempt to disguise this modification to his theology. He openly describes this modification in his theological method as natural theology, "a theology developed solely by rational interpretation of common experience." He clearly understands this as a proof for the existence or reality of God, defining such a proof as "uncovering the necessary connections of an

remainder of *Reaping the Whirlwind* as well: e.g., see Gilkey, *RW*, 246-70, 300-18.

[111]Gilkey, *RW*, 129, 240, 255, 301-302; idem, *SAS*, 31, 36, 37 (emphasis mine); idem, *ME*, 78, 103.

[112]See the following appearances of this threefold argument in Gilkey's thought: Gilkey, *RW*, 124-25, 249-52, 303-306; idem, *ME*, 78-81, 85n.1, 103; idem, *SAS*, 31-33; idem, "God," in *Christian Theology: An Introduction to Its Traditions and Tasks*, ed. Peter C. Hodgson and Robert H. King (Philadelphia: Fortress Press, 1982) 83-85; repr. as chap. 5, "The Christian Understanding of God," in *TT*, 85-87; idem, *NRS*, 200-204; cf. idem, "God: Eternal Source of Newness," 151-66. In their republication of Gilkey's "Christian Understanding of God," Musser and Price did not include the relevant portions of Gilkey's original essay: see "God," in *A New Handbook of Christian Theology*, ed. Donald W. Musser and Joseph L. Price (Nashville: Abingdon Press, 1992) 198-209.

assumed aspect of an ontological structure with other aspects" [of that structure].[113] Most certainly, with this change in his theological perspective, Gilkey had begun to "comprehend the mysteries of the Chicago school" and had effectively dissolved, with his genuine argument if not plea "for a new natural theology," his own strict distinction between his original neoorthodoxy and the tradition of empirical theology in the University of Chicago Divinity School. As Gilkey expressed it, "[t]he ontological structure of historical being . . . *proclaims* the rationality of theism."[114] With the introduction of this element into his theological method, Gilkey quite clearly, finally, and fully (despite his retention of some neoorthodox reluctance—as I will indicate in following discussions) entered the community of empirical theologians, the so-called "Chicago school."

Even though Gilkey's argument for the reality of God identified the theistic foundation for Christian faith, one *necessary* to establish the intelligibility of the temporal process itself, Gilkey still did not regard this argument (and others like it, or natural theology as a whole, of course), as alone *sufficient* to establish the validity of theological claims about that process.[115] As a result, Gilkey assigned to this argument for God or this

---

[113]Gilkey, *ME*, 9; idem, *SAS*, 37. In 1989, during the conference on Gilkey's thought (on the occasion of his retirement) at the University of Chicago Divinity School, Lois Gehr Livezey delivered a paper on Gilkey's theology in which she commented on the place of natural theology in his works. In his responses to those papers, Gilkey related how, to his surprise, he had changed his mind about natural theology, having been, as he described himself, "one of the leading opponents of natural theology for a good number of years" (Gilkey, "Theology and Culture: Reflections on the Conference," 3). He narrates this same story in *Nature, Reality, and the Sacred*, beginning the narrative quite honestly: "[m]y relation to the tradition of natural theology has been a puzzle, especially to me" (Gilkey, *NRS*, 243n.1).

[114]Gilkey, *SAS*, 33; emphasis mine. In the previous stage of his methodological development, Gilkey had claimed that, although arguing for a philosophical anthropology as a prolegomenon to theology, he was "not pleading for a new natural theology" (Gilkey, "Dissolution and Reconstruction in Theology," 137). Furthermore, during his earliest years as a professor at the University of Chicago Divinity School, Gilkey had distinguished himself "from the 'Chicago school,' in that to [him] a study of culture, while essential to theology, reveals more of man's problems and situation than it does of the surprising answers he may hope for" (Gilkey, "If There Is No God," 6).

[115]Gilkey employed the term, "foundation," precisely with the meaning of "foundationalism" currently available in theological discussion. For example, foundationalist theologians "interpret Christian believing in relation to universally available facts, principles, or structure" (Ottati, "Between Foundationalism and Nonfoundationalism," 27; cf.

example of natural theology only one role in a series of arguments in his interpretation of Christian symbols: "to show the intelligibility and so the reality of a theistic interpretation of that structure" [the ontological structure of history, the polarity of destiny and freedom or actuality and possibility]. Beyond this role, this argument could not proceed.[116]

Although Gilkey had discovered this argument through his efforts to construct a Christian theology of history or divine providence, as a theistic foundation implied by the ontological structure of actuality and possibility or destiny and freedom, it became foundational for understanding the entire system of Christian beliefs or symbols. This argument for God's reality, based as it is on the ontological structure of freedom and destiny implicit to human experience of historical process (with the same characteristics as his analysis of secular experience: contingency, temporality or transience, relativity, and autonomy or freedom), essentially extended Gilkey's previous accomplishment in *Naming the Whirlwind*: his establishment of the meaningfulness of God-language through his disclosure of the dimension of ultimacy in ordinary experience. Nevertheless, due to the derivation of this argument for God's reality from the abstract ontological structure of finitude, this argument for or proof of God's existence remained abstract as well, separated from the polarity of destiny and freedom as experienced in the ambiguities of life itself: "[a] metaphysical understanding of the structure of history leads, mysteriously, to an abstraction from the concrete actuality of history; and thus, in large part, away from its object rather than toward it."[117]

C. Sin as Obscuration of Theistic Rationality: Divine Reality as Incredible

According to Gilkey, an ontological analysis of finitude, with its emphasis on "the essential ontological structure of destiny and freedom," "overlook[s] history's self-contradiction and its tragedy," the actuality of history as concretely characterized by "sin and fate, categories not derivable from the structure of history, and so not metaphysically 'provable,' but categories essential to the understanding of history's actuality." In other words, the warping and distortion of finitude, of the ontological structure of destiny and freedom, do not occur necessarily.

Lints, "The Postpositivist Choice: Tracy or Lindbeck," 655-77).
    [116]Gilkey, *RW*, 127-28, 254-55.
    [117]Gilkey, *RW*, 126.

Nevertheless, the actuality of history, in which the realities of freedom and destiny interact concretely, "challenges the rationality" of the natural theology that the ontological structure of finitude entails. The misuse of freedom has warped and estranged the ontological structure of destiny and freedom, actualizing freedom as sin and converting destiny to fate. Thus, according to Gilkey, not only does the distorted character of human history obscure the ontological structure of destiny and freedom or actuality and possibility, but it also obscures the reality of God, its ground, as implied in that structure, thus making God into "the *deus absconditus*." Gilkey uses a nautical metaphor to illustrate this situation. On a clear day, a sailor in a small boat can easily navigate the seascape by sight, following the structure of the scene with the shoreline, familiar islands, landmarks, and buoys, neither requiring nor envisioning any special means by which to navigate other than by sight. When a fog covers the bay, however, the fog obscures the landmarks and buoys, necessitating navigation by other means, such as by compass or radar. Although the structure of the shoreline and its familiar landmarks remain, the fog has obscured or hidden them, thus making its familiar rocks and shoals into possible menace rather than blessing. In Gilkey's characterization of this warped, fallen, or estranged actuality as "this strange fog," he retains a theme that has accompanied his theological method from his earliest days as a Niebuhrian neoorthodox theologian.[118]

With the retention of this awareness, Gilkey thoroughly qualifies any naïve or arrogant approach to Christian foundationalism. Although he adopts natural theology as a moment in his even heavier apologetic theological method, he does so with a humility tempered by historical experience and awareness of freedom as sin and destiny as fate. Consequently, Gilkey acknowledges that positive theological knowledge and construction depend on still one more warrant beyond the results of his ontological analysis of temporality.

D. Redemption as Illumination of Theistic Rationality: Divine Reality as Credible

Despite the obscuration of the ontological structure of finitude (the polarities of destiny and freedom, or actuality and possibility) that results

---

[118]Gilkey, *RW*, 125-28, 253-65; idem, "Dialectic of Christian Belief: Rational, Incredible, Credible," 74-78; idem, *SAS*, 33-37; idem, *ME*, 104-105; idem, "God: Eternal Source of Newness," 161-62.

from its distortion and warping through human estrangement, Gilkey says that, in that same ordinary experience (both personal and social), one may discern experienced clues to, "intuitions" of, or "warrants for the search for a deeper meaning," "*ontic*" (as distinct from ontological) grounds for claiming that "there might be a meaning to history, a meaning whose concrete shape is to be discovered by inquiry." This meaning to history Gilkey describes as "an order transcendent to human intentions and surface conditions," yet "within the events" of human experience. Gilkey refers to three areas of life in which people experience these "clue[s]" or "intimation[s] of meaning." He characterizes these three areas of experience in the following ways, although I will not supply full discussions of them here: (1) "the experience of the creativity of the unwanted given in personal life and history"; (2) "the proximate intelligibility of much of the tragic"; and (3) "the possibilities of the new in history despite the tragic character of the present." According to Gilkey, each of these experiences empirically and practically "points to a thread of meaning, the hidden working of some principle of order within the ambiguity of time and change, that undergirds both our confidence and our autonomy." Christian symbols, then, thematize "this series of intuitions" into a Christian interpretation of life or history.[119]

Even though such intimations of meaning occur in ordinary experience, the presence of sin or estrangement and its resultant distortion of destiny into fate still render history deeply ambiguous, an ambiguity that accumulates to such an extent that "the potential nemesis grimly reappears." Because of this ambiguity, Gilkey claims that the symbol of providence as possibility or creativity requires supplementation with the symbols of redemption: incarnation, atonement, and eschatology. Although Gilkey does not characterize the system of Christian symbols as *rational* (in the way that he does characterize his argument for God's reality as rational—"philosophically demonstrable"), he does describe that system as *credible*. By "credible," Gilkey means that the system of Christian symbols "can satisfy the mind as a valid symbolic thematization of the totality of concrete experience as no other global viewpoint can." In this way, Gilkey claims that "[a]n intuition of fundamental order, itself no more than credible, grounds and establishes the possibility of metaphysical inference and of theistic rationality." Gilkey, thus, also

---

[119]Gilkey, *RW*, 130-33.

proposes several criteria of credibility for the theological use of the Christian symbol system: (1) coherence within the system of symbols; (2) adequacy of the symbolic system and its interpretation to the contours of experience as a whole; (3) appropriateness or fidelity of the interpretation to the symbolic tradition, including scripture and the history of its interpretation by the Christian community; and (4) a participatory sense of divine work in human life—in a twofold sense: first, a sense of one's consciousness of sin and, second, a sense or experience of the gospel's reality, "commitment to its demands and promises," and "enactment of its implications in praxis."[120]

Thus, with this point, Gilkey qualifies in a second major way his late and positive employment of, confidence in, and dependence on natural theology generally and his own threefold argument for the reality of God more specifically. The necessary appearance and use of natural theology in Gilkey's apologetic (even *foundational* apologetic) approach finally depend on the credibility of the system of Christian symbols. In this way, Gilkey remains still deeply within the neoorthodox tradition with its Protestant principle, while invoking simultaneously a Catholic substance of a sort, albeit one radically different from the Platonic, Neoplatonic, and Aristotelian philosophical foundations of historic Catholicism.

E. Postliberal Foundational Theological Method

Insofar as Gilkey's modification of his phenomenological hermeneutic of ordinary experience (to include ontological as well as ontic analyses) led him empirically to discern an argument for the reality of God, then religious symbol or doctrine and theological method merge for Gilkey, even though the experienced estrangement and fatedness of history obscure and humble the results of that stage in theological method.

---

[120]Gilkey, *RW*, 265-70; idem, "Dialectic of Christian Belief: Rational, Incredible, Credible," 78-83; idem, *SAS*, 37-41. At this stage in the evolution of his theological method, Gilkey calls for "more" than providence or the supplementation of a theology of providence with eschatology, explicitly emphasizing the opposite of his response to the eschatological theologians: "Eschatology must be tempered by Providence if either social or revolutionary action is to be meaningful" (Gilkey, *NW*, 346n.24). Rather than a reversal in his thought, however, this emphasis expressed his fuller recognition of the dialectical relationship between a theology of providence and eschatology, a dialectic reflected in chapters of *Reaping the Whirlwind*: chap. 10, "Providence and Eschatology: A Reinterpretation"; and chap. 11, "Eschatology and Providence: The Future of God" (Gilkey, *RW*, 239-70, 271-99).

During this most mature period in the operation of his theological method, Gilkey carefully integrates the previous moments of this discussion: his adoption of natural theology, its obscuration by estrangement, and the intimation as well as Christian message of redemption. He describes this as the "dialectic of Christian belief," a dialectic between rationality, incredibility, and credibility.[121]

The remainder of Gilkey's work reflects the contours of this dialectic and the methodological stages connected with it. Although I have discussed various theoretical aspects of Gilkey's method in this section, the operation or practice of this method deserves one final look. Here I will refer, however, only (and very briefly) to Gilkey's principal systematic theological constructions during this period in the operation of his theological method: *Reaping the Whirlwind* and *Message and Existence*.

1. *Reaping the Whirlwind*. In *Reaping the Whirlwind*, Gilkey applies his theological method to a neglected or thinly treated theme in the theology of the early twentieth century: the doctrine of divine providence. He claims, through a complex series of studies and arguments, "that historical change can neither be intellectually comprehended, existentially borne, nor politically and ethically dealt with, without a theological and a Christian interpretation of it."[122] The structure of Gilkey's book follows the various stages of method as he had outlined them in *Naming the Whirlwind* and modified them *en route* in *Reaping the Whirlwind*. His theology remained thoroughly, and perhaps even more deeply, correlational and apologetic, now even foundational—yet, though more modestly, still neoorthodox. Gilkey supplied this book with a threefold structure.

In part 1, "Historical Passage: A Prolegomenon," Gilkey begins with a phenomenological hermeneutic of the secular experience of historical passage in four chapters. This first part also reflects a substructure, in that

---

[121]Gilkey developed this dialectic first in *Reaping the Whirlwind*: e.g., in chap. 10, "Providence and Eschatology: A Reinterpretation." There, the dialectic of Christian belief appears in three sections: (1) "The Sovereignty of God Reinterpreted: God as Being and Logos" (rationality); (2) "The Estrangement of History, Nemesis and Judgment" (incredibility); and (3) "Redemptive Forces in History" (credibility) (Gilkey, *RW*, 246-53, 253-65, 265-70). Also, see the three moments of this dialectic in chap. 5 of *Reaping the Whirlwind* (Gilkey, *RW*, 124-25, 125-28, 128-30). See his slightly later summaries and sharpening of this dialectic: Gilkey, "Dialectic of Christian Belief: Rational, Incredible, Credible," 65-83; idem, *SAS*, 26-41.

[122]Gilkey, *RW*, 34.

the first two chapters examine contemporary human *experiences* of historical passage, while the second two chapters examine contemporary theories about or *reflection* on historical passage. Chapter 1 describes the situation of social change in contemporary experience, identifying the major areas or factors of social change in terms of the characteristics of secular experience. In chapter 2, Gilkey addresses this situation with an ontic analysis, as he had performed on individual experience in *Naming the Whirlwind*, to uncover in this situation the religious dimension or ultimacy implicit to contemporary historical experience. Here, however, Gilkey introduced something new into his prolegomenon: an ontological analysis of the contemporary experience of historical passage. Through this new analysis, Gilkey discovered the ontological structure of destiny and freedom, actuality and possibility, an ontological structure in which he discerned evidence of an argument for the necessity of God—natural theology. Turning from his examination of existence itself, to contemporary reflection on historical passage, in chapter 3, Gilkey studied contemporary scientific interpretations of history in order to uncover their own weaknesses and the implicit religious dimension to them. With the same goal in chapter 4, Gilkey subjected contemporary philosophies of history (those of Ernst Bloch and A. N. Whitehead) to similar analysis.

With part 2, "Entre' Acte," Gilkey introduced two chapters on methodological issues (chaps. 5 and 6). As I have mentioned previously, he placed these chapters between parts 2 and 3 in order to formalize his distinction between his prolegomenon and constructive theology proper.

Part 3, "The Christian View of History: A Reinterpretation," moves from the first pole in Gilkey's correlational method (existence or the contemporary situation) to the second pole (the Christian message). This part of Gilkey's book reflects a threefold substructure. *First*, chapters 7, 8, and 9 represent Gilkey's *eidetic analysis* of Christian symbols. Chapter 7, "Traditional Views of Providence: Augustine and Calvin," examines the theologies of providence from two of the most prominent classical and reformation figures. With chapter 8, "Modern Historical Consciousness," Gilkey studies developments during the advent and flowering of modernity in the 17th and 18th centuries, to which Christian theology responded and which challenged and began to alter the classical and reformed Christian paradigms. In chapter 9, "Gilkey surveys the major theological responses to modern historical consciousness in the 19th and 20th centuries: nineteenth-century liberal theology, early twentieth-century Krisis or neoorthodox theology, and the eschatological theologies of the

1960s and 1970s. *Second*, in chapters 10 and 11, Gilkey performs his *analyses of the moral and political meaning* of providence: in chapter 10, examining the meaning of providence in terms of the more individual experiences of historical estrangement and transformation; and, in chapter 11, elucidating the political praxis of providence and eschatology. *Third*, in chapter 12, "The God of Process, of Possibility and of Hope," Gilkey draws the several strands of his study together into an *ontological elucidation* of the Christian symbol of providence, with which he concludes *Reaping the Whirlwind*.

2. *Message and Existence*. *Message and Existence*, though equally sophisticated, does not reflect the complexity of *Reaping the Whirlwind* due to its condensed size. Although the practice of theological method in this book deserves a fuller treatment, I will abbreviate my remarks about *Message and Existence*. With *Message and Existence*, Gilkey offers a short, summative interpretation of the entire system of Christian symbols, following the major structural moments or articles of the *Apostles Creed*. As a result, this supplies *Message and Existence* with a fourfold structure, preceded by an introductory chapter: first, examining the creed's "I believe"; second, interpreting God as creator; third, interpreting the article on Jesus as the Christ; and, fourth, discussing the creed's article on the Holy Spirit. Thus, with the exception of the first part, Gilkey's book reflects a trinitarian structure, due to his efforts to follow the contours of this basic Christian creed.

Disregarding his distaste for beginning with methodological consider-ations, in the introductory context of chapter 1, Gilkey roughly outlines his correlational method for theological construction. His methodological reflections follow, though with less complexity and distinction, the methodological pattern that he developed in *Naming the Whirlwind* and deepened in *Reaping the Whirlwind*. Each part contains two chapters: the first chapter focusing on a Christian symbol of human experience, life, or history (human existence, question, or situation); and the second chapter interpreting a Christian symbol of the divine life and activity (divine message, answer). (1) In part 1, Gilkey devotes chapter 2 to the nature of human faith and chapter 3 to the character of divine self-revelation. (2) Part 2 begins with chapter 4, Gilkey's examination of essential human life (the characteristics of finitude, as distinct from estrangement or sin), and concludes with chapter 5, his interpretation of God as creator. (3) In part 3, Gilkey begins with an interpretation of human estrangement and sin in chapter 6, answered by chapter 7 on Jesus Christ and salvation. (4) With part 4, Gilkey concludes the book: beginning by interpreting the symbol of human community in chapter 8 and concluding with his interpretation of the Holy Spirit in chapter 9. Gilkey has correlated or paired Christian symbols with one another: one of human experience or existence, which asks a question, with one of divine activity, which offers the answer to the human question.

Furthermore, Gilkey even builds this same pattern into each chapter: beginning with actual human experience as related to the symbol under consideration, then moving to the Christian tradition's witness to that aspect of human life.[123] Thus, each chapter contains all four of the major forms of analysis, as developed by Gilkey previously: (1) analysis of the religious dimension in ordinary experience, both ontic and ontological interpretations; (2) eidetic analysis of the Christian tradition; (3) ontological elucidation of the symbols; and (4) moral and political appropriation of the symbols. By virtue of the Christian symbols examined by Gilkey in the respective chapters, some of these analyses appear more prominently in some chapters than in others. Furthermore, due to the condensed character of the book, to which Gilkey refers as his "baby systematic," these layers of meaning do not as clearly distinguish themselves from one another.[124] Nonetheless, with care, one can discern the same series of moves in this book as in *Reaping the Whirlwind*, although here I cannot demonstrate this claim thoroughly.

V. Beyond Liberalism, Postliberalism, and Foundationalism: Correlational Theological Method and the Relative-Absolute

As I have stated previously in this chapter, with this final section, I isolate another period in the development of Gilkey's theological method. This period, however, does not distinguish itself from the previous period as much chronologically as it does qualitatively. In many but not all respects, the previous period and this period coextend, or at least overlap one another, across the same chronological span. For that reason, I will argue that Gilkey's perspective in this most recent phase of his thinking remains *largely* consistent with much of his most mature neoorthodox perspective in the previous period or stage of his career. Nonetheless, a

---

[123]Gilkey, *ME*, 7-19, 70.
[124]Gilkey, *ME*, 2; idem, "Retrospective Glance at My Work," 26.

gradual shift in Gilkey's theological strategy does appear during the previous period in the development of his method, more specifically in terms of how he has done theology in light of the new parity of religions; and, although Gilkey employs this newer strategy tentatively, he has done so ever-increasingly. More than ten years ago, Gilkey even noted the conclusion of the previous period of his thought—perhaps even the end of that basic methodological strategy so characteristic of his thought.

> This effort to articulate a theological interpretation, a "revised Christian theology," on the basis of the method of phenomenological prolegomenon and existential correlation—ordinary experience providing the ultimacy, the crisis of anxiety, and so the "question," and the reinterpreted theological symbol providing the answer—was continued (*and concluded*) in a short ("baby") systematic theology called *Message and Existence* (1979).[125]

In this light, then, I have chosen to address this additional modification in Gilkey's theological method in a separate section altogether. I refer to the methodological shift occasioned by Gilkey's encounter with the plurality of religions. This most recent period in the development of Gilkey's theological method also originates, as in the previous periods as well, in light of the results from his employment of correlational theological strategy. More specifically, this most recent change in theological strategy has resulted from his assessment of and response to the contemporary situation or his persistent, alert, and sensitive theology of culture.

Several factors from previous stages in the evolution of Gilkey's theological method relate directly to the present form of Gilkey's theological method in its engagement with religious plurality. A brief review of those factors will help to contextualize the present character of Gilkey's theological method—especially its significant differences from his previous perspective on other religions. I will follow that review with two further discussions: first, a brief account of Gilkey's understanding of religious plurality; and, second, a discussion of Gilkey's theological method in the face of this new situation.

---

[125]Gilkey, "Retrospective Glance at My Work," 26; emphasis mine.

A. Factors in the Evolution of Gilkey's Present Theological Strategy

1. *Religions and Niebuhrian Postliberalism.* As a young Niebuhrian postliberal theologian, Gilkey's posture toward other religions remained reserved—at least, by comparison to many neoorthodox theologians, for whom religion and the religions (as contrasted with Christian faith) represented human *efforts* to reach God, opposed divine *grace*, and therefore constituted rebellion and idolatry.[126] During this period, Gilkey did not take an aggressively conflictual approach in his understanding of the relationship between Christianity and other religions. Nonetheless, in his early concern with "correct" theology, he occasionally placed other religious perspectives into categories with concepts that contradicted or undermined basic Christian symbols or doctrines, clearly considering Christian faith to be the most adequate answer to the questions of the human condition. Most often, however, Gilkey referred to other religions in comparisons to various aspects of Christian religion.[127]

---

[126]See Gilkey's reference to the "unrelieved critique of religion at all levels" in Karl Barth's theology: Gilkey, "Appreciation of Karl Barth," 154. Note also Gilkey's use of Barth's distinction between revelation and religion elsewhere: Gilkey, *SAS*, 164-65. Gilkey considers this aspect in Barth's thought, "paradoxically, very helpful (if analogically used) in the present encounter of and dialogue between religions"—specifically, I suspect, although Gilkey does not mention it in this brief article, as a resource against that which Gilkey describes elsewhere as "the intolerable," the appearance of demonic absolutes in history. As I mentioned earlier, however, Gilkey did regard *natural theologies* as idolatrous (as themselves also human efforts to reach God) during his earliest period as a postliberal.

[127]For example, in *Maker of Heaven and Earth*, Gilkey cited a text from the Hindu *Upanishads* as an example of pantheism, a perspective antithetical to the reality and goodness of creation; he also referred to Mahayana Buddhism (along with Neoplatonism and nineteenth-century idealism) as representing "a denial of the reality and value of individual creaturely existence," also something affirmed by the Christian doctrine of creation; and he referred to the monism of Hinduism as opposed to the Christian affirmation of the distinction between God and world in the doctrine of creation (Gilkey, *MHE*, 58n.8, 59, 61, 93). Also see Gilkey's comparative references to Hinduism and Buddhism, e.g., in his discussions of the nature of religious language (e.g., Gilkey, *MHE*, 337-39, 358; idem, *NW*, 285, 290n.34). In one respect, in his earliest neoorthodoxy, Gilkey's approach to understanding the relation of Christianity to other religions *resembled* (at least in principle) his understanding of the relationship between philosophy and theology. He illustrated that relationship with a parable about two teams of climbers aiming for the same peak on the same mountain. "The mountain they are climbing is

2. *Dialogue and Tillichian Neoorthodoxy.* During the period of his Tillichian modifications to his original Niebuhrian neoorthodoxy, Gilkey continued to deepen his thinking about the implications of the cultural situation for Christian theology. Two factors in Gilkey's work during this period appear to prepare the way for the shift in his theological account of other religions: first, Gilkey's understanding of the dialogue between church and the larger culture; and, second, Gilkey's theological reflection on the meaning of ecumenical dialogue, as he experienced it with Roman Catholicism.

In the years immediately prior to and following the publication of *Naming the Whirlwind,* Gilkey also began to study contemporary Roman Catholic theology. This engagement in ecumenical dialogue, as subsequently reflected in *Catholicism Confronts Modernity,* led him to consider the implications of a secular culture for the Roman Catholic church and its theology. In that context, Gilkey developed the concept of "the Spirit as manifest in and through dialogue, dialogue of the Church with culture on the one hand and dialogue within the whole Church on the other."[128]

---

necessarily the same if each of them is, in his own way, aiming for the highest peak. Therefore it is *far better* for the climbers *to compare* approaches, to use both as far as possible, to see how each supplements the other, and *then* (the most significant decision) *to take the better path to the summit,* than to go each his own way muttering that the other is a fool or a liar. Since the goals of philosophy and theology are likewise ultimately the same, they will, like the climbers, proceed much *more successfully in cooperation than in conflict*" (Gilkey, *MHE,* 31; emphasis mine).

[128]Langdon Gilkey, "The Spirit and the Discovery of Truth through Dialogue," in *Experience of the Spirit,* ed. Peter Huizing and William Bassett, vol. 9, no. 10, *Spirituality, Concilium: New Series* (New York: Seabury Press, 1974) 58; also published under the same title in *Leven uit de Geest: Festschrift for Edward Schillebeeckx,* ed. Paul W. Brand (Hilversum, The Netherlands: Gooi en Sticht, 1974); also published in French as "L'Esprit et la découverte de la vérité dans le dialogue," in *L'Expérience de L'Esprit: Melanges E. Schillebeeckx,* ed. Paul W. Brand, Le Point Theologique Series, vol. 18 (Paris: Beauchesne, 1976) 225-40. Gilkey mentions, as one of the factors during this same period that contributed to his "growing interest" in interreligious dialogue, his "wife's increasing devotion to yoga," through which Gilkey's family "became involved with the Sikh movement in America"; in 1974, his wife even entered "the Sikh Khalsa as one of its members" (Gilkey, "Retrospective Glance at My Work," 31). Gilkey later wrote a paper (to my knowledge, never published), reflecting on his participation with his wife in the activities of the Sikh Khalsa: Langdon Gilkey, "The Khalsa Goes West," July 1980, TMs (photocopy) 1-30, Personal Files of Langdon Gilkey, Charlottesville, Virginia. Gilkey also mentions another factor that increased his interest in dialogue with other religions: a term of teaching at Kyoto University in 1975, during which time, he

a. *Dialogue between Church and Culture*. Gilkey identified the central feature of culture's new historical situation as "the new realization of the *historicity* of human being in its totality, and so the historicity of the thought and the action of men, women and so of their communities." This new awareness, an expression of secular consciousness itself, held two implications: (1) all Christian theology and ethics participate in the relativity of all other cultural productions and have no absolute status; and (2) Christian theology, to be relevant, "can only discover *its own* truth in explicit dialogue with its cultural setting." This situation entails the relativity of both partners in dialogue: the church's perspective experiences this relativity as much as the culture. Gilkey, thus, affirms the "universal work of the Spirit in human culture," even though he still maintains an ecclesiological criterion for this universal divine pneumatological activity: "[a]s in the early Church the criterion for the use of the universal logos was the logos made flesh, so for the Church now the criterion of the Spirit at work in the world is and must be the Spirit revealed in and through the originating symbols of the Church's life; the Spirit within the Church's life is the criterion of the Spirit at work in the world." According to Gilkey, affirmation of the universal work of the Spirit in culture supplies the basic principles for dialogue with other religions, as also aspects of culture themselves: "We can enter into a constructive dialogue with them, recognizing the validity and power resident in them, with openness and yet with confidence because we know that the same Spirit that we know is at work in its own ways, often strange to us, in them."[129] Similarly, in *Reaping the Whirlwind*, Gilkey admits his belief that God has not confined the divine "healing, reconciling work" to "the Jewish and the Christian dispensations." Rather, Gilkey says, "[i]t appears to a more or less degree in all religions, and in many secular arts as well." Again, whereas he supplied an ecclesiological criterion for his concept of God's universal pneumatological activity, here he supplies a Christological criterion for his concept of God's universal soteriological activity. "For Christians, however, the criterion of this universal reconciling work of God is manifested in Jesus: *wherever* the judgment, the love and the promises of God *as* they are known and defined by him are evident elsewhere, there we know the universal

---

conversed frequently with the Buddhist philosopher, Takeuchi Yoshinori (Gilkey, "Retrospective Glance at My Work," 30).

[129]Gilkey, "Spirit and the Discovery of Truth through Dialogue," 59-63.

redemptive activity of God to be at work."[130] Thus, as early as the mid-1970s, on the basis of his developing theology of providence, Gilkey had also begun to develop a concept that would soon lead him nearer to his notion of the *parity of religions*, but still stopped far short of Gilkey's present understanding of that concept.

    b. *Dialogue within the Whole Church.* Second, a similar situation exists for dialogue within the whole church. When Gilkey mentions the "whole" church, he refers to an *ecumenical* community, a community of communities, not merely all of the members of one local congregation. Gilkey refers to "the ecumenical movement" as "the *new* locus for the Holy Spirit and for our faith in the continuity of Christian truth." Gilkey argues that Christian communions within the larger or whole church need one another, not in spite of their divergent perspectives or opinions, but precisely because of those differences. This Christian variety, even plurality, provides "the way to the fullness of divine truth," rather than the dissolution of the absolute truths affirmed by one communion's relative viewpoint. According to Gilkey, from the divine side, "the promise of the Spirit within our fragmentary perspectives" relates communions to the wholeness of truth; from the human side, "the reality of our dialogue with one another" achieves that relation to the wholeness of truth. Accordingly, Gilkey argues, this concept implies that "freedom of theological debate" with its "apparent tolerance of error" represents the "essential condition for truth within the community." Only through dialogue—even as it issues in argumentation or debate—can the wisdom and strength of communions balance the errors or deficiencies in other communions, and all communions have errors or deficiencies of some kind. As Gilkey says in *Catholicism Confronts Modernity*, "[v]ariety of opinion is the sole human way of achieving the truth: it respects individual conscience, and it balances the relativity of each position with the correction of other points of view." Gilkey brilliantly observes—here reflecting his developing notion of divine providence—that this understanding of truth, as achieved through dialogue among divergent and equally relative perspectives, itself represents "an example of a gift to the Church of the Spirit as it worked 'hiddenly' in culture; for this understanding of truth as approximation rather than possession, and an

---

[130]Gilkey, *RW*, 267-68, 421n.84.

approximation that grows through criticism and debate, is an interpretation of the truth that the scientific community has given to us all."[131]

Clearly, Gilkey discerns *dialectical* relationships between church and culture. On the one hand, through the church, the divine Spirit supplies criteria to the culture, in order to discern both authentic creative and genuine redemptive divine activity in culture—and, by implication, in other religions as expressions of culture. On the other hand, through the culture, God supplies the church with gifts to aid in its own humility—and, by implication, such gifts have also come from the Spirit to the church through other religions as aspects of culture themselves. Gilkey's methodological posture here depends significantly on a theology of providence, one which he published in *Reaping the Whirlwind*.

3. *Religious Criterion of Religion: Christianity's Covenants with Culture and Other Religions*. Around the time of and shortly after the publication of *Reaping the Whirlwind*, Gilkey began to borrow historic models of Christianity's relation to culture as analogies with which to propose a relationship between Christianity and other religious communities or traditions. He referred specifically to two models: first, " 'a covenant of God with the Greeks,' " a model used by some early Christian theologians to refer to God's work in the world "prior to the Christian revelation," which then legitimated for those theologians "a synthesis of Christian revelation with Hellenistic culture"; and, second, "a 'divine covenant' with modern culture," or "the covenant with the modern West," employed by liberal and postliberal theologians (at least implicitly) to legitimate "current theological efforts to reinterpret the Christian tradition in the light of modern science, modern social theory, modern psychology, and so on."[132] Gilkey proposed to employ this model in two ways in relation to religious phenomena.

First, Gilkey proposed a *covenant between Christianity and the religious substance or dimension of culture* itself. This covenant, of course, implies a covenant with the larger life of culture itself—a covenant in which Christianity and a given culture engage in mutual exchange of

---

[131]Gilkey, "Spirit and the Discovery of Truth through Dialogue," 66-68; idem, *CCM*, 81-82, also 174-77.

[132]Langdon Gilkey, "Toward a Religious Criterion of Religion," in *Understanding the New Religions*, ed. Jacob Needleman and George Baker (New York: Seabury Press, 1978) 136, 137; idem, "A Covenant with the Chinese," 181, 182 (later included as chap. 10, "Revelation and an Ancient Civilization," in *SAS*, 139 140, 141-42).

political, social, economic, philosophical, and moral values, resources, and creativity, especially at those points where either one has resources and the other has needs. The deeper and more problematic aspect concerns the expression of this covenant with culture in Christianity's more focused covenant with the culture's religious dimension: the cultural "vision of what is ultimately real, true and valuable," those ideals that a culture actualizes in all of its forms and from which it lives. As Gilkey notes, given the difficulties, "only when each side has something to offer," does such a covenant or "synthesis" become "possible and necessary." Gilkey specifically proposed such a covenant with the religious dimension of Chinese culture, which illustrates his vision of that which Christianity can offer in covenant with a culture's religious dimension.[133]

Second, Gilkey proposed various *covenants between Christianity and other religious traditions or communities*, as aspects of culture and explicit expressions of its religious substance. One of Gilkey's earliest publications of this idea even invokes the concept of a covenant with another religion, specifically referring to Buddhism, as (suggestively, however) the work of divine providence or the universal work of the Spirit: "long ago a covenant unknown to us may have been prepared in the Orient as well as in Greece."[134] In his small systematic theology, *Message and Existence*, Gilkey mentions the possibility of such covenants with Buddhism, Hinduism, and Islam. In the context of his discussion of the nature of theology, he discusses the body of other religious traditions as one of four resources for the theological task—including the Christian scriptures, Christian traditions, and the contemporary situation as well.[135] On the basis of two principles or presuppositions, Gilkey suggests an

---

[133]Gilkey, "A Covenant with the Chinese," 184-87. See Gilkey's discussion in this article of the distinction between sin (distorted freedom) and fate (distorted or fallen destiny), as the basis for his distinction between liberation from unjust institutions and the solution of the more basic cause of fate, overcoming sin itself. Christianity should participate in the political liberation of people, inasmuch as warped and oppressive institutions defy the divine purposes for creation. Christianity must also address the problem of sin itself, however, since that effort deals with the cause behind those warped institutions and distorted destiny. Also see Gilkey, *ME*, 42-43.

[134]Gilkey, "Toward a Religious Criterion of Religion," 137.

[135]Gilkey, *ME*, 54-63. He also refers to the possibility of covenants with religions of Asia, specifically Buddhism, elsewhere: Gilkey, "Toward a Religious Criterion of Religion," 137.

approach to using other religious traditions as resources for Christian theology. (1) First, divine revelation extends to the entire world and has not limited itself to the Christian religion alone; one may find truth in other religious communities and traditions. (2) Second, as a *human* response to divine activity, Christian tradition is "both partial and fallible." Because of both presuppositions, "the width" or universality of divine revelation and "the narrowness" or partiality of human reception of it, other religious traditions function as "a creative and authentic resource" for Christian theology.[136] Here Gilkey's point remains consistent with his earlier position on the necessity of dialogue among different Christian communions, in order to approximate the fullness of truth, since each communion experiences divine revelation—yet both partially and fallibly. Through this concept of covenant with other religions, Gilkey invites critique and deepening of the Christian's understanding of her own tradition by viewing the Christian tradition from the perspective of another religious tradition.[137]

Gilkey seems to struggle during this period with whether or not these covenants between Christianity and other religions constitute religious *syntheses*. Clearly, Gilkey admits quite readily that Christianity's covenants with the larger cultures of Hellenism and Modernity constituted syntheses for Christian theology and religion. For example, he begins his discussion of Christianity's covenant with Chinese culture by interchangeably employing the terms "covenant" and "synthesis." Thus, he at least *implies* that the covenants between Christianity and other religions (as expressions of those cultures) constitute *syntheses* as well. Nonetheless, he later explicitly shrinks from this claim in *Message and Existence*: for example, he states that Christianity's covenant with Buddhism "does not represent a *synthesis*."[138] In light of Gilkey's continued dialogue with other religions and his theological formulations in light of those conversations, this issue in Gilkey's thought remains open and worthy of consideration. Do the results of such covenants for interreligious dialogue, as expressed in theological construction, qualify as syntheses or not?

---

[136]Gilkey, *ME*, 18, 61.
[137]Gilkey, "Toward a Religious Criterion of Religion," 137; idem, *ME*, 63.
[138]Gilkey, "A Covenant with the Chinese," 181, 185; idem, *ME*, 63; emphasis mine.

B. Time of Troubles and the New Understanding of Religious Plurality

1. *Religions in the New Situation.* In the early 1980s, Gilkey began to record his then most recent assessments of the newer cultural situation, describing it following Arnold Toynbee as a "time of troubles," with its cluster of questions and problems to which Christian theology would need to respond, if that theology would hope to offer a new relevant word to a world in crisis. From Gilkey's interpretation of culture during that period, originates his deepened insight into the plurality of religions.

Although I will not outline his entire interpretation of the new and larger cultural situation, I note two features of most immediate importance for his understanding of religious plurality. First, having written two of his largest, most complex, and most well-known books (*Naming the Whirlwind* and *Reaping the Whirlwind*) in direct response to the problems and issues produced for Christian faith and theology by a secular culture, one of the biggest surprises to Gilkey occurred in that which Gilkey has called "the reappearance of the religious." By the early 1980s, many varieties of fundamentalist religion had appeared and begun to flourish in the secular West, as well as numerous imported forms of competing religions from the East, in spite of the still prevailing secularism in culture as a whole. Second, in addition, Gilkey identified another major factor that directly affected the status and self-understanding of other religions in the world: the Western world's loss of dominance over the remainder of the earth. More recently, Gilkey has identified this factor even as the "major" or "main" cause of the new parity among religions. Resulting from the upheavals of revolutions and two global wars, the West has lost its political power and ideological influence over most of the world. This loss of influence has extended to Christianity for a variety of reasons, one of the most important of which concerns Christianity's close identification with the West's political and ideological imperialism around the world (one might even say here, Christianity's covenant with Western culture). So, along with the loss of Western political dominance, and the consequent appearance of "the historical relativity of the West," went the dominance and sense of superiority once enjoyed by Christianity as the religion of dominant Western colonials. These two factors especially shed new light for Gilkey on the ancient plurality of religions.[139]

2. *Plurality of Religions as Parity.* Many strands from Gilkey's previous thinking about other religions and the many Christian communions began to merge as Gilkey considered the plurality of religions in this new situation. Nevertheless, in certain essential respects, Gilkey's perspective changes radically here.

---

[139]Langdon Gilkey, "Theology for a Time of Troubles: How My Mind Has Changed," *Christian Century* 98 (29 April 1981): 474-79; repr.: "Theology for a Time of Troubles," in *Theologians in Transition*, 29-36; cf. idem, "A New Watershed in Theology," *Soundings* 64 (Summer 1981): 119-28; cf. revision also, chap. 1, "The New Watershed in Theology," in *SAS*, 4-12; idem, "The Pluralism of Religions," in *God, Truth and Reality: Essays in Honor of John Hick*, ed. Arvind Sharma (New York: St. Martin's Press, 1993) 115; idem, "Theological Frontiers: Implications for Bioethics," in *Theology and Bioethics: Exploring the Foundations and Frontiers*, ed. Earl E. Shelp (Dordrecht: D. Reidel Pub. Co., 1985) 131; idem, "Culture and Religious Belief," in *The Life of Religion: A Marquett University Symposium on the Nature of Religious Belief*, ed. Stanley M. Harrison and Richard C. Taylor (Lanham MD: University Press of America, 1986) 89; idem, "The Paradigm Shift in Theology," in *Paradigm Change in Theology: A Symposium for the Future*, ed. Hans Küng and David Tracy, trans. Margaret Köhl (New York: Crossroad Pub. Co., 1989) 371-82; idem, "Theology of Culture and Christian Ethics," in *Annual of the Society of Christian Ethics*, ed. Larry L Rasmussen (Vancouver: Society of Christian Ethics, 1984) 361; also under the same title, as chap. 9, in *TT*, 154; idem, "Events, Meanings and the Current Tasks of Theology," *Journal of the American Academy of Religion* 53 (1985): 726-28; also under the same title, in *Trajectories in the Study of Religion: Addresses at the Seventy-Fifth Anniversary of the American Academy of Religion*, ed. Ray L. Hart (Atlanta: Scholars Press, 1987) 184-86. Although in more recent publications Gilkey has stressed the loss of Western political and spiritual dominance as the principal cause of the new parity among religions, earlier he considered this new encounter among religions to be "a function of three factors" (although each of these may find their center in the major cause mentioned previously): "ambiguity of the modern scientific consciousness, the loss of Western political and spiritual dominance, and the death of the Western deity of progress" (Gilkey, "New Watershed in Theology," 128-29). Elsewhere, Gilkey adds theological changes to the cultural changes, as causes for this appearance of religious parity—though he clearly subordinates their importance to the major cause, the loss of Western cultural and political dominance as a whole: Langdon Gilkey, "Plurality: Our New Situation," in *The Pastor as Servant*, ed. Earl E. Shelp and Ronald H. Sunderland (New York: Pilgrim Press, 1986) 102-22, 131; also published as chap. 2, under the title, "Plurality: Christianity's New Situation," in *TT*, 21-34; idem, "Plurality and Its Theological Implications," in *The Myth of Christian Uniqueness: Toward a Pluralistic Theology of Religions*, ed. John Hick and Paul F. Knitter (Maryknoll NY: Orbis Books, 1987) 37-50.

Gilkey acknowledges, of course, that the awareness of religious plurality or the plurality of religions is not new: people have always known of many different and competing religions. Rather, Gilkey identifies the appearance of a very different, "new form of the encounter of Christianity with other religions," a new understanding of the relationships among religions. He describes this new relationship among the religions as a "continental or epochal shift," even as "a monstrous shift," in the cultural situation. Because Western culture has experienced the loss of its own position of political and intellectual superiority and has experienced a forced shift to a position of equality with other cultures, experienced its own cultural relativity, so too has Christianity descended from its assumed superiority over the other religions to a new situation of equality with (if, often, not inferiority to) other religions.[140]

Gilkey's writings supply the elements for a rough typology of perspectives on Christianity's relation to other religions. This typology, though of limited historical and philosophical value, serves well to specify more precisely the viewpoints that Gilkey has abandoned or repudiated and helps to sharpen an understanding of Gilkey's own theological location in this new situation. Gilkey supplies six major categories. (a) First, Gilkey identifies and refuses an obviously problematic perspective: "clear exclusivism," largely the traditional, orthodox, conservative, and even fundamentalist Christian perspective, for which "the other [religions] are simply false, if not blasphemous," while Christianity represents "the only way to salvation"—and, without which, "[t]here is neither truth nor grace." Hence, this first Christian perspective at best aims to convert the other. (b) Second, Gilkey refuses a liberal strategy that tones down or eliminates some Christian symbols to which other religions might object (such as revelation or Christ) (Gilkey's representative of this view—John Hick). Gilkey argues quite correctly that the problem between religions involves entire systems—all symbols or doctrines not just some of them. (c) A third perspective represents a philosophical approach, in its effort to transcend the particularities of religions, in order to "achieve a universal standpoint," a perspective "above and so neutral to the fundamental differences between religions" (Gilkey's examples of this strategy—Whitehead and Hegel). Gilkey also

---

[140]Gilkey, "Paradigm Shift in Theology," 379; idem, "Theology of Culture and Christian Ethics," 360; also in chap. 9, idem, *TT*, 153; idem, "Plurality and Its Theological Implications," 39.

rejects this approach, since even philosophical systems disclose their own particularities as well—in this case, the rationality of Western culture. (f) Gilkey identifies a fourth approach in the typology as an inclusivist strategy: all religions express a religious or mystical core, the particularities of which (laws, rituals, doctrines, liturgies, and so forth) the divine reveals for the sake of different cultural needs; as a revelation for a particular community, each religion is true, yet "relative to other true revelations and to other communities, and relative to the Absolute that each only partially and so somewhat distortedly manifests" (Gilkey's example of this view—Frithjof Schuon). Gilkey also finds this approach unsatisfactory, since it "raises an *aspect* of religion (mysticism) and its philosophical equivalent to supreme status over other aspects of the religious." (e) Gilkey includes a fifth type of approach, also an inclusivist strategy: the liberal and neoorthodox traditions generally affirmed that, because God works universally, other religions disclose "some measure of truth and grace, even a saving measure," though the "final revelation" occurs in the "Christian revelation" or Christ—"the criterion" by which to evaluate all other religions. Gilkey mentions Schleiermacher, Tillich, and Reinhold Niebuhr as representatives of this perspective; he also notes that, methodologically, Hinduism and Buddhism employ this strategy as well, though with their own religious categories and symbols. Although Gilkey openly admits that he has used this strategy himself (following his teachers), at this point he describes it as "unsatisfactory" and "inadequate to the new situation." By finally raising "a particular tradition above all the others," this fifth type of approach "incorporates others into its own world," interpreting and defining them "from an alien perspective": hence, "in seeing the other through its own eyes," a proponent of this strategy "can never hear what the other has to say." (f) Gilkey distinguishes all of the previous strategies or types of approaches from the sixth approach that he advocates and describes with the concept, *plurality of religions as parity*.[141]

---

[141]In one slightly earlier version of this typology, Gilkey describes three stages in the history of the relation between Christianity and other religions: orthodoxy or exclusivism; liberal and neoorthodox views of Christ as the criterion of the partial revelation in other religions; and the present phase of plurality of religions as parity (Gilkey, "Plurality: Our New Situation," 117-18; also in chap. 2, "Plurality: Christianity's New Situation," in *TT*, 30-31). In a later typology, Gilkey discusses several other strategies of relating the religions to one another to overcome the conflicts (Gilkey, "Plurality and Its Theological

With the term "parity," Gilkey suggests "not an assessment of all relevant religions," but rather "an 'heuristic principle' " or "a method of *approach* to the other religions, a way of meeting them and relating to them," that "abjures and denies the claim . . . of superiority." Gilkey describes the claim of religious superiority as "the quiet confidence of the hidden possessor of an absolute standpoint, and with it a tolerant but secure certainty that one really understands the other on one's own terms better than they understand themselves on their terms." Instead, Gilkey proposes a "new attitude" that "denies such a superior vantage point," one which "recognizes, however painfully, its own perspective as relative and not universal—and thus it can listen to the other in order to learn and not just in order to take notes on them or to gain time to argue."[142]

Gilkey describes this new understanding of the relationships among the many religions as rough equality or parity.[143] The *plurality of religions as rough parity*, however, does not refer only to each religion's achievement of social or political equality—the right to exist alongside all other religions as an equal—although that may be (and hopefully is) true also. Rather, rough parity among the many different religions refers to something much more radical. Gilkey describes it as an awareness that has grown from the experience of perceiving the "spiritual power (truth and grace, as we would say it in Christian terms)" in other religious communions and traditions.[144] Most pointedly, rough parity does not mean either that one wants to study the other religions, that one aims to convert the adherents of different religions, or that one communion expresses

---

Implications," 41-44, 48). I have conflated these two accounts, since several of his categories overlap, in an effort to illustrate Gilkey's attempt to locate his own most recent perspective. Gilkey also, as he admitted, borrowed with significant qualification during the early 1980s the mystical approach to truth in other religions (Gilkey, "Plurality and Its Theological Implications," 42; cf. idem, *SAS*, 162-66). Gilkey also refers to the conversionist aims of an exclusivist perspective (Gilkey, *SAS*, 158).

[142]Gilkey, "Pluralism of Religions," 115.

[143]Gilkey, "Plurality and Its Theological Implications," 37, 39; idem, "Paradigm Shift in Theology," 379.

[144]Gilkey, "Retrospective Glance at My Work," 31-32; idem, "Paradigm Shift in Theology," 382; idem, "Toward a Redefinition of Universal Salvation in Christ," in *SAS*, 157; idem, "The Meaning of Jesus the Christ," in *The Christ and the Bodhisattva*, ed. Donald S. Lopez, Jr. and Steven C. Rockefeller, SUNY Series in Buddhist Studies, ed. Kenneth K. Inada (Albany: State University of New York Press, 1987) 207; also under the same title as chap. 7, in *TT*, 113; idem, "God," in *Christian Theology*, ed. Hodgson and King, 85; idem, also as chap. 5, "Christian Understanding of God," in *TT*, 87.

some sort of friendly interest in the other religions. Rather, rough parity or equality among the religions means that one considers their methods, even their viewpoints about reality, to be "as good" as one's own, that one recognizes the other religions "as bearing *power* and as embodying vital, healing, redemptive forces providing unique illumination and grace to our ailing cultural life and our somewhat impoverished existence," that the many religions also bring a "plurality of revelations." This new understanding of the many religions as equal, then, relativizes not only every person's religious faith, not only the human response to revelation, not only doctrines and dogmas, but, most significantly, "the *referent* of that faith, the revelation" on which faith depends, "the revelation to which we are responding."[145]

In his initial thoughts about the new situation of religious pluralism, the rough parity or equality of religions, Gilkey responded with genuine personal and theological perplexity, referring to the situation as "an uncharted sea" or "a sea with no maps." He stated his perplexity as a paradox or a puzzle. This paradox originated from his attempt to answer a question that initially appeared through his own encounter with persons in other religious communities: how do I affirm the presence of truth and grace in another's tradition and continue to affirm the truth and grace in my own very different tradition? According to Gilkey, when a person of faith perceives "the truth and grace, the spiritual power, of another faith" (as surely one must), "[h]ow does such recognition, necessary for one's own honesty as well as for dialogue, feed back on our own theological understanding of our faith?" Although Gilkey did not make extensive proposals in his earliest struggles with this problem, nevertheless, he did establish one solid point of reference. In order to maintain *genuine dialogue among equals*, the participants must meet two conditions: (1) each participant must stand in a tradition, affirm a perspective of her or his own, maintain a commitment to that "absolute" perspective; yet, (2) each participant must simultaneously acknowledge the equality of the other partner in dialogue and, thus, the "relativity" of her or his own faith

---

[145]Gilkey, "Theology and Culture: Reflections on the Conference," 7; idem, "Toward a Redefinition of Universal Salvation in Christ," in *SAS*, 157; idem, "God," in *Christian Theology*, Hodgson and King, 85; idem, also as chap. 5, "Christian Understanding of God," in *TT*, 87; idem, "Plurality and Its Theological Implications," 39, 40-41; idem, "Plurality: Our New Situation," 119; also in chap. 2, "Plurality: Christianity's New Situation," in *TT*, 31.

and religious tradition.[146] With this, Gilkey's paradoxical category appears: *the relative absolute.*

C. Voyage on "a Sea with No Maps": Postliberal Foundational Theological Method and the Problem of Religious Plurality as Parity

In light of Gilkey's response to the plurality of religions, one wonders just exactly what remains for Gilkey. In the preface to *Reaping the Whirlwind*, Gilkey had alerted readers to those theologians whose work most served as resources in his efforts to address the problem of providence in that book. Gilkey mentioned his indebtedness, in that connection, to three theologians and one philosopher, by their names, and to one group of theologians, by the name of its theological perspective. In addition to Augustine and the eschatological theologians of the 1960s and 1970s, Gilkey acknowledged his most extensive theological indebtedness to three others: Reinhold Niebuhr, Paul Tillich, and Alfred North Whitehead—to the former two of whom, he had dedicated the book. In this radically new situation of cultural and religious parity, however, Gilkey seemed to jettison precisely those most dependable and hard-won resources of his theological approach, as represented both by his teachers, Niebuhr and Tillich, and by his most recent philosophical ally, Whitehead. Facing the requirements of this new situation, in one paragraph in another essay and referring specifically (again, by name) to these three formative influences on his own perspective, Gilkey set aside Whitehead, Niebuhr, and Tillich: "no cultural logos is final and therefore universal (even one based on science) [Whitehead]; no one revelation is or can be the universal criterion for all the others (even, so we are now seeing, Christian revelation) [Niebuhr and Tillich]."[147] Gilkey has embarked on an uncharted sea, going beyond sight of all familiar shorelines. Moreover, even any new shorelines that might appear only briefly before

---

[146]Gilkey, "New Watershed in Theology," 129-30; idem, *SAS*, 13-14; idem, "Theology for a Time of Troubles," 479; idem, "Theology for a Time of Troubles," in *Theologians in Transition*, 38-39; idem, "Dimensions of Basic Faith and the Special Traditions," 119; idem, "Plurality: Our New Situation," 119; idem, *TT*, 32. On Gilkey's concept of the relative absolute, see Mark Kline Taylor, "Religion, Cultural Plurality, and Liberating Praxis: In Conversation with the Work of Langdon Gilkey," *Journal of Religion* 71 (April 1991): 145-66.

[147]Gilkey, *RW*, viii-ix; idem, "Plurality and Its Theological Implications," 48.

him recede just as quickly or disappear as effectively behind the banks of plurality's rolling mist and dark clouds of history's storms.

Given Gilkey's most recent methodological orientation, has the new situation of parity among religions completely set Gilkey adrift in unknown and stormy waters with no help? How has this new situation affected Gilkey's theological method, if it has not caused him to heave every thing from his theological vessel, leaving it bereft of provisions, sails, even rudder, or even to scuttle the vessel itself? As others embark on theological voyages across this same seascape, with either no maps or still very inadequate charts, will they merely discover in Gilkey's previous work, as admirable as it may be or might have been, a ghost ship adrift and derelict in dark night on those open, stormy, and still poorly if not entirely uncharted seas? These questions remain difficult to answer. Gilkey himself has asked such questions of his own work and has proposed provisional answers. Gilkey's work in the last several years, as a result, holds promising possibilities in his responses (even if highly tentative) to those questions.

1. *The Question(s) of Theology in This New Situation?* In the early 1980s, during the symposium, "Paradigm Change in Theology," sponsored jointly by The University of Chicago Divinity School and the University of Tübingen, Gilkey concluded his address, "The Paradigm Shift in Theology," with two questions about this new situation in the encounter of religions. (1) First, Gilkey asked, "[h]ow is one to understand *theologically* this 'relative absoluteness' I have described?" (2) For Gilkey, this question implied a second question: "[w]hat does it ["relative absoluteness"] do to revelation, to Christology, to justification and/or sanctification, to the doctrine of the church, to eschatology and to social praxis?" In that setting, Gilkey clearly understood the second question as an elaboration of the first question. Although these two questions relate closely to one another, however, they do not make the same sort of inquiry. The first question seeks to discover how Christian theology might understand the parity of religions from a Christian theological perspective. The second question really inquires into the effects of this new encounter of the religions on the content of Christian theology itself.[148] In that

---

[148]Langdon Gilkey, "Der Paradigmenwechsel in der Theologie," in *Das neue Paradigma von Theologie: Strukturen und Dimensionen*, ed. Hans Küng and David Tracy (Zurich: Benziger; Gutersloher Verlagshaus G. Mohn, 1986) 144; idem, "Paradigm Shift in Theology," 383. I am not certain that Gilkey perceived a genuine difference between

address, appearing in German first in 1986, Gilkey concludes with questions and makes no proposals. Nevertheless, this essay remains important, in that one may interpret Gilkey's subsequent efforts to respond to this new encounter among the religions as falling into two categories. In Gilkey's earliest thinking about this problem, he seems to pursue answers to the first question, while his more recent reflection about this problem seems to answer the second question—at least as I have distinguished the two questions from one another. Although Gilkey does not differentiate between these two questions initially, the genuine difference between them appears eventually to account for a shift between his earliest efforts to work through the theological implications of this problem and his different more recent approaches to the parity of religions.

2. *General Revelation and Divine Covenant with Other Religions.* In this first phase of his thinking about plurality of religions as parity, Gilkey extended his understanding of the notion of Christianity's covenant with other religions, as developed in the late 1970s. Gilkey's employment of this strategy appears significantly in *Society and the Sacred.* Within the typology described previously in this most recent period of his work, at this stage in his approach to the problem of religious plurality, Gilkey adopts a carefully qualified form of what he calls the "mystical" approach, in which he describes a "union of the absolute and the relative." According to Gilkey, for this mystical approach, as seen in Buddhism and Hinduism, although many revelations have appeared in other religions, the mystical perspective retains "an unmovable standpoint or core of interpretation," which "is not relative and that becomes the hermeneutical principle for assessing the relative truth and efficacy of other faiths." There is a union of the relative with the absolute; but not all religions are equally relative in this view. Gilkey largely adopts this view, with some qualifications. According to Gilkey,

---

these two questions. In his intellectual autobiography, he remembered his initial engagement with this theological problem and seems still to interpret the first question in terms of the second question: "The new task, therefore, was to understand this *theologically*; that is, to understand my own faith all over again in the new light of this incontestable 'plurality' " (Gilkey, "Retrospective Glance at My Work," 31-32). In any case, the movement in his thought from his initial efforts (centering, as they do, around his notion of "covenants" with other religions, analogous to Christianity's covenants with various cultures—Hellenism, Modernity) to his more recent efforts (centering as they do around interpreting one's religion as seen through the eyes of other religious traditions) seem to suggest this difference between the questions themselves.

the presence of "redemptive force" and truth in other religions clearly and unavoidably indicates that "not only is the creative and providential activity of God present and manifested throughout nature and history, but also the *redemptive* work of God that culminates (for us) in the Christ is universally present." On this basis, Gilkey affirms the presence of "divine covenant" with the other religions. Accordingly, "because there is a 'divine covenant' with each form of faith and so genuinely healing truth there, each tradition can encounter another tradition in real dialogue, not only learning from them new truths about the mystery of the divine, but also finding new insight into, criticism of, and even deeper respect for elements of our own tradition." Thus, Gilkey lists three foundations for dialogue among the religions: (1) "a strong doctrine of general revelation," (2) "a clear sense of the relativity of all that has been characteristic of our own religion and culture as human forms," and (3) "a respect and gratitude for the elements of genuine revelation that can come to us out of the 'covenant' that God has made with them [the other religions]."[149]

Although Gilkey claims that Christians in dialogue with other religious traditions can discover much about their own tradition, can learn about themselves through the eyes of others, the mystical approach—which Gilkey later repudiated as I noted earlier—still raised one aspect of its own religious tradition *above* the other religious traditions, using that aspect as its hermeneutical principle. Hence, as his own nonrelative, absolute, or "unmovable standpoint or core of interpretation," Gilkey clearly employed a twofold hermeneutical principle from the Christian tradition: (1) his theology of providence (general revelation) and (2) his Christological soteriology (special revelation).[150]

3. *Christian Theology through the Eyes of Other Religions.* Gilkey soon realized the limitations, even the imperialism, of his mystical perspective. With the mystical approach, Gilkey tended to interpret other religions through his own Christian eyes—the unmovable core of its own

---

[149]Gilkey, *SAS*, 162-67. On this basis in 1986, Gilkey referred to Barth's "universalism" as "endlessly inspiring." "To me, something like this represents the only possible way to interpret Christian faith, that is in terms of the universality, the priority, the all-encompassing character, and the triumph of God's redeeming love. It is also *the only basis* on which a Christian can genuinely enter into dialogue with other religions—although this was (I am sure) hardly what Barth had in mind!" (Gilkey, "Appreciation for Karl Barth," 154-55). Note also that, by this time, the three conditions or foundations of dialogue had become one.

[150]Gilkey, *SAS*, 162-63, 166-67.

tradition—thereby reducing the particularity of the other religious tradition. As Gilkey put it, "[o]ne can hardly carry on a dialogue on this basis—for each, seeing the other through its own eyes, can never hear what the other has to say."[151] This realization led Gilkey to a different proposal. In his own way, therefore, not only did he finally divide the original question practically, but he also clarified both questions. Rather than pursuing a Christian theological interpretation of religious plurality as parity (as the mystical path certainly did), now Gilkey works to answer a different question. Previously, Gilkey posed his original question in a second form: How does this new situation of religious encounter affect Christian doctrines and practice? As early as 1983, Gilkey initiated a different sort of proposal on the implied basis of this or a similar question. Here he develops one strand in particular from the previous approach. He describes the "baffling paradox of any genuine dialogue":

> by listening to the other not only with regard to the character of *her* faith but even more to the character and interpretation of *my own*, I am participating not only as outsider but also as concerned *insider*. Thus, through the faith and perspective of the other, the dialogue suddenly becomes itself a medium of truth and possibly of grace for me. *We* now not only understand *them* better but also existence itself, the divine itself and destiny itself.[152]

Thus, Gilkey has reversed the entire situation. Rather than seeing the other through one's own eyes, one must come to see oneself through the other's eyes. Rather than interpreting the other religious tradition, through listening to the other tradition, the other partner in dialogue reinterprets her or his own life and religious tradition.

4. *The Problem of Religious Parity: The Intolerable and Theological Praxis.* Gilkey has not naïvely proposed *mere* dialogue, with toleration as its condition, as *the* solution to the problems between cultures in general and among the religions in particular. As a consistent analyst of culture

---

[151]Gilkey, "Plurality and Its Theological Implications," 42. As Gilkey says it elsewhere, he considers it "impossible in this new epoch to interpret other religions from the perspective of our own" (Gilkey, "Events, Meanings and the Current Tasks of Theology," 725; also under the same title, in *Trajectories in the Study of Religion*, 183).

[152]Langdon Gilkey, "Responses to Ross Reat's Article, 'Insiders and Outsiders in the Study of Religion,' " *Journal of the American Academy of Religion* 51 (1983): 485. This approach, in similar language, though developed more completely, appears in most of Gilkey's more recent discussions of religious plurality as parity: Gilkey, "Plurality and Its Theological Implications," 42; idem, "Pluralism of Religions," 120.

and history, Gilkey has persistently noted the appearance in the twentieth century of the negative religious dimension in historical realities, that which Gilkey has described as the appearance of "the demonic possibilities of religious absolutes at every level," or "a 'hierophany' of an apparently transcendent evil"—as experienced in the examples of the Jewish Holocaust, the imminent threat of nuclear annihilation, and even the rising political power of fundamentalist religion in the Religious Right of the United States. He has even characterized the twentieth century "politically, economically, socially, as well as religiously, as the age of idolatries, or, in more secular language, of pervasive and lethal *ideologies*." Thus, Gilkey declares boldly yet honestly that the plurality of cultures and religions has "another face" in addition to "ecumenical tolerance," "a face fully as terrifying as is the relativity" that he has described. "For within the plurality of religions that surround us are forms of the religious that are intolerable, and intolerable because they are demonic." Thus, Gilkey points to the "ambiguity of plurality," again rejoining to his theological method an even deeper recognition of sin and fate.[153]

Consequently, according to Gilkey, "toleration is here checked by the intolerable; and plurality means *both*." The category of "the intolerable" introduces another paradox into the plurality of religions as parity. On the one hand, all religious perspectives are relative to one another, on an equal level even in terms of divine revelation, thus requiring toleration and even humility for the sake of dialogue—genuine allowance of the existence and operation of those alternative ways of life. On the other hand, appearances of demonic absolutes, with their "radically destructive" qualities, require resistance and mark the limits of toleration. As Gilkey unreservedly declares, "we *must* resist, and we must liberate ourselves and others from them" ["intolerable forms of religion and the religious"]. Thus, Gilkey introduces the category of "the intolerable," a category that requires one to "stand somewhere," to "assert some sort of ultimate values," which, Gilkey rightly emphasizes, "is to assert a 'world,' a view of all of reality." Accordingly, Gilkey claims, not only does "any practical political action, in resistance to tyranny or in liberation from it," presuppose "ultimate values and an ultimate vision of things, an ethic and

---

[153]Gilkey, "Pluralism of Religions," 118; idem, "Plurality and Its Theological Implications," 44-45; idem, "Events, Meanings and the Current Tasks of Theology," 720-21, 726-28.

so a theology," but it also "presupposes an absolute commitment to this understanding of things." Thus, "[t]he necessity of action, liberating action, calls first for the relinquishment of all relativity and secondly for the assertion of some alternative absolute standpoint." Gilkey admits that, in order to avoid imperialism of one religious perspective over another, the conditions and practice of dialogue must occur. Yet, he realizes that appearances of demonic absolutes threaten that very situation and, thereby, require resistance to those idols, the refusal to tolerate such destructive and oppressive forms of the religious and religion. As Gilkey says it, "puzzled immobility before a contradiction or indifferent acceptance of a plurality of options must both cease." Such appearances of the intolerable move one beyond dialogue to resistance. Gilkey calls this a *"forced* option, one that cannot be avoided." In order to *"think* as well as act on this new basis," Gilkey returns to a familiar category in his thought, the notion of symbol. "A symbol or criterion points beyond itself and criticizes itself if it would not be demonic; but it also points *to* itself and *through* itself if it would not be empty, and if we would not be left centerless." Thus, in order to maintain both the possibility for "liberating praxis" and "creative reflection," Gilkey claims that such an understanding of symbols both relativizes the manifestation of the absolute ("and so all incarnations of the absolute") and yet manifests *"through* the relative an absoluteness that transcends it."[154]

5. *Theological Method and Interreligious Dialogue.* As Gilkey has admitted, however, "[i]t is by no means easy—though it is surely interesting—to try to do constructive theology in this atmosphere."[155]

---

[154]Gilkey, "Plurality and Its Theological Implications," 44-49. Precisely the dynamics at the basis of this most serious paradox of plurality as parity (dialogue on the basis of revelational equality with other religions, yet necessary resistance to demonic absolutes) motivated my own previous theological efforts to expose and resist demonic religious absolutes, hierophanies of transcendent evil, or lethal ideologies in the policies, actions, and their fundamentalist theological/biblical/doctrinal legitimations both within Southwestern Baptist Theological Seminary (see Jeff B. Pool, "Conscience and Interpreting Baptist Tradition," in *Sacred Mandates of Conscience: Interpreting the Baptist Faith and Message,* ed. Jeff B. Pool [Macon GA: Smyth & Helwys Publishing, 1997], 1-36) and within the larger political goals of the Southern Baptist Convention itself in North American society and government (see Jeff B. Pool, *Against Returning to Egypt: Exposing and Resisting Credalism in the Southern Baptist Convention* [Macon GA: Mercer University Press, 1998] esp. 271-310).

[155]Gilkey, "Events, Meanings and the Current Tasks of Theology," 725; also under

Nevertheless, the difficulty of the task did not prevent his constructive labors. In his most recent publications on this cluster of problems, Gilkey has thought carefully, if still not extensively, about other methodological issues that he has previously addressed and their relationships to the parity of religions.[156] Most importantly for the task of systematic theology, however, Gilkey has produced numerous interpretations of various Christian symbols in light of his dialogue with other religions, most notably through his dialogues with Buddhism—although I now have exhausted both time and space for discussion of even one of Gilkey's formulations as an illustration. Nonetheless, these interreligious dialogues have resulted in Gilkey's reinterpretations of the symbols of God, creation, Christ, ethics, spirituality, suffering, the problem of evil, and a variety of other related themes and symbols.[157] The challenge of this new

---

the same title, in *Trajectories in the Study of Religion*, 183.

[156]See esp. Gilkey, "Events, Meanings and the Current Tasks of Theology," 723-34; also under the same title, in *Trajectories in the Study of Religion*, 181-92; idem, "Plurality and Its Theological Implications," 44-50; idem, "Pluralism of Religions," 111-23.

[157]In *Reaping the Whirlwind*, Gilkey began to consider dialogue with Buddhism, especially developing the category of divine self-limitation, in light of the Buddhist category of nothingness in God (Gilkey, *RW*, 432n.19). See the following on various doctrinal themes developed by Gilkey in dialogue with other religions: Gilkey, "God," in *Christian Theology*, ed. Hodgson and King, 86; also published as chap. 5, "Christian Understanding of God," in *TT*, 88; idem, "Creation, Being, and Non-Being," in *God and Creation: An Ecumenical Symposium*, ed. David B. Burrell and Bernard McGinn (Notre Dame IN: University of Notre Dame Press, 1990) 226-41; also published as chap. 6, "Creation: Being and Nonbeing," in *TT*, 89-100; idem, "The Meaning of Jesus the Christ," in *Christ and the Bodhisattva*, 193-207; also published under the same title as chap. 7, in *TT*, 101-13; idem, "Ethics in Christianity and Buddhism," *Dialog* 28 (Winter 1989): 37-42; also published under the same title as chap. 10, in *TT*, 157-65. Also on ethics, see Gilkey, "Christian Congregation as Religious Community," 128-30; idem, "Plurality: Our New Situation," 108-16; also published as chap. 2, "Plurality: Christianity's New Situation," in *TT*, 24-30; idem, "Theology of Culture and Christian Ethics," 360-64; also under the same title, as chap. 9, in *TT*, 153-55; idem, "Theodicy and Plurality," *Archivio di Filosofia* 56 (1988): 707-20; also published under the same title, as chap. 12, in *TT*, 181-93; idem, "The Christian Understanding of Suffering," *Buddhist-Christian Studies* 5 (1985): 49-65; also published under the same title, as chap. 14, in *TT*, 215-31; idem, "Meditation on Death and Its Relation to Life," *Archivio di Filosofia* 49 (1981): 19-32; also published as chap. 15, "Death and Its Relation to Life," in *TT*, 233-46. Also see his explorations of the relationships between Tillich's thought and Buddhism: Langdon Gilkey, "Tillich and the Kyoto School," in *Negation and Theology*, ed. Robert P. Scharlemann, Studies in Religion and Culture Series, ed. Robert P. Scharlemann (Charlottesville: University of Virginia, 1992) 72-85.

situation seems to have inspired Gilkey's doctrinal explorations, rather than stifling them. Still, Gilkey's present perspective leaves many questions about its relationship to his method as developed prior to the appearance of religious plurality as parity in his theology.

As I have noted from the beginning, however, the correlational style of Gilkey's method remains, in spite of the reflexivity of its work even on itself. Theologically, Gilkey's basic Christian commitment—defined principally by his original Niebuhrian orientation—also remains solid, as the basis for his own place in dialogue. That postliberal perspective, however, sounds far more Tillichean in its language now, as Gilkey has engaged in both open dialogue with Buddhism and, as a consequence, active reinterpretation of the central Christian symbols especially in light of the Buddhist concept of nothingness. Nevertheless, as various examples attest, he does not appear to eliminate Whitehead's influence on the dynamic character of reality as a whole, which includes God for him.[158] Still, the argument for God that Gilkey found so foundational for his dialectic of Christian belief in his theology of providence (as seen most prominently in *Reaping the Whirlwind*) does not appear in his dialogues with other religious traditions. Has he abandoned that aspect of his former methodological perspective or has it simply lost its effectiveness as a basis for dialogue? I do not know the answer to this question, but suspect it to be the latter alternative. Gilkey's explorations of the basic symbols through his encounters, especially with Buddhism, do suggest that he remains a postliberal foundationalist, one knowingly afloat on an ocean of pluralism, but through which he hopes to navigate.

Conclusion: Sounding the Depths

My previous analyses have demonstrated the validity of the first and guiding thesis of my study of Gilkey's theological method. *Gilkey has altered key features of this correlational theological approach across the course of his career, in light of the results from his continual employment*

---

[158]See, as one example, an interpretation of the book of Job by Gilkey from the early 1990s, in which he discusses the symbol of God as self-limiting (in terms of creating humanity as cocreator with God), as suffering with humans to redeem them, and as the transcendence of divine grace and love over distinctions between good and evil: Langdon Gilkey, "Power, Order, Justice, and Redemption: Theological Comments on Job," in *The Voice from the Whirlwind: Interpreting the Book of Job*, ed. Leo G. Perdue and W. Clark Gilpin (Nashville: Abingdon Press, 1992) 165-71.

*of that correlational theological strategy, thus disclosing a reflexive char-
acter or mechanism in his theological method.* With that reflexive
mechanism, Gilkey has consistently submitted even his own method to
critical scrutiny and revision, as he has continually refashioned the tools
with which ever more effectively to deliver a relevant transcendence to
his own epoch. Gilkey has altered his theological method, therefore, in
light of discoveries both from his analyses of culture and from his interpretations of Christian symbols. Furthermore, in my effort to demonstrate
the validity of the guiding thesis of this chapter, this study has also
demonstrated that *Gilkey's theological method has developed (through the
reflexive mechanism in that method) in five major stages: (1) from a
liberal, Baptist, Christian social matrix, to (2) a Niebuhrian postliberal
or neoorthodox theological method, through (3) a Tillichian deepening
of his initial postliberal perspective, through (4) a Whiteheadian transformation of his Tillichean perspective into a postliberal foundationalism,
and finally to (5) the chastening of both the postliberal and foundational
elements of his theological method in light of religious plurality as parity.*

The previous map of Gilkey's methodological voyage marks several
cumulative gains in the movement of Gilkey's methodological practice
and reflection. In some of these marks, Gilkey developed latent aspects
in his method during its various periods of evolution. In other respects,
he continued to carry certain explicit aspects of his method through to
fuller form or more consistent expression. In the following summary, I
will mention only a few, among many others, of the most prominent
marks in his methodological development.

(1) The liberal Baptist Christian character of the social matrix for
Gilkey's early life supplied him with a variety of resources that would
serve him theologically: emphases on human freedom, the priority of
experience to doctrine, the two major social values of peace and justice,
even the revisionist (rather than the conservative) character of religion
itself. (2) Initially, among many factors in Gilkey's experience as a young
adult, one major factor altered significantly and permanently Gilkey's
inheritance from his initial religious and social matrix: his discovery of
the reality of sin in human experience and the corresponding answer to
it from the Christian gospel. Gilkey, following the pattern of his neoorthodox teachers, incorporated this Christian doctrine or symbol of the
human condition into the very heart of the earliest forms of his theological method. In a variety of ways, Gilkey never surrendered, and actually
extended and deepened, this insight—as especially seen most recently in

his category of the intolerable. (3) Furthermore, through his expansion of theological method with an ontic analysis or a phenomenological hermeneutic of secular experience, Gilkey discerned the religious dimension in all ordinary experience. Although Gilkey understood this as a prolegomenon to theology (and not theology itself), insofar as this step established the meaningfulness of religious language for human experience (thereby providing a preliminary answer, or at least its possibility, to the meaninglessness threatened by the human experience of relativity), this step in Gilkey's method made possible his next step toward a theology of providence. (4) In spite of Gilkey's consistent rejection of natural theologies as viable or legitimate forms or aspects of theological method during the previous periods of his career, Gilkey discovered and adopted a threefold argument for the reality and necessity of God as an essential step in his theological method toward the development of his theology of providence. Here method and theology appear to converge for Gilkey, arising from his ontic analysis and developing into an ontological analysis, thus supplying both his method and his theology of providence with a kind of foundation in common human experience that he had hitherto denied. Thus, whereas his previous stage of thought had led him to demonstrate the necessity of God-language, in this period, he discerned an empirical rationale for the necessity of divine or ultimate reality itself. Nonetheless, because Gilkey retained a strong understanding of the Christian symbol of sin, this symbol continued to function methodologically to prevent a relapse of Gilkey's new foundationalism into the false confidence and optimism of liberal natural theologies. Furthermore, Gilkey's lifelong commitments to the social values of peace and justice reappear again, conditioning his foundationalism as the even more substantial basis of criteria for praxis or practical social action. (5) Finally, Gilkey's continuing careful analyses of the ever-changing contemporary situation yielded an understanding of the parity of religions, which directly affected both his approach to other religions with Christian theology and his interpretation of Christian symbols in light of that dialogue. Although his new foundationalism with its emphasis on the necessity of God for the experience of temporality prepared the way for Gilkey to address the plurality of religions as parity, his recognition of the relativity even of the rationalities (ontologies, epistemologies, axiologies) of all cultures, including Western culture, finally prohibited his application of criteria (either from Western culture or from Christianity) in evaluations of other religions. Thus, his new understanding of how to approach other religions emphasized gleaning the insights about one's own religion through the eyes of other religious traditions. Again, the thread of his commitments to the social values of both justice and peace also reappeared here: specifically, in his efforts both to define the situation of dialogue among religions and to clarify the necessity of resistance to the appearance of the intolerable or demonic absolutes.

The flow of the previous examples indicates that Gilkey's theological method has oscillated in its dependence on and borrowing from aspects of both cultural insight and Christian revelation. Thus, in order to understand Gilkey's theological method most adequately, one must carefully compare studies of his practice of theology with his less extensively developed theory of theological method.

I have characterized Gilkey's theological method as *postliberal foundationalism*, obviously juxtaposing two terms that, in contemporary theological discussion, find themselves on opposite poles methodologically. Even though Gilkey employs both of these terms in ways resembling the contemporary usages of this language, he has never designated his perspective as postliberal foundationalism. Nonetheless, I have drawn these two terms together, despite their contemporary conflictual relationships, for one very important reason. Due to the instability of their relationships with one another in contemporary discussions of theological method, holding these two terms together in this characterization points to the basic character of Gilkey's theological method (as well as to the character of his overall perspective) to which I referred at the beginning of this chapter: the reflexive character of his method. Gilkey continually scrutinizes his own method, in the course of his theological work, for the sake of a more adequate approach to understanding both the Christian message and the contemporary situation. This characterization indicates a self-critical instability in Gilkey's theological style, one that willingly changes direction or alters approach when the conditions necessitate such corrections in course.

Given the components in the evolution of Gilkey's theological method, an interpreter might characterize Gilkey's theology in other ways, of course. Those construals might include at least three other possibilities: postfoundational liberalism, foundational postliberalism, and liberal postfoundationalism.

An interpreter might describe Gilkey's method, especially following his development of the concept of the relative-absolute, as *postfoundational liberalism*. Such an interpretation of Gilkey's method might

construe the absence of his natural theology (the universal basis for interreligious dialogue) from his most recent methodological practice and
reflection as the return to a form of liberal theology, but liberalism
without its confidence in Western forms of rationality, ontology, or
natural theology. Although even Gilkey has referred to his more recent
work on the pluralism of religions as his return to liberalism of a kind,
he does not adopt liberal theological approaches in their classic forms.
Thus, he refuses universal rationalities as ways to explain other religions
and how they "fit" within a theological or philosophical system; he also
refuses to ignore the serious limitations to such interpretations that result
from the distortions of both freedom (sin) and destiny (fate). Given the
most recent forms of Gilkey's theological method in dialogue with other
religions and given his criticism of Whitehead's approach to encountering
other religions, this approach possesses some, though not quite enough,
plausibility as an interpretation of Gilkey's most recent practice and
theory of theological method.

An interpreter might also understand Gilkey's theological method,
emphasizing a slightly different dimension in the development of Gilkey's
method, as *foundational postliberalism*. In this perspective on Gilkey's
theological method, the interpreter might perceive Gilkey's postliberalism
as the aspect of his thought that most dominates his theological method.
Thus, this view, in the evolution of Gilkey's method, highlights the
continuity of his Niebuhrian and Tillichian postliberal approach, admitting
its modification with a soft foundationalism. Most certainly, one can
plausibly interpret Gilkey's dialectic of Christian belief as support for this
perspective.

Finally, one might interpret Gilkey's theological method as *liberal
postfoundationalism*. In this view, both the disappearance of natural theology from Gilkey's theological method and the reappearance of his criticism of Whitehead's philosophy—especially as the basis for understanding the present encounter of religions—justify interpretation of Gilkey's
thought as again rejoining a sort of contemporary antimetaphysical
community composed of deconstructionists and contemporary postliberals.
This postfoundationalism, however, would have a liberal rather than a
postliberal character. Here the interpreter might emphasize the extent to
which Gilkey's problems and solutions remain within modern rather than
postmodern paradigms. From my perspective, this last alternative seems
the least plausible interpretation of Gilkey's theological method.

Instead, I have described Gilkey's theological method as *postliberal foundationalism*, rather than as *foundational postliberalism, postfoundational liberalism*, or *liberal postfoundationalism*. Gilkey's theological method has evolved significantly since he began as a devout Niebuhrian postliberal, and even since his extensive and intensive Tillichian modifications to that postliberalism. Although Gilkey's earliest perspective has much in common with contemporary forms of postliberalism, the foundationalism of his more recent theological strategies (however modest and tentative they remain) does not fit categorically with the ideology of contemporary postliberalism. For those reasons, I have preferred instead to categorize his theological strategy as a form of foundationalism rather than as a form of postliberalism, although I am well aware that one could easily make other arguments about Gilkey's basic theological strategies.

Gilkey's more recent dialogues, as a committed Christian, with other religious traditions, and his characterization of that encounter as rough parity, however, do raise a variety of questions about his basic perspective: particularly about the ground purchased from Whitehead and the revelation received from his postliberal teachers, Niebuhr and Tillich. As important as his argument for God was in establishing his theology of providence as one moment in his dialectic of Christian belief, one wonders how these interreligious dialogues have affected that foundation. The virtual absence of Gilkey's natural theology from his thought about religious plurality as parity may suggest that Gilkey has abandoned his Whiteheadian foundationalism altogether, and returned to his more skeptical stance in *Naming the Whirlwind*, though not perhaps to his most enthusiastic rejection of natural theology (as idolatry) in *Maker of Heaven and Earth*. Certainly, Gilkey abandoned Whitehead's rationalism as a criterion; but so too does he appear to abandon his theological symbols of providence (as the support for his notion of the divine covenant with other religions) and Christ as the criterion of the genuine work of God in other religions. Insofar as he remains Christian, I assume that he retains his trust, in some sense, in both providence and Christ—especially since, as he claims, one must remain committed to the absolute as manifested through the symbols of one's own religious tradition, in order to remain an equal partner in dialogue with other religions. On that analogy, then, perhaps one can conjecture that Gilkey has also retained his foundationalism. Perhaps one can only say with certainty that Gilkey has at least bracketed or silenced both his foundationalism and its postliberal character, in order to protect other religious traditions from imperialisms that inhibit genuine dialogue.

Still, if Gilkey only brackets his Whiteheadean foundationalism for the sake of genuine interreligious dialogue, his retention, as well as his initial adaptation, of Whitehead's metaphysics still raises questions—at least in relation to his own thought. For example, in *Naming the Whirlwind*, Gilkey's neoorthodox faith shared the opinion of secularity about metaphysics, and specifically about natural theology.

> The heart of modern secularity is that human experience, secular or religious, is devoid of relation beyond itself to any ground or order, and that there is no form of human thought that can by speculation come to know of such a ground or order. Consequently, for this mood, philosophical analyses of the ontological structures of reality as in Whitehead, or of general religious experience as in Otto, of even moral experience as in the Kantian tradition, or of value experience as in Wieman, are themselves infinitely suspect and so contain no immediate bases for theological discourse. Clearly, for such a view, the philosophical sources of liberal religion, be they moral or religious experience, metaphysical speculation, or an analysis of either cosmic or human history, are as moribund as is the revelation which was the basis of Christianity's older dogmatic formulations. Thus to seek to build thereon a natural theology for the contemporary world is futile, since that which is to be a bridge to the modern man—the natural theological effort of liberalism—itself defies every basic tenet of modern spirituality.[159]

In that light, should one consider the absence or silence of his Whiteheadean argument for God in his interreligious dialogues as evidence of his repentance for all aspects of his own perspective—whether based on postliberal concepts of revelation or on process philosophical metaphysics—that might operate imperialistically in dialogue with other religious traditions? By contrast, one might also draw the opposite conclusion: that perhaps Gilkey has finally capitulated to culture and has abandoned not only metaphysics, but revelation as well, as meaningful and intelligible categories. Clearly, not only for secular culture, but even in interreligious dialogue, these categories or perspectives remain problematic.

I would like for Gilkey to explore this cluster of issues and questions about his own theological strategies. Clarifying some of these issues in

---

[159]Gilkey, *NW*, 188; cf. idem, *RW*, 118-19.

Gilkey's thought would help to suggest the potential and promise of Gilkey's theological strategies for future work.

A vast number of questions remain to ask of Langdon Gilkey's theology. As lengthy as this chapter may be, it only roughly surveys the diverse and broad terrain of Gilkey's comprehensive vision. Somehow Gilkey seems to have discovered the secret to theological method. He has made the variety of category, symbol, and argument fit the complexity of that which he has tried to understand. Yet, he has always done so without allowing methodological issues to seduce him from the theological content itself. Moreover, where method has occupied his theological interest, he has often shown how those methodological issues and problems arise from and even generate doctrinal or theological themes themselves. Methodological concerns and doctrinal themes have merged, often due to the very topics under discussion.

After surveying the various kinds of methodological rigging and sails employed by Gilkey during his diverse theological voyages, one sees exactly the reasons for Gilkey's methodological changes. Gilkey has expressed far more concern to address the issues of contemporary life, than to remain bound ideologically to a perspective because he developed it. When other theologians relax as they near retirement from teaching, remaining content to repeat the formulations made in the exuberant youth of their careers, Gilkey has courageously engaged new issues, left behind outmoded or insufficient methods, searching always for those tools with which to disclose both the distortions of and the healing power within life and culture. In Gilkey's willingness to make changes, to take risks, to admit false starts, one beholds simultaneously in him both boldness and humility.

Langdon Gilkey's father, Charles Gilkey, also enjoyed sailing. Furthermore, he also often employed nautical metaphors as illustrations in his own sermons and books. One of his illustrations aptly applies to the exploratory, bold yet humble, theology of his son, Langdon.

> Every boatman knows that in quick water it is dangerous, if not fatal, to drift; the swift current will bear him onward fast enough, but it may equally fling him on a rock or upset him in a rapid. Only a quick eye for the deep water, a firm hand to push into it, and a stout heart that does not lose its courage and confidence, will bring him safely through.[160]

---

[160]Charles Gilkey, *Jesus and Our Generation*, 13-14.

Langdon Gilkey has not allowed his theology to drift in the dangerous quick water of history. His quick eye in discerning the deepest cultural and religious problems and in knowing instinctively when to push into them, his firm hand pushing into that deep water, and the stout heart of his own still courageous and confident faith have carried him thus far through many swift currents in this time of troubles. Those of us who have served as his theological apprentices have learned perhaps as much from this example as from his specific methodological and theological proposals.

Part 2

Gilkey's Interpretations of Culture

Chapter 4

Becoming Langdon Gilkey:
The Theological Significance of *Shantung Compound*

Joseph Bessler-Northcutt

Introduction

A vital aspect of Langdon Gilkey's contribution to a genuinely public Christian theology is his concern to speak as "secular Christian." Convinced early on that theologies starting from the assumptions of revelation or ontology were no longer convincing or persuasive to Christians living in a secular culture, Gilkey explored the depth of secular experience to disclose a dimension of human experience in need of religious symbolization. The point of that method, I take it, has been to argue not only that religion is intrinsic to human experience, but that the value of a specifically Christian faith must be persuasively argued in terms broadly intelligible and accessible to a particular culture at any given time.

In this chapter, I attempt to explain in a partial way, as well as critique, the textual strategies by which Gilkey *became* Gilkey, which is to say *how* he developed a theological method that begins with human experience. While the origins of that method are to be found, broadly speaking, in his correlating the discussions of a scientific worldview and religious faith in *Maker of Heaven and Earth*, as well as in his correlation of social-science research and the language of faith in *How the Church Can Minister to the World without Losing Itself*, the decisive turning point in Gilkey's development of his own theological methodology occurs in *Shantung Compound*.[1] In what follows, I first discuss the underwhelming reception of *Shantung Compound* by the theological academy, as well as some of the theological and methodological issues Gilkey was grappling with at the time. I then propose a tropological method of reading *Shantung Compound* that can illuminate and retrieve its pivotal role in Gilkey's theological development, showing how the work's textual strategies resolve those methodological problems. The bulk of my essay, in turn, performs an analysis of the text that illumines Gilkey's strategies

---

[1] Langdon Gilkey, *Shantung Compound: The Story of Men and Women under Pressure* (New York: Harper & Row, 1966); hereafter cited as *SC*.

in a way that praises Gilkey's rhetorical skills but also calls into question his implied epistemological, or foundational, claims. I conclude the chapter by arguing for a more thoroughgoing rhetorical approach to Christian theology.

I. A Fear of Rhetoric:
The Scholarly Reception of *Shantung Compound*

In an interview in November 1991, Gilkey rehearsed a long-standing complaint with the publisher of *Shantung Compound*, Harper & Row.

> I suspect they had the Sunday-school trade in mind. This was always for them a religious book. And I objected to that and objected to it, and I couldn't get anywhere with it. I said, "This is not a religious book." "Well, you're a theologian." I said, "Forget that. It's the story of a camp." "Well, you end up with rel. . . . " I said, "All right you end up with Freudian or Marxist I end up with that, that doesn't make it a religious book. It's about a secular experience." "No, no, no." So, they always put it under religion, which really disappointed me very much. And I think they made a mess of it.[2]

Gilkey's expressed disappointment with Harper & Row might have also been aimed at theologians who never glimpsed what Gilkey was up to in the book, and, who, in fact, dismissed it. Bernard Meland, for example, in the introductory essay from a volume published in 1969, *The Future of Empirical Theology*, did not even mention *Shantung Compound*, urging readers to see "Gilkey's *major* publications: *Maker of Heaven and Earth*, *How the Church Can Minister to the World without Losing Itself*, and *Naming the Whirlwind*."[3] And, in a brief review (one of only five written about the book), Keith Watkins gives *Shantung Compound* high marks as a Christian "apology," calling it "an amazing book"; yet this very praise severely limits the book's theological significance.

---

[2]See the text of my interview with Mr. Gilkey: "Appendix B: New Orleans Conversation," in "Shantung Trilogy: The Rhetorical Shaping of Langdon Gilkey's Theology of Culture and History," by Joseph Bessler-Northcutt (Ph.D. diss., University of Chicago, 1996) 399-417.

[3]Bernard Meland, "Introduction: The Empirical Tradition in Theology at Chicago," in *The Future of Empirical Theology*, ed. Bernard E. Meland, vol. 7, *Essays in Divinity*, ed. Jerald C. Brauer (Chicago: University of Chicago Press, 1969) 58n.70; emphasis mine.

It is the nature of an apology to present an appealing and convincing testimony to one's point of view. This much Gilkey has accomplished. An apology, however, is quite different from a systematic theology and this latter task Gilkey has not given us. It is hoped that the author's next writing will combine the systematic and analytical strength of his earlier *Maker of Heaven and Earth* and the existentially based conviction of *Shantung Compound*. We then would really have something.[4]

Suggesting that *Shantung Compound*'s basis in personal experience is not adequate for *real* theology, Watkins' assumptions about genre actually prevent him from being able to see how *Shantung Compound* contributes anything more than "conviction" to Gilkey's theological enterprise. Watkins assumes a difference or gap between apology's *conviction* and systematic theology's *analysis*, a gap that parallels an epistemological split between rhetoric and science. Categorizing *Shantung Compound* in the weaker, rhetorical genre of apology, Watkins argues that it needs the completion of systematic theology's stronger and more detached analysis. He misses entirely the "empirical," secular character of the writing and the theological significance of that style.

The academy overlooked *Shantung Compound* for at least two related reasons. First, since Karl Barth's rejection of Schleiermacher, appeals to personal experience, especially secular experience, had become deeply suspect in theological circles. Watkins was only expressing a consensus view that appeals to experience might be helpful apologetically, that is, persuasive to those "outside" the church, but not as an approach to the more scientific work of theology per se. As we will see, Gilkey's narrative voice in *Shantung Compound* shows that Gilkey himself was extremely attentive to avoid giving any impression of a purely personal or subjective account. Second, *Shantung Compound* makes its theological contribution in the nontraditional form of a narrative. To understand fully the significance of *Shantung Compound* in Gilkey's theological development, one needs a theory of reading and a literary analysis of the work's

---

[4]Keith Watkins, review of *Shantung Compound*, by Langdon Gilkey, in *Encounter* 28 (Spring 1967): 182.

form, not simply the author's theological conclusions.[5] Such approaches to theological texts were still in their infancy.

II. Background Theological Issues

What theologians of the time missed, and more recent Gilkey scholars as well, is that *Shantung Compound* provides the methodological strategy for Gilkey's own reclaiming of experience for theology, laying the basis for a correlational theology that begins with the analysis of secular experience.[6] A brief article from 1958, entitled "Neo-Orthodoxy," illustrates Gilkey's concern with connecting the language of empirical, or historical, fact to theological symbols. Gilkey first summarizes the neoorthodox view regarding doctrinal statements:

> . . . to the contemporary thinker theological doctrines are statements containing symbolic rather than literal truth, propositions pointing to the religious dimensions of events rather than propositions containing factual information about events (See Niebuhr's use of "myth," Tillich's use of "symbolic language" and Dodd's "fact and interpretation").

He then notes the existence of a continuing problem:

> The intricate relation between the historic fact and the religious, "mythical" or symbolic interpretation of the fact remains as an important and as yet unresolved problem for neo-orthodoxy.[7]

By 1964–1965, Gilkey's concern with resolving the fact/interpretation dilemma developed into a deeper suspicion about his teachers' (Niebuhr's and Tillich's) starting points for theological reflection. In a now famous essay, "Dissolution and Reconstruction in Theology," Gilkey argues that

---

[5]William Thompson supplies a good example of the problem in his "Theology's Method and Linguistic Analysis in the Thought of Langdon Gilkey," *The Thomist* 36 (July 1972): 363-93. Thompson was a rather lone voice in finding *Shantung Compound* a serious book in Gilkey's theological development. Thompson's approach, however, relied heavily on Gilkey's last chapter, which turned more explicitly to theological issues, and failed to analyze the narrative structure of the book.

[6]In both *Naming the Whirlwind* and *Reaping the Whirlwind*, Gilkey claims that human, secular experience opens onto the ground of the sacred. In each work, he includes footnotes directing readers to *Shantung Compound* for an account of his own experience of that dimension of depth.

[7]Langdon Gilkey, "Neo-Orthodoxy," in *A Handbook of Christian Theology*, ed. Marvin Halverson (New York: Meridian Books, 1958) 256-61.

"the winds of change, fresh and strong are blowing through the theological world."[8]

> Our theological task is not that of "scholastics" working out the implications of firm theological systems inherited from a more creative past. We must go back to the very beginning, must defend the reality of God and the possibility of language about him in a world in which no longer prior assumptions, metaphysical or religious, can be taken for granted, and in which ordinary experience seems swept clean of cosmic coherence and ultimate meaning alike.[9]

In the context of a secular culture, suspicious of any claim to the existence of a transcendent reality, Gilkey argues that theology must "reveal" or "uncover" a religious dimension in common experience that relates the person to an ultimate or transcendent ground. Such a study will accept the terms of secular culture, on the one hand, while suggesting the inadequacy of that culture's own presuppositions of reality, on the other: "My own feeling, therefore, based on the most vivid and convincing elements of my own experience of life, is that a 'secular' account of man's existence is too thin, too lacking in the dimension of depth and mystery."[10] When Gilkey writes here of the most "vivid and convincing elements" of his own experience, he is actually in the midst of rewriting and attempting to publish *Shantung Compound*! To show how *Shantung Compound* itself enacts, and thereby resolves, the movement from surface to depth, from fact to interpretation, one needs to attend less to its explicit claims than to its figurative or tropological structure.

III. A Theory of Tropes and the Analysis of Narrative

In "A Theory of Autobiography," James Olney explains the significance of an organizing metaphor within a text.

> In the given, whether it be external reality or internal consciousness, there is nothing to be called meaning: the world means nothing; neither does consciousness per se. Our sense that there is a meaning in something—in a poem, in experience—comes only when the elements that go to make up that thing take on a relation to one another; in other words, the meaning emerges

---

[8]Langdon Gilkey, "Dissolution and Reconstruction in Theology," *Christian Century* 82 (3 February 1965): 135-39.

[9]Gilkey, "Dissolution and Reconstruction in Theology," 136.

[10]Gilkey, "Dissolution and Reconstruction in Theology," 137.

with our perception of a pattern, and there can obviously be no pattern in chronologically or geographically discrete items and elements. We must connect one thing with another and finally assume the whole design of which the element is only a part. Metaphors supply such a connection, relating this to that in such and such a relevant way.[11]

The use of a particular metaphor is neither obvious nor natural to experience itself. One's choice of fundamental metaphors in a text, therefore, illuminates not only the experience in question but a strategy, perhaps even an unconscious one, of construction. In the context of auto-biography, Olney's analysis of metaphor cuts through the illusion of a "speaking self," and raises the question of how metaphorical constructions of the self function strategically to project a set of interests.

In a more broad-ranging theory of discourse, Hayden White argues for the importance of rhetorical tropes in providing the fundamental bases of narrative construction. Attempting to undo a positivistic approach to history, White willingly grants that historical events differ from fictional events. The problem of the historian, as White sees it, is that "the facts do not speak for themselves." Rather, "the historian speaks for them, speaks on their behalf, and fashions the fragments of the past into a whole whose integrity is—in its *re*presentation—a purely discursive one."[12]

These fragments have to be put together to make a whole of a particular, not a general, kind. And they are put together in the same ways that novelists use to put together figments of their imaginations to display an ordered world, a cosmos, where only disorder or chaos might appear.[13]

The narrative strategies by which such fragments are linked together, argues White, are themselves *pre*figured "by the original description (of the "facts" to be explained) in a given dominant modality of language use: metaphor, metonymy, synecdoche or irony."[14] In another essay, White explains the meaning of this point for the historian:

---

[11]James Olney, *Metaphors of Self* (Princeton NJ: Princeton University Press, 1972) 30-31.

[12]Hayden White, *The Tropics of Discourse: Essays in Cultural Criticism* (Baltimore MD: Johns Hopkins University Press, 1978) 121-35.

[13]White, *Tropics of Discourse*, 125.

[14]White, *Tropics of Discourse*, 128.

This means that the *shape* of the *relationships* which will appear to be inherent in the objects inhabiting the field will in reality have been imposed on the field by the investigator in the very *act of identifying and describing* the objects that he finds there. The implication is that historians *constitute* their subjects as possible objects of narrative by the very language they use to *describe* them.[15]

Taking seriously both Olney's and White's attention to the figurative patterns of a text will enable me to analyze *how* Gilkey "moves" from surface to depth, from fact to interpretation in *Shantung Compound*. The use of this analysis, however, will also lead me to challenge Gilkey's implicit claim that *Shantung Compound* demonstrates a depth dimension to experience as such.

IV. Beginning with Metaphor

In the reading of *Shantung Compound* that follows, I argue that Gilkey's first tropological move is metaphorical. He claims that the internment camp was like a small civilization. He then extends that metaphor metonymically, developing two, overlapping strands of narrative that correspond to two disciplines of "anthropology," one cultural and one theological. Those two strands function to suggest a surface level and a deeper, more hidden, level of experience. While the tropes of irony and synecdoche are also structurally significant to *Shantung Compound*, I will focus in this chapter on the structural use of metaphor and metonymy in Gilkey's development of a theological method.

Announced in the preface, Gilkey's organizing metaphor, the camp as a "small civilization," is crucial to the structure of the work.

This was a life almost normal, and yet intensely difficult, very near to our usual crises and problems, and yet precarious in the extreme. Thus my story relates an experience within which one of those rare glimpses of the nature of men and of their communal life is possible. In our internment camp we were secure and comfortable enough to accomplish in large part the creation and maintenance of a *small civilization*; but our life was sufficiently close to the margin of survival to reveal the vast difficulties of that task.[16]

---

[15]White, *Tropics of Discourse*, 95.
[16]Gilkey, *SC*, ix; emphasis mine.

By describing the camp as a "small civilization," Gilkey informs readers that the account they are about to read is not about a private experience but about a public one, not only about what happened to him but what happens in a society.

What differentiates the camp *from* ordinary life—its marginal character—is precisely that which makes the camp a *normative* site for the study of "all" societal life. According to Gilkey, internment provided a threshold-like perspective from which to "glimpse" the "nature of men and their communal life." To explain his "glimpse," however, Gilkey turns to the scientific language of the laboratory.

> Thus, as the laboratory reveals the structure of what is studied by reducing it to manageable size and subjecting it to increased pressure, so this internment camp reduced society, ordinarily large and complex, to viewable size, and by subjecting life to greatly increased tension laid bare its essential structures.[17]

Gilkey's analogy of the camp to a laboratory does not negate the more fundamental metaphor of the camp as small civilization. Rather, his turn to the image of the laboratory suggests a certain set of assumptions about the "study" of culture, and how its fundamental, underlying structures are "revealed."

While Gilkey's image of the laboratory is indebted in a general way to the laboratory work of the chemical and biological sciences as well as to philosophers like John Dewey, who use the laboratory as an image of a new kind of knowledge, neither of those sources captures his use of the laboratory as an analogy for the study of civilization or culture. In his work from 1944, *A Scientific Theory of Culture*, Bronislaw Malinowski tried to set out those constants of cultural systems that would ground a science of culture. Writing about the methodological procedures of this science, Malinowski says:

> Again anthropology, especially in its modern developments, has to its credit the fact that most of its votaries have to do ethnographic field work, that is, an empirical type of research. Anthropology was perhaps the first of all social sciences to establish its laboratory side by side with its theoretical workshop.[18]

---

[17]Gilkey, *SC*, ix.
[18]Bronislaw Malinowski, *A Scientific Theory of Culture* (Chapel Hill: University of

Gilkey's use of the laboratory image evokes this association with the empirical methods of the anthropologist, suggesting that the years in the camp were analogous to time spent in field work.

Moreover, Gilkey's claim that the simple structure of the camp reveals the "anatomy" of the human community is also indebted to an assumption common in anthropology. In *The Elementary Forms of the Religious Life*, Emile Durkheim writes about the importance of studying "primitive" religions.

> That which is accessory or secondary, the development of luxury, has not yet come to hide the principal elements. All is reduced to that which is indispensable, to that without which there could be no religion. But that which is indispensable is also that which is essential. . . . Primitive civilizations offer privileged cases, then, because they are simple cases.[19]

Durkheim develops his point by turning to both "experimental" and "scientific" analogies. Noting that primitive religions are both "rudimentary and gross," he writes:

> But even their grossness makes them instructive, for they thus become convenient for experiments, as in them, the facts and their relations are easily seen. In order to discover the laws of the phenomena he studies, the physicist tries to simplify these latter and rid them of their secondary characteristics. For that which concerns institutions, nature spontaneously makes the same sort of simplifications at the beginning of history.[20]

Gilkey's basic metaphor of the camp as civilization, and his supplemental metaphor of the camp as a laboratory, both suggest indebtedness to a disciplined form of social analysis that one could describe as either sociological or anthropological. Through these images, fundamental to the theory of the social sciences, Gilkey suggests quite subtly that he participates in the authority of those disciplines.

North Carolina Press, 1944) 11.

[19]Emile Durkheim, *The Elementary Forms of the Religious Life*, trans. Joseph Ward Swain (Glencoe IL: Free Press, 1947) 6.

[20]James Clifford adds this support: "In a practice not essentially different from that of Herbert Spencer, Henry Maine, Durkheim, Engels, or Freud, it is assumed that evidence from 'simple' societies will illuminate the origins and structure of contemporary cultural patterns" (James Clifford, *Writing Culture* [Berkeley: University of California Press, 1986] 110).

V. Metonymy—Extending the Metaphor

In their book *More than Cool Reason*, George Lakoff and Mark Turner provide a helpful discussion of how metonymy differs from metaphor.[21] While in metaphor "there are two conceptual domains, and one is understood in terms of the other" (as in the internment camp understood *as* a small civilization), metonymy "involves only one conceptual domain." In metonymy, "one can refer to one entity in a schema by referring to another entity in the same schema." One thinks of the example in which the sailor calls out that he sees "fifty sails" on the horizon. The fifty sails are a metonymy for fifty ships; from one element of the field, one can deduce other elements of the field or the field itself.

Metonymy works by a kind of intrafield implication. By naming only a characteristic of an object, it leaves unstated the explicit object of its trope. The hearer or reader must supply the other object, or frame of reference, implied by the speaker or text.

While seldom discussed, metonymy also functions with respect to intellectual or academic disciplines. If, for example, one is reading a story and one encounters a telling "slip of the tongue," and/or an interpretation of a character's dream that hinges on an oedipal analysis, one could infer metonymically that a kind of Freudian theory of psychology was in some way (perhaps seriously, perhaps satirically) operating within the story.

In *Shantung Compound*, Gilkey's emphases on (1) the *empirical* nature of his account, (2) the quality of his narrative voice, and (3) his arrangement of chapters and their topics, all imply a cognitive domain similar to that of cultural anthropology. The effect of these relatively hidden, yet structurally significant, metonymies is to suggest that *Shantung Compound* is an empirical, social-scientific account of a small civilization, which is to say of a distinctly knowable "world."[22]

---

[21]George Lakoff and Mark Turner, *More Than Cool Reason* (Chicago: University of Chicago Press, 1989).

[22]Gilkey intentionally sought to establish an "empirical" tone in *SC*: "The third [book] (*Shantung Compound*), based on an internment-camp experience, argued that liberal optimism about human rationality and goodness was a false and 'unempirical' view and that only the traditional symbol of original sin could make sense out of our ordinary individual and communal behavior" (Langdon Gilkey, "Responses to Peter Berger," *Theological Studies* 39 [September 1978]: 189).

A. *Shantung Compound as an Empirical Account*

Shaped by the assumptions of neoorthodox theologies, Gilkey is painfully aware in *Shantung Compound* of his own discipline's suspicion about personal experience as a basis for theology. His troping of cultural anthropology is designed to show that his account is not merely subjective. The anxiety of subjectivity, however, is one that has haunted the discipline of anthropology itself. Clifford Geertz, in his book *Works and Lives*, discusses how the anxiety of authority underlies much of anthropology's ethnographic literature:

> The question of signature, the establishment of an authorial presence within a text, has haunted ethnography from very early on, though for the most part it has done so in a disguised form. Disguised, because it has been generally cast not as a narratological issue, a matter of how best to get an honest story told, but as an epistemological one, a matter of how to prevent subjective views from coloring objective facts.[23]

Like Malinowski, who, according to anthropologist James Clifford, struggled in *Argonauts of the Western Pacific* (1922) "with the rhetorical problem of convincing his readers that the facts he was putting before them were objectively acquired, not subjective creations," Gilkey subtly arranges an impressive array of supporting materials as evidence of his "being there," securing thereby his authority as interpreter.[24] He is quick to mention in the preface that his account is not based on memories of events now twenty years passed. He kept a "rather lengthy journal," wherein, he claims that he "set down every fact and happening, every problem and its resolution, that came to my attention." To prove the existence of the journal, there is a photocopy from one of its early pages. In addition, one finds a map of the compound and drawings depicting scenes from camp life, all sketched by Gilkey. These items are included not only for aesthetic, but for authoritative, reasons. They metonymically imply the anthropological authority of field notes, of "being there," of studying and mapping the relations of a cultural world.

---

[23]Clifford Geertz, *Works and Lives: The Anthropologist as Author* (Stanford CA: Stanford University Press, 1988).

[24]James Clifford, *The Predicament of Culture* (Cambridge MA: Harvard University Press, 1988) 29.

B. *Shantung Compound and the Topics of Anthropology*

Melville Herskovits's work from 1964, *Cultural Anthropology*, includes a series of chapters under the heading, "The Aspects of Culture": "The Universals in Culture," "Technology and the Utilization of Natural Resources," "Economics and the Fulfillment of Wants," "Social Organization and the Educational Function," "Political Systems: The Ordering of Human Relations," and "Religion: The Problem of Man and the Universe."[25] In *Shantung Compound*, Gilkey is preoccupied with just these kinds of problems. Gilkey's second chapter, for example, "Learning to Live," introduces a range of difficulties from the technical problems of sanitation and labor distribution, to problems of social class in the living quarters, to the first round of political maneuvering in which a variety of charismatic leaders vie for power. Throughout the book, Gilkey describes the institutional structures of the camp and the importance of these institutions for a coherent sense of political organization and security.

> In this bumbling way, the official camp organization was formed. From that time on, there were nine internee committees, each with a chairman and one or two assistants who negotiated directly with the Japanese. The job of each committee was, on the one hand, to press the Japanese for better equipment and supplies and, on the other, to manage the life of the camp in its area. Thus the needs of the camp began to be dealt with by designated men. The amorphous labor force was organized; the problems of equipment and of sanitation were handled by the engineers; supplies were distributed more fairly and efficiently; the complex problems of housing began to be tackled; and schools were started for our three hundred or more children.[26]

In other chapters, Gilkey also studies the allocation of space within this cultural compound. He describes disputes arising over the just distribution of housing, how families of different sizes and ages were accommodated, how space was divided in the barracks for single persons, and so forth. In addition, he undertakes a study of camp commerce, focusing in particular on the black market and its surprising practitioners, the Belgian Trappists! Assigned as a kitchen helper and later as manager of one of the kitchens, Gilkey provides a fascinating depiction of food

---

[25]Melville J. Herskovits, *Cultural Anthropology* (New York: Alfred A. Knopf, 1964); an abridged revision of *Man and His Works: The Science of Cultural Anthropology* (New York: Alfred A. Knopf, 1948).

[26]Gilkey, *SC*, 33.

preparation and its division of labor, noting, among other things, the space of the kitchens, the various kinds of equipment and their use, and specific cooking breakthroughs.

It is not experience alone that makes Gilkey's narration persuasive. His analyses and observations have authority because he organizes his analyses and observations into chapters that conform to the topical structures of an empirical discipline like anthropology.

C. The Narrator as a Participant-Observer

While autobiographical in the sense that it is "about" Langdon Gilkey's two and a half year experience, the narrative style of *Shantung Compound* does not focus directly on Gilkey himself, but on the various cultural situations that he observes. One does not find here the strong, first-person "I" of the diary or the autobiography. Nor is the narrative voice simply that of a storyteller. Rather, one finds a voice that is at once involved in, yet also objectively removed from, the experience of the text. It is the voice of what James Clifford calls the fieldworker-theorist.

> The authority of the academic fieldworker-theorist was established in the years between 1920 and 1950. This peculiar amalgam of intense personal experience and scientific analysis (understood in this period as both "rite of passage," and "laboratory") emerged as a method: participant observation.[27]

This new combination of the fieldworker-theorist, says Clifford, ushered in a "powerful new scientific and literary genre, the ethnography," which he describes as a "synthetic cultural description based on participant observation."[28]

> "Participant observation" serves as a shorthand for a continuous tacking between the "inside" and the "outside" of events: on the one hand grasping the sense of specific occurrences and gestures empathically, on the other stepping back to situate these meanings in wider contexts. Particular events thus acquire deeper and more general significance, structural rules and so forth. Understood literally, participant observation is a paradoxical, misleading formula, but it may be taken seriously if reformulated in hermeneutic terms as a dialectic of experience and interpretation.[29]

---

[27]Clifford, *Predicament of Culture*, 34.
[28]Clifford, *Predicament of Culture*, 30.
[29]Clifford, *Predicament of Culture*, 34.

Like Clifford's dialectic between experience and interpretation, Gilkey's narrational style moves between observation and interpretation of camp experience. Gilkey's narrator nearly always indicates his critical distance from a particular conflict in order to justify his interpretation of a certain person's or group's behavior. In his chapter, "Learning to Live," for example, Gilkey uses the first-person singular to describe several specific scenes, taking care to emphasize his observational point of view. "I recall, . . . *as a member of the Quarters Committee*, being called in to pacify a dorm of twenty-one single women about a month after the camp began."[30]

After describing another problem in the women's dorm, in which Gilkey, "was called in to mark off in chalk on the floor the exact space belonging to each resident," he describes how he and others wrestled to *interpret* these problems: "Often in those first months we in the quarters office puzzled about why the explosions were always generated in female rather than male dorms."[31] The explanation which Gilkey offers in this particular case is a kind of sociological analysis of gender, discussing the implications of gender formation in situations of social pressure. More important than the explanation itself is the tacking that one observes between the depiction of events and his interpretation of them.

The narrative's rhetorical movement between experience and interpretation also results from the interplay of two voices in the text, that of the young Gilkey who undergoes the experience of the camp, and that of the older Gilkey, now a theologian and author of the narrative. The presence of these two Gilkeys, one diachronic, the other synchronic, provides a powerful illusion in which Gilkey is both character and author, both inside and outside the narrative. What results is not merely a tacking between experience and interpretation, but a narrative that shows the development and transformation of the naïve, optimistic Gilkey into a more mature and realistic theologian. Here, too, as part of its participant/observer narrative style, *Shantung Compound* overlaps the genre of cultural ethnography. Pertinent to this point, Clifford comments about ethnography:

> They [early incidents of an ethnography] normally portray the ethnographer's early ignorance, misunderstanding, lack of contact—frequently a sort of

---

[30]Gilkey, *SC*, 18; emphasis mine.
[31]Gilkey, *SC*, 19.

childlike status within the culture. In the *Bildungsgeschichte* of the ethnography these states of innocence or confusion are replaced by adult, confident, disabused knowledge.[32]

From its metaphorical assertion of the camp *as* a small civilization, to the metonymical extension of that metaphor in the tropes of cultural anthropology, Gilkey's emphasis on the "empirical" nature of his account develops a surface level of cultural experience—a level for which the methods and languages of the social sciences are appropriate. The telos, however, of Gilkey's *Bildungsgeschichte* is found not in a secular form of social knowledge such as anthropology, but in the movement toward a realistic theological anthropology.

VI. A Niebuhrian Anthropology: Metonymy, Level Two

In "The Historical Text as Literary Artifact," Hayden White uses the following diagram to illustrate how historical texts are rhetorical in character.[33] Suppose, he argues, that there is a set of events (a, b, c, d, e, . . . , n) that is chronologically ordered. This chronological ordering does not yet explain *how* the events are related to one another. Interpreting the interconnections among the events and arranging them in the form of a plot or argument is the task of the historian. The historian structures the text, therefore, not only chronologically but also *syntactically*. "Now, the series can be emplotted in a number of different ways and thereby endowed with different meanings without violating the imperatives of the chronological arrangement at all."[34] In the following graph, each line suggests an alternative plot structure with the capitalized letters indicating how a historian uses certain particular events in the narrative to interpret the whole.

A, b, c, d, e, . . . , n
a, B, c, d, e, . . . , n
a, b, C, d, e, . . . , n
a, b, c, D, e, . . . , n

---

[32]Clifford, *Predicament of Culture*, 40.
[33]White, *Tropics of Discourse*, 81-100.
[34]White, *Tropics of Discourse*, 92.

The historian cannot escape choosing to emphasize the importance of one event over another and, therefore, cannot escape the work of interpretation and rhetoric.

Readers of *Shantung Compound* are familiar with the pivotal story of the parcels in chapter 6, "A Mixed Blessing."[35] In terms of the previous illustration from White's work, this incident in the narrative from *Shantung Compound* is capitalized. Clearly it occupies a central point in the narrative. But *how* does it become so? The incident of the parcels is pivotal to *Shantung Compound* because Gilkey's description of the event and its placement in the narrative are parts of a broader figurative pattern. There exists in *Shantung Compound* a second metonymical structure overlapping the first. This metonymical structure is theological in character and conforms in its basic outline to the theological anthropology of Reinhold Niebuhr, as presented in the first volume of *The Nature and Destiny of Man*. This second metonymical strand does not compete with the first as much as it provides, in Gilkey's terms, a "deeper," theological interpretation of it.

In the narrative action of *Shantung Compound's* first eight chapters, Gilkey subtly encodes the activity of his "small civilization" in terms of the three basic moments of Niebuhr's theological anthropology. In chapter

---

[35]In January 1945, 1,550 large parcels arrived at Weihsien from the American Red Cross. Facing serious shortages due to Japanese losses in the war, the entire interned community was thrilled with the arrival of the packages. Three feet long, a foot wide and eighteen inches high, each parcel weighed fifty pounds and represented not mere survival but "real wealth." Addressed to the remaining 200 Americans in camp, this would have meant that each American would receive seven to eight parcels each! On the other hand, not counting Americans, there were 1,250 other internees. The Japanese commandant decided that each American would receive one and one-half parcels while every other person would receive one parcel. Seven Americans, however, went to the commandant and demanded that, unless otherwise authorized by the Red Cross, all of the parcels should be distributed to Americans only. Gilkey uses this story to illuminate (a) the human propensity for self-concern, (b) the complicity of reason in justifying the interests of the self, and (c) the ambiguous character of wealth in a society. Quite contrary to the liberal assumption that reason could illuminate and resolve the conflicts caused by competing desire, Gilkey found that, under pressure, reason defends the self-interests of desire. Amidst these realizations about human nature, Gilkey returns to a theological theme. "Having found these truths about human existence enacted before my eyes, I began to recall some of the theological ideas I had almost forgotten in the bustle and activity of camp life. Among the most relevant, it now seemed, was the old idea of original sin" (Gilkey, *SC*, 115).

1, *Shantung Compound* first enacts the experience of overwhelming *anxiety* that accompanies the experience of being "placed" in an internment camp. In chapters 2 through 4, Gilkey documents the early successes of the camp in its *creativity* and order; and, in chapters 5 and 6, he describes the disintegrating effects of *self-centeredness*. Moreover, in chapters 7 and 8, Gilkey depicts the "corruption" of the camp civilization that follows from the contagious character of self-centeredness. By mapping his narrative action to a Niebuhrian theory of *human nature*, and only gradually revealing its presence in the narrative, Gilkey creates the illusion of a discovery of an insight or truth that has been hidden from view.

A. Enacting The Condition of Anxiety: Chapter 1

If the walls of the Weihsien camp served, as we saw in the first chapter, to define a specific cultural territory in need of ethnographic description, these same walls also allow Gilkey to develop another kind of space—the peculiarly human setting of existential anxiety. In the opening chapter, the young Gilkey and other American nationals, following Japanese orders, gather at the former U.S. embassy compound in Peking. The Americans know that the embassy is but the first stage of a process that will take them to a "Civilian Internment Center" near Weihsien, a city about two hundred miles south of Peking. Gilkey writes about the internees:

> The only thing we all seemed to have in common . . . was a queer combination of excitement and apprehension. Were we bound for a camping vacation or the torturer's rack? Because of the uncertainty, our emotions seesawed, voices were loud and tempers short.[36]

The double-edged emotion of excitement and apprehension is repeated when Gilkey's group of new internees arrive at the gate of the camp. "At this sudden confrontation with total strangers, I felt excitement as well as antipathy."[37] Entering into the camp itself, Gilkey experiences a deeper sense of anxiety.

> . . . a sense both of complete change and of utter reality came over me. Suddenly I felt what it was like to be *inside* something, and stuck there; . . . With this awareness I could feel my world shrink: the countryside beyond the walls receded and became unreal—like the pictured scenery of a stage

---

[36]Gilkey, *SC*, 2.
[37]Gilkey, *SC*, 6.

set. The reality in which I had now to exist seemed barely large enough to stand on, let alone large enough to live in. With a feeling of genuine despair I thought, "How can anyone *live* enclosed in this tiny area for any length of time?"[38]

Gilkey's anxiety in the passage—his claustrophobia of being inside the walls that define *reality*—is part of a larger figurative sequence. The metaphor of the internment camp as small civilization is now being metonymically interpreted through a contiguous elaboration of a particular theological model. The walls, which define the situation of internment, represent not only a cultural reality, but the reality of human finitude as such.

In *Maker of Heaven and Earth*, Gilkey first discussed the problem of *anxiety* in terms of the disintegration of meaning brought about by the external events of fate, or *Fortuna*.

> Existence and its meanings *are* dependent and insecure. They are dependent upon and conditioned by great forces beyond our control—the forces of life and death, of nature, society, and history. As Tillich remarks, creaturehood "from the inside" is experienced as anxiety, the anxiety which comes from an awareness of this basic dependence. Whenever, therefore, . . . the forces that we cannot control seem to thwart our every hope, then in desperation we ask, "what possible meaning can this dependent existence of mine have?"[39]

Gilkey's discussion in *Maker of Heaven and Earth* is profoundly similar to one found in *Shantung Compound's* chapter, "Living for What?" In that chapter, Gilkey is portrayed thinking through a difficult issue with his friend Matt. The latter raises an important question:

> Isn't this internment camp, though, quite atypical of the normal course of life where things *do* go on? Here ordinary goals—the struggle for money, for social development, prestige, and success—stopped dead at the gate.

Gilkey responds:

> No, I disagree. Situations like internment camps, though rare for most of us, are a part of life and far more prevalent than we in the West like to think. History, as we like to call it—though the ancients were more realistic and

---

[38]Gilkey, *SC*, 7.

[39]Langdon Gilkey, *Maker of Heaven and Earth: A Study of the Christian Doctrine of Creation* (New York: Doubleday, 1959) 169.

called it fate or *Fortuna*—continually does strange things to those who live within it.[40]

By emphasizing the continuity of the internment camp with other problems of fate associated with "living within history," Gilkey suggests that the *anxiety* of being "within the walls" of the camp is, if marginal, analogous to the felt anxiety of living "within" history and its finite character. The walls of the camp may serve in laboratory fashion to exaggerate or heighten this anxiety—applying increased "pressure" to what is normally felt—but they also help to illuminate the more fundamental existential problem of anxiety.

If, in terms of the first metonymic strand, Gilkey emphasized the camp as a distinct and different world, this second metonymic strand emphasizes an *underlying continuity* across cultural boundaries. While Gilkey used the *external* camp walls to demarcate a cultural world, he draws on the *internal* response to those walls (that is, the felt anxiety) to develop a universal and existential "situation."

B. Creativity and Self Transcendence: Chapters 2–4

In keeping with Niebuhr's model of theological anthropology, Gilkey's narrative moves from anxiety to creativity. Near the conclusion of chapter 1 in *Shantung Compound*, "Into the Unknown," Gilkey places himself at the *origins* of a small civilization:

> If this great crowd of people were to survive, much less to live a passable life, a civilization of some sort would have to be created from scratch. Gradually the nature of the problem facing our community dawned on me. As it did so, everything took on an intensity and excitement I had not known before.[41]

Unlike Boas and other anthropologists who understood their work as belated preservers of cultures about to disappear, Gilkey's "dawning civilization," suggests the theological idea of a virtual creation out of chaos.[42] From toilet facilities, to the division and upkeep of living quarters, to the development of a kitchen with sanitary food preparation and efficient distribution, Gilkey describes the various facets of the camp's organizational crisis in chapter 2, "Learning to Live." The

---

[40]Gilkey, *SC*, 200.
[41]Gilkey, *SC*, 12.
[42]Gilkey, *SC*, 33.

meeting of these basic needs began to occur through a rather *ad hoc*
division of labor.

> Jobs which had to be done were at first taken in hand by experienced people
> who alone knew how to handle them, and therefore alone saw the real need.
> Later, when work was organized and every able person was assigned a task,
> inexperienced people were trained in the new crafts. Thus bank clerks,
> professors, salesmen, missionaries, importers, and executives, became bakers,
> stokers, cooks, carpenters, masons, and hospital orderlies.[43]

Within the first weeks of this process, a sense of routine developed:

> Work of this sort, largely voluntary at first, was soon organized so that in
> a short while everyone had a set job with a routine and regular hours. With
> such a thoroughgoing organizational plan, the most vital needs of these two
> thousand people soon began to be met. The first rude form of our camp's
> civilization started to appear.[44]

The creation of order and organization out of chaos is experienced by the
narrator as an amazing and profoundly good accomplishment: "Suddenly
we had all become equally workers of the world, and although many of
us were not apt to admit it then, most of us enjoyed it."[45]

While Gilkey's discussion of camp organization recalls the metonymic structure of cultural anthropology, these early chapters also enact
the creative aspect of the human capacity for self-transcendence that one
finds in Niebuhr's Christian anthropology. Human beings can work
together to create a common future and pursue a common goal—such is
the power and goodness of human reason, creativity, and will. As in
Niebuhr's discussion, the positive goodness of human skills and
capabilities is affirmed. There are numerous reprises of this theme
throughout the first four chapters; the following few sentences from the
middle of chapter 4 will conclude my argument on this point.

> Day in and day out, the camp was a small hive of activity, most of it
> manual and vigorous. Everyone became more efficient in dealing with the
> practical problems of life than he had been when he came in. . . . After we
> had been there a year or so, an exhibit was held of the artifacts that
> ingenious people from all professions had made. . . . The display drove

---

[43]Gilkey, *SC*, 15.
[44]Gilkey, *SC*, 15.
[45]Gilkey, *SC*, 16.

home to me the truth that no practical situation, however unwieldy or difficult, was too much for human ingenuity. This group of humans had been faced with the total lack of all the comforts to which they had been accustomed, and for once they were unable to purchase gadgets ready made. Thus all the intense technical activity that resides in any group of men became active. Each in his own way embarked with energy and skill on the task of raising ever higher our level of material comfort.[46]

C. The Fallen Community: Chapters 5 and 6

Gilkey's impressive hymn to ingenuity is followed in the fifth chapter, "A Place of One's Own," which begins to enact the other side of Niebuhrian anthropology: "Gradually, however, as I encountered more and more unexpected problems in my work in housing, I began to realize that this confident attitude toward things simply did not fit the realities of camp life."[47] What the young Gilkey-as-character begins to discover amidst the camp is a kind of moral ambiguity. Faced, in one case, with a recalcitrant dorm, unwilling to listen to reason, Gilkey writes:

> But in block 49 men understood—they understood fully. They understood that a "reform" meant their own loss, and so they fought that reform, whatever its rationality and justice, as if it were a plague, a poisonous thing. Self-interest seemed almost omnipotent next to the weak claims of logic and fair play.[48]

Interestingly enough, the first time that Gilkey takes up the familiar topos of sin, or self-concern, he does so in the context of talking about the human need to have a "place." Earlier, in chapter 3, Gilkey had noted the adaptability of human persons to a strange and even hostile environment:

> How quickly man makes his life—whatever its character may be—into what he calls "normal." What would have seemed a fantastic deprivation to a man comfortable, well fed, and serene in an easy chair at home, had by the end of a few short months become just "life" to us. We recognized Weihsien as the accepted framework of our existence, and so the familiar context *within* which we reacted emotionally to things.[49]

---

[46]Gilkey, *SC*, 68.
[47]Gilkey, *SC*, 75.
[48]Gilkey, *SC*, 79.
[49]Gilkey, *SC*, 48; emphasis mine.

The theme of adaptability to the enclosed "framework" of the camp as the space *within* which life was lived, finds its more personal application in chapter 5.

> Somehow each self needs a "place" in order to be a self, in order to feel on a deep level that it really exists. We are, apparently, rootless beings at bottom. Unless we can establish roots somewhere in a place where we are at home, which we possess to ourselves and where our things are, we feel that we float, that we are barely there at all. For to exist with no place is to fail to exist altogether.[50]

In these passages, Gilkey links his discussion of cultural "place"—the camp itself—to that of personal "place." Moreover, he connects this need for a place with the need for self-preservation, and thereby to the depths of one's existential anxiety.

> Thus lonely and isolated people in our dorms would cling to every inch of space as if it were the very foundation of their being—and indeed it was. They would lavish on it and its sacred dimensions the same fanatical love that a nation will lavish on the boundaries of its territory. And in the wider world, each of us driven by the fear of never "being" at all, is eager to "make a place for himself" by almost any method available. And it is for this reason that we will defend our present status with all our ferocity if we should feel it threatened.[51]

By connecting the objective need for place to existential anxiety, Gilkey subtly connects a topos of cultural anthropology with Niebuhr's Christian anthropology. Gilkey can now appropriate the image of "laboratory" from his preface for his Niebuhrian anthropology: the "pressure" of the camp illuminates a fundamental structure, the human problem of anxiety. In the aftermath of a bitterly intractable fight over housing priorities, Gilkey is particularly despondent.

> "Out of those forty-four families, everyone saw only the logic of his own case," I reflected. "If that is at all typical of human affairs, then what sort of reality *is* there to the concept of 'impartial reason'? For when it is needed most desperately, that is, when the stakes are high for both parties and they begin to be overwrought, then impartial reason is sadly conspicuous by its absence! Does it fly away every time it is needed, to return only when

---

[50]Gilkey, *SC*, 80.
[51]Gilkey, *SC*, 81.

harmony reigns, when the conflict is over? If that is so, then surely reason is more a symptom or effect of social harmony than it is a cause—and if *that* is so, from whence can we expect social health to come?"[52]

The problem of self-centeredness does not leave reason unscathed, but shows it to be intimately involved in the defense of one's own territory.[53] In the face of such recalcitrance, Gilkey's view of human nature undergoes a dramatic change. I quote here at some length.

> The ordinary social relations fostered in college or country club seemed continually to validate the modern liberal estimate of man as rational and moral, able to see what is right and willing to pursue it for the common good.
>
> Certainly this is the way we all like to think of ourselves. Unless some crisis explodes in our family or in our communities, there is little on the polite surface of things to contradict this opinion. In this padded environment of friendliness, good cheer, and generosity, at least one thing seems as sure to everyone as it was to the liberal Rev. Mr. White: the old pessimism about a "fallen existence," about "original sin," or about a fundamental selfishness in man is either antiquated monastic gloom or the twisted view of modern novelists and playwrights. . . .
>
> The revelatory value of life at Weihsien camp, I decided, was that this false estimate, based on the surface pretensions of a secure society, was cut down to size. . . .[54]

In this passage, Gilkey connects the language of "ordinary social relations" to that of "surface pretensions." The camp experience is *revelatory* precisely to the extent that it allows Gilkey to see *beneath* the pretension to a deeper, underlying reality: "I now understood that beneath this surface harmony lay the reality I had just discovered."[55] In the wake of the incident about the parcels, where he rediscovers the importance of original sin, Gilkey writes of this deeper dimension:

> The reality to which the symbols of the "Fall" and of "Original Sin" point is not really the particular and dubious act of Adam. Rather it is this fundamental self-concern of the total self which, so to speak, *lies below* our

---

[52]Gilkey, *SC*, 84.

[53]See Niebuhr's discussion of *self-deception*: Reinhold Niebuhr, *The Nature and Destiny of Man*, vol. 1, *Human Nature* (New York: Charles Scribner's Sons, 1941; repr.: New York: Charles Scribner's Sons, 1964) 203-207.

[54]Gilkey, *SC*, 91.

[55]Gilkey, *SC*, 91.

particular thoughts and acts, molds them, directs them, and then betrays us into the actual misdeeds we all witness in our common life.[56]

VII. A Breakthrough in Method

The movement from the metaphor of the camp as a small civilization to the dual metonymies of cultural and theological anthropology represents a fundamental breakthrough in Gilkey's theological method. The two metonymic levels of *Shantung Compound* provide for Gilkey an analogue for resolving the series of methodological dichotomies discussed earlier: (1) surface/depth, (2) fact/interpretation, and (3) secular experience/religious language. The first metonymic strand lays out "what happened." It is a kind of factual report, more scientific than subjective in character, and clearly public or secular in its orientation. One does not have to be a religious person in order to follow the narrative. Gilkey's second metonymic strand, which develops the same metaphor of the camp as a small civilization, is less obvious. The second strand plays off the first and develops a simultaneous secondary level of analysis that, over the course of the text, interprets the more obvious experiential strand. By lacing the early part of *Shantung Compound* with religious themes of anxiety, creation, and so forth, Gilkey subtly develops the Niebuhrian anthropology that breaks into the text's foreground only in chapters 5 and 6. In the latter chapter's discussion of the parcels, the theme of original sin seems to dawn on the young Gilkey (and the reader!) as a discovery of the truth about human beings. By structuring that narrative moment as a kind of revelation, Gilkey-as-author shows the connection and fit between secular experience and religious language. The religious symbol of original sin, implies Gilkey, while not obvious to a secular culture, is finally the most adequate language to name what happens in cultural experience.

The young Gilkey's discovery of the relevance of theological language to his experience in the camp is the pivotal breakthrough of the narrative's *Bildungsroman*, the insight that moves Gilkey-as-character from naïve ephebe to a more mature, realistic, and disabused theologian. It is also the moment that convinces not only the young Gilkey, but the reader, that religious or theological language is necessary to interpret fully our human experience. For Gilkey-as-author, however, the real break-

---

[56]Gilkey, *SC*, 116; emphasis mine.

through of *Shantung Compound* occurs in his rhetorical pacing of the theological insight, subtly and metonymically, building the Niebuhrian anthropology in *Shantung Compound* to its moment of "revelation." By "starting" with human experience, Gilkey-as-author displays the development of his own theological voice. Developing a fundamental narrative theology that goes beyond his teachers' starting points in revelation and ontology, Gilkey constructs in *Shantung Compound* a kind of "empirical myth"—a narrative that both accurately portrays the facts of human experience and that illumines a depth of meaning unintelligible apart from religious language. While *Shantung Compound's* theological anthropology is not yet explicitly theological, insofar as it does not yet rely on revelation, its narrative structure enacts a two-fold depth that demonstrates, for Gilkey, the reality of a depth-dimension to human experience, and thus anticipates his discussion of the religious symbol in *Naming the Whirlwind* and his own approach to correlational theology.

VIII. Forgetting Rhetoric: The Problem in Gilkey's Method

In his essay, "Historicism, History and the Imagination," White discusses the relation of two terms that one finds throughout Gilkey's methodological reflections, fact and interpretation.

> In most discussion of historical discourse, the two levels conventionally distinguished are those of the *facts* (data or information), on the one side, and *interpretation* (explanation or story about the facts), on the other. This conventional distinction obscures the difficulty of discriminating within the discourse between these two levels. It is not the case that a fact is one thing and its interpretation another. The fact is presented where and how it is in the discourse in order to sanction the interpretation to which it is meant to contribute.[57]

White goes on to describe how the literary construction of "facts" occurs simultaneously to the construction of an interpretation of those facts.

> The facts and their formal explanation or interpretation appears as the manifest or literal "surface" of the discourse, while the figurative language used to characterize the facts points to a deep-structural meaning. This latent meaning of an historical discourse consists of the generic story-type of

---

[57]White, *Tropics of Discourse*, 107.

which the facts themselves, arranged in a specific order and endowed with different weights, are the manifest form.[58]

In the case of *Shantung Compound*, the "latent meaning" of the narrative consists in working through the differing moves of Niebuhr's theological anthropology. Insofar as "understanding" such narratives is equated with the reader's grasping the secondary level of meaning, as White argues, Gilkey structures the text so that the reader experiences the same kind of deep persuasion about the importance of religious language that the young Gilkey does.[59]

White's analysis of historical discourse proves immensely helpful in getting at the rhetorical structure of a book like *Shantung Compound* and in showing how arguments and texts are figurative compositions. While helpful in illuminating the theological significance of *Shantung Compound*, however, such a method of analysis also raises serious concerns about the kind of claims Gilkey hoped to establish in the work. Certainly, one conclusion of White's rhetorical analysis of historical texts is that *meaning* does not dwell within experience, but is a construction about experience. As one would expect, Gilkey does not see it that way.

In my interview with Gilkey in 1991, he used the image of archeology to explain the relationship between fact and interpretation.

> I prefer Ricoeur's image of archeology here. . . . And I've treasured that image. . . . It's basic to *Reaping the Whirlwind*. There are different levels: there's the event, there's the newspaper report, there's certain political reflection, there's a moral and philosophical reflection, and there are theological symbols that finally make sense of the thing. . . . That's what I was dealing with in *Shantung Compound*, facts and interpretation, events and interpretation. But the interpretation of the events was doing an archeological task of getting at the richness of the fact.[60]

Gilkey's archeological metaphor attempts to provide a secure foundation in experience to ground the discipline of theology. The image

---

[58]White, *Tropics of Discourse*, 110.

[59]White, *Tropics of Discourse*, 110. In *Shantung Compound*, the young Gilkey (as well as the reader) can be said to understand the camp experience only insofar as he grasps its deeper revelations about the character of sin. Indeed, in the final chapters of the narrative, the young Gilkey is still learning that the structure of sin that he discovered at work in the camp applies to the "ordinary" culture of American life.

[60]"New Orleans Conversation."

suggests that there is an objective structure—what he calls in *Shantung Compound* an "anatomy"—to human experience that can be thematized by differing forms of discourse. By assigning differing forms of intellectual discourse (for example, the political, the moral, and so forth), Gilkey gives theology at once a voice that is both comparable to and more important than the other disciplines. In a secular culture suspicious about theology, securing a place for the discipline at the intellectual table is an important task in itself. In Gilkey's archeological model, theology is comparable to the other disciplines insofar as it, too, addresses a particular level of meaning in an event. Theology is more important than the other disciplines insofar as it thematizes the "deepest," most profound level of meaning.

In addition to there being an objective structure to existence, the image of archeology also suggests that the content of interpretation is present in the fact/event itself. Gilkey explains this fullness of the fact by arguing that it takes time for the different levels of an event to become clear to reflective consciousness.

> This is what Hegel means when he says the "Owl of Minerva flies at sunset." That is to say, when the events are over there comes reflection upon it. And in that sense philosophy is a reflection upon events. . . . What you find in *Shantung Compound* is a description of events and analysis of the structure of the events. Say the political structure of the kitchen or something like that—that's a certain abstraction. An analysis of the description of the moral content of it, and then a theological level below that. These got stretched out a little bit. The moral came almost immediately, . . . but the theological was a good deal later.[61]

The task of the theologian is to reflect upon human experience in order to discern the deep pattern present in the experience itself.

Gilkey would be willing to agree that any interpretation is a construction, insofar as it is only a partial attempt to get at the richness of a fact. But I would agree with White: the "richness of the fact" is itself a construction, not a given. Gilkey's archeological theory of interpretation allows the theologian to mask or hide his or her rhetorical power, and to claim that s/he is expressing only what is already there in experience. When Gilkey in his lectures and later books refers to *Shantung Compound*, he always refers to what he learned there. He refers to the work

---

[61]"New Orleans Conversation."

in terms of what the young Gilkey-as-character discovered. This way of reading *Shantung Compound* fits his theory of interpretation. Yet, while he underscores the figure of the young Gilkey diachronically moving through the text from naïveté to maturity, Gilkey seems to forget that *he* authored the text, synchronically arranging his young Gilkey's discovery.

Gilkey purchases a theological commitment to the depth of experience by the denial of his rhetorical power. Rather than acknowledge that theology is a discourse that constructs or shapes experience, Gilkey insists that theological discourse is representative, that it "discovers" or "uncovers" what was present all along, but at a deeper level, forgotten or hidden from view. His position allows him to retain an objective order, or depth, of reality, while acknowledging that the "surface" of human experience is radically contingent. Yet, a careful reading of *Shantung Compound* illuminates not a depth-dimension to human experience, but the tropological character of theological construction. Theologies illumine because of their rhetorical force in shaping and reshaping the way we "word" our lives, not because they point to a truth that stands outside of language. The task for a more fully committed rhetorical theology is to retrieve Gilkey's empiricism not as a foundational argument but as a public appeal.

Chapter 5

History, Society, and Politics: Gilkey's Theology of Culture

Brian J. Walsh

"Time of Troubles": Cultural Chill, Betrayal, and Precariousness

The following comment is one of the most memorable lines in the writings of Langdon Gilkey: "An autumnal chill is in the air; its similarity to the chill in other periods of cultural decline is undeniable."[1] Gilkey is a theologian for a culture in decline.[2] Furthermore, as a testimony to the prophetic insight of Gilkey's cultural analysis, it now feels as if our chill is no longer autumnal, but that we have entered into the depths of a cultural winter.

Indeed, winter is an apt metaphor. In his apocalyptic description of the end of modernity, the poet/songwriter Leonard Cohen wrote:

Things are going to slide, slide in all directions
Won't be nothing
Nothing you can measure any more
The blizzard, the blizzard of the world
has crossed the threshold
and it has overturned
the order of the soul.[3]

Like a snowstorm on a freeway, the blizzard of the world takes away all normative points of reference, any ability to measure life or to measure ourselves, and the resulting anomie is personally and culturally deadly. Cohen tells us that this blizzard has crossed the threshold, overturning the order of the soul. I take this as a double entendre. The blizzard has crossed the threshold—it has entered into our homes, our inner sanctums, indeed, into our souls. The blizzard, however, has also

---

[1]Langdon Gilkey, *Society and the Sacred: Toward a Theology of Culture in Decline* (New York: Seabury Press, 1981) xi; hereafter cited as *SAS*.

[2]Hence, the subtitle to my book: Brian J. Walsh, *Langdon Gilkey: Theologian for a Culture in Decline* (Lanham MD: University Press of America, 1991).

[3]Leonard Cohen, "The Future," from *The Future* (audio recording and lyrics booklet) (©Sony Music Entertainment Corp, 24 Nov 1992).

crossed the threshold in the sense of going over the top, there is now no turning back. No wonder Cohen concludes this chorus by saying, "When they said Repent / I wondered what they meant." What could the religious language of repentance possibly mean in a culture for which neither measurement nor turning back are possible?

Gilkey often uses Arnold Toynbee's notion of a "time of troubles" to describe the present cultural situation.[4] Following Toynbee, Gilkey refers to a "time of troubles" not as a fated necessity but as a "period when the *possibility* of collapse or of radical decline appears for the first time on the scene."[5] Modernity is in crisis, Gilkey claims, because the Enlightenment has not fulfilled its promises to control the natural forces that threaten human life, end poverty through economic abundance, and eradicate religious superstition by establishing rational and moral political structures in history: "What was promised has either not in fact occurred, or, if it has occurred, new problems, even contradictions, even lethal dilemmas have resulted." We are witnessing, therefore, "an ending of the Enlightenment," because "the Enlightenment dream has been falsified."[6] This ending necessarily entails, says Gilkey, an end to unlimited technological expansion, the domination of science, unfettered human autonomy, and confidence that humankind can realize earthly blessedness through its own progress: "All of these beliefs in man and his vast potentialities in history through knowledge and the control it brings that characterize the 'modernity' created by the Enlightenment have been proved to the hilt not to have established and secured human life on earth—as had been promised."[7]

---

[4]Arnold Toynbee, *A Study of History*, vol. 1 (London: Oxford University Press, 1934) 53; idem, *A Study of History*, vol. 4 (London: Oxford University Press, 1939) 1-5.

[5]Langdon Gilkey, *Through the Tempest: Theological Voyages in a Pluralistic Culture*, ed. Jeff B. Pool (Minneapolis: Fortress Press, 1991) 149; hereafter cited as *TT*. See also idem, "Theology for a Time of Troubles: How My Mind has Changed," *Christian Century* 98 (20 April 1981): 474-80; and idem, "Theological Frontiers: Implications for Bioethics," in *Theology and Bioethics*, ed. E. E. Phelp (Dordrecht, The Netherlands: D. Reidel, 1985) 118-19.

[6]Gilkey, *SAS*, 4-5. Similar to Gilkey's analysis of a "time of troubles," Robert Heilbroner describes the present cultural mood as a "civilizational malaise," in which "the values of an industrial civilization, which has for two centuries given us not only material advance but also a sense of *élan* and purpose, now seem to be losing their self-evident justification" (Robert Heilbroner, *An Inquiry into the Human Prospect* [New York: W. W. Norton, 1974] 21).

[7]Langdon Gilkey, "Robert Heilbroner's Vision of History," *Zygon* 10 (September

Again, as a witness to Gilkey's insight, these unfulfilled promises find their strongest echoes in the poetry and music of our time. Artists identified with so-called Generation X illustrate both this sense of ending and the betrayal that such broken promises necessarily entail. Furthermore, they have in view precisely an ending of Enlightenment modernity. In "tales of a scorched earth," on the aptly titled double album, *Mellon Collie and the Infinite Sadness*, The Smashing Pumpkins sing, "farewell goodnight last one turn out the lights / and let me be, let me die inside." Cultural darkness and personal dissolution are integrally related. This band knows that the present cultural malaise is rooted in broken promises. In the same song they sing "and we're all dead yea we're all dead / inside the future of a shattered past."[8]

We live inside the future of a shattered past because that past told grand stories that have proven to be destructive lies. The grand story of a Marxist utopia collapsed along with the Berlin Wall. The heroic tale of technological progress blew up with the Challenger. The progress myth of democratic capitalism, which promised economic prosperity and social harmony, strains under the weight of economic contraction, ecological threat, and a never-ending and ever-widening gap between the rich and the poor both domestically and internationally. It is no wonder, therefore, that in their Grammy award-winning song, "bullet with butterfly wings," The Smashing Pumpkins confess that "the world is a vampire, sent to drain / secret destroyers, hold you up to the flames / and what do i get, for my pain / betrayed desires, and a piece of the game."[9] As members of the first generation of this century in the Western world that cannot expect a standard of living that exceeds or is equivalent to that of their parents, members of Generation X (and those younger) frequently give voice to a deep sense of betrayal. Someone has told them a story, spun them a line, about the good life; it has proven to be a lie. When the lie runs as deep as this, not surprisingly, they experience the world not as a place of safety and opportunity, but as a vampire that sucks the very lifeblood out of them. The world is decidedly malignant and dangerous. The best that one can expect in this world of betrayal is simply to get a piece of the game; but even this cannot be guaranteed. Any sensitive

---

1975): 218.

[8]The Smashing Pumpkins, "tales of a scorched earth," from *Mellon Collie and the Infinite Sadness* (audio CD) (©Virgin Records America, 1995).

[9]"bullet with butterfly wings," from *Mellon Collie*.

reader of Gilkey's theology of culture is not surprised by any of this—only grieved.

Following in the tradition of Reinhold Niebuhr, Gilkey has argued from his earliest writings that modern culture was in crisis and in decline.[10] In such a context, the very normative ground on which one stands is uncertain, sliding "in all directions." The old answers and the old stories are no longer convincing; and ultimate questions that once had some form of ultimate, faith-committed answers are reopened. Such reopening is usually horrific. Gilkey summarizes our situation well: "Everything seems to slip: our landscape, our institutions, our values, our way of life—and so the security and meaning, the sense of being at home in a world we can understand and deal with that they brought."[11] A "time of troubles" aptly describes this cultural state of affairs. Such times, however, are not just troublesome; they are also dangerous. Gilkey notes that "an old culture, like an old bear, can suddenly whiff the dank odor of its own mortality; and then it is tempted, and tempted deeply, to sacrifice its ideals for the preservation of its life—and thus to hasten the very demise in history that it fears so much."[12] Although Western liberal modernity may have felt a sense of euphoric ideological vindication with the collapse of Soviet communism, the inherent vulnerability of liberal modernity to a similar demise cannot be concealed for long.[13] Peter McLaren, puts it well.

---

[10]See Langdon Gilkey, "A Christian Response to the World Crisis," *Christianity and Crisis* 15 (8 August 1955): 107-11. Whereas Reinhold Niebuhr's theological anthropology (Reinhold Niebuhr, *The Nature and Destiny of Man*, 2 vols. [New York: Charles Scribner's Sons, 1941, 1943]) decisively shaped Gilkey's view of the fundamental ambiguity of the human subject and therefore of all cultural formations, Niebuhr's interpretation of modernity (Reinhold Niebuhr, *Reflections on the End of an Era* [New York: Charles Scribner's Sons, 1934]) functions as the precursor to everything Gilkey says about the decline of modernity.

[11]Langdon Gilkey, *Reaping the Whirlwind: A Christian Interpretation of History* (New York: Seabury Press, 1976) 16; hereafter cited as *RW*.

[12]Gilkey, "Theology for a Time of Troubles," 478. For similar comments, see Langdon Gilkey, *Gilkey on Tillich* (New York: Crossroad, 1990) 193-95; hereafter cited as *GOT*; idem, "Religion and the Technological Future," *Criterion* 13 (Spring 1974) 6-7; and idem, *SAS*, 95.

[13]For an example of post-Berlin-Wall-liberal-self-congratulatory euphoria, see Francis Fukuyama, "The End of History?" *The National Interest* (Summer 1989): 3-18, and idem, *The End of History and the Last Man* (New York: Free Press, 1992). See my theological/biblical critique of Fukuyama's position: Brian J. Walsh, *Subversive Christianity: Imaging God in a Dangerous Time* (Seattle: Alta Vista College Press, 1994) chap. 3.

We live at a precarious moment in history. Relations of subjection, suffering dispossession, and contempt for human dignity and the sanctity of life are at the center of social existence. Emotional dislocation, moral sickness, and individual helplessness remain ubiquitous features of our time.[14]

This emotional dislocation and sense of helplessness, says McLaren, is the result of late modernity's "dehydrated imagination that has lost its capacity to dream otherwise."[15]

Without life-empowering dreams and an ability to imagine and hope that life might be different than the present broken status quo, cultural life is precarious indeed. Funding such an imagination and dreaming such dreams, however, are inescapably religious matters.[16] This has been Langdon Gilkey's abiding claim. The essential drive of Gilkey's theology of culture has been a concern for a religious answer to the crisis of modernity. In one of his more blunt moments, he wrote that our over-whelming need is for "a credible myth that does not lie to us about ourselves and our future."[17] We need a credible myth because the crisis of modernity is fundamentally a crisis for the myth of progress.

According to Gilkey, a theology of culture, like all theology, has two foci. First, the theology of culture is an "analysis of the current socio-political-cultural situation with regard to its religious dimensions and issues."[18] Gilkey develops his own cultural analysis on the basis of four resources: (1) a Tillichian understanding of the religious substance of culture; (2) a phenomenology of ultimacy in historical and political experience; (3) a Niebuhrian critique of the myth of progress; and (4) a prophetic discernment of the decline of this myth and its culture. In the next section of this chapter, I will offer a brief exposition of these dimensions of Gilkey's theology of culture.

---

[14]Peter McLaren, *Critical Pedagogy and Predatory Culture: Oppositional Politics in a Postmodern Age* (London: Routledge, 1995) 1.

[15]McLaren, *Critical Pedagogy and Predatory Culture*, 2.

[16]In a context explicitly indebted to Gilkey's cultural analysis, Walter Brueggemann speaks of the need for theology to "fund, feed, nurture, nourish, legitimate and authorize, a *counterimagination of the world*" (Walter Brueggemann, *Texts under Negotiation: The Bible and Postmodern Imagination* [Minneapolis: Fortress Press, 1993], 20).

[17]Langdon Gilkey, *Religion and the Scientific Future* (New York. Harper & Row, 1970) 97; hereafter cited as *RSF*.

[18]Gilkey, *TT*, 148.

Theology of culture, however, also presumes to propose new patterns of sociocultural-political life. This is its second focus. In the context of a declining culture, Gilkey supplies a mythic alternative with two primary qualities: (1) it embodies a dialectical character; and (2) it offers resources for freedom in the midst of historical fatedness and alluring hope in the face of cultural despair. After an exposition of these dimensions of Gilkey's thought, I will conclude by situating Gilkey's theology of culture in relation to certain themes of postmodern thought.

I. Society and the Sacred

A *theology* of culture is only a meaningful mode of analysis, if one begins with a broad functional definition of religion as referring to an ultimate dimension of life rather than to certain specified cultic activities or beliefs. Employing the resources of sociology and anthropology, Gilkey argues that "any community or society is held together in sharing in, expressing and devoting themselves to, something sacred and ultimate—or a sacrality and ultimacy—that permeates their life together, holds them together, directs their common life, and makes that common life possible."[19] Tillich described this as the religious substance of a culture, the deepest soil or "ground" out of which a culture grows, providing it with passion and vision, determining its overall style and mood.[20] Gilkey describes such a religious substance as follows:

> Social existence involves and depends on a shared consciousness, a shared system of meanings [which] is structured by symbols that shape or express the understanding of reality, of space and time, of human being and its authenticity, of life and its goods, of appropriate relations, roles, customs and behavior, symbols which together constitute the unique gestalt, the identity or uniqueness, of that social group.[21]

Because social existence is experienced and formed in the context of historical passage, any symbolic system of meanings necessarily assumes

---

[19]Gilkey, *SAS*, 19.

[20]Paul Tillich, *Systematic Theology*, vol. 3 (Chicago: University of Chicago Press, 1963) 59-61. Gilkey refers to a cultural mood as a "fundamental attitude toward reality, toward truth, and toward value which characterizes an epoch, and within whose terms every creative aspect of life . . . expresses itself" (Langdon Gilkey, *Naming the Whirlwind: The Renewal of God-Language* [Indianapolis: Bobbs-Merrill, 1969] 34); hereafter cited as *NW*.

[21]Gilkey, *SAS*, 43.

the form of myth that "tells us who we are in history and why we are here."[22] Any global vision of history or metanarrative entails "a mythical structure providing for those who are committed to it an understanding of their own role in the global history of good and evil, an ultimate norm for cultural life, and a sense of meaning and of hope for the unknown future."[23]

While Jean-François Lyotard describes postmodernity as "incredulity toward all metanarratives" and Terry Eagleton claims that the "secretly terroristic function" of all such metanarratives "was to ground and legitimate the illusion of a 'universal' human history,"[24] Gilkey's phenomenological analysis is more nuanced. Recognizing the inherent ambiguity of all symbolic-mythic structures and noting that such total visions can have both conserving/legitimating as well as critical/revolutionary functions in social life, Gilkey also demonstrates that myth, symbol, and total visions are phenomenologically constitutive to human sociopolitical life.[25] Because political action "seeks basically to evade fate, to transform the given in all historical life into a destiny which our freedom can in some measure control and direct," such historicopolitical experience is only adequately thematized by myths which "function as essential answers to the deepest, desperate questions of historical being,

---

[22]Gilkey, *SAS*, 24. I suspect that Gilkey would concur with the contention of Alasdair MacIntyre: "I can only answer the question 'What am I to do?' if I can answer the prior question 'Of what story or stories do I find myself a part?' " (Alasdair MacIntyre, *After Virtue* [Notre Dame IN: University of Notre Dame Press, 1981] 201). For a reflection on the narrative nature of Scripture and its implications for understanding biblical authority, see Brian J. Walsh, "Reimaging Biblical Authority," *Christian Scholar's Review* 26 (Winter 1996): 206-20.

[23]Gilkey, *SAS*, 61-62.

[24]Jean-François Lyotard, *The Postmodern Condition: A Report on Knowledge*, trans. Geoff Bennington and Brian Massumi (Minneapolis: University of Minnesota Press, 1984) xxiv. For an insightful critique of Lyotard's perspective, see J. M. Bernstein, "Grand Narratives," in *On Paul Ricoeur: Narrative and Interpretation*, ed. David Wood (London: Routledge, 1991) 102-23. David Harvey quotes Eagleton's comment from Terry Eagleton, "Awakening from Modernity," *Times Literary Supplement* (20 February 1987) (David Harvey, *The Condition of Postmodernity: An Enquiry into the Origins of Cultural Change* [Oxford: Basil Blackwell, 1989] 9).

[25]On religion as conserving and revolutionary, see the following: Gilkey, *SAS*, 22; idem, *RW*, 19, 61-62, 290-91; and idem, *Message and Existence: An Introduction to Christian Theology* (New York: Seabury Press, 1981) 214; hereafter cited as *ME*. On the ambiguous and demonic nature of ultimate myths and symbols, see Gilkey, *RW*, 68-69.

to human being in passage, and so . . . provide the grounds for the possibility of human freedom in that passage."[26]

Although Lyotard, Eagleton, and others are undoubtedly right to note that totalizing myths can legitimate the violence of the powerful over marginalized others, Gilkey insists that mythic legitimacy is a constitutive dimension of political life precisely because "legitimacy is established by relating governmental power to what is conceived to be the ultimate sovereignty in history, to the grain and texture of the movement of historical time."[27] Without some ultimate answers to questions of the ground of human freedom and the grain and texture of historical time, political action is paralyzed and history is rendered meaningless. Human life in historical passage together with the ability to guide that passage, however, "create together the necessity of giving to the sequences of time a *logos,* a structure of order and meaning in terms of which both understanding and purposive action become possible." Because creative political action presupposes a vision of the structure and meaning of the total sequence of historical events, myths or symbolic visions of reality as a whole "appear as basic to all important political speech" and "a general vision of history is presupposed in all historical understanding."[28] Such an ultimate vision invariably encompasses not only the *structure* of historicopolitical life, but also its *norm.* Indeed, structure and norm form an indissoluble unity for Gilkey, because "no political action is possible unless what is regarded as ultimately authentic and good is also regarded as the most real."[29] Gilkey's phenomenology of political life discloses a dimension (or horizon) of ultimacy constitutive to political life, a religious substance as the very ground of cultural formation, myth as the foundation of history making.

The credibility of Gilkey's model needs to be established, not just by the heuristic value of his phenomenology of historical and political experience, but also by the fruit it bears in analysis and interpretation of that experience.[30] This analysis initially attracted me to Gilkey's work.[31] While

---

[26]Gilkey, *RW,* 51, 54.

[27]Gilkey, *RW,* 54.

[28]Gilkey, *SAS,* 60.

[29]Gilkey, *RW,* 67. Gilkey continues with the following comment: "For every moral norm by which we judge the present, and every moral hope by which we bear in anticipation the unknown future, is taken by us to be an aspect of the ultimate grain of history itself, to be ultimately real as well as ultimately good."

[30]See my more detailed exposition of Gilkey's phenomenology of ultimacy: Walsh,

undoubtedly the influences of Tillich and Niebuhr are "so thoroughly intertwined" that it is "impossible to clearly disentangle the strands," it is perhaps not too simplistic to suggest that the theoretical model for Gilkey's theology of culture is Tillichian, while the content of the analysis itself tends to be Niebuhrian.[32]

Rooted in a phenomenology of ultimacy, Gilkey's theology of culture attempts to discern and describe the dimension of ultimacy inherent in the very defining characteristics of modernity. Gilkey's central strategy in *Naming the Whirlwind* was to demonstrate that the actual life of modern secular people discloses a religious dimension, replete with its own secular myths, in total contradiction with the secular self-understanding.

Gilkey's Niebuhrian roots are clearly exposed in his naming and analysis of those myths. In *Faith and History,* Niebuhr argued that a "single article of faith has given diverse forms of modern culture the unity of a shared belief. Modern men of all shades of opinion agreed in the belief that historical development is a redemptive process."[33] Gilkey could not concur with his former teacher more. The "a-religious" and "wholly secular" self-understanding of modernity is a façade. Following Niebuhr, Gilkey argues the following.

> Despite all its positivism and empiricism . . . at the deepest level modernity has been founded on a new philosophy of history, a philosophy built on faith in knowledge and its power to control, on the triumph through knowledge of human purposes over blind fate, and on the confidence that change, if guided by intelligence informed by inquiry, can realize human fulfillment in this life.

Langdon Gilkey, chaps. 6 and 7.

[31]As a personal note, in 1982, Langdon Gilkey presented the annual "Christianity and Scholarship Lectures" at the Institute for Christian Studies (ICS) in Toronto. What intrigued me about those lectures was that he offered a historical and cultural analysis that was, in many ways, remarkably similar to the "Kuyperian" Dutch reformational tradition of thought represented by the ICS; yet, he came to this analysis on the basis of the very different Niebuhrian and Tillichian theological traditions. I chose to do my own doctoral research on Gilkey's theology of culture, both in order to deepen my own historical and cultural analysis and in order to broaden the theological traditions that could be resources for my developing theology of culture.

[32]Gilkey, *RW*, viii.

[33]Reinhold Niebuhr, *Faith and History* (New York: Charles Scribner's Sons, 1949) 1-2.

This is "the implicit religion of the West."[34]

This religion, like the Christianity it rejects, is a historical religion. Modernity, however, replaces the Christian notion of providence with the belief in progress. Providence is no longer necessary if the autonomous human can "provide for himself."[35] Modernity shows its Judeo-Christian heritage in the historical character of its fundamental mythos. The ideal of progress is nothing less than a secularized, autonomous, progressive salvation-history.

Gilkey has described this myth in various ways and in numerous writings. In a characteristic text, he describes the myth of progress, which

> sees history, beginning way back with Egypt and Greece, as a story of cumulative development leading up to modern times temporally, and to Western culture, and especially America, spatially. Here and now, with us, the goal towards which this story has led, and so the goal in which it culminates, is represented by our culture. Thus, in terms of this story, do we know who we are, what we are to do, and what we can count on. This story has been one of cumulative learning and cumulative techniques, leading up to the scientific and technological world we so clearly represent.

This myth is engraved in our grade school textbooks, the lifestyle portrayed in the popular media, and in the attitudes we have toward the so-called "underdeveloped" world. A myth governs our common existence:

> It helps us determine what is creative and what is not in the world, and what our own priorities are or should be. It tells us what to defend and why we defend it. It gives meaning to our work, confidence in the midst of failure, and hope in the face of tragedy or of temporary discouragement. It helps us to distinguish good from evil forces in the world around us, and gives us confidence in the ultimate victory of good over evil in history. Above all, it tells us who we are in history and why we are here. It forms the ultimate set of presuppositions for most of our aims and so our patterns of education.[36]

---

[34]Gilkey, *SAS*, 94-95.

[35]See Bob Goudzwaard, *Capitalism and Progress: A Diagnosis of Western Society* (Grand Rapids: Eerdmans, 1976) chap. 3; and Karl Löwith, *Meaning in History* (Chicago: University of Chicago Press, 1964) chap. 4.

[36]Gilkey, *SAS*, 23-24.

Progress is both the foundation and utopian vision of modernity. But, says Gilkey, the foundation is structurally flawed; the vision is myopic; and the religious substance is in crisis.

The crisis of modernity is multifaceted. It is political, social, economic, and environmental. At heart, however, it is a failure of vision. It is a crisis of the religious substance, the mythos of modernity. A cultural vision rooted in the salvific power of autonomous science and technology promised a progressive future of increased freedom, but delivered a "technological imperative" that subjects us to the fate of an unstoppable expansion of technology beyond "any measure of rational determination or control." This transmutation of progress into fate is immediately apparent in the nuclear arms race, which provided a "transcendental" threat to the very conditions of life on this planet. In such a context, "[n]ormal history has become madness; normality has become pathology."[37]

According to Gilkey, modernity is in decline due to profound contradictions within its own religious substance. The ambiguity of human autonomy is demonstrated in the careers of Enlightenment science and technology and in the transfiguration of human autonomy into its antithesis, fate. The nuclear threat demonstrates both this ambiguity and fatedness. Although a nuclear holocaust would be the ultimate refutation of modernity's faith in progress, however, it remains only a threat. Gilkey identifies the ecological crisis as a present process of disintegration of the fabric of life that demonstrates the ambiguity of science and technology, evidences the decline of modernity, and is, perhaps, more difficult to avert than a nuclear crisis.

Like the nuclear threat, the ecological crisis is something new in history, a unique product of Enlightenment culture. This does not suggest that humans have not previously polluted the environment. Rather, Gilkey's point is that, "for the first time, our freedom in history menaces not only our fellow humans but nature as well," because "now civilization and history have become so dominant in their power that they threaten to engulf nature in their own ambiguity."[38] Human freedom in history has always been ambiguous; but the expansionism entailed in modernity's imperial, autonomous self raises that ambiguity to new and more lethally

---

[37]Gilkey, *RSF*, 93-94; idem, "On Thinking about the Unthinkable," *The University of Chicago Magazine* 76 (Fall 1983): 7.

[38]Gilkey, *SAS*, 99.

dangerous heights. The modernist self may be imperial and expansionist, but the nature which is the arena for that expansion is itself finite and limited. The combination of nature's finitude and the infinity of human greed and concupiscence, as we are now witnessing, has disastrous consequences.[39]

The inherent contradictions of modernity's religious substance, together with the arrogant destructiveness of its guiding myth, have understandably resulted in the loss of Western influence in the world community. A people has cultural power, says Gilkey, when "their symbols grasp others, when their goals and intentions are shared and supported by other wins." That is decreasingly the case with the social ideals of the Enlightenment. Indeed, such ideals as individual rights, political freedom, and democratic processes now appear suspect to a growing segment of the world community, "as ideologies that are covers for special privileges and for selfish materialism—an assessment that is hard to argue with."[40]

In the face of such lost symbolic hegemony, one can discern a shift in the cultural rhetoric of the West from a preoccupation with progress and conquest to an almost neurotic concern with survival. The language becomes concerned with "holding the line" or "defending our kind of world" against aggressors. "The salvation history of progress seems to have disintegrated as *future progress* into a quest for historical survival, for ways of avoiding historical extinction. Implicit here is a quite different vision of history's career."[41] Rather than responding to this loss of Western hegemony by attempting to forge a more creative and humble vision of history we tend toward either a cynical postmortem paralysis or a strident entrenchment of modern imperialist ideals.

Gilkey says that, at the end of modernity, we have become aware of the "imminent deconstruction of the centrality, universality and permanence of the Western consciousness and so of the universal validity of its varied forms."[42] In this new cultural situation, we must acknowledge *both*

[39]Gilkey often suggests that Tillich's notion of concupiscence, as the attempt to "attain and devour unlimited abundance," discloses "the main face of estrangement for a consumerist goods-society, scrambling for money, for place, for possessions" (Gilkey, *GOT*, 129, 130; also see Gilkey, *ME*, 150-53). For Tillich's view of concupiscence, see Paul Tillich, *Systematic Theology*, vol. 2 (Chicago: University of Chicago, 1957) 51-55.
[40]Gilkey, *RW*, 25; idem, *SAS*, 7.
[41]Gilkey, *SAS*, 11.
[42]Langdon Gilkey, "Events, Meanings, and the Current Tasks of Theology," *Journal*

the relativity of Western consciousness as representing only one limited, finite and partial perspective on the whole of life *and* that other religious traditions embody genuine alternatives to our consciousness, which clearly manifest a truth, grace, and spiritual power that is not found in either secular modernity or Christianity. For Gilkey, the demise of the superiority of the Western worldview and the unavoidable acceptance of the essential equality or "parity" of the religions are parallel phenomena.[43] In a context where there is no universal standpoint, each particular standpoint must reinterpret itself in the light of pluralism. For a culture that has enjoyed political, economic, and cultural dominance in the world, this situation necessarily entails the end of that epoch of superiority and domination and ushers in a new, and often frightening, cultural reality. This leads us to the second, more constructive, focus of Gilkey's theology of culture. At the end of modernity, in a context fraught with danger and anxiety and chastened by the pluralist reality of a postmortem parity of religions, what is the nature of Gilkey's theological proposals? What is his credible myth that will not lie to us about ourselves? Furthermore, is this a theology that animates a renewed imagination in the face of late modernity's dehydration?

II. Theology for a Culture in Decline

The declining culture of modernity needs a new myth, a new religious vision, because our cultural malaise is ultimately religious in character. Therefore, not surprisingly, Gilkey boldly argues that, from religion alone, we can find the norms to "prevent manipulation of people and dehumanization of society." From religion alone "can come the vision or conception of the human that can creatively guide social policy," and "from religion alone can come a new understanding of the unity of nature, history and humankind" that can creatively respond to the ecological crisis.[44]

Which religious vision, however, should replace the declining religious substance of modernity? Which kind of faith is the most creative? What criteria are applicable to choosing from among the plethora of reli-

---

of the American Academy of Religion 53 (December 1985): 726-27.

[43]See Gilkey, *TT*, chap. 9; idem, *GOT*, chap. 10; idem, "Theology for a Time of Troubles"; and idem, "The AAR and the Anxiety of Nonbeing," *Journal of the American Academy of Religion* 48 (March 1980): 5-18, esp. 14-15.

[44]Gilkey, *SAS*, 102-103.

gious options available? Gilkey suggests three requirements that must be met if a faith is to be creative in the present cultural crisis. The first criterion is breadth. In a declining culture, a creative faith "must be able to comprehend, shape and deal with all of those basic religious issues and their corresponding religious dilemmas which a scientific culture produces."[45] Faith must provide creative answers to social questions of power and justice, metaphysical questions of the meaning of history and nature, and existential questions of estrangement and mortality. The greater the breadth of the religious vision, the more adequate it is.

The second requirement or criterion Gilkey borrows from Tillich's distinction between autonomy, theonomy, and heteronomy. Gilkey says that "a creative faith must undergird and not constrict, repress or oppress our autonomous intellect, our autonomous decisions, our own artistic creativity and our legal/political structures and actions: it must be *theonomous* and not *heteronomous*."[46] A purely autonomous culture divorces itself from its divine ground, is unaware of its religious substance, and therefore loses touch with that which Tillich described as the "Catholic substance." A heteronomous culture, however, allows its religious substance to become absolute and, therefore, has no ability for self-critique—it has lost the "Protestant principle." The goal is to strive for a theonomous culture, which is "at once autonomously creative and yet dependent upon, and so affirmative of, its unconditional ground, its religious substance."[47] Only a theonomous religious vision will be a creative one.

The third criterion goes significantly beyond the first two criteria and raises a characteristically religious issue, though not raised in my earlier discussion about the role of a religious substance in culture. A creative faith must not only have breadth and be theonomous; it must also communicate the truth about our own ambiguity and evil, and address that ambiguity redemptively. While such a faith must be able to criticize even our highest cultural achievements, recognizing their demonic potentialities, it must also "offer a grace that can transmute these demonic potentialities into actions genuinely creative of higher community." A credible myth that will tell us the truth about ourselves can be creative

---

[45]Gilkey, *SAS*, 118.

[46]Gilkey, *SAS*, 119. Also see Tillich, *Systematic Theology* 1:83-94; idem, *The Protestant Era*, trans. James Luther Adams (Chicago: University of Chicago Press, 1948; abridged ed., 1957) chaps. 3, 4, and 9; and Gilkey, *GOT*, chap. 3.

[47]Gilkey, *GOT*, 143.

only if it can lead us to reconciliation beyond and through the truth of our estrangement. We need a myth that includes forgiveness.[48]

What kind of theology can meet these kind of criteria? Only a dialectical one. The criterion of breadth requires a dialectical interaction of message and existence, the symbols of the Christian *Weltanschauung* and the present *Lebenswelt*.[49] Fostering theonomous cultural forms and practices requires a dialectical relation between human autonomy and divine sovereignty. Even more importantly, however, if we are to tell the truth about the inherent ambiguity of our own cultural forms and provide hope for a redemption and renewal beyond our cultural brokenness, then we will need a theology of culture that can account mythically for the dialectic process by which cultures believe in their own authenticity and even divine constitution and yet share crushing experiences of estrangement, guilt and judgment. This would appear to be the condition of the culture of betrayal experienced at the end of modernity.

According to Gilkey, this pattern of ultimate constitution and eventual judgment is common to all cultural history. If cultural historians and analysts do not account for this dialectic, then "they either emphasize the positive structure and harmony of passage and the possibilities of historical life . . . in an unwarranted and soon-to-be falsified optimism, or, concentrating so heavily on the actuality of evil, they speak only of fatedness, failing to discern new possibilities and forces of reconciliation latent in historical experience."[50] The way beyond the starkness of this either/or is to affirm both options by recognizing a third stage or moment in cultural history, namely, the experience of a promised renewal. All movements of revolution and reform imply such an experience of promise. For a culture to be sustained in history, it must always be in a

---

[48]Gilkey, *SAS*, 119. Gilkey says, "In every epoch of our history, then, we need to discover not only moral standards by which we may judge ourselves and the social world we live in, but also forgiveness somewhere for what we and our world are, an assurance of the ability to accept ourselves and our world, even in the ambiguity that we know to characterize them when we are aware of the truth. For only thus are we enabled to go on with our worldly work for a better and juster world than we now have" (Gilkey, *RSF*, 97).

[49]"In this interaction the symbols give that world of experience ultimate coherence, order, illumination, and healing—in turn, experience in its contemporary form provides the symbols with relevance, reality, and validity" (Langdon Gilkey, *Catholicism Confronts Modernity: A Protestant View* [New York: Seabury Press, 1975] 114); hereafter cited as *CCM*.

[50]Gilkey, *SAS*, 64-65. One might discern in these two options the contrast between a "Great Books" tradition in education and its postmodern, deconstructive nemesis.

dialectical tension of divine or ultimate constitution, prophetic deconstruction of that constitution—thus exposing the estrangement that permeates all cultural life—and prophetic hope of a pathway beyond estrangement, beyond deconstruction.[51]

One of Gilkey's most radical theological claims is that this dialectic, common in all cultural history, is also the underlying structure of Christian faith. The structure of the gospel manifests "a dialectic of affirmation, of negation, and then a higher reaffirmation that, in overcoming the negative, also transmutes the original positive." For example, the Christ manifests God but in weakness, a manifestation that his passion negates. Only by moving from affirmation ("This is my beloved Son with whom I am well pleased") through negation ("My God, my God, why have you forsaken me?") does the Christ receive reaffirmation in the resurrection: "The originating affirmation is true, but, taken undialectically, it is false; the negative represented by estrangement is also true, but taken undialectically it too is false." Therefore, Gilkey argues that "this dialectic persists . . . as the fundamental formal structure of Christian symbolism, what it is that is *unique* to the Christian understanding of reality and of existence."[52]

This dialectic of affirmation, negation, and reaffirmation is rooted in the overall pattern of creation, fall, and redemption that encapsulates the biblical worldview.[53] Our most primordial reality and our most foundational myth is that of a creation unambiguously affirmed as good. This affirmation, however, is compromised by the negation of the fall. If our essentially good nature as creatures functions as the thesis in this dialectic, then the antithesis is the estrangement of human creatures and the despoliation of creation. Therefore, a new moment is necessary, if the goodness of creation is to be reaffirmed and estrangement overcome—this is the moment of redemption.[54]

---

[51]Gilkey, *SAS*, 47, 67-71; idem, *RW*, 262-66

[52]Gilkey, *ME*, 182, 183.

[53]Richard Middleton and I have discussed the relation of creation, fall, and redemption at greater length: Brian J. Walsh and Richard Middleton, *The Transforming Vision: Shaping a Christian Worldview* (Downers Grove IL: InterVarsity Press, 1984).

[54]See Gilkey, *TT*, 218-31. Clearly, Gilkey's understanding of dialectic is stamped by both Tillichian and Niebuhrian influences: Gilkey, *GOT*, chap. 4; idem, "Reinhold Niebuhr's Theology of History," *Journal of Religion* 54 (October 1974): 364.

In light of the criteria that Gilkey establishes for creative religion and the way in which Christianity understood dialectically meets these criteria, not surprisingly Gilkey has the courage (audacity?) to proclaim that "only a theological understanding of history, structured in the categories of Christian faith, is . . . adequate to the interpretation of the ambiguity that is history as we experience it." Indeed, he claims that the Christian interpretation of history is a myth that is validated "as the most coherent and adequate mode of interpreting our common experience of historical passage."[55] *How* does this interpretation of history and its concomitant theology of culture offer resources for freedom in the midst of historical fatedness and alluring hope in the face of cultural despair?

Despair, whether experienced personally, politically, or culturally, is always a consequence of fate. In the face of mounting crises and a loss of personal or historical confidence, despair is the only response available if there is no way out, no way forward, no personal, political, emotional, or historical room for fresh agency or new options. Fatedness, however, like the sin that gives birth to it, is always a distortion of the fundamental ontological structure of human life in historical passage. A central feature of Gilkey's philosophy of history and a pervasive theme in his thought is the phenomenological conviction that "the fundamental ontological structure for groups and so for historical passage is the polarity of destiny and freedom, the inherited 'given' from the past on the one hand, and the present human response in the light of possibilities for the future on the other."[56] Whereas destiny refers to the actuality of our present "given" historical condition, freedom uncovers new possibilities inherent in that actuality. Freedom captures the essence of human intentionality. Therefore, "the new in historical action arises out of the union of destiny

---

[55]Gilkey, *RW*, 294, 153. Such claims for the superiority of Christian faith are not rare occurrences in Gilkey's corpus. For example, consult the following texts: Gilkey *SAS*, 39-40; idem, *CCM*, 11, 93, 136, 163; idem, *ME*, 47, 247, 250; and idem, *Maker of Heaven and Earth: A Study of the Christian Doctrine of Creation* (New York: Doubleday, 1959) 17, 181, 287. That such statements of the superiority of Christian symbols to thematize the world are in some tension with other more pluralistic dimensions of Gilkey's thought there can be no doubt. It is not in the purview of this chapter, however, to address this question, although I address this question at some length elsewhere: Walsh, *Langdon Gilkey*, 158-67.

[56]Gilkey, *RW*, 43. Gilkey also says that, although the given conditions of actuality (destiny) are the *necessary* conditions for any event to occur, they are not the *sufficient conditions*. For this, we need to attend to the radical contingency of all historical events. That contingency is rooted in the freedom of historical response (Gilkey, *RW*, 96).

with freedom, of given actuality with relevant possibility." Destiny "sets the stage for our response, and is thus the ground and limit of our freedom."[57]

Estranged freedom, however, transmutes historical destiny into fate. Under the conditions of fate, "we experience the given and the ongoing changes it represents as overwhelming and oppressive, as destructive of our powers and so of our freedom."[58] The "time of troubles" known as late modernity or postmodernity is a destiny, a historical given, to which we must respond. This time of troubles, nonetheless, seems to be suffused with a sense of fate. Recall Leonard Cohen's line: "the blizzard of the world has crossed the threshold." Also, in "tales of a scorched earth," The Smashing Pumpkins lament that, in a world in which "the dye is cast," history is experienced as "the same old things keep on happening." The result is a pervasive cultural numbness ("beyond my hopes there are no feelings"), historical paralysis ("so fuck it all cause i don't care"), and a resigned loss of historical confidence ("so what somehow somewhere we dared / to try to dare to dare for a little more").

Gilkey's understanding of the ontological structure of destiny and freedom provides some intellectual foundation to assert that "no determined future is the truth."[59] In a historical context in which we face the future as an oppressive weight because of the seemingly unstoppable processes of ecological destruction, nuclear threat, economic globalization, genetic engineering, and an unquestionable technological imperative, however, it becomes necessary to move beyond an ontological *structure* to an ontological *horizon of ultimacy*.[60] Beyond the ambiguity of human freedom, an open future requires the possibility of promise. If the shattered promise of the progress-myth has devolved into fate, then we need a new, credible myth that reopens history. Gilkey claims that, "such faith in a nonfated future, in the continuity of open possibility, and in the divine completion of our every abortive creation is now more necessary

---

[57]Gilkey, *RW*, 44.

[58]Gilkey, *RW*, 49.

[59]Gilkey, *RW*, 90. Gilkey's debate with Heilbroner best illustrates the implications of the freedom/destiny polarity for his cultural analysis: see Gilkey, *RW*, 79-90; idem, "Robert Heilbroner's Vision of History"; and idem, "Robert Heilbroner's Morality Play," *Worldview* 17 (August 1974): 51-55.

[60]Gilkey, *RW*, 119.

than ever."[61] This is the immediate cultural context for Gilkey's reinterpretation of providence.[62]

Free self-actualization in history depends upon a future that is open, characterized by real possibility. Gilkey argues, however, that "possibility, which can be effective only in relation to actuality, must be in relation to an actuality of transcendent scope, an actuality that is capable of holding within its power of envisionment the entire and so open realm of possibility."[63] This transcendent actuality, says Gilkey, is the ontological ground for novelty, openness, and future possibility. A primordial actuality can envision all possibility as possible. Gilkey refers to this transcendent and primordial actuality as the envisioning providence of God. In a fated present, with a dehydrated imagination and a constricted freedom, more than ever, we need a transcendent ground of possibility—a sovereignty that delegitimates the status quo that requires things to remain the same. If we are to escape the fatedness of the same old things happening over and over again, if we are to engage in history as free agents, there must be a sovereignty that envisions newness.[64]

The Smashing Pumpkins, in describing their own paralysis and numbness, sing "beyond my hopes there are no feelings" and later, "beyond my hopes there are no reasons."[65] Historical agency requires passion and moral direction. Historical fatedness strips both passion and moral direction from us. A transformed and renewed imagination is, therefore, a historical necessity if we are to experience history as open and our lives as agents.[66] Such an imagination, nonetheless, understands that human historical agency and moral direction are intimately related. Historical agency is free; we saw previously that such freedom is necessarily related

---

[61]Gilkey, "Robert Heilbroner's Vision of History," 232.

[62]My discussion will be brief. Kyle A. Pasewark addresses Gilkey's doctrine of providence in some depth later in this volume. Specifically, because I am concerned with the late modern experience of fatedness in history, my exposition will only address that which Gilkey calls "envisioning providence," leaving to Pasewark Gilkey's understanding of preserving and concurring providence.

[63]Gilkey, *RW*, 305.

[64]This appropriation of Gilkey's understanding of envisioning providence is significantly different, and more appreciative, than my previous critique of his view (Walsh, *Langdon Gilkey*, 257). I recant. Gilkey is right. We do need God as a primordial actuality to envision possibility as possibility!

[65]From "tales of a scorched earth."

[66]Walter Brueggemann calls this a "prophetic imagination" (Walter Brueggemann, *The Prophetic Imagination* [Philadelphia: Fortress Press, 1978]).

to ultimacy as the source of the norms that guide its actualization. Novel possibilities must be ordered in terms of graded options that are more or less relevant to present actualities and desired future actualities. Gilkey wisely notes that "possibility enters history with a moral tone, as a claim on our integrity and responsibility." The source of this claim on us and the ground of this morality is the envisioning providence of God. "One of the creative roles of God . . . is that he gives to each occasion, and so to each person and community, an ordered vision of possibility, a leap beyond the present actuality yet one in relation to it. Thus is our creativity possible."[67] Through participation in this envisionment, we apprehend the possibilities that are relevant to our situation and freely actualize (or fail to actualize) these possibilities. Thus, envisioning providence is both the ground of possibility and that which guides self-actualization.

Envisioning providence anticipates, then, its own eschatological fulfillment: "As providence is the historical presupposition for eschatology, so is eschatology the defining and controlling symbol for providence."[68] To have hope not only beyond our present fatedness, but also beyond the very ambiguity of human agency in history, requires a vision centered on a referent transcendent to history. This is the ultimate content of envisioning providence. The Christian name of this transcendent hope is "the kingdom of God." In the ministry of Jesus, Gilkey argues, the kingdom is revealed as the *logos* of history that functions as both the lure and norm of that history. In providing the norm for social relations, the kingdom "both challenges the warped relations of the present and 'lures' our social, that is, our political action into a more creative future."[69]

The lure of this eschatological kingdom is the foundation of Christian praxis because it "reveals the alienation and so the injustice of the present," and "opens the present to new possibilities in contrast with what is." Because sin is estranged freedom, the kingdom of God is a metaphor of restored freedom and, therefore, also a metaphor of the redemption of historical destiny over against fate. In a context of numbed historical fatedness in which we have no "reasons" or "feelings," this affirmation that "the kingdom is the divine goal toward which the future points . . . grounds the eros of all political action and political hope in what is taken to be the most real in history." In addition, while language of the "most

---

[67]Gilkey, *RW*, 252.
[68]Gilkey, *RW*, 287.
[69]Gilkey, *ME*, 233.

real in history" can be (and usually is!) a self-justifying ideological cover for systems of totality that legitimate oppression and marginalization, Gilkey prophetically notes that "eschatology provides the only continuing ground for radical criticism," because "the kingdom transcends those who seek to bring it in." Eschatologies that legitimate clear us/them polemics and engender a praxis of the oppressed outsider and the self-justification of the insiders clearly distort the kingdom of God that Christian theology envisions.[70]

Conclusion: Gilkey and Postmodernity

In a historical context of crisis, any theology of culture is at least partially judged by its ability to illumine critically the religious roots of the cultural malaise. Gilkey agrees with Karl Marx that the critique of religion is the beginning of all critique, because "no social order can be challenged and refashioned unless its religious substance, the sacrality of its institutions, symbols and myths, is itself first challenged."[71] Only such a critique is radical enough to address adequately our civilization's crisis. One of Gilkey's enduring contributions to theology at the end of the twentieth century has been to provide such a religious analysis of our plight with prophetic insight and historical wisdom. The illuminating power of the analysis demonstrates the validity of his theoretical model for a theology of culture.

Gilkey is a theologian for a culture in decline. In this sense, he is also a "postmodern" theologian who recognizes the literal bankruptcy of the modernist project. Yet, Gilkey's postmodernity takes some interesting turns that merit some consideration. If postmodernity is a cultural context characterized by a loss of center, the collapse of all grand narratives, and the deconstruction of all totalizing claims of universal applicability, then Gilkey's is a theology that discerns cultural meaning and normativity in terms of a religious center at the heart of social forms and necessarily

---

[70]Gilkey, *RW*, 294-95. For a brilliant discussion of the nonideological ethic of the kingdom in the face of postmodern tribalism, see Miroslav Volf, *Exclusion and Embrace: A Theological Exploration of Identity, Otherness, and Reconciliation* (Nashville: Abingdon Press, 1996).

[71]Gilkey, *SAS*, 20. See Karl Marx and Friedrich Engels, *On Religion* (New York: Schocken Books, 1971) 41. Frederick Sontag and John K. Roth demonstrate the relevance of Marx's dictum for theological analysis of American culture: Frederick Sontag and John K. Roth, "The Premise of Criticism," *Andover Newton Quarterly* 17 (January 1977): 195-200.

articulated in terms of global myths and overarching symbol systems. Metanarratives and symbol systems that aspire to comprehensive universality may well be fundamentally ambiguous and in need of radical deconstruction when they take idolatrous forms; but they are also anthropologically constitutive of social life. Postmodern suspicions notwithstanding, Gilkey's theology of culture reminds us that humans constitutionally need metanarratives and universal perspectives that allow them to understand their place in the world and give them guidance for living in the world. Indeed, without a coherent metanarrative, we are left morally adrift, at the mercy of random violence and brutality.[72] The issue at the end of modernity is the demise of one particular worldview or mythic vision of life—the Western myth of progress. This catastrophe is not adequately addressed simply by deconstructing mythic visions per se, but by seeing the inherent ambiguities and fatal flaws of *this* worldview and proposing a creative and credible myth in its place.

The content of Gilkey's credible myth is richly multifaceted and is the subject of a number of other chapters in this book. In the context of Gilkey's theology of culture in decline, I have attended only to the transcendent sovereignty in history that he discloses as necessary for history to remain open. Sovereignty, however, is also a concept that is open to postmodern deconstruction. Sovereignty implies rule, lordship, kingdom. Michel Foucault has argued, however, that all aspirations to sovereignty are sociohistorical power moves characteristic of all "regimes of truth."

> Truth is a thing of this world: it is produced only by virtue of multiple forms of constraint. And it induces regular effects of power. Each society has its regime of truth, its "general politics" of truth: that is, the types of discourse which it accepts and makes function as true; the mechanism and instances which enable one to distinguish true and false statements, the means by which each is sanctioned; the techniques and procedures accorded value in the acquisition of truth; the status of those who are charged with saying what counts as true.[73]

---

[72]J. Richard Middleton and I have argued this point at greater length: J. Richard Middleton and Brian J. Walsh, *Truth Is Stranger Than It Used to Be: Biblical Faith in a Postmodern Age* (Downers Grove IL.: InterVarsity Press, 1995) esp. chap. 4.

[73]Michel Foucault, *Power/Knowledge: Selected Interviews and Other Writings, 1972–1977*, ed. Colin Gordon, trans. Colin Gordon, Leo Marshall, John Mepham, and Kate Soper (New York: Pantheon Books, 1980) 131.

Gilkey's theology of culture could be seen as both affirming and radically opposing Foucault's observation. Truth is, indeed, a thing of this world and there are undoubtedly regimes of truth that employ multiple forms of constraint. The hegemony of the secularism of Western culture with its myth of autonomous progress is such a regime; Gilkey has devoted a good part of his professional career to deconstructing precisely that mythic-symbolic framework because it lies to us about ourselves and legitimates cultural, political, economic, ecological, and personal violence and meaninglessness.

Nonetheless, Gilkey believes that human beings cannot live without truth or sovereignty. Undoubtedly, truth is no longer the possession of any particular group or tradition in a pluralist world. Nor is truth established by various forms of constraint—even the constraint of rational argumentation. Fully aware of the epistemological circle, Gilkey acknowledges that there is no independent set of universally acknowledged criteria for establishing the truth of any claim. Rather, the affirmation of truth requires "a religious mode of relating to the truth."[74] To know the truth of a religious symbol is to participate in it: "Religious symbols function as religious symbols and so are known to be true by those to whom they communicate a religious meaning, i.e., an awareness of the ultimate ground to life's passage and an ultimate answer to life's crises."[75] But there is the rub! *Can* there be ultimate answers to life's crises? Or is any talk about an ultimate ground, even a sovereignty transcendent to history, merely an ideological nostalgia for a now lost totality?

Foucault is right about regimes of truth and their hegemonic violence. Gilkey asks, however, what are our resources for opposing such regimes? Here the question of truth will not go away. In order "to combat what one takes to be a virulent false truth, some approximation to and possession of a healthier truth . . . is necessary as a basis for disengagement, for protest, and for dissident political action." Without some such approximation of a "healthier truth," we are left with the powerlessness and paralysis of postmodern undecidability. Therefore, "a transcendent point of criticism, of judgment and certainty, of hope of renewal is necessary in political action and in political theorizing as well as in

---

[74]Gilkey, *RW*, 147.
[75]Gilkey, *NW*, 464.

theological reflection on events, whenever idolatry is abroad in the land."[76] Creative praxis, in response to an oppressively idolatrous ideology, requires an alternative sovereignty in history, thematized in the form of a centered vision.

Here Gilkey takes his stand. Faced with either postmodern anomie or the heteronomy of a regime of truth we must act. That action, however, requires a center which one wagers will be healthier and more liberating for human culture. By wagering, we take a stand somewhere that provides us with "a ground for the apprehension and understanding of reality," "criteria for judgments," and " priorities in value."[77] But how will such a stand avoid the absolutism of heteronomy, while also being centered enough to animate a praxis in the face of undecidability? Only by standing at the cross. Here is a particularity, a center, that deconstructs all regimes of truth by inviting us into a kingdom of love. Indebted to Tillich, Gilkey says that "self-negating and continually self-negating particularism, if religious, if related to ultimacy . . . is, therefore, the only human path or way to universality."[78] Here is a sovereignty ruling from a cross. Only such a sovereignty can open up history, engender renewed imagination, provide orientation in the midst of the blizzard of the world, and animate our life with a promise of resurrection, even for this scorched earth.

---

[76]Gilkey, "Events, Meanings, and the Current Tasks of Theology," 722.

[77]Gilkey, "Events, Meanings, and the Current Tasks of Theology," 728-29. Gilkey borrows the notion of a wager, of course, from Paul Ricoeur, *The Symbolism of Evil*, trans. Emerson Buchanan (Boston: Beacon, 1967) esp. 308, 355. This stand, or wager, is the "absolute" in Gilkey's formulation of a relative absolute. For further discussion of this dialectic, see Mary Ann Stenger's chapter in this book.

[78]Langdon Gilkey, "Tillich: Master of Mediation," in *The Theology of Paul Tillich*, 2nd ed. Charles Kegley (New York: Pilgrim Press, 1982) 55-56.

Chapter 6

Sovereigns Past and Present:
The Sciences and the Religious
in the Theology of Langdon Gilkey[1]

Donald W. Musser

The major philosophical and theological task of our time is represented by this question: How are the many diverse ways of thinking in a culture—its technical and scientific thought, its social and political thinking, its artistic and moral experience and reflection, and its deepest or religious convictions—to find *unity*, that is, together to achieve coherence, mutual credibility, and effectiveness?[2]

Introduction

To assume that science and theology have much, if anything, in common runs counter to a dominant strain in Western theology and science, and in popular culture where the so-called "creationist-evolution controversy" continues unabated. A common view of these two spheres of intellectual pursuit does not consider them likely candidates for pleasant or fruitful intellectual interchange. Their fields of interest are as different as heaven and earth, and their methods of inquiry are unrelated: science utilizing disciplined reason; theology relying on faith in revelation. The sounds from several centuries of combat between scientists and theologians have settled in academe, and one can describe the situation generally as an "uneasy truce between science and theology."

Chief among the proponents of a gaping chasm between the "two cultures" are neoorthodox theologies and analytical philosophies.[3]

---

[1]I want to thank D. Dixon Sutherland and D. Gregory Sapp, my colleagues in the Department of Religious Studies at Stetson University, for their criticisms and suggestions on this chapter.

[2]Langdon Gilkey, *Creationism on Trial: Evolution and God at Little Rock* (Minneapolis: Winston Press, 1985) 207-208; hereafter cited as *CT*.

[3]C. P. Snow popularized this notion of a gaping chasm between the "two cultures," when he wrote of "a gulf of mutual incomprehension" between literary scholars and scientists: see C. P. Snow, *The Two Cultures and the Scientific Revolution* (New York: Cambridge University Press, 1959). See Langdon Gilkey, "Neoorthodoxy," in *A New Handbook of Christian Theology*, ed. Donald W. Musser and Joseph L. Price (Nashville:

Neoorthodox theologian, Karl Barth, for example, represents a widely held position, which denies that the languages of theology and science have anything in common. For Barth, theology proclaims a Word of God that comes from "a strange new world." This Word is unrelated to human words, including those of science.[4] Therefore, science and theology for Barth have no point of contact, because they refer to such entirely different things that they can neither support each other nor conflict with each other. Analytical philosopher, Ludwig Wittgenstein, from a quite different and nontheological perspective, represents an important position that militates against any conversation between science and religion. He argues that religion and science are autonomous language games. Because they speak different languages and play by different rules, they have no ground for a cognitive relationship.[5] An alternative to the neoorthodox theologies and analytical philosophies, which claim that science and theology have nothing to discuss with one another, is the view that science and religion are related in important and significant ways, that they indeed can be brought into conversation, and that it is crucial for both the church and the wider culture that they talk. The representatives of this alternative perspective often consider the development of natural science as a vitally important new factor in Western culture. They also believe that creative religious activity is vital and indispensable for society. Langdon Gilkey is an important proponent of this dialogue.[6]

Abingdon Press, 1992) 334-37. On analytical philosophy, see Jerry H. Gill, "Language—Religious" in *New Handbook of Christian Theology*, 279-82. An excellent study of the "separatist" position is William L. Austin, *The Relevance of Natural Science to Theology* (New York: Barnes and Noble, 1976).

[4]See Karl Barth, *The Word of God and the Word of Man*, trans. Douglas Horton (New York: Harper & Row, 1956; repr.: Gloucester: Peter Smith, 1978) 33, 37, 40, 45. These references come from his essay entitled "The Strange New World within the Bible," which forms his book's second chapter. He originally delivered this chapter as an address in the church at Lentwil in 1916.

[5]Anders Nygren finely represents a neoorthodox theologian who utilizes Wittgenstein's philosophy: see Anders Nygren, *Meaning and Method: Prolegomenon to a Scientific Philosophy of Religion and Scientific Theology*, trans. Philip S. Watson (Philadelphia: Fortress Press, 1972). Others who wall off theology and science as separate realms include Hans Frei, George Lindbeck, Rudolf Bultmann, and an earlier generation influenced by Søren Kierkegaard.

[6]Among the host who bring science and theology into creative dialogue, although in a variety of ways, and in some cases ways that contradict one another, are Philip Hefner, Robert John Russell, Arthur Peacocke, John Polkinghorne, Ralph Wendell Burhoe, Stanley

I. The Two Tasks of Theology

Entrance into the complex world of Langdon Gilkey's view of the relation of science to religion can be facilitated by a brief statement of his overall intellectual horizon. Gilkey approaches the topic from the perspective of a Christian theologian. Because the meaning of "Christian theologian" is not entirely obvious in an era of competing theological methods,[7] we need to observe his understanding of the role of a theologian, particularly since his engagement with science has been specifically from his stance as a theologian.[8]

For Gilkey, a theologian has two primary roles: (1) an ecclesial role as a systematic theologian; and (2) a public role as a theologian of culture or public theologian.[9] The systematic theologian seeks to interpret the message of a religious community for the contemporary situation. A constructive theology re-presents the classic religious symbols for today. "Its job is, therefore, to reflect on the Christian message in relation to the human situation, personal and social, and in the light of the present cultural situation."[10] Theology of culture proceeds from the assertion, firmly established for Gilkey by Tillich, that "every aspect of culture has its ground in the culture's religious substance."[11] His root assumption is

---

Jaki, John Haught, Eric Rust, Teilhard de Chardin, Holmes Rolston III, and Ian Barbour.

[7] For the major varieties of theological methods, see Werner G. Jeanrond, "Theological Method," in *New Handbook of Christian Theology*, 480-86.

[8] For several windows of entry into the place of science in Gilkey's view of theology, see especially the following: Langdon Gilkey, *Religion and the Scientific Future: Reflections on Myth, Science, and Theology* (New York: Harper & Row, 1970; repr.: ROSE 2, Macon GA: Mercer University Press, 1981) (hereafter cited as *RSF*); idem, *Society and the Sacred: Toward a Theology of Culture in Decline* (New York: Crossroad, 1981) 73-120 (hereafter cited as *SAS*); idem, *CT*; and idem, *Nature, Reality, and the Sacred: The Nexus of Science and Religion* (Minneapolis: Fortress, 1993); hereafter, cited as *NRS*.

[9] See John Macquarrie, "Systematic Theology" in *New Handbook of Christian Theology*, 469-74. Langdon Gilkey, "The Role of the Theologian in Contemporary Society," in *The Thought of Paul Tillich*, ed. James L. Adams, Wilhelm Pauck, and Roger Shinn (New York: Harper & Row, 1985) 331-50; rev. ed. in *Gilkey on Tillich* (New York: Crossroad, 1990) 177-96. This important article delineates the Tillichean framework for Gilkey's analysis and assessment of science in contemporary culture.

[10] Langdon Gilkey, *Through the Tempest: Theological Voyages in a Pluralistic Culture*, ed. Jeff B. Pool (Minneapolis: Fortress Press, 1991) 38; hereafter cited as *TT*.

[11] Gilkey, "Role of the Theologian in Contemporary Society," 333.

that God, the supreme object of religion, is the ground of all that is finite. Therefore, everything in existence related to the divine has a religious ground or depth, as Tillich put it. Because all cultural forms ultimately have a religious ground since they are rooted in Being and therefore in God, the public theologian can penetrate the questions asked and the answers propounded by the art, philosophy, politics, science, technology, and law of a particular culture. This would include, of course, a culture's science, technology, and modes of reasoning. The public theologian analyzes these essential cultural assumptions and assesses their actual status within a culture.[12]

In both theological roles, as both an ecclesial theologian and a public theologian, the theological thinker critically interprets the church's traditions *and* the culture's foundational assumptions. Traditional meanings assigned to the church's symbols are rethought "in the light of the present cultural situation."[13] Contemporary assumptions of modern culture with regard to science, often unreflective and confused assertions, are critically tested. In both roles, the theologian is never purely an apologist, for example, only defending religious symbols against scientific assertions or merely interpreting religious symbols purely by the criteria of a culture. The theologian, rather, operates critically and dialectically at the intersections of religion and science. Theology, thus, has a polar character.

> On the one hand, it must express the original and central message of the faith and thus point us beyond our immediacy in our cultural present to God's presence in the event of Jesus Christ and subsequently in the means of grace related to that event. On the other hand, it must bring that message to us, to our understanding and our modes of thinking and thus express that message in a form intelligible, credible, and relevant to us—that is, in the form of modern concepts, categories, standards, and aims.[14]

Gilkey has produced significant works that have engaged theological and scientific themes. *Maker of Heaven and Earth* (1959) inquires about what "creation" has meant traditionally and essentially to Christian faith. *Naming the Whirlwind* (1969) investigates the meaning of "God" in a culture dominated by reductionistic philosophies heavily indebted to science. *Reaping the Whirlwind* (1977) brings "providence" and

---

[12]Gilkey, "Role of the Theologian in Contemporary Society," 334-42.
[13]Gilkey, *TT*, 38.
[14]Gilkey, *TT*, 42.

"eschatology" under scrutiny with particular attention to that which one can say theologically about God's activity in an advanced scientific culture. *Creationism on Trial* (1985) revealed the stresses that "scientific creationism" posed for a democratic society dominated by science. *Religion and the Scientific Future* (1970) examines the enormous impact of science on theology's form and content. His most recent work, *Nature, Reality, and the Sacred* (1993), provides a mature statement of the various themes that he has delineated over three decades with particular attention to a theology of nature.[15]

Both as a systematic theologian and as a theologian of culture, then, Gilkey has addressed science's enormous impact on modern culture and on the church's understanding of its symbols and, as well, provided a critique of science's quasi-religious status. To that critique we now turn.

II. Public Theology:
Analysis of an Advanced Scientific Culture

Gilkey believes that for at least three centuries natural science has been a two-pronged cultural force. *Theoretically*, science has provided the culture's model for knowing—its epistemology. Indeed, for many, science is the *only* cognitive method. *Practically*, the application of scientific knowledge to nature has resulted in massive technological and industrial development. Gilkey playfully but seriously has pointed out that the airplane, automobile, and air conditioner, have reshaped modern life.[16]

One consistent motif in Gilkey's theology is his theological analysis of our "advanced scientific and technological culture."[17] By "advanced," he refers to the fact that science and technology are "thoroughly established" in our common life. In many ways, they define culture. By

---

[15]Langdon Gilkey, *Maker of Heaven and Earth: The Christian Doctrine of Creation in the Light of Modern Knowledge* (Garden City NY: Doubleday, 1959; repr.: Lanham MD: University Press of America, 1985); idem, *Naming the Whirlwind: The Renewal of God-Language* (Indianapolis: Bobbs-Merrill, 1969); idem, *Reaping the Whirlwind: A Christian Interpretation of History* (New York: Seabury, 1976); idem, *CT*; idem, *RSF*; idem, *NRS*.

[16]He expounded on this frequent theme on a sultry summer day when I flew into Chicago, with colleague Joe Price rented a Buick Park Avenue, picked up Gilkey at his home, and drove him in air-conditioned comfort around the South end of Lake Michigan to the centenary Tillich Conference at Hope College in Michigan.

[17]Gilkey, *CT*, 162.

"established," he means that science rules our cultural institutions, wields massive power over our budgets, dominates as sovereign in academia, and permeates all aspects of society.[18] It "has become the utterly necessary theoretical basis for every essential aspect of our common social life."[19]

The thorough establishment of science and technology in culture has brought to science a "religious aura" or "sacred status." Scientists, physicians, and engineers have become the new priests because they possess "sacred" knowledge to predict and determine the future, to heal deadly diseases, and to build a culture of comfort and convenience. Science has effectively become the "religious" substance of culture for those who acknowledge its power. By "religious," Gilkey refers to what is taken to be the ground and source of truth and value. Science provides this ultimate foundation for us—financially, intellectually, and spiritually.[20]

Science has become the way we know: it provides our epistemology (how we know). It also determines what is real by the extent of the powers of its inquiry: it provides our ontology (what we consider to be real). Gilkey concludes that science as revelatory "represents the *only* form of knowledge, the only reliable clue we possess to what is real."[21]

The enthronement of science in our culture has brought all the benefits of royalty to the scientific establishment—prestige, power, and money. During the reign of science, ignorance has dissipated, the mysteries of nature have been revealed, and disease has received a deadly blow. The culture has embraced the new sovereign with ebullient excitement—new ideas, new possibilities for life, and a new future. This new power has made possible control of hitherto chaotic and uncontrollable natural forces. No longer victims of nature's forces, humans believe they can now shape their own destinies. Science, thus, has emerged as *the* salvific force in history.[22]

---

[18]Gilkey has frequently confounded lecture audiences who scowl skeptically at the assertion that science is sovereign, especially conservative religious folks who deny conceptually science's power and who view that scientific power as a demonic intrusion, with the claims that, if you travel by air, check with your physician, use plastic, refrigerate food, and cook with gas, you "participate in the results of science (willingly or unwillingly)" (see Gilkey, *NRS*, 69).

[19]Gilkey, *TT*, 145.

[20]Gilkey, *TT*, 145.

[21]Gilkey, *CT*, 177.

[22]Gilkey has sometimes been misunderstood as being "antiscience." On the contrary, he thoroughly understands and accepts the knowledge about nature harvested by modern

A. Science's Difficulties

1. *Difficulties with Culture.* At the same time, Gilkey points out the difficulties that an elite science has faced, much to its own surprise and chagrin. Deviant forms of science damaged the prestige and power of the scientific establishment. Powerful science was corrupted to serve ideological ends in the regimes of Hitler and Stalin.[23] More recently, scientists with legitimate credentials perverted science in the name of fundamentalist theologies, with the creation of "creation science," which Gilkey views as "a response to the arrogant claim of science that it represents the only mode of knowing and so that only what it speaks of is real."[24] Another difficulty arose because the creative power of science had bred lethal weapons of mass destruction, which threaten the very culture that freely gave birth to them. A further difficulty for science is the ambiguous results of its technologies that arose from the free and creative human use of science for our benefit. Although enormously beneficial, occasional lethal results of these same technologies threaten our very existence. Unbridled industrial expansion consumes limited natural resources voraciously and leaves a path of pollution and despoliation in its wake. In short, the powers of science frequently become wed to philosophies, theologies, and ideologies that redirected those energies in dangerous ways. The "lordship" of science in culture has a demonic underside.[25]

2. *Difficulties within Science Itself.* Gilkey also chides scientists for their ignorance about the history and limits of their own discipline. He frequently appeals to the story of the previous, now deposed, regal discipline of theology to bring scientists out of their elitist naïveté. With penetrating and chilling insight, he copiously illustrates how haughty theologians from several past centuries, ignorant of science and isolated

---

science. See his *Nature, Reality, and the Sacred* for a summary of his perspective on that which science tells us about nature (Gilkey, *NRS*, 87-91). He also expresses great appreciation for the practical results of science. "Science is our most reliable and, on one level, our most fruitful way of knowing. It is a wondrous power and creation of the human spirit or mind" (Gilkey, *NRS*, 15).

[23]See Gilkey, *TT*, 147. Gilkey predicts deviance in Iranian science under Shiite hegemony.

[24]Gilkey, *TT*, 146. See his fascinating story and analysis: Gilkey, *CT*.

[25]In Tillich's terms, it had become "heteronomous." See esp. Gilkey, "The Creativity and Ambiguity of Science," in *SAS*, 75-89.

from the cultural revolutions spawned by science and the Enlightenment, undermined themselves and quietly vacated the throne. By this assessment, Gilkey has sought to alert scientists to these dangers.

The first internal difficulty that ultimately confounds scientists is that they frequently adopt a naturalistic worldview without fully acknowledging that they have done so, claiming, for example, that reality is limited to the natural realm. By "naturalistic worldview" or "philosophical naturalism" or, simply, "naturalism," Gilkey refers to the position that considers nature the sole source of all things and the only end of all things. Naturalism denies any reality that transcends nature. The ideas of mind, soul, and spirit, for example, are all reducible to bodily, and hence, natural phenomena. Gilkey, of course, recognizes the long and rich history of naturalism.[26] His critique of scientists at this point is that they often unreflectively assume a naturalistic metaphysics. Thus, in the name of science, they make claims about nature that are really veiled speculations and, hence, unscientific assertions. The phrase, "only study nature," describes the core of scientific investigation; to claim that "nature is the only object of study possible" is the core of metaphysical naturalism. This unrecognized assumption leads to further internal confusions in science.[27]

A second internal difficulty for science in culture derives from the first. Frequently, scientists assume that the scientific method is the only valid source of knowledge about nature. It is the only valid epistemology or source of truth. This nonempirical assumption creates a paradox that raises the question about science as the sole way to the truth. In science, Gilkey observes, the self is understood to be free, autonomous, and creative, having the power to remake the future. This human subject, however, can never become an *object* in scientific inquiry. Science, by its own well-defined limits, can know the human only in biochemical and physical terms: that is, in terms of nature where ideas like freedom and creativity dissolve. The terms "freedom," "autonomy," and "creativity" never come under the microscope of investigation. The knower who

---

[26]Gilkey, *NRS*, 225. His deep understanding of naturalism was nurtured at Columbia University where he engaged the thought of John Dewey and John H. Randall, Jr., among others.

[27]Although Gilkey has adequately construed this argument alone, he has frequently acknowledged the correlative position of Stephen Toulmin: see Toulmin's introduction (parts 1 and 2) in *The Return to Cosmology: Postmodern Science and the Theology of Nature* (Berkeley: University of California Press, 1982).

knows scientifically cannot be known by the same method![28] Gilkey concludes, in opposition to this epistemological reductionism, "that the reality which is experienced and known by the scientific community itself in doing science is much wider than the 'reality' which the objectifying net of the scientific method itself can capture."[29] Therefore, that which science finds to be true cannot be taken to represent the full reality of the object known.[30] To take the case of human beings, Gilkey fully accepts the conclusions of science about our biophysical makeup; science cannot and does not say "all" that can and must be said about humans with regard to our unique character. A complete understanding of humanity must include theological and philosophical claims.

Science's third internal difficulty results from naturalistic and epistemological assumptions that go beyond the limits of legitimate science. Science assumes a metaphysical naturalism with three chief premises: (1) science is the sole way to knowledge; (2) the proper object of science is nature; and (3) knowledge is limited to natural phenomena. Insofar as science holds these assumptions, it has reduced the real to the natural. No sacred or divine ground or human person is found when science makes these assumptions (unless the divine is identified with the natural processes, as in religious naturalism; or unless the divine is identified with human beings, as in naturalistic humanism). In a study of scientific cosmologies,[31] Gilkey finds these unexamined assumptions in the metaphysics, epistemology, and ontology of Heinz Pagels, Carl Sagan, Steven Weinberg, Richard Dawkins, John Barrow, and Frank Tipler. For example, in his book, *Cosmos*, Sagan claims that "[t]he Cosmos is all that is or ever was or ever will be"; Gilkey notes that Sagan's claim signals clearly a reductionistic dogmatism.[32]

---

[28]"Such a conception of a deterministically ordered reality finds no place for the scientific mind that has conceived it, for the intentional will that has, in persistent scientific inquiry, uncovered it, or for the purposes that obviously prepare and then use this knowledge" (Gilkey, *NRS*, 129).

[29]Gilkey, *SAS*, 81.

[30]Gilkey believes humans can know what is real "through interior self-awareness, through personal and communal awareness of the other, and through intuitions of external reality that are much wider and deeper than either sensory experience or inquiry based on sensory experience" (Gilkey, *NRS*, 86).

[31]Gilkey, *NRS*, 43-57.

[32]Gilkey, *NRS*, 50-51.

As the dominant and pervasive substance of culture, science has affected all other cultural forms, just as theology did in a previous epoch. When science mutates through a reductionistic metaphysics and episte-mology, however, the results produce a "scientific mythology"[33] that is lethal for the humanities in general and theology in particular. To take a salient example, Gilkey observes that where scientific knowing has become the supreme and only form of knowing, other modes of inquiry are conceived as purely subjective in that whatever they aim to say has no bearing on our understanding of truth and falsehood about reality. Theology, for example, becomes anachronistic, innocuous, or both. Religion becomes purely subjective and irrelevant, superstitious and/or pathological. Alleged revelations of truth about transnatural phenomena are replaced by "the knowledge [of the natural or real] guided by science . . . and . . . technology in its broadest sense *replaces* the benefits brought by religious devotion and practice."[34] In this situation, theology becomes anachronistic, an artifact of a past and passing prescientific culture because it is no longer believable. It becomes innocuous because it advances no true understanding of reality. These descriptions of religion and theology in an age of scientific dominance are pervasive.

What is somewhat surprising is the persistence of religion in an advanced scientific culture. The problem, Gilkey claims, lies in the ambiguity of science. For, while science has opened new vistas of human possibility, at the same time the bitter fruit of its technologies menace our future. Science and technology, our chief cultural achievements, threaten the very culture that nurtured them. The threats come in a variety of forms:

> the endangering of the quality of life . . . by the spread of a technological, industrial civilization; the apparently uncontrollable population explosion generated by scientific medicine, agricultural improvement, and industrial expansion; the seemingly unavoidable crisis of the environment, the depletion and exhaustion of its resources, brought about by expanding technology and industrialism; and the ultimate terrors of a nuclear conflict bringing with it an apparent end . . . to both nature and history.[35]

---

[33]Gilkey borrows this phrase from Stephen Toulmin.
[34]Gilkey, *CT*, 180.
[35]Gilkey, *SAS*, 199.

In this time of multiple threats and apparent decline and disintegration of our culture, Gilkey believes that people are turning away from science to new religions for security, meaning, and hope. This, he asserts, accounts for the rise of myriad cults, the religious right, and surging fundamentalism, all forms of heteronomous religion.

B. *The Future of Science and Religion*

"Science and religion are essential aspects of our common life, necessary for that life and for each other."[36] The ambiguities of science—its promise and its threats—that Gilkey exposes, however, pose a critical dilemma for our culture and require a new relationship between science and the humanities, one based on mutuality and interdependence.[37] As a theologian of culture, he has analyzed science as the "religious" substance of our society and revealed its promises and threats; he turns now from diagnosis to proposed treatment. Gilkey believes that his analysis of our common life has portrayed a crisis that threatens our security, meaning, and future. These are undeniably religious issues. As a Christian theologian, he addresses the religious issues of a scientific culture.

Gilkey believes that the menace of the future can be addressed if our culture shifts its attention away from the accumulation and technical application of knowledge to the persons who use the knowledge. The creative and destructive use of scientific knowledge is in human hands; therefore, the character and values and aims of the people who employ this knowledge is crucial. Since human values are, in Western culture, the province of religion, Gilkey believes that a religious renewal that fosters self-control and self-sacrifice is necessary in order to make appropriate and responsible use of our knowledge.

Both religion *and* science, however, are ambiguous because both can be creative and demonic. Both have a dark side; both are ambiguous. Therefore, great care must accompany the construction of desired mutuality and interdependence. Already, our century has witnessed the wedding of science and religion under the ideologies of Progress and Marxism. Furthermore, presently, more than half of the American population, according to Gallup polls, believes that creationism deserves "equal time" in the biology classes of public schools. Gilkey presently foresees

---

[36]Gilkey, *NRS*, 9.
[37]Gilkey, *NRS*, 9; also, idem, *CT*, 201-208.

the threat of the possibility of a destructive joining of science and religion under the imperialism of religious ideology.

> Scientific knowledge and the technology it makes possible are not . . . purely benevolent. Rather, they can both be terribly ambiguous, creating evil as well as good, instruments of self-destruction as well as of survival. Thus they and their use are *dependent* on other aspects of culture: on its political and legal structures and processes, its moral integrity and courage, the forms of its religious faith. Correspondingly, . . . our century has also shown the persistence, the permanence, the ever-renewed power, as well as the deep ambiguity, of religion. . . . Religion . . . is and will be there, like science, and it will be there in demonic or in creative form. Thus the relations between these two essential and permanent elements of culture represent a recurrent and foundational problem.[38]

The central cultural question for the future, then, is this: will science and religion unite in a theocratic or ideological form, or in a form where the autonomy and creativity of each is respected?

Both communities, Gilkey observes, must rethink their roles in society in a dialogue based on mutual respect. As theology has had to do in light of the challenges placed before it by an advanced scientific culture, Gilkey believes that science must reassess the ways it has been used and misused. He offers three suggestions. First, because science is a human activity relative to its historical context, it needs to understand that it does not represent a "pure" or totally objective form of knowing. Second, science must come to see that it is only one method of valid cognitive activity. Third, we need to realize that the application of science in technology requires human manipulators who are *moral* human beings, persons who employ the vast power of science with wisdom.[39] Religion must likewise reassess itself in a scientific culture.

Both science and religion need to reassess their pervasive and dominant "unyielding dogmatism." Naïve realism needs to give way to critical realism; literal language needs to step aside for symbolic language; and the Cartesian quest for pure knowledge needs to be replaced by a dialectical quest between the knower and known—in both science and theology!

---

[38]Gilkey, *CT*, 204-205.
[39]Gilkey, *SAS*, 85-87.

Modern philosophy of knowledge has noted with much clarity the contextual nature of all knowing. Gilkey has recognized this.[40]

First, "both science and religion proceed on the assumption, or 'faith,' that their discourse and so their knowing is a response to what is real; but both recognize the inadequacy, the perspectival character of their articulations—and the consequent mystery of the object of their knowing."[41] Thus, the sense of absolutism and dogmatism about their claims is mellowed. Second, modern epistemology recognizes that the "knower" "plays an essential role in the knowing process."[42] Therefore, any claims of complete objectivity and cognitive certainty are inappropriate. Third, because science and theology both seek to know and understand the real through symbols, they share an often unrecognized mutuality.[43]

Gilkey believes that the Christian faith is *credible* and *most adequate* to address the needs of our scientific culture. As "credible," Christianity "can satisfy the mind as a valid symbolic thematization of the totality of concrete experience as no other global viewpoint can."[44] Moreover, "a Christian interpretation provides a clearer, more illuminative, and more complete access to the full character of personal and historical experience than any other viewpoint."[45] Gilkey holds this view of Christianity on the basis of two criteria: (1) the coherence of Christianity's major symbols; and (2) its adequacy to interpret our lived experience.[46]

Gilkey also maintains that Christianity is most adequate to the needs of a scientific culture.[47] As "adequate," he means that Christian theological claims "fit" the shape of the experience they claim adequately to thematize.[48] First, he holds that Christianity deals with all the basic

---

[40]Gilkey frequently acknowledges the work of Thomas Kuhn, Richard Bernstein, Stephen Toulmin, and Michael Polanyi.

[41]Gilkey, *NRS*, , 31.

[42]Gilkey, *NRS*, 31.

[43]Gilkey, *NRS*, 32.

[44]Gilkey, *SAS*, 39.

[45]Gilkey, *SAS*, 40.

[46]Langdon Gilkey, "The Dialectic of Christian Belief: Rational, Incredible, and Credible," in *Rationality and Religious Belief*, ed. C. F. Delaney, University of Notre Dame Studies in the Philosophy of Religion 1 (Notre Dame IN: University of Notre Dame Press, 1979) 65-83. Also published as chap. 3, "The Dialectic of Christian Belief," in *SAS*, 26-41.

[47]Gilkey, "The Dialectic of Christian Belief," 65-83; also see Gilkey, *SAS*, 118-19.

[48]Gilkey, *SAS*, 39.

religious issues of a scientific culture, whereas many other faiths and ideologies do not. Second, Christianity at its best—as theonomous—values those elements most prized by science: "independence of thought and speech, the freedom to criticize old formulations and inherited goals; the freedom to experiment with new hypotheses, new methods, new values; and the willingness to appreciate and to learn from viewpoints that differ fundamentally from our own."[49] Third, Christianity includes the realism to deal with the dark, ornery side of humanity. Cognizant of our demonic potentialities, Christian faith can be constructively critical of the reigning sovereign—science—and offer grace as well.[50]

III. Ecclesial Theology: Systematic Theology and the Sciences

In his role as a theologian of culture, Gilkey has assessed the pervasive impact of science on our culture and, thus, science's impact on religion. Gilkey also critically evaluates science. Additionally, Gilkey examines the influence of science on systematic theology.

As indicated previously, Gilkey holds that the systematic theologian has both ecclesial and public roles. As servant of a religious tradition, the theologian seeks to render intelligible the meaning of that tradition's symbols: as examples, the meaning of the symbols of God, sin, creation, and providence. At the same time, the theologian's attempt to retrieve and re-present those meanings is public, in that any contemporary language that is meaningful addresses believers who think in terms of ideas prevalent within a culture. In other words, the meaning of language, including the language of systematic theology, is culture laden. Moreover, the religious community has a mission to bear its perception of the "truth" to the culture. Thus, the language of belief must be publicly understandable.

Science, more than any other cultural force, has affected the contemporary theologian. Gilkey indicates this in two ways. The first manner in which science affected theology concerned the scope of the language of systematic theology. Prior to the nineteenth century, theological language had two foci: (1) a universal, transcending element usually conceptualized in philosophical language; and (2) a concrete, matter of fact

---

[49]Gilkey, SAS, 119.
[50]See Gilkey's more extensive discussion of "credibility": Gilkey, SAS, 26-41.

element expressed in historical terms. Science, Gilkey claims, has eradicated all mundane references from theological language.[51]

Science, then, has taken as its province the delineation of facts with regard to nature. We know about the created order, for example, through geology, geography, biology, and physics. Religious truth contains no information about geology, astronomy, or botany. Further, religious language is now seen as symbolic and analogical, claiming nothing factual about sacred reality or the cosmos.[52] For example, no longer do theologians, except perhaps creationists, hold that the meaning of "creation" entails any content about mundane facts. No longer do theologians conclude on the basis of religious traditions that the world began on a certain date, that the present order of the world was established in six days, that a certain couple lived in a particular garden, or that evils befell the created order on a particular date. "Creation," for the contemporary theologian, is a religious symbol and not a scientific concept. As religious, the symbol "creation" entails nothing about matters of fact that are established by science. What "creation" does entail religiously and theologically includes the following: (1) that God is the source or ground of existence; (2) that the created order is meaningful and valuable due to the care of God; (3) that human beings as "created" are valuable and creative; and (4) that, because God is a caring creator, one can be hopeful that creation and history have meaning.[53]

Although Gilkey clearly distinguishes between scientific meanings and theological meanings, he does not separate them into realms isolated from one another. Science deals with finite existence; theology treats religious meaning. He expounded this admirably in his testimony at the trial in Little Rock in 1981 where, with regard to the created order, he distinguished between science's interest in proximate origins (how changes occurred within nature) and religion's concern with ultimate origins (how nature came into being, from whence, and why).[54] In this sense, then, science has affected systematic theology indirectly in an important way. Science has taken from theology the ability to say anything "factual" about nature. Theology is limited to religious meanings. To be sure, Gilkey does not lament this intrusion of science

---

[51]Gilkey, *RSF*, 6.
[52]Gilkey, *NRS*, 20.
[53]Gilkey, *CT*, 225-27; and idem, *RSF*.
[54]Gilkey, *CT*, 48-53, 103-16.

upon theology. Indeed, this event has entailed at least two positive benefits. First, theology no longer has to defend the facticity of the sun standing still, axheads that float, and human lives that span hundreds of years. Second, theology can now focus its attention more directly on its central interest; namely, the religious meanings of the symbols, meanings that Gilkey believes are credible and relevant.

So, the *form* of theological language has been changed directly and dramatically by the establishment of science. Science has also affected contemporary theology in a second manner with regard to the *content* or substance of theological symbols.[55] For example, the meaning of the theological affirmation, "God is creator of the earth," has been modified. No longer, because of science, is a recent and sudden creation tenable. Theologians now view God as creating the earth through a long and slow process. Science has similarly evoked a change in the meaning of "God as providential" or "sustainer." Theologians now conceive of God as working *within* the created order (immanently), rather than *beyond* the creation (transcendentally).[56] Correlatively, notions of God's power in creation and God's interaction with the created order, especially the idea of "miracle," have been reframed. God, the Christian symbol for sacred reality, is no longer conceived as a static and changeless concept, but rather in dynamic and encounter terms.[57] Thus, Gilkey attributes the pervasive changes in the understanding of theological language and the religious content of the Christian symbols directly to science.[58]

The content of theological anthropology is likewise revisited and reformulated in light of modern science. In a recent essay, Gilkey clearly demonstrates how science and theology relate in their views of human being.[59] Rather than seeing humans as created apart from the natural (as in older theologies, which held to a "special creation," that set them on a higher plane), he asserts with modern biology that humans are thoroughly natural. "*All* our possibilities are in the end genetic; our physical, psychological, moral, and spiritual similarities, as well as all our

---

[55]Gilkey, *NRS*, 21.

[56]Gilkey, *NRS*, 21.

[57]Langdon Gilkey, "God," in *New Handbook of Christian Theology*, 198-209.

[58]Gilkey, *NRS*, 20-21.

[59]Langdon Gilkey, "Biology and Theology on Human Nature," in *Biology, Ethics, and the Origins of Life*, ed. Holmes Rolston III (Boston: Jones and Bartlett Publishers, 1995) 163-90.

differences, have their patterns set in our genetic endowments."[60] Yet, and in contradistinction to the reductionism that Gilkey finds in the writings of many evolutionary biologists, the results of biological and sociobiological investigation are "not the whole story."[61] Gilkey argues that both biology and theology are necessary for an adequate understanding of human being, concluding that "human existence is a baffling mixture of being conditioned and of self-determination, of an inherited 'given' and a chosen self-direction for the future, of being objectively determined and of living as a centered, subject-spirit."[62]

In summary, theological language that *faithfully* bears the content of a religious tradition "must be united with contemporary discourse about nature, society, and individual persons if our active existence in the world is to be morally creative, consistent with itself, and genuinely expressive of its religious center."[63]

Conclusion

In a career spanning four decades of cultural turbulence, Langdon Gilkey has addressed issues at the intersection of nature, humanity, and the sacred. From his first book (*Maker of Heaven and Earth*, 1959) to his most recent work (*Nature, Reality, and the Sacred*, 1993), he has consistently brought the natural sciences and contemporary theology into dialogue. He has provided a model for engaging these two cultural giants that C. P. Snow lamented were hopelessly isolated from one another. Although science and religion have distinct methods, languages, and provinces that should not be confused,[64] Gilkey does not consign science and religion to separate realms, isolated from one another.[65] Rather,

---

[60]Gilkey, "Biology and Theology on Human Nature," 168.

[61]Gilkey, "Biology and Theology on Human Nature," 169.

[62]Gilkey, "Biology and Theology on Human Nature," 169-70. Gilkey very specifically states this thesis. "Evolutionary science has taught us how we humans have appeared in all facets of our being *in and through* the processes of nature; hence, a theological understanding of human being must also be informed by a biological understanding. Correspondingly, a historical and theological understanding of all the aspects of culture must be informed by a sociobiological understanding of the biological roots of culture" (Gilkey, "Biology and Theology on Human Nature," 172).

[63]Gilkey, *CT*, 224.

[64]Gilkey, *CT*, 108-16. In his testimony during the trial in Arkansas, Gilkey clearly distinguished science from religion.

[65]In his outline of ways to relate science and religion, Ian Barbour overemphasizes

Gilkey views them as polar disciplines that can be brought into necessary and creative dialogue.

Gilkey fears the hegemony of either an established science or an established theology in culture, citing the foibles of a once-regnant sovereign, theology, and the more recent troubles that afflict an advanced scientific culture in the postmodern period. Like unfettered sovereigns who invoke divine rights, neither science nor religion should be granted unchecked power. Alone, they are either dangerous or incomplete or both.

Thus, Gilkey desires to bring science and religion into dialogue, into mutual appreciation and critique, without violating their unique purposes and scope.

> What is needed is not only brilliant, articulate defense of what one knows in one's own discipline, but also humility about the limited character of what one knows and about its cooperative place in the entire panorama of human understanding. What is called for is a *synthesis* of all these perspectives, each of which sheds its own light on the larger mystery.[66]

Science, theology, and philosophy, Gilkey declares, are the three interdependent yet distinct disciplines, mutually distinct but mutually dependent, that are the tools for our understanding of nature, ourselves, and the sacred.[67]

Gilkey's attempt to distinguish the two realms from one another. Barbour considers Gilkey as illustrative of the perspective that sees science and religion as *independent*, in that they have contrasting methods and differing languages (Ian Barbour, *Religion in an Age of Science*, vol. 1 [San Francisco: HarperSanFrancisco, 1990]). Gilkey, rather, holds that the two realms are *distinct* and not independent. Science and religion are definitely in "dialogue" and can be "integrated" (Barbour's favored categories) through philosophical discourse.

[66]Gilkey, "Biology and Theology on Human Nature," 189.

[67]Gilkey, *NRS*, 75-76.

Chapter 7

Relative Absoluteness:
Langdon Gilkey's Approach to Religious Pluralism

Mary Ann Stenger

Introduction

Rooted in experience and extensive theological reflection, Langdon Gilkey's approach to the plurality of religions attempts to balance the absoluteness of personal commitment and the relativity of being open to truth in other faith traditions. Rather than demanding that absolute personal commitment be sacrificed for relativism, or openness for the absoluteness of one's own tradition, he holds these two foundational attitudes together in a dynamic paradox and dialectic. In encounters between Christians and non-Christians, the paradox allows participants to hold the absoluteness of their faith tradition in tension with the relativity implied in an acknowledgment of truth in other faith traditions. The dialectical dimension points to the "back-and-forth" relationship between absoluteness and relativity that enables challenge, growth, and renewal within their own faiths. This chapter will explore the significance of Gilkey's theory of relative absoluteness in relationship to his own theological understanding as well as to other approaches to religious pluralism.

I. Personal Encounters and Historical Context

For many religious theorists who write about religious pluralism, the interest in and direction for their theories stem from personal encounters with people from diverse religious faiths.[1] Similarly, Gilkey's personal experiences and the changing historical and cultural context intersect in ways that compel him to rethink traditional Christian attitudes of religious superiority and absoluteness. He describes his theology as "existential and

---

[1] See the following examples: John Hick, *God Has Many Names* (Philadelphia: Westminster Press, 1982) 13-28; Wilfred Cantwell Smith, *Towards A World Theology: Faith and the Comparative History of Religion* (Philadelphia: Westminster Press, 1981) 4, 11, 29-31; Diana Eck, *Encountering God: A Spiritual Journey from Bozeman to Banaras* (Boston: Beacon Press, 1993); Paul Knitter, *One Earth Many Religions: Multifaith Dialogue and Global Responsibility* (Maryknoll NY: Orbis Books, 1995) 1-22.

historical-cultural," reflecting a "correlational" approach that accepts truth validated by historical-cultural events and personal experiences.[2]

Gilkey credits his parents for teaching him that racial and religious prejudice are "anathema to a genuine Christianity." Experiences in China (both teaching English and as a prisoner in a Japanese internment camp during World War II) countered that tolerance with a general Western arrogance and an attitude of "unquestioned superiority" over against the Chinese. Although he experienced both positive and negative effects of that arrogance, internment prevented him from developing an intellectual critique of it. Nor did these experiences challenge the absoluteness of his Christian faith and commitment.[3]

Extensive dialogues with Takeuchi Yoshinori in 1975 and personal experiences with the American Sikh community reinforced his early attitude of tolerance and also brought recognition of the spiritual power in non-Christian traditions and a desire to learn from them.[4] Gilkey began to affirm the rough parity of world religions although he remains challenged by its personal and theological implications:

> Can one at the same time affirm and articulate a genuine and viable spiritual commitment, an existence centered on the relation to the divine beyond relativity, and yet also recognize, as now apparently we must, the "particularity" of one's own stance with that of others and so the relativity in some sense of all our affirmations?[5]

Gilkey's affirmation of other religions as legitimate bearers of truth deepened the personal, intellectual challenge to acknowledge both his own personal religious commitment and the authenticity of others' religious faiths. Theologizing on these issues meant rethinking religious pluralism and reinterpreting traditional Christian doctrines. For Gilkey, that process of reinterpretation must be understood not only as personal but also as connected to the larger scientific and political contexts, as major influences on Christian theology.

---

[2]Langdon Gilkey, "A Retrospective Glance at My Work," in *The Whirlwind in Culture: Frontiers in Theology: In Honor of Langdon Gilkey* (Indianapolis: Meyer-Stone Books, 1988) 2, 13.

[3]Gilkey, "Retrospective Glance at My Work," 4, 9-11.

[4]Gilkey, "Retrospective Glance at My Work," 31-32.

[5]Gilkey, "Retrospective Glance at My Work," 33.

One important theological effect of scientific developments in the nineteenth and twentieth centuries, Gilkey argues, is a change from a more literal understanding of religious truth to a symbolic approach.[6] While recognizing that many religious people still do theology from a literalist, realistic, and absolutist interpretation of the Bible, Gilkey criticizes that approach and argues that a more symbolic and constructionist understanding of religious truth fits best with contemporary science and culture.[7]

Related to scientific developments and to this shift toward a more symbolic understanding of truth are the historical critiques of scriptures and doctrines that occurred within religious scholarship.[8] These critiques relativize and humanize the basic doctrines and texts of faith, thereby undermining them as absolutist bases of faith. Both the symbolic understanding of religious truth and the relativization of doctrines have helped to open Christian thinkers to the possibility of equality or parity among religions.

This shift away from an assumed superiority of Christianity is not, according to Gilkey, simply a theological issue, but arises also because Christian superiority was historically connected to a sense of Western superiority.[9] Perhaps because his experiences in China during World War II led him to be particularly sensitive to Western arrogance, Gilkey emphasizes the important impact of the decline of Western dominance and the revitalization of non-Western cultures and religions on the issue of religious pluralism.[10] Gilkey notes that the case for Christian superiori-

---

[6]Langdon Gilkey, *Nature, Reality, and the Sacred: The Nexus of Science and Religion*, Theology and the Sciences series, ed. Kevin J. Sharpe (Minneapolis: Fortress, 1993) 18; hereafter cited as *NRS*.

[7]Gilkey, *NRS*, 12, 30, 31.

[8]Gilkey notes that theologians "are loath to admit such an influence of science on theology; they prefer to talk about 'in-house' influences, such as new interpretations of Scripture or new modes of religious experience" (Gilkey, *NRS*, 18). Gilkey argues that these new, more humanized interpretations of scriptures and doctrines are an effect of the Enlightenment and an important factor in changing Christian understanding about religious plurality (Langdon Gilkey, "Plurality and Its Theological Implications," in *The Myth of Christian Uniqueness; Toward a Pluralistic Theology of Religions*, ed. John Hick and Paul F. Knitter [Maryknoll NY: Orbis Books, 1987] 37-38).

[9]Langdon Gilkey, *Society and the Sacred: Toward a Theology of Culture in Decline* (New York: Crossroad, 1981) 13; hereafter cited as *SAS*.

[10]Gilkey, "Retrospective Glance at My Work," 32.

ty had been argued from the standpoint of cultural dominance, rather than with theological arguments. The dogmatic claims of Christian superiority had been relativized by critiques of Enlightenment philosophers; liberal Christianity, however, responded with interpretations of itself as "enlightened" and as culturally superior as "the religion of the civilized West."[11] Since 1945, however, cultural changes, such as decolonization, new non-Western centers of power, and the diminished global power of Europe, have undermined Western cultural superiority and are slowly beginning to change our academic and cultural understandings toward a position of cultural parity.[12] These changes do not just demand modernization of old cultural or intellectual positions or revision of traditional religious doctrines; rather, values and symbols of values are radically relativized.[13] The assumed superiority of the West was tied to its cultural values, such as "historical and this-worldly consciousness, its humanitarian ideals, its democratic morality, its monogamous family, its autonomy, its high evaluation of the person."[14] As these values have been challenged and relativized by cultural pluralism within the West as well as by increased appreciation for non-Western values, Gilkey sees Western culture on more equal footing with other cultures. Similarly for religions, there has been an increase in the availability of non-Christian religious options in Western cultures, and Christianity's assumed self-understanding as the absolute religion has been undermined and relativized.

Gilkey also argues that the Western "deity" of progress was tied not only to a sense of the West's cultural superiority, but also to some form of "salvation history."[15] The various versions of salvation history (Jewish, Christian, Enlightenment, and Marxist) posit some vision of progress that will eliminate social evils.[16] Various historical and cultural events such as wars, cultural movements against racial, sexual, and economic oppression, and awareness of injustices and violence within our families, our religions, and our cultures, however, have challenged the truth of these visions and have reduced the hoped-for progress to more realistic,

---

[11]Gilkey, *SAS*, 13.
[12]Gilkey, "Plurality and Its Theological Implications," 40.
[13]Gilkey, "Plurality and Its Theological Implications," 41.
[14]Gilkey, *SAS*, 13.
[15]Gilkey, *SAS*, 7.
[16]Gilkey, *SAS*, 10.

pragmatic goals. The effect of this for religious pluralism is, once again, a relativizing of Western and Christian salvation histories.

In addition to these cultural and political factors, Gilkey notes a religious shift, arising out of Protestant liberalism, that emphasizes love more than defending the faith.[17] Love is to be shown, not only to other Christians; rather, God's love includes *all* humans, not only Christians.[18] Not only should Christians develop a strong ethic of love for their (now global) neighbors, but in relationship to *God's* love for humanity, those who belong to one religious community are put on a par with other human groups.

Thus, both cultural and religious factors reinforce Gilkey's personal experience, leading him to new theological thinking about the plurality of religions and to reinterpretations of traditional Christian doctrines, such as the doctrines of God and Christ. The challenge for Gilkey is to reflect theologically on the questions raised by non-Christians about Christian doctrines and to formulate an approach that takes the other seriously while affirming his own religious commitment.

II. Gilkey's Theological Response to Religious Plurality

A. Implications for the Understanding of God

A major challenge to Gilkey's understanding of God stems from his encounter with Buddhism. He calls for a "covenant with the Buddhists" parallel to the early Christian "covenant with the Greeks." A key issue for Gilkey is the mystery of being and nonbeing, including whether they are or are not, whether being or nonbeing is primary, and how they relate to becoming. Whereas Western thought assumes the primordial character of being, Buddhist thought holds that nothingness is the ultimate transcendence—and unity—of both being and nonbeing. Upon reflection, Gilkey argues that the Buddhist approach "better represents our own deepest and reflectively most coherent interpretation of our gospel than does our traditional 'being-centered' form." He suggests understanding being and

---

[17]Gilkey, "Plurality and Its Theological Implications," 38. This shift has affected not only the relationship between Christians and Jews, but also the Christian responses to racism and sexism. He notes that churches which are not connected to Protestant liberalism have experienced more difficulties when dealing with issues of religious pluralism, racism, and sexism.

[18]Gilkey, "Plurality and Its Theological Implications," 38-39.

nonbeing not as ultimate terms, but as "dialectically related symbols each in its own way expressive of the mystery of ultimacy, of the self, and of its destiny." Once again, Gilkey opts for a relationship of both/and rather than either/or.[19]

On the side of being, Gilkey notes that Western Christian cultural and religious life affirms the value of the individual person, including personal freedom, individual creativity, the responsibility of one person for others, and the possibility of love between individuals. Those affirmations are more fully ascribed to the divine who is seen as the one who brings individuals and the world to their fulfillment. Such a view, which stems from Gilkey's concern with concrete life, is biblically grounded.[20]

Gilkey also notes that this view of God and God's connectedness to our world can lead toward a strongly heteronomous understanding of God, whose power overwhelms human freedom and creativity. In such cases, individuals, then, are seen as struggling against God rather than being empowered by God. Such an omnipotent God of pure being can become "idolatrous," which leads to valid protests—such as those of Karl Marx, Sigmund Freud, Friedrich Nietzsche, rationalist thinkers, and others—against that God in favor of the individual and/or the concrete world. The Buddhist conception is one form of that protest; but its argument is deeper, objecting not only to heteronomous divine being, but also to autonomous individual being, because the Buddhist question is rooted in the "sacrality of nothingness."[21]

On either side of the affirmation of being, whether a heteronomous understanding of God who thereby becomes demonic or an autonomous understanding of selves who themselves become "imperial demons," ambiguity is denied; the dialectic of being and nonbeing is lost; and being is "overaffirmed." Such overaffirmation of being, however, is only one piece of Christian theology. Rather, "God is being qualified dialectically and yet essentially by nonbeing, and so the divine mystery transcends the categories of both being and nonbeing."[22] This understanding of the divine mystery reflects Buddhist doctrines of ultimacy and also fits with Christian doctrines of creation, providence, and incarnation, wherein finite

---

[19]Gilkey, *SAS*, 124-26.
[20]Gilkey, *SAS*, 127.
[21]Gilkey, *SAS*, 128.
[22]Gilkey, *SAS*, 129, 134.

being is connected to the divine ground and these divine activities occur through both being and negation of being within the divine itself.

> The divine *being* can seemingly only create and sustain finite being by continually negating itself, by uniting being and nothingness in its own self. Correspondingly, and on a deeper and more significant level, the divine *love* can only manifest itself effectively in the mode of the negation not only of being but of becoming as well: by weakness, suffering, and death. To redeem our being, the divine must negate its own.[23]

Thus, the challenge of sacral nothingness presented by Buddhist thought leads Gilkey to reevaluate understandings of being and nonbeing in Christian traditions. The goal is not to make Christian thought Buddhist, but rather to answer questions raised by the Buddhist understanding of ultimacy as nothingness. Nor was the result to make Christianity more palatable to Buddhists, but to rethink more deeply Christian understandings in light of Buddhist approaches.

B. Implications for the Understanding of Christ

In the last chapter of *Society and The Sacred*, Gilkey proposes an inclusivist understanding of Christ that still attempts to be pluralist in its effects. The impetus for rethinking the doctrine of Christ in relation to other religious traditions is not just a theoretical push for understanding plurality from a Christian standpoint but, more importantly, a recognition of "the reality of powerful, healing spiritual forces embodied in these non-Christian traditions." Genuine dialogue stems from accepting, on all sides of the dialogue, truth and the possibility of salvation within each of the traditions, as well as partiality and error. If one accepts that view, however, then what of the Christian claim of universal salvation in Christ? At the very least, the special knowledge that roots the claim is relativized. As we saw earlier, however, abandoning that special knowledge would end the dialogue rather than enhancing it: "Some fixed and therefore quite particular starting point for each member of the dialogue is essential if a real conversation about salvation, or about the extent of religious truth, or about the extent of the divine love, or other central issues in religious dialogue, is to be possible." Otherwise, the dialogue is no longer religious but secular and philosophical.[24]

---

[23]Gilkey, *SAS*, 136.
[24]Gilkey, *SAS*, 158, 160, 161.

If one begins with a Christian stance, then, is the center in Christ necessarily exclusivist or can one still acknowledge other means of knowing about and participating in salvation? Gilkey's response is to affirm that "the redemptive work of God that culminates (for us) in the Christ is universally present."[25]

First, in working out the theological dimensions of this universally present redemptive activity, Gilkey affirms a strong doctrine of general revelation as the basis of genuine interreligious dialogue. This doctrine of general revelation is expressed in the language of "covenant," suggesting a divine covenant with Buddhism, parallel to the patristic suggestion of a "divine covenant with the Greeks," or parallel to the implied but unstated assumption of a "divine covenant with modernity." Particular revelations, thereby, are relativized in relationship to God but also accepted as valid, which allows for recognition of genuine revelation in religious forms outside one's own tradition.[26]

Second, Gilkey argues that the Cross needs to be understood as a broad, nonexclusive manifestation God's love and will for all creatures. This view maintains the freedom of God's activity and grace, rather than restricting it to one community. Here, too, Gilkey maintains the tensions and paradox of universality and particularity. He affirms the disclosure of God's "loving and saving will" in Christ—a particular claim of salvation and truth—and interprets that revelation more universally as demonstrating God's saving will and love for all.[27]

Third, Gilkey maintains that the depth of the divine love (*agapé*) is inclusive, surmounting cultural and religious barriers. Drawing from Paul's first-century claim of inclusivity (neither male nor female, Jew nor Greek, etc.), Gilkey argues that the use of cultural and religious relativities to divide and exclude misunderstands and trivializes the divine redemptive will and love.[28] In other words, Christian absolutism uses human differences and divisions to restrict God, rather than using the revelation of God's saving love to challenge human exclusions and limits.

Fourth, Gilkey addresses ambiguities in all religions (they contain sin *and* grace, truth *and* untruth) as a vital basis for God's—and therefore

---

[25]Gilkey, *SAS*, 161, 163.
[26]Gilkey, *SAS*, 166, 167.
[27]Gilkey, *SAS*, 168, 169.
[28]Gilkey, *SAS*, 169.

Christians'—inclusive love.[29] Gilkey accepts Barth's distinction between revelation and religion, which recognized the humanity, conditionedness, and ambiguity in all religion, including Christianity.[30] Gilkey also personalizes this understanding to emphasize the presence of sinful human faith and works in Christians, Buddhists, and others. The parity of sin, in tandem with his earlier affirmation of the priority and inclusivity of God's love, leads Gilkey to affirm "universal salvation in Christ."[31] Once again, Gilkey's view leaves the judgment about salvation and acceptance to God, rather than to fallible humans.

Finally, Gilkey argues that the gospel proclaims God's final victory, noting that it is God's redemption, not retribution against all beings; this victory, therefore, should not be confined to those who acknowledge a particular form of that promise. One reason for Gilkey's strong stance on God's redemption as inclusive is that sin and idolatry are primarily inward, rather than based on external acts alone. Thus, the external acts of hearing or acknowledging the promise in Christ are not the basis of God's redemption.[32] Ultimate power, will, and redemption are God's victory; this forfeits human self-righteousness in external actions and communities.

C. Implications for the Understanding of Other Doctrines

In addition to dialogue with Buddhists, Gilkey also reflects on the mutual benefits of encounters with Chinese culture that center on the relationships between the individual, the community, and nature. On the one hand, Gilkey's sense of the need for a new synthesis of individuality and communal responsibility in the West increases his appreciation for Chinese efforts to harmonize the needs of the community, the importance of nature, and the roles of individual persons. On the other hand, he believes that Christianity is capable of reshaping the religious aspects of Chinese culture, although the details of this transformation are not fully explicated. Gilkey is quite clear that this is not an imperialistic effort to remake Chinese culture in a Western-Christian image. Rather, the

---

[29]Gilkey, *SAS*, 170.
[30]Gilkey, *SAS*, 164; similarly, also see idem, "An Appreciation of Karl Barth," in *How Karl Barth Changed My Mind*, ed. Donald K. McKim (Grand Rapids MI: Eerdmans, 1986) 154-55.
[31]Gilkey, *SAS*, 170.
[32]Gilkey, *SAS*, 170.

Christian church must put its own culture and religion under God's word of judgment and grace in order to witness to that Word for China. Gilkey tries to counter the traditional Western Christian approach of self-superior imposition on other cultures such as China. Still, he looks at the relationship more in terms of what Christianity can offer China (however humbly) than in terms of what China can offer Western Christians (the latter is mentioned briefly but not fully developed).[33]

Christianity, Gilkey believes, is particularly valuable, because it can offer a vision of transcendence that would enhance Maoism in the same way that Christian transcendence reshaped Hellenism. Gilkey envisions several benefits: greater creativity within the culture, major restructuring of government, property, and social relations, with Christian liberation theology becoming a primary influence. To prevent such influences from being just another form of Western domination, Gilkey argues that the church must be willing to sacrifice "what it is in the world— in culture, in religion, in theological formulations, and in ecclesiastical might—in favor of the transcendent to which it seeks to witness." In other words, Gilkey sees the transcendence in the Christian message as the source of liberating transformations. True, the particular structures of Western Christianity may not be liberating in other cultural contexts; thus, he demands that Western Christianity relativize its own structures in relationship to the transcendent and, thereby, allow the liberating power of transcendence to work.[34] In *Society and the Sacred*, then, Gilkey presents a strongly inclusivist Christian theology of religions, along with an equally strong relativizing of all religions (including Christianity) and an affirmation of the parity of religions.

D. Relative Absoluteness

In his effort to affirm the particularity and relativity of all religions as well as his own absolute religious commitment, Gilkey proposes a dialectical paradox of "relative absoluteness."[35] He is quick to recognize

---

[33]Gilkey, *SAS*, 146, 149, 155-56.
[34]Gilkey, *SAS*, 149, 151, 156.
[35]For another response to Gilkey's theory of relative absoluteness, see Mark Kline Taylor's analysis in relationship to cultural pluralism: Mark Kline Taylor, "Religion, Cultural Plurality, and Liberating Praxis: In Conversation with the Work of Langdon Gilkey," *Journal of Religion* 71 (April 1991): 145-66. Taylor finds "relative absoluteness" helpful in its affirmation of relativity, but insufficient in its claim of absoluteness.

that the new cultural and religious situation should not result in religious persons (Christian or non-Christian) giving up their claims of truth and faith for a pure relativism, for then neither dialogue nor a religious stance is possible. His strategy to avoid both absolutism and relativism is to "adopt a strangely paradoxical stance, namely, that at one and the same time we affirm our own stance and faith, and yet also recognize theirs—a not impossible and quite creative *personal* attitude but a difficult if not contradictory *theoretical* one."[36] The challenge for Gilkey is to understand such a personal paradoxical stance *theologically*, in relation to issues of truth, theological understandings of God, Christ, humans, nature, and diverse practices.

Gilkey's concern for holding to one's individual religious claims as absolute does not arise merely from his honest appraisal of the nature of religious commitment; it also stems from his analysis of culture, which indicates a need for "an illuminating, healing and transcendent Word."[37] Theological discourse must reveal an absoluteness that transcends contemporary suffering and questioning, yet relativizes all theology and faith in their encounters with other religious faiths and theologies.

Because he sees the whole system of religious symbols as relativized by the current context, Gilkey does not agree with thinkers who have tried to resolve the tensions of religious plurality by pulling out one religious doctrine as universalizable for all religious faiths, such as the doctrines of God or humanity, which are subject to widely differing cultural and religious interpretations. Similarly, he rejects efforts to suggest a universal philosophical standpoint as neutral and transcending all particular religious differences.[38] He does find somewhat helpful those theological efforts to interpret religious symbols in ways that can include diverse religious faiths (such as Schleiermacher's or Tillich's Christian efforts, or some recent Hindu and Buddhist theories that include all religious developments as part of the movement toward a higher religious consciousness). Useful as these latter attempts are, however, Gilkey argues that they are inadequate to our present situation, because "each incorporates others into its own world, interprets and defines them from an alien perspective."[39] Such theories are inclusive, but do not fairly

---

[36]Gilkey, *SAS*, 14.
[37]Gilkey, *SAS*, 14.
[38]Gilkey, "Plurality and Its Theological Implications," 41.
[39]Gilkey, "Plurality and Its Theological Implications," 42.

represent the perspectives of other faiths. Similarly, Gilkey finds interesting those approaches that interpret all religions as particular manifestations of a perennial philosophy or theology, but he declares them inadequate because they elevate one aspect of religion, the mystical, over the nonmystical aspects.[40]

Yet, the alternative appears to be a relativism without grounding, which reduces each religious expression to a cultural, individual projection that is empty of any saving content and cannot be evaluated. The plurality of religions demands tolerance, but tends to a relativity that can include the intolerable and the demonic.[41] It is necessary both to be tolerant and yet able to critique the intolerable. Critique, however, must be based on some ultimate values, Gilkey argues. "Our view of existence as a whole gives locus in reality to the values we defend. Consequently any practical political action, in resistance to tyranny or in liberation from it, presupposes ultimate values and an ultimate vision of things, an ethic and so a theology. And it presupposes an absolute commitment to this understanding of things." Thus, Gilkey argues that both absoluteness and relativity are needed in order to meet intellectual/theological and practical/political concerns.[42]

At this point, Gilkey sees the praxis of interreligious dialogue as making possible that which is nearly impossible to resolve in theory—the dialectical paradox of relativity and absoluteness. In dialogue, one affirms one's religious commitments as unconditional in one's life, and yet relative in relationship to the others at the table of dialogue: "What to reflection is a contradiction, to praxis is a workable dialectic, a momentary but creative paradox." Analysis of these issues, then, must stem from the experiences of actual dialogue, rather than preceding the dialogue. In the practice of interreligious dialogue, the absolute is "*relatively* present in the relative."[43]

---

[40]Gilkey, "Plurality and Its Theological Implications," 43. This more recent article reflects a shift within Gilkey's own thinking—from a more inclusivist approach in *SAS* to this more equalized approach.

[41]The term "demonic" refers to that which claims ultimate truth and goodness, but results in destruction and radical evil. Placing all religions on an equal level, without some ultimate grounding or ultimate values, removes any basis for critique of religions or aspects of religions; thus, actions that many would call radically evil are allowed in the name of religious tolerance.

[42]Gilkey, "Plurality and Its Theological Implications," 43-44, 45.

[43]Gilkey, "Plurality and Its Theological Implications," 47.

Gilkey acknowledges that this dynamic, dialectical relationship of absolute/infinite and relative/finite parallels the theoretical efforts of G. W. F. Hegel, Søren Kierkegaard, Paul Tillich, and Reinhold Niebuhr. Insofar as those thinkers saw their own standpoints of meaning as less relative than others, as more objective and universal, however, Gilkey's approach differs. Hegel, Kierkegaard, Tillich, and Niebuhr, therefore, were still limited to a Western view of rationality and universal structures of meaning that did not take seriously the plurality and relativity of religions and cultures.[44]

Still, Gilkey's proposal is strikingly close to Tillich's perspective. The absolute participates in the relative; the relative is not completely relative. Gilkey maintains that "[t]he infinite *is* in the concrete, the absolute is unavoidably in the particular—that is, it cannot be approached except through the particular and the relative."[45] Particular reflection and praxis, however, need some absolute grounding and, therefore, are not completely relative. With considerable affinity to Tillich's theory of religious symbols and critique of idolatry, Gilkey offers the following formulation: "A symbol or a criterion points beyond itself and criticizes itself if it would not be demonic; but it also points to itself and through itself if it would not be empty, and if we would not be left centerless."[46] For Tillich and Gilkey, a symbol both points beyond itself to the infinite or unconditioned and must be transparent to that infinite without being identified as absolute.[47] The absolute or infinite relativizes the particular symbol or manifestation of itself, but also manifests that absolute infinite through its relativity.[48]

This approach implies practically that a religious person can remain within the theological circle of her own religious commitments— affirming absoluteness within various relative symbols and structures, while recognizing the relativity of her position in relationship to other religious approaches. "The relative here participates in and manifests the absolute. As relative it thus negates and transcends itself. It is final and yet not the only one; it is definitive and yet so are other ways."[49]

---

[44]Gilkey, "Plurality and Its Theological Implications," 48.

[45]Gilkey, "Plurality and Its Theological Implications," 48.

[46]Gilkey, "Plurality and Its Theological Implications," 48.

[47]See Paul Tillich, *Dynamics of Faith* (New York: Harper & Row, 1957) 97.

[48]Gilkey, "Plurality and Its Theological Implications," 49.

[49]Gilkey, "Plurality and Its Theological Implications," 49.

Thus, Gilkey argues that multiple, genuinely valid manifestations of religious meaning can exist in rough parity with each other, not just as cognitive theological perspectives, but as real existential positions and liberating praxis. The task is "to hold on with infinite passion to both ends of the dialectic of relativity and absoluteness."[50]

Gilkey illustrates this approach with several theological points. First, as in his earlier discussion, the symbol of God is relative in relationship to the infinite mystery—a mystery that is manifested concretely in other symbols.[51] He also reiterates a Buddhist-influenced understanding: the infinite mystery embraces both nonbeing and being.[52] Second, as he suggests in *Society and the Sacred*, the Christ is the revelation of the infinite as absolute *agapé*/love. So also, he now argues, can other manifestations and symbols be revelations of that infinite love (for example, bodhisattvas). Third, Gilkey argues that redemptive power and grace characterize the concrete experience of the infinite mystery—both within Christian faith and in varying symbols and manifestations. In other words, others are not included simply within Christian redemption, as in *Society and the Sacred*; instead, parity is *fully* acknowledged.

> To understand God in relation both to a mystery that transcends God and to the nonbeing that seems to contradict God; to understand revelation in relation to other revelations that relativize our revelation; to view Christology and gospel in relation to other manifestations of grace; anthropology in relation to *anatta* (no-self) and identity—this is the heart of our present baffling but very exciting theological task.[53]

The challenge expressed here reflects Gilkey's dialogue with Buddhists as well as his broader respect for diverse religious faiths. The basic categories of Christian theology (God, revelation, Christology, and human identity) are opened by Buddhist understandings.

In summary, Gilkey's theological response to religious pluralism includes four major concerns. First, because all religious forms are ambiguous in relationship to the infinite mystery, particular manifestations have no absolute claim. Yet, critiques of religious structures and of

---

[50]Gilkey, "Plurality and Its Theological Implications," 49-50.

[51]Gilkey, "Plurality and Its Theological Implications," 49-50.

[52]Note the similarity to Tillich's understanding of being and nonbeing in the God above the God of theism: Paul Tillich, *The Courage to Be* (New Haven CT: Yale University Press, 1952) 178-90.

[53]Gilkey, "Plurality and Its Theological Implications," 50.

theology need some basis in absoluteness in order to reject particular forms and structures that prevent liberation. Relative absoluteness, then, can become the basis of critiques of religious ideas and forms.

Second, Gilkey affirms that grace and salvation are experienced through various non-Christian religious forms. As a result of his ongoing participation in Buddhist-Christian dialogues, Gilkey becomes increasingly explicit about the basic parity of religious traditions. Perhaps in part because Buddhist categories seem directly counter to Christian ones, Gilkey extends his acceptance of revelation, grace, and so forth, within Buddhism to include other traditions.

Third, Gilkey takes seriously the personal absolute religious commitment that characterizes faith. Thereby, he recognizes the psychological dimension of relativizing religious truth and accepting religious parity. Rather than dismissing it as closed-minded or exclusivist, he realizes its importance while setting that commitment within the larger global context of religious diversity.

Finally, Gilkey supports rethinking traditional Christian understandings in relation to ideas from other religious traditions. For example, he acknowledges the seeming contradiction of no-self and yet self-identity made concrete in Buddhist-Christian dialogue as an important challenge to traditional Christian anthropology. Dialogue does not just exchange understandings, but enables and stimulates personal and theological transformation.

III. Comparisons, Evaluations, and Conclusions

Just as Gilkey's theology of religious plurality is rooted in a historical-cultural context, it is also part of the theological context that has produced numerous theologies dealing with the interrelationship of diverse religions. Like Gilkey's theology of religious plurality, many of these theologies have a Christian basis, but some arise from Hindu, Buddhist, Jewish, and Muslim contexts. Comparisons with several Christian thinkers and with one Buddhist theorist will help to reveal Gilkey's contributions to the theological discussions of religious pluralism.

In "Plurality and Its Theological Implications," Gilkey attempts a new approach for dealing with religious pluralism. He both rejects traditionalist, exclusivist approaches and criticizes the imperialism of inclusivist approaches, which subsume non-Christian ideas and practices into Christian terms and actions. Gilkey argues that, not only does the experience of interreligious dialogue relativize one's own faith, but that experience also relativizes "the *referent* of that faith."[54] The *whole system* of theological symbols and doctrines, *not merely specific doctrines or symbols*, must be reinterpreted. Simply to eliminate focus on Christ or to move from Christocentrism to theocentrism, alternatives explored by John Hick and Wilfred Cantwell Smith, is not radical enough for Gilkey; the remaining theology is too Western and, therefore, not fully inclusive.[55]

Gilkey also tries to move away from Schleiermacher's and Tillich's forms of inclusivism, because both perspectives rest on an assumed final revelation in Jesus as the Christ, accepting other faiths within the Christian interpretation rather than on their own terms. Moreover, he rejects Hindu and Buddhist theories that include other faiths within their own versions of absoluteness and mysticism. Gilkey admits to using similar strategies in his earlier approaches to religious pluralism, but now he finds such universalist approaches "parochial" and "inadequate to the new situation." Because such approaches deny true legitimacy to the particular perspectives and forms of the diverse religions, he offers a similar criticism of perennial philosophy or theories centered in a mystical core. Perennial and mystical approaches do radically relativize forms of revelation and theology—all except the mystical.[56]

In spite of his critiques of these approaches, Gilkey maintains some parallels with these thinkers in his effort to transcend the duality of absoluteness and relativity. For example, Gilkey's analysis shows strong influence from Tillich's approach to religious pluralism. Although moving away from Tillich's inclusivism, Gilkey follows Tillich's understanding of symbols, paradox, the need for absoluteness, the critique of idolatry, and the claim that the ultimate or unconditioned is manifest in the relative and the conditioned. Symbols reflect that ambiguous and sometimes paradoxical manifestation; they point beyond and criticize themselves and yet manifest the unconditioned within themselves.[57] Gilkey maintains,

---

[54]Gilkey, "Plurality and Its Theological Implications," 41.

[55]Gilkey, "Plurality and Its Theological Implications," 41. See John Hick, *God Has Many Names: An Interpretation of Religion; Human Responses to the Transcendent* (New Haven CT: Yale University Press, 1989); idem, *A Christian Theology of Religions: The Rainbow of Faiths* (Louisville KY: Westminster/John Knox Press, 1995); and Smith, *Towards a World Theology.*

[56]Gilkey, "Plurality and Its Theological Implications," 42, 43, 48.

[57]Gilkey, "Plurality and Its Theological Implications," 48; cf. Tillich, *Dynamics of Faith,* 97.

with Tillich, the necessary affirmation of absoluteness *both* as a kind of limit point to the relative manifestations *and* as a real presence within the relative (and, thus, not a purely formal ultimacy). The dialectic between the relative and the absolute prevents absolutization of the finite and relative (idolatry); the absolute also provides a ground from which injustice and the demonic can be opposed, thus enabling liberation and creativity.[58] The intersection of the relative and the absolute implied in this dialectic is paradoxical, as is Gilkey's formulation of relative absoluteness. In the end, whereas Tillich maintains an inclusivist approach to religious plurality that allows finality to the Christian revelation, Gilkey's later writings more radically subject his own approach to the relativizing effects of the dialectic and paradox.

Like Hick and Smith, Gilkey affirms the infinite (the transcendent—Smith; or the Real—Hick) that is beyond and yet connected to finite religious symbols and forms. Also like Smith, Gilkey is concerned to recognize the personal, lived dimension of faith—the sense of commitment and the centrality of faith within the lives of religious persons. Hick and Smith would agree with Gilkey that the infinite mystery cannot be comprehended from a human standpoint. Unlike Hick and Smith, however, Gilkey does not think his own theology can be universally applied to or include all religions. Yet, like Hick, Smith, and Tillich, Gilkey does propose his theory as applicable beyond Christianity and, therefore, as holding some universality, even if not absolute. Gilkey's approach, like Smith's effort to develop a world theology, is rooted in a particular religious tradition with openness to other religions and to the impact from dialogue with those religions.

Several other recent theories of religious pluralism attempt, as does Gilkey, to take the particularity of religious traditions more seriously than Hick, mystical theories, or inclusivism. Both S. Mark Heim and Paul Knitter argue that religious faiths should be relativized in relationship to one another, rather than in relationship to one God or one transcendent goal.[59] They too are concerned to retain the importance of specific religious faiths, but assert more clearly than Gilkey a diversity of redemptions (although that conclusion would fit with Gilkey's theory).

---

[58]Gilkey, "Plurality and Its Theological Implications," 48-49.
[59]S. Mark Heim, *Salvations: Truth and Difference in Religion* (Maryknoll NY: Orbis Books, 1995); Knitter, *One Earth Many Religions*.

The Buddhist philosopher, Masao Abe, like Gilkey, focuses on the historical, cultural context in his approach to religious pluralism. Abe stresses more than Gilkey, however, the irreligious and nonreligious dimensions of contemporary technology, Marxist politics, and secularism as important reasons for interfaith dialogue and analysis of pluralism. Abe's theoretical basis for religious pluralism, although strongly rooted in the Kyoto school of Buddhism, shares with Gilkey a concern for not absolutizing any particular form and a dialectic of relativity and ultimacy. Gilkey affirms the dialectical unity of being and nonbeing, while Abe pushes that dialectic to a nondualistic oneness, preceding the duality of being and nonbeing.[60] Gilkey continues to maintain more priority for being, creating some asymmetry of being and nonbeing, while Abe wants to maintain a symmetry as well as a prior nonduality. Gilkey and Abe have engaged in dialogues that bring them almost to agreement on some Christian understandings expressed in light of Buddhist views.[61] For example, Abe and Gilkey basically agree on the understanding of the self-emptying of God as part of the character of the divine itself.[62] Nonbeing, no-self, creation, redemption, and suffering are among the topics where serious discussion and intellectual challenges have occurred.[63] For example, Gilkey accepts Abe's critique of the Christian view of nature, acknowledging Buddhism's more positive view of nature. Similarly, Gilkey suggests that Christianity should learn from the Buddhist approach of holding finite life (*samsara*) and liberation (*nirvana*) together as interdependent and begin to think of creation, the fall, and redemption as interdependent in any one moment, rather than as distinct moments.[64] Clearly, Gilkey's approach to religious pluralism deepens as his encounters and dialogues with people of diverse faiths increase. His Christian commitment does not decrease, but his sense of Christianity in relationship to other religions clearly changes, as does his understanding of Christian doctrines.

---

[60]Gilkey, *SAS*, 126, 136-37.

[61]Masao Abe, *Buddhism and Interfaith Dialogue*, ed. Steven Heine (Honolulu: University of Hawaii Press, 1995) 11-12, 18-20, 205-22.

[62]Abe, *Buddhism and Interfaith Dialogue*, 216-17.

[63]See discussions in *Buddhist-Christian Studies* 5 (1985) and in Abe, *Buddhism and Interfaith Dialogue*, chap. 18.

[64]Gilkey, in *Buddhism and Interfaith Dialogue*, by Abe, 214.

Gilkey has made several major contributions to the discussion of religious pluralism: (1) to retain the importance of personal religious commitment, with its connection to absoluteness; (2) to insist on the importance of the particularity of religious traditions, even while maintaining their relativity in relation to each other and to absoluteness; and (3) to respond to non-Christians not only with tolerance and respect, but also with a willingness to have one's own theology transformed by the encounters.

Although "relative absoluteness" does hold together dialectically the experienced oppositions of the relativity of all religions and the absoluteness implied in religious commitment, the doctrine keeps Gilkey balanced precariously on a boundary point between the two poles of the dialectic. To the extent that he is able to hold both in a dynamic, paradoxical center, the paradox can simultaneously present both the oneness of a particular religious commitment and the multiplicity of truth in all religions.

Koen DePryck asserts that paradoxes show the limits of our knowledge as well as of our expressions of knowledge.[65] Particularly in relation to absoluteness, paradoxes point to the element of uncertainty in our present level of knowledge and can push us to a more complex level of knowledge. For Tillich, the paradox is connected to the breaking in of the Unconditioned in the conditioned—a kind of primal paradox that grounds all theology.[66] "Relative absoluteness" corresponds to this kind of primal, ontological paradox; it expresses the manifestation of ultimacy as well as the lack of ultimacy within one's experience.

The tension of the paradox can become a criterion against absolutization of a finite form or meaning.[67] In the midst of the dialectic within the paradox, ultimacy and absoluteness are experienced, but one cannot claim ultimacy for one's expression of that experience. The paradox of relative absoluteness, then, can be used to combat approaches that assert absoluteness in one locus, excluding the validity of any other manifestations.

---

[65]Koen DePryck, *Knowledge, Evolution, and Paradox: The Ontology of Language* (Albany: State University of New York Press, 1993) 80, 152, 154.

[66]See Paul Tillich, "The Conquest of the Concept of Religion in the Philosophy of Religion," in *What Is Religion?* ed. James L. Adams (New York: Harper & Row, 1969) 122-23.

[67]See Mary Ann Stenger, "The Significance of Paradox for Theological Verification: Difficulties and Possibilities," *International Journal for Philosophy of Religion* 14 (1983): 171-82; and idem, "The Problem of Cross-Cultural Criteria of Religious Truths," *Modern Theology* 3/4 (1987): 315-32.

Such a description may seem too abstract for the existential experience of religious commitment and encounters with other religious faiths. Yet, the experience of such encounters contains the paradox, often reflected as an existential conflict between the absoluteness of one's own religious faith and the desire to be open to and even transformed by other religious faiths. Gilkey's approach does resonate with the experiences of many people engaged in interreligious dialogue.

Finally, Gilkey tantalizes his readers with suggestions of how Christian doctrines might be transformed and reconceptualized by the encounter with Buddhism. Because the foundational concepts of Buddhism stand in apparent opposition to their Christian counterparts, this transformation is the most challenging and the most exciting. We await a more complete discussion of this new theology, developed through ongoing interreligious dialogues and reflections.

Chapter 8

Theology, Submission, and Language in the Thought of Langdon Gilkey

Charles E. Winquist

What has Athens to do with Jerusalem,
the Academy with the Church?
—Tertullian *De praescriptione haereticorum* 7

Introduction

The theology of Langdon Gilkey has to do with both Athens and Jerusalem and also with the Academy and the Church. I do not think it would be an exaggeration to claim that Langdon Gilkey and Gabriel Vahanian are the only two major theologians who have consistently sought, since the 1960s, to develop fully secular theologies that are deeply rooted in the traditions of Athens and Jerusalem, the Academy and the Church.[1] Gilkey has written that "any current theology . . . that does not recognize and seek reflectively to deal with this presence of secularity, of doubt, of skepticism, and so of a sense of the meaninglessness of religious language inside the Church as well as outside, and so inside the theologian and believer, is so far irrelevant to our present situation."[2] More recently, Vahanian has written that, "with the secular, theology recovers its integrity and becomes at last autonomous."[3] He alludes to a religious authority no less than Jesus whose parabolic preaching likens the kingdom of God to what occurs in the world, in the *saecula saeculorum.*[4] What is the image of theological thinking that is either operating or implied in these statements? I am not suggesting that Gilkey and Vahanian are saying the same thing theologically. Their works, however, both posit

---

[1]Robert Scharlemann clearly works in both traditions, but it would be difficult to understand his work as fully secular. Thomas J. J. Altizer's apocalypticism defies restriction to a plane of immanence. Mark C. Taylor and I are clearly outside the church.

[2]Langdon Gilkey, *Naming the Whirlwind: The Renewal of God-Language* (Indianapolis and New York: Bobbs-Merrill, 1969) 10; hereafter cited as *NW.*

[3]Gabriel Vahanian, "The Denatured Nature of Ethics: In Praise of the Secular," in *Philosophie de la religion entre ethique et ontologie*, textes reunis par Marco M. Olivette, Biblioteca dell' Archivio Filosofia 14 (Padova [Padua], Italy: CEDAM, 1996) 514.

[4]Vahanian, "Denatured Nature of Ethics," 514.

an important question: What does it mean for Christian theologians to give an epistemological priority to the secular spirit and yet not fall into a simpleminded atheistic secularism? It would seem that, in both of their works, what is intelligible is fully inscribed on a plane of immanence. Intelligibility means inscription on a plane of immanence. Intelligibility, however, is not coextensive with reality. Even within a theological circle of thinking, there are affects that elude or are more than propositional sense. Not only can theological thinking formulate limit-questions that reach beyond its own sensibilities, but there are felt realities that can challenge the adequacy of any particular formulations or thematizations.

I. A Secular Image of Theological Thinking

I do not want to fixate reflections on the theologies of Gilkey and Vahanian in the work of the 1960s; at that time, nevertheless, Vahanian was writing the death of God in his work and Gilkey was grappling with the meaning of theological thinking that could write the death of God. I mention them together because they both affirmed the secular and continued to write Christian theology after the death of God. This was a time for negotiating an image and meaning for theological thinking that neither abandoned theology nor retreated into an evangelical orthodoxy. Clearly, the death-of-God movement marked a crisis in theological traditions coming from both Athens and Jerusalem. The voice of Nietzsche's madman was being heard. Theology had to learn how to think itself in ways that understood the exigencies of a gay science. Nietzsche's notion of a gay science deracinates the Greek metaphysical tradition as well as Judeo-Christian historical and revelatory traditions.

One may misread Gilkey's theology by oversimplifying Tillich's method of correlation and applying it to Gilkey, so that the metaphysical/ philosophical tradition raises questions about the human situation that can be answered by Christian revelations and symbol systems. What is important in Gilkey's diverse publications is that he reads these theological traditions in their integrity.

Although Aristotle equates first philosophy, the science of *being qua being*, wisdom, and theology, Gilkey refers back to Anaximander's move to the limits of intelligibility in a notion of a primordial undifferentiated stuff, in order to see the genius of Greek theological thinking as it then comes forward in complexes of ontological and epistemological questions and concepts that are especially visible in the distillations of the crises of epistemology in the transcendental philosophy of Kant. Gilkey reads the history of philosophy with the sensibilities of a transcendental interrogation. What are the conditions that make knowledge possible? This can be a general philosophical question, but Gilkey also asks a specific theological question. What are the conditions that make theological knowledge possible? The answer will not be simply metaphysical because, in the trajectory of that which we have conveniently called the Greek tradition, the declaration of the end of metaphysics by Nietzsche and Heidegger or the closure of the ontotheological tradition of a philosophy of presence in deconstructionist thought parallels the death of God in Judeo-Christian theologies. Theology as a science of *being qua being* is as hard to sustain in the positivist spirit of the twentieth century as are historical theologies of proclamation and revelation. The epistemic dominance of the secular makes this era postmetaphysical and post-Christian. This is not the same as saying that this era is unmetaphysical or un-Christian. The theological streams flowing from Athens and Jerusalem are just thought differently. Thinking thinks itself differently because of the tremendous development of the physical sciences and technology, because of the hermeneutics of suspicion, and because of a history of abjection that has characterized so much of the twentieth century. The shift is ethical and moral, epistemic and linguistic.

The most important issue in *Naming the Whirlwind* is the definition and assessment of contemporary images for thinking theologically. As a question, this issue is not fully resolved and reappears with different appropriations in Gilkey's subsequent works. As he wrote, "[t]he theological debate has moved from the question of the character of God to the more radical question of his reality, and from the question of the nature and form of religious language to the more radical question of its possibility as a mode of meaningful discourse"; or, the "current questions concern more the meaning than the validity of theological discourse."[5]

The image of thinking, and this includes theological thinking, is only secondarily philosophical or epistemological. Thinking is always involved in negotiations; in a book by this title, Gilles Deleuze has written that "the image of thought is what philosophy as it were presupposes; it precedes philosophy, not a nonphilosophical understanding this time but a prephilosophical understanding. . . . It's the image of thought that guides

---

[5]Gilkey, *NW*, 13.

the creation of concepts."[6] What is very complicated in reading Gilkey's theology is that the prephilosophical image of thought has to do with both Athens and Jerusalem. It is as if there are two images and, thus, two trajectories that form a double helix coiling around each, resonating with each other, intersecting each other in specific historical moments, but never resolving their doubleness in a durable fusion. There is wisdom which is theology and there is revelation which is theology. In both trajectories, there is the creation of concepts. Both trajectories confront the secular with their own characteristic losses, metaphysics, and God.

Gilkey neither rescues Athens with a neoorthodox or neoevangelical reaction, nor rescues Jerusalem by sacrificing Christ to a humanistic Jesus. Instead, he addresses the secular and increasingly makes explicit a concept of secular theology. The secular is the realm of the *logos*. With the references to Vahanian in writing about Gilkey, I aim to help clarify the meaning of the secular; for Vahanian confronted theology with the secular as a fundamental epistemic transformation, not as a problem or inconvenience for theological thinking. Vahanian never equated the death of God with atheism, or thought of atheism as a condition for the secular meaning of Christianity, for he realized that the secular is not contrasted with the sacred. Rather, the profane is contrasted with the sacred. The secular replaces the sacred epistemically in the determination of conditions for thinking intelligibility and reality. The secular is the transcendental ground for thinking ultimate reality. These are the circumstances in which Gilkey images theological thinking and creates theological concepts.[7]

Following this double trajectory of theology, Gilkey writes that "the loss of metaphysics in philosophy and the loss of God-language in theology are alike symptoms of what we shall call the 'radical secularity' of our culture." The question for theology, whether it has roots in Athens or Jerusalem, is if it can be a meaningful discourse: "What 'meaninglessness' implies, we submit, is a sense of the total disrelation of a given set

---

[6]Gilles Deleuze, *Negotiations, 1972–1990*, trans. Martin Joughin (New York: Columbia University Press, 1995) 148.

[7]Gilkey equates Vahanian's position with an untroubled neoorthodoxy but also refers to his excellent descriptions of the secular spirit (Gilkey, *NW*, 27, 70). Now, clearly, the biblical dimensions of Vahanian's theology are understood in a profoundly secular milieu. With the secular, theology recovers its integrity (Vahanian, "Denatured Nature of Ethics," 514).

of concepts or a language game to experience and to life." Gilkey equates the secular with the cultural spirit (*Geist*) of our time, a cultural spirit marked by the characteristics of contingency, relativism, transience, and autonomy. The gods are dead. Familiar structures of coherence, order, and value have vanished: "Darwin and Nietzsche, Russell and Freud, not Marx and Kierkegaard, are the real fathers of the present Geist." This secular spirit is the deepest background of the theological ferment of the late twentieth century. Experienced reality is marked by these secular characteristics; the question for theology is whether its talk has anything to do with this reality.[8]

Does theology have anything to do with the stuff of life? If not, can it be a matter of ultimate concern? This is both a matter of the definition of faith and a matter of the assessment of the possibility for theological thinking. Gilkey is very much aware that we cannot beg the question of God-language in a secular age. Traditional or "recognized methods of theological construction . . . presuppose precisely those affirmations which that [the secular] age finds it impossible to grant." Gilkey deliberately goes outside "the walls of the Church into the broad arena of the world, where our own deepest attitudes about what is real and true are formed."[9] In *Shantung Compound*, that which he called the wisdom of the household budget is in fact a variation of theological exigency for thinking in a fully secular milieu. In order for theology to address an ultimate concern, it must be related to life.

Gilkey sees that the theological task or at least the prolegomenon to theological thinking is the development of a hermeneutic of secular experience: "Our task, then, is to investigate in the broad range of secular experience what function and use, and therefore what meaningfulness and intelligibility, the realm of discourse called 'religious language' may have." Fascinatingly, in this secular prolegomenon, the loss of God, the silence of the sacred, and the end of metaphysics tell us about dimensions of ultimacy. "One of the most striking things about human existence in this epoch," Gilkey notes, "is that we notice this relation to an unconditioned as much by its absence as by its presence."[10] It appears that the secular prolegomenon is not simply a prolegomenon; it is itself a modality of theological thinking.

---

[8]Gilkey, *NW*, 14, 18, 71.
[9]Gilkey, *NW*, 201, 231, 232.
[10]Gilkey, *NW*, 234, 301, also see 309.

The language of the death of God is God-language. The thinking of the end of metaphysics is a metaphysical thinking. The prolegomenon is an empirical rather than apophatic negative theology: "A secular prolegomenon to theology, therefore, is one which begins in our ordinary experience of being in the world and elicits hermeneutically the meanings for religious language and its symbolic forms latent within that experience."[11] Absence can be as important as presence in these experiences. Limits or limit-questions tell us much about the quality and meaning of experience. We might not know much about the sea by mapping the shore of an island, but we know something of what the island is not and what the sea is not. Gilkey understands that theological exigencies in thinking are such that the range of what we can ask can exceed the range of what we can answer.

This discrepancy between the excess of inquiry and the limitation of answerability is a real experience on a plane of immanence within the secular domain: "To us, the modality of our secular existence—in terms of both the positive and the negative character of the tone of our modern being in the world and so of our felt meanings and resultant behavior—is out of relation to the symbolic forms of its self-understanding." Gilkey, thus, challenges the adequacy but not the necessity of secular theology or a secular understanding of existence "on its failure to provide symbolic forms capable of thematizing the actual character of its own life." He says that the "unalterable requirement" of the secular mood for any relevant theological thinking is that it "be related to this worldly life, evident within it, and creative for it."[12] It increasingly appears that the challenge to secular thinking, based on its failure to thematize and articulate the complexities and ambiguities of actual living, is that it recognize within itself a theological exigency. In 1969, Gilkey saw traces of ultimacy within secular experience as a nonsecular interloper, but he paradoxically defines and locates this interloper within the language and space of the secular. In the midst of the ordinary relative realities of worldly life, we meet presuppositions that are limits, demands, or ultimate questions.

Gilkey thinks of these traces of ultimacy, whether marked by presence or absence, as being different in kind from ordinary worldly experiences; but I fail to see why they should be thought of as nonsecular. They manifest themselves on a plane of secular immanence.

---

[11]Gilkey, NW, 260.
[12]Gilkey, NW, 249, 250.

Thinking's capacity to formulate extreme expressions of ultimacy or limit-questions is not a counterinstance to Wittgenstein's famous opening sentence of the *Tractatus*: "the world is all that is the case."[13] Even Anselm's formulation, of "that than which nothing greater can be conceived," falls within the formulative capacity of secular thinking.

Again, that which Gilkey calls a secular prolegomenon to theology is itself theological thinking.[14] It may not be easily identified with Christian theology or with an Aristotelian metaphysical theology; but, it is a worldly theological thinking. It is a matter of ultimate concern. This assertion does not beg the theological questions of metaphysical or revelatory theologies. It stays within the world that is the case. "A *secular prolegomenon to theology*, therefore, is one which begins in our ordinary experience of being in the world and elicits hermeneutically the meanings for religious language and its symbolic forms latent within that experience. . . . We must begin as best we can with the concrete character of secular experience and defend religious experience *only* in terms of what we find there."[15] That we can do this is a witness to the possibilities for a secular theology. The exclusive language of "only" keeps theology honest to what is actually experienced; but, in no way, does it force experience to be less than what it is. Gilkey claims that there is an experience of ultimacy that belongs to ordinary experience. Even if it is on a boundary, there is always an inside as well as an outside to a boundary.

Gilkey understands *meaning* functionally and pragmatically. Linguistic symbols have meaning and use, including a religious meaning and use, only if they "thematize some significant area of common, ordinary experience; and conversely if they *do* so function, then *ipso facto* they have, or can have, significant meanings in the life of even a secular age."[16] He appeals to felt immediate experience and avoids a linguistic positivism by acknowledging that these experiences require elucidation

---

[13]Ludwig Wittgenstein, *Tractatus Logico-Philosophicus*, trans. D. F. Pears and B. F. McGuinness (London: Routledge and Kegan Paul, 1961) 7.

[14]My claim is a conscious misreading of *Naming the Whirlwind*: "This has been an ontic prolegomenon to theological discourse, not an example of theological discourse" (Gilkey, *NW*, 413). I am arguing that secular theology is not Christian theology, but it is theological because of the interrogative theological exigency (the possibility of unrestricted inquiry) that it embodies.

[15]Gilkey, *NW*, 260-61; emphasis mine.

[16]Gilkey, *NW*, 272.

of a hermeneutic of experience. The basic unit of intelligibility is more than the word or the sentence, if we are to grasp the affect in experience. He clearly recognizes that eliminating meaning from meaning does violence to the integrity of experience. The repression of meaning is a methodological and a psychological pathology.

There is no pure speech and there can be no pure logic for speech. Gilkey can make no metaphysical assumptions that are outside of the impure and entangled voices of secular discourse in the development of his prolegomenon. Just as he has no simple access from within secular experience to revelation, he has no access to a pure ontology. He says that the analysis in his secular prolegomenon will be ontic rather than ontological. His analysis will search for the relation of *words* to lived experience. It is Gilkey's belief that there is a "latent but pervasive and immensely significant dimension of ultimacy and sacrality which forms the continual horizon of man's being in the world. . . . [W]e shall, therefore, conduct an 'ontic' analysis, hoping to uncover the sacral dimension in man's secular life, the shape or character of the horizon of our existence as this is directly apprehended and experienced in our actual life."[17]

This ontic analysis is not a specific methodology as much as it is a strategy for uncovering dimensions of ultimacy within the secular. I am not sure there is any gain in calling such dimensions sacred and, thereby, segregating them from the integrated experiences in which they were discerned. I would like to characterize Gilkey's strategy for thinking within the secular as metonymical. That is, he posits formulations of religious traditions, questions of ultimacy, and other limiting questions next to and within the fluxes and flows of ordinary experience. This forced metonymical pressure unsettles and defamiliarizes the ordinariness of experience and denies its thinking any simple closure. The ordinary, then, is a witness to the extraordinary. The ordinary is intensified in its openness. The ordinary is no longer only ordinary and certainly is not dreary or drab. The becoming of the future is indeterminate because of the conceptual valuations and reversions that mark its emergence. Gilkey's strategy can enfranchise a transvaluation of values and a *yes* to the meaning of secular life, as it fissures the ordinary with new possibilities for the actualization of the ordinary/extraordinary. A secular theology has

---

[17]Gilkey, *NW*, 275, 280-81.

a certain grasp on what might be called, in the language of Huston Smith, a divine ordinariness.

The juxtaposition of theological formulations of extremity can create interference patterns that fissure ordinary discourse and ordinary expectations within experience. Such juxtapositions can mark a void or create a hope for a coherence of meaning within the ordinary. In theological thinking, we experience ourselves as unfinished women and men. Gilkey suggests that the secular spirit is in tension with actual existence and out of relation to the symbolic forms of its self-understanding.[18] Fissuring the surface of discursive practices opens experience to the intensity of its actuality.[19] On the level of felt existence, secular thinking has failed to articulate and thematize the character of its own life, and "it is on this basis that we shall argue that religious discourse is meaningful in the midst of secular life."[20]

Strangely, the experience of *meaninglessness* may be *meaningful*. The death of God, the loss of God, or the silence of that which had been sacred may reveal to us dimensions of ultimacy in the secular realm: "our experience reveals as often as not the absence of God and so a sense of loss, of a Void where we are looking for something; but it is a special kind of a Void and a loss which, like our experience of sacrality, participates in the general character of this region of experience. . . . Here we experience our own ultimate incapability." Here we experience an anxiety about the absence in secular life of symbols or other constructs that concern our identity, values, and destiny. Here our love of life is challenged existentially. Gilkey says that, without consistent and profound religious symbolism, secular experience is blind: "Its joys are left uncelebrated and so unexperienced, and its terrors uncomprehended and so unconquered."[21]

If secular theology holds promise, it will enable us to "begin to notice, to see, and to feel the immense creativity of the 'given' in life, those aspects of our being which neither we nor anyone else can create

---

[18]Gilkey, *NW*, 248-49.

[19]Gilkey is deeply informed by Whitehead's understanding of the value and intensity of the actual in the primary mode of causal efficacy and the diminishment of intensity in the secondarily conscious mode of presentational immediacy. Causal efficacy is the primary mode of feeling.

[20]Gilkey, *NW*, 250.

[21]Gilkey, *NW*, 301-302, 306.

and yet which are the foundation of all that we are and love."[22] There is terror and the threat of meaninglessness in the secular world filled with contingencies. There can be an *unbearable lightness to being*. Gilkey, however, also indexes common aspects of our secular experience that are positive: a deep joy in living, the pulsating vitality and strength of life, awe at the wonder and beauty of life. There is a positive creativity in the given. There is something rather than nothing, and there is always the threat of nonbeing.

Secular theology lives in this tension between the creativity of the given and the threat of nonbeing. The problem has been set before us. The felt actuality of reality is incommensurate with the ability to give expression to its depth and complexity. Human beings, nevertheless, "must think and conceive what they feel if they are vividly to apprehend it, fully to appropriate it, and especially if they are communally to share and perpetuate it."[23] We desire to think theologically but are not free to choose the conditions, mood, or tonality of dominant experiences that determine how we think. In our time, we must think in relation, with or against, the dominant figurations of the secular spirit: contingency, relativity, transience, and autonomy.

II. A Christian Symbolic Theology

Gilkey never lost sight of the epistemic problematic that he defined in *Naming the Whirlwind*. It explicitly resurfaces in his studies of religion and science, but it is also strategically interwoven into his specifically Christian theological studies. The image of theological thinking as a double helix now has a slightly different meaning than the heuristic formulation that I used to introduce Gilkey's theology. Gilkey now writes a secular theology, which he calls a prolegomenon, that can coexist with and coil around the interpretation of religious or theological classics of Athens or Jerusalem, pressuring the experiences of meaning, but not violating the integrity of either secular or traditional thinking. Theology is a practice or symbolic activity. This activity gives form to definite regions of our lifeworld.[24] This thinking is specifically located and, therefore, perspectival. As with science, the truth of theology is a symbolic

---

[22]Gilkey, *NW*, 311.

[23]Gilkey, *NW*, 419.

[24]Langdon Gilkey, *Reaping the Whirlwind: A Christian Interpretation of History* (New York: Seabury Press, 1976) 144; hereafter cited as *RW*.

perspective on the real: "the role of symbols is crucial; the expression of what is known appears in metaphors, models, and analogies rather than in literal, univocal descriptions."[25] The mechanisms for action are tropic figurations within textual productions. In the coiling of traditional and secular thinking, each thinking has a perspective on the other that can contribute to its own development.

Gilkey's strategy for thinking allows him to speak of different levels of meaning and truth. There can be what he calls the historical and the *eidetic* meaning of traditional symbols. These are not enough. Meaning must be related to the lifeworld existentially and reflectively. It is possible, however, for these meanings to coexist on different textual trajectories. The *eidetic* meanings derived from the *Bible* and the historical Christian traditions "give 'Christian' form to our understanding of God, of ourselves, our world, our history, and our future."[26] The reflective meanings derived from a secular theology give immediate relevance to thinking in the lifeworld. They pressure and complement each other *per*spectively. The *eidetic* meanings of Christian theology, with its retention of mythology, allow ultimacy to "be expressed in determinate and not merely in negative terms."[27] This contrasts with secular theologies that are fundamentally negative theologies. Gilkey can recognize dimensions of ultimacy in the experience and proclamation of the death of God and at the same time recognize the human capacity symbolically to express dimensions of ultimacy in a determinate language.[28]

Gilkey has deeply founded his understanding of the secular in his understanding of the Enlightenment and its epistemic entailments. In particular, the Kantian problematic or maze is very important to him; indeed, he entitles a chapter in his recent book on science and religion, "Whatever Happened to Immanuel Kant?" Kant's *maze* does not hover in the background of his thinking as it might in many of the popular con-

---

[25]Langdon Gilkey, *Nature, Reality, and the Sacred: The Nexus of Science and Religion*, Theology and the Sciences series, ed. Kevin J. Sharpe (Minneapolis: Fortress Press, 1993) 18, 31; hereafter cited as *NRS*.

[26]Gilkey, *RW*, 140, 143.

[27]Langdon Gilkey, *Religion and the Scientific Future: Reflections on Myth, Science, and Theology* (New York: Harper & Row, 1970) 116.

[28]See examples of Gilkey's theological writings that give a determinate form to ultimacy and, yet, can coexist with the epistemic undecidability and indeterminacy of his writings on the secular and scientific worlds: e.g., Gilkey, *RW*; and idem, *Message and Existence: An Introduction to Christian Theology* (New York: Seabury Press, 1979).

temporary cosmological reflections of some scientists; rather, it is always front and center in his thinking.[29] He realizes that the Kantian problematic is no less a problem for cosmology than for theology and metaphysics. To brush philosophical problems aside by accepting a "cultural atmosphere" that embraces the "plausibility structures of positivism" is too obviously a sleight of hand to be a matter of ultimate concern in an interrogative framework of unrestricted questioning.[30]

Gilkey discerns the internal meaning of external relations that is an experiential confrontation with Kant's *Critique of Pure Reason*. He writes that "the common methodological thread that guides Whitehead, Tillich and Santayana out of the subjectivity of the Kantian maze is the notion of 'participation.' . . . The process manifests itself in us, as well as in those objects 'outside' of us. . . . In us, 'being' comes to self-awareness and self-consciousness (Tillich); prehensions change to apprehensions, consciousness, and intellection (Whitehead); the rush of matter becomes the awareness of spirit (Santayana)."[31] This internal relatedness is meaning, the self-consciousness of meaning. It is the constitutive character of thinking—philosophically, theologically, or scientifically—and not an accident or by-product of thinking: "Self-awareness, knowledge of the subject from the inside of her own experiencing, reflecting and judging— that is, from the inside of her knowing and the meanings she knows—is as constitutive of science as are sensations and measurements."[32] The self-awareness in cognitive participation is self-authenticating. You would have to decide against yourself, diminish the intensity of your feelings and generally make yourself smaller, if you choose not to think reflexively the felt qualities of your own experience. Gilkey has a confidence in life that makes this decision untenable but not inconceivable. It is possible to be victims of our own thinking.

Our thinking is a participation in nature. This is our nature and Gilkey will affirm that nature, as life, is a realm of meanings: "the cosmos, as providing the conditions of life, is indirectly such a realm; its order over eons of radical change, a puzzle; and its itinerary toward our world of explicit meanings over almost endless improbabilities, an

---

[29]Gilkey cites several examples: Pagels, Sagan, Weinberg, Dawkins, Barrow, and Tipler (Gilkey, *NRS*, 44).

[30]Gilkey, *NRS*, 45.

[31]Gilkey, *NRS*, 71.

[32]Gilkey, *NRS*, 38.

astonishment." In understanding nature, we can speak of traces of the sacred: power, life, and order. Gilkey emphasizes, however, that in nature or the silence of the cosmos we *only* have traces of meaning and value. All is not well: "Throughout experience, natural and historical, these traces of value seem to become continually submerged by some antithetical force; for power wanes; life is wounded and dies, vanishes; and order becomes threatening disorder."[33] These polarities between meaning and its negation, good and evil, pose the most profound questions of religion and theology. That we are finite and will die is evidently real. How we think and stand in relation to the power of life and its negation is an elementary definition of religion. That we think and stand in relation to the power of life and its negation is the peculiar nature of the privilege of consciousness. This thinking is a *natural theology* or, as Aristotle suggests, *first philosophy* and *wisdom*.

For Gilkey, there is, problematically, an unfinished quality to any natural theology: "The effort of natural theology to understand and articulate the whole of experience, it seems to me, never represents the initiating source of 'religious knowledge'; hence this effort cannot function as the final criterion of this knowledge." Instead, the locus of "religious knowledge," knowledge of God, is historical and existential. Here Gilkey is deeply Christian in his affirmation of a religious knowledge: "The important knowledge of God is not philosophical; it is 'religious,' that is, it is on the one hand existential and on the other communicated through symbols to the community that acknowledges the most fundamental disclosure and witnesses to that knowledge." He affirms the singularity of an event or events of disclosure to which there can be witnesses.[34]

Gilkey, therefore, affirms the reality of a God who acts in history. He affirms covenanted communities that have a special clarity in the knowledge of a God who acts in history: "If in nature the divine power, life, and order or law are disclosed through dim traces, and if the divine redemptive love is revealed only in ambiguous hints in and through the tragedy of suffering and death, it is in the life of the peoples of God that all this is disclosed in much greater certainty, clarity, and power." The historical disclosure of God intensifies the traces of the divine in nature, so that they become "genuine signs of the power, of the order, and of the will of God." Thus, that which Gilkey called a prolegomenon in *Naming*

---

[33]Gilkey, *NRS*, 134, 135.
[34]Gilkey, *NRS*, 194.

the Whirlwind, and in his later work a natural theology, Gilkey thinks to be very important for, but not the vital center of, Christian theology. It is important because it expands and deepens our knowledge of the self and the world. The traces of God appear at the limits of our finite analyses. There are limit-questions to which Gilkey believes that "God remains the sole reasonable answer." It, however, does appear that God is a credible word in our theological thinking because of the historical manifestation of God. If there is not a credible historical witness to the manifestation of God in history, then theology is left only with traces of the divine.[35]

There is a tension in Gilkey's theology for which I cannot find a simple resolution. His detailed articulation of the secular spirit makes some of us hesitate with a certain incredulity when we are hearers of the word of Christian proclamation. The recognition of contingency in secular thinking applies to the disclosure of God as well as to all the other singularities of experience. I have experienced a revelation of God or I have not. I have to be at the right place, perhaps in the right community, at the right time.

It is possible that there can be an aesthetic justification for thinking in a Christian symbolic framework even without a historical justification. It may be, and I think this is consonant with Gilkey's theology, that thinking the Christian symbol system next to a secular inquiry can intensify the traces of the divine within the ordinary and, in this way, bring about assent to the Christian God now reinscribed on the secular plane of immanence: "As John Calvin put it, when one puts on the spectacles of Scripture, the signs of God in creation are seen truly for what they are." What is seen is the creation.[36]

As the legacy of his theology, Gilkey has established the credibility of a secular frame for thinking theologically that, at the same time, allows a thinker to attend to the particular singularities of experience when they witness to the manifestation of an incarnate God. Within this secular frame, the death of God can be addressed next to the manifestation of God. Gilkey enfranchised the language of an ultimate concern within the domain of the secular spirit. There are traces of ultimacy even in a realm that is contingent, relative, transient, and autonomous. If there are special

---

[35]Gilkey, *NRS,* 195, 201.
[36]Gilkey, *NRS,* 195.

revelations within the realm of the world, these are singularities that can be celebrated and enhanced or missed. Gilkey shows that there is an urgency to thinking theologically as an expression of our humanness. Gilkey's Christian theology is a gift and not a necessity.

Part 3

Gilkey's Interpretations of Christian Symbols

Chapter 9

Navigating in the Whirlwind:
Langdon Gilkey's Doctrine of God[1]

Eric H. Crump

Some went down to the sea in ships,
  doing business on the mighty waters;
they saw the deeds of the LORD,
  his wondrous works in the deep.
For he commanded and raised the stormy wind,
  which lifted up the waves of the sea.   (Psalm 107:23-25 NRSV)

Introduction

Any explication of Langdon Gilkey's doctrine of God must recount his theological voyage in order to give an account of his articulation of the doctrine of God. Because Gilkey (alas!) has not written a "systematic" theology that one could easily consult for an authoritative statement of his position, an exposition of his doctrine of God must arise from an examination of his prolific body of writings that have "dealt either with particular issues or symbols in theology (creation, Church, providence) or with the relationships of theology to aspects of cultural life (for example, to modern secularity or to science)."[2] Yet, more important, in contrast to

---

[1]According to Charles Sanders Peirce, "A book might be written to signalize all the most important of these guiding principles of reasoning. It would probably be, we must confess, of no service to a person whose thought is directed wholly to practical subjects, and whose activity moves along thoroughly beaten paths. The problems that present themselves to such a mind are matters of routine which he has learned once for all to handle in learning his business. But let a man venture into an unfamiliar field, or where his results are not continually checked by experience, and all history shows that the most masculine intellect will oftentimes lose his orientation and waste his efforts in directions which bring him no nearer to his goal, or even carry him entirely astray. He is like a ship in the open sea, with no one on board who understands the rules of navigation" (Charles Sanders Peirce, "The Fixation of Belief," in *Writings of Charles S. Peirce: A Chronological Edition, 1872–1878*, ed. Christian J. W. Kloesel [Bloomington: Indiana University Press, 1986] 3: 245-46).

[2]Langdon Gilkey, *Message and Existence: An Introduction to Christian Theology* (New York: Seabury Press, 1979) 1; hereafter cited as *ME*. He also notes that "[t]he effort to express on a grand scale the whole faith results, of course, in a 'systematic theology,'

many theologies which begin with the doctrine of God, Gilkey's doctrine of God must be seen as the result of a process of reflective inquiry pertaining to the questions of the intelligibility, meaningfulness, and truth of the central religious symbols of the Christian tradition in their relationships to human existence and of contemporary human existence as interpreted through those symbols.[3] Since theology is "faith seeking understanding" in terms of those symbols, a formulation of a doctrine of God may be seen best as the relative and partial culmination of such a process of reflective inquiry. It seeks to explicate the intelligibility, meaningfulness, and truth of the two assumptions that configure the task of theology: (1) that "God is present decisively and for us . . . fully through the life and work, past and present, of Jesus who is the Christ"; and (2) that "God is also manifested, as an unconditional and ultimate creative presence, in the world and thus in culture, as the source or ground of creativity, of judgment, and of new possibility in ongoing historical life."[4]

Yet, as Charles Sanders Peirce noted, inquiry, if it is real inquiry, is a struggle.[5] For Gilkey, this inquiry commenced with the "steady dissolution of all these certainties, the washing away of the firm ground on which our generation believed we were safely standing."[6] In this chapter,

---

the massive summation of the theologian's lifework. As the major recent examples of this genre (for instance, the works of Barth, Brunner, Tillich, and Rahner) show, however, such works presuppose on the part of their authors an immense range of scholarship and a rare originality of thought with regard to every major area or issue within Christian doctrine. An unavoidable realism about the level of my own present learning and capacities, and the length of time remaining to improve either one, have together cautioned against such an ambitious and demanding project" (Gilkey, *ME*, 1-2). Gilkey's most concise exposition of a doctrine of God is his essay, "The Christian Understanding of God," in Langdon Gilkey, *Through the Tempest: Theological Voyages in a Pluralistic Culture*, ed. Jeff B. Pool [Minneapolis: Fortress Press, 1991] 69-88; hereafter cited as *TT*; also as "God," in *Christian Theology: An Introduction to Its Traditions and Tasks*, ed. Peter C. Hodgson and Robert H. King [Minneapolis: Fortress Press, 1985] 62-87; and as "God," in *A New Handbook of Christian Theology*, ed. Donald W. Musser and Joseph L. Price [Nashville: Abingdon Press, 1992] 198-209).

[3]See Gilkey, "Theology: Interpretation of Faith for Church and World," in *TT*, 38.

[4]Gilkey, *TT*, 36.

[5]See Peirce: "The irritation of doubt causes a struggle to attain a state of belief. I shall term this struggle *inquiry*. . . . The irritation of doubt is the only immediate motive for the struggle to attain belief. . . . With doubt, therefore, the struggle begins, and with the cessation of doubt it ends" (Peirce, "The Fixation of Belief," 247).

[6]"The winds of change, fresh and strong, are blowing through the theological world. No more than five years ago, the 'younger theologians' seemed to have a comfortable

I will explicate the logic of Gilkey's theological voyage culminating in his doctrine of God.[7] I then will summarize his doctrine of God as "trinitarian panentheism." This chapter will conclude with questions about Gilkey's formulation of God as being, logos, and love, in light of the renewal of trinitarian theology and the advent of postmodern "antitheism." I will contend that Gilkey's doctrine of God requires an articulation of the triunity of God in terms of the primacy of love.

I. Dissolution in the Whirlwind

Gilkey's classic article, "Cosmology, Ontology, and the Travail of Biblical Language" (1961), an analysis of the "biblical theology" movement, posed troubling questions for that theology. His essay did not stem from a repudiation of that theological point of view. "Speaking personally, I share it, and each time I theologize I use its main categories; but I find myself confused about it when I ponder it critically, and this paper organizes and states rather than resolves that confusion."[8] The embarrassing problem results from the recognition that no specifiable content or meaning can be given to the main categories and words used in the so-called "biblical theology of the mighty acts of God." This

---

basis for their task, fashioned by the great theologians of the '20s, '30s, and '40s. To the question 'How are you making up your mind?' the young theologian would probably have replied, 'I have already done so'—and it would have been in a neo-orthodox, a Bultmannian, or a Whiteheadian direction. Or if he were more honest than most he would have said, 'My mind has already been made up for me'—by Barth, Niebuhr, by Tillich or by Hartshorne. For most of us felt that our theological task was to show the intelligibility of the particular theological stance we had imbibed from our great teachers. We saw ourselves a generation of 'scholastics' whose function would be to work out in greater detail the firm theological principles already forged for us. We knew from our teachers what theology was, what its principles and starting point were, how to go about it, and above all we were confident about its universal value and truth" (Langdon Gilkey, "Dissolution and Reconstruction in Theology," *Christian Century* 82 [3 February 1965]: 135).

[7]In order to follow the logic of the path leading to his formulation of a doctrine of God, I shall focus on the following texts from Gilkey's works: "The Concept of Providence in Contemporary Theology," *Journal of Religion* 43 (July 1963): 171-91; "Cosmology, Ontology, and the Travail of Biblical Language," *Journal of Religion* 41 (July 1961): 194-205; *Naming the Whirlwind: The Renewal of God-Language* (Indianapolis/New York: Bobbs-Merrill, 1969) (hereafter cited as NW); and *Reaping the Whirlwind: A Christian Interpretation of History* (New York: Seabury Press, 1976) (hereafter cited as *RW*).

[8]Gilkey, "Cosmology, Ontology, and the Travail of Biblical Language," 194.

theology failed to recognize the analogical character of its language concerning "acts of God" and, hence, could not escape from equivocations; it was unable to articulate the meaning of analogy, how the word was used, and that to which an analogy refers or points. The "uneasy" posture of biblical theology, as half liberal and modern and half biblical and orthodox, results in this quandary because biblical theologians continued to use the biblical and orthodox theological language of divine activity and speech, but dispensed with the wonders and voices that gave univocal meaning, and thus content, to the theological words "God acts" and "God speaks."[9] The awareness of this confusion gives rise to the question of the intelligibility and meaningfulness of the theological language of "mighty act" and revelation.

For Gilkey, without an ontological basis, the language of biblical theology remains equivocal, neither univocal nor analogical, hence, empty, abstract, and self-contradictory. Without the articulation of a theological ontology that provides intelligibility and credibility for the analogical language of divine activity and divine self-manifestation through events, the language of special "acts of God" collapses, given biblical theology's half-liberal posture of accepting modern cosmology.

> When we use the analogies "mighty act," "unique revelatory event," or "God speaks to his people," therefore, we must also try to understand what we mean in systematic theology by the general activity of God. Unless we have some conception of how God acts in ordinary events, we can hardly know what our analogical words mean when we say: "He acts uniquely in this event" or "this event is a special divine deed."[10]

An understanding of God's relation to the world and general experience is required in order to give content and specificity to the theological language of special divine action. One might say that, for Gilkey, God's general activity without God's special activity is soteriologically insignificant and, conversely, that God's special activity without God's general activity is meaningless and blind. "Put in terms of doctrines, this means that God's special activity is logically connected with his providential activity in general historical experience, and the understanding of the one assumes a concurrent inquiry into the other."[11]

---

[9]Gilkey, "Cosmology, Ontology, and the Travail of Biblical Language," 199.
[10]Gilkey, "Cosmology, Ontology, and the Travail of Biblical Language," 204-205.
[11]Gilkey, "Cosmology, Ontology, and the Travail of Biblical Language," 205.

Yet, Gilkey found the doctrine of providence to be remarkably absent from theological discussions, despite its prominence in Reformation and liberal theologies.[12] Similarly, as in the case of Biblical Theology's "mighty acts of God," theology's affirmations of an "Arminian" belief in freedom and the nexus of finite causality present more difficulties in making reaffirmations of God's objective rule and action in nature and history. "We need some constructive thought about God's providential relation to ordinary events," Gilkey maintains, "lest our theological words become empty, emptied by our own Arminian and naturalistic qualifications."[13] He highlights three interconnected reasons for problems that confront reaffirmations of God's objective rule and providential action in nature and history. These perplexities involve the meaning of theological words.

First, neoorthodox methodology was insufficient. Unless theology provides some specification to clarify neoorthodox epistemological confusion, terms like "sovereignty" and "lordship" remain empty. For Gilkey, neoorthodox theology has a limiting rule:

> [T]here are no doctrines about God's activity or being which are not at once doctrines *about* our personal, cognitive relation to God. From this basic principle stems one of the main characteristics of contemporary theology, namely, that in its view epistemology and theology are one; or, put another way, that all theology is about our knowing of God and not about God. . . . Here . . . is also the source of that strange "epistemological bias." . . . this "bias" consistently confused the order of being with the order of knowing, rejected almost a priori any discussion of God's action beyond the sphere of encounter, and did so on the epistemological grounds that any such discussion *must* involve an objective biblicism or an objective natural theology.[14]

Despite its affirmation of providence, neoorthodox theology found itself methodologically restricted; hence, it could not adequately make providence the topic of specific theological inquiry. Its methodological structure of thought, based on the correlation of revelation and faith, did

---

[12]"Our problem, therefore, is: Why has Providence in our generation been left a rootless, disembodied ghost, flitting from footnote to footnote, but rarely finding secure lodgement in sustained theological discourse?" (Gilkey, "Concept of Providence in Contemporary Theology," 171).

[13]Gilkey, "Concept of Providence in Contemporary Theology," 181.

[14]Gilkey, "Concept of Providence in Contemporary Theology," 183.

not apply to God's relation to the world and events "beyond the scope of the faith relation."[15] Second, without some understanding of God's ordinary activity in history, theological discourse concerning God's special acts in history as the locus of saving revelation "tends also to dissolve into ambiguity and thus to undermine the very views of revelation and of God this phrase ["mighty acts of God"] seeks to express."[16] Third, the existential significance of providence for the "meaning of historical existence" becomes vacuous or merely humanistic "if the relation of God to the historical structures in which we seek to live meaningfully is not in some way comprehended."[17]

Compounding these theological issues and their intellectual treatment was the lurking phenomenon of secularism, which exacerbated the problem of the intelligibility of theological language at a visceral level. The challenge of secularism necessitates a fundamentally "radical" reconstruction of the theological task; not only is the intelligibility of the phrase "mighty acts of God" called into question, but also the logically prior intelligibility of the reality of God.

> The question of the reality of God and so of the possibility, meaningfulness, and validity of any religious faith and of any theological discourse at all, forms the center of our present ferment—which is as fundamental a question as theology can raise. Furthermore, the question of God is radical as well as fundamental. For, in essence, to debate the question of God in theology means that in that debate no theological assumptions can usefully be made, or any theological authorities invoked—since every such assumption or authority presupposes the reality of the divine. One cannot begin, for example, with the presupposition of the presence of the Word of God, if one is asking the question of God—nor, as we shall argue, can one begin with the assumption of a divine Logos which makes metaphysics possible. If the question of *God* is raised, theology literally must begin from the beginning, it must deal with its own most basic foundations.[18]

Reconstructing the theological task in light of secularism's challenge necessitates a prolegomenon: a hermeneutic of secular experience, in which secular experience is investigated in order to ascertain the intelligibility and meaningfulness of religious discourse. To be relevant,

---

[15]Gilkey, "Concept of Providence in Contemporary Theology," 184.
[16]Gilkey, "Concept of Providence in Contemporary Theology," 186.
[17]Gilkey, "Concept of Providence in Contemporary Theology," 186.
[18]Gilkey, *NW*, 11.

the prolegomenon cannot make any nonsecular assumptions; it cannot import anything into its analysis not found or already affirmed in secular experience.[19] This hermeneutic seeks to discern "what religious dimensions there may be [in secular experience], and so what usage and meaningfulness religious discourse has in ordinary life. It is *this* meaningfulness which provides a large part of the answer to the question, 'What do your Christian theological symbols *mean*?' "[20] This prolegomenon will not provide a sufficient ground for positive theological assertions. At best, it can show two things: (1) how theological symbols can explicate and illumine ordinary existence in the world; and (2) how human experience of being in the world can give meaning and reality to theological discourse. In addition, this prolegomenon will be an "ontic" analysis, which prepares for subsequent ontological and theological discourse. Through the discernment of dimensions of ultimacy in ordinary human experience, ontic analysis points beyond itself to an analysis of the ontological structures of either human being or Being; but the methodological possibility of ontological analysis depends upon these dimensions.[21]

---

[19]See Gilkey's important qualification in *NW*, 249-50: "This does not mean, however, that we need to accept all there is in the secular understanding or account of that existence, *if* that account does not accord with the lived character of secular life. In our prolegomena, in other words, the secular spirit can be criticized only in terms of the essential characteristics of secular life itself. To do this, we shall consider each of the elements of the secular spirit which both defined its unique shape and also which made such difficulty for religious language: its sense of contingency, relativity, temporality, and its affirmation of autonomy." See also Gilkey's *Auseinandersetzung* with Peter Berger in "Responses to Peter Berger," *Theological Studies* 39 (September 1978): 486-97.

[20]Gilkey, *NW*, 234.

[21]Cf. the following comments by Gilkey: " . . . the possibility of ontological analysis is itself based on ontic experiences and decisions in the region of ultimacy, namely the confidence in a universal logos in existence generally. Such a confidence cannot usefully be assumed in our day; prior to it, the possibility of language about such an ultimate order must be shown, and thereby the sources of such a confidence uncovered. Thus, logically as well as prudentially, an ontic analysis must precede the ontological as the latter's possibility." Also, "thus just as theological language about God has been impaired through secular experience, so has metaphysical language about an ultimate order. And correspondingly, just as theological language about God can begin, not by assuming *ab initio* the meaningfulness or validity of its religious symbols, but only by unearthing the grounds in ordinary experience for these symbols, so metaphysical or ontological language in theology must start with the foundational experiences of order in ordinary experience— with that 'revelation' of the ultimate order which grounds thought—if such language is

[This ontic analysis is also a] phenomenology of religious apprehension within secular life; it has not asked or answered questions about the "reality" or the ontological structure of the ultimate or the sacred that "appears" there. It has sought only to show that it does appear, and how and where it does appear. Only indirectly and, so to speak, in brackets have we made positive or "Christian" reference to God or to doctrines about him.

This has been an ontic prolegomena to theological discourse, not an example of theological discourse. . . . A prolegomena, in other words, is just that: it prepares for Christian theological discourse by establishing the meaningfulness of religious discourse in general in relation to experienced characteristics of human existence in the world, and thus by providing for the meaningful and relevant use of the specifically Christian symbols in a secular age. It can neither establish by itself the truth of that faith nor even provide the symbols within which that faith expresses itself.[22]

On the basis of such a prolegomenon, an explicitly Christian theological discourse represents formally one among many answers to the questions that secular experience and existence raise. If "the sacred is apprehended in and through the structural elements of secular life, and if its symbolic expression is to be *meaningful*," then "religious symbols must be understood as answers to the questions of ordinary life."[23] For Christian theology, this formal requirement (of the correlation between secular questions and the Christian answers mediated through its symbols) entails that "in Christian reflection each theological symbol, each facet of Christian theology, each 'doctrine,' is to be understood, reflected upon

---

to be possible today. A modern theology using metaphysical or ontological discourse itself depends upon a contemporary reception of the revelation of such an order if it is to be possible; such a theology will only be intelligible and valid if those grounds are established by some such prolegomenon to a metaphysical language as our own in this volume" (Gilkey, *NW*, 306-307n.1, 436).

[22]Gilkey, *NW*, 413. Compare with the following statement elsewhere. "In a secular prolegomena, however, when we merely look into these depths, we find as yet nothing so definite as the God of Christian faith. At this point, the referent for this particular Christian symbol has not yet appeared. Rather, we are here only in the region of our experience where 'God' *may* be known, and so where the meaningful usage of this particular symbol can be found, but also where, as we have noticed, not only may many other symbols be used to conceptualize our experience, but even more where the sacred may be experienced as totally silent or hidden" (Gilkey, *NW*, 301).

[23]Gilkey, *NW*, 456.

and clarified in relation to that same question which human existence in the world has raised."[24]

Yet, Christian theological discourse will also be quite distinct from such a prolegomenon. That discourse seeks to explicate the reality of God by also correlating ontological inquiry and the Christian religious symbols in light of contemporary experience. One might characterize Christian theological discourse as that which emerges in light of the progression from the ontic to the ontological and from the ontological to the theological. For Gilkey, Christian theology must contain ontological elements (1) in order to articulate the ontological uniqueness, universality, and decisiveness of God to the world so that God may be properly conceived and (2) so that "the universality and the decisiveness of the problem to which religion addresses itself and of the resolution which is offered be expressed, that is, in order that its *salvation* be properly conceived."[25]

Theology is more than ontology, however, because it retains mythical elements for two reasons: first, in order to give positive determination to the articulation of the ultimacy, freedom, and transcendence of the divine; and, second, in order that its "understanding of the transcendence and the sacrality of the divine is grounded in particular past events within the general stream of temporal passage and contains promises for the particularity of history in the future." For Gilkey, "God here is related thus to *particular* events, and at the most *concrete*, phenomenal level."[26]

This complex interrelation between the ontological and the mythical is characterized by a dialectic of Christian belief that moves from

---

[24]Gilkey, *NW*, 456.

[25]Gilkey, *Religion and the Scientific Future: Reflections on Myth, Science, and Theology* (New York: Harper & Row, 1970) 115; hereafter cited as *RSF*.

[26]Gilkey, *RSF*, 116-17. Cf. the following statement by Gilkey: "When, moreover, theological symbols are referent to historical passage and are clustered together so as to form a theological interpretation of history, then inescapably they take a 'story' form: they describe the 'mighty acts of God' or the 'divine economy.' All theological symbols in our tradition, I believe, relate to our life in time and seek to explicate a divine activity which transcends in some sense that temporality, and yet is in relation to that temporal life. Thus all theological symbols take this story form—be they symbols of creation, of providence, of revelation or of eschatology. They express the relation of God to temporal passage and so speak of God as an 'actor' in temporal affairs. In short, they take a 'mythical' form, a form which is unavoidable in a theology centered in history and in what it knows of God in and through history, whose God, therefore, transcends history and yet is *known* because he is in continual and diverse relations to historical life" (Gilkey, *RW*, 149-50).

rationality via incredibility to credibility.[27] Gilkey characterizes the ontological and the mythical (rational and credible respectively), although having distinct grounds and warrants, as dialectically interdependent, "such that the rationality of the one and the credibility of the other disappears if either element is separated or isolated from one another."[28] For Gilkey, this dialectical interdependence of the ontological and the mythical, the rational and the credible, overcomes the seeming antithesis between natural theology and a purely kerygmatic theology.

> Thus, while a natural theology is an integral and essential moment in the total dialectic of Christian belief, it is a part within a wider, credible whole, an aspect of the total viewpoint of faith. Its rationality, while defensible and significant, is therefore itself in the end dependent on the more elusive, less rigorous, and scarcely "natural" intelligibility and meaning characteristic of the faith as a whole.[29]

---

[27]The term "incredibility" designates the status of the theistic claim (that finitude has its source in a divine ground), as seen in light of the estrangement and alienation of concrete historical existence. It is the result of the experience of meaninglessness, suffering, and despair "at the point *deus* becomes radically *absconditus*, and the theistic claim begins now to seem incredible and the arguments that ground it irrational. The concrete reality of historical being as both temporal and estranged now challenges the rationality and meaningfulness of finite existence, the sense of the reality of God, and as a consequence the rationality of religious or of Christian belief" (Gilkey, "The Dialectic of Christian Belief," in *Society and the Sacred: Toward a Theology of Culture in Decline* [New York: Crossroad, 1981] 29; hereafter cited as *SAS*.

[28]Gilkey, *SAS*, 28.

[29]Gilkey, *SAS*, 28. For further discussions in relation to David Tracy's *Blessed Rage for Order*, see the following: Gilkey, *RW*, 370n.17, 371n.19, 373n.1. This affirmation of natural theology is a revision in Gilkey's thought. "My relation to the tradition of natural theology has been a puzzle, especially to me. As an enthusiastic younger supporter of the so-called neo-orthodoxy (non-Barthian wing), I represented a strongly argued anti-natural theology position, as my books from *Maker of Heaven and Earth* to *Naming the Whirlwind* show. Then, when writing *Reaping the Whirlwind*, a volume on providence and the philosophy of history, I found it incumbent in developing that 'doctrine' to think out an 'ontology of historical passage.' Further, it was necessary, if that ontology was to serve as the basis for conceiving an ontology of providential action (i.e., what do we *mean* by an ordinary and universal act of God?), to articulate an intelligible relation between that 'empirically' derived ontology and a 'biblically' derived interpretation of providence—if the former was to be 'Christian' and the latter 'credible.' Once this relation was seen to be defensible and intelligible from the biblical side, it became clear that it was also defensible and intelligible from the empirical and ontological side to be biblical; that is, there appeared arguments as to why the mind moved—even if it did not want so to

Natural theology or ontological analysis presents a necessary, but not sufficient, condition for the determination of the validity of the Christian symbol-system. Yet, the critical and constructive ontological explication of a theological symbol concerning God's general relation to the world and history is an intrinsic moment of systematic theology. The ontological explication endeavors to think the divine activity in history, in order to exhibit the coherence of the symbols expressive of the activity with an ontology of historical process.

Whereas *Naming the Whirlwind* primarily focused on the development of a prolegomenon in light of the challenge of secular experience and indicating a progression from the ontic to the ontological and, thus, to the theological, only indirectly broaching Christian theological claims, only in *Reaping the Whirlwind* does Gilkey supply a sustained execution of the methodological program. *Reaping the Whirlwind*, presents a doctrine of God through the dialectical interdependence of the ontological and the theological. Chapter 1, "Change, Politics and the Future: The

---

move!—from an ontology based on general experience to the reality and efficacy of God" (Langdon Gilkey, *Nature, Reality, and the Sacred: The Nexus of Science and Religion*, Theology and the Sciences series, ed. Kevin J. Sharpe [Minneapolis: Fortress Press, 1993] 243-44n.1; hereafter cited as *NRS*).

Possible objections to the affirmation of natural theology as an integral moment within the larger theological task should be made after pondering the following statement from Regin Prenter. "Der wirkliche Gegensatz ist nicht der zwischen *theologia revelata* und *theologia naturlis*, sondern der zwischen *theologia crucis* und *theologia gloriae*. Eine vermeintliche Offenbarungstheologie, die von der Herausforderung der natürlichen Theologie (des Zeugnisses der Philosophie von Gott) völlig absieht, kann gerade dadurch eine Herrlichkeitstheologie werden. Umgekehrt kann der Wille, das Zeugnis der Vernunft nicht offenbarungspositivistisch zu unterschlage, sondern gerade ernstzunehmen, davon zeugen, daß Kreuzestheologie getrieben wird. Der fanatische Kampf gegen jede natürliche Theologie verbindet sich nicht selten mit herrlichkeitstheologischen Tendenzen" ("The real antithesis is not that between *theologia revelata* and *theologia naturalis*, but rather that between *theologia crucis* and *theologia gloriae*. A reputed revelational theology, that altogether disregards the challenge of 'natural theology' [of the testimonies of philosophy of 'God'], can precisely become thereby a theology of glory. In contrast, the intention not to suppress the testimony of 'reason' in a 'revelationally positivistic' manner, but rather precisely to take it seriously, can testify that a theology of the cross is carried on. The fanatic war on 'any' natural theology is connected not unseldomly with 'theology of glory' tendencies" [my translation]) (Regin Prenter, "Der Gott der Liebe ist: Das Verhältnis der Gotteslehre zur Christologie," in *Theologie und Gottesdienst: Gesammelte Aufsätze*, Teoligiske Studier 6 [Århus: Forlaget Aros, 1977] 291n.11).

Historicity of Human Being," analyzes the temporality of social and historical existence as the fundamental structure of human experience. The peculiar character of modernity lies in its sharpened apprehension of temporality in the experience of change. The historicity of human being and historical events is marked by a union of destiny and freedom.

> Human temporality in its changing historical context sets the conditions for the way we are human; it thus also sets the conditions for the way we are or are not religious. Our humanity, our action, our religiousness and thus our theology are essentially intertwined with our historicity.[30]

Chapter 2, "Ultimacy in Historical and Political Experience," argues that a dimension of ultimacy appears at every level of historical and political life in temporal passage as the horizon of secular communal experience, such that the Christian theological symbols of providence and eschatology possess relevance and meaning in political existence. The ontological structure of history as temporal passage involves not only (1) the polarity of destiny and freedom as constitutive of finite being in time, but also (2) that polarity's transcendent ground, which unites actuality and possibility and provides the dimension of ultimacy to the experience of destiny and freedom.

The ontological explication of the structure of history as temporal passage, however, still represents an abstraction from the concrete actuality of history. Other concepts than those of actuality and possibility are necessary in order to comprehend history theologically.[31] Whereas the religious symbols of creation and providence are relevant to the polarities

---

[30]Gilkey, *RW*, 9.

[31]For Gilkey, the ontological analysis, e.g., in Whitehead's and Bloch's speculative philosophies of history, "must be reinterpreted and in part refashioned, not adopted *en bloc*, by theology. A reflective examination of history on the grounds of ordinary experience alone, to which secular philosophy is confined, cannot provide the final vision elucidating our historical experience. For as nonspeculative, critical philosophy of history has emphasized, we do not yet stand at the end of history, and thus its most basic structures and principles are not yet quite clear to us. In uncovering the significant ontological structures of our present, and then elucidating for us in clarified form our own contemporary experience of history and its movement, philosophy can illumine those fundamental religious and theological symbols by which we may think out the wholeness of historical experience in all its creativity, its vast contradictions, and its hope. Thus are we driven beyond science and even critical philosophies of history to ontology, so are we driven beyond speculative philosophy to embark on the theological question of history" (Gilkey, *RW*, 114).

of actuality and possibility, of destiny and freedom, the symbols of sin, Christology, and eschatology are relevant for an account of the warped and estranged character of historical existence, its incoherence and tragedy, and its redemption. In *Reaping the Whirlwind*, Gilkey explicates the dialectical interdependence of the ontological and the theological principally in terms of the mutual interdependence of the symbols of providence and eschatology: exemplified in the coupling of Chapter 10, "Providence and Eschatology: A Reinterpretation," and Chapter 11, "Eschatology and Providence: the Future of God." The Christian interpretation of history proposed involves reinterpreting the classical doctrine of providence through an ontological analysis that coheres with the sense of contingency, relativity, transience, and autonomy in temporal passage characteristic of modern historical consciousness. This revised understanding of providence overcomes what Gilkey regards as the deficiencies of neoorthodox, liberal, and political-eschatological theologies for the historical consciousness of the modern world.

> [I]n some essential aspect each has been found wanting, each finally let the mystery of history as a creative and yet ambiguous union of destiny and freedom escape rather than inform its interpretation. Perhaps the reason is that each emphasized one theological symbol to the exclusion of others. For liberalism providence provided the sole clue to the meaning of history; for neo-orthodoxy it was christology; and for the contemporary political theologies it has been eschatology. Possibly, therefore, a union of all of these symbols—providence, christology and eschatology in combination—will provide a better theological clue to the mystery of history.[32]

II. Providence, Eschatology, and the Doctrine of God

Gilkey retains several elements from the classical doctrine of providence, as exemplified in Augustine and Calvin: (1) the affirmation of God's sovereignty over history, such that God's providential activity is directed and defined by God's eschatological goal; (2) that the work of providence extends to events, both natural and historical, cosmological and social; (3) the establishment of freedom through the providential transformation of fate into destiny; (4) that providential activity of God works through, not against, human freedom in order to reach the eschatological goal; and (5) that God works in and through the domain of secondary causality, the

---

[32]Gilkey, *RW*, 238.

creaturely forces and dynamic factors in history. Gilkey does not retain, however, emphases upon the immutability of God and God's consequent foreknowledge and foreordination of all events. Instead, he reinterprets the classical model's absolutist view of divine sovereignty in terms of modern historical consciousness.

The key to Gilkey's theology of providence lies in modernity's understanding of the temporality of being and the correlative new understanding of the relation between actuality and possibility: "[t]he movement of time is modal, the movement from possibility into actuality; time is the locus of the becoming of actuality and so the locus of being."[33] If temporal passage as the movement from possibility to actuality is creative of actuality, then the "openness of the future" is the ontological category related to the reality of the creative freedom of self-determination. Following Whitehead, Gilkey maintains that freedom is a necessary, but not sufficient, factor in the determination of relevant actuality. Freedom is not only in relation to destiny, but also in relation to "genuine alternatives and not-already-decided actualities in its future."[34] The ontological basis for the future's openness is that the future is constituted by as yet unrealized possibilities; and the self-creation of entities and events in time is that which realizes projected possibilities into concrete actuality.

Thus, Gilkey's theology of providence avoids "supernaturalistic" explanations of history;

> [rather, the] "naturalistic" principle of historical explanation on the level of direct, historical causation is not abrogated, that God can be intelligibly said to "act" in and through the secondary "causes" of destiny and freedom . . . and yet to have a constitutive, critical and renewing role in that process.[35]

God's providential work is found and experienced within our contingency, relativity, temporality, and freedom as that which makes them possible. God's creative providence as the ground of our being as temporal passage is "*essentially* active, dynamic and related, present in all of changing time, sustaining and driving forward all that is, and

---

[33]Gilkey, *RW*, 200.

[34]Gilkey, *RW*, 201.

[35]Gilkey, *RW*, 247. Gilkey's theology of providence is indebted to Gerhard von Rad's exposition of God's hidden work in history, as attested in the Old Testament.

creative of the new."[36] If God is the source of the totality of being, then God is essentially self-limiting; divine self-limitation guarantees the genuine freedom of the creature in bringing freedom into being. The creature is "capable of and called to self-constitution" and consequently "capable of original, novel action and so is 'free' to sin and/or to accept grace—that is, free to act in ways neither determined nor predetermined by God."[37]

In light of the temporality of being, God's *providentia*, comprising conservation (*conservatio*), concursus (or *cooperatio cum causis secundis*), and governance (*gubernatio*), are retrieved from the classical model of the sovereignty of God as Absolute Being. Each essential aspect of providence is related to the relations between past, present, and future. Because God is the creative source of all being, Gilkey interprets the symbol of *creatio ex nihilo* in process terms of the temporality of being: God is the power of being that originates and sustains continuing existence through the conquest of passingness of time, preserving the continuing being of achieved actuality as destiny in relation to the present, so as to make the process of becoming possible. Preservation of the creature over time, the movement from a vanishing past actuality into the new coming to be of the present as self-actualizing actuality, is the first aspect of providence. Second, through divine self-limitation, providence is the ground of both possibility and freedom's creativity in the present. To each occasion, divine creativity gives the power of self-creation out of its destiny. Third, divine providence is directive, as the envisioning power relating an ordered vision of unrealized possibility to the actual present as process moving into the future. In contrast to the classical model, *gubernatio* is understood as *directio*: "[p]rovidence does not determine historical creativity; it makes it possible, gives it relevance and so limits and guides it. . . . Providence is the sustaining and creating work of God within the ambiguity of historical life that leads to the divine eschatological fulfillment as the latter's presupposition and ground."[38]

Providence, understood in light of the ontological structure of history, receives an additional characterization in light of the concrete actuality of history. Freedom can and does misuse both the destiny given to it from

---

[36]Gilkey, *RW*, 248.
[37]Gilkey, *TT*, 82.
[38]Gilkey, *RW*, 252, 253.

the past and the new possibilities provided for the future. The temptation for the misuse of human freedom in sin arises from the ontological situation of freedom's contingency. The actual emergence of sin results in movement of humans "*beyond* ontological structure to warped actuality, and so correspondingly *beyond* the gifts of continuity and of new possibility that providence brings into the deeper need for redemption."[39] The misuse of freedom in sin transforms destiny into the form of fate. In light of sin, divine providence is the principle of judgment in and through history. Judgment includes destruction of what had been created and preserved through destructive fate, "the 'hidden' or 'alien' work of God in the destruction of what is itself destructive, the negation of the negative, the conquest of that in human history which is experienced as fate ('the footprint of His wrath,' as Barth put it)."[40]

Yet, the divine *providentia* —as the principle of the continuation of finite being, freedom, new possibility, and judgment—does not exhaust the entirety of divine action within history. Providence must be supplemented by Christology and eschatology. According to the Christian understanding of history, the universal reconciling and redemptive work of God is decisively manifest in the person of Jesus as the Christ.

> Thus while the sanctifying grace, as well as the creative and the judging providence of God are universal in historical life as the salvific will of God is universal, still the central manifestation of the reality and the character of that redemptive grace entered history in a particular tradition and in a particular person.[41]

In the decisive manifestation of redemption in Jesus Christ, there is a Christological coincidence of providence and eschatology in the life, death, and resurrection of Jesus.

> [T]he *goal* of history is manifested in the proclamation, the existence and the transcendence of Jesus over sin and death alike. He is the beginning of the end and in him the promise of God for history is manifest. . . . He is the embodied promise, the criterion and the first example of the future of God; here God's eschatological goal of authentic humanity and authentic community receive definitive form. Thus it is in him, and the eschatological goal of the kingdom he represents, that the goal of *providence*—hidden

---

[39]Gilkey, *RW*, 258.
[40]Gilkey, *RW*, 264.
[41]Gilkey, *RW*, 268.

amidst the waywardness of human freedom—is revealed within the ambiguity of time.[42]

Hence, for Gilkey, the Christian interpretation of divine action in relation to history is manifold, articulating distinct, but interrelated "levels" or dimensions: creative providence, redemptive grace, and eschatological fulfillment. Despite the ambiguity of history, each of these dimensions, distinguishable and indivisible, is universal in scope, operative everywhere in history: recall the classic canon in trinitarian reflection—*opera trinitatis ad extra sunt communio, indivisa*. Moreover, "the character and goal of all three levels of the divine activity in history are known most fully in Jesus, and thus the possibility of our certainty about them and of our inward acceptance of and participation in them is fullest there."[43]

For Gilkey, the symbol of God provides the overarching framework for the theological interpretation of both the ontological structure of temporal passage as the union of actuality and possibility and the ambiguity of its concrete actuality. The symbol of God is explicated in light of the divine activity as that which gives to temporal passage its ontological possibility, its final intelligibility, and its redemptive significance. "We can speak of God at best," according to Gilkey, "only in terms of our relations to him and so in terms of his activity in and on us and on our world."[44] This correlation makes Gilkey's conceptual explication of the symbol of God panentheistic (in contrast to the absolutist classical model of God). Whereas the classical model affirmed the absoluteness of God's being as utterly unrelated, changeless, and eternal, Gilkey's position diverges in affirming three interrelated

---

[42]Gilkey, *RW*, 270. Also, "thus the goal of providence, the character of God's hidden work within the ambiguity of social existence, is defined and so clarified both eschatologically and christologically. It is defined eschatologically because it is the promised kingdom as the community of humans that is in general history the purpose of God's providential work. And in turn the eschatological kingdom is defined christologically because the solitary and yet sublime figure of Jesus, alienated from history and yet sharing all of history's suffering and terror, is as the Christ transparent to the ultimate power, meaning and love of God and so gives in promise the character of the kingdom as a community of the fullness of being, meaning, and love. In eschatology and christology, therefore, are unveiled for us the logos that lures history, and so the *norm* for history—the purpose guiding God's creative and providential work" (Gilkey, *RW*, 288).

[43]Gilkey, *RW*, 284.

[44]Gilkey, *RW*, 310.

elements: the self-limitation of God, the temporality of God, and the mutability of God.

I have discussed the self-limitation of God previously. Gilkey's process understanding of temporal passage entails the temporality of God. Because temporal passage involves the modal distinction between actuality and possibility, which God grounds, God is related to the past as achieved or accomplished actuality, the present as self-achieving actuality, and the future as possibility. God knows the future as possibility, not as already actual, through the envisionment of infinite possibility and the relevant gradation of that possibility in relation to achieved actuality and God's ultimate intentions. Hence, while God is transcendent to process as the necessary ground of temporal passage, God participates in and is really related to the passage of possibility to actuality and, hence, can be termed temporal in this sense. God "may, as in the classical tradition, be said to be eternal, unconditioned and necessary as the continuing, creative ground of all of process; and yet as the moving ground of process, he is essentially, not 'accidentally,' in relation to the flux of becoming."[45] This essential relatedness of the divine being itself to temporal passage means that God is living and dynamic.

The affirmation of divine temporality entails the final element of change from the classical conception, the mutability of God. Because God is essentially related to actuality as actuality and to possibility as possibility, God's providential envisionment of future possibility and ordered gradation of that possibility change as temporal passage occurs. In addition, God's knowledge of actualized actuality changes in the transition from self-actualizing actuality in the present to achieved and determinate actuality in the past. "History, and with it finite being, is self-creative under God, not determined by God. As history changes, therefore, so inescapably God changes, for God is in essential relation to a world he does not in its final and determinative form ordain or make."[46]

Gilkey's reflective explication of the symbol of God in a doctrine of God is, hence, a panentheistic theological articulation of the relation between God and the world (in terms of the temporality of being) within a trinitarian framework of God as being, logos, and love, which includes creation and providence, redemption, and eschatology. Gilkey's brilliant presentation of a Christian understanding of history culminates in "the

---

[45]Gilkey, *RW*, 309.
[46]Gilkey, *RW*, 310.

rethinking of that most fundamental affirmation of all, namely, that God is being, truth, and love, and that on this threefold divine activity all our possibilities for the future depend."[47]

III. Retrospective Questions
concerning the Center of the Whirlwind

Langdon Gilkey's formulation of a "doctrine" of God in the final chapter of *Reaping the Whirlwind* is the constructive "culmination" of a constant process of inquiry that began in dissolution. The final chapter, "The God of Process, of Possibility and of Hope," arises as the fitting closure to a masterful dialectical interweaving of perspectives in a series of arguments wherein "attention has been directed primarily at interpreting history rather than conceiving God."[48] That chapter focuses principally upon an explication of history's ontological meaning rather than upon its existential significance in terms of salvation, though Gilkey rightly points out that "no clear and certainly no definitive separation can be made between ontology and ethics, ontology and meaning, between the nature of God, the responsibilities of faith and the promise of salvation."[49] He also acknowledges that, with regard to the ontological categories utilized in interpreting history and providence, "despite the fact that no effort has here been made to show that universal applicability, it is here recognized as an obligation—as yet unredeemed—if these categories are valid."[50]

Yet, one can see the significance of Gilkey's position for future articulations of a doctrine of God when considering two more recent developments in systematic theology that Gilkey has not explicitly addressed: (1) the revival of interest in the doctrine of the Trinity; and (2) suspicions concerning theistic claims advanced in relation to metaphysical or ontological questions concerning being. Both developments respond to challenges from postmodernity and oppose in varying degrees theological positions (such as Gilkey's) that responded to challenges from modernity.

The first development, the renaissance of trinitarian theology in the work of Eberhard Jüngel, Jürgen Moltmann, Wolfhart Pannenberg, and

---

[47]Gilkey, *RW*, 318.

[48]Gilkey, *RW*, 300.

[49]Gilkey, *RW*, 300.

[50]Gilkey, *RW*, 430n.2. Gilkey's insightful development of an ontological and theological interpretation of nature in *NRS* can be profitably seen as an effort to satisfy this obligation.

others shows a renewed interest in interpreting the Christian symbol of God by retrieving the doctrine of the immanent Trinity from its "relative neglect." Many contemporary theologians share the conviction that "the doctrine of the Trinity simply *is* the Christian doctrine of God," to the extent that "any doctrine of God which has ceased to be trinitarian in character has thereby ceased to be Christian."[51] Ingolf U. Dalferth designates this revival of trinitarian theology as *Antitheismus*, seeking to overcome the "sterile alternative of theism and atheism" in modernity.[52]

The second development is also hostile to "theism." It seeks to overcome the approach to the symbol of God that gives priority to the question of being. Edward Farley formally characterizes this movement as "religio-philosophical anti-theism" that (1) refuses to entertain the question of God as the question of being, (2) refuses to think the being of God, and (3) refuses to think the relation between God and world.[53] It

---

[51]Cf. Nicholas Lash, "Considering the Trinity," *Modern Theology* 2 (1986): 183-96, esp. 193.

[52]Ingolf Ulrich Dalferth, *Der auferweckte Gekreuzigte: Zur Grammatik der Christologie* (Tübingen: J. C. B. Mohr [Paul Siebeck], 1994) 189.

[53]Edward Farley, *Divine Empathy: A Theology of God* (Minneapolis: Fortress Press, 1996) 45. Cf. Jean-Luc Marion, *God without Being: Hors-Texte*, trans. Thomas A. Carlson, Religion and Postmodernism series (Chicago: University of Chicago Press, 1991). Marion rearticulates the Pascalian differentiation between the "God of Abraham, Isaac, and Jacob" and the "God of the philosophers" by thinking God without Being and "outside of the text." More specifically, Marion's meditation situates itself philosophically within postmodernity's questioning of metaphysics and its ontotheological determinations of God, presupposed by both theism and atheism, in order to unmask as idolatrous all thought of God within the constraints of either ontotheological metaphysics or the Heideggerian ontological difference explicated upon the primacy of the postmetaphysical *Seinsfrage*. Negatively, the critique of metaphysical and postmetaphysical understandings of "God" allows for the emergence of the possibility of thinking God without Being. To this situation, Marion proposes theologically the "essential anachronism" of charity that "belongs neither to pre-, nor to post-, nor to modernity" (Marion, *God without Being*, xxii). Marion's essay is the attempt to articulate "the absolute freedom of God with regard to all determinations, including, first of all, the basic condition that renders all other conditions possible and even necessary—for us, humans—the fact of Being" (Marion, *God without Being*, xx) by thinking "God as love." For, if "God is love," that which is *norma normans, sed non normata*, then God loves before being and can be thought of "only in letting God be thought starting from his sole and pure demand" of charity, "the *agape* properly revealed in and as the Christ" (Marion, *God without Being*, xxi). "God can give himself to be thought without idolatry only starting from himself alone: to give himself to be thought as love, hence as gift; to give himself to be thought of as a thought of the

endeavors to think love or the "ethical" as beyond being (*Jenseits von Sein*).

How might one relate Gilkey's project to these positions? Gilkey's doctrine of God would concur with these two positions in terms of their critiques of classical theism and its claims. With regards to religiophilosophical antitheism, Gilkey might argue that there cannot be a disjunction between the ontological and the ethical, love and being, or the ontological and the theological. Rather than a disjunction, there is an intimate unity in difference between love and being, such that love is the beyond of being (*das Jenseits des Seins*).[54] One would be able to affirm both that

---

gift" (Marion, *God without Being*, 49). Theologically, for Marion, the order of charity and the economy of the gratuitous excess of the gift are prior to and beyond the order of Being/beings. The donation of charity as the "crossing of Being" renders the ontological difference indifferent only by the excess of the gift. For Marion, God is *Jenseits von Sein* (beyond being).

[54]I borrow this terminology in light of Tillich's formulation of the relation between the ontological and the theological. See the following comments: "Das Ontologische ist in ihr gebrochen und zum Theologischen geworden. Gegenstand ist nicht das menschliche Sein, sondern das Jenseits des Sein, erscheinend im menschlichen Sein. Daß so etwas möglich ist, muß vorausgesetzt werden. Es kann nicht anders als vorausgesetzt werden. Denn Prolog ist Vorwegnahme, ist Reden von der Sache vor der Sache. . . . Im Prolog führt der Weg von der Ontologie zur Theologie. In Wahrheit ist das Theologische die Voraussetzung des Ontologischen. Das[s] die Ontologie bis zu dem Punkt führt, wo sich die Frage erhebt nach dem Jenseits des Seins: das ist nur möglich, weil hinter ihr die schon vernommene Antwort steht. Nach dem Jenseits seiner selbst kann der Mensch im Ernst nur fragen, wenn das Jenseits schon gesprochen hat. Dieser Spruch kann abgeklungen sein, aber er wirkt nach in jedem Schritt der Ontologie. Das menschliche Sein so sehen, daß es zu der Frage treibt nach seinem Jenseits, das kann nicht rational erzwungen werden, das ist nur möglich auf dem Boden ursprünglichen Zeugnisses vom Jenseits des Seins. Der methodische Weg des Prologs schlägt also die entgegengesetzte Richtung ein als der sachliche Weg des Lebens. Und das bedeutet: nicht das Ontologische auf das Theologische, wenn auch der Weg der Hinführung notwendig der umgekehrte ist. Denn nicht das Sein, auch nicht das menschliche Sein ist das erste, sondern das Jenseits des Seins ("The ontological is broken in it and becomes the theological. The object is not human being, but rather the other of being appearing in human being. That something thus is possible must be presupposed. It cannot be other than presupposed. For the prologue is anticipation, speaking of the subject matter before the subject matter itself" [my translation]).

("In the prologue the way leads from the ontology to theology. In truth the theological is the presupposition of the ontological. That ontology leads up to the point where the question arises concerning the beyond of being [*das Jenseits des Seins*], that is only possible because behind it stands the already received answer. The human can only seriously

"God is being" and that "God is more than being as love." Methodologically, then, it is useful to distinguish between *priority* and *primacy*. The question of being has *priority* methodologically in thinking the relation between God and the world in the movement from the ontological to the theological. The theological has *primacy*, however, in relation to the ontological, in that love is more than being as the beyond of being—as the beyond of being, the sole theological reason for there being a world.[55]

---

ask about the beyond of himself if the other has already spoken. This claim can be abated, but it is at work in every stage of ontology. Seeing the human being such that it is impelled to the question concerning its beyond cannot be rationally coerced; it is only possible on the basis of the primordial witnesses of the beyond of being. The methodical path of the prologue strikes out in the opposite direction than the material way of life. And this means not from the ontological to the theological, even if the way of introduction is necessarily the reverse. For not being, also not human being is the first, but rather the beyond of being" [my translation]) (Paul Tillich, "Die Gestalt der religiöse Erkenntnis [1927–1928]," in John Powell Clayton, *The Concept of Correlation: Paul Tillich and the Possibility of a Mediating Theology*, Theologische Bibliothek Topelmann 37 [Berlin/New York: Walter de Gruyter, 1980], 274).

[55]See the following: "Der Liebe wird . . . nicht als eine der Eigenschaften Gottes, sondern als sein tieffstes Wesen bezeichnet. Was von Gott auszusagen ist, das muß nicht nur mit der Liebe Gottes vereinigt, sondern aus ihr verstanden werden. Aus der Liebe Gottes müssen die Schöpfung, die Offenbarung und die Erlsung abgeleitet werden. Wenn sich das Bekenntnis, daß Gott Liebe ist, auf die Offenbarung Gottes gründet, so soll damit nicht gesagt sein, daß sich Gott nur in seiner Offenbarung als Liebe bettigt, sondern es soll bedeuten, daß alles Wirken Gottes, seine Weltregierung aus seiner Liebe fliet, daß aber diese im Weltlauf verborgen und nur in der Offenbarung offenbar ist" ("Love is not designated as one of God's attributes, but rather as his deepest essence. That which is to be asserted of God must not only be united with God's love, but rather must be understood from it. Creation, revelation, and redemption must be derived from God's love. If the confession that 'God is love' is grounded upon God's revelation, then it should not be said thereby that God actuates himself only in his revelation as love, but rather it should mean that all of God's works, his world governance flows out of his love, that this, however, is hidden in the course of the world and only manifest in revelation" [my translation]) (Wilhelm Lütgert, *Schöpfung und Offenbarung: Eine Theologie der ersten Artikels*, mit Einführung von Werner Neuer, Zweite Aufl. [Giessen/Basel: Brunnen Verlag, 1984] 375-98, esp. 376-77). See also Gilkey's comments. "In Christian faith the claim is made to know the nature of the will of God who created the world and to know why He did so. In its communion with God in Christ, the Christian community has encountered the Almighty Power from which all of finitude has come, and it has found that the final nature of that creative will is love" (*Maker of Heaven and Earth: A Study of the Christian Doctrine of Creation* [Garden City NY: Doubleday, 1959] 71; hereafter cited as *MHE*.

In terms of the divine attributes, one could even say that the "physical" attributes have priority, but that the "ethical" attributes have primacy.[56]

This distinction between priority and primacy accords with Gilkey's affirmation of the supralapsarian emphasis of Calvinism even apart from its classical formulation.[57] If love is the beyond of being, a modification or clarification of the divine self-limitation in Gilkey's modification of the doctrine of God is necessary in order to alleviate suspicion that the ontological approach to thinking the relation between God and the world ignores the "ethical." The notion of the self-limitation of divine being, apart from love as the beyond of being, can too easily be understood as mere permission. More appropriately, self-limitation must be seen as rooted in the self-impartation of divine love, as the divine affirmation of creation that does not come to full expression in the ontological explication of the symbol of God in Gilkey's doctrine of God. Gilkey himself noted something similar in *Maker of Heaven and Earth*.

> If God is love, and it is thus that we know Him in the gospel, and if therefore the purpose of His creation of the creature man is that he may have personal fellowship with God, then the reality of a finite being alongside an infinite power becomes intelligible. Considered in the personal categories where He is most deeply known, God can be understood as a self-limiting Creator who desires to give being to another free person. For if it is God's

---

[56]See Issak August Dorner, *Divine Immutability: A Critical Reconsideration*, trans. Robert R. Williams and Claude Welch, Fortress Texts in Modern Theology (Minneapolis: Fortress Press, 1994). Surprisingly, given the parallels between their critiques and revisions of classical theism, Gilkey does not utilize Dorner's work. Dorner argues, on the basis of God as love, for the complexity of God's being as simultaneously actual and potential, universal and particular, eternal and temporal, and immutable and mutable.

[57]"No ultimate division between persons who are sheep and persons who are goats, those who participate in God and those who are condemned to hell, is admissible if the divine power is to be ultimately sovereign and the divine love the ultimate quality of that power. Orthodox Calvinism was correct in its supralapsarian emphasis: God's will to re-deem was *not* made in the light of either the fall or of our fallible individual efforts to regenerate or to fulfill ourselves." "The most important consideration in this connection is that the essence of the divine love, as portrayed throughout the New Testament, seems denied or negated by the traditional doctrine; that love is viewed in the New Testament as (a) the central character of God's will, and (b) as directed in mercy at the unworthy in order to redeem *them*. Such a view of the divine love in turn seems *denied* or *negated* either by (a) an arbitrary choice of some for salvation and others for retribution . . . or (b) by a view that some are chosen by their 'faith' or 'obedience' " (Gilkey, *RW*, 298, 429n.58).

will to be "Lord" in a personal sense, then this self-limitation of His almighty power and being is required.[58]

Yet, if love is the beyond of being (*das Jenseits des Seins*) as the strictly theological reason for creation and providence, redemption, and eschatological fulfillment, this requires the reformulation of a doctrine of the immanent Trinity in light of a panentheistic understanding of the trinitarian framework of God as being, logos, and love. More specifically, this requires thinking a doctrine of the immanent Trinity in terms of love in order to account for the gift character of creation itself. To say that God as being is the transcendent condition of the possibility for the existence of beings is certainly necessary in order to account for the givenness of beings. Is it theologically sufficient, however, in order to account for the specification of that givenness of being as being utter gift? Does not one need to think the complex unity of God as being, logos, and love in terms of the immanent *Dreieinigkeit Gottes*? Does not an "economic" articulation of the divine activity in relation to the world in terms of being, logos, and love need to be supplemented with an account of the immanent triunity of God as love? Classical theism's absolutism debilitated post-Nicene theology, resulting in the separation of the economic from the immanent Trinity. Gilkey's reinterpretation of God in panentheistic terms, however, provides a basis for retrieving the doctrine of the immanent triunity of God.

Given Gilkey's theological method and its progressive stages, it would be fair to say that a full exposition of the Christian doctrine of the Trinity could be developed as a postlegomenon to a systematic theology,

---

[58]Gilkey, *MHE*, 229. Compare this to Dorner's comments. "In the living, God posits a self-positing, an effect which is self-effecting, an act which becomes active. And this is far removed from the notion . . . that God limits his omnipotence when he grants an actual causality also to that which he is not; rather, he first becomes active causality through this alleged self limitation, which in truth is manifestation of his power and extension of his sphere of power. . . . Only if the finite beings, in particular the free ones, were *given* to him, would the granting of a proper causality for them, that is, their existence, be a limitation for God's creative power. Thus again the now commonly heard expression of God's self-limitation is to be excused only as figurative, whereas in truth God without the free beings would prove himself not more but less in his creative power, as having a smaller than a larger sphere of power and government." Further, according to Dorner, "the self-impartation to the actual other, the creature, is in no way a loss of self, a giving up of self by God; it is rather the power of love to be in the other itself and to be itself in the other" (Dorner, *Divine Immutability*, 144, 178).

in light of his theological epistemology and with a systematically articulated Christology and pneumatology informed by an eidetic explication of the "trinitarian" grammar of the Christian symbol-system.[59] Gilkey would agree, I believe, with Schleiermacher, Tillich, and Ebeling that the doctrine of the Trinity is to be formulated as the capstone [*Schlustein*] to a systematic theology.[60] It would be the capstone as second-order discourse of theological reflection. This discourse presupposes the first-order discourse of the economic Trinity of being, logos, and love, and making explicit that which is already implicit in that first-order discourse.[61] The economic and the immanent Trinities would then treat the same theme, but only according to different aspects—as, for example, in Karl Rahner's famous thesis: "The 'economic' Trinity *is* the 'immanent' Trinity and the 'immanent' Trinity is the 'economic' Trinity."[62] The affirmation of the economic Trinity would assert then that the workings of the triune God are not only undivided, but also indivisible, namely, that "*each* activity of God participates without restriction in God's divinity *and* in God's unity."[63] Each of the divine activities (creation, providence, redemption, eschatological fulfillment) are modes of divine love.

Yet, as Tillich noted, the doctrine of the Trinity remains open: it can be neither discarded nor retained in its traditional form. The charting of the whirlwind requires further navigation. Langdon Gilkey's work still aids us greatly in that navigation. He has taught and exemplified why one

---

[59]For an exposition of the *trinitarische Grammatik* of Christian *bildliche* discourse concerning God, see Dalferth, *Der auferweckte Gekreuzigte*, 210-36.

[60]Friedrich Schleiermacher, *Der christliche Glaube nach den Grundsätzen der evangelischen Kirche im Zusammenhange dargestellt*, Bd. 2, hrsg. Martin Redeker, Siebente Aufl. (Berlin: Walter de Gruyter, 1960) 458-73; Paul Tillich, *Systematic Theology*, vol. 3 (Chicago: University of Chicago Press, 1963) 285; and Gerhard Ebeling, *Dogmatik des christlichen Glaubens*, Bd. 3, *Der Glaube an Gott den Vollender der Welt* (Tübingen: J. C. B. Mohr (Paul Siebeck), 1982) 529-46.

[61]On this character of trinitarian discourse, namely, as second-level discourse, see Wilfried Härle, *Dogmatik* (Berlin/New York: Walter de Gruyter, 1995) 386; and Dalferth, *Der auferweckte Gekreuzigte*, 218-25.

[62]"Die 'ökonomische' Trinität *ist* die immanente Trinität und umgekehrt" (Karl Rahner, *The Trinity*, trans. Joseph Donceel [New York: Seabury Press, 1974] 22; "Bemerkungen zum dogmatischen Traktat De Trinitate," in *Schriften zur Theologie*, Bd. 4 [Zürich/Kln: Benziger Verlag Einsiedeln, 1964] 115).

[63]"*Jedes* Wirken Gottes partizipiert uneingeschränkt an seiner Göttlichkeit *und* an seiner Einheit" (Härle, *Dogmatik*, 396-97).

can sail into the whirlwind in confidence, for at the heart of the motion of whirlwind there is God, and "God is love" (1 John 4:9, 16).

> They mounted up to heaven, they went down to the depths;
>   their courage melted away in their calamity;
> they reeled and staggered like drunkards,
>   and were at their wits' end.
> Then they cried to the Lord in their trouble,
>   and he brought them out from their distress;
> he made the storm be still,
>   and the waves of the sea were hushed.
> Then they were glad because they had quiet,
>   and he brought them to their desired haven.
> Let them thank the Lord for his steadfast love,
>   for his wonderful works to humankind.   (Psalm 107:26-31 NRSV)

Chapter 10

Power, Freedom, and History:
The Symbol of Divine Providence
in Langdon Gilkey's Theology

Kyle A. Pasewark

Introduction: The Postmodern Eclipse of Providence

Langdon Gilkey is one of the few late twentieth-century American theologians to give sustained focus to the Christian symbol of providence; he is the only one to give it a central place in a theological system. Contemporary theology's lack of attention to what traditionally had held an honored place at the doctrinal table is not surprising. After all, philosophies of history, the parallel philosophical enterprise, have also receded from attention. One reason for this weakened pulse in efforts to account for the course of history is noted by Gilkey himself: throughout the nineteenth and early twentieth centuries, philosophies of history were constructed under the aegis of a reflexive "faith in progress," the belief that history was moving toward a final culmination, and that the signs of advance toward that goal could be read in and through the events of history.[1] This dominant myth was, Gilkey notes, related intrinsically to the Western sense of progressive cultural hegemony. Western values, Western technology, the West in all its glory would bring history home, in ever-ascending progress toward truth, goodness, and beauty.[2]

It is, Gilkey says, an "unanswerable certainty" that those days are behind us.[3] Gilkey recognized the loss of Western dominance earlier than most Americans, a perpetually optimistic and sanguine people. As the Westerners who were to be interned in Shandong compound made their way clumsily to the trains that would carry them to captivity, Gilkey knew that the imprisonment signaled not only the internees' loss of

---

[1]See, e.g., Langdon Gilkey, *Reaping the Whirlwind: A Christian Interpretation of History* (New York: Seabury, 1976) 9, 10; hereafter cited as *RW*.

[2]Langdon Gilkey, *Through the Tempest: Theological Voyages in a Pluralistic Culture*, ed. Jeff B. Pool (Minneapolis: Fortress Press, 1991) 16; hereafter cited as *TT*.

[3]Langdon Gilkey, "A Retrospective Glance at My Work," in *The Whirlwind in Culture: Frontiers in Theology: In Honor of Langdon Gilkey*, ed. Donald W. Musser and Joseph L. Price (Bloomington IN: Meyer-Stone Books, 1988) 32; reprinted in this book.

freedom for the foreseeable future; it also symbolized the end of Western imperialism in the East.[4] Most Americans could and did maintain pleasurable ignorance about the death of the Western era and maintained their progressive mindset for several decades. The failure of American military force in Vietnam, Watergate, the oil embargo, a period of slow economic growth and "stagflation"—all occurring or coming to a head in the 1970s—however, brought American confidence crashing down. In academic circles, Robert Bellah's *Broken Covenant* captured this sense of loss; in popular music, Stephen Stills' "Do You Remember the Americans?" poignantly spoke to the nearly overnight reversal of American consciousness.[5] To be sure, Americans swaggered through the Reagan era, but the embrace of Reagan's "morning in America" had the feel more of desperation than confidence. Our great military victories were over the mighty Grenada and later Iraq, variations on a new theme of "conquest-lite"; even the collapse of the communist archenemy failed to bring Americans much joy or serenity.

Never has American confidence had a shorter shelf life. George Bush, with ninety-percent-plus approval ratings in public opinion polls after the war with Iraq in mid-1991, suffered electoral defeat less than twenty months later. Bill Clinton, presiding over a healthy economy and lacking disastrously unpopular foreign entanglements, failed to secure popular majority support in his reelection bid. However much we announce it with our lips, the myth of progress has surely died in our hearts.

The dominant American philosophies of history and, with the substantial exception of the Niebuhrs, theologies of providence were, however, based on that myth. With the collapse of the myth of progress, American theology and philosophy seemed to have nothing to say about history. Gilkey remarks in another connection that intellectual shifts in theology are only partly the result of in-house doctrinal or religious pressures. In a fundamentally secular culture, "cultural changes that our century has witnessed . . . have represented the major causes" for theo-

---

[4]Langdon Gilkey, *Shantung Compound: The Story of Men and Women under Pressure* (New York: Harper & Row, 1966); hereafter cited as *SC*.

[5]Robert N. Bellah, *The Broken Covenant: Civil Religion in a Time of Trial* (Chicago: University of Chicago Press, 1975); Stephen Stills (composer, performer) and Manassas (performers), "Do You Remember the Americans?" *Down the Road* (audio recording) (New York: Atlantic, ©1973) track 6.

logical shifts.[6] The same is true of philosophy. At least one of the reasons for the popularity and fashion of postmodernism in America is that it chronicles and celebrates the collapse of cultural hegemony and the notion of progress (while, to be sure, maintaining the sanctity of freedom, perhaps the most Western and modern concept of all). Moreover, postmodern thought both confirms and authorizes the elimination of traditional philosophies of history and, by extension, theological accounts of history's meaning. It is true that theologies of providence and philosophies of history were in eclipse long before Michel Foucault, Jean-François Lyotard, and Richard Rorty asserted that philosophies of history are at best delusion, at worst hegemonic, grand narratives that license oppression by suppressing the validity of "local knowledges."[7] Postmodernism, however, accurately caught the mood, the feeling that universal claims about the course and meaning of history are no longer possible. Additionally, to accept the claims of these postmodern thinkers is to close the road to constructive theologies and philosophies of history based on a hypothesis of progress.

This context provides one angle from which both the achievement and the shortcomings of Langdon Gilkey's theology of providence can be examined. On the one hand, the very effort to recover the symbol of providence for the late twentieth century is remarkable for its boldness and Gilkey's dexterity of execution. On the other hand, notwithstanding his incisive criticism of one form of modernism (the myth of progress), Gilkey remains undeniably modern in his understanding of the divine activity in history.[8] If one accepts the core convictions of modernism, among them that there must be, historically or eschatologically, a single overarching power or truth that holds everything within itself (including, in Gilkey's case, possibility), then Gilkey's understanding of providence

---

[6]Langdon Gilkey, "Plurality and Its Theological Implications," in *The Myth of Christian Uniqueness: Toward a Pluralistic Theology of Religions*, ed. John Hick and Paul F. Knitter (Maryknoll NY: Orbis Books, 1987) 39.

[7]On local knowledge, see Michel Foucault, "Two Lectures," trans. Kate Soper, in *Power/Knowledge: Selected Interviews and Other Writings, 1972–1977*, ed. Colin Gordon (New York: Random House, Pantheon, 1980) 82-93; on "grand narratives," see Jean-François Lyotard, *The Postmodern Condition: A Report on Knowledge*, trans. Geoff Bennington and Brian Massumi (Minneapolis: University of Minnesota Press, 1984).

[8]There are impulses in his later work on pluralism that tend to move away from this modern understanding, but Gilkey has not reformulated his conception of providence in their light. I examine this issue below.

may be the best solution available. Gilkey's concept of providence, however, generates its own internal tensions that are not overcome easily, that tend to exceed the very framework he establishes, and that invite us to revisit understandings of providence that Gilkey prematurely rejects. I contend that Gilkey asks both too much and too little from history: too much, in that he expects history to exhibit universal, unconditioned, absolute meanings in particular, conditioned, relative forms; too little, in that finally the power of God can be secured definitively only beyond history, in the eschatological consummation.

The path to these conclusions is complex, as is Gilkey's theology of providence. I proceed in several stages: (1) an examination of the scope, significance, and placement of providence within Gilkey's theology; (2) an account of why Gilkey thinks that a *theological* (rather than secular) account of history is both necessary and desirable; (3) an exposition of the understanding of God and the divine activity in and beyond history that emerges, with emphasis on Gilkey's understanding of divine self-limitation; and (4) an evaluation of the successes and shortcomings of Gilkey's understanding of God and providence.

I. Providence in the Theology of Langdon Gilkey

Gilkey's theology of providence retains two important continuities with the dominant Christian traditions: it maintains an interest in theodicy and retains the classical theological structure of creation/providence/eschatology.[9] With respect to theodicy, the classical double interest in justifying God's seemingly odd ways asserted—often with considerable difficulty—both the notion of divine omnipotence so central to any monotheistic tradition and the emphasis on the perfect goodness of God. In the classical traditions, both Augustine's apology in *The City of God* and Luther's great debate with Erasmus stand as paradigmatic instances of the struggle. This paired interest was retained generally by Christian theologians and philosophers of religion after the Enlightenment. The Enlightenment, however, added a new wrinkle by postulating "freedom" as a high—perhaps the highest—human good, so that now (*contra*

---

[9]See an excellent brief presentation of Gilkey's theology of providence in Gilkey, *TT*, 115-39.

Augustine and Calvin) divine omnipotence *itself*, irrespective of whatever external evils omnipotence failed to protect us against, became suspect.[10]

The classical question was on the order of Harold Kushner's inquiry: Why do "bad things happen to good people" (if God is omnipotent and omnibenevolent)?[11] The post-Enlightenment question (admirably anticipated by Erasmus) was different: How can we speak of *human* good or evil at all, if God is all-powerful and therefore all-controlling?[12] The presupposition for moral evaluation became the postulate of free choice, the capacity to reject divine power, a startling shift from the now nearly discarded notion of effective grace so decisive in the edition of Calvin's *Institutes* from 1559. With this understanding of freedom as requiring autonomous personal choice, the difficulty of preserving both divine omnipotence and divine goodness became even more complicated than it had been. Gilkey too is involved in a kind of post-Enlightenment theodicy. As we will see, the problem of squaring divine omnipotence with God's beneficence, in light of human freedom, persists as a background issue in Gilkey's theology of providence.

Second, for the most part, Gilkey's thought retains a traditional triadic structure for historical interpretation: creation, providence, and the eschatologically centered moment of re-creation. As in the thought of most of his predecessors, Gilkey does not conceive these three moments as temporally or theologically separate moments; although each moment tends to distinct emphases, each flows into the others. There are, however, two ways to conceive the ordering of creation, providence, and eschatology: one emerges from the "historical" order of beginning (creation), persistence (providence), and *telos* (eschatology), the other from the standpoint of the theologian who asserts her or his claims about this trinity.

Gilkey's initial theological foray, *Maker of Heaven and Earth*, was, appropriately enough, centered on the doctrine of creation.[13] In compari-

---

[10]Gilkey, *RW*, 159-87.

[11]Harold S. Kushner, *When Bad Things Happen to Good People* (New York: Schocken, 1981).

[12]See Erasmus of Rotterdam, *De Libero Arbitrio*, trans. and ed. Philip S. Watson, in *Luther and Erasmus: Free Will and Salvation*, ed. E. Gordon Rupp and Philip S. Watson (Philadelphia: Westminster Press, 1969) esp. 74-96.

[13]Langdon Gilkey, *Maker of Heaven and Earth: A Study of the Christian Doctrine of Creation* (Garden City NY: Doubleday, 1959; repr.: Lanham MD: University Press of America, 1985); references herein are to the reprinted edition; hereafter cited as *MHE*.

son to religious and philosophical conceptions of creation from preexistent matter, Gilkey argued that the Christian notion of creation out of nothing was vital.[14] Gilkey claims that "dualist" conceptions of creation

> contradicted two basic affirmations about God and his world which lay at the very foundations of Christian convictions. The first of these was that God was the Almighty Sovereign of all existence. . . . Secondly, a metaphysical dualism in which one principle is "divine" and the other principle not, always tends to become a moral dualism in which all good comes from the divine and all evil from the opposing principle.[15]

The principles at stake are those of traditional theodicy: the power of God and the goodness of divine creation. The former is the necessary affirmation of monotheism. Christian thinkers "had discovered that in order to express the traditional monotheism of the Jewish and Christian religions, they must, in speaking of creation, insist on creation out of nothing," asserting that God "is the sole sovereign Lord of existence" and that "every aspect of existence must be essentially dependent on His power as the ground and basis of its being." With respect to the latter, the goodness of God implies "that since all that is comes from God's will as its sole source, nothing in existence can be intrinsically evil."[16]

Clearly, the doctrine of creation has bled over into providence; the myth of origin has implications for history and the present. Why? Consider an alternative, a doctrine of creation that understands the biblical accounts of creation as historical records that describe an accomplished fact that "happened" at some time in the past. For Gilkey, such a conception is not only irresponsible intrusion of theology into a realm properly belonging to science, but—exactly to the extent that creation is reduced to "original history"—also irrelevant.[17] One significant contribution of theological liberalism, Gilkey contends, was to restore the significance of the "immanence of God . . . and the belief that God's creative activity was not just 'once upon a time' in the remote past, but a continuing

---

[14]Gilkey also asserts the superiority of *creatio ex nihilo* in relation to creation myths that posit creation of the world out of the divine substance (Gilkey, *MHE*, 58-66). These arguments, however, neither are relevant for my purposes nor does Gilkey emphasize them in his later work.

[15]Gilkey, *MHE*, 47-48.

[16]Gilkey, *MHE*, 49-50.

[17]Langdon Gilkey, *Creationism on Trial: Evolution and God at Little Rock* (Minneapolis: Winston, 1985); hereafter cited as *CT*.

factor in the ongoing life of nature and of culture."[18] That continuing divine activity can be conceived equally well as creative providence or providential creativity. "[T]his is the way the divine creates: in and through this providential story of cosmic and evolutionary development."[19] Without such an interrelation, creation is likely to sail too close to a deism that removes God from history subsequent to the "days" of creation.

On grounds of divine sovereignty in history, providence initially contains two aspects: "the principle of the continuation of finite being [and] the principle of new possibility."[20] We must be careful, however, not to think of these two aspects as limited to ontological structures of the world that God continually creates and upholds. Rather, both are suffused with providence "as the principle of judgment," made necessary because of human sin.[21] Judgment requires theology to surpass exclusively ontological accounts of divine activity. Gilkey, borrowing a phrase from Reinhold Niebuhr, maintains that purely ontological accounts cannot account for the "dramas" of history.[22] The basic ontological structure in which history appears is the ontological polarity of destiny and freedom, which includes (and is sometimes identified with) actuality and possibility.[23] Each historical moment pulses into existence out of the past, providing human action with a finite range of alternative actions and perspectives in relation to it. These are components of our destinies: to be here and nowhere else, now and no time else, of one sex, a specific racial and national heritage, and so forth. We are not free to choose our inherited destiny. Destiny, however, is not closed to the future; every destiny, in pulsing toward the future, leaves open possibilities. "Destiny" that is utterly closed, without opportunity for human freedom to act

---

[18]Gilkey, *MHE*, 11.

[19]Langdon Gilkey, *Nature, Reality, and the Sacred: The Nexus of Science and Religion*, Theology and the Sciences series, ed. Kevin J. Sharpe (Minneapolis: Fortress Press, 1993) 100; hereafter cited as *NRS*.

[20]Gilkey, *RW*, 265-66.

[21]Gilkey, *RW*, 266.

[22]See Reinhold Niebuhr, *The Self and the Dramas of History* (New York: Charles Scribner's Sons, 1955).

[23]Gilkey, *RW*, 49. Several contributions in this book discuss the priority of this polarity, especially my own contribution in chap. 2. What follows here is a brief summary of Gilkey's understanding of this polarity.

creatively with respect to the future is, Gilkey says, no more destiny but "fate." Gilkey approaches destiny

> as a given on which our present freedom, our judgment, decisions and actions can work and so in some measure shape and control toward our own ends. . . . As malleable to freedom, this destiny in turn becomes *fate* for us when we experience the given and the ongoing changes it represents as overwhelming and oppressive, as destructive of our powers and so our freedom. . . . Those who are conquered or enslaved, those who are oppressed and exploited . . . experience no freedom to shape their life; they experience destiny as fate.[24]

Destiny is transmuted to fate primarily through the very same ontological pole that provides us with the capacity to fulfill our destiny: freedom. That "the pot of human evil seems to be bottomless" is neither a necessity of the ontological structure of finitude nor a necessary consequence of created freedom.[25] Here Gilkey returns to the sovereignty and goodness of God: if finitude and freedom are creations of God, they must be essentially good.[26] Sin is not a necessary consequence of freedom, but is a universal one: "we continually, actively distort the possibility of the moment and thus fundamentally despoil the harmony of the process."[27] We are, individually and socially, "motivated by self-interest," a "lust for power," "inordinate self-love and love of [the community's] own," and so forth.[28] Fallen freedom, not created freedom, invites and receives divine judgment; individually and especially culturally, "what is created by the ambiguity of this freedom is sinful and sick, always and in part, and thus, speaking theologically, under the judgment of God."[29] We cannot describe this judgment nor, therefore, can we describe divine providence, exclusively through ontological categories, because "ontology knows only structure and not its misuse."[30]

---

[24]Gilkey, *RW*, 49.

[25]Langdon Gilkey, *Message and Existence: An Introduction to Christian Theology* (New York: Seabury Press, 1979) 115; hereafter cited as *ME*.

[26]Gilkey, *ME*, 125.

[27]Gilkey, *ME*, 124-56; Langdon Gilkey, *Naming the Whirlwind: The Renewal of God-Language* (Indianapolis: Bobbs-Merrill, 1969) 385-86n.11; hereafter cited as *NW*.

[28]Gilkey, *NW*, 386, 387; idem, *ME*, 142.

[29]Gilkey, *NW*, 389.

[30]Gilkey, *RW*, 256.

Providence as judgment must be described ontically, in terms of the actual activity of the divine and human within and through the events of history: "history is event, a compound of destiny . . . with freedom."[31] This constitutes the dramatic character of history as well as the immanence of God and the perpetuation of human freedom. Yet, judgment should not be understood as simply a negative act; rather, the judgment contained in providence connects with the third traditional moment of Christian theology, redemption from sin.[32] Envisioning providence "lures" the present on the basis of an expectation of fulfillment. If the present is not the fulfillment of history, if it is trapped in sin, Gilkey asks, "What then is our eschatological hope in its ultimate shape? What is it that we ultimately hope *for* in the ambiguity of individual and historical life as they move into the future?"[33] Providence provides possibilities, visions for the future, which are the content of history's meaning and purpose. Providence is teleological, directed toward future fulfillment and conquest of the ambiguities of sin.

Providence's purposive character includes judgment. Following a long tradition exemplified by Augustine, sin is sin because it damages the created order, "destroys relations with others, the natural world around it, and ultimately itself; it leads inexorably to the loss of self, the loss of the other, and the loss of world."[34] Sin is not sin because God "says so"; rather, God says so, because sin, "ultimate religious devotion to a finite interest," violates the fulfillment that is proper to creatures within the created order.[35] For Gilkey, the chief effect of sin is to skew the polarity of destiny and freedom, limiting the possibilities available for the actualization of destiny, increasing the intensity of "fatedness" and destroying freedom. This is the case not only with social oppression, but also with the domination of nature, which both endangers the possibilities of nature itself and increasingly threatens to destroy the same humanity that is so intent on dominating it.[36] Gilkey argues that especially self-

---

[31]Gilkey, *RW*, 293.

[32]Langdon Gilkey, *Society and the Sacred: Toward a Theology of Culture in Decline* (New York: Crossroad, 1981) 54-55; hereafter cited as *SAS*.

[33]Gilkey, *RW*, 295.

[34]Gilkey, *TT*, 208.

[35]Gilkey, *SC*, 233.

[36]Gilkey, *NRS*, 143-57.

giving love allows renunciation of domination and, therefore, the expansion of the possibilities of freedom for all in history.[37]

Our failures to love others place individuals, cultures, and perhaps the species under the specter of divine judgment. This judgment, however, is not merely retributive, but is intended to call us back to—and provide possibilities for—freedom's expansion. Gilkey's use of the Hebrew prophets as paradigmatic announcers of divine judgment is instructive. Although the prophets proclaimed the judgment of God (especially upon the privileged), they also announced a new promise. Gilkey describes the cycle of promise, betrayal, and a judgment that produces new gifts in this way:

> First, Israel experiences divine election and gift. . . . Then rebellion, rejection, and betrayal are followed by destruction and catastrophe or nemesis. But then (the continuing surprise) is offered the promise of a new act to come, a gift of new possibilities from the divine creativity. . . . The main message for us, besides the judgment on the mighty and the affluent, is that in a situation of apparently inevitable destruction, new social and historical possibilities are there. . . . To believe in divine providence is to expect such a *kairos*.[38]

To be sure, sin will frustrate these new promises also (hence, history retains something of a cyclical character) and, therefore, "Providence . . . is not enough"; an eschatological consummation beyond the ambiguities of history will be necessary.[39] The *content* of that consummation, however, *is identical with the demand placed on history*. In this sense, the eschatological theologians did not entirely miss the mark. Eschatological content is "the lure of new possibility [that] inspires that historical activity which shapes a recalcitrant history in the direction of the ultimate kingdom."[40]

---

[37]Gilkey relates the importance of self-giving, sacrificial love to his construal of sin as principally inordinate self-love, which constricts—as did Reinhold Niebuhr—Augustine's category of "pride." Throughout his works, Gilkey contrasts self-love, therefore, with its solution, self-sacrifice. Gilkey develops it as the major theme in *Shantung Compound* (also see Gilkey, *ME*, 172-73, 192-93, 213; idem, *TT*, 199-200; and idem, *NRS*, 138, 149, 169, 183, 191-92).

[38]Gilkey, *TT*, 120-21.

[39]Gilkey, *TT*, 121.

[40]Gilkey, *RW*, 287.

Providence, therefore, is in doctrinal contact with both creation and redemption. Situated between them "temporally," it is the historical switching yard that connects the whole of history together, beginning to end. Another vantage point, however, indicates the overriding importance of conceptions of providence in relation even to the doctrine of creation—on which, Gilkey suggests, "logically depends all that Christians say about their God"—and eschatology, which defines the ultimate purpose of both creation and providence.[41] Although in a theological system providence may be one among equals, existentially it is primary. The reason is straightforward: only from the present can the traces of the divine be read into the past, the future, and our ultimate meanings. However the theological *system* begins, the *theologian* has no choice but to begin in the arena of providence. The doctrine of creation may be the logical presupposition for the rest of that which Christian theology has to say, but divine "traces" in creation must be read from present existence, which is principally a matter of divine providence.[42] Gilkey recognizes this, noting that, in ancient Israel, "it was the historical experience of the providential creation of the covenant people in conjunction with their own human misuse of the divine covenant that probably lay in back of the dialectic of creation and fall expressed in Genesis 1–3."[43] Similarly, the content of human fulfillment, all "direct intuition of the possibility of improvement in history" and even consummation beyond history, can be read only prospectively from this moment, our moments, in history.[44] We have no direct intuition of what healed structures of existence would be except as we project them from here. Providence, therefore, carries an existential priority because its emphasis concerns our existence immediately. At its fullest, Gilkey's theology of divine providence is an account (not an explanation) of the whole of history—from whence we came, our current condition, that toward which we are going, and how, roughly, we might get there.

It is not clear, however, why a theology of providence is necessary to account for history or to give impetus to human efforts in history. The necessity of providence, of course, depends on the necessity of divine activity in history. I already drew a parallel between philosophies of

---

[41]Gilkey, *MHE*, 4.
[42]Gilkey, *NRS*, 175.
[43]Gilkey, *SAS*, 47.
[44]Gilkey, *RW*, 287.

history and theologies of providence. Both endeavors attempt to give an account of history, outline the possibilities for the future, and provide visions of fulfillment that motivate human action toward the future. Philosophies of history, however, appear to accomplish these tasks more economically, without the hypothesis of God's immanence in history. Moreover, in a secular culture, the hypothesis of God's action in history seems not merely superfluous but inconvenient. Gilkey is not only aware of the difficulty involved in being a theologian in secular culture; it is as such a theologian that he understands himself. He defines himself in that way because he is convinced that a theological account of history is necessary in secular culture. I turn to that claim.

II. Why Theology? Why God?

A. The Theological Imperative

One suspects that this theological die was cast irrevocably for Gilkey in the internment camp in Shandong province. One of the many striking features of Gilkey's account of prison life is that life proceeded relatively smoothly at the beginning, when basic necessities had to be provided by organizations that did not yet exist, when all were equally desperate, in short, when the internees stood at the margins of existence. When Gilkey arrived in Shandong, he was a "convinced Christian," but

> those first months of camp raised the most urgent and devastating of questions: What's so important about the way a person looks at life? . . . The real issues of life are surely material and political. . . . Those matters are resolved by practical experience and by techniques, not by this or that philosophy or religious faith. . . . It was not that I thought religion wrong; I simply thought it irrelevant.[45]

When the prisoners had become comfortable (relative to a general situation of deprivation), however, bickering, theft, hypocrisies, and threats of anarchy, appeared in full force. Not only does this say much about the character of human sin; it also speaks to the need for religion. As the camp's social fabric disintegrated, as hopelessness about the future took hold, Gilkey realized that no practical experience or technique had sufficient power to stave off the demons of meaninglessness. Rather, "the only hope in the human situation is that the 'religiousness' of men find

---

[45]Gilkey, SC, 73.

its true center in God, and not in the many idols that appear in the course of our experience."[46] As for Tillich, for Gilkey religion is an "ultimate concern." Following Tillich and Augustine, Gilkey claims that every person and culture have "religion" in this sense. Thus, "the presence of this dimension more than anything else renders false any purely secular account of man's problems and hopes."[47]

Everyone muddles through life with errors, many of them benign, some fortunate. Gilkey argues, however, that secularism's error is malignant. Secular philosophies of history (and some theological ones) tend either toward a cyclical or toward a progressive conception of history; put theologically, they tend to sacrifice either God's immanence or transcendence. Cyclical theories of history, classically propounded by the Greeks, have a largely accurate understanding of the human predicament. These theories recognize the fallenness of freedom, the inevitable and universal perversion of the good by historical actors, and consequently, the inability of history to embody a single, enduring answer to the question of human meaning. All historical fulfillments are imperfect and impermanent; consequently, what human meaning there is can be had only beyond and outside history. The divine does not providentially intervene in human history. The result of cyclical theories of history, Gilkey says, is resignation and discouragement with respect to the possibility of meaning in history; all history is equally meaningless, a "fundamental alienation of creativity from the iron laws of history," correspondingly "with no purpose and no permanence."[48] Even if provisional meaning is achieved, the distorted structures of human evil—and time itself—will conspire to destroy it. The cyclical interpretation of history, which discourages concrete historical involvement because of its apparent hopelessness, has not been absent in Christian theology. Early Christian theologies such as gnosticism, Arianism, and Manicheanism were tinged with this conception of history. Otherwise dissimilar contemporary religious ideologies, from Heaven's Gate to the political resignation in much orthodox Lutheranism, the contemporary fascination with escapist mystical religious feeling and, Gilkey points out, some *krisis* theologies, also find little meaning in history.[49] Whatever fulfillment exists is beyond the

---

[46]Gilkey, *SC*, 234.
[47]Gilkey, *SC*, 233.
[48]Gilkey, *RW*, 87, 205.
[49]Gilkey, *RW*, 273.

world *and only there*. The divine resides high above us, having abandoned the world to its own corrupt devices.

Still, elements of this resigned worldview are true, which is perhaps why it persists. A culture with frustrated utopian hopes (like America after the collapse of the progressive myth) may feel these truths more sharply than others. The truth of the cyclical view is its recognition that history cannot provide a permanent answer or consummation, that judgment or its analogue is immanent in all historical process. The permanence of judgment and the inability of history autonomously to generate and stabilize its completed meaning is not, however, recognized in the second major beat of the secular historical heart: progressive and ontological interpretations of history.

Readers familiar with Gilkey's thought will notice that the linkage of progressive and ontological philosophies of history expands Gilkey's more typical either/or: either cyclical or progressive. Especially in *Reaping the Whirlwind*, however, Gilkey examines and criticizes ontological philosophies of history. Our reason for linking the two lies in Gilkey's understanding of the universality of sin. Neither progressive nor ontological theories of history recognize that humans inevitably distort the possibilities offered by destiny, that is, that all humans are fallen and that there is no reason to believe that we will suddenly refrain from miscreancy. Because they deny this, either explicitly or implicitly, ontological and progressive theories of history retain the hope of a time in which the ambiguities of history and freedom are overcome, when, as Marx said, the end of history is reached. History has an end in two senses: (1) as *telos*, history's purpose is fulfilled; and (2) as *finis*, time reaches a stasis, has nothing else to do—history and eternity merge.

In North America, progressive and ontological conceptions of history cut across the political spectrum. They are present in "conservative" and "liberal" circles. The point of difference lies in the content of the conception of the meaning of history and the temporal direction of their outlook. Ontological conceptions, for their part, in which progressivism participates to some extent, locate a special present structure (the church, a form of government, natural law) in which the meaning of history is retained in relatively complete and perfect form. That structure of order is surrounded and threatened by the chaos of fallen humanity, and must conquer the latter in order to remove the ambiguities of history. Despite Augustine's development of the doctrine of original sin, he exemplifies this ontological approach. The doctrines of the church were not brought under the purview of original sin. Although sin remained within the will of the church's members, the teachings of charity, humility, the Trinity, and so on, revealed truth without significant taint of sin. Consequently, Augustine approached the church's intellectual enterprise as unfallen, the historical place where the content and means of redemption were given. The church, therefore, was the chief locale of God's constructive providence, both intellectually and morally. All advancement, whether of persons or cultures, depended on obedience to the church. In such ontological conceptions, there is an existent avant-garde that can bring the remainder of the world to its senses, if only the world will listen.

Although in Augustine the dominating possibilities of this ontological vision are balanced somewhat by the recognition of the distorted wills even of those who announce doctrine correctly, this is only a partial counterweight to the domination that such institutions can inflict on their subjects. Moreover, those who truly merit the appellation "fanatic," religious or otherwise, do not retain Augustine's emphasis on the corruption of the individual will, assuming rather that they, their associates, their nation, are historical meaning incarnate; they are the messengers of history's final unity of destiny and freedom. The annals of church history certainly and amply reflect the dangers. Lest we believe that the ontological interpretation of history has disappeared, we need only consider the U.S.A's mission of making the world safe for (North American) democracy and the imperialism it creates. As Gilkey notes, American progressivism participated in this ontological conception—whatever was wrong with the world, Western values were available to correct it—and neither those values nor their agents, as the culmination of history's meaning in germ, were subject to criticism from others.

Progressivism often participates in an ontological conception of history. Still, its impetus is somewhat different. The essential claim of progressivism (and, as Gilkey points out, of the eschatological theologians of the 1960s and 1970s) is that the structures of destiny and freedom *will be* united in history, even though they are not yet so joined.[50] The warping of freedom and the distortion of destiny into fate are incidental in history, not universal; there is nothing deeply diseased about freedom that historical progress cannot cure. The oppression of the past occurred either because freedom was undeveloped or distorted by external

---

[50]Gilkey, *RW*, 226-38.

structures, whether economic, political, geographic, technological. The first of these interpretations, of which John Dewey sometimes can be accused, tends to a sanguine attitude toward sin—if we continue to develop without interference, evil and fate will gradually disappear. The second interpretation is more militant; it was found in the social-gospel theologians, early liberation theology, Marxism, and the eschatological thinkers. The demand is to reform the external structures that have perverted and victimized human freedom.

Progressivism is not always "liberal." Liberal progressivism tends to look at the past with disdain and the present with distrust, while the future is the arena of unbridled possibilities of fulfillment. Conservative progressivism, on the other hand, often conceives of a moment of the past as a golden age, followed by a fall from grace that infects the present. The battle cry of this progressivism is "Forward to the past!"[51] Such golden-age thinking is not necessary for conservative progressivism, however. Without the necessity of a previous economic golden age, the radical free-marketeers of the 1980s held that the progress of the free market would finally solve our economic, moral, and spiritual problems. The division between these economic progressives and the golden-age "traditional values" camp is one of the major fault lines in the Republican Party.

Despite his emphasis on social and cultural sin, and despite his corresponding sympathy with political and liberation theologians, Gilkey believes that progressive and ontological theories of history ignore the character of the polarity of destiny and freedom in two ways. First, progressive and ontological theories of history are, in the end, not historical; they ignore the complex of destiny *and* freedom that makes history possible. History always offers possibilities; humans are always transcendent in relation to their historical circumstances. The "end of history" would also be the end of the self-transcendent spirit of freedom, which always sees beyond its present.[52] Gilkey appropriates the Augustinian insight that human desire, for better and worse, cannot be contained. Second, these conceptions of history refuse to recognize the ambiguity of human freedom. No political or social arrangement can be satisfactory or

---

[51]In North American religious movements, this tendency is outlined by Richard T. Hughes and C. Leonard Allen, *Illusions of Innocence: Protestant Primitivism in America, 1630–1875* (Chicago: University of Chicago Press, 1988).

[52]Gilkey, *RW*, 278.

final for human beings in history, and part of the reason is that every structure is capable of being perverted by self-love. Again, Gilkey is Augustinian. Social structures do impede or encourage sin, but they neither force us to engage in it to the extent that we do nor compel us to take the pleasure in it that we do. Freedom appropriates and perpetuates sinful structures, and those are the inward actions of distorted freedom. Sin is both inward and external, but its origin in each moment is inward.[53] To paraphrase The Eagles, evil "can't take you anywhere you don't already know the way to go."[54] Human freedom perpetually perverts productive destinies into fate and domination. Consequently, ontological and progressive theories of history fail to recognize that *all* history, not just specific moments, are subject to God's judgment. If cyclical theories of history sacrifice divine immanence, progressive and ontological conceptions tend to ignore God's transcendence.

If history is understood in a solely secular manner, Gilkey is convinced that history's meaning is necessarily stretched on a rack by cyclical theories, on one end, and progressive philosophies, on the other. Gilkey summarizes the alternative that secularist conceptions leave us:

> On the one hand, we may believe against history's evidence that one social act, one creative political construction, one new political form may rid history of its estrangement and so of the grim cycle of destruction and decay. . . . [T]his is to say that the estrangement that besets history lies alone in the fate that threatens freedom . . . and not in the corruption of freedom itself, in the human beings who, in our present and for our future, construct and defend those institutions. On the other hand, if this historical perfectionism seems to us naïve, we are left with that grim cycle itself as the final clue to history and the final coup de grace of history's meaning.[55]

The secular problem is that "[o]nce the problem of history has been driven into the heart of the human beings who make and remake history, as the evidence seems to indicate it should be, then apparently there is from within history no answer to the problem of history."[56] It is true, of course, that theological interpretations can and have participated in these errors; but theological interpretation is also, according to Gilkey, the way

---

[53]Gilkey, *ME*, 142, 246-47; idem, *SAS*, 152-53.
[54]The Eagles, "Peaceful, Easy Feeling," *The Eagles: Their Greatest Hits, 1971–1975* (audio recording) (Elektra, ©1976).
[55]Gilkey, *RW*, 265.
[56]Gilkey, *RW*, 265.

out of the difficulties. Only theological interpretation of history can appreciate simultaneously the fallenness of human freedom (which precludes history from embodying its own meaning finally) and *the meaning of historical life despite human fallenness*:

> if this tragic element is taken seriously as recurrent, and therefore as a possibility for our future. . . . it is only on theological grounds that hope can be brought back into history. For such a sense of history in which fate seems continually to engulf freedom, only a God transcendent to these now overwhelmed human powers can break the power of that inexorable fate.[57]

B. The Necessity of God

Theological interpretation of history is required, then, because God is necessary to an understanding of historical process and meaning. History's ambiguities prevent it from autonomously providing an adequate guarantee of its own meaning, and therefore of grounding faith. Gilkey provides several arguments for the necessity of a principle transcendent to history. First, drawing from Whitehead, Gilkey argues that the "continuity of existence" itself calls for the divine. How, Gilkey asks, is the past available to the present at all?

> How is it that achieved actuality, if it is constituted by events and not by enduring and so determining substances or essences, presents itself in each moment as a given, a destiny over time from the now receding and vanishing past? How can the past *be* in the present . . . ? If all is temporal and contingent, if all passes into a vanished and so ineffective past in coming to be, how is the continuity of existence possible?[58]

To these questions, Gilkey answers. "Some principle of necessary being or of 'creativity' must be there as the principle of transition, as what Whitehead calls 'the ultimate' in any philosophy. . . . For finite being to be and to be contingent in passage, there must be a power of being transcendent to that contingency and to that continual passing away." God is, therefore, the *ultimate cause*, the "creative 'preserving' or 'sustaining' " agent, the "condition of the *possibility* of secondary causality."[59]

---

[57]Gilkey, *RW*, 254.
[58]Gilkey, *RW*, 303.
[59]Gilkey, *RW*, 303.

Gilkey accomplishes a number of things with this claim. Initially, with Tillich and Whitehead, he affirms that God is the "infinite power of being." God is omnipotent in this sense, namely, that God is the condition for the possibility of all finite, creaturely power. On the other hand, Gilkey advances a theodicy in which God is not responsible for the distortions of freedom and the transformation of destiny into fate. This is because, although God is the condition for secondary causality, God is not the "*sole* 'cause' of the given from the past."[60]

Moreover, the post-Enlightenment problem of theodicy is also taken into account: far from being the negation of human freedom, divine causality is the condition for the possibility of freedom. This claim merges with Gilkey's second argument for the necessity of God, a "creative 'accompanying' or 'concurring' providence of God." This is God's bringing into being "the present as self-determining in each present." God is the ground of present possibilities. Third, God embraces all possibility and, therefore, is the condition of the future's possibility. Gilkey argues that possibility must in some sense "be," but cannot be "solely by means of its relation to the finite and so already achieved actuality—lest the future merely repeat the limited forms of the past." Again following Whitehead, Gilkey argues that this "power of envisionment" relates the possibilities of the new

> to actuality in terms of relevance, in terms of an ordered structure of graded options in continuity with the past. . . . [B]oth the being and the order necessary for relevant possibility require some actuality that spans achieved actuality and infinite possibility alike. . . . Such a transtemporal actuality is God. On the one hand, he is transtemporal in the sense of transcendence over passage, a transcendence that reaches from its seat in present actuality infinitely into the unactualized future. On the other, he is "temporal" in the sense that the very movement of actuality into new possibilities and so into the future is an aspect of the role and so the being of that transcendence.[61]

God is the condition for both actuality and possibility; both have being and are underlain by the power of being. Moreover, in envisioning providence, freedom is given a range of possibilities upon which it can act. Still, this is an ontological account which, we have seen, is not adequate as a guarantee of meaning because "freedom corrupts these

---

[60]Gilkey, *RW*, 303.
[61]Gilkey, *RW*, 305.

possibilities in enactment." God's providence does not simply keep history in business; it also "has its own telos or goal" that "has been manifested to us in Jesus who is the Christ," manifested as reconciliation through love and the unity of divine transcendence and immanence. This is grace and redemption, fragmentarily available in history, fulfilled only beyond it. Without the promise of final fulfillment, and without faithful confidence in it, we could not avoid the despair of the cyclical interpretation of history, on the one hand, or the twin outcomes of historical progressivism, fanaticism or passivity, on the other. To the contrary, "[t]he Christian confidence in the creative sovereignty of God over history—the final ground of our hopes—means that the ambiguous future, with all its manifold uncertainties, can be faced with serenity and courage."[62]

Before leaving this account of Gilkey's theology of providence, we should note with additional concentration Gilkey's neat answer to the problem of theodicy. Gilkey attempts to give the same answer as Christian theology has traditionally given, namely, that God is both omnipotent and omnibenevolent. Gilkey, however, cannot repeat the solutions of his pre-Enlightenment theological favorites, Augustine and Calvin, to this problem. Both lacked what is essentially a post-Enlightenment understanding—and valorization—of freedom. Calvin's (as well as Luther's) argument for irrefusable grace in the name of divine omnipotence sacrifices human freedom to divine power and makes the problem of evil inexplicable as both Luther and Calvin recognized. Gilkey, like Augustine, posits a secondary causality. Augustine (like Kierkegaard), however, does not place the external effects of freely willed action within the purview of freedom. For Augustine, God turns evil to good despite the intentions of free actors in history. Freedom tends not to extend to being able to effect human purposes.[63] Such roads are closed to Gilkey; rather, he must allow a freedom of choice, both inwardly and externally, that his predecessors did not require. Freedom includes both the ability to will autonomously and the ability to determine, to some extent, results or outcomes of that will.

The problem that arises is power itself, or rather, power's opposition to freedom. The God who would eliminate freedom would be a tyrant. Gilkey, in consonance with the Enlightenment and most postmodern

---

[62]Gilkey, *RW*, 315, 316, 321.
[63]Gilkey, *RW*, 165-73.

thought, places the highest possible value on human freedom as the capacity to choose.[64] Indeed, we have already seen that the transmutation of destiny into fate, the real evil of the world, is defined exactly by fate's eradication of freedom, even though fate is the product of freedom's misuse. Thus, God's sovereignty over history cannot mean God's control of history and of the human beings who produce it. Rather, the divine relation to history "is one of self-limitation. At no point does God overwhelm or determinatively direct our freedom; he does not ordain us to will what we will. Rather, it is we who actualize our own being in each present out of the destiny given us."[65] Only in this way, Gilkey argues, is freedom protected:

> This self-limitation in God, and so the reality of our created freedom, is . . . an almost inescapable implication of the modern historical consciousness. It is thus that future possibilities are genuinely possible, that freedom is real, and the future open [against Augustine], i.e., that history is history. But if this divine self-limitation be constitutive of history, as essential an ontological structure as the polarity of destiny and freedom, then God will have to act in the future as he has in the past, namely, *through* our freedom and *limited by* our freedom [against the eschatological theologians]. History in the future, therefore, will remain open to the wayward as well as the creative possibilities of freedom.[66]

Like Jesus the Christ, the Trinitarian role in history is that "[t]he divine *being* can seemingly only create and sustain finite being by continually negating itself. . . . To redeem our being, the divine must negate its own."[67]

The opposition between power and freedom is created because divine power is not only the power of being, but also implies control of finite being.

> A God constituted by unrestricted being tends . . . to threaten the being, the autonomy, the creativity, and the meaning of all else in the universe. An actively omnipotent being . . . can drain of their reality and value the world

---

[64]Gilkey, *RW*, 139, 297; idem, *ME*, 233. Gilkey's most sustained discussion of freedom is *NW*, 365-413.

[65]Gilkey, *RW*, 279.

[66]Gilkey, *RW*, 279.

[67]Gilkey, *SAS*, 136.

and the life of creatures. As a consequence, freedom, finite value, and authenticity must struggle against God rather than on God's basis.[68]

The consciousness of contingency and freedom is "*not* compatible with an understanding of events as transcendentally ordained or caused from eternity (or from the future)."[69]

The self-limitation of God forces Gilkey to maintain "omnipotence" in a weaker sense than the tradition; it is not clear what omnipotence means if it is not "active." To be sure, Gilkey thinks that God remains the *condition* for all power and meaning, but precisely Gilkey's desire to maintain God as the condition for all meaning drives him to deny that God is all power. With this, we are in a position to evaluate the significance of Gilkey's theology of providence.

III. Gilkey's Theology of Providence: A Critical Appraisal

One of Gilkey's objectives in constructing his theology of providence was to evade what he saw as inevitable shortcomings of secular philosophies of history. Those alternatives tend to be despairing cyclical theories, on one hand, or progressive or ontological theories that can be either sanguine or dominating. Neither is much help to concrete historical struggles. In their more sanguine versions, progressive and ontological theories of history fail to generate an impulse for justice on behalf of those who are suffering now; in their crusading moments, progressivists, unable to recognize that they also are trapped in sin, create new oppressions of their own that are frequently as bad or worse than the oppressions inflicted by their predecessors. Yet, if one eschews such utopian thinking and affirms the inevitability of sin, Gilkey believes that the only alternative is the despairing, cyclical attitude of The Who: "Meet the new boss, same as the old boss."[70] That attitude refuses historical involvement, because it is aware that the promised land of peace and justice for all is out of history's reach. Gilkey, however, is convinced that the way between the Scylla of despair and the Charybdis of utopianism is a theological understanding of history that recognizes that final meaning cannot be actualized in history, but that the content of such

---

[68]Gilkey, *RW*, 128.
[69]Gilkey, *RW*, 243.
[70]The Who, "Won't Get Fooled Again," *Who's Next* (audio recording) (MCA, ©1995).

meaning is given in history, can be partly actualized there, and is finally victorious beyond history. How successful are these claims? As important, because Gilkey holds that a theological interpretation is *required* because God is *necessary*, is he successful in establishing the demand for a theological interpretation of history?[71]

Surely, Gilkey deserves praise for his searing diagnosis of the tendencies of secular (and some theological) interpretations of history, particularly in its American forms. People who harbor hopes of realizing a grandiose historical utopia should have Gilkey's work slipped into their reading. Perennially naïve American youth, who seem never to lose hope in the infinite perfectibility of the species (until they get older, when they are increasingly prone to exactly the despair that Gilkey warns against), would profit from an inoculation with Gilkey's theological medicine.

Still, one suspects that Gilkey is able to realize his project successfully because of a certain fuzziness in his concepts and a predominantly modern conception of meaning. The imprecision of Gilkey's notion of divine sovereignty is one issue. I claimed, on the one hand, that Gilkey's notion of the self-limitation of God's power means that, in order to preserve freedom, God is not "actively" omnipotent. On the other hand, the condition for our historical "serenity and courage" was exactly that God *is* sovereign over history. There are two possible meanings of divine sovereignty "over history." Does Gilkey mean that, because God is transcendent to history, (1) God is also sovereign *in* history, or (2) God is sovereign in another arena, that is, one "over" or beyond history? The first claim is unsustainable for Gilkey. God could not be sovereign (in Gilkey's sense) in history without destroying history and freedom. This means in turn that the *content* of future history, whether it will conform to divine purposes more or less than it does now, is open. This much Gilkey grants, as he must in order to retain the human freedom that is a presupposition of all achieved historical meaning. Such meanings must be *ours*. "Active" omnipotence is restored, it seems, only beyond history, where God reestablishes divine sovereignty and can fulfill divine objectives. Moreover, God's *transcendence* and not divine immanence allows Gilkey the confidence that there is a victorious, stable *content* of divine

---

[71]My concern is with Gilkey's theology of *providence*, not with his entire theological project. Therefore, although I will maintain that God's transcendence is not necessary for an adequate interpretation of history, it may be helpful or necessary for other theological endeavors.

love that overcomes one cause for the despair of cyclical theories of history, namely, that whatever provisional meaning is achieved is impermanent, subject to decay, loss, and change.

This leaves a quandary with respect to providence, which concerns history and this world, not another. In this world, God's immanent power is limited to providing (1) the formal conditions for the possibility of history and (2) the content of the divine will, which acts as lure, vision, and demand on present historical action. The formal condition establishes the necessity of God, whereas the luring content of self-giving love establishes the moral desirability of God and theological interpretation. The formal claim can be dealt with quickly. It is true that the possibility of temporal transition, the availability of the past to the present, the sustenance of the present itself, and the continuation of history into a future of possibility and destiny, require power (irrespective of how one conceives of power). Why would it, however, require a power transcendent to history? Do not quite immanent powers, either by themselves or in concert, create power beyond the precise moment in which they exist and act? All these powers, of course, may be finite, but finitude implies some duration and durability of its own, not instantaneous dissolution. If one wishes to call all these powers—or power itself—manifestations of God, that is certainly an arguable case.[72] It is not clear, nonetheless, that the existence of the historical process requires power transcendent to that process. It is a metaphysical leap without clear justification to assert that "[s]ome deeper, more permanent power must exist and continue from moment to moment if this 'temporal power' . . . is to be possible."[73]

One suspects that the process itself, although important, is not Gilkey's central concern. Rather, one senses that, like his theological predecessors, Gilkey thinks that God's transcendence over history is necessary in order that *meaning*, which cannot be guaranteed or stabilized within history, is nonetheless assured of ultimate victory. This is not so much because the majesty of God requires vindication as it is due to faith's assurance that what we do here—feebly attempting to achieve some measure of integrity for ourselves, gentleness for our culture, and conformity with the purposes of God—is not all vanity, as the lamenta-

---

[72]See my book for a more complete argument, that such a notion is an ontologically helpful conception of omnipotence: Kyle A. Pasewark, *A Theology of Power: Being beyond Domination* (Minneapolis: Fortress Press, 1993).

[73]Gilkey, *NRS*, 201.

tion of Ecclesiastes suggests, nor will become, like the futile memorial of Ozymandias to his timeless majesty, a "colossal wreck, boundless and bare."[74]

In this effort to assure meaning's triumph, more than anywhere else, Gilkey is rooted firmly in modernity. Gilkey may say more than he intends, when he claims that "[t]he result" of his constructive theology "should be a *Christian* interpretation of *modern* experience."[75] Courage is only possible if we can believe in the stable, final victory of the definitive meaning of history, given in God's revelation of Jesus the Christ.[76] Why must we rest our hope for meaning, however, on the eternal being of a single, overarching truth that is vouchsafed beyond history and is therefore eternally stable? Indeed, should we do so? Why is it necessary to assume that self-giving and self-limiting love, revealed in the Christ-event, must be eternally guaranteed in order to avoid the despair of cyclical theories of history? The answer, it appears, is that all the theories of history that Gilkey seriously considers also assume what Gilkey does, namely that, unless a final meaning is guaranteed and stable, it is no longer meaning but futility. Progressivism finds the guarantee, erroneously, at the conclusion of history; moreover, were that meaning to be reached, as Marx argued, history would be at an end. Cyclical theories despair less of present meaning than of its future—whatever is achieved now, however important or majestic, will inevitably disappear. For both, only eternity can provide meaning; history cannot. This is why history and eternity merge in the end of history in progressivism, and why cyclical theories are prone to despair. Gilkey, for his part, works his way between these two alternatives, but does not question their common assumption. For Gilkey, too, history means something only insofar as it fragmentarily actualizes meanings that are *guaranteed elsewhere, namely, in eternity.*

But why should this be so? Why are fragmentary meanings insufficient? Why would it not be possible to reverse the traditional Protestant prioritization of faith over hope, and say that, rather than taking faith as the "evidence" and assurance of "things not seen," we may hope that

---

[74]Eccles 1:2-11; Percy Bysshe Shelley, *Ozymandias,* in *Romanticism: An Anthology,* ed. Duncan Wu (Oxford: Blackwell, 1994) 860.

[75]Gilkey, *ME,* 60.

[76]The conformity of this position with Gilkey's later reflections on pluralism is discussed below.

there is enough meaning in our historical lives to overcome the equally real times of meaninglessness? Why must meaning be transcendent in order to be meaningful, rather than local, limited in time and space, that is, historical? There are two points to consider here: first, why Gilkey believes that localized, fragmentary meaning is not sufficient; second, whether parts of Gilkey's own project, including the significance of history and his later emphasis on pluralism, incline us to precisely such a localized, partial, hopeful, but not assured understanding of meaning.

Gilkey's argument against the limitation of meaning to localized, immanent meaning was staked out as early as *Maker of Heaven and Earth*, and remained remarkably constant throughout his corpus. In *Maker of Heaven and Earth*, Gilkey confronts the question directly. "Naturalism," Gilkey says, asserts that "[o]ur life is involved in 'small meanings,' local fulfillments and achievements, partial victories over those things that resist our human purposes. Surely those are enough for us." Naturalism asks, "why search for an ultimate meaning?" Gilkey's response is an existential one, but one that substantially begs the question. Two examples suffice. First, Gilkey maintains that "the local meanings of life float on the surface of the vast river of historical destiny whose course largely determines their possibility. The question, therefore, of the nature and direction of that river is scarcely an irrelevant one." But why must we assume that we do float on a river that has an irreversible direction from eternity? The metaphor itself picks the pocket of progressivist assumptions, and leads to a second claim: that, if "these local values rest on a blind nature and an undirected history, then this necessary sense of fundamental coherence has no footing—nor does the secularist faith that these small meanings will always 'be there' to make life good have any ground."[77] The *grounding* of faith is, therefore, the crucial issue and that grounding, in turn, requires a "fundamental coherence" and "directedness" to history's meaning. Otherwise, Gilkey asserts,

> To depend for our sense of meaning upon . . . observable victory . . . is to be easily vulnerable to pessimism and despair. There are times in history when our confidence in the meaning of life must be grounded in faith, and not in observation alone. But here the naturalist is caught, for in his world there is nothing but observable progress on which he can found his courage.

---

[77]Gilkey, *MHE*, 190, 191, 192.

This is the reason that secular cultures, and the people within them, tend to fluctuate between optimism and pessimism.[78]

These two responses beg the question. It should be noted that Gilkey quickly identifies "naturalism" and "localism" with "progressivism." It is true that the disappointed progressivist tends to despair, but is that not because the progressivist, like Gilkey, interlocks meaning and permanence? Is it not, in short, because the progressivist is not finally directed to *historical* meaning but to eternal meaning, the end of history? The cyclical theorist, the progressivist, and Gilkey all carry a common presupposition; historical meaning is not sufficient meaning without a nonhistorical guarantee. If one accepts that assumption, then Gilkey's theology of providence represents a decided improvement. One need not accept it, however. Although assuredly difficult, one can maintain with integrity a quite different attitude toward historical meaning: it is what we have and, as long as we have it, we must cherish and nurture it. We do not have an assurance of faith (though we may have hope) that *this* meaning will continue, nor need the content of this historical meaning be a fragmentary expression of the final content of meaning-itself. In fact, it probably is not, for, as history changes the character of reality, our meanings can and probably should be altered. Finally, what is most meaningful in one place on the globe (even in contemporaneous time) may not carry similar weight in another, so that meaning is variable temporally and spatially. On this reading, divine power communicates power to historical entities, and one hopes that this power is sufficient to produce *enough* meaning to make history—and life in history—on the whole worth our participation.[79] We do not need to project a final, definitive import of history in order to maintain this hope.

Indeed, there are reasons not to rely on an eschatological assurance of faith in order to give meaning to history. Three deserve mention, two of which bring Gilkey's theology of providence into some tension with his broader theological project. I have already alluded to the first reason:

---

[78]Gilkey, *MHE*, 193. On the question of local meanings in Gilkey's later theology, see Gilkey, *SAS*, 61, 144, 150, 160-70. There do not seem to be substantial differences in the argument.

[79]This hypothesis also has the advantage of avoiding the need to assert the "self-limitation" of God's omnipotence, which does not go far enough in overcoming the philosophical, political, and theological identity of power with "domination." On this point, see Pasewark, *Theology of Power*, 200.

despite Gilkey's attempt to take the reality of history seriously, in the end his thought remains partly ahistorical. Gilkey goes to the edge of the waters of history but refuses (theologically more than existentially) to dive in the deep end. He does not permit history to create the really new, despite his intention to allow precisely that. Rather, his metaphysical claim that God must contain all possibilities within God's self (related to the formal assertion that God's transcendence is the condition of historical possibility) means that possibility "is" actual in some way. The really new is rendered impossible; it is simply the old come out of hiding, eternally possible in God. Gilkey is beholden, as was Whitehead, to the Aristotelian categories of actuality and potentiality as exhaustive of all reality. Aristotle, however, was not a historical thinker; and, if we are to take history seriously, we must give it scope to produce meaning and events that are really new, that are not encompassed by the nonhistorical category of eternal potentialities.[80]

That problem is related to a second: Gilkey's theology of providence stands in some tension with his later emphasis on pluralism and the rough parity of religions.[81] Gilkey rejects the claim of Schleiermacher, Barth, Tillich, and others that "other religions are included as valid and effective within a Christian theology of revelation and incarnation. In all of these, however, Christian revelation remains 'final and definitive,' to use Tillich's words."[82] Gilkey cannot follow this solution, because what has changed in the contemporary world is that "[t]o recognize . . . the presence of truth and grace . . . in another faith is radically to relativize not only one's religious faith [which Schleiermacher, et. al., also did] but the *referent* of the faith, the revelation on which it is dependent."[83]

Still, Gilkey maintains that *any* valid religious claim "presupposes an absolute standpoint." "Whether we refer to the Buddhist, the Christian, the Marxist, or the Freudian hope of salvation, none can speak of salvation at all without presupposing the cognitive solidity and efficacy of its starting point and so the validity of the knowledge gained thereby."[84]

---

[80]Pasework, *Theology of Power*, 207-21, provides a more extended argument for this position.

[81]For extensive treatment of Gilkey's theology of pluralism, see especially the chapters in this book by Jeff B. Pool, Mary Ann Stenger, and James O. Yerkes.

[82]Gilkey, "Plurality and Its Theological Implications," 42.

[83]Gilkey, "Plurality and Its Theological Implications," 40-41.

[84]Gilkey, *SAS*, 160.

The paradox of the "relative absolute," however, is not necessitated by the requirements of thought (which acknowledges the conditioned and particular nature of all claims to truth) but because of the demands of action, in which necessarily absolute stands (I do this and not that) are taken on the basis of now nonabsolute claims to meaning.[85] So far, so good. Why must Gilkey continue to say, however, that "[t]here seems to appear here as a requirement of authentic being a relationship . . . to some stable and assumed, and in that sense, *absolute* standpoint, a participation in it, and commitment to it"?[86] This claim is not about the necessary decisiveness of action, but precisely about the absolute, unconditioned character of the definitive cognitive meanings in which those actions participate. It tends, then, to cut against the pluralism which Gilkey wants to foster. As an alternative, we can say that the issue is not absolute, stable, eternal meaning at all; rather, our responsible action and thought are placed under the demand of formulating and responding to the true, good, and beautiful—the powerful—as those are available to us in this time and place. This is not "relativism" in the usual sense, because we can evaluate better and worse historical alternatives. Nonetheless, we need not assume that historical meanings are only vouchsafed if they are removed from history and immune to its course. Christian revelation may be a force for creativity in late twentieth-century America, but that implies neither that it will continue to be so into the future nor that it is a creative force for late twentieth-century Bosnia. These are questions that must be argued and discerned; that is, they are historical truths; and it is unlikely that historical truths would be anything but plural in character. If God acts historically, if we are really to take history seriously, then history actually alters *what truth is* and *what is true* across time and space, not merely the embodiments or human apprehension of truth.

Indeed, the need to guarantee meaning eternally can, in certain circumstances, damage historical meaning. This is a third related issue: summarily, it is not only the *referent* of revelation that is called into question, but also its *content*. The problem can be illustrated through an example much-discussed elsewhere. Gilkey has argued throughout his career that the definitive meaning of the divine revelation in Christ Jesus is the necessity of self-giving love. In conformity with Reinhold Niebuhr and Paul Tillich, the demand of Christ—and his example—is *agapé*. Here

---

[85]Gilkey, "Plurality and Its Theological Implications," 47-50; idem, *TT*, 191-93.
[86]Gilkey, "Plurality and Its Theological Implications," 46-47.

again, one suspects that, in addition to his theological predecessors, Gilkey draws from his time in Shandong. Can one say or should one say, however, that this is the "unconditioned" content of Christian revelation? Certainly, most feminist and liberation theologians think it is not so. Indeed, the notion of self-giving love is an excellent instance of localized meaning and truth. One need not deny the significance of measures of sacrifice entirely to deny its desirability, let alone its duty, for all. It may well be that self-giving love is *an* answer and *a* meaning in history. That is a long way from asserting that it is *the* definitive meaning of revelation and history. Yet, if one persists in speaking about "unconditioned," "eternal" meaning, those cognitive, moral, and aesthetic debates about the circumstances in which any mode of historical action serves the power and efficacy of the actor and others tend to be obscured. The contents of truth are products of history and it is better to recognize that, in order that they be debated, reformed, and altered in the realm in which alone providence can operate: the arena of history.

Langdon Gilkey's theology of providence, like all theologies, is a historical product. It, too, is part of the providence and power of God, insofar as it serves to orient us toward the present and the future. It can, however, better perform that task in this time and culture if claims about the necessity of stable eternal guarantees of meaning are overcome by concentrated reflection on the divine immanence within history. Indeed, aspects of Gilkey's own project—and his theological generosity—are better advanced by retrieving and developing theologies of providence that take historical meaning as sufficient. That approach retains the value of Gilkey's criticisms of both progressive and cyclical theories of history. Gilkey is correct that history does not allow us to infer a final shape to history's meaning, much less our progress toward that goal, from within history. But that recognition need not lead to the despair that Gilkey fears. Rather, that historical despair is arguably more likely if, like Gail Godwin's Father Melancholy, one feels that the meanings we have striven to achieve and in which we participate are really only significant if they are eternal.[87] Similarly, Shelley's "Ozymandias" has the power to make us recognize vanity and despair only because Ozymandias labored under the foolish illusion that his greatness would remain forever remembered. That is too much to ask. We can hope that the meanings that appear in

---

[87]Gail Godwin, *Father Melancholy's Daughter* (New York: Avon, 1991) 35-36.

our time mean enough to make our participation in them worthwhile; we can hope that what we do and say will ease some burdens now and in the future. We need not ask more, nor probably should we. To insist that history really only attains its meaning if it is guaranteed by eternity also makes too little of history; it prevents us from appreciating the radically new in history, the plurality of truths, and can discourage timely and needed alterations in the truths we proffer. The meaning of historical achievements lies *in* their contingency and particularity, not in elimination of these features.[88] Charles Winquist strikes exactly the right chord when he concludes that "Gilkey's Christian theology is a gift and not a necessity."[89] To that, it is necessary only to add that Gilkey's theology—and the man himself—are gifts for which I am immensely grateful. And perhaps—though the thought, the man, and their effects are historical through and through—that is enough.

---

[88]For this formulation, I am indebted to Jeff B. Pool.

[89]See Charles E. Winquist's contribution to this book.

Chapter 11

Contingency, Tragedy, Sin, and Ultimacy:
Trajectories in Langdon Gilkey's
Interpretations of History and Nature

Larry D. Bouchard

Many are the wonders [*deina*],
none is more wonderful than what is man.
This it is that crosses the sea,
with the south winds storming and the waves swelling,
breaking around him in roaring surf.   (Sophocles, *Antigone*)

Can you draw out Leviathan with a fishhook,
or press down its tongue with a cord?   (Job 41:1 NRSV)[1]

Introduction

How is the tragic a dimension of ultimacy? In an appreciative yet ironic discussion of Robert Heilbroner's *Inquiry Into the Human Prospect*, Langdon Gilkey projects a view of the tragic that is distinctively biblical and resonately Greek. It is the view that tragic fate, as it comprehends the suffering of the relatively powerless, is the objective *effects and consequences* (social, historical, and environmental) *of the sins* of the relatively powerful.[2]

In other of Gilkey's writings—and in other theologies that interpret the witnesses of tragic art—there is, however, another trajectory toward understanding the tragic: sin, idolatry, and harm to people and nature are *responses to the tragic*, understood as contingency and suffering, among other possible responses. The second trajectory passes through more variations on the tragic than the first, and the two are not the only trajectories imaginable. Neither, for instance, points to sin as being ultimately *caused* by tragic contingency, a Manichean-like position. Yet,

---

[1]Sophocles, *Antigone*, ll. 332ff., trans. David Grene, *Sophocles* 1, 2nd ed. (Chicago: University of Chicago, 1991) 174. Biblical citations are from the New Revised Standard Version (New York: Division of Christian Education of the National Council of Churches of Christ in the United States of America, ©1989); hereafter cited as NRSV.

[2]Langdon Gilkey, *Reaping the Whirlwind: A Christian Interpretation of History* (New York: Seabury, 1976) 84-89, 253-65; hereafter cited as *RW*.

neither discounts the import of prior conditions for understanding moral evil. Neither considers the tragic to be illusory, nor a false, totalizing view of reality, nor primarily an aesthetic form. And neither trajectory seeks to explain definitively suffering and evil. Nor are these trajectories wholly incommensurate, for both learn from Søren Kierkegaard's analysis of anxiety.[3] On the first trajectory, "the tragic" is the consequence of sin. On the latter, tragic suffering and contingency are the prior conditions, to which sin is an irresponsible "response" (which, to be sure, generates more suffering and contingency). The differences between the trajectories are not merely definitional; they bear upon how the created good and the moral life are envisioned.

While these trajectories for theologically interpreting the tragic are not the only two, they remain especially significant. My own view—nurtured by Gilkey as teacher, colleague, and theologian—is that, while both are required, it is hard to "combine" them. They pursue different intuitions about God's association with suffering and evil. But one can, as Gilkey does, move now along one and now along the other. While the tragic effects of sin are often more explicit in Gilkey's thought, both trajectories are evident, especially when he writes about science and nature. Hence, his theology provides a pliable medium for constructive interpretation.

By "tragedy," I refer to a literary and critical family of resemblances, a heuristic tradition, that poses questions by dramatizing stories. By "the tragic," I mean the various questions and interpretations disclosed in the art and criticism of tragedy. The tragic in life, by this account, is identified and given to language by the tragic in art. Tragedies, ancient and modern, function as inquiry: they ask about suffering and the limits of understanding that arise from entanglements of chance or fate with evil or moral accountability. As a pluralistic genre, tragedy generates numerous versions of the tragic, a term not simply synonymous with "evil."[4]

---

[3]See Edward Farley, *Good and Evil: Interpreting a Human Condition* (Minneapolis: Fortress Press, 1990) esp. chap. 6, "Idolatry." Anyone at all indebted to existentialism is likely to have learned, directly or indirectly, from Kierkegaard's analysis of anxiety (Søren Kierkegaard, *The Concept of Anxiety*, ed. and trans. Reidar Thomte and Albert B. Anderson [Princeton: Princeton University Press, 1980]), as well as from G. W. F. Hegel's reading of tragedy as conflicting goods and from Friedrich Nietzsche's reading of tragedy as erupting, Dionysian passion.

[4]See Larry D. Bouchard, *Tragic Method and Tragic Theology: Evil in Contemporary Drama and Religious Thought* (University Park: Pennsylvania State University Press,

And, as a tradition, tragedy proffers language, themes, and analogies we often use, deliberately or not, when speaking or asking about suffering and evil. The heuristic character of this tradition gives us room to explore the tragic provisionally. For theology, "the tragic" allows questions about God's relations to suffering, evil, and accountability to remain—for a time—open questions. So, as an example of Gilkey's use and interpretation of this tradition, let us linger over his exegesis of Heilbroner in *Reaping the Whirlwind*. For both writers, the tragedy of Prometheus is global in its import and harbingers an ecological nightmare.

In 1974, Heilbroner told of modern civilization approaching the limits to its exponential growth. He observed how the earth's resources are inequitably distributed and rapidly dwindling, while the desires of its human inhabitants are unabated. Our virtually unlimited freedom has created the conditions of our own extinction, and perhaps has done so inevitably. What's more, we have missed the chance for irenic remedies. Human survival in any form will require economic and political changes of such magnitude as to be "forced upon us by external events rather than by conscious choice, by catastrophe rather than by calculations. . . . Nature will provide the checks, if foresight and 'morality' do not."[5] Heilbroner reluctantly believed that there must emerge authoritarian, static societies of the sort that oppose Enlightenment freedom. "The new, unfree world," writes Gilkey glossing Heilbroner, "will not be willed by freedom but created by fate—even though a wise freedom, were it *really* free,

---

1989) 8, 36. *Evil*, in traditional parlance, comprises moral evil, natural and supernatural misfortunes, and severe suffering. While these matters are configured in many ways in literary tragedy, here I must keep them distinguished. I will reserve the term "evil" for culpable dispositions and deeds of accountable agents ("moral evil," "sin"). *Suffering, contingency, finitude*, and other locutions refer to possibilities prior to assessments of culpability. I do not distinguish necessary from contingent suffering here; often "necessity" in tragedy is the unfolding of contingencies, such as the oracle in *Oedipus the King*; it is, but might have been otherwise. *Tragic* is the odd-job word, qualifying understandings and limits of understanding encountered with severe suffering and moral accountability. "Tragic accountability" is the awareness that one must respond to actual suffering or evil irrespective of one's own or another's guilt or innocence: before the tragic, I must give account.

[5]Robert Heilbroner, *An Inquiry into the Human Prospect* (New York: Norton, 1974) 132.

would have willed its own unfreedom. Theology has never, even in the hands of Reinhold Niebuhr, produced more intriguing paradoxes!"[6]

At the end of his book, Heilbroner proposes that we abandon the myth of Prometheus, with its spirit of "conquest and aspiration" and "intellectual daring," for the myth of the resolute Atlas, who bore "with endless perseverance the weight of the heavens in his hands."[7] Gilkey observes that Heilbroner misconstrues the Prometheus myth, yet credits it more than he knows. Like most moderns, Heilbroner "understands myth as merely a moral ideal or example, an imaginative projection of those powers and virtues of man which we admire or should admire." As such, Prometheus extols challenging freedom and creativity; because these virtues have proven self-destructive, Heilbroner judges Prometheus to be an outmoded moral paradigm. To the ancients, however, myths were not only moral ideals but fundamentally references to nature, the cosmic order, and the place of humanity therein. "Myth was a vehicle for religious and even ontological understanding," Gilkey writes, "not of moral self-improvement, and on this score the Promethean myth seems to have been painfully accurate."[8] Heilbroner's projections of the future imply a new and more accurate reading of Prometheus, in which enlightened humanity's "titanic creativity"—its science, industry, and politics—condemns "men and women to future chains," to the judgment of implacable reality imposed by "Zeus." "I find no point at which Heilbroner's argument disputes the Promethean interpretation of human history, or its understanding of the tragic link between creativity and self-destruction."[9]

Gilkey's tone is appreciative, which may make his ironic demurrals at first hard to specify. But Heilbroner seems unaware of the religious and biblical antecedents to his own interpretation; and, more importantly, while granting that it was Heilbroner who exposed the ecological and political dark age threatening us (which other contemporary futurologists failed to see), Gilkey cautions against certainty. We are too enmeshed in history to be objectively certain about history, and history invariably surprises us with novelty. Thus, Gilkey does not share Heilbroner's near fatalism. Whereas Heilbroner unwittingly affirms the truth of the Prometheus myth—a myth that indeed tells much truth—he does not tell the

---

[6]Gilkey, *RW*, 84.
[7]Heilbroner, *Inquiry into the Human Prospect*, 142-44.
[8]Gilkey, *RW*, 88.
[9]Gilkey, *RW*, 89.

whole truth. It is not human creativity that causes our self-destruction, but rather "the pride, the greed, and the lust for gain and security which accompany that creativity in historical life."[10] The truth of Prometheus is the self-alienation of the human spirit from nature, an estrangement which the Bible and the Greek tragedians understood, albeit differently.[11] Further, the Christian vision of tragedy rooted in sin makes a moral distinction between creativity and fault, which Heilbroner seems at times aware of and which undoes his ontological determinism. "Our creativity in itself," Gilkey writes,

> has not caused our present dilemma; it is rather our insatiable gluttony in our use of the earth, our unwillingness to share, our resistance to equitable distribution, our frantic use of power to grasp and to maintain security, that will in the end destroy us if we are destroyed. But if the "fault" is a taint in our creativity, not the creativity itself . . . then perhaps the punishment has a different character, the perpetuator of the punishment a different role, and the issue a different possibility.[12]

As suggested at the outset, in certain recent theologies, we can see two trajectories for understanding the tragic in human experience. Along one, the tragic originates in sin and proliferates in the oppressive effects of idolatry, selfishness, and self-deception in structures of injustice and cruelty. Along another trajectory, the tragic is associated primarily with suffering and the contingencies of humanity's natural, temporal, and social situation; idolatry and sin are then responses to tragic contingency and suffering. Gilkey, like Reinhold Niebuhr, especially follows the effects-of-sin trajectory when writing about history and politics. When writing about nature, however, he, like Paul Tillich, approaches the contingency trajectory.[13] While Tillich can speak of tragic *hubris* as sin

---

[10]Gilkey, *RW*, 89.

[11]Gilkey, *RW*, 87.

[12]Gilkey, *RW*, 89.

[13]In *RW*, "tragedy" and "the tragic" invariably refer to fate as the objective consequences of sin. More recently, with the term "tragedy," Gilkey refers to the negating contingencies of nature, whereas the term "fate" designates the effects of technology (Langdon Gilkey, *Nature, Reality, and the Sacred: The Nexus of Science and Religion*, Theology and the Sciences series, ed. Kevin J. Sharpe [Minneapolis: Fortress Press, 1993]; hereafter cited as *NRS*). Some of Gilkey's earliest discussions of fate, sin, and death also refer to "tragic" contingency: see Langdon Gilkey, *Maker of Heaven and Earth: A Study of the Christian Doctrine of Creation* (Garden City NY: Anchor Books,

in its "total form,"[14] sin itself is possible only in the prior condition of "universal tragedy" or "estrangement" and in the ontological contact between the myths of creation and fall. Heilbroner himself is close to the contingency trajectory, for it seems that he considers the self-contradictory aspect of freedom and creativity to be less the *fault* of human creativity than its *inherent* implication.

To speak of two trajectories follows from distinguishing between the "internality" and "externality" of sources of suffering, a self-world distinction. Inward culpability and external contingency, however, are thickly entangled. Mircea Eliade suggests that, for *homo religiosus*, construing suffering as punishment can make it meaningful and tolerable.[15] Our "pain" is rooted in the Greek *poinè* ("penalty," "punishment"); and in Christian tragedy guilt may pain one's conscience—as in *Hamlet's* Claudius—and attract divine judgment upon the whole social complex of motives and retaliations. Alternatively, Clifford Geertz sees the problem of evil as an aspect of a more general "problem of meaning." There arise anomalous contingencies, not necessarily culpable, which "baffle" our frames of reference.[16] And tragedy can be said to explore the baffling complications of contingency and culpability. As a pluralistic and heuristic tradition, it does not reduce to a singular "vision," but can juxtapose incommensurate witnesses. In Greek tragedy, people suffer fates and contingencies not of their own devising; or commit hubris or culpable negligence; or suffer others' or deities' acts of witting or unwitting impulse (*atè*); or perish in knotted webs wherein victims are also perpetrators. Analogous tangles appear in Scripture—though reflecting Israel's

---

1965) 192-93, 225, 228; hereafter cited as *MHE*. Gilkey implies that contingency and sin are distinguishable among the threatening aspects of existence: "We have tended in America to look upon the *radical contingency* and the *inner perversion* of our life as exceptional, and to use a screen of technological gadgets to hide from our gaze the inevitable sorrows, frustrations, and turmoil of life" (Gilkey, *MHE*, 172; emphasis mine). See also Gilkey's comments on fate as Void: Langdon Gilkey, *Naming the Whirlwind: The Renewal of God-Language* (Indianapolis: Bobbs-Merrill, 1969), discussed below (hereafter cited as *NW*).

[14]Paul Tillich, *Systematic Theology*, vol. 2 (Chicago: University of Chicago, 1957) 50.

[15]Mircea Eliade, *The Myth of the Eternal Return*, trans. Willard Trask (Princeton: Princeton University Press, 1971) 96-98.

[16]Clifford Geertz, *The Interpretation of Cultures: Selected Essays* (New York: Basic Books Publishers, 1973) 100-108.

covenantal relation to the God who opposes chaos.[17] What these traditions have "in common" are depictions of suffering or evil that resist and test conceptual understanding; this resistance gives tragic stories much of their power to probe experience across historical and cultural distances.[18] That they resist our understanding, or pull us up short, is a clue to their realism.

I. The Tragic as Disclosed in Sin

The first trajectory, sin as the source of tragic fate, offers, *first*, a powerful psychological description of anxiety and temptation, which, for Reinhold Niebuhr, "validates" the myth of original sin. Although Niebuhr does tend to reduce the tragic to sin, sin itself is an irreducible category. Living at the juncture of nature and spirit, we find ourselves tempted to imagine our contingent condition otherwise than it is. Our embodied finitude makes us anxious, but our spirits can imagine more possibilities than we can possibly realize; indeed, we can imagine ourselves infinite and self-sufficient. Further, the sources of our temptation are not entirely in our own anxiety, but also in false interpretations of finitude that precede us, symbolized by the plausible serpent of Eden: "The situation of finiteness and freedom in which man stands becomes a source of temptation only when it is falsely interpreted by the 'serpent' . . . by a force of evil which precedes his own sin." And, "sin can never be traced merely to the temptation arising from a particular situation or condition."[19] "Sin presupposes itself," wrote Kierkegaard; sin follows prior

---

[17]See Jon Levenson, *Creation and the Persistence of Evil: The Jewish Drama of Divine Omnipotence* (San Francisco: Harper & Row, 1988) esp. chaps. 2–4; and Patricia Wismer, "Narrating Creation," in *The Whirlwind in Culture: Frontiers in Theology: In Honor of Langdon Gilkey*, ed. Donald Musser and Joseph Price (Bloomington IN: Meyer-Stone, 1988) 183-99. See also discussions of Greek *hamartia* (errors or mistakes, be they innocent or culpable) and divine *atè* (striking, blinding, maddening), and sources cited, in Bouchard, *Tragic Method and Tragic Theology*, chap. 2.

[18]On "resisting," see Paul Ricoeur, *The Symbolism of Evil*, trans. Emerson Buchanan (Boston: Beacon Press, 1967) 211-12. On "testing the limits of culture" and moral understanding, see James Redfield, *Nature and Culture in the Iliad: The Tragedy of Hector* (Chicago: University of Chicago Press, 1975) 68, 73.

[19]Reinhold Niebuhr, *Nature and Destiny of Man*, vol. 1, *Human Nature* (New York: Charles Scribner's Sons, 1941) 180-81, 254. See esp. chaps. 7 and 9. The analysis follows Kierkegaard's.

sin.[20] For Gilkey, contingent situations and conditions certainly contribute to the anxieties that tempt us to sin but they cannot by themselves account for the perversity and the irrationality of our deciding to "center our lives on ourselves" and, by our own meager powers, secure ourselves against an infinite future. We rationalize, then, like this:

> How can I help stealing from my neighbor if my children must be fed? How can I help accumulating money when all the bills for education are going to arrive? How can we help annexing new territory and building new bases when our enemies might attack us from just over there?[21]

Anxiety is human, arising in our finitude and spiritual freedom; while it is the precondition of and can be the temptation to sin, it is not the necessity of sin. Sin, unlike anxiety, is only superficially intelligible and is deeply contradictory. Its destructive, corrupting, and oppressive consequences are what are truly tragic. Ideally, when facing a future of contingencies, we center our imaginations on the ultimate source and limit of our being, God; moreover, our anxiety can spur us to create finite structures that ease misery and enhance the meaning of our lives and the lives of others. We indeed do this, and we will see shortly how Gilkey accounts for how we do so. But also, inevitably, we try to "depend entirely on our power—or that of our group—to provide security and meaning to all we are and love." Anxiety, at those times, "leads to aggression" and becomes virtually identified with original sin. "It is, then, as the story reminds us, the prior 'sin' of unbelief, of lack of trust, the rebellion against God by making the self the center of the world, that is the root of sin."[22]

It follows, *second*, that this first trajectory toward the tragic offers a critique of the sufficiency of any reductive analysis of history. Humanity's capacities for alienation and sin (together with human destiny and freedom seen against a transcendent horizon) mean that history is a

---

[20]Kierkegaard, *Concept of Anxiety*, 32, 57.

[21]Langdon Gilkey, *Message and Existence: An Introduction to Christian Theology* (New York: Seabury Press, 1979) 140; hereafter cited as *ME*.

[22]Gilkey, *ME*, 141. There may seem to be a contradiction here, if anxiety is assumed to be part of natural finitude yet "leads to," or virtually causes, sin. If anxiety, however, as Gilkey says (Gilkey, *ME*, 140), arises out of the juncture of nature and spirit, then it is itself not merely a natural but a human possibility; as such, anxiety is inevitably (not necessarily) liable to sin and figures in how sin presupposes sin. Anxiety is not itself sinful but can be configured in sin.

source of mystery that confounds thought. Sin is an aspect of history that provides a negative-dialectical moment in theology related to neoorthodoxy, a powerful critique of the rationalizing and moralizing pretenses of power and intelligence. The powerful, for Niebuhr and Gilkey, are not more sinful than others but they do accrue more guilt and responsibility.[23] Power means that we can do more damage with our imaginations, ideologies, and institutional practices. We create for others (and eventually for ourselves) structures of suffering or, as Tillich termed it, "fate"—that is, a destiny bereft of possibilities and hope.[24] Gilkey speaks of "tragic" fate as destiny warped by sin and experienced as evil: "Fate is the situation where the accumulated sins of the past have built a social and historical situation and structure where freedom is historically bound. . . . In these historical structures men and women are fated because they have no freedom; the given in their lives allows no room for their own determination of it."[25]

Power not only enhances our destructive potency; it also leads to the uneasy conscience that can prompt us to rationalize wrong as right. As did Niebuhr, Gilkey writes often of demonic, godlike postures, but perhaps nowhere more piercingly than in his allegory of the American Red Cross parcels in *Shantung Compound*.[26] One winter day in 1945, cartloads arrived unexpectedly, enough to give one parcel, a four month extra food supply, to each of the 1,450 souls in the civilian internment camp. But, to Gilkey's lifelong chagrin, the protests of seven of the 200 Americans in the camp delayed the Japanese from distributing the parcels equitably, and even more of the Americans defended the protests of the seven. Some were forthrightly jingoistic—American sandwiches only for

---

[23]See Niebuhr, *Nature and Destiny of Man*, 1:219-27; and Gilkey, *RW*, 259.

[24]Langdon Gilkey, *Society and the Sacred: Toward a Theology of Culture in Decline* (New York: Crossroad, 1981) 51; hereafter cited as *SAS*. See also Gilkey's discussions of fate: e.g., Gilkey, *RW*, esp. chaps. 10–11.

[25]Gilkey, *RW*, 257. Fate, or "bad fortune," does not have this essential association with sin in *MHE*, but refers to arbitrary, negating events that evidence no intelligible order and "threaten our basic sense of meaning. . . . The contingency of man in the face of fortune calls for the Providence of God if life is to have meaning" (Gilkey, *MHE*, 174). In the Christian view, " 'Fateful' events cannot disturb this good [human fulfillment that comes with trust in and commitment to God], but only give it new opportunities" (Gilkey, *MHE*, 263).

[26]Langdon Gilkey, *Shantung Compound: The Story of Men and Women under Pressure* (New York: Harper & Row, 1966); hereafter cited as *SC*.

Americans! Some appealed to legal and property rights, and some to "moral" principles of individual holiness. One man carefully explained that, although sharing was a fine thing, it would not be moral unless each shared voluntarily, and not as directed by the enemy. So Gilkey asked how many parcels the Americans were likely to give the other internees.

> "Why," said Grant with satisfaction, "I'm sure that most of the Americans will give away at least two of their packages."
> At this answer I quickly phrased my rejoinder:
> "That would mean that each non-American would get, on the most optimistic guess, less than one-fourth of a parcel instead of one parcel apiece. Would that be moral sharing when all of us are equally hungry and in need?"
> Grant looked at me in bafflement. This was not at all what he meant by "moral." . . .
> The advantage of Grant's view was that on its terms, "being moral" allowed us to eat our cake and have it too. For as was plain from his argument, if I were good and shared two of my parcels with our British neighbors, I would not only gain moral credit . . . but even more, I would be able to keep five whole parcels for myself![27]

The first trajectory toward understanding the tragic, *third*, also functions as a modest *theodicy*, modest in that it describes the "mystery" of evil more than justifies or explains a "problem," though the description itself asserts a coherence against the impression of incoherence.[28] So Niebuhr, in describing God's ironic, providential ways, distances God from the origins of sin. When fate is the objective consequences of sin, then the tragic originates in human insecurity and freedom, not in God. In that we are all implicated in this insecurity, unbelief, and misdirected freedom, we are all both tragic perpetrators and victims. None are wholly innocent, all are partly responsible, though to vastly different degrees. Human being falls "inevitably," Reinhold Niebuhr insisted, but not "necessarily." To suggest that creaturely finitude "causes" sin, or that the

---

[27]Gilkey, *SC*, 109-11.

[28]In his earlier work, see Gilkey's citation of Gabriel Marcel on mysteries and problems (Gilkey, *MHE*, 19). Also see his earlier treatments of theodicy (Gilkey, *MHE*, 220-23). For example, "Christian symbols, such as that of the devil and the fall of Adam, are not attempts to rationalize evil [but] seek to point to and express the mysterious possibilities of human freedom, which we cannot fully explain but which we can in part understand" (Gilkey, *MHE*, 223).

fall is ontologically necessary (as Niebuhr believed Tillich thought), would implicate creation, hence the Creator, and dissipate human responsibility. Yet, to say that sin arises anew with each moral lapse ignores social structures of evil and their historical momentum. As Gilkey writes, the Hebraic view that the parents' sins are visited upon their children's children may well have been "primitive, but unfortunately it was also true."[29] So tragic victims neither "reap what they sow" nor "get what they deserve." When a tyrant invades weaker neighbors, or when parents abuse their children, countless innocents suffer. The more one's power, the more suffering one can cause, and the greater one's objective guilt. But there remains the sense that, on the whole, "we"—collective humanity—do reap quite a bit of what we sow, and a rough, inexorable pattern of divine justice can be cautiously discerned.

Sin in history is inevitably self-contradictory (and frequently self-destructive), so the structure of sin is also revealed as a structure of judgment upon sin, like a precarious tower that collapses under its own weight. Yet, only rarely does Gilkey compose a sentence about providential judgment not contextualized by "the lure of new possibility" in historical change, appearing in contingency and freedom.[30] Without this lure, divine judgment would look too much like the *nemesis* of Zeus upon Prometheus:

> [C]hange brings to the surface both the decay of life and the injustice lying back of that decay. Change opens up the festering sores of history's body and lays the raw flesh bare—in our cities, in Asia, in Africa, in South America. Through the instrument of change, the divine judgment in history, a crucial aspect of God's providence, does its destructive and creative work. Correspondingly, change claims from us the political response of concern, courage and action to transform the social reality that is ours. It instigates the call to mission; it evolves and requires the symbol of the kingdom. . . . Change and movement in time, therefore, relate us "christianly" to our world: to God's work in that world of constitution and new possibility, of judgment and of liberation, of justice, peace and human authenticity.[31]

Fourth and finally, this initial trajectory offers a *religious and moral vision* that goes "beyond tragedy." It finds history more shadowed by

---

[29]Gilkey, *SAS*, 48.
[30]Gilkey, *RW*, 287.
[31]Gilkey, *RW*, 33.

tragic meaning than by tragic meaninglessness—both in terms of why there is fate and that it must be resisted. It is a little ironic, however, that this vision can be viewed as either too optimistic or too tragic. One critique of Niebuhr is that he saw so clearly the selfish taint in every moral endeavor as to inspire resignation or quietism despite his own agitations for justice. But Gilkey employs the eschatological symbolism of the Kingdom of God, Tillich's creative *Kairos*, and a qualified appreciation for Whitehead's metaphysics, to valorize moral achievement. God participates in human praxis that lessens the objective burden of fate and strengthens sources of meaning and caring. Such achievements are real and gracious. They reveal the lure (as well as the norm) of God toward our realizing novel possibilities of transformation. There is no progress toward sinlessness in history, but we do make religiously significant achievements that resist the objective effects of sin, that is, tragic fate.[32]

II. The Tragic as Disclosed in Contingency

The difference between the first and second trajectories might appear merely definitional. For the one, sin is the source of tragic fate; for the other, sin responds to tragic contingency. That which we name "the tragic," however, reveals intuitions that are not merely semantic. These may arise from a sense that the first trajectory is incomplete, both as a reading of "tragedy" and a description of experience. Whereas the first correlates with an ancient tradition that says tragedy is about terrible *choices*, the second fits an equally ancient witness that tragedies are about *suffering and terror*. The sufferings and evils that tragedies explore are located in the contingent stories of fallible persons and communities, anxiously beset by configurations of nature, society, and cosmos.

First, like the previous trajectory, the second trajectory offers a compelling *description* of the psychology of sin, arising from contingency, suffering, and anxiety. Edward Farley, who in describing idolatry as the primary sin also cites Kierkegaard, associates various types of suffering (vulnerability, benign and ontological alienation, and anxious discontent) with the tragic condition prior to sin: "Altogether, these sufferings constitute the tragic condition of human agents, an intolerable condition that opens them to the dynamics of evil."[33] To say that this

---

[32]Gilkey, *RW*, 286-88.
[33]Farley, *Good and Evil*, 122.

prior condition is tragic is not to say it is evil, but intolerable. Thus, "it becomes something that forces from us a response" which, negatively, can entail "a refusal or denial of the condition itself."[34] This refusal of the human condition is, in traditional terms, idolatry. Here our sinning is less a response to Adam's sin than to Eden's limits. By defining idolatry as a response to tragic finitude, Farley allows questions of the origins of evil just barely spoken in classical Christian lore. "The issue of context and motivation, the issue of sin as a response to something, is not entirely absent from the old stories. The lure of the tree of knowledge hints at a response to the limitations of finite knowledge."[35] Other thinkers would have us recognize what Martha Nussbaum calls "the fragility of goodness." Those things which we primarily value (such as friendship, health, aesthetic enjoyment, justice) are matters concretely subject to loss; further, if such goods are incommensurate, they can come into irresolvable conflict; and, further still, these goods often entail the emotions and appetites, which are subject to irrationality and loss of control.[36] Thus, the tragic dimension of moral life is not rooted in perversity; rather, perversity is a possible response to the fact that being virtuous is contingent, in part, upon chance and circumstance.

Gilkey sometimes follows this trajectory. Although he rarely mentions tragedy explicitly in *Naming the Whirlwind*, he discusses contingency and fate at length in his phenomenological descriptions of "ultimacy in secular experience." He writes of times when we find within us and beyond us "nothing" in the way of meaning, order, and value. This absence "becomes the infinite Void threatening all we are and do. . . . When the coldness and infinity of the Void is felt, we look rather desperately for some means to fill up this infinite cavern or emptiness."[37] Ideally, such an experience might prompt us to appreciate "the immense creativity of the 'given' in life," the given which we do not create yet which founds "all that we are and love." Nonetheless, there is little in Gilkey's description, to this point, to say that the Void or "Fate" is perverse interpretation:

---

[34]Farley, *Good and Evil*, 132.

[35]Farley, *Good and Evil*, 129.

[36]Martha C. Nussbaum, *The Fragility of Goodness: Luck and Ethics in Greek Tragedy and Philosophy* (Cambridge: Cambridge University Press, 1986) 3-7.

[37]Gilkey, *NW*, 310.

We can only understand the shape and character of our inner anxieties and of our patterns of public behavior if we comprehend our contingency within this dimension or framework of the ultimate, both as the ground of our own reality . . . and as the unconditioned threat of Fate which, paradoxically, appears as that which rules over us.[38]

As he continues to describe ultimacy in ontic experience, however, Gilkey widens the phenomenological brackets to include freedom and human being's communal and moral dimensions. In this broader context, the bondage of the will is discovered.[39] Experiences of ultimacy include that of being morally obligated to follow a norm or ideal, to be—in Christian terms—like Jesus in the world. Yet, "something in ourselves, that we perhaps did not know was there, prevents our enactment of this image; we seem unable, perhaps even strangely unwilling, to become what we thought we really wanted to be."[40] "Despite our best intentions, we do something else . . . ; an evil that was not part of our purpose—or the purpose we told ourselves was ours—appears from nowhere as an aspect of what we have done."[41] What is this "something"? It is the demonic, or idolatry, now appearing not as awareness of the Void but as the project of an embodied, spiritual being that finds its contingent self ultimately threatened. "Its will becomes a will to its own security, power, prestige and glory. . . . And for this reason it is unable to affirm with all its power the model or ideal it thought it cherished with its mind, because it is in bondage to its own well-being."[42] The brackets now widened, one wonders: was our prior awareness of contingency as Void or Fate already a perverse interpretation, a harkening to the lies of the serpent; or is the ultimate truly both depth and abyss, both gracious and tragic—to which idolatry is, then, a perverse response?

Second, this latter trajectory offers a *critique* of theologies that locate the source of the tragic in the deeply contradictory choice to deny one's nature and make a god of oneself or one's group. Rather, such perverse

---

[38]Gilkey, *NW,* 320.

[39]In an essay from 1926, Tillich follows a similar structure, from the demonic arising in the depth and abyss of being to the demonic as an idolatrous possibility of human existence: Paul Tillich, "The Demonic," in *The Interpretation of History,* by Paul Tillich, trans. N. A. Rasetzki and Elsa L. Talmey (New York: Scribner's, 1936) 77-121.

[40]Gilkey, *NW,* 385.

[41]Gilkey, *NW,* 388.

[42]Gilkey, *NW,* 390-91.

choosing is responsive to prior suffering, to natural and social contingencies (such as scarcity, accident of birth), or to the contingencies of the ethical (such as intractable moral dilemmas, unintentional harming). One line of this critique has been that the neoorthodox vision of sin as pretentious self-sufficiency corresponds mainly to evil as experienced by the socially or personally powerful. This vision of sin may ignore the tragic contexts and dimensions of fault and sorrow among the relatively powerless, disenfranchised, or despairing.[43] In terms of sin, for instance, the neoorthodox perspective notices little of the self-enslaving resignation that can overcome women in sexist societies, of the constricted imaginations of some whose poverty obscures or destroys structures of hope, of the moral enervation that can afflict the chronically ill or depressed, or of the thoughtless abnegation of humanity in that which Hannah Arendt called the banality of evil. The second trajectory demands of the first both a thicker analysis of sin under the conditions of fate and a more variegated recognition of what fate comprises (that is, not only the effects of sin but other contingencies not reducible to sin).

Third, when the second trajectory approaches questions of *theodicy,* it more willingly describes creatureliness as tragic and among the sources (though not really the "cause") of moral evil; and it is less interested in distancing God from those sources. Wendy Farley's theodicy of "divine compassion" understands God's loving to be incarnate in human resistance to evil and solidarity with suffering.[44] For Jürgen Moltmann, theodicy is taken up into the narrative of the crucified God, who undergoes the Godforsakenness of the world, and so abides in solidarity with

---

[43]See the following studies: Valerie [Saiving] Goldstein, "The Human Situation: A Feminine View," *Journal of Religion* 40 (1960): 100-12; Daphne Hampson, "Reinhold Niebuhr on Sin: A Critique," in *Reinhold Niebuhr and the Issues of Our Time,* ed. Richard Harries (London: Mowbry, 1986) 46-60. Both Wendy Farley and Kathleen Sands make related observations: Wendy Farley, *Tragic Vision and Divine Compassion: A Contemporary Theodicy* (Louisville KY: Westminster/John Knox, 1990) 42-52, 78; Kathleen Sands, *Escape From Paradise: Evil and Tragedy in Feminist Theology* (Minneapolis: Fortress Press, 1994) 26-29, 68-69. Some objections to Niebuhr in particular may be mitigated by attending to his discussion of sin as sensuality in *Nature and Destiny of Man.* On this point, see Robin Lovin, *Reinhold Niebuhr and Christian Realism* (Cambridge: Cambridge University Press, 1995) 142-57.

[44]Farley, *Tragic Vision and Divine Compassion,* 113-33. For many theologians, of course, retrieving the biblical God becomes impossible; this is true for Sands, though she seeks to argue with theistic theologies (see Sands, *Escape From Paradise,* 112-13).

the fate of the Godforsaken. Also, in the theocentric ethics of James Gustafson, God's involvement in the *whole* of reality (including the natural processes of life and cosmos) means that, while God is properly *our* ultimate concern, and while we are *part* of God's purposes, human well-being may not be God's *final* purpose for the whole of reality. It is not that God is distant from our sinning or well being; God is, indeed, our source, sustainer, even redeemer. But God does not order reality to guarantee the final well-being of our species or planet—not historically, socially, or naturally. Hence "God will be God" and we cannot justify God's ways on our terms. In Jewish religious thought, there is a much greater willingness to hold God in part accountable for the natural and moral aspects of catastrophe; we find this accountability, for example, in the narratives of Elie Wiesel and in Jon Levenson's restatement of biblical Judaism.[45]

Fourth, the overall implication of the second trajectory is, arguably, a *religious and moral vision* less interested in going "beyond tragedy." Rather, the meaningfulness of the world, including its resources for hope and comedy, is inseparable from its tragic contingency. There is, however, as much temptation to quietism on this trajectory as on the first. For, one might ask, if all choices are tragic, what is the point in moral choosing? And this appears to be the temptation Gilkey perceived in Heilbroner's perspective, and which others face in problems of allocating scarce resources.[46] The trajectory's answer to this temptation, however, is the moral and religious imperative to resist fate, to participate in solidarity with God's solidarity with suffering. This resistance is realized not only through memory and heightened awareness of and living with

---

[45]See Jürgen Moltmann, *The Crucified God: The Cross as the Foundation and Criticism of Christian Theology*, trans. R. A. Wilson and John Bowden (New York: Harper & Row, 1974); James M. Gustafson, *Ethics from a Theocentric Perspective*, vol. 1, *Theology and Ethics* (Chicago: University of Chicago Press, 1981); idem, *Ethics from a Theocentric Perspective*, vol. 2, *Ethics and Theology* (Chicago: University of Chicago Press, 1984); Elie Wiesel, *The Gates of the Forest*, trans. Frances Frenaye (New York: Holt, Rinehart, and Winston, 1966); Levenson, *Creation and the Persistence of Evil*; and Wismer, "Narrating Creation." Wismer's Christian theological analysis of "tensions" in Genesis 2–3 resembles Levenson's perspective.

[46]On the moral and political dilemmas of allocating scarce natural and medical resources, see Guido Calabresi and Philip Bobbitt, *Tragic Choices* (New York: Norton, 1978).

those who suffer, but also in seeking in the contingencies of nature and culture creative resources for alleviating pain, cruelty, and fate.[47]

III. Two Moments of Irreducibility

As we have seen, along the second theological trajectory, some theologians have been more willing to associate God with horizons of tragic contingency. The implications are not a desire to conceive God perversely, nor to resolve the puzzle of theodicy by jettisoning God's goodness. Rather, the second trajectory recognizes that, where "the sacred" and "the tragic" have been discerned, they perennially have been discerned together. Mysteries of suffering and evil are recognized not only to be mysteries of the human but also of the divine, and Gilkey addresses this recognition in his most recent writings on nature, especially *Nature, Reality, and the Sacred.* We may restate the trajectories in terms of limits to understanding. The first pursues the irrationality of sin in the context of anxiety, and discovers that the question "why sin?"—why does the will contradict its very nature—resists reduction. Sin is already there, however far we trace its histories, and yet sin remains inevitable but not necessary. The second trajectory agrees that anxiety occasions moral evil. But it pursues the plethora of anxious possibilities impinging on human being, some destructive, some creative, some old, some new, many boding new configurations of suffering—and asks, not "why contingency" but "why these contingencies?" This question also resists reduction: we cannot pursue its probabilities very far into the future before we are surprised by novel threats (and novel resources).

Along the trajectories, we discover two moments of irreducibility: (1) tragic ultimacy disclosed in sin and (2) tragic ultimacy disclosed in contingency—though in actual discernment, the distinctness of these "moments" is rarely observed. On one hand, while as embodied beings we participate in creaturely finitude, we experience but few uninterpreted, naked contingencies.[48] This is one meaning of the serpent preceding

---

[47]On cultural and natural resources for resisting fate, see the following studies: Elaine Scarry, *The Body in Pain: The Making and Unmaking of the World* (New York: Oxford University, 1985); and *Encyclopedia of Bioethics*, rev. ed. (New York: Macmillan, 1995) 5: 2490-96, s.v. "Tragedy," by Larry D. Bouchard. On memory and solidarity, see Johann Baptist Metz, *Faith in History and Society: Toward a Practical Fundamental Theology,* trans. David Smith (New York: Seabury Press, 1980).

[48]We may encounter some uninterpreted contingencies—if we follow Geertz on

anyone's sin: nature and its contingencies come to us clothed in culture, woven of interminable histories of interpretation. So that which makes us anxious has always already been interpreted, both falsely and wisely, and this coarse mix of lies and wisdom tempts our own interpreting. So sin is irreducible to naked contingency; contingency usually arrives pervaded by anxious interpretation. On the other hand, contingency is something else than interpretation and is irreducible to sin.[49] And further, the effects of sin—novel, structural, ideological—are always contingent effects. They contribute to horizons of destiny or fate and become virtually inseparable from other contingencies in our cultural and natural milieux.

During the twentieth century, there arose a novel confluence of possibilities for sin and contingency, the global ecological crisis. For Gilkey, the ancient threats of nature *to* history became newly threatening, insofar as nature is now threatened *by* history.[50] Nature and history are converging disastrously, threatening the future as a source of present meaning, value, and hope. To understand this threat, theology must interpret the two moments of irreducibility in their distinctiveness yet together.

If one cannot synthesize them—that, I suspect, would require "explaining" God—then what one can do is to recite these moments in terms of two interpenetrating stories: the story of history (preeminently a story of sin and creativity) and the "story of life," of humanity coming to be through slow change over vast eons of time. Gilkey argues that "[t]he influence of this cosmic and evolutionary story—passed on to us through our genes, through DNA—is immense, almost beyond comprehension. . . .To speak theologically, this is the way the divine creates: in and through this providential story of cosmic and evolutionary development."[51]

---

bafflement. What baffles us is what we cannot "interpret," making bafflement an exceptional hermeneutical "experience." Martin Buber offers another example: the moment in which we encounter the other as Thou is prior to interpretive experience (*Erfahrung*): see Martin Buber, *I and Thou*, trans. Walter Kaufmann (New York: Scribner's, 1970) 55-56.

[49]Gilkey concludes his discussion of natural evil in *MHE* with the following admission: to understand *that* God does not explain *why* God "created natures of such a character that their systematic interactions result in tragedy. In that sense natural evil remains ultimately unexplained in God's creation" (Gilkey, *MHE*, 228).

[50]See Gilkey, *NRS*, 169; also, see the appendix to *RW*, "The Theological Understanding of Humanity and Nature in a Technological Era" (Gilkey, *RW*, 319-22).

[51]Gilkey, *NRS*, 100.

Gilkey has always understood God as creator to mean that God transcends the "whole of reality," the whole realm of secondary causation.[52] Here he finds, however, the divine implicated in aspects of nature—its dimensions of power, life, order, and meaning—that confront us with a plenitude of contingent possibilities. And the language of tragedy thematizes such contingency, in part because it is among the participatory "modes of knowing" required by these dimensions of nature. (Other modes include the arts, philosophy, and especially "archaic" religion.) Sin remains at issue here. For, if we rely exclusively on technical modes to know nature, biological nature is not likely to survive on this planet. To know nature only as means, never as an end, is to abuse nature's "integrity," in which we may see "an image of God."[53]

Nature is a medium through which God creates and sustains providentially. Everything we are, including our cultural and spiritual being, arises within this natural milieu. Through our various modes of knowing (including science when augmented by other modes), we encounter nature as *power, life, order,* and most fully as *meaning, value,* and *unity.* These dimensions are well known to *homo religiosus* and are implicitly known to modern science, Gilkey argues, though scientistic ideologies typically ignore or deny them. They are discerned through encounters with nature as *Thou,* whose integrity is also the proximate source of our own embodied integrity. For those who view nature through the lens of revelation—itself a mode of encounter—these dimensions should be acknowledged as "traces" of the divine.[54] As matters of

---

[52]See Langdon Gilkey, *Creationism on Trial: Evolution and God at Little Rock* (Minneapolis: Winston, 1985) 49, 212 (hereafter cited as *CT*); and Gilkey, *MHE,* 16-25. The much thicker account in *NRS* of God's creative immanence in nature—still bounded by the distinction between ultimate and proximate origins (Gilkey, *NRS,* 18)—may have become possible after the cautious appropriation of Whitehead in *Reaping the Whirlwind*: Gilkey, *RW,* 110-14, 250, 414n.34. Gilkey retrieves the apparatus of prehension and concrescence as a kind of conceptual narrative. He criticizes Whitehead for inconsistently and incorrectly employing the "principle" of creativity as a cause; only actual entities or occasions can cause, not abstract principles. For Gilkey, only the Creator can order the passage between possibility and actuality; this divine ordering is known through revelation, not conceptual reason alone.

[53]Gilkey, *NRS,* 150, 152.

[54]The thought is from Calvin. That the "traces" are really "there" is evident through various modes of knowing, including scientific modes. Insofar as the traces are "sacred," they are known through the history of religions. But to see them as "images" or "signs" of God requires acts of faith and obedience (Gilkey, *NRS,* 4, 175).

ultimate concern, these traces import promise, moral imperative, and threat. The threats are discerned most obviously when nature rebounds upon our hubristic disregard and abuse. But these primordial traces are themselves fraught with contingency apart from the effects of human *hubris*: nature manifests contingency both in the sense of giving rise to particular powers, life forms, orders, and meanings, and in the tragic sense of entailing their perishing. Power in nature threatens, destroys, and also wanes. Life arises dialectically with death, which makes room for and nurtures subsequent life. Order appears with disorder. With meaning comes tragic negation, though Gilkey never calls this meaninglessness. Rather, the meaning and value of nature require of us, as of *homo religiosus*, self-discipline and sacrifice.[55]

With these threatening aspects of nature, sin is entangled. The most global threat of nature to humanity has now become humanity's global threat to nature, much as Heilbroner said.[56] Promethean creativity—that is, empowered sin—turns nature into fate. If anyone ever doubted the relevance of the theme of sin to the ecological crisis, Gilkey is a powerful corrector. But the point here is that nature is also acknowledged as having "tragic" aspects.[57] Nature is a source of our primordial anxiety; and this thicker analysis of nature makes clearer why the temptations that arise as we face ultimate horizons seem so intelligible—though as temptations to infinity they remain contradictory to our own nature, hence intelligible but not rational. Ultimacy and contingency, and implicitly the divine, are discerned in nature as tragically threatening as well as empowering, before the temptation to respond idolatrously. This analysis also shows how through power, order, life, and meaning God is with us as the ultimate, empowering depth of our pretensions as well as of our moral achievements.[58] So Gilkey interprets the tragic along both trajectories, sometimes emphasizing the priority of sin, sometimes contingency.

---

[55]On the trajectory of sin, we must sacrifice pretentious needs that we do not really need. On the trajectory of contingency, we must sacrifice matters of real value—aspects of freedom, affluence, life—entailing regrettable loss, in behalf of ultimate value. Which does Gilkey mean? In *Nature, Reality, and the Sacred* and in the appendix to *Reaping the Whirlwind*, he implies both, confident that with sacrifice the planet will sustain human flourishing (Gilkey, *NRS*, 137-41; idem, *RW*, 319-22).

[56]Interestingly, here Gilkey appreciates Heilbroner, without irony: Gilkey, *NRS*, 150, 171.

[57]See references to the tragic in Gilkey, *NRS*, 134-36, 155, 189.

[58]The implication resembles Tillich's explorations in his study, "The Demonic."

We have seen how the two trajectories are closest, *first*, in their *descriptions* of anxious finitude and culpability. Together, they imply that we cannot decide between the priority of sin and that of contingency in tragic experience. Since these moments of irreducibility resist synthesis, I suggest that the turning from one to the other may be mediated by fragmentary, contingent witnesses which we can juxtapose, drawing only provisional lines between them.

The literary witnesses that resonate with Gilkey's descriptions of ultimacy in human experience[59] would be those not of meaningless horrors but compelling mysteries, some associated with depths of the self, others with its farthest horizons—as in the epigraphs to this chapter. The first epigraph, from Sophocles' *Antigone*, interprets *anthropos* as *deinos*, a word meaning both wonder and fearsome strangeness. Sophocles deemed human craft a strange-wonder, by which we span the seas, plow the earth ("oldest of gods"), master the beasts, resist the elements, cure illness, and shape the world by language, thought, and feeling. But the choral ode ends in anxiety. Though one faces the future with all sorts of contrivances, "only against death / can he find no means of escape." Against contingency one applies *technè* to ironic effect: "With some sort of cunning / inventive beyond all expectation / he reaches sometimes evil, sometimes good." Likewise, Gilkey describes the irony of technology in terms of creativity, sin, and fate. The strange wonder that is human being, however, Gilkey sets beside the strange wonder that is God, Job's God, whose creative power is incommensurate with human craft. Leviathan—the limit-experiences of nature in which God may be discerned—will not be caught, will not be tamed, will not supplicate us:

No one is so fierce as to dare to stir it up.
　　Who can stand beside it?
Who can confront it and be safe?
　　—under the whole heaven, who? (Job 41:10-11)

Both of these fragments capture something of Gilkey's sense of the tragic, especially if we bring to them other fragments: "Come, let us

---

[59]See Gilkey, *NW*, chaps. 3–4. The title of these chapters ("The Dimension of Ultimacy in Secular Experience") is misleading if Gilkey's distinction between "secular" and "secularist" (that is, ideologies about secularity) is not followed. He means that human experience is pervaded by intimations of ultimacy, be it that of *homo religiosus*, or of a medieval monk, or of a modern banker.

make ourselves a city, and a tower with its top in the heavens, and let us make a name for ourselves; otherwise we shall be scattered upon the face of the whole earth" (Genesis 11:4).

Second, sin and contingency *critique* both understanding and virtue. For poststructuralists, the limits of understanding are developed (a) in deconstructions of signification (anticipated in Tillich's analysis of the idolatrous temptation of finite symbols) and (b) in the claim that language is rhetoric always implicated in violence (which can recall Niebuhr on original sin). The force of this critique is against theory that naively thinks itself sufficiently rational and referential. And it can be objected that the critique is itself an ideology that hypostatizes "difference."[60] A more serious objection, however, is that in deconstructing signification, supposedly in behalf of difference, we may trivialize actual suffering. Historical catastrophes that "rupture" meaning would be only the most notable instances of the rupture inherent in all discourse. Thus, the Holocaust—which in distinctive ways is incommensurate with language—would lose its particular meanings to the universal pathos of signification.[61] One might also say that to view sin as so inevitable as to be the explanation of all such horror also homogenizes suffering. But Gilkey's analysis of sin and fate insist on being rooted in historical particularity. What confounds understanding is both the finitude of thought—which includes human finitude and the limits of language—and actual evils and contingencies, novel emergences of disorder and pretensions.

Neoorthodox views of sin are also criticized for understanding only the *hubris* that afflicts the powerful. Gilkey could be so criticized, in that he wants to expose the pretensions of insecure nations, institutions, and their rationalizing defenders. His view of fate as the historical and social effects of sin, however, contextualizes other forms of sin and suffering,

---

[60]Gilkey observes that philosophies never establish their own presuppositional grounds, and their founding intuitions arise in contingent communities of discourse (Gilkey, *MHE*, 142-48; idem, *NW*, 436-38). But he also insists that any philosophy or science assumes that its contingent intuitions do somehow point to "reality," which can be known only through risky engagement. So rhetoric about God as "ground," "norm," and "lure" is qualified by the double critique of contingency and fault—and further, these qualifications themselves must be so qualified. Without critique, there can be no confidence in disclosure.

[61]See Susan E. Shapiro, "Failing Speech: Post-Holocaust Writing and the Discourse of Postmodernism," *Semeia* 40 (1987): 65-91; David Hart "Beauty, Violence, and Infinity: A Question Concerning Christian Rhetoric" (Ph.D. diss., University of Virginia, 1997).

particularly those of the powerless.[62] There is hardly any contingency or suffering in the historical-cultural realm that does not relate to some, and usually many, structures of sin and fate. (So while our genes may predispose some of us to heart disease, the tobacco economy and fatty diets remain the inherited faults of lots of folks.) Here, there is a strong, emancipatory implication. Gilkey's view of God as providential lure to courageous moral achievement opens ways to a religious interpretation of material culture. Through practical arts and sciences, as well as through politics employed in behalf of compassion and justice, humanity can resist objective fates and the habits of violence. Technologies usually do, but need not only, mask pretensions.[63]

Third, that God works providentially through tragic horizons of sin and contingency involves Gilkey in *theodicy*. Paul Ricoeur, writing of Greek tragic theology (where transcendence is not benign but inscrutably malevolent), suggests that the tragic "resists" thought and thought the tragic,[64] especially thought that explains misfortune—the thought, for instance, of Job's comforters. Theodicy, however, may be as unavoidable as it is problematic. The illusion of theodicy is to think it can write an algebra for God, suffering, humanity, and evil. But if it knows this illusion to be its temptation, then theodicy can resist in another way; it can become a practical resistance[65] that seeks to be honest both about

---

[62]On Christian complicity in the Holocaust, see Gilkey, *RW*, 260-61. The nemesis of the ecological crisis may be "even vaster," in that technology threatens the total "extinction and not deliverance of mankind" (Gilkey, *RW*, 261).

[63]Scarry, in both her publications and her recent lectures on reasoning in emergencies, offers possibilities for such a line of interpretation (e.g., Scarry. *The Body in Pain*, especially chap. 4). See Gilkey's observations about fate being "vastly reduced" through politics and social reform (Gilkey, *RW*, 286-87). Typically, he views technology as a Promethean symbol of fate: e.g., Langdon Gilkey, *Religion and the Scientific Future* (New York: Harper & Row, 1969) 92-95; and idem, *NRS*, 164-65. But providence and the religious significance of moral achievement imply that caring, just, and disciplined uses of technology can also resist fate (e.g., Gilkey, *SC*, 71—a discussion to which Gilkey referred me after I despaired of finding one).

[64]See Ricoeur, *Symbolism of Evil*, 211-12.

[65]On cognitive resistance being transformed into practical resistance, see the discussion of resistance during the Holocaust, especially that of a German philosopher, Kurt Huber: see Emil Fackenheim, *To Mend the World: Foundations of Future Jewish Thought* (New York: Schocken, 1986) 266-79. See also Kenneth Surin's distinction between theoretical and practical theodicies: Kenneth Surin, *Theology and the Problem of Evil* (Oxford: Basil Blackwell, 1986).

tragic accountability and about its own confession of God who resists evil. If I rail against theodicy as pretentious, or blind wishful thinking, then my railing itself resists suffering and evil, and hence can become a practical theodicy that resists evil as the final thing to be enacted of creation.[66] Tragedy itself invites us to make theodicies, for the artifices of tragedies or tragicomedies contain and hold at some distance, though without resolving, both terror and care. Tragedy insists, however, that we not rest secure in the forms we make, and so should theology.

Thus, *fourth*, what follows now is less criticism of Gilkey's *religious vision* than collaboration. In *Nature, Reality, and the Sacred*, Gilkey envisions a dialectical theodicy of life and death. Sin remains irreducible, contextualized, but not caused, by anxiety and contingency; but tragic contingency is now described as the prior condition for life:

> If God is all powerful and all good, how can there be an experience of evil? If God created and rules the world, how is the tragedy of death possible? Is God the ground of death as well as of life, of that which threatens value as well as that which creates and increases it?[67]

> In nature the patterns of life, death, and new life issued in the appearance of life and its meanings; in the "story" of nature, the dialectic of life and death issued in the appearance and increase of values evident in animal and human existence.[68]

> The strange fact is that the dialectic of life and death spreads out from its natural origin into the very midst of human, personal, ethical existence; nature in this sense leads us into the very deepest levels of spirit. We cannot live truly and with integrity unless we are willing to die.[69]

---

[66]See Arthur Cohen, *The Tremendum: A Theological Interpretation of the Holocaust* (New York: Crossroad, 1981) 49. That tragic configurations of suffering and accountability are "ultimate" means they are ontically discerned within and at the farthest horizons of existence and thus can be, though not necessarily are, associated with the divine. "Finality" connotes an ontological or metaphysical judgment about ultimate reality or God. For caution in interpreting limit experiences in light of a prior metaphysical judgment, see Susan E. Shapiro, "Recovery of the Sacred" (Ph.D. diss., University of Chicago, 1983); and idem, "Hearing the Testimony of Radical Negation," *Concilium* 175 (October 1984): 3-10. Her distinction informs my discussion: see Bouchard, *Tragic Method and Tragic Theology*, 242-51.

[67]Gilkey, *NRS*, 189

[68]Gilkey, *NRS*, 190.

[69]Gilkey, *NRS*, 191.

God creates and rules both the realm of life and the realm of death: for it is out of death that life and new life arises. Life is the supreme value for life; all of nature discloses this. But the condition of life is dying, and with consciousness this condition becomes the ultimate willingness to die.[70]

Ultimacy is manifest in experiences of novel possibility, abundant meaning, and renewed value. Ultimacy also appears, when our centers and horizons are negated—including experiences hedged by suffering and evil. God, in such moments, is *"deus absconditus* whose mystery within this dialectic [of life and death] is impenetrable."[71] Before quoting Gilkey's next, redemptive sentences, I must clarify that to listen to tragedy is not a simply a matter of "agreeing" or "disagreeing" with any singular witness, nor of abandoning beliefs, but of remaining perplexed. Tragedy perplexes, and holds its questions in forms to be shared. And to say with Gilkey that God is lord of life and death does not relax the perplexity or "impenetrable mystery" that such Lordship gives. That which one can do is hold fragmentary witnesses in contingent juxtaposition, and observe that, in the gaps between them—here between the testimonies of sin and nature—questions appear that are not resolved, and so more fragmentary witnesses are to be sought.

To say that God is lord of life and death does not resolve the perplexity of fate. To be sure, meaningless fate—be it fates of contingency or of sin—cannot be a concept of totality. In similar fateful places, people live and die in despair and in hope; we hear their different testimonies without attempting their synthesis. My concern is not with meaninglessness as a category, but with felt abandonment, with particular personal and social horizons so utterly opaque that some never see out nor others in. Gilkey speaks of such voids, wherein providential histories of fault and judgment are eclipsed and people perish in anguish, horror, or numb indifference.[72] Once attentive thought knows that these horizons

---

[70]Gilkey, *NRS*, 192.

[71]Gilkey, *NRS*, 192.

[72]"Meaninglessness, like contingency, when it is felt in all its power, is a messenger of an ultimate Void, of terrifying nonbeing, and quite blankets out the apprehension of the relative, finite self, its world, its future, and the community within which alone it can really exist" (Gilkey, *NW*, 347-48). See also Gilkey's comments on *both* empty horizons of fate and despair *and* on salvation and God's "rescue of the lost" (Gilkey, *ME*, 154, 191-92).

have existed and will again exist, it can never proceed without this broken, breaking knowledge.

To say that God is lord of life and death does not resolve perplexity before nature's limits and scarcity. Scarcity is inevitably exploited by greed, so episodes of famine and overpopulation are compounded by political and economic oppression.[73] Yet, the fateful dimensions of scarcity in nature do not reduce to such structures.

To say that God is lord of life and death does not resolve the perplexity of nature's integrity. By integrity, Gilkey refers to nature as an *imago dei*, as a Thou and valued as end and not as means. But ethically, to approach another as Thou, one must be willing to part in peace when meeting cannot endure. To meet nature as Thou must imply that, while nature abides *with* us and we with nature, nature cannot always abide *for* us.[74] Contemporary cosmology sometimes suggests—as in the "anthropic principle"—that the constants of nature are fine tuned *for* life and even meaning.[75] They certainly are not tuned, nonetheless, to guarantee *our* life and meaning. So, as we meet nature as Thou, nature may well part our company. And if our medium, in its integrity, parts our company—which is the destiny of our star and planet—might we not be gripped, for a moment or a lifetime, by "pointlessness" rather than peace?[76] Given this alterity of nature, another meaning of *imago dei* comes to mind: to be a

---

[73]On sin and scarcity, see Gilkey, *RW*, 418n.63; and on technology's threat to human viability, see Gilkey, *NRS*, chap. 11.

[74]On I-Thou relations with nature, see Donald L. Berry, *Mutuality: The Vision of Martin Buber* (Albany NY: SUNY Press, 1985) 1-38. James M. Gustafson explores the thought that nature—and if nature, then nature's God?—may be with us but not finally for us: Gustafson, *Ethics from a Theocentric Perspective*. In my view, only a theology of exile or a *theologia crucis* can approach the apparent disjunction between Gustafson and biblical faith on this issue.

[75]See John D. Barrow and Frank B. Tipler, *The Anthropic Cosmological Principle* (Oxford: Clarendon, 1986); Gilkey, *NRS*, 67-68, 133.

[76]See the comment by the physicist, Steven Weinberg, that the more we understand the universe's expansion toward heat death, "the more it also seems pointless" (Steven Weinberg, *The First Three Minutes* [New York: Bantam, 1979] 144). The comment is ontically valid as a witness to meaninglessness; I agree with Gilkey that it is philosophically no more warranted than had Weinberg said the opposite (Gilkey, *NRS*, 1, 185). Incidentally, Weinberg concludes that, if "the fruits" of such research are unconsoling, "there is at least some consolation in the research itself. . . . The effort to understand the universe is one of the few things that lifts human life a little above the level of farce, and gives it some of the grace of tragedy" (Weinberg, *First Three Minutes*, 144).

fellow ruler or steward with God.[77] And to contemplate the rule of nature, in light of ecological limits, is again to imagine nature parting our company. Nature suffers. Its rebound upon our history will likely manifest a divine judgment catastrophically harsh—for reasons Heilbroner and Gilkey well understand.

If nature viewed as *imago dei* now bodes nemesis upon human viability, however, we might yet place beside it another view of nature as *sacramental*.[78] Christian warrants for doing so are the material forms of baptism and eucharist: water, bread, and wine, products of the earth and of human labor. At the table, Christ chooses these elements—and not the slain lamb—to identify his embodiment and sacrifice. For the church to acknowledge nature as sacramental would mean that nature, bearing traces of God, is an icon transparent to God's creating and transforming grace. It would also mean that, in living with nature, as well as with humanity, we may discern and participate in Christ's suffering, resisting evil, and dying—especially the kenotic Christ poured out in the world and in the form of a slave (Philippians 2:6-8). To unite nature with human suffering and divine sacrifice, however, would be intolerable for nature without a third implication. To confess nature as sacramental is to be transformed, in responsible community with nature, by the promise that God loves in solidarity with suffering—ours, the world's, and nature's—and seeks to transform death and life within the newness of God's own life and love.[79]

> But this God has disclosed an even deeper dialectic: that of the call to life and its values; that of life, death, and beyond death new life; and that of mercy, forgiveness, and eternal grace. God is not only power and life and so life and death; God is grace, life, eternity . . . [who has] in the covenant with Israel and the life and death of Jesus, disclosed the divine participation in our suffering and death and thus provided in the divine power and grace the means to unite and overcome the dialectic of life and death.[80]

---

[77]See Levenson, *Creation and the Persistence of Evil*, 112-13.

[78]See Alexander Schmeman, *For the Life of the World* (New York: National Student Christian Foundation, 1963) 3-5.

[79]See Gilkey's early discussion of the Eucharist: Langdon Gilkey, *How the Church Can Minister to the World without Losing Itself* (New York: Harper & Row, 1964) 122-27.

[80]Gilkey, *NRS*, 192.

When the trajectories of tragedy are juxtaposed with the dialectic of death and resurrection, then Christian discourse of hope needs such limits as these: To confess God's participation in suffering, guilt, and loss is first to confess that God is discerned with those who perish in the hell of meaningless despair; their perishing remains a restless disturbance for those who discern both God and despair. It is also to witness that, while we may lose our words beside those who die without hope, in their irreparable loss we encounter an embodied, divine command to resist restlessly their fates and ours.

Theologies willing to hold contingent fragments of experience and tradition, deferring their correlation, can risk narrating a redemptive future. Theologies of God entering exile with the exiled or entombment with the entombed can risk disturbing confessions of abiding covenant and resurrection with the dead. To survive an internment camp, Gilkey has written, is not to survive a death camp.[81] The former intensifies and exposes the stress and sins of our mutual camping, the latter negates the whole idea of "our" camp. In the former, to rise with the dead has an apocalyptic irony and joy captured near the end of *Shantung Compound*, as American paratroopers dropped from the sky. In the latter, to be passed over by death may bode a haunted, incongruous survival and exile. Both witnesses are fragments. Theology tries to hold our fragments. Gilkey's theology is so finely attuned to biblical and creedal paradigms, philosophical methods, and horizons of experience as to give a generous medium for interpreting the tragic. The traditions of tragedy know people and their horizons to be sometimes occasions of despair and also of fear, wonder, and strangeness. Gilkey evokes these latter traits most powerfully, the traces of nature and humanity as *mysterium*, traces discerned in the drama of Sophocles and the poetry of Job. They are ultimate, not final things to be said of history and nature.[82]

---

[81]Gilkey, *SC*, ix.

[82]I am grateful to my colleagues, Charles Mathewes and Eugene Rogers, for their critical comments and suggestions regarding this chapter.

Chapter 12

"A Sharp Turn":
Christology in a "Time of Troubles"

James O. Yerkes

Introduction

Before I began to write this essay, it would never have occurred to me
that I would find myself a shipmate at sea with both Langdon Gilkey and
John Updike. Fingers poised for the first strike on the keyboard, I was
suddenly struck by the fact that both writers employ a "hugging the
shore" simile to explain their critical reflections as contemporary writers
and as creative interpreters of the human condition. Looking back on their
efforts as cultural critics, though in different genres, both Gilkey and
Updike see a strategy which helps explain why their reflections have
taken the form they did and do. The comparison is worth noting
carefully. "Writing criticism," says Updike,

> is to writing fiction and poetry as hugging the shore is to sailing in the open
> sea. At sea, we have that beautiful blankness all around; hugging the shore,
> one can always come about and draw even closer to the land. . . . A fervent
> relation with the world: I suppose this is my critical touchstone. I find
> myself, in these pieces, circling back to man's religious nature and the real
> loss to man and art alike when that nature has nowhere to plug in. . . . At
> all times, an old world is collapsing and a new world arising; we have better
> eyes for the collapse than the rise, for the old one is the world we know.[1]

"Quite unintentionally," says Gilkey,

> my thought has reflected a "correlational" approach: as when a sailboat hugs
> a massive but variegated shoreline, its course has been determined by the
> twists and turns of twentieth-century events. . . . But that formal method is
> a symptom of a more basic pattern of thinking, namely, to ponder the
> character of our existence, both personal and historical, before God in the
> light of the historical and social situation, the massive contours of events, in
> which we find ourselves.[2]

---

[1]John Updike, *Hugging the Shore* (New York: Knopf, 1983) xv, xviii-xix.
[2]Langdon Gilkey, "A Retrospective Glance at My Work," in *The Whirlwind in
Culture: Frontiers in Theology: In Honor of Langdon Gilkey*, ed. Donald W. Musser and

How strikingly similar are these two perspectives. As sometime seagoing New Englanders, both emphasize the dynamic correlation between cultural turbulence and critical insight—*their* insight, literary and theological: culturally speaking, no pain, no gain; religiously speaking, no God, no Ground.

Gilkey repeatedly emphasized, in the last essays written prior to his retirement from the University of Chicago Divinity School, that the dramatically new situation now roiling the waters of the Christian theologian's reflective task is "a new consciousness with regard to plurality," which entails "a feeling of rough parity, as well as diversity, among religions." And the theological implication of such feelings of parity and diversity he finds pretty bracing, Christologically speaking. The problem is this: "It is not just our response to revelation [in the event of Jesus Christ] that is relative; it is the revelation to which we are responding that is now roughly equal to the others. This is the new situation, a new and deeper interweaving of the relative and the absolute."[3]

Gilkey shares with Updike the realization that "at all times, an old world is collapsing and a new world arising" and that "we have better

---

Joseph L. Price (Bloomington IN: Meyer-Stone Books, 1988) 1.

[3]Langdon Gilkey, *Through the Tempest: Theological Voyages in a Pluralistic Culture,* ed. Jeff B. Pool [Minneapolis: Fortress Press, 1991] 21, 31; hereafter cited as *TT*; cf. Langdon Gilkey, "Plurality and Its Theological Implications," in *The Myth of Christian Uniqueness: Toward a Pluralistic Theology of Religions,* ed. John Hick and Paul F. Knitter (New York: Orbis, 1987) 37-50. To get some initial perspective here on how different is this new point of view, consider Gilkey's previous work. Gilkey describes "Christology" as "the Christian witness to God's presence and activity in and through the event of Jesus." Furthermore, "to be a Christian, at least in belief . . . [is] to center one's understanding and existence on this total event (of Jesus as the Christ) as uniquely revelatory of God's power and love" (Langdon Gilkey, *Message and Existence: An Introduction to Christian Theology* [New York: Seabury Press, 1979] 180; hereafter cited as *ME*). Gilkey suggests that his book, *Message and Existence,* and its still essentially neoorthodox perspective "concluded" a way of thinking that focused on "the method of phenomenological prolegomenon and existential correlation" (Gilkey, "Retrospective Glance at My Work," 26). His correlational method in theology remains, but the focus of analysis has changed to matters of cultural and religious relativity. Although Brian Walsh supplies an otherwise helpful analysis of Gilkey's thought, he does not understand the radical change in Gilkey's Christological views that developed after *Message and Existence* (Brian Walsh, *Langdon Gilkey: Theologian for a Culture in Decline* [Lanham MD: University Press of America, 1991] 162-63).

eyes for the collapse than the rise, for the old one is the world we know." Right now, Gilkey thinks that we especially need a new theology of religions, one which responds to the shoreline tug of the pluralistic cultural consciousness that attends honest and unprejudiced dialogue with other religious traditions. He also recognizes that we sail here on uncharted seas.[4] With this essay, I intend briefly to trace the effects of this "sea change" of sentiment on Gilkey's earlier Christological interpretations and, then, carefully to consider whether the position he now advocates is properly warranted in its new correlation of existence and message. In some ways, the latter goal is necessarily tentative, because theological reconstructions based on this new dialectic of a relative absolute are still in process.[5] On occasion, I have wondered if Gilkey sees our current situation as waiting for a new Kairos, somewhat as did Paul Tillich in *The Religious Situation*. In passing and not incidentally, one needs to emphasize that no other theologian since Tillich has worked harder, written more brilliantly, and shown more imaginative

---

[4]Langdon Gilkey, "Theology for a Time of Troubles: How My Mind has Changed," *Christian Century* 98 (20 April 1981): 479.

[5]Notwithstanding, earlier tentative proposals in outline form have been followed by some substantive essays that show the new application of this dialectic to traditional theological issues: as examples of earlier proposals, see Langdon Gilkey, "Events, Meanings, and the Current Tasks of Theology," *Journal of the American Academy of Religion* 53 (1985): 728-34; and idem, "Plurality and Its Theological Implications," 46-50. Gilkey's *Through the Tempest* contains a number of his more recent proposals: Gilkey, *TT*, 21-34, 89-100, 101-13, 143-55, 157-65, 181-93, 215-31. The latter proposals contain richly suggestive discussions that include correlative insights from Eastern traditions, especially Buddhism. Gilkey characterizes his new way of doing theology as "affirming and articulating one's own position in the light of its relation to other positions, developing its own uniqueness in dialectical relation to the Others. This means . . . interpreting, for example Christianity, primarily in the light of its own sources in scripture and tradition, in using its own historic symbols: God, Christ, creation, fall, incarnation, and the call to liberation" (Langdon Gilkey, "The Pluralism of Religions," in *God, Truth and Reality*, ed. Arvind Sharma [New York: St. Martins, 1993] 120; also see Gilkey, *TT*, 193). As he mentions in several contexts, the difficulty of working theologically with such a new theological vision leaves the mind "stunned," "silenced," and "puzzled" (Langdon Gilkey, "The AAR and the Anxiety of Nonbeing: An Analysis of Our Present Cultural Situation," *Journal of the American Academy of Religion* 48 [March 1980]: 16; idem, "Events, Meanings and the Current Tasks of Theology," 730; idem, "Plurality and Its Theological Implications," 46). The clear public harbinger of this "sharp turn" was Gilkey's Presidential Address to the American Academy of Religion in November 1979 (Gilkey, "AAR and the Anxiety of Nonbeing," 5-18).

courage in tackling life on the open sea of modernity—and now postmodernity—than Langdon Gilkey. On the present issue, this again remains impressively so.[6]

I. The Interpretation of Culture

I begin by assessing the perspective on culture that informs Gilkey's present Christological position. Gilkey sees the culture of the West in impending, incipient decline: "An autumnal chill is in the air; its similarity to the chill in other periods of cultural decline is undeniable" and "it *feels* as if we are reaching the end of a historical era." Gilkey's book, *Society and the Sacred*, carries the subtitle, *Toward a Theology of Culture in Decline*.[7] Numerous times, borrowing from Toynbee, he refers to the present situation in the West as a "Time of Troubles," a time of social disintegration when, after four centuries of self-assured dominance and superiority in all spheres of human endeavor, the specter of anxious self-doubt haunts Western self-consciousness.[8] Intellectual colonialism began to vanish along with political colonialism, beginning roughly in 1945, right after the second world war. "The era of Western military dominance and cultural superiority (and not just *Europe's* empires) is over. A new parity of cultures and powers is upon us."[9] East meets West on increasing terms of parity in all those spheres of human endeavor— militarily, scientifically, industrially, politically, socially, morally, and, most importantly for Gilkey's argument, religiously. And with this

---

[6]See Paul Tillich, *Die religiöse Lage der Gegenwart* (Berlin: Ullstein, 1926); idem, *The Religious Situation* (New York: Henry Holt, 1932). David Tracy's respectful comment deserves repeating. "It is difficult to think of a major theological or cultural issue not addressed in the theology of Langdon Gilkey. In his extraordinary theological career he has consistently spotted, formulated, and addressed the questions demanding Christian theological attention in our ever-changing cultural and historical situation" (David Tracy, "The Question of Criteria for Inter-Religious Dialogue: A Tribute to Langdon Gilkey," in *Whirlwind in Culture*, ed. Musser and Price, 246).

[7]Langdon Gilkey, *Society and the Sacred: Toward a Theology of Culture in Decline* (New York: Crossroad, 1981) xi, 3; hereafter cited as *SAS*.

[8]Gilkey, *SAS*, xi; idem, "Theology for a Time of Troubles," 474; idem, "Events, Meaning and the Current Tasks of Theology," 718; idem, "Retrospective Glance at My Work," 2, 27, 29; idem, *TT*, 148-53.

[9]Gilkey, "Retrospective Glance at My Work," 32; also see idem, "Plurality and Its Theological Implications," 39-40; idem, "Events, Meaning and the Current Tasks of Theology," 723-28.

cultural sense of acute relativism in values has arrived, right on schedule, acute *intellectual* relativism.

Ever the theologian of culture, having taken the mantle of his mentor Tillich, Gilkey sees a clear parallel of relativism in the development of Western theology—what he terms the growing sense of the "co-validity and co-efficacy of other religions."[10] The early theological liberalism of both Europe and America at the turn of the century, he reminds us again and again, was heavily progressivist in its view of cultural history. It optimistically took for granted that the rise of the West was the leavening emergence of a cultural progress that would furnish the world with its "higher" values in all spheres of human endeavor, including, of course, religion. The political derailment of this faulted assumption began in Europe in 1914 and ended catastrophically for Americans in 1941—even though, as Gilkey says, this second conflict came to be considered "the good war" because of the evils it fought.[11]

Owing to the sense of relativism intellectually implicit in the rise of historical and literary criticism, however, theological liberalism also generated a more ecumenical attitude both inside and outside the Christian tradition. Thus, Gilkey suggests, "the most important development . . . is the shift in the balance between . . . the requirements of faith and those of love":

> In the modern period—largely with the help of the Enlightenment . . . the doctrines of faith—creeds, confessions and even the words of scripture itself—began to be seen as human . . . and hence relative expressions of a truth that transcended any single expression. Their defense is no longer the defense of God—and [such a defense] becomes morally dubious.[12]

This "liberal" perspective of historical relativism was carried over directly into the neoorthodoxy of Reinhold Niebuhr and Tillich, Gilkey's first theological mentors after he returned from his time of imprisonment in China in 1945.[13] Though each maintained the finality and uniqueness

---

[10]Gilkey, "Plurality and Its Theological Implications," 37.

[11]Gilkey, "Events, Meaning and the Current Tasks of Theology," 719.

[12]Gilkey, "Plurality and Its Theological Implications," 38.

[13]At the conference organized in his honor in 1988, Gilkey agreed with Lois Gehr Livezey's characterization of his thought as "using Tillichian categories with Niebuhrian sentiments." He noted, "Only I would add a name and call it a movement from Niebuhr to Tillich to Eliade—who is much closer to who I am at the present time" (Langdon Gilkey, "Theology and Culture: Reflections on the Conference," *Criterion* 28 [Autumn

of Christian revelation, they, along with Emil Brunner, Karl Barth, and Rudolf Bultmann, insisted that "salvation came neither through perfection of life nor perfection of faith."[14] We are not justified by any work of Christian belief, but solely by the gracious *agapé* of God. This religious courtesy they also understood to be extended to believers in other traditions. Truth is one thing, salvation quite another.[15]

Further, all of the major neoorthodox figures, together with their liberal theological forebears, operated on the assumption that divine self-revelation had taken place elsewhere, in addition to the Christian revelation. However, they also presumed that this Christian revelation was the criterion by which to measure the religious validity in truth and experience represented in other religious traditions. That is, they stressed what Friedrich Schleiermacher affirmed and Ernst Troeltsch denied as "the Absoluteness of Christianity." Gilkey contends that they thus practiced, perhaps quite unself-consciously, an intellectual imperialism in the realm of religion which was a matching image of the cultural imperialism of Western military, educational, and economic institutions.[16] It was assumed that other religions were indeed included in the realm of truth and grace, in revelation and salvation, but without their epistemic and ethical misunderstandings, which all agreed are correctly adjusted in the central Christian revelatory event of Jesus as the Christ.

For most of his theological career, Gilkey understood this to be the religious message implicit in the theology of the church. The intellectual and cultural changes in modernity required it. Changes in his own

---

1989]: 3). In some more fundamental sense, however, Reinhold Niebuhr remains what Gilkey has named his "spiritual father." "My conversion—and that is the right word—was quick and complete. I heard him, as did hundreds more [at Harvard in 1939], twice again that day, afternoon and evening; and I bought, read and reread all his books then in print (up to *Beyond Tragedy*, 1936)" (Gilkey, "Theology and Culture," 7). Gilkey's narration of events and ideas in the widely read book about his life of imprisonment in China (1943–1945) rings uncompromisingly with Niebuhrian sentiments about our "fallen" human condition and our consequent need of grace and forgiveness to restore personal and communal hope (Langdon Gilkey, *Shantung Compound: The Story of Men and Women under Pressure* [New York: Harper & Row, 1966] see esp. 229–42; hereafter cited as *SC*). Gilkey has recently reflected on the abiding significance of that experience: Langdon Gilkey, "From Shantung to Sarajevo," *Christian Century* 112 (16-23 August 1995): 782-86.

[14]Gilkey, "Plurality and Its Theological Implications," 38.

[15]Gilkey, *TT*, 181-82.

[16]Gilkey, *TT*, 188-89.

personal existence also seemed to confirm it and raise the ante of relativism's intensity on that side of his theological correlation. His wife's commitment to the Sikh movement in 1974, and his attendant involvement in its yogic and communal activities, together with his visit to Kyoto University and conversations with Buddhist philosopher Takeuchi Yoshinori in 1975, began to shift his perspective sharply.[17] The *lived* spiritual power of these Eastern religious traditions startled him, however, not simply their alternative religious *beliefs*: "What I have later called the new experience in our time of the rough parity among religions came to me with unanswerable certainty in these experiences and has set for me the major theological task of the next years."[18] It is indeed no small task. In seafaring words that he uses to describe the venturesome efforts of Wilfred Cantwell Smith, "there are as yet no charts, nor even (as he well knows) a true north by which to steer; and in all probability hidden rocks, lurking monsters and heavy gales are omnipresent—but we don't yet know where."[19] What is required in this situation, he contends, is "speculative courage."[20]

The importance of Gilkey's sentiment about the West's incipient intellectual and cultural decline in shaping his more recent Christological

---

[17]Gilkey mentions Yoshinori's comment as the personal moment when he realized that he was being faced with quite a new situation as a Christian theologian: "One afternoon, walking in a Zen temple garden, we talked about our talking, about dialogue. I murmured a kind of apology that I always spoke from a Christian position. 'Do not for one moment consider in our conversations ceasing to speak as a Christian,' he said. 'Do you wish me to cease to speak as a Buddhist? Then we could no longer teach each other anything— and, above all, our conversation together would become a bore, like those secular philosophers in Tokyo who stand outside every position and so stand nowhere at all.' And he concluded with the paradox, 'Remain what you are, and then and only then can we converse' " (Gilkey, *TT*, 192). All the essays in *TT*, save two, were written or published between 1981 and 1990. This personal experience obviously becomes the paradigm by which he thinks interreligious dialogue should take place and in terms of which he forged his concept of a "relative absolute."

[18]Gilkey, "Retrospective Glance at My Work," 31-32.

[19]Langdon Gilkey, "A Theological Voyage with Wilfred Cantwell Smith," *Religious Studies Review* 7 (October 1981): 298.

[20]Gilkey, "AAR and the Anxiety of Nonbeing," 15. As he mentions in several contexts, the difficulty of working theologically with such a new theological vision leaves the mind "stunned," "overwhelmed," "silenced," and "puzzled" (see Gilkey, "AAR and the Anxiety of Nonbeing," 16; idem, "Theology for a Time of Troubles," 474; idem, "Events, Meaning and the Current Tasks of Theology," 730; idem, "Plurality and Its Theological Implications," 46).

statements can hardly be overstressed: "An autumnal chill is in the air" and he senses the gathering of ominous forces.[21] One feels the powerful, if not gloomy, shadow of Augustine's reflections about the fall of Rome cast over his discussions. Gilkey is clearly groping for a new way of finding a center of meaning for Christian and human existence, where "an old world is collapsing and a new world arising"—precisely as is Updike. The startling new Christological turn here, however, is, as we have seen, his insistence that "it is the revelation to which we are responding [in the event of Jesus as the Christ] that is now roughly equal to the others. This is the new situation." Indeed, he says, this "seems to represent a sharp turn toward the 'liberal' side of my intellectual history, *if not a step beyond that*."[22] Earlier he had declared quite another sentiment: "Only in the event of Jesus as the Christ is clarity with regard to ultimacy manifest."[23] Now he is left with the conviction: "No cultural logos is final and so universal . . . , no one revelation is or can be the universal criterion for all others," including "one based on Christian revelation."[24]

II. The Theological Trajectory

It will help at this point to review more specifically the theological trajectory which has brought Gilkey to this "sharp turn" in reconceiving the theological meaning of revelation in Jesus as the Christ. This second exploration is especially important because Gilkey is very clear that, as far as he is concerned, it is the cultural crisis which has rendered previous theological solutions to religious relativism inadequate, not the other way around. Being clear about that trajectory of development, which he himself personally has transversed, helps to understand why he now feels impelled to veer rather sharply in another direction.

This trajectory was, of course, already implicit in our discussion of the interpretation of culture as a "time of troubles." Here I want to make

---

[21]In a dark, powerful simile, Gilkey writes, "An old culture, like an old bear, can suddenly whiff the dank odor of its own mortality; and then it is tempted, and tempted deeply, to sacrifice its ideals for the preservation of its life—and thus to hasten the very demise in history it fears so much" (Gilkey, "Theology for a Time of Troubles," 478).

[22]Gilkey, "Retrospective Glance at My Work," 30; emphasis mine.

[23]Langdon Gilkey, *Catholicism Confronts Modernity: A Protestant View* (New York: Seabury Press, 1975) 93; hereafter cited as *CCM*.

[24]Gilkey, "Events, Meaning and the Current Tasks of Theology," 731-32; cf. idem, "Pluralism of Religions," 116.

it explicit. Gilkey's intellectual history has moved from (1) what he called a rather "hardheaded" naturalistic humanism (à la Santayana at Harvard),[25] to (2) a centrist, sometimes called apologetic neoorthodoxy[26] strongly influenced by both Reinhold Niebuhr and Tillich, to (3) a modified post-"death of God" neoorthodoxy which recognized a "much needed ground or base in common experience" that begins to take the shape of a kind of "natural theology,"[27] to (4) what he now characterizes as that "sharp turn" back to a more liberal or what might in fact be called a postmodern orientation. At this latter stage, the strong influence of Mircea Eliade emerges in conjunction with courses jointly taught with David Tracy.[28] Gilkey insists that the issue for him in this radically new

---

[25]Gilkey, "Retrospective Glance at My Work," 8.

[26]Recently, Gilkey has observed the following about variations within neoorthodoxy. "Despite their many and important differences, Tillich and Barth (and also Brunner) reveal here some unexpected similarities, namely, that all knowledge of God and of the *true* status of the self, its problems, and possibilities, and especially of history, come via revelation and thus under the criterion of special revelation in Jesus as the Christ. . . . I would prefer to label this common *ultimate* dependence on revelation as characteristic of 'neoorthodox' or 'dialectical/*Krisis*' theology rather than as 'Barthian.' This, along with the correlated emphasis on estrangement/sin, was what united that epoch of theology despite their real differences, with Barth on the far right, Tillich (and Bultmann) on the left, and Brunner, Aulén, and Nygren somewhere in the middle" (Langdon Gilkey, *Gilkey on Tillich* [New York: Crossroad, 1990] 141n.20; hereafter, cited as *GOT*). Interestingly, Gilkey does not include Niebuhr in this list. "In any case," he says, "since 1964 my reflective work, while still very much shaped by the original influence of Niebuhr, as well as by my own experience, has been fundamentally Tillichian in form" (Gilkey, *GOT*, xiv). Ever honest, Gilkey also observes that in his early neoorthodox emphasis on transcendence, sin, revelation, and grace—which he notes in his retrospection even after the sharp turn, "is still my general orientation"—he was "as an erstwhile liberal . . . tolerant of every view except liberalism, and . . . orthodox about what was in fact a very unorthodox way of doing theology!" (Gilkey, "Retrospective Glance at My Work," 13-14).

[27]Gilkey, "Retrospective Glance at My Work," 25.

[28]Gilkey, "Theology and Culture," 3. The influence of Eliade is particularly marked in Langdon Gilkey, *Nature, Reality, and the Sacred: The Nexus of Science and Religion*, Theology and the Sciences series, ed. Kevin J. Sharpe (Minneapolis: Fortress, 1993); hereafter cited as *NRS*. In that collection of essays (prepared or published between 1987 and 1991), there are four direct references to Jesus, three of which are substantive in interesting contexts. The first context notes that "the unity of life and death, of nonbeing with being, is perhaps most clearly articulated in archaic religion." Gilkey states, "This is scarcely an objective comment, but as the church long viewed the history of the covenant with the Hebrews as a 'preparation' for the new covenant in Jesus, so one might view this strange dialectic of fertility and immortality as a preparation for the dying and

"situation" is deeply theological—how can one think *theologically* about Jesus as the Christ in a time of the recognized rough parity of all religious traditions and their conflicting claims to special revelation? Gilkey feels that he is compelled "to understand my own faith all over again in the new light of this incontestable 'plurality.' "[29]

It will be helpful for our purpose to review briefly the categories that Gilkey has used over the years to identify the significance of the revelation of God in Jesus as the Christ—what it was that he earlier understood to be "special" about it. Only then, I feel, will the later "sharp turn" be appreciated for what it is. We begin epistemically, or with revelation. On the matter of God's relation to this event, generally speaking, Gilkey shared an epistemically inclusivist understanding of the revelation of God in Jesus as the Christ for most of his career, until the

---

rising of the Christ." Further, he observes that "this paradox—the enjoyment of life and of its values within the courageous acceptance of death—represents a spiritual achievement of impressive magnitude." His closing observation for the chapter is that "God has in many symbols and modes, but above all in the covenant with Israel and the life and death of Jesus, disclosed the divine participation in our suffering in death and thus provided in the divine power and grace the means to unite and overcome the dialectic of life and death" (Gilkey, *NRS*, 192). Finally, citing only the ambiguous hints and traces of God's power, life, order, and law found in nature, he affirms that "it is in the life of Israel, in the life and death of Jesus, and in the historical pilgrimage of the peoples of God that all of this is disclosed in much greater certainty, clarity, and power"—noting again with approval Calvin's view that, "when one puts on the spectacles of Scripture, the signs of God in creation are seen truly for what they are" (Gilkey, *NRS*, 195). These texts suggest to me the kind of theologizing Gilkey thinks can continue to be done even in a "time of troubles." If Eliade appears prominently in such discussions, frequent visits from the Reformers can also still be expected.

[29]Gilkey, "Retrospective Glance at My Work," 31-32; also see idem, "AAR and the Anxiety of Nonbeing," 16; idem, "Events, Meaning and the Current Tasks of Theology," 731; and idem, "Plurality and Its Theological Implications," 48-50. Gilkey's refreshingly honest self-reflection about these changes is best laid out in "Retrospective Glance at My Work," and is supplemented by "Theology and Culture," 2-9. Jennifer Rike provides a fine summary of this same biographical and developmental information (Jennifer Rike, "Langdon Gilkey" in *A New Handbook of Christian Theologians*, ed. Donald W. Musser and Joseph L. Price [Nashville: Abingdon, 1996] 158-70). Gilkey's "Retrospective Glance at My Work" reminds one of Tillich's autobiographical reflections in tone and temper (Paul Tillich, *On the Boundary* [New York: Scribners, 1966]). Gilkey has often been encouraged to write a more detailed autobiography, not only because of the fascinating details of his own personal development, but also because of the span of theological history he has witnessed from a vantage shared by few others in our century. He has said that he intends to do that.

1980s—at least in his published materials. That is, this personal event of God's self-revelation provided the criterion of religious truth by which other claims to revelation in other traditions were to be evaluated. The claim was not the exclusivist assertion that God revealed to and saved only Christians. The liberal inheritance of neoorthodoxy on this issue, as noted above, was firmly in place at the outset of his thinking. In *Maker of Heaven and Earth*, he notes that Jesus Christ is "the only clear clue" to God's will for us, a clue found only in the "biblical revelation," which "corrects our mistaken views of the nature of God."[30] In *Religion and the Scientific Future*, Gilkey argues that there is a "unique uniqueness" to the event of Jesus which "*God* gives it," and it is this which determines for us its "normative significance over other events."[31] In *Catholicism Confronts Modernity*, he continues to insist that "Only in the event of Jesus as the Christ is clarity with regard to ultimacy manifest." He argues that neither nature, history, nor a descriptive analysis of human being, however much they reveal hints of ultimacy, can be taken "as the conceptual clue, the grounding model," for Christian theology, "lest the divine be made either too immanent or too transcendent."[32] In *Message and Existence*, Gilkey states that "to be a Christian, at least in belief, . . . [is] to center one's understanding and existence on this total event (of Jesus as the Christ) as uniquely revelatory of God's power and love" and that Jesus' "life and person were unique, decisive, and utterly extraordinary, an unequivocal, though hidden, manifestation of God."[33] But, true to the inclusivist tradition, he insists that the "finality" of revelation in Jesus of Nazareth means "not that Christian revelation is the sole or exclusive revelation. Rather it indicates that for those committed to it and participating in it, it provides the all-determining criterion and measure for the reality and nature of God, for what is in the end taken to be real, to be true and to be of value."[34] Thus, in *Society and the Sacred*, Gilkey,

---

[30]Langdon Gilkey, *Maker of Heaven and Earth: A Study of the Christian Doctrine of Creation* (New York: Doubleday, 1959) 227, 233n.24; hereafter, cited as *MHE*.

[31]Langdon Gilkey, *Religion and the Scientific Future* (New York: Harper & Row, 1970) 180n.19; hereafter cited as *RSF*.

[32]Gilkey, *CCM*, 93.

[33]Gilkey, *ME*, 180, 182.

[34]Gilkey, *ME*, 41. In Gilkey's earlier book, *Reaping the Whirlwind*, the same perspective is emphasized: "It should also be noted that the issue whether Christ reveals God decisively and uniquely need not be the same issue as the issue of the exclusiveness of salvation in and through Christ; in these pages we try clearly to separate these two

emphasizing the credibility of faith, can still insist that Christianity as a total system of symbols "can satisfy the mind as a valid thematization of the totality of concrete experience as no other global viewpoint can" and that "Christian interpretation provides a clearer, more illuminative, and more complete access to the full character of personal and historical experience than any other viewpoint."[35]

We move next to soteriology. Gilkey argues that Jesus defines God's will for us in ethical terms in his role as Lord: "Thus the personal re-creative love of God in Christ . . . is the one unsymbolic and direct idea of God that Christians possess."[36] In *Reaping the Whirlwind*, Gilkey insists with Tillich that Jesus as the Christ is to be understood as "essential manhood under the conditions of existence," as "the Second Adam or true humanum," the "final criterion of all other manifestations of the New Being."[37] Jesus reveals not only "the authentic possibilities of human existence" but also the nature and purposes of God in grace: "we must be granted as well a new relationship to the divine favor—both as individuals and as a race."[38] But Christ's redemptive work is to be understood as a *criterion* of God's redemptive action, not an exclusive *locus*: "it is only with regard to the deeper character, intent and goal of that work that a uniqueness is claimed, not with regard to the universal presence of grace or to its efficacy." Sacrificing himself as a medium of grace, Jesus as the Christ becomes the criterion, "the final (criteriological)

---

issues, and affirm the first and deny the second" (Langdon Gilkey, *Reaping the Whirlwind: A Christian Interpretation of History* [New York: Seabury Press, 1976] 422n.86; hereafter cited as *RW*).

[35]Gilkey, *SAS*, 39, 40. There are no notations in *SAS* that date individual chapters, but I was told by Gilkey that he had presented chap. 3, "The Dialectic of Christian Belief," as a paper for a conference in 1979 at the University of Notre Dame. That paper was included in a collection of essays entitled *Rationality and Religious Belief*, ed. C. Delaney (Notre Dame IN: University of Notre Dame, 1979) 65-83. Since by 1980 Gilkey was making his "sharp turn," these comments fall within 1979, the year which he later says "concluded" the earlier, more distinctly neoorthodox phase of his thought with *ME*. The publication date of *SAS* in 1981, therefore, should not confuse us. Even if Gilkey may consider it now passé, given his present theological perspective, that chapter remains one of the finest essays on theological method written in the twentieth century.

[36]Gilkey, *MHE*, 359-60.

[37]Gilkey, *RW*, 480n.81, 422n.88.

[38]Gilkey, *RW*, 482n.86.

manifestation of New Being," of God's redemptive activity always and everywhere present—before, during and after his earthly life.[39]

Gilkey can even insist that "In Jesus, for Christians, an answer, a model, a paradigm of authentic existence has appeared: the possibilities of human existence are here defined and enacted, and thus the requirements of being fully human *for the first time are made plain.*"[40] These possibilities are also *achieved* for the first time. Amidst the ambiguities of history, through his "complete love and self-surrender for others . . . he manifested a new form of human reality, and yet the essential form of our reality."[41] This "for the first time"-emphasis is drawn, I think, from the conviction that, as Tillich emphasized, there is a perfection of *being*, not just a perfection of *knowing* which radically changed human history in Jesus.[42]

Gilkey's confidence in the "perfection" of Jesus as a human being seems to stem from two sources. One is the point made by both Philip Melanchthon and Schleiermacher that Christian confidence in Jesus as the Christ stems from a present salvific experience of his "benefits." That is to say, for Schleiermacher, it is an argument *from* a Christian's transformed consciousness *to* the therefore necessary perfect God-consciousness of Jesus as its antecedent cause. The experience of New Being points to the emergence in history of a new *humanum*, as noted earlier, and creates an epistemic, soteriological, and eschatological "center" for history.[43]

Second, Gilkey seems to assume that the biblical witness requires the attribution of such human and moral perfection. On the issue of historical inquiry into the life of Jesus, Gilkey affirms that what knowledge we have owing to the canons of modern historical inquiry is "relatively reliable," but he is equally clear that "no biography of Jesus tracing his life's development, exploring his inner consciousness, or even outlining systematically his philosophical and ethical teachings, is possible."[44] Still, for all that, one is puzzled to run across references to "the perfection of Jesus' humanity and the character of the divine love manifest in and

---

[39]Gilkey, *RW*, 421n.84; also see 422n.86.
[40]Gilkey, *ME*, 189; emphasis mine.
[41]Gilkey, *RW*, 269-70.
[42]Gilkey, *GOT*, 142-49.
[43]Gilkey, *RW*, 168; idem, *ME*, 166.
[44]Gilkey, *ME*, 161-62.

through him" and to the fact that "his life was totally pure in its devotion to his own cause and calling."[45] Moreover, we are told that Jesus "lived in devotion to God; in courage, serenity and inner integrity; in utter self-giving and sacrifice to others."[46] This assertion of total and inner perfection, however, seems to require the kind of historical, indeed even psychological, knowledge that Gilkey denies is methodologically available to the contemporary theologian.

This drive beyond the "facts" of biblical history is a function of Gilkey's deeply soteriological conviction that Jesus did not just *show* us what God wanted us be in our full humanity, as if without him we could achieve it on our own, but that Jesus *achieved* this perfection. This is why he communicates a redemptive possibility for our fallen humanity today in the experience of faith. "Unless [Jesus] was actually loving, committed, self-giving, serene, in a word 'authentic,' " in his historical actuality, Gilkey argues, the Christian witness remains at best abstract, unrealized, and at worst irrelevant in the human quest for spiritual fulfillment.[47] Still, unless I misunderstand Gilkey, this is more a retrojected fact of faith experience within the Christian community than a fact of the sort a

---

[45]Gilkey, *ME*, 113, 164.

[46]Gilkey, *ME*, 189.

[47]Gilkey, *TT*, 104. The essay from which this quotation is taken, "The Meaning of Jesus the Christ," was written in 1986–1987 and published in *The Christ and the Bodhisattva*, ed. Donald S. Lopez, Jr. and Stephen C. Rockefeller (Albany NY: SUNY Press, 1987) 193-207. What is interesting is that these comments are made some time after Gilkey's "sharp turn." In context, he is arguing for a Christian view that affirms the world; and so, clearly, the point is that Jesus, like the Bodhisattva in Mahayana Buddhism, was one who, manifesting spiritual perfection or enlightenment, compassion-ately sought the salvation of others. "In him what is taken to be the highest human possibility appears in fulfillment, in actuality. What we only might be has in him become, an existence fully like ours but without distortion, frustration, meaninglessness, hostility, and destructiveness that dominate our own lives and tear us apart from ourselves and from one another. Jesus represents, therefore, *true humanity, essential humanity,* or *authentic humanity....*Thus he represents not only a final definition of human perfection, although he does.... But, even further, he represents hope, a real possibility for this life unknown and unrealized by us before." Indeed, Gilkey argues, "All of this dissipates if the historical actuality of Jesus dissolves. ... How this historical actuality is either established or defended is a complex matter; but its centrality is undoubted" (Gilkey, *TT*, 103-105). The insistence on the moral and religious perfection of Jesus has apparently survived the "sharp turn." See also the same emphasis much earlier in his work: Langdon Gilkey, *Naming the Whirlwind: The Renewal of God-Language* (Indianapolis: Bobbs-Merrill, 1969) 380-81, 457-58; hereafter cited as *NW*.

modern secular historian could underwrite by investigating the New Testament documents. It is a *kerygmatic* fact which, to use Schubert Ogden's suggestion, is existential-historical in character, not empirical-historical.[48]

What then is the *terminus ad quem* of the essentially neoorthodox and hence implicitly liberal trajectory of Gilkey's theology prior to the 1980s? It is clear that the publication of *Message and Existence* marks the end of a theological era for him. In that book, he recalls, "the effort to articulate . . . a 'revised Christian theology,' on the basis of the method of phenomenological prolegomenon and existential correlation—ordinary experience providing the ultimacy, the crisis of anxiety, and so the 'question,' and the reinterpreted theological symbol providing the answer—was continued (and concluded)."[49] What was concluded, and in what sense? If it still remains true for him—and I believe it does—that Christology must be understood as "the center of Christian witness and understanding," where "each mode of life and obligation, each rite and each institutional form, and each pattern of thought and hope must be justified and molded by reference to this figure," how can this now be done since, after the sharp turn, we can no longer speak as if Jesus of Nazareth as the Christ represents "the definitive and decisive event of revelation in which God's power, will, and ultimate purposes are manifested in a unique way to human beings?"[50]

---

[48]Schubert Ogden, *The Point of Christology* (New York: Harper & Row, 1982) 39-40. Gilkey's *kerygmatic* intentions notwithstanding, I find his emphasis on the human moral and social perfection of Jesus unconvincing as both historical and theological arguments. In some ways, it is a holdover from liberal views of Jesus at the turn of the century, and it is found in evangelical circles expressed in the same language, though for different theological reasons. Both perspectives, however, suffer from the same very questionable assumption, which is, in Ogden's words, that "Jesus is understood to be God for us, finally, because, unlike us, he perfectly actualized the possibility of authentic faith and love" (Schubert Ogden, "The Point of Christology," *Journal of Religion* 55 [October 1975]: 390). Gilkey articulates a form of "consciousness Christology" which he has agreed cannot be provided by modern historical inquiry. It is not that Gilkey thinks Jesus' moral perfection makes him God, but that without it he could not be Savior as the Christ. For more on this issue as central in many attempts to develop modern "revisionist" Christologies, see the following: Ogden, "Point of Christology"; idem, *The Point of Christology*; and James Yerkes, *The Christology of Hegel* (Albany NY: SUNY Press, 1983) 219-26.

[49]Gilkey, "Retrospective Glance at My Work," 26.

[50]Gilkey, *ME*, 158-59. It is clear that Gilkey saw this Christological exposition as fulfilling the commitment made in *Reaping the Whirlwind*: "The author must freely

As we proceed to answer this question, we need to be very clear about the rather careful logic by which Gilkey has understood his task as a Christian theologian. From the beginning of his career, Gilkey insisted that "Christianity is credible only as a *total* system of symbols," and that Christology as a doctrinal symbol—eidetically, hermeneutically, and ontologically interpreted—organizes the religious hermeneutic of the whole system.[51] This total system of Christian symbols, as we noted before, can be shown to be credible—though not provable in a philosophical sense—in such a way "that a Christian interpretation provides a clearer, more illuminative, and more complete access to the full character of personal and historical experience than any other viewpoint."[52] Christian symbols express the way in which ultimacy forms and manifests itself for us as Christians. They name the totality and mystery in which we exist and "only in the event of Jesus as the Christ," as we saw, "is clarity with regard to ultimacy manifest."[53] Further, "the uniqueness claimed by traditional Christianity for its founder as the unique and irreplaceable locus of special divine activity" is "the central and ultimate Kairos of a history made up of unique particulars."[54]

Review of Gilkey's trajectory through 1979 allows us to set the stage for a discussion of the methodological proposal that he articulates as his "sharp turn" in facing the issue of the plurality of religions. We need to understand carefully what has changed and what has remained the same in his theological perspective as it affects Christology. And so we can do no better now than to turn to his own more recent reflections on theological method to pursue that distinction.

---

admit—what will be evident to many readers—that in these few pages no fully conceived, worked out, or adequately documented Christology is presented. The present volume is on history and providence, and . . . as neither can be understood without Christology, Christology appears—but in markedly inadequate form. . . . Hopefully a more adequate presentation will appear in the future, and one enough in line with what is here sketched out so as not to be embarrassing" (Gilkey, *RW*, 421n.85). It was consistent, but in a form over against which Gilkey makes his "sharp turn."

[51]Gilkey, *SAS*, 28. For example, "The doctrine of creation . . . is a 'Christological' doctrine through and through, and must always be understood in the closest relation to what we know of God in Christ" (Gilkey, *MHE*, 227).

[52]Gilkey, *SAS*, 39-40.

[53]Gilkey, *CCM*, 93.

[54]Gilkey, *CCM*, 206n.4.

III. The Dialectical Proposal

Gilkey has consistently followed a correlational approach in all of his theological reflections, the correlation of message and existence, of "situational issues . . . in direct relation to all of the major Christian symbols."[55] The "sharp turn" he admits to have taken in connection with the issue of religious pluralism is just another example of this method in action. As a Christian theologian, Gilkey feels compelled to develop a theology of religions because something "situationally" emergent in the cultural experience of the West and in his own personal religious experience is driving toward a crisis of understanding and praxis. In this connection, several items deserve mention.

A. Christianity as a Total System of Symbols

First, as noted previously, "Christianity is credible only as a *total* system of symbols," and Gilkey regularly is at pains to suggest that this conviction accounts for a significant difference between what he calls his own more "relatively jumbled" method and that of both Tracy and Ogden.[56] For Gilkey, the whole structure of constructive theology—the concluding "moment" of his system where "message" and "existence" culminate in a new articulation of faith for a given historical moment—has, as we also just saw, a Christological norm.[57]

This is the case, first, because the *phenomenological* analysis of common human experience and the *ontological* analysis of finite

---

[55]Tracy, "Question of Criteria for Inter-Religious Dialogue," 246.

[56]Gilkey, *RW*, 373n.1; cf. 371n.17; 372n.19; 378n.33.

[57]Thomas E. Hosinksi helpfully describes four moments of Gilkey's theological program: "(1) a phenomenological analysis of common human experience to uncover its religious dimensions (which provides the 'ontic' meaning of Christian symbols); (2) an ontological analysis and argument to establish the theistic implications of the religious dimension of common human experience (which provides the ontological meaning of Christian symbols); (3) a hermeneutical analysis of Christian religious experience, symbols, and tradition to establish the historical and eidetic meanings of Christian symbols, including their meaning for praxis (their ethical and political meanings); and (4) the constructive moment attempting to 'correlate' the Christian symbols with our common human experience" (Thomas E. Hosinksi, "Experience and the Sacred: A Retrospective Review of Langdon Gilkey's Theology," *Religious Studies Review* 11 [July 1985]: 233-34). In judging the validity of the constructive theological proposals, the criteria are to be eidetic fidelity, reflective coherence, and existential appropriateness. These general criteria have remained constant in Gilkey's considerations (see, e.g., Gilkey, *NW*, 460-64).

existence in nature and history remain rationally abstract over against the radical ruptures of sin and evil which characterize that existence. Hence, only with the redemptive experience of grace as New Being, the symbol of which is Jesus understood as the Christ, are those analyses properly appropriated theologically: "Thus the God present in creation and in providence is finally known and finally trusted as redeemer, and life [known and trusted] as meaningful, only when that God is known as redemptive love"—which is precisely what is revealed in Jesus as the Christ.[58]

This Christological emphasis is necessary, second, because Gilkey understands the Christ-event (life, death, and resurrection) to provide a dialectical pattern of development to which all theological reflection and preaching should conform. That dialectic is formally defined as the movement from affirmation, to negation, and then to "a higher reaffirmation that, in overcoming the negative, also transmutes the originating positive." "This dialectic persists," he suggests, "as the fundamental formal structure of Christian symbolism, what it is that is unique to the Christian understanding of reality and existence." Thus, "to reinterpret creatively this fundamental dialectic in and for each age is the major task of theology." Gilkey continues, "I suspect that it is more crucial for a theology, or for preaching, that it is faithful to this dialectic than that it adopt any particular philosophical scheme."[59] Nothing suggests that Gilkey has changed his mind about this.

A Christological emphasis is required, third, because the one key category in Gilkey's theology which has not moved one centimeter off

---

[58]Gilkey, *RW*, 372n.19. Gilkey's argument with Hick and others working toward a new theology of religions derives directly from this assumption about the interlocking relation between Western theism and its inextricable Christological shading. They suggest that we can set aside Christology and Western conceptions of revelation, and work with a purged, more liberal doctrine of God or the Sacred that will meet Eastern objections. No, says Gilkey, "Each system of religious symbols forms a coherent, interrelated whole; and each *Gestalt* of symbols is particular, at variance with, other *Gestalten*. Thus each doctrine or symbol within any given systems differs significantly from analogous symbols in other systems" (Gilkey, "Plurality and Its Theological Implications," 41).

[59]Gilkey, *ME*, 181-84. For a discussion of how one may read G. W. F. Hegel's philosophical attempt to appropriate the reflective meaning of the Christian religion in exactly this manner, see Yerkes, *Christology of Hegel*, 207-19. This is not meant to suggest, of course, that Gilkey is a Hegelian, only that there is a similar recognition that creative reflection follows an existentially dynamic rather than a statically analytic pattern. There must be "movement" in the logic by which reality is understood.

center—from the outset of his more centrist neoorthodoxy after Union Seminary through his more leftist post-death-of-God neoorthodoxy at Chicago—is the doctrine of sin as pervasive existential evil. "The fact of evil," he says, "intervenes both existentially and epistemologically" in our ability to discern the meaning of human existence.[60] In fact, I shall shortly argue that the "sharp turn" that he has taken recently in theology has been away from Christology as the organizing epistemic *dynamic* of his system, to a position where the doctrine of sin fulfills this role. Startling as that proposal may seem, the point here I wish to make is that Gilkey understands deeply—both personally and historically—the irrational rupture which existential evil engenders in the human mind and within human cultures. It is solely because of the radically transforming power of redemption by the love of God in the gift of grace that this power of sin can be broken. That redemptive experience of grace, beyond all expectation because of the radical rupture occasioned by sin and evil, is what allows him in another context to state the Christian theological dialectic epistemically as a movement from rationality to incredibility, and then to credibility.[61] Jesus of Nazareth as the Christ is the "incredible" manifestation of this restorative grace. It is not incidental that, both early and late, Gilkey appeals to Calvin's "spectacles" of God's grace in special revelation through the Holy Spirit to help us "see" what would otherwise appear distorted to unaided human reason.[62]

B. Situational Convictions

The second point to emphasize is that, since the 1970s, two "situational" convictions have continued to focus his attention, even as the earlier neo-orthodox theological trajectory was concluding. These convictions were that western culture "appeared to be more and more in a situation of crisis," as we saw, "a 'Time of Troubles,' " and that "however secular it may still consider itself to be, modern culture continued to be 'religious' in its essential existence."[63] Hence, both new and newly virulent religious and political mythologies—orthodox and unorthodox—have been spawned that appeal to the anxious concerns for personal and historical meaning awakened by these troubles. Both Gilkey's bout with the crea-

---

[60]Gilkey, RW, 372n.19.
[61]Gilkey, SAS, 27-29.
[62]Gilkey, MHE, 236n.24; idem, RW, 431n.16; Gilkey, NRS, 241n.10.
[63]Gilkey, "Retrospective Glance at My Work," 27.

tionists in Little Rock in 1981 and his encounter with new spiritualities in Japan, as well as in this country beginning in 1975, provided him with the new situational realities in experience that fed the momentum for the "sharp turn" toward the liberal side of his intellectual history.[64]

C. Destination of the Turn in a Time of Troubles

So now, finally, where exactly has that turn in a "time of troubles" taken Gilkey? *First*, as mentioned at the outset, to what he calls "the new experience in our time of 'the rough parity' among religions," an experience he says which "came to me with unanswerable certainty."[65] This involves a common consciousness that other religions possess their own spiritual power, their own truth and grace—"and by 'grace' I mean healing power."[66] The direct theological consequence of this awareness is to call in question "the finality and *Einmaligkeit* of the event of Jesus Christ."[67] What previous Christian liberal and neoorthodox theologians, including his teachers Niebuhr and Tillich, accepted as a relativizing of the human responses to final revelation in Jesus as the Christ, now has to

---

[64]Gilkey has written about his role in that historic trial: Langdon Gilkey, *Creationism on Trial: Evolution and God at Little Rock* (San Francisco: Harper & Row, 1985) hereafter cited as *CT*. Gilkey develops the substantive philosophical and religious arguments especially in chaps. 5–8.

[65]Gilkey, "Retrospective Glance at My Work," 32.

[66]Gilkey, "AAR and the Anxiety of Nonbeing," 16. The powerful impression of such an experience is reflected at the precise time of his "sharp turn," in his presidential address to the AAR in 1979. "Each tradition lives on its experience and affirmation of the unique presence of truth and of healing power within its own life; if this experience and this affirmation dissipate, the tradition dies. . . . Anyone who encounters another religion in and through those of its members who genuinely and creatively embody that tradition can hardly claim any longer that his or her tradition alone possesses truth or healing power. And yet precisely for the reason that it has been through the medium of their tradition that those persons can be seen to embody truth and grace is their own stance not merely a relativistic one. In their very embodiment, and as the *condition* or *possibility* of that embodiment, they stand *there*, in *that* tradition, undergirded by that form of consciousness, and understanding themselves and their world through that set of symbolic forms. In encountering us so powerfully, they do not leave or desert their tradition, lest their embodiment of it cease" (Gilkey, "AAR and the Anxiety of Nonbeing," 15-16).

[67]Gilkey, "AAR and the Anxiety of Nonbeing," 16. Gilkey poses the options faced at this point quite succinctly: "are these two components of the religious—truth and grace—then present in *all* traditions; or are they present in *none*—and so present only in a humanistic, nonreligious culture—or are they present in *all*, but *more* so in one than in the others?" (Gilkey, "AAR and the Anxiety of Nonbeing," 16).

be extended to the event of Jesus as the Christ itself. "They had no sense of the relativity of that revelation or event of revelation among other revelations. . . . It is not just our response to revelation that is relative; it is the revelation to which we are responding that is now roughly equal to others."[68] The dilemma here is that "every faith proceeds theologically on the basis of some central starting point, from which all else is viewed and understood. For Christians, this is the event of Jesus Christ," which now has to be relativized in relation to God's revealing activity in the world and throughout history.[69] This judgment, however, is democratic: it applies to "any philosophy" or "any theology," including those of the East.[70]

There seems to be no firm ground to stand on, either in a given tradition and its symbols, or in religious experience and its various aspects. And note, this

---

[68]Gilkey, *TT*, 31. This is one of Gilkey's generalizations that I find impossible to accept. He suggests that they really did not, as he and we now do, truly understand and see the profound problems of cultural and historical relativity, including that of the West. To say that Tillich and Niebuhr, among others named, were really *blind* to and "had *no* sense of" the relativity in *all* epistemic judgments, including religious ones shaped in the West, is to claim a point of elevated "gnosis" for our present which not only seems unfair but inaccurate. One can surely argue that, yes, "each of them saw clearly the dialectic of infinity and manifestation, of absolute and relative, of unconditioned mystery and conditional meaning" and that they perhaps, "true to their cultural and religious epoch, saw their own particularity, their concrete scheme of meaning . . . as somehow privileged, as final, as less relative, as the clue to the mystery that transcended it." But to say that, as Western thinkers, "this defies an awareness of the plurality and relativity of all cultures," including the "plurality and relativity of religions" (Gilkey, "Plurality and Its Theological Implications," 48) begs the question. They saw the problem clearly, as I read them, but did not choose to elevate the dilemma to a solution. After all, skepticism and relativity is not all that new. Plato and Aristotle struggled with Pyrrho, Protagoras, and Gorgias of Leontini. And Augustine struggled with the "Academicians" led by Carneades. It is not that these theologians and philosophers literally did not *see* the options of total agnosticism or parity of truth claims; it is just that they did not accept their relativistic implications, if for no other reason than that to claim "there is no universal standpoint" presumes a universal standpoint. It would be rude to suggest that Gilkey does not understand this. As a superb historian of theology, he does understand, and he is honest enough to own that this is a conceptual struggle which continues to go on in him. What is being questioned here is his claim that, because Niebuhr and Tillich did not choose the more relativistic position of parity, they either did not or could not *see* the problem epistemically as we now do.

[69]Gilkey, *TT*, 31.

[70]Gilkey, "Plurality and Its Theological Implications," 48.

is *real* relativism: if they are relativized, God, Christ, grace and salvation, higher consciousness, *dharma*, nirvana, and mukti alike begin to recede in authority, to take on the aspect of mere projections relative to the cultural and individual subjectivity of the projectors, and so in the end they vanish like bloodless ghosts.[71]

Theologically, the turn seems to be into a blind alley.

Second, the turn is toward the fearful recognition of the social dangers in this sort of epistemic pluralism. If it promotes ecumenical toleration, it also tends to paralyze moral action and to encourage the demonically intolerable elements of both religion and politics so regularly evident in human history. From the beginning, Gilkey has argued that there is an awareness of ultimacy latent in all human experience that will not be denied attention, so that, if the human spirit will not find a secure resting place for the hopes and fears of its common life in a sacred reality beyond itself, it will *create* the idols necessary to serve its own greedy and oppressive interests. Hence, in order to resist such political and cultural idolatries, we must have some place nonrelative to stand, some values to affirm without qualification.

> That is, we must assert some sort of ultimate values. . . . And to assert our ultimate value or values is to assert a "world," a view of all reality. For each affirmed political, moral, or religious value presupposes a certain understanding of humankind, society, and history, and so a certain understanding of the whole in which they exist. . . . Consequently, any practical political action, in resistance to tyranny or in liberation from it, presupposes ultimate values, an ultimate vision of things, an ethic and so a theology.[72]

But how can one do this personally and socially without a nonrelative, fixed, "absolute" place to stand, without a criterion by which to distinguish between the sheep and the goats, the possessing demons and the angels of mercy? Another blind alley seems to appear.

Gilkey's theological solution is well known and it is as simple as it is ingenious and surprising: we proceed with a praxis which allows us room for an epistemic dialectic of relative absoluteness: "A dialectic or paradox combining and interweaving both one part absoluteness and two parts relativity, a *relative absoluteness*, represents a posture essential to

---

[71]Gilkey, "Plurality and Its Theological Implications," 43-44.
[72]Gilkey, "Plurality and Its Theological Implications," 45.

public and political praxis, again whether humanistic or theological."[73] Here he appeals to the American intellectual tradition of John Dewey and William James in terms of pragmatic procedure, and to Paul Ricoeur in terms of an enacted wager.[74] What thinking cannot do in advance of a resolution—that is, solve the intellectual paradox here—can be done in the lived experience of cooperative dialogue and action: "What to reflection is a contradiction, to praxis is a workable dialectic," so "reflection must not, because it cannot, precede praxis; on the contrary, it must be begun on the basis of praxis. The basic principle of such a theory is that what is necessary to praxis is also necessary for reflection and theory—though the reverse is not true."[75] This is the task, as we noted earlier, which Gilkey says requires "speculative courage."[76]

In specifically religious dialogue, this means that we do not cease to be, or try not to be, Christian by relinquishing our own standpoint or starting point, i.e., our commitment to Jesus as the Christ, as one among many revelations of the Sacred. Rather, in this dialectic of the infinite and finite, one insists that the absolute *is* present, but *relatively* present in the relative and particular. "The relative here participates in and manifests the absolute. As relative it thus negates and transcends itself."[77]

A symbol or a criterion points beyond itself and criticizes itself if it would not be demonic: but it also points to itself and through itself if it would not

---

[73]Gilkey, "Plurality and Its Theological Implications," 47; also see idem, "Events, Meaning and the Current Tasks of Theology," 730; idem, *TT*, 191-93; idem, "Pluralism of Religions," 120. The discussion of this constructive proposal is nearly word-for-word identical in the concluding section of the essays from both 1985 and 1987.

[74]Gilkey, "Events, Meaning and the Current Tasks of Theology," 728-29. Paul Ricoeur says that the hermeneutic of symbols performed by the philosopher requires that one "wager" his or her "belief and . . . lose or win the wager by putting the revealing power of the symbol to the test of self-understanding." One wagers and then tries to verify the wager by "saturating it, so to speak, with intelligibility" (Paul Ricoeur, *The Symbolism of Evil*, trans. Emerson Buchanan [Boston: Beacon, 1967] 308, 355). Gilkey seems to have some such similar intention in his dialectical proposal for reflection about a "relative absolute," an attempt to experience a kind of postcritical "second naiveté," a critical point of view "no longer reductive, but restorative" (Ricoeur, *Symbolism of Evil*, 350-52). As James puts it, however, the wager is forced—that is, if one is to do theology today in serious interreligious dialogue, Gilkey argues that one must wager that dialectic and paradox will assist reason to modify and/or clarify its function.

[75]Gilkey, "Plurality and Its Theological Implications," 47.

[76]Gilkey, "AAR and the Anxiety of Nonbeing," 15.

[77]Gilkey, "Plurality and Its Theological Implications," 49.

be empty, and if we would not be left centerless. The dialectic works both ways; relativizing the manifestation of the absolute, and yet manifesting as well through the relative an absoluteness that transcends it—else again there be no liberating praxis and no creative reflection possible.[78]

Clearly, this is precisely the dialectic of the symbol of New Being which Tillich articulated, a symbol that "negates itself without losing itself," and which Gilkey exegetes so cogently and splendidly.[79] Gilkey is at pains, however, to suggest that even here Tillich's concept of Jesus as "*the* clue" to the divine mystery, which nonetheless transcends his life and death as the embodiment of New Being, is a function of "a Western logos, and this defies an awareness of the plurality and relatively of cultures."[80]

IV. A Critical Evaluation

In two key essays, Gilkey makes suggestive proposals about how a Christian theologian might try with this dialectic, especially in the context of Eastern traditions, to think about the reality of God: God-as-symbol mystery, God as *agapé* in Christological terms, and thus God as redemptive power and promise.[81] At this point, however, the need to evaluate these proposals Christologically interests me. What is abidingly valuable and religiously problematic about his theological proposal as we head into the next century? Is such a Christological proposal adequate for Christian praxis in such a "time of troubles"?

The first comment must emphasize that Gilkey's sense of the incipient decline of the West is deep and tinged with a hint of apocalyptic warning. And this experiential sensitivity, as our present existential situation, sets the correlational context for his theological rethinking of the Christian message. The strict correlation that he repeatedly draws between the imperialism of Western powers and the imperialism of Western thought—scientific, political, economic, religious, and philosophical—shows how his theological reflections in recent years hug the shore of this

---

[78]Gilkey, "Events, Meaning and the Current Tasks of Theology," 732.

[79]Paul Tillich, *Systematic Theology*, vol. 1 (Chicago: University of Chicago Press, 1951) 133, see also 135-37; Gilkey, *GOT*, 154-57.

[80]Gilkey, "Plurality and Its Theological Implications," 48.

[81]Gilkey, "Events, Meaning and the Current Tasks of Theology," 732-34; idem, "Plurality and Its Theological Implications," 49-50. Gilkey's later studies fill out this basic agenda: Gilkey, *TT*; idem, *NRS*.

cultural sensitivity so closely. The strong winds blowing from offshore toward his "small sloop named 'Dialogue' " portend a difficult sail ahead.[82]

Perhaps others are like me. I have the eerie feeling that, one hundred years from now, theological students and pastors may be reading Gilkey, as Augustine was read by the Popes in Rome and Kierkegaard by Barth. Granted, as Gilkey strongly emphasizes, there are also life-affirming possibilities and creative surprises that are always ingredient in such momentous cultural transitions. A religion like Christianity, built on the *agapé* of God, cannot be hopeless; and Gilkey's theology is so built. There is no whine of despair here. Human freedom makes possible deviations from fates which may at some moments seem ineluctable. Still, illustrations of past historical catastrophes and biblical examples of judgment move like waves of distant thunder throughout these later writings. A cultural storm is gathering in the West and no other living theologian, I think, has made the point so convincingly.

This calls for a second comment. It has to do with Gilkey's attitude toward the Enlightenment. On the one hand, he states quite clearly that the Enlightenment was one among many cultural *Weltanschauungen*, the insights of which must now be recognized as relative and particular, along with the relativity of religious claims to universal significance. This is the basis of his critique of the "Western" Christological inclusivism in both liberal and neoorthodox theologies, which draw so heavily on the self-indulgent Enlightenment frame of mind. On the other hand, some valid insights abide, of course, such as Lessing's Enlightenment dictum "that from a historical event, no universal proposition can be derived." Gilkey notes, "we can't live without assenting to the validity" of such insights.[83]

But this dependence is selective, given different interests. Early liberals were taken in by the naïve assumption of cultural progress, energized by critical reason applied in the sciences and historical inquiry. The neoorthodox, children of the two world wars, were less sanguine about cultural progress because of the personal, social, and epistemic reality of sin; but they did agree that the relativizing deliverances of modern historical inquiry required a rethinking of the role of biblical authority, both for personal faith and for the authority of fixed (read

---

[82]Gilkey, "Theological Voyage with Wilfred Cantwell Smith," 298.
[83]Gilkey, "Theology and Culture," 7.

"orthodox") creeds in the life of the church. Gilkey was the child of this neoorthodox child of liberalism.

Quite clearly, further, Gilkey presumes as self-evident that certain values affirmed by Enlightenment *political* reason remain not only valid, but one might also say sacrosanct. Indeed, when he argues that pluralism's shadowside in the emergence of demonic forms of political and religious life must be resisted, he insists that, as a counterbalance, "we must assert some sort of ultimate values . . . in this case, the values of persons and their rights, and correspondingly, the value of the free, just, and equal community."[84] At the occasion organized to celebrate his life and thought, when he was about to retire from the University of Chicago Divinity School, he observed about some of the continuity in his thought that "the defense of autonomy—the autonomy of culture and of the person—has been a consistent theme." Indeed, he went on to say, "I came to the realization a few years ago that—although I had been extremely critical of the Enlightenment for very good reasons—if I were to go out into the streets for anything, it would be for an Enlightenment idea, and that I had better wake up to that fact."[85]

Here is the point to consider: on what epistemic grounds does one choose as valid the insights of any cultural epoch—the Enlightenment, our own, or any other? For example, if Lessing and the Enlightenment announce "that from a historical event, no universal proposition can be derived," is *that* then a judgment that is universally true and not culturally relative? How does one know that to be true without qualification? Furthermore, why are not the values of "persons and their rights" and of a "free and equal community" also simply Enlightenment, Western, and relative? Is our investment in *those* values—and I candidly admit along with Gilkey that those are values for which I think *I*, *too*, could go to the barricades—not subject to the critique that they are merely and peculiarly Western? What if other cultures, let us say in the East, tend to feel quite differently about the universal value of free, just, and equal communities, of the autonomy of culture and of the person? And what if religions instantiated in those cultures insist that the revelation of their founding event requires social values which move in quite the opposite direction? That, of course, Gilkey himself chillingly demonstrates has happened. How does one know which values the Absolute, the Sacred, the

---

[84]Gilkey, "Plurality and Its Theological Implications," 45.
[85]Gilkey, "Theology and Culture," 3.

Surrounding Mystery prefers and supports if one *in advance* of critical reflection accords status of parity for all traditions? How *could* one know that, unless one already knew, at least implicitly, the conditions of what would count for or against the truth of the Absolute? Perhaps one needs to pursue that adjective "*rough* parity." How does one know epistemically what outside the "rough" does not count as parity?[86] Put yet another way, by what criteria other than the Enlightenment *political* values of the

---

[86]Gilkey's use of the term "parity" in different contexts is puzzling. On the one hand, he says the following about the concept of parity. "Certainly this is neither an empirical nor a theoretical judgment of equality, the equality of all religions or standpoints. Such a judgment would require a criterion of religions that itself transcends all of them. . . . No, by parity we suggest not an assessment of all relevant religions but what is called an 'heuristic principle': a method of *approach* to the other religions, a way of meeting them and relating to them. It abjures and denies the claim—which, though diplomatically repressed, is frequently present—of superiority, the quiet confidence of the hidden possessor of an absolute standpoint, and with it a tolerant but secure certainty that one really understands the other on one's own terms better than they understand themselves on their terms" (Gilkey, "Pluralism of Religions," 115). Here "parity" as heuristic refers to a technique taken in dialogue which provides direction in the solving of a problem, but which is otherwise unjustified. Parity is here an *attitude* by which one enters dialogue. Sometimes he just emphasizes that we *experience* these religions as parity—it is a matter of cultural and historical self-evidence in our time and this is what calls for the new attitude (Gilkey, "AAR and the Anxiety of Nonbeing," 15-16; idem, "Retrospective Glance at My Work," 30-33). On the other hand, Gilkey clearly does employ the term in a way by which it serves as a theoretical criterion of judgment, indeed one which involves "revelational authority": "Rough parity is loath to claim definitive, final, and absolute validity and efficacy for our own [religion]; our religion, even our revelation, does not define what is true and of value in theirs" (Gilkey, *TT*, 182). So, "a theologically based theodicy," such as he had written in *RW*, "is challenged at the very center of its authority by recognition of parity with other modes of revelation or—as in Buddhism and most of Hinduism—other modes of religious consciousness in which ultimate reality is encountered and by which it is known" (Gilkey, *TT*, 186). Here parity does involve an epistemic judgment. It does indeed seem to be "a theoretical judgment of equality" about revelational authority. What else would it mean to say, "our religion, even our revelation, does not define what is true and of value in theirs"? How can the parity here be only about claims and not a matter of substance? Moreover, if parity were not intended to be so interpreted, why does Gilkey regularly associate claims to parity with the issue of relativism in judgments about founding events in religion, and then immediately speak of the need for a new Christological reformulation in which its revelational "finality" is denied (see Gilkey, "Plurality and Its Theological Implications," 40-41; idem, *TT*, 31)? My fundamental disagreement with Gilkey is not that I think he assumes all foundational events are equal, but that he assumes *ab initio* that none could be, or be assessed, more revealing of the Sacred than another.

autonomy of culture and personal freedom, which he implies are universally valid, does one know how to identify what is the "one part absolute" from the "two parts relative" in claims made about founding events and religious traditions?[87]

A point to be pondered in this connection is that, from what I can see, many leaders of other religious traditions with whom one experiences the genuine spiritual power of "truth and grace" usually have had significant educational exposure to Western ideas, either in Western cultural contexts or through Western literature—a reverse cultural perspective, I am embarrassed to note, not true of most clergy and theologians in the West.[88] I have wondered, at times, if perhaps it is in part or in significant measure *because of* and not *in spite of* some Western ideas and ideals that they are as open religiously and politically as they are. Lest that sound unbearably chauvinistic, I certainly must add that many striking modifications in Western values regarding the environment, animal rights, personal health, and communal obligations are owed to the corrective insights derived from Eastern and Native American religious traditions. Western ideas and values must never be uncritically idolized, but they should at least be allowed democratic footing among historical contenders in the moral and religious quest for truth. Gilkey says relatively little about this issue.

My point is to question whether Lessing's Enlightenment dictum, "that from a historical event, no universal proposition can be derived," is necessarily true. What if history is the cumulative cultural process through which humanity painfully winnows through to some *virtually* universal propositions? Why may one not argue, with the help, say, of Hegel's master/slave dialectic, that our moral and religious awareness is not at all developed on a purely individual or ahistorical basis. This view would insist that it requires the give and take of human moral and religious transactions over time, within the broad range of other forms of

---

[87]See Gilkey, "Events, Meaning and the Current Tasks of Theology," 730; idem, "Plurality and Its Theological Implications," 47; Walsh, *Langdon Gilkey*, 165-67.

[88]I believe this judgment about Eastern religious leaders is true of Gilkey's dialogue partner, Buddhist Professor Takeuchi Yoshinori in Japan; and it is certainly true of the Dalai Lama. One also thinks of Mohondas Gandhi. Fortunately, Gilkey, John Cobb, Jr., John Hick, Paul Knitter, Schubert Ogden, David Tracy, Huston Smith, and Wilfred Cantwell Smith—some who come quickly to mind—are the grand exceptions to this Western problem.

knowledge in cultural history, to shape and sharpen our collective moral and religious sensitivity. This is how one might explain why the emancipation of slaves and the liberation of women appear "later" in our common history. Other things simply had to happen first. Reflective method in determining truth is certainly not static. As Bernard Lonergan observes, "The wheel of method not only turns, but also rolls along."[89]

And this is why—*very* carefully qualified—one could even argue that there is, in fact, moral and religious progress, as well as positive moral and religious evolution, in cultural history, a development in our awareness about what constitutes a more mature and expanded moral responsibility among human beings. This way of understanding moral and religious development is what makes cross-cultural criticism possible— and necessary. It explains *why* Gilkey feels, quite properly I believe, that some Enlightenment political ideals *are* indeed sacrosanct. I believe that a credible argument can be mounted to suggest that humans possess an innate sense for truth, moral and religious—an intuition of a "horizon" to our consciousness which both grounds and evokes our sense of uncondi- tional moral and religious obligation.[90] But, like Kant's categories of the understanding and Chomsky's linguistic universals, this sense for truth remains a potential awareness until sensory and cultural experience, individually and as a species, activates its discriminatory powers. I am more inclined to speak of an emergent consensus of *universal principles of judgment* rather than *universal truths*, principles of insight concerning what now seem *virtually* settled conclusions—something like a high-level scientific theory, which is not at all absolute, but the best consensus of responsible and respected persons to date, given the information one has available. Furthermore, like Lonergan, I believe that such intellectual conversion is both possible and necessary in all truth seeking over time.[91]

The difference between this point of view and Gilkey's is that universal principles of truth are *emergent through history not*, as Lessing announced, *forever obstructed because of history*. Such principles are not delivered once and for all by some authoritative fiat, religious or political. They emerge through the tortured travails and inexplicable ecstasies of human cultural history, including religious history. Moreover, some events are more crucially determinative of the resultant insights than

---

[89]Bernard Lonergan, *Method in Theology* (New York: Herder and Herder, 1972) 5.
[90]Lonergan, *Method in Theology*, 235-53.
[91]Lonergan, *Method in Theology*, 130-32.

others. So I cannot see why it is epistemically improper to suggest that some religious revelatory events are more determinative of universally true religious insights, beliefs, and praxis, than are others: say, maybe, Jesus of Nazareth whom some people call the Christ; maybe the Buddha; maybe Moses; maybe Muhammad. Time may tell more clearly. Reasons can be discussed. In addition, this view does not presume ever upward, ever onward cultural progress led by the West. If one may judge from what Hegel called "the slaughter bench of history," there will always be abject and abundant cultural tragedies in our human future. What impressed Hegel about all this carnage, he said, was not the repeated fall of empires to moral, political, and religious corruption, but the fact that new empires continue, in moral hope, to arise.

The problem with Gilkey's view is that, based on genuinely wonderful personal relationships with those committed to other religious revelational centers, he simply announces that all revelatory claims *are* of roughly equal validity. I have wonderful personal relationships, nevertheless, with persons who hold and teach foundational ideas and values that I consider to be incorrect. They *might* be correct, but deciding that would require the very kind of personal dialogue—perhaps over our lifetimes and by others beyond our lifetimes—which Gilkey correctly argues to be so essential in all truth seeking. To make Gilkey's epistemic claim stick, which claim denies that any revelatory event could actually be arguably demonstrated a better religious clue than some other, one would already have to know, at least implicitly, what the character of the Absolute is and thus why each event is in some way deficient.

There is a final point. I do not see why the inclusivist position of any religion, East or West, is necessarily imperialistic. There are ways such positions *can* be, and *have* been, so expressed.[92] For most of us in the

---

[92]On this matter, I am persuaded by a position that Schubert Ogden has recently articulated. He has proposed a distinction between "monistic" and "pluralistic" inclusivism, with correlatively quite different Christologies. The former implies that Christianity requires one to hold that the event of Jesus as the Christ uniquely *constitutes* the conditions for developing the criterion of formal validity for authentic religious witness, whereas the latter understands the event of Jesus as the Christ to *represent* the conditions of such truth. As he nicely puts it, "All that one has to affirm . . . is that there *can* be other religious traditions that are formally valid, even if it should turn out, as a matter of fact, that Christianity is the only such tradition there is." The Christ-event in such a pluralistic inclusivism "serves to declare a possibility of salvation that is already a possibility prior to the event's occurring to declare it" (Schubert Ogden, "Some

Western Christian tradition, however, commitment to Jesus as the Christ simply means, this is the best, even if also sometimes the only, satisfying clue to religious truth we have so far found. We are not imperialistically closed. We are not overly concerned about who will get the brass ring on the historical merry-go-round of world religions, since we are at this point convinced by Jesus of Nazareth that God saves by unmerited grace and not by intellectual works. Gilkey explained this point well in the liberal inheritance. Honesty also requires us to admit, however, that, if there is not much to fear at the final judgment in this regard, there is much to fear in the decisions of history when moral claims are at stake. Gilkey makes this very clear, too. But the praxis issue, as far as I am concerned, is not that no one knows what is *absolutely* true from the standpoint of God, but how one may determine what is a *relatively better* moral or religious judgment than some proposed alternative. In classes of philosophical ethics, students often ask me: "Who are you to judge?" My reply is, "Who else in history besides us humans *is* there to judge?"[93]

Our task in history is to be as *relatively* correct as we can be given the information and skills that we possess, not to claim to be *absolutely* right about anything, including religion. Nonetheless, we are obliged to be as correct as we can be through the kind of dialogue that Gilkey urges. Appeals to disciplined reason and the deliverances of common human experience seem to me to be the minimal criteria that we have for such dialogue, each sharing religiously what feels genuinely true and each listening for what can purify, enlarge, or replace what already had been thought to be so. This seems to be the commonsense epistemic point of George Fox's answer to William Penn, when Penn, son of an English admiral, asked if he should continue to wear a sword. Pacifist Fox's reply was, "Wear it as long as you can."

Thoughts on a Christian Theology of Interreligious Dialogue," *Criterion* 33 [Winter 1994]: 8-9). I subscribe to the latter position. Thus, my point here is that there is no necessary imperialism of mind at all in assuming that one's own tradition meets the formal criteria for authentic religious witness, even if one is clear that this awareness of such a witness was in fact mediated by that tradition, rather than another, and that one's own tradition is judged to stand closer to that awareness than do other traditions.

[93]The event which sealed this point of view for me, in an unforgettable way, was when Judge Clarence Thomas told Senator Joseph Biden that the hearing prompted by Anita Hill was just another "nigger lynching" and concluded his protest by stating, "God is my judge, Senator Biden." Biden calmly and wisely replied, "Well, Mr. Thomas, I presume that is true for all of us. But that is not why we are here."

Let us be clear here. Gilkey presumes divine revelation is *universal*, as is salvation, and both are based in the *agapé* of a God seeking to be present to and the redeemer of humankind in all religious traditions. What is denied is that there can be true judgments in history about which revelational center in religion is clearer or in some sense normative. Further, he is not denying, at least as I read him, that *for Christians* all theological judgments regarding Christianity's doctrinal symbols should retain a Christological ordering. What he is denying "at the moment" or "in our time" is that theological judgments made by any religious traditions have demonstrable validity concerning the mystery of the Sacred outside those traditions.[94] Is *this* judgment, however, really compatible with one of the three key criteria of Christian theology, namely, Gilkey's insistence that doctrines must be eidetically faithful to biblical tradition? Could Jesus be the *biblical* Christ on Gilkey's terms? Even granted certain necessary hermeneutical difficulties and loopholes, there are real problems that require systematic clarification.[95]

Let me stop this train of thought here to emphasize the basic methodological point behind my critique. It is one thing to be personally committed to a revelational event as such an epistemic Archimedean point, and another thing to discuss the possible grounds of its formal validity as a criterion for all religious truth claims. Rather than declare at the outset, as does Gilkey, that all claims *are* equally valid—and how could one *know* that for sure unless, as we noted earlier, it were at least already implicitly understood what such validity must entail—why not insist that one may enter dialogue with the conviction that all claims to validity, including one's own, must be worked out in the context of rational appeals to common human experience at all epistemic levels in cultural history? For example, Schubert Ogden observes, "Christians today can, and should, frankly acknowledge that the only way in which

---

[94]Gilkey, "Plurality and Its Theological Implications," 47; idem, *TT*, 192.

[95]Examples of the way Gilkey now presents his Christological position follow. "Perhaps all we can say is that Christ reveals the mystery of God, a mystery that transcends, though it does not negate, even the clarity and reliability of what is even there manifest. But that sense of the mystery of the divine beyond all we can say or know is hardly as new as it sounds" (Gilkey, *TT*, 113). Again, "Christians know that in and through Christ we experience the truth, and yet there are other truths; that the revelation we live from is a true revelation, and yet there are others" (Gilkey, "Pluralism of Religions," 121). One notes the change from "the truth" to "a true revelation," intending to signal the dialectic of the relative ("a") absolute ("the").

they can continue to be Christians at all is to accept the possibility, and the risk, of ceasing to be such in face of experiences and reasons that, on the whole, tend to invalidate their claim instead of validating it."[96] My basic disagreement with Gilkey can be framed in the following way: To enter religious dialogue without the assumption of unquestioned *a priori* superiority is not the same as saying that the event on which we base our religious commitment is therefore or necessarily relative. I believe that Gilkey consistently collapses this distinction and, thus, confuses the epistemic question.

Gilkey wants to argue that so circular are all value judgments in the context of human discourse, religious and otherwise, that such hope in critical judgment is bound to founder: but founder because of limitations of finitude or sin? Is this our situation only "at the moment" or is it permanent? Read in one way, his argument about relativity between cultural systems reduces to the view that the problem is finitude.[97] There *cannot* be cultural transcendence for anyone, ever—or at least as far as we now can see. Every person, theologian or politician, is ineluctably imprisoned in her or his own cultural conditioning and limited powers of reason. I would argue, however, that such a position seems at odds with the way by which, in fact, a partial transcendence of human understanding and reason makes possible not only linguistic, literary, scientific, and moral transfer of ideas between cultures, but also engenders interest in

---

[96]Ogden, "Some Thoughts on a Christian Theology of Interreligious Dialogue," 7. Ogden's position on this issue is also very persuasive: "Many argue that one cannot really allow that the other's religious tradition can be valid without conceding that one's own tradition is somehow incomplete or defective, in need of completion or complementation by the other's. . . . But just as I do not have to grant that the other's tradition is valid in order to allow for its possible validity, so I do not have to grant that there must be something invalid or otherwise amiss in my own tradition in order to make the same allowance. All I have to do is to allow that the other's claims to validity are as deserving of validation as mine are and that my own claims to validity are as much in need of being validated as are the claims of the other" (Ogden, "Some Thoughts on a Christian Theology of Interreligious Dialogue," 7). By validity, he means "formal validity" in contrast to "substantial validity": "a religious tradition is substantially valid if, or insofar as, it agrees in substance with every other valid religious tradition. To be formally valid, however, a religious tradition must be a tradition with which every other has to agree in substance if it is to be correctly affirmed to be substantially valid" (Ogden, "Some Thoughts on a Christian Theology of Interreligious Dialogue," 6).

[97]Gilkey, "Pluralism of Religions," 116.

and respect for "the other" as "the bearer of truth of grace" in religion, as Gilkey puts it.[98]

There is another issue, however. It has to do with what has been called the noetic effect of sin. I suggested earlier that one might be able to argue that the organizing dynamic of Gilkey's theology of religions is now the doctrine of sin and fall rather than Christology. I want to say this *very* carefully so it is understood *only* as a heuristic proposal for understanding the tone and shifted emphases of his more recent reflections. Formally, it is my judgment that he still believes that all specifically Christian doctrinal symbols are Christologically normed. Nevertheless, in his more liberal "sharp turn" through the 1980s, there are major shifts in emphasis which connote, I believe, a major shift in doctrinal presuppositions.

Gilkey's powerful critique of the colonial and intellectual imperialism of the West, for example, displays his critique of abused power and the *hubris* of self-importance. This Western attitude is not, or no longer is, a question of ignorance, but a function of *hubris*. Its political, educational, and scientific energies are fueled with a sense of its own importance and its own destiny as a superior cultural world power. Further, his critique of Western religion is not simply that finite creatures cannot ever encompass the meaning and truth of the transcendentally mysterious infinite, but that the dominant religion of the West—Christianity—has, out of a sense of imperialistic *hubris*, claimed a revelational superiority over other traditions.[99]

So is the epistemic problem finitude or sin? Is it that humans *cannot* transcend their religious particularity, or that they *will not*? A case can be

---

[98]See Gilkey's response to Robin Lovin's similar suggestion. "I agree . . . that analogy is crucial between cultures. Our particular viewpoints are incurably particular. But they are analogous to one another and this, I suggest, is a subject ripe for fruitful reflection in the next years, both in terms of culture and in terms of religion" (Gilkey, "Theology and Culture," 7).

[99]It should be noted here that Gilkey is especially and increasingly critical of the modern university as the place where the *hubris* of the Western presumption of superiority is robustly displayed and deeply ensconced: "The University, although everything within the scope of its inquiries becomes *ipso facto* relative, is not *itself* relative to itself; nor are its methods of inquiry, the ontology they imply, and the values on which all this rests held to be relative." When some day to come *real* relativity hits, he says, "there will be as much excitement and hustle, accompanied by angst (!) . . . as there is beginning to be now in our seminaries and divinity schools" (Gilkey, "Pluralism of Religions," 114, 123).

made for both in Gilkey's theology, and as not necessarily in conflict. After "the turn," however, it more regularly appears to be the sin of *hubris* which causes humans to refuse to acknowledge the relativity of their cultural values and religious claims to uniqueness. This persistent perversity of the human spirit to turn power to ends of unjust self-interest is another truth of "unanswerable certainty" in Gilkey's experience. This emphasis seems to dominate the discussion when he speaks about the way that Christological assumptions must be recast in Western theology. But, to be fair, Gilkey's charge is again democratic. Other religions, including Buddhism and Hinduism, are just as wont to develop an "inclusivist" criterion of truth around their center of revelation.[100] At least the sin of inclusivism seems to be universal! So, behind the sin of inclusivism stands the sin of imperialism, and behind the sin of imperialism stands the noetic disruption caused by *hubris*. This perception, I think, accounts for the theological *energy* behind his new Christological critique. The reflections are *moved* by moral indignation.

In his new emphasis on God's relation to us as more radically immanent, this equation of revelation and salvation, it seems to me, has

Here one still may ask, however, why the imperialist abuses of religious claims to uniqueness authorize one to conclude that all must be assigned a "rough parity" in revelational significance. There is yet another dynamic at work in Gilkey's theology here which bears consideration. His self-acknowledged "movement from radical transcendence and separation—emphasizing the freedom of God—to immanence and the universal presence of the divine" has had a major impact on his theology of religions. The relativizing of the Christ-event is serious theologically, because his view is epistemically skeptical at the center of what is supposed to be normative for all doctrinal judgments. Gilkey has been clear that we need to distinguish between revelation and salvation in God's relationship with humanity. This was *de rigeur* in the theology of most liberals and neoorthodox thinkers, as we noted earlier. In God's freedom to elect, the epistemic center of revelation was Jesus as the Christ, and, in God's freedom to love, all are included in God's redeeming grace. The first was a free act of grace in view of the noetic effect of sin and the second was a free act of grace in view of the priority of mercy over judgment.

In his new emphasis on God's relation to us as more radically immanent, this equation of revelation and salvation, it seems to me, has

---

[100]Gilkey, "Plurality and Its Theological Implications," 41-44.

shifted on both sides in Gilkey's thought. It turns out that God is less able to work around our finitude and freedom to sin, and humanity is more captive to God's limitations owing to that freedom. Paradoxically, as humans become more epistemically capable (able to know for sure what cannot be known and cannot be done), God becomes less soteriologically free (hampered by the intractable limitations of both our finitude and sin).

In other words, strangely enough, one could argue that Gilkey's theology has seemed to move back to the tendencies which crippled the old liberalism theologically. That liberalism was too self-assured in its knowledge about what constituted human limits and possibilities in culture and history—including religion, and too presumptive about the limitations of God's power and purposes in working his redemptive purposes through them. Granted, this *formal* shift in the equation of God's freedom and human powers does not alter Gilkey's clear and continuing *non*liberal *substantive* conviction that the major problem in humanity's relation to God is *not* the limitation of ignorance, which ever more education and moral conditioning can mitigate. Nor is it simply finitude. Rather, it is the more radically disruptive problem of personal and social sin rooted in exploitation and injustice. Gilkey continues firmly to insist that only God's coming to us in grace can redeem us from sin's self-destructive and demonic consequences.

This said, it still seems that the change in this equation of God's freedom and human limitation made it both possible and acceptable for Gilkey to propose the epistemic and thus soteriological relativization of the Christ-event in religious history. The problem is that God for the new, more liberal Gilkey has become too trapped by ontological immanence, just as God for the earlier, more neoorthodox Gilkey was too isolated by radical transcendence. This seems to characterize his sharp turn back toward the liberal side of his intellectual heritage, and, with the radical relativizing of the Christ-event in religious history, it is clear he has gone "a step beyond even that."[101]

These are some of the problems which seem to be at work in both the method and content of Gilkey's Christological position in a "time of troubles." Little has been said about the enormous courage and generosity of spirit with which Gilkey has always worked as a theologian *of*, and not

---

[101]Gilkey, "Retrospective Glance at My Work," 30.

just *in*, the Christian community of faith. He has insisted with typical and brutal honesty that "at the moment," and "stunned" by the impact of this new cultural situation, his proposal for a praxis operating with the epistemic dialectic of "relative absolutism" is simply the only way he sees for going forward in Christian theology.[102] I do not agree that it is the most promising way for reasons I have suggested. Reinhold Niebuhr somewhere once remarked about critics of Tillich's theology, particularly his ontology, that, given the intellectual power he demonstrated in performing such a profoundly creative theological high-wire act, it was not surprising that those who lacked all such skill should attack him. The careful reader will note that my critique has mostly amounted to nay-saying about Gilkey's hardworking and courageous efforts. One may qualm at his own proposal but he is dead right. The cultural and theological issue of plurality in religion cannot be avoided. As his fellow seaman, Updike, well put it, "At all times, an old world is collapsing and a new world arising; we have better eyes for the collapse than the rise, for the old one is the world we know."

Gilkey has always been a master at helping the Church squint through the cultural fog toward a future which cannot be avoided. Nothing has changed, except, of course, that everything has changed. Sextant in hand and charts at ready on the small sloop "Dialogue," he is still trying, indefatigably and faithfully, to help us hug the shore. And The Shore.

---

[102]Gilkey, "Events, Meaning and the Current Tasks of Theology," 730.

Chapter 13

Langdon Gilkey's Theology
of the Servant Church

H. Frederick Reisz, Jr.

Introduction: Voice within the Church

Langdon Gilkey is usually called a "theologian of culture." Is Gilkey's theology, however, "of" or "for" the church in any intentional fashion? At first thought, Gilkey's theology would not be called an "ecclesial theology" in the conventional sense. That label is used often to designate what is really a "denominationally" based theology or a theology specifically written only for Christian believers to clarify their faith. In a real sense, however, Gilkey's theology has been a sustained plea addressed to the Christian church from within the ecumenical Christian church. He has himself defined Christian theology as a theology of and for the church.

> Clearly, first of all, then, theology is a function of the church, of the Christian community. It represents that community's effort to understand itself and its message, to define what it is in the area of belief, of fundamental conviction, that is to say, what basic symbols or sets of symbols constitute that community, that distinguish it from other communities, and that therefore guide and empower its life, its decisions, its actions and policies, and its rites and customs.[1]

Gilkey is a theologian within the tradition, seeking the meaningful communication of that faith in the modern world for the sake of intelligible proclamation, faithful existence, and transformative living toward the community of love.

Certainly, many of Gilkey's works have addressed the secular world, the scientific community, or Western culture in its various manifestations. Some of his writings have been dialogues with other non-Western religions, especially Buddhism. Particularly in the former writings,

---

[1]Langdon Gilkey, "Theology: Interpretation of Faith for Church and World," in *Through the Tempest: Theological Voyages in a Pluralistic Culture*, by Langdon Gilkey, ed. Jeff B. Pool (Minneapolis: Fortress Press, 1991) 38; hereafter cited as *TT*. Gilkey published this essay originally in 1985.

however, there is always the sense that, in part, Gilkey addresses women and men who are scientists and often Christian; women and men who are modern secularists but also historically Christian.

Gilkey reminds us and himself about the relativity of theology to its cultural context, even as it reaches toward universal horizons of meaning. Thus, he is clear about the context from which he writes his own theology. In this cultural sense, Gilkey's theology is Western and Christian, and thus of the Christian church.

In a deeper sense, Gilkey's thought has been a sustained plea for the Christian church to reconceive its religious symbols and theology in the contemporary context and with contemporary terms. From his standpoint within the church, Gilkey has regularly spoken to groups of clergy and laity. He has published, not just in academic journals, but in those journals read by clergy. He has written not a comprehensive "systematic" theology, but one in a form which clergy and laity can read and discuss—most powerfully in his book, *Message and Existence*.[2] In the preface to this book, Gilkey writes that his purpose is "to introduce interested beginners, not into the pursuit of theology as an academic discipline, but into the various views or beliefs about life and destiny held by the community of Christians, that is, into the contents of the Christian faith as it can be understood today."[3] In Gilkey's sustained work on a "prolegomenon" to theology in many books and lectures, he lays a foundation upon which to build his argument that the church and the modern world are not separable realms; rather, the Christian church is a community of modern people. The assumptions, worldview, language, secular symbols, communal associations, culturally bound horizons of the West, and modes of action of the modern twentieth-century West are inescapably part of the mentality and feelings of persons sitting in the pews and preaching from the pulpits of churches. Thus, Gilkey's hermeneutics of the western mentality is at the same time a reading of the congregation. His incisive analyses of finitude, relativity, historical contextuality, contingency, rationality, and the demonic are analyses of modern people who are the church. Gilkey's analyses are not critical bombs lobbed at the world "out there."

---

[2]Langdon Gilkey, *Message and Existence: An Introduction to Christian Theology* (Minneapolis: Seabury Press, 1979); hereafter cited as *ME*.

[3]Gilkey, *ME*, 3.

From one of his earlier works in which he formulates a mission for the Protestant Church, *How the Church Can Minister to the World without Losing Itself*,[4] to a later book suggesting reforms and mission for the Roman Catholic Church, *Catholicism Confronts Modernity: A Protestant View*,[5] Gilkey's theological reflections attempt to show Christian communities how they must reformulate theological conceptions from the tradition into contemporary terms, seriously confront their responsibilities to proclaim and show forth the Holy in the contemporary world, be responsible critics of the ideology of scientific secularism, intelligibly utilize the salient gifts of modernity, and be active communities within the world for the forming of communities of reconciliation and love. The theologian has the task of helping the community through a theology that attempts "to ponder the character of our existence, both personal and historical, before God in the light of the historical and social situation, the massive contours of events in which we find ourselves."[6]

Gilkey was nurtured in a liberal, cultured, academic, Baptist family in Chicago. Gilkey's father, Charles W. Gilkey, was the acclaimed minister of Hyde Park Baptist Church, which functioned as "the" university church. Gilkey has recounted the role of Christianity in his home life and the pietistic practices of his family (Bible reading, prayer) even though they were "liberal." During his college years at Harvard, admittedly not involved in "Chapel" or "church", Gilkey fell into an enchantment with Reinhold Niebuhr's theology after hearing him preach a sermon at Harvard's Memorial Chapel.[7] Gilkey was deepened through reading Niebuhr's theology. After a life-defining experience (for good or ill) in an internment camp in China, Gilkey returned to Union Theological Seminary to study with Niebuhr. Other defining events in his life, by his own summary, include a courageous stand with faculty at Vanderbilt

---

[4]Langdon Gilkey, *How the Church Can Minister to the World without Losing Itself* (New York: Harper & Row, 1964); hereafter cited as *HCCM*. The title of this book illustrates Gilkey's experience with publishers picking titles other than his own: the rather long title comes from the first sentence of the book.

[5]Langdon Gilkey, *Catholicism Confronts Modernity: A Protestant View* (New York: Seabury Press, 1975); hereafter cited as *CCM*. Gilkey originally entitled this book *Crisis and Promise* (Langdon Gilkey, "A Retrospective Glance at My Work," in *The Whirlwind in Culture: Frontiers in Theology: In Honor of Langdon Gilkey*, ed. Donald W. Musser and Joseph L. Price [Bloomington: Meyer-Stone Books, 1988] 22).

[6]Gilkey, "Retrospective Glance at My Work," 1.

[7]Gilkey, "Retrospective Glance at My Work," 6-7.

Divinity School against the expulsion of an African-American student from the school, his divorce from his first wife, his discovery and joy in his second marriage, his encounter with the Second Vatican Council, his encounters with Buddhism, and then through his wife his experiences with the disciplines of Sikhism. What appears in these admittedly summary reflections on life-shaping experiences is that Gilkey's theology is shaped by the Christian tradition, contemporary experience, and modernity's currents of thought. Clearly, except perhaps in his youth, regular participating membership in specific Christian congregations have not served as the explicit generating sources of his theology. While participation in congregations may be a source and nourishment of his personal faith, Gilkey does not refer to these specific congregations in his writings. His understanding of congregations, however, is evident in his writings. He places worship as central to the life of Christian church. Clearly, writing out of the Christian traditions and to Christians, Gilkey has addressed most of his speeches and writings to the contemporary Christian church, its clergy, and people.

Gilkey explicitly communicates a desire to speak from within the Christian tradition as his abiding place in several of his later writings. In the "Preface" to *Message and Existence*, Gilkey speaks of his intent to write a relatively short introduction to Christian theology for "beginners in theology."[8] He states that he is not writing an academic theology or a complete theology, but writes to communicate how Christians express their beliefs in the contemporary world in which they live in part as communities of Christians. In his writings within the last decade or more, Gilkey has been increasingly concerned with other religions. Gilkey, however, adamantly claims not to create a philosophy of religion or theology that simply blends these traditions. Rather, he emphasizes specificity, contextuality, and the meaningfulness of doctrinal or theological "positions" for people. Gilkey explores options for Christian theology that can more comfortably speak of references to its theological assertions as "relative absolutes." Equally, he urges that Christian theologians genuinely can dialogue with other religions and reinterpret Christian religious symbols within the context of a rough "parity" with some other religions. In his explorations of this new territory, one can sense Gilkey's struggle

---

[8]Gilkey, *ME*, 1-3.

to be explicit and clear about his "Christian" commitment. He continues to speak from *that* community.

More than twenty years ago, in an impassioned manner, Gilkey defended himself and his colleagues, David Tracy and Schubert Ogden, against charges of heresy made by Avery Dulles.[9] Gilkey exposed how Dulles had misrepresented Gilkey's theology at critical points. Gilkey almost shouted back at such implied charges: "My work also represents an effort—however successful or unsuccessful!—to interpret the whole range of modern existence in terms of a *Christian* understanding, and so to provide a modern interpretation of the classical symbols of the Christian tradition."[10]

Gilkey's theology has not been a "church" theology in a narrow sense, but it has clearly been a theology speaking from within the Christian tradition and, most often, speaking in the midst of communities of Christian clergy and laity. His theology has affirmed the role of Christian communities, churches, as the locus of the Holy, the Body of Christ, the bearer of the tradition, the locus for the reinterpretation of the symbols of that tradition in light of modern experience, and the agency for the expression of those symbols and that formulated "truth" in worship, proclamation, and service for the renewal of the world. Gilkey articulates several major challenges from modernity that face the church and its theologians in the following summary:

> the relation of Christian truth to science and to the world order that science studies, the relation of biblical and doctrinal history to historical studies, the relation of divine authority and grace to personal autonomy and freedom, the relation of grace to natural goals in life, and, perhaps most important, the relation of the purposes of God and the calling of the church to the political and social developments of the world, of God's promise of salvation to "this worldly liberation."[11]

In the preceding paragraphs, I have established that Gilkey takes the "church" seriously, indeed that his theology in major part has been a pleading with the church to be the community of Christ in the modern world, and that his theology is an exploratory breaking of ground for the

---

[9]Langdon Gilkey, "Anathemas and Orthodoxy: A Reply to Avery Dulles," *The Christian Century* 94 (9 November 1977): 1026-29.

[10]Gilkey, "Anathemas and Orthodoxy," 1028.

[11]Gilkey, *CCM*, 13.

church in its mission. Now I want to extract and explicate from Gilkey's writings that which Gilkey says about the "church" theologically, his ecclesiology.

I. Church as Sacramental Servant

Gilkey directly addressed two major books to naming the nature and mission of the "church" in the modern world, one for Protestants and one for Roman Catholics. In *Catholicism Confronts Modernity*, Gilkey appears to refer back to the earlier book, *How the Church can Minister to the World Without Losing Itself*, as his address to the Protestant churches.[12] Only in his writings from the last decade or so do we begin to get a hint that more may be required in light of his experience of religious pluralism. How that might reshape his ecclesiology is not yet clear.

I will extrapolate from Gilkey's theology the sketch of a general theological view of the Christian church. This effort will concentrate on a theology of the church, rather than on issues of structure or the "practical" exercise of ministry, ordained or lay. The mission of the church will be addressed as part of this theology of the church.

Throughout his work, Gilkey carefully identifies himself as a Western, Protestant Christian theologian. Clearly, however, he thinks that both Protestant and Roman Catholic communities have much to learn from one another. In this short essay, insofar as I speak of a theology of the church, I usually will not distinguish these two communities from one another. Gilkey, however, clearly thinks both that the Protestant church has lost much of its passion for evoking the Holy as well as its sacramental depth and that the Roman Catholic Church has not been able as a church to reinterpret its theology and traditional symbols in terms meaningful for the contemporary world—a world from which Roman Catholic clergy and laity think and feel, even if they do not acknowledge that context fully. The hierarchical structure and assumptions of clerical and magisterial authority as they are exercised in the Roman Catholic Church, Gilkey believes, are not adequate, truthful, or effective. Gilkey believes that, truthfully, even the clergy have a gnawing sense that this hierarchical structure has no enduring foundation in the modern world. To retreat from modernity, however, Gilkey asserts would be neither feasible

---

[12]Gilkey, *CCM*, 202n.10.

nor credible in terms of the church's life and mission in the modern world.

For Gilkey, on the one hand, the Protestant church has too easily vitiated the depth and ground of its religious symbols for God and God's activity by capitulation to an unholy secularity. On the other hand, the Roman Catholic Church has been unable to reconceive its unyielding and uncritical authority in a manner that recognizes and responds to the realities of what we know and experience in history, namely relativity, contingency, and finitude. The Protestant church has failed to fulfill a mission to the world that speaks distinctively, utilizing its Christian symbols and their authentic religious depth. The Roman Catholic Church has failed to fulfill its mission to itself speaking distinctively and meaningfully from and to the modern experience of its people. Thus, the dilemma of the Christian church in the Western world can be better addressed by these two communions speaking and ministering to one another as complementary sisters and brothers in Christ open to mutual admonition and affirmation.

Gilkey, with incisive and remarkable consistency, indicts the Protestant church in his writing. He describes the "evident weakness of present Protestantism as a form of communal church life."

> Related essentially to the bourgeois middle-class worlds of Europe, Britain, and America, and in the last two to the "Wasp" worlds of small towns and suburbs, Protestantism seems, despite its conservative and neo-conservative theologies of transcendence, to have been so engulfed in that world as merely to reproduce the individualistic, quantitative, moralistic, nonemotional, and in many respects, naturalistic, bourgeois world in ecclesiastical form. Its sense of community is weak, or else defined entirely by its middle-class, white parameters; its liturgical life and its experiential potential are almost nonexistent; its experience of the holy in sermon, sacrament, or common prayer is fleeting at best; and its ethical existence is largely an anachronistic individual moralism subscribed to by all in theory but practiced only by its clerical leaders.[13]

Gilkey's indictment is stinging. It comes from a love of the faith and a passion for the church's mission in the world. In this case, as in many of his writings, he clearly writes for a particular "slice" of the Protestant, and perhaps of the Roman Catholic, community. The Pentecostal

---

[13]Gilkey, *CCM*, 14.

churches, African-American churches, Eastern and other Orthodox communions, and churches in the third world would not find themselves in the previous characterization. Gilkey has written elsewhere of the Pentecostal and particularly the fundamentalist churches.[14] Generally, however, Gilkey addresses "mainline" Protestantism.

The Second Vatican Council energized Gilkey. He saw light there for Protestants. Gilkey has given his theological life to the reformulation of a "Protestant" theology that he thinks can contribute to Roman Catholic reflection. His massive and relentless work on a "prolegomenon" to theology and a hermeneutics of modernity serve all religions.

Gilkey's theological views on the Christian church are scattered throughout his works. Nonetheless, a remarkable continuity pervades his convictions about the theological meaning of "church," although his phenomenological examination of modernity has deepened the warrants and backings for those convictions through the years. In his writings of the last decade, we begin to experience more of a challenge for the church to listen more intently to other religious traditions. This listening is not merely to hear about successful techniques or to indulge in the exotic ventures of observing "foreign" practices, but is to engage as a full partner in dialogue, learning from the works of God in other religions. While Christian, Gilkey is not an exclusivist. Perhaps he would say that God is not that small.

In the concluding paragraph of his essay, "The Political Dimensions of Theology," Gilkey hints at the reach of his conception of the Christian church. He mentions various roles of the church.

> The implications of the religious dimension of community life for the priestly role of the church in society; the implications of estrangement and sin of community life for the prophetic role of the church in the world; the implications of the resurrection for the hopes of the church in the future; and the implications of the Kingdom for the constructive politics of the church.[15]

---

[14]Gilkey, *HCCM*, 17ff., 30n.3, 31ff., 109ff.; idem, *Creationism on Trial: Evolution and God at Little Rock* (San Francisco: Harper & Row, 1985); hereafter cited as *CT*; idem, *TT*, 8-10, 144-48.

[15]Langdon Gilkey, "The Political Dimensions of Theology" in *Society and the Sacred: Toward a Theology of Culture in Decline*, by Langdon Gilkey (New York: Crossroad Publishing Company, 1981) 56; hereafter cited as *SAS*.

For Gilkey, the church is not an incidental or accidental reality. It is not merely instrumental, a creation of sinners to have a place for communal feeling. The church is a creation of God and a part of the intentionality of God for God's creation. It is one of the great gifts of grace, extending the new Israel.[16]

Gilkey's theological views of the church identify and call communities of Christians to be the church as *sacramental, Christological, dialectical, proclamatory/prophetic, and transformative.* In this theology, such a church is a servant church, both the servant of God in Christ through the Spirit and the servant of God's world for the relative but more fulfilling actualization of meaning, justice, hope, and love.

It is critical to keep reminding oneself that Gilkey does not radically separate the church from the world. Indeed, God is not separated from the world as in supernaturalism; rather, God is sacramentally present and active in the midst of the world for the sake of the world, granted in a flawed and finite manner. What is to be perfected is not an individual "soul," but the world as the dwelling place for both ourselves and God.

II. Method and Ecclesiology

Gilkey often has stated that he did not form his theology by developing first of all a method. He has even been critical of the reputed obsession with method at the Divinity School of the University of Chicago where he taught.[17] As a "systematic" theologian, however, Gilkey's thought is coherent and there is a perceivable method to his thinking. In a previous paper on Gilkey's theological method, I have described theology as a "tensive 'system' of reflection on experience and tradition, argumentation

---

[16]Gilkey, *HCCM*, 60-61.

[17]Langdon Gilkey, "Theology and Culture: Reflections on the Conference," *Criterion* 28 (Autumn 1989): 3-4. Gilkey's remarks were reflections on an extended paper that I had given, in which I dissected his "theological method." He was kind and gentle in his insistence that he did not have in his mind a highly articulated method that he then proceeded to apply. In a marvelous summary, Gilkey stated, "In other words, be as careful as you can, as wise as you can, and only *then* think about what it is you've just done" (Gilkey, "Theology and Culture," 4). Of course, he has a method for his theology and an effective one!

and expression."[18] Gilkey's theological method is a "trialectic" or "quadralectic," even though it would more commonly be called "dialectical":

> There is (1) a rational interrogation of experience, tradition, culture, history; (2) a critical moment of estrangement and incredibility; (3) a complex ingression of grace which discloses reality in a transcending presence of incredible redemptive grace which is expressed; (4) theologically in credibly warrantable assertions.[19]

The resulting systematic theology presents coherent meaning that both aids celebration, uniting both the depths of feeling and convicted thought, and then effective praxis in the service of God and God's world.

For Gilkey, the Christian theologian carries forth this existential and reflective project not just "in" the modern world, but also within and from the community bearing the Christian symbols and thought. The church is a principal bearer of these symbols and the community of engendering sustaining worship, a discipline of being in the divine presence. Because God is "in" the world, God is not "only" in the Christian church ecumenical or in a Christian church. The community of believers in the Spirit of Jesus Christ, however, exist in that Spirit. A major responsibility of the church is to make that Holy reality wholly evident, not in the sense of completely and unambiguously evident but in the sense of inescapably before us and with us.

Starting with a hermeneutical phenomenology of experience, Gilkey's "method" begins with the "presence" of the Holy, of God, in the church as powerfully communicated through symbols.[20] His method then is critical and dialectical.[21] He interrogates the reality of the church and its symbols in terms of their meaningfulness and relevance to the common human experience of the contemporary world. The symbols of the church are questioned both in terms of their continuing power in our day and in terms of their meaningfulness for modern people. Then, these symbols either are affirmed in their power to interrogate and deepen modern experience or they must be discarded or reinterpreted to enable them to

---

[18]H. Frederick Reisz, Jr., "The Task of Theology: Reflections on Langdon Gilkey's Writings" (unpublished paper presented at the conference in Gilkey's honor, on his retirement from the University of Chicago Divinity School, 14-15 April 1989) 26.

[19]Reisz, "Task of Theology," 26.

[20]Gilkey, ME, 19.

[21]Gilkey, "The Dialectic of Christian Belief," in Gilkey, SAS, 30.

speak anew in a new context—being revelatory in a new way. The church is called to such reinterpretation of its symbols. Gilkey admits the power of the authentic symbols and of the Spirit of Jesus the Christ to break through skepticism, doubt, finitude, despair, and quandary. Thus, as an example, the symbol of the cross exhibits our finitude and the participation of God with us in suffering. At the same time, it shows us the brokenness of our lives and the limited nature of our knowledge of God. The scandal of the cross powerfully conveys to us the hiddenness of God in the midst of every revelation, and the presence of God in the context of all suffering. It also conveys the judgment and forgiveness of God when combined with the resurrection.[22] As another example, most powerfully, Gilkey utilizes the testimonies to the resurrection of Jesus the Christ to exhibit how humans are ultimately thrown back upon both trusting God to be God and receiving the heartening proclamation of ultimate hope.[23] This ingression of grace as power and meaning enables theology to continue in a new but not ungrounded reflection on God and Christ through being grasped by the Spirit. The church can provide the opportunities, disciplines, consolations, conversations, and settings to enable the working of grace and the fructifying of meaning. In Jesus Christ, we experience and know the revelation of love that impels us toward expression in the community of love, the church as servant of the world. The Spirit of Jesus the Christ commissions the church for praxis in order to enlarge the community of justice, mercy, and love. This is participation in the work of the fulfillment of God's creation. On this hopeful horizon, Gilkey calls for a balanced emphasis on God's providence and eschatological hope.

Gilkey summarizes his manner of applying theology to the Christian faith, in his essay, "The Dialectic of Christian Belief."

> There is a dialectic of rationality, incredibility, and credibility that constitutes the formal structure of Christian belief, with the negative, estrangement, initiating the movement from one moment to the other. If these moments are separated, each one loses its status, and Christianity dissolves as a total interpretation of life. If they are not distinguished, then untold confusion results. If they are held in distinction and yet tension, then rationality and

---

[22]Gilkey, *ME*, 192-93.
[23]Gilkey, *ME*, 252-54.

credibility join to make intelligible the incredible grace and promise which Christian faith proclaims.[24]

In a very real sense, the life and mission of the church recapitulates the form of Gilkey's theology. This is not surprising, since the theological form sacramentally recapitulates the life of Jesus the Christ. The lived-incarnation itself is tensive and dialectical. The life of Jesus the Christ as divine revelation in finite form, partaking in the ambiguities and realities of history and yet incarnating God, is a sign of the life of God's people and the church.[25] Gilkey's theological method follows the path of immersion in experience, interrogation of it, critique, prophetic insight through religious symbols and tradition, and loving reformulation for the sake of service to the church and to the world. Here the style of the life, death, and resurrection of Christ, and the style of the life of God's people are mirrored.[26] These connections will be further aided by consideration of the sacramental nature of the church in the following section.

III. The Church as Sacramental

The servant church is also a church that so forms its worship and life that the Holy manifests itself. Gilkey often implies that the church must be "transparent" to the divine.[27] Here he utilizes Tillich's theories and words concerning religious symbols.[28] I prefer the word "translucent" to convey the continuing reality of the veiled God and ambiguity within finitude. This is consonant with Gilkey's thought. The sacramental nature of the church has three major aspects: the church is that community (1) through which God works, (2) in which God is disclosed, and (3) whose members become, in a sense, the sacramental carriers of the presence and activity of God. None of these assertions means that God is not also working, represented, and served by nonchurch actualities in the "world." The church, however, has a sacramental reality and an intentional mission. Gilkey describes the continuous and binding elements of the Christian church as the presence of the divine Spirit, faith, hope, and love

---

[24]Gilkey, *SAS*, 30.

[25]Gilkey, *ME*, 218, 238-39.

[26]Gilkey, *ME*, 9ff.

[27]Gilkey, *ME*, 234ff.; idem, *CCM*, 8-9.

[28]Gilkey, *ME*, esp. chap. 3, "Revelation and Theology," 39-65; idem, "Symbols, Meaning, and the Divine Presence," in idem, *TT*, 49-65; idem, *Gilkey on Tillich* (New York: Crossroad, 1990) 48-53; hereafter cited as *GOT*.

expressed in the common symbols around which this communal life in history fashions itself: these symbols express the ground of her life in the divine activity and the goal of her life in the divine purpose. Such essential symbols provide the basis for the beliefs and reflection of the community, its modes of worship and behavior, its social and political forms of life, its ethical decisions, and the shape of its mission.[29]

These basic and grounding symbols are sacramental. In his earliest writings, Gilkey criticized especially the Protestant church for losing this sacramental reality. Speaking of the Protestant church, he writes, "the secular social values which were always present in the life of the church have now come to the fore and replaced religious values as the primary bonds of loyalty and support."[30]

Gilkey explicitly does not confine God to the church. "The religious or holy, then, is properly not a category either totally separated from the secular or completely identified with it. Rather it is that which relates us to the source of our life and the goal of its meaning."[31] Throughout the years, Gilkey has called the church to be the church. Fundamentally, Gilkey has called the church, first of all, not to be defined on the basis of its culture, but to be in part countercultural, since the church is rooted in the Holy. Gilkey has been careful, however, to say that the church must both communicate in language or symbols that are meaningful for its time and actively disclose to the culture its own religious depth. According to Gilkey, the loss of the Holy in contemporary culture and the church, especially in its worship, is the root experiential problem which must be addressed, in the wake of which will then come solutions to other problems—such as those of the meaningfulness and relevance of the church's symbols.[32]

Using Tillichian language, Gilkey speaks about the "theonomous" potential of a culture." "Theonomy . . . represents precisely the viewpoint expressed . . . namely, that the fulfillment of the powers, capacities, eros, and goals of the human (or of any creature) are realized only in, with,

---

[29]Gilkey, *CCM*, 8-9.

[30]Gilkey, *HCCM*, 145.

[31]Gilkey, *HCCM*, 53.

[32]Gilkey, *HCCM*, 145; idem, *CCM*, 178ff., 185, 210n.2-3; idem, *Reaping the Whirlwind: A Christian Interpretation of History* (New York: Seabury Press, 1976) 290-91; hereafter cited as *RW*.

and through an essential relation to the divine."[33] Gilkey advocates a theonomous interpretation of all human existence. However, especially the church must manifest its grounding depth in God, the Holy. The church is a sacramental sign of the more veiled theonomous depth of culture. The church must manifest the Holy or it fails its mission.

The church's servanthood of theonomous humanity and culture begins in powerfully expressive and meaning-filled worship. Here the depth and power of the fundamental Christian symbols are not to be obscured. Preaching must disclose the Gospel, even when it is intent on social commentary or prophetic critique of the culture. The world and the church are to hear, see, and feel the Holy. Humanity and the world are to be called to their ground and depth by the community which is the church. Gilkey defines worship as

> primarily related to this presence of the divine throughout the human creature's existence. Its central purpose is to bring to awareness and celebrate that universal presence, to shape that awareness into Christian form and, through that shaping of our natural existence by sacrament and word, to elicit gratitude, contrition, recommitment, and transformation of that natural existence. It is the holy as it permeates our entire life as creatures, and at every level of that life, to which worship primarily responds.[34]

Gilkey understands this sacramentality as present in the church in Word and sacrament. The Word is necessary, because God is transcendent and the world is finite. Thus, as God uses the media of the finite world to be present, proclamation (pointing to) and interpretation (pointing out—making meaningful) are necessary. Gilkey defines a threefold function of the Word: the Word interprets, the Word judges, and the Word announces proleptically that which is sacramentally experienced as inward and private—it makes the Holy public and social.[35]

The Holy is to be evident in the whole life of the church. In the sacraments of the church, that presence must be immediately and sensuously real.[36] The sacraments are, thus, always in a sense creative. They create or evoke the presence of the Holy that, while already there, has been veiled or submerged; and they create a deepening of reality's

---

[33]Gilkey, *ME*, 256.
[34]Gilkey, *TT*, 56.
[35]Gilkey, *TT*, 61-62.
[36]Gilkey, *CCM*, 196-97; idem, *ME*, 234.

grounding or meaning. This creative nature of the sacraments criticizes us, brings us to judgment, and empowers us—bringing us to our actuality grounded in God. For Gilkey, the sacraments are sacramental in both their power for participation in the Holy and their functionality for the impact and impress of the Holy (to use my own words). They are life changing as they place us before the face of God and revelatory of the Holy and our own lives. They also are, however, the media of the Spirit to forgive, reconcile, renew, and extend the community of service and love.

Rationality and secularism have invaded the churches, undercutting this sacramental service. In this respect, Gilkey has been critical of conservative and liberal Protestantism alike. He describes the ethos of many of these churches as "nondenominational, noncreedal, nonsacramental, nonliturgical."

> If, then, shorn of tradition, they have also rejected the Bible as an absolute authority over their life, they can represent merely the spiritual and moral life of their social environment, expressing in their own life whatever that spiritual content may be. The goals of such churches are almost entirely the products of the hopes and aims of the surrounding community.[37]

Gilkey counters such a culturally determined congregation by advocating that, in part, the church is marked by the power and revelatory meaning manifested in word and sacraments. His view of the Eucharist illustrates this. Gilkey describes the sacrament of the Eucharist or Communion as that activity in which the church surely makes present Jesus the Christ and recapitulates his meaning. In addition, the action of the Eucharist calls us to, and makes real, the unity of the community of humanity, creatures of God, both inside and outside the church. Gilkey advocates a broadening of the reach of the symbols of the sacraments through allowing the Christian symbols embodied and enacted in them to evoke powers and meanings that are relevant to wider arenas of modern life.

The church also has a sacramental function in deepening the spirituality of the people the Christian community. This emphasis on the disciplined practices of Christianity or religions has grown more prominent in Gilkey's work since the 1980s, as he has both encountered other religions seriously, especially Buddhism, and also as he has been drawn into some of the practices of yoga and Sikhism through his wife.

---

[37]Gilkey, *HCCM*, 50.

The church is called to be a source for "common spiritual strength."[38] In an essay from 1986, "Plurality: Christianity's New Situation," Gilkey notes the need for pastors to be "spiritual" leaders and educators for their congregations.[39] He urges pastors to begin their servanthood of both church and world by starting in the area of spirituality, "the care and nurture of souls." The pastor must become comfortable with and able to engender in others techniques to help people deepen their spiritual existence, their awareness of and life in the presence of and service of God. In this regard, Gilkey chides the Protestant Reformation's tendency to avoid disciplines and practices as works-righteousness that undercut the actuality of grace.[40]

Gilkey's emphasis on the servant church as first sacramental may be summarized as he himself did in the conclusion of his early book on the ministering church.

> When the Word is heard in the congregation in real repentance and in faith—then the sacraments become the medium of the presence of that Word of Christ to each of us in his own immediate situation—then the church can be the new People of God, related to Him in confession and trust, and so related to one another and to their social environment in love and service. . . . For only God is holy, and only He can work wonders through His instrument, the church.[41]

IV. The Church as Christological

The servant church's sacramentality is Christological. Although Gilkey refers to the church as the community in which the divine Spirit is present, basically this is the Spirit of Jesus the Christ. The model for the servant church is her Lord. The life, death, and resurrection of Jesus the Christ, taken together, are the basis for the faith, hope, and love of the church. The cross is the symbol of contingency and triumph, sacrifice and service, dialectic and renewal, finitude and divine depth. In a sense, the

---

[38]Gilkey, *TT*, 178.

[39]Gilkey, *TT*, 21-34.

[40]Gilkey, *TT*, 29-30.

[41]Gilkey, *HCCM*, 126-27. The editors have retained Gilkey's own terminology in reference to God. The changes in his use of terms to refer to God themselves signal some of his changing perspectives. In Gilkey's more recent writings, he employs other pronouns or terms for God, such as "parent" rather than "father," and Gilkey refers to God not as "him" but as "him/her."

ontogeny of the church recapitulates the phylogeny of the life, death, and resurrection of Jesus the Christ. He is the accomplishment of salvation. The presence of the Spirit of Jesus Christ is the grounding and empowering reality of the church.

> The primary role of the Christian community, the ecclesia, in the continuing history of men and women is to provide a locus for those redemptive forces that God's action in Christ had introduced into history. . . . That role is to be the bearer of "dependent revelation," witnessing to, re-presenting, and thereby renewing in the successive moments of time the event of Jesus as the Christ and its recreative effects.[42]

Of course, Gilkey makes a trinitarian assertion. In God as father or parent, Son, and Spirit, we discover our own humanity: "our courage to be temporal, our openness to possibility, our faith and trust in acceptance, our hope in the future, and for the love which alone can recreate community among all creatures."[43] Jesus the Christ revealed all of this as lived within finitude.

When Gilkey discusses the life of Jesus, he includes the teachings and promises of Jesus the Christ. These elements reveal the judgment, love, and providence of God. Jesus also shows us the way of faith, courage, and hope in the midst of adversity, temptation, and sin, in living within finitude. The church as the community of love has a life that includes these realities of the people of God. The church is fully a human community and fully an historical institution, yet within it divine depth and transcending values are evident. Jesus as the Christ also manifests this ingression of the infinite in the finite. The historicity of Jesus is important theologically in many ways for Gilkey. The relativity of history, as a fact crucial for modernity, however, does impact the church's life through its understanding of its Christological base and that base's implication for the church's life and mission:

> if we understand the purpose of the Incarnation as the gift of the possibility of loving one another in historical community—not the gift of absolute doctrine or propositions leading to a supernatural level of life—we shall be able to see in this modern principle [historical relativity] something creative

---

[42]Gilkey, *ME*, 234.
[43]Gilkey, *ME*, 216.

for our Christian life, a strange preparation, if not for the Gospel, at least perhaps for its historical enactment.[44]

In a more radical sense, Gilkey has hinted that the incarnation has revealed to us that "vulnerability, suffering, contingency, and death—nonbeing in all its terrors for us as a sacral nothingness—are characteristics of deity."[45] Thus, as Christological, the servant church may be called in mission to risk its very life and in some parts of its mission to negate itself for love. Gilkey has applied this perspective to defining the "Protestant principle" of the church, a principle that must risk and reform. More radically, Gilkey has stated that Christ "manifests" God and the freedom of divine grace, rather than "creating" God's expansive grace.[46] Thus, the church must not limit its mission or its soteriology, which, for Gilkey, extends toward universalism. Salvation should not necessarily and only be tied to assent regarding Christological dogma, although Gilkey can still speak of this breadth as salvation "in Christ."[47] We must note here that Gilkey takes the finitude of Jesus, as well as his status as the Christ, seriously. Jesus the Christ is the manifestation of God, but not the whole of God.[48] God has a freedom that is not first of all bound by Jesus the Christ. With regard to the people of God in the church or the Body of Christ, Gilkey's later writings extend this theme by indicating that the church, while in Christ, also has a freedom not completely bounded by Jesus.[49] In these theological probings, we begin to glimpse what Gilkey might mean by "relative absolutes."[50]

The servant church is Christological as it proclaims the being of all under the creation of God, the meaning of life grounded in its depth in God, and the loving community as an impossible possibility generated on the basis of the empowerment of the divine Spirit with us, the Spirit of Jesus the Christ. The eschatological dimensions of Jesus' teaching and resurrection ultimately exhibit our final dependency on God and enliven our creative living as participation in the preparation of the Kingdom,

---

[44]Gilkey, *CCM*, 74.

[45]Gilkey, *SAS*, 136.

[46]Gilkey, *SAS*, 169.

[47]For a detailed exposition of Gilkey's Christology on many of these issues, see the chapter in this book by James O. Yerkes.

[48]Gilkey, *ME*, 99-100; idem, *SAS*, 136, 169.

[49]Gilkey, *SAS*, 169.

[50]Gilkey, *SAS*, 14; idem, *TT*, 191ff.

about which Jesus declares that we will not know the time or place. This Kingdom is wholly God's. The church is a servant of that Kingdom through Christ.

V. The Church as Dialectical

The servant church is a community and institution in history. Thus, it has a dialectical existence. Gilkey does not refer to the church in terms of its unalterable structures or its static truths. Rather, Gilkey says, "[i]t was a quite *different* promise that founded the *ecclesia,* namely the promise to provide the grace to create *new* forms of life in each successive age, forms more capable than the older ones of ministering authentically to each new age."[51] Ontologically, the dialectic of being and nonbeing, not just in finite existence but even in God's life, means that the fullness of the church's life will be dialectical. Theologically, the church always stands under divine judgment and is continually called to reformation. Hermeneutically, the church must periodically reinterpret the texts and symbols of the faith, so that they are relevant, meaningful, and compelling in each new historical situation.[52] Phenomenologically, the church will be strongest as it remains both open to hearing words of judgment and flexible structurally to allow celebration, proclamation, and mission to be shaped by the community of love.[53] Thus, hierarchical structures of clergy and authority must submit to the creative divine presence of the Spirit of Jesus the Christ and allow a dialectical sharing of leadership within the community. Historically, the presence of other religions and the depth of meaning and life which they enable have motivated Gilkey more recently to speak about both "relative absolutes" in religion, including Christianity, and a rough "parity" of religions.[54] Accordingly, Gilkey identifies the development of a dialectical relationship between the Christian church and other religious communities.

Gilkey finds one model for this dialectical life of the church in the covenant people of Israel, whom the searing ministries of the prophets called to "create" new forms of the covenant for faithful existence in different times.[55] Gilkey's theology has always called the church to live

---

[51]Gilkey, *CCM,* 4.
[52]Gilkey, *HCCM,* 79-80.
[53]Gilkey, *ME,* 226-27, 250.
[54]Gilkey, *SAS,* 168-69.
[55]Gilkey, *HCCM,* 62, 146.

on the edge, by being a loving community of risk for the sake of the world.[56] The "arts" of ministry for pastors and priests includes discernment of the times, clarification of the Gospel, sensitivity to the "kairos," and courage to risk for the sake of the Holy and redemption.[57] Nevertheless, in some periods of history, the church has failed to be faithful to that to which it is called.

Gilkey has observed how in some periods of history, primarily but not exclusively premodern, the church has moved into the culture but only selfishly, to form the culture in order to enhance the prestige and maintain the stability of the church's present structure. In the Western developed and secularized modern world, this is less a possibility, except for enclaves within the culture. For Gilkey, however, these are never authentic strategies for the church. Such selfish and protective strategies are unfaithful and undialectical. Gilkey offers a stern warning here. "As history shows, an absolutized culture and an absolutized religious community feed on one another: They breed, encourage, and support each other in baffling interunion. An absolutized religion tends inexorably to absolutize its cultural base. . . ."[58] In such situations, the transcendent grace and judgment of God will come upon both the church and the culture. By contrast to such inauthentic forms of the church, the servant church will be a dialectical reality, which may be unsettling, but ultimately will deepen and broaden participation in the intentions of God and the promises of the Kingdom.

VI. The Proclaiming and Prophetic Church

God calls the servant church to proclaim the Gospel and to be a prophetic presence in the power of the Spirit of Jesus the Christ. Modern culture especially, for its own integrity, requires grounding in the divine; paradoxically, however, that which the culture most needs it also most fears and suppresses. The church's message for existence will have to be intentionally proclaimed in word and action; but often that proclamation will not be received. Proclamation will involve a prophetic activity that declares the presence of the Holy as creative ground, judging and sustaining presence, and fulfilling possibility. Such proclamation includes

---

[56]Gilkey, ME, 226, 235f.; idem, HCCM, 64ff., 66.

[57]Gilkey, HCCM, 100-103; idem, ME, 234; idem, "Plurality: Christianity's New Situation," in idem, TT, 28ff.

[58]Gilkey, TT, 176.

at least three basic elements: (1) the Word that witnesses to the "originating event" of divine revelation; (2) that event or presence sacramentally re-presented; and (3) the disclosure of the event through the actual lives or witness of persons in the community of love—the church.[59]

For Gilkey, the church's proclamation flows from all of those elements in the church that I have previously described. The church interprets its central symbols through the experience of faith, honest interrogation of life in the world, the creative but faith-constrained use of imagination, and prayerful constancy in the Spirit of Jesus the Christ. As God continues to do, the church calls humanity and nature to their true groundedness in God. For Gilkey, the church grounded in Jesus the Christ is the new humanity, albeit in finite form.[60] Thus, the church is a new reality that requires interpretation and proclamation. Its very existence is prophetic, governed in part by the promises of the future Kingdom. The structure of time and being themselves seem to move into the "new." This movement aims toward the dimension of life that is humanity, focusing and directing the church through the Spirit of Jesus the Christ with us. The church's proclamation will then always contain a prophetic element. As Gilkey writes, "One critical task of theology and proclamation is, thus, to discern the signs of the times, to be 'without the law' in this sense, to enact the prophetic role: to see what it is that the Lord's creative and judging action in history requires of us now."[61]

For Gilkey, the prophetic role includes both judgment and envisionment. This ecclesial role is to shake up the present. The church also exercises the proclamatory role or priestly role. The church's priestly role is to recover the Kingdom's symbols of forgiveness, healing, reconciliation, and renewal. Then, the priestly task entails reinterpretation of those symbols both in terms and with a coherent organization which will have meaning and power for the contemporary world. The Spirit, then, can work through them toward redemption. This priestly role does not seek merely to preserve that which is treasured and was meaningful from the past; rather, the church exercises this role also to deliver those treasures relevantly and meaningfully to the present. Gilkey refers, not to the infallibility of the church, but to, using a term defended by Hans Küng,

[59]Gilkey, *ME*, 234.
[60]Gilkey, *HCCM*, 59ff., 62ff.
[61]Gilkey, *TT*, 121.

the church's "indefectibility."[62] The prophetic and the priestly roles of the church go hand and hand. There is a dialectical wholeness in their partnership.

Of course, prophetic judgment, envisionment, and proclamation are never only from the church to the world, but also from the church to the church (even, at times, from the world to the church). In his more recent work, Gilkey has been more moved by the meaningful aspects of non-Christian religious traditions. The church's proclamation in the contemporary pluralistic world is not just a periodic judgment on the form of the church or its lack of theological integrity. Gilkey has turned a corner in his theology, to say now that there is a rough "parity" of religions and Christianity itself theologically must learn to speak of "relative absolutes."[63] Thus, for Gilkey, there is a deeper and more serious prophetic word being proclaimed to the church in our day by other religions and cultures. Theologically, the church is called neither to a protectionist denial nor to an imperialistic and bombastic proclamation of exclusivism. The church is called to live honestly in this pluralistic world, celebrating the divine depth of creation and the breadth of the divine love, living the servanthood of the Cross of Jesus the Christ, and trusting the providence of God.[64] This, according to Gilkey, is the heart of the church's proclamation.

VII. The Church as Transformative

The servant church participates in God's providential sustaining, reforming, and re-creative work to realize the Kingdom. Gilkey resists identifying "mission" as the primary means of characterizing the church's work. "Mission," as he uses it in this context, means "evangelism." Here his Baptist background, and much of what he fought against as a young theologian, becomes visible. Gilkey resists such a concept of mission, first, because he believes that Christians who primarily, and perhaps only, focus on "bringing others to Christ" in time forget about their own lives

---

[62]Gilkey, *CCM*, 82-83; see Hans Küng, *Infallible? An Inquiry* (Garden City NY: Doubleday, 1971) 181-85; idem, *The Church* (Garden City NY: Doubleday/Image Books, 1964) 440-43.

[63]Gilkey, "Plurality: Christianity's New Situation," in *TT*, 33; idem, "Theodicy and Plurality," in *TT*, 191-93; idem, "Theology and Culture: Reflections on the Conference," 7.

[64]Gilkey, *ME*, 238-39, 250.

as Christians, their call to be people of Christ. Second, the primary focus on evangelism as "bringing people in" can lead the church not to be concerned with that which it has to share with others—the Holy, the Gospel, the Word and sacraments, the community of love.[65] If it merely concentrates on bringing others "in," the church can be distracted from its primary missions of Gospel proclamation through word and sacraments and being of service as the community of love in the world as activities of sharing with others. Gilkey also argues that, if the church primarily and almost exclusively concentrates on bringing others in or quantity as the church's mission, it will miss its mission to and in the world as the transforming community of love.[66] By the grace of God, the church is the new humanity in Christ.

By its nature as a community of love, the church seeks to transform the world. Such transformation, however, is for the sake of bringing nature and humanity to themselves. This retrospective and prospective mission of the church was evident in the early Christian community. "For the earliest church understood itself as a people in two ways: first, as the New Israel—that is, the continuation and renewal of the covenant community, the chosen people of God, the Jews; and secondly, as embodying a new humanity, the renewal of a total creation that had fallen in Adam but had now risen to new life in Jesus Christ."[67] For Gilkey, the Holy Spirit is alive and active in the church. This Spirit of Jesus the Christ is a transforming Spirit. This Spirit is also the grounding, sustaining, and redeeming depth of the world. The church's servanthood, as transformative, is toward the goal of theonomous life in all its dimensions.

The transformative dimension of the church's life is both internal and external. The church must continually renew itself and the world, as participation in God's creative work through the Spirit of Jesus the Christ. Gilkey describes the Christian gospel and the redemption that it promises as "both spiritual and political, involving both an inward healing of sin and an outward transformation of history's institutions."[68] Openness to a variety of viewpoints that are discussible and tested in the praxis of living aids the church's internal transformation. The church must be a communi-

---

[65]Gilkey, *HCCM*, 63-64n.6.
[66]Gilkey, *HCCM*, 32ff., 41ff.
[67]Gilkey, *HCCM*, 60.
[68]Gilkey, *ME*, 126.

ty of celebration and deliberation. The internal transformation of the church involves a reinterpretation of the grounding symbols and a reexamination of all the church's structures, in order to fulfill the call of God in the present time, for the sake of the future, under the symbol of the Kingdom. Moreover, this internal transformation may involve a restructuring of the role of the pastor or priest. As Gilkey advises Roman Catholics, in the community of love where the Gospel is truly in the midst of the people, priests will be advisors, counselors, and friends, "open" theologians more than legislators or judges.[69] He has urged ministers to become spiritual leaders who aid their congregations in the disciplines of spirituality.[70] Much of what we have spoken of previously in this essay has illuminated the internal transformative mission of the church or the people of God.

The external transformative work of the church is not wholly external, since the dimensions of life designated by "church" and "world" interpenetrate one another. Gilkey asserts that religious institutions "reproduce the culture religiously."[71] The outward thrust is minimally toward justice and maximally toward a social manifestation of the community (or communities) of love. Gilkey often refers to this goal as the creation of an ordered, just, and creative world. The transformation administered through the church is always to center life around and in God. It is toward a deepening of the sacramental or theonomous life in all dimensions. This redeeming activity is always a participation in the Spirit, even if only fragmentarily. Following Tillich, Gilkey calls for a theonomous church in a theonomous culture.[72] Gilkey willingly asserts that the church cannot be the church without the world and the world cannot be the world without the church. Both of these dimensions of life are dynamic, interpenetrating, fragmentarily manifested, renewable, and redeemable!

From the evidence of history, Gilkey fears that a church which does not involve itself in the politics, debates about policy, and formation of a culture is doomed simply to mirror the culture.[73] Such a Christian

---

[69]Gilkey, *CCM*, 77.
[70]Gilkey, "Plurality: Christianity's New Situation," in *TT*, 28-30; idem, *HCCM*, 100-103.
[71]Gilkey, *TT*, 169.
[72]Gilkey, *ME*, 243.
[73]Gilkey, *HCCM*, 306.

community will be more of a heteronomous cultural product than a theonomous community.[74] If that church is to be an agent for transformation the church, however, must have a critical edge toward its culture.[75] The life of the church again is lived in a dialectical process of support, criticism, healing, proposal, and redeeming renewal.[76] The awareness of the present ministry of Christ and the vision of the theological symbol of the Kingdom are both critical for the faithful life of the church as agent of transformation. The ministry of Jesus the Christ exhibits a style and intent of social transformation.[77] The Spirit of Jesus the Christ empowers us. The Cross is a reality which may mean sacrifice and not always evident success.[78] The symbol of Kingdom inspires us, lures us, challenges us, and testifies that the "end" will only be accomplished by God.[79] Trust and hope are placed in the constancy of God.

For the survival of humans in societies that enable individual and communal fulfillment, for the sake of the fuller life of all classes, and for the ability of the church to exist in a society truly open to its existence and ministrations, Gilkey advocates the necessity of fostering critical virtues: respect for other humans, personal freedom within limits, concern for community, justice, compassion, communal responsibility, courage, confidence, serenity, sacrifice, and love.[80] Members of the church, Christians, are "personal, ethical, and religious beings in our historical situation."[81] God grounds the possibilities of these virtues, and calls us to their fostering. Jesus the Christ is the redemptive force in the Spirit, active in the church and the world towards the Kingdom. In the social praxis of the church, humanity's historical destiny in the Spirit of Jesus the Christ is called forth, so that the church and the world may be liberated from fatedness. Gilkey boldly claims that, in social praxis, "church and theology *become*, become real, redemptive, and effective."[82] In the church's involvement in the social order for the sake of redemptive

---

[74]Gilkey, *ME*, 236n.3.

[75]Gilkey, *ME*, 238ff.; idem, *HCCM*, 26-27.

[76]Gilkey, *ME*, 183-84; idem, "Theology for a Time of Troubles," *Christian Century* 98 (29 April 1981): 478.

[77]Gilkey, *ME*, 193-94; idem, *HCCM*, 27.

[78]Gilkey, *ME*, 183.

[79]Gilkey, *ME*, 217-56, esp. 252.

[80]Gilkey, *TT*, 130.

[81]Gilkey, *TT*, 123.

[82]Gilkey, *TT*, 131.

transformation, God's Word becomes incarnate in our world for its future. The church is to minister both grace and liberation, to participate in God's healing and God's renewing fulfillment. In this social perspective, the church enacts a threefold mission. (1) As sacramental, the church mediates the Holy through word, sacraments, and communal life in a community of love; thus, the church actualizes forgiveness, promise, and hope. (2) As a social institution with social power and a community of people capable of social praxis, the church works for liberation into a more just society, freeing people from their fatedness to poverty, injustice, and political-social impotence. (3) As the bearer of the Spirit of Jesus Christ and grounded in the Creator, the church contributes creative envisionment of fulfilling possibilities for the society, by risking itself in the midst of the societal discourse, political processes, and cultural expressions.[83]

Gilkey concludes one of his essays, "The Church and Public Policy," with six "Guidelines for Ecclesial Praxis." He acknowledges that hard and fast "rules" are inappropriate for the church's public activity, since historical contexts change. Guidelines, however, indicate a style of life in the "polis." These six guidelines may be summarized in this way. (1) The church must clearly conceive those grounding realities in which it is rooted and also know its "bases" in the society, in order to be enabled to specify its concern for "justice, peace, equality, order, and freedom." (2) The culture already has one or many "moral" stances; the church joins in some of these. (3) The church needs sophisticated analysis and acute discernment of where the ideals, roots, and meanings of its social ethic converge with or criticize the society's ethos, ideology, or social ideals. (4) The church must remember and guard against the ambiguities of finitude, both within the church and in the broader society. (5) The church must know that every community needs a supportive and critical conscience; the societal conscience will not be generated by the state, but can arise through the ministries of private institutions in the community, especially the church. (6) The church must be a constant source for the virtues of spiritual strength needed socially; Gilkey lists courage, confidence, norms, compassion, faith, and hope. He is also clear that the church is called both to be a community of love and to engender analogous social communities of love.[84]

---

[83]Gilkey, *TT*, 133.
[84]Gilkey, *TT*, 178.

In considering the church as transformative, I have delineated both internal and external missions. Theologically, along with the symbols of God's sustenance, providence, and Kingdom, the church's transformative task also verges on the theological symbol of "eternal life." This theological concept does not result from rational reflection, but arises as a consequence of the whole of Christian thought and existence. This symbol springs from trust in God, even in the face of death, whether personal or communal. Thus, "transformation" itself is grounded in the power and meaning of the divine life. Our ultimate confidence in the possibilities of transformation are grounded in our relationship to God in Jesus the Christ. The church must proclaim and celebrate the purpose of the creation and the destiny of the creature in "the reunion of God with his/her creation, the establishment of communion of God with each of us, then that sharing of the eternity of God's own divine life."[85] The church's transformative mission as servant church expresses and points to the love of God especially as manifested, made real, actualized in Jesus the Christ. The acquisition of eternal life does not motivate the church's social praxis; but eternal life is the proleptic vision evoked by that confidence in God which enables the church's courage in transformation even when facing the Cross.

Conclusion. Theologian of the Church

It is abundantly clear that Langdon Gilkey is a theologian of and for the Christian church. He has a comprehensive and challenging theology of the church, its substance, life, mission, and hope. Such a realization must challenge the more common label of Gilkey as a "theologian of culture." It would violate his roots, his work, his passion, his impact upon so many clergy and laity in the church, and the intended audience of many of his writings, if that label was interpreted too narrowly or used exclusively to characterize this theologian. Langdon Gilkey is a theologian of church and culture.

Gilkey calls the church to a risky, yet ministering and caring, servanthood. The church must be conscious of how its own "norms and aims" are related to its "own ecclesiastical, social and political structures, habits and forms of behavior." In this respect, Gilkey calls the church to be "prophetic, critical and transformative." The church must discern

---

[85]Gilkey, *ME*, 253.

"those aspects of the wider cultural life in which it shares and which support and are supported by its own Christian norms and aims." Here Gilkey calls the church to be "priestly and conserving." Finally, the church must honestly assert "those aspects of its cultural life that are antithetical to its own norms and aims." Then, the church must be "prophetic and radical."[86]

In his theological project, Gilkey addresses both churches and world. Because women and men in the church are creatures of God's creation and thus "worldly" people, historical beings in communities, clearly the life in God that Gilkey illuminates also is a proposal to all people. Thus, it is appropriate to conclude with that call as the summons to fuller life for church and world.

> [H]uman response is an essential aspect of the divine work: in acceptance of our destiny, in affirmation of our freedom; in the courage to dare new possibilities; in repentance for our sins; in new trust in God's mercy and love; in the risk of loving relations with others; and finally in the courage, wisdom, and self-giving required for creative politics.[87]

The servant church is called to empower such living through faithful evocation of, celebration of, and participation in the mission and ministries of the Spirit of Jesus the Christ.

---

[86]Gilkey, *TT*, 238-39.
[87]Gilkey, *TT*, 250.

Part 4

Gilkey's Practice of Theology

Chapter 14

From Liberalism to Postmodernism:
The Role of Integrity
in the Thought of Langdon Gilkey*

Jennifer L. Rike

Introduction

Langdon Gilkey describes himself, in terms often quoted from Arnold Toynbee, as a theologian living in a "time of troubles." Born in Chicago in 1919, to a future dean of Rockefeller Chapel at the University of Chicago, he initially eschewed following his father into the ministry for the allure of a stint teaching English in China. His subsequent, now famous internment along with other suspect foreigners in a camp in Shantung (now Shandong) Province by the Chinese during the Second World War compelled him to acknowledge the inadequacy of his prior liberal, humanist convictions, and led to his undertaking a course of theological studies and a career as a theologian. This career has spanned five decades (and counting) of cataclysmic intellectual, social, and political change, from the 1940s through the 1990s.

Throughout this half-century, Gilkey has wrestled philosophically with the naïveté of humanist and modernist perspectives and the cynicism of postmodernist perspectives; theologically, with the worldly hopefulness of nineteenth-century liberalism and radical theologies, and the other-worldly tempering in twentieth-century neoorthodox theologies. His enduring project has been to develop a theological vision and method adequate to these changing times and perspectives, a new synthesis responsive to this radically secular, postmodern world entering the new millennium. His vision and method have evolved in ways typical of one variety of postmodern theology, with modernist tendencies resulting from his own methodological insistence upon the requirements of integrity. I shall argue that this insistence remains, in the final analysis, systematical-ly ambiguous: it enables him to avoid one pit into which the variety of

---

*Portions of this essay previously appeared as "Langdon Gilkey," in *A New Handbook of Christian Theologians*, ed. Donald W. Musser and Joseph L. Price (Nashville: Abingdon Press, 1996) 158-70. Copyright ©1996 by Abingdon Press. Revised and reprinted by permission.

postmodern theology most often associated with postmodernism—the total relativism of deconstructivist postmodern theology—has fallen but impels him toward another pit typical of late modern theology, making claims with greater claim to universality than is fully warranted. To clarify the dynamics of his admittedly complex position as it has developed through the decades, I must first establish the issues and perspectives key to the modern and postmodern alternatives, and in this way, render these terms more precise.

I. Modernity Gives Way:
The Path from Premodern to Postmodern Theology

The meanings of the terms "modern" and "postmodern" are a matter of endless debate, but discussions usually focus on how each perspective relates to foundationalism. Generally speaking, the term "postmodern" describes the state of Euro-American culture after the nineteenth century, a state that reflects major transformations in the disciplinary self-understandings and operations of science, literature, and the various arts. Far from being a radical departure from modernity, however, these transformations were themselves the result of the very Enlightenment quest that had *created* modernity—the quest to question radically the foundations that traditional, premodern authorities had used to validate their claims to knowledge and to legitimate their claims to power. Initially, in modernity, this questioning substituted one set of foundations for another: it dethroned the Bible and ecclesiastical authorities as the final arbiters of truth, in favor of what could be determined through reason and experience, and it set up new rationally and empirically established foundations by which to validate knowledge and legitimate power.[1] These foundations consisted of a specific worldview, developed initially from seventeenth-century science by virtue of the theories of Galileo, Descartes, Bacon, and Newton, and later, through the nineteenth and into the early twentieth centuries, by virtue of Darwin's theory of evolution. Carried over from modernism into postmodernism, however, the originally Enlightenment posture of radical questioning forever undermined modern confidence in

---

[1]"Modernity is understood as the condition in which society must legitimate itself by its own self-generated principles, without appeal to external verities, deities, authorities, or traditions" (John McGowan, *Postmodernism and Its Critics* [Ithaca NY: Cornell University Press, 1991] 3).

modernity's ability to build reliable foundations. For, in postmodernism, the posture of radical questioning has become surcharged by the conviction that it is essential to get beyond modernity before we annihilate ourselves. Ironically enough, even when empowered with tools wrought by the scientific, technological, and industrial revolutions, modernity did not indisputably succeed in improving the human lot. The expressed purpose of its proponents was to harness the Enlightenment impetus toward greater knowledge and put it to the task of creating a more prosperous, humane, and just world for all. But modernity's initially sanguine expectations of success in changing the world for the better were shattered by the violence and mounting environmental disasters of the twentieth century whose proportions, ironically enough, were made gargantuan by the very scientific and technological advances that had been expected to create a more humane world.

Many current proponents of postmodern perspectives manifest the desperation of idealists whose utopias have disclosed the seeds of more destructiveness than the most oppressive of traditional authorities. For many, little remains in which to invest hope but the originating, courageous impulse to pursue truth, even though this impulse has reduced itself to attacking any position that pretends to express any truth but that which is purely relative and subjective. Consequently, Jean-François Lyotard, in his renowned study, *The Postmodern Condition*, defines as modern "any science that legitimates itself with reference to a metadiscourse of this kind making an explicit appeal to some grand narrative, such as the dialectics of Spirit, the hermeneutics of meaning, the emancipation of the rational or working subject, or the criterion of wealth," while postmodernism exhibits a singular skepticism toward all such metanarratives presuming to offer foundations that legitimate various disciplines and sciences.[2] In contrast, John McGowan argues that postmodernism should not be simply identified with a rejection of foundationalism, but rather with "a distinctive response to the lack of foundations, . . . [a response that] is the attempt to legitimate knowledge claims and the moral/political bases for action, not on the basis of indubitable truths, but on the basis of human practices within established communities."[3]

---

[2]Jean-François Lyotard, *The Postmodern Condition: A Report on Knowledge*, trans. Geoff Bennington and Brian Massumi (Minneapolis: University of Minnesota Press, 1979) xxiii, xxiv.

[3]McGowan, *Postmodernism*, 24.

In my project, to locate Gilkey's thought on the contemporary theological map, McGowan's perspective on postmodernism, as a series of responses to the radical undermining of all foundations, proves far more helpful than Lyotard's now widely accepted identification of postmodernism with antifoundationalism. Clearly, theologians will rapidly self-destruct if they simply swallow postmodern antifoundationalism whole, for what is a religious faith if not a response to the foundation(s) of the world as we know it (them)? Traditionally, the very nature of theology has been to ascertain and witness to the foundations of the world, foundations in which we might place our trust and hopes in troubled times. Given the massive destructiveness of the twentieth-century world, theologians have had their hands full defending the validity of faithfully relying upon a (presumably) beneficent Creator and Redeemer. Nearly all have registered the recent seismic shaking of foundations—some (fundamentalist, evangelical) by clinging tenaciously to premodern methods and certainties; others (the genuinely postmodern) by increasingly intense scrutiny of the warrants for positing foundations, and by exercising extreme caution in recommending them to anyone else.

Historically, premodern theology tended to appeal to scriptural, theological, and institutional authorities to excuse experiential and rational incoherence in their views. It simply accepted as itself a tenet of faith that the truths of faith transcended and often contradicted the truths of reason and science. Hence, premodern theology promoted a dualistic supernaturalism in which God and world remained unrelated—even opposed—to one another. Consequently, knowledge based on experience became disconnected from and so largely irrelevant to theological reflection, while the reverse was also true: theological claims about the nature of God and salvation were too often divorced from concrete lived experience.[4] In its contemporary manifestations, premodern theology continues to live in a split world: its proponents believe in science when they turn the keys in the ignitions of their cars, and look to the vast industrial, technological, and military complexes of their nations to give their lives comfort and safety. When it comes to belief in God and God's Word,

---

[4]David Ray Griffin, *God and Religion in the Postmodern World: Essays in Postmodern Theology* (Albany NY: SUNY Press, 1989) 1; David Tracy, *Blessed Rage for Order: The New Pluralism in Christian Theology* (New York: Crossroad, 1975) 24-25.

however, reason is left behind: against all evidence to the contrary, the world and all that is in it was created in six days.[5]

The move from premodern to modern theology initially seemed to force a choice between rejecting science in order to retain traditional beliefs in God, transcendently grounded values and free spirit, or accepting science and losing them. Postmodern theologians sorted through this apparent conflict between faith and theology, on the one hand, and reason and science, on the other, by recognizing how the sciences approached reality differently than the various humanities, including theology, in search of different kinds of truth. Most importantly, modern and postmodern theologies reject, in principle, any appeal to authorities that cannot be validated on the basis of some analysis of experience. The development of modern and postmodern theologies can be traced by examining their appeals to increasingly expansive, complex, and pluralistic accounts of subjective and objective experience. The attempts of early modern (especially Deist) theology to construct a theology that was universally valid for all who believe in God, as a basis for moral, social, and political action, worked from so limited an understanding of humanity and science that the resulting theology eliminated the mysteries of the divine so intrinsic to the biblical faith and left Christian communities with little foundation for their existence. Later modern attempts to render science and faith harmonious by embracing natural science, particularly the Darwinian theory of evolution, offered a more materialistic worldview, while proposing that salvation will come through material progress in creating a more economically, socially, and politically just world. The views of most late modern or liberal theologians (such as Albrecht Ritschl, Wilhelm Herrmann, and Adolf von Harnack) were more widely accepted, but ultimately proved too sanguine to withstand the challenge of historical events.

The shift to postmodern theology began in 1919, with Karl Barth's lambasting the self-serving naïveté and pride of liberalism in light of the

---

[5]The term "to split," when used in a technical psychoanalytic context, means forcibly to separate off some psychic contents and block them from full consciousness: see Jennifer L. Rike, "Loving with Integrity: A Feminist Spirituality of Wholeness," in *Spirituality, Creativity, and Relationship: The Emotional and Philosophical Challenges of Adulthood*, ed. Melvin E. Miller and Alan N. West (Madison CT: International Universities Press/Psychosocial Press, 1999). Here I use the term to suggest that this happens when someone sharply divides their ways of reasoning in the everyday world from their ways of reasoning in religious matters.

horrors of World War I's bloody trench and chemical warfare in his
Römerbrief (1919), and gained momentum through the twentieth century.
Not Barth's call to return to the foundations of the Reformation faith, but
his challenge to liberalism's ultimately arrogant and destructive optimism
reverberated throughout postmodern theology. Embracing the pivotal role
of experience in theological reflection, the task of postmodern theology
has become the development of methods and visions that, first, reflect the
strictures placed upon what humanity can really know by virtue of its
innate structures and limited but diverse modes of experience and, second,
avoid any self-serving and ultimately oppressive distortions of the truth
by making false universal claims on the basis of that limited experience.
Much postmodern theology, then, strives to be public in two senses: first,
it believes that all theological claims to truth must meet criteria of appropriateness of Scripture, adequacy to experience, and internal coherence;
second, it believes that theological claims must be relevant to public
policy.[6] Precisely insofar as it tries to be public, postmodern theology
retains the emphasis of modern theology upon experience as an authoritative source in theological reflection.

Langdon Gilkey came of age both personally and theologically in the
intense upheaval of the early twentieth century, and found himself sorting
through the issues confronting those who were likewise moving from
modernism into postmodernism: how to adjudicate between the frequently
conflicting claims of empirical experience and scientific investigation, on
the one hand, and religious and theological authorities, on the other; how
to engage in philosophical reflection upon the Christian faith, particularly
in light of recent advances in scientific and social-scientific knowledge
of humanity and the world, without forsaking its biblical foundations;
how to render theological reflection relevant to the religiously committed
without sacrificing the distinctive identity of the Christian faith and traditions or, alternatively, how to mine the profound insights into the human
condition that Christianity offers, without sliding back into oppressive
authoritarianism. Gilkey ultimately stands with postmodern theology, as
distinct both from contemporary evangelical or fundamentalist theology
(themselves essentially premodern), and from modern liberal theology. He
strives to articulate a genuinely theological vision of the world on the
basis of a more nuanced understanding of the relationship between reason

---

[6]Some postmodern theologies eschew the concern to be public. See the discussion on
the confessional approach of the Yale School of Theology that follows.

and science, on the one hand, and faith, on the other, than either premodern or modern theologies achieved. He has also developed a more realistic perspective upon the ability of human scientific, moral, and spiritual endeavors to achieve progress than modernity.

David Ray Griffin's fourfold typology of postmodern theology—liberationist, deconstructive, constructive or revisionary, and restorationist—is especially helpful in evaluating the dynamics of Gilkey's final vision and method. *Liberationist* theology concerns itself primarily with constructing a worldview that liberates its proponents from the oppressiveness of premodern pieties, by developing theologies that reflect their distinctive gender-specific, sociopolitical, and economic locations. Such theologies focus upon the chief criterion of truth in postmodern theology: that it liberates and does not oppress its practitioners.[7]

Deconstructive theology carries through the implications of Jacques Derrida's deconstructive method to argue that objective analyses of reality lead inevitably to the conclusion that no true objectivity is possible, hence radically undermining the modern faith that reason does attain reality. Such a postmodern worldview will be radically relativistic, even self-negating; theologically speaking, its proponents (most notably, Mark C. Taylor) argue that all theology must become a/theology, and deny the existence of God, objective values, and the self-determining free soul. Griffin argues that, far from being truly postmodernist, deconstructive theology is really "mostmodernist," because it carries the radically skeptical impetus behind modernism through to its most nihilistic conclusions.[8]

Constructivist theologians, like Griffin himself, do agree with deconstructive theology that the rational-empirical approach to establishing a view of reality no longer supports a modern worldview (particularly in its drive to achieve universality), so that all claims to truth are relativized by the context that created them; nor does it support optimism about the human condition. Constructivist theology, however, resists nihilism by remaining convinced of the validity of scientific investigation and expanded conceptions of experience, and integrates insights drawn from science and experience into its theological method. In contrast to the modernist ten-

---

[7]David Ray Griffin, "Introduction: Varieties of Postmodern Theology," in *Varieties of Postmodern Theology*, by David Ray Griffin, William A. Beardsley, and Joe Holland (Albany NY: SUNY Press, 1989) 4-5.

[8]Griffin, *God and Religion in the Postmodern World*, 8; idem, "Introduction: Varieties of Postmodern Theology," 3-4.

dency to think that naturalism and personal belief in a Creator-God are mutually exclusive, constructivist postmodern theology maintains a naturalistic theism in which both the integrity of the natural order and its groundedness in another dimension are affirmed. It also affirms the validity of nonsensory modes of perception which, far from being derivative from sensory perception, ground it, and through it, moral and spiritual values, forming their deepest and abiding presupposition.[9] In effect, various accounts of nonsensory, but nevertheless perceptual, experience offer an access to the transcendent Creator God. Consequently, religion and science are not in contradiction, but offer different, complementary perspectives on reality. Constructivist theology also asserts that ultimate reality is fundamentally creative, and humanity realizes itself insofar as it too is creative.[10]

Gilkey's vision contains all of these elements of constructive postmodern theology, even as it operates within the classical Christian framework to establish its meaningfulness and validity to the citizen of postmodernity. In that sense, it is also restorationist. Restorationist theology responds to postmodernism's shaking of foundations, primarily by mining those foundations for their profound insights into the human condition, in order to defend and reconceptualize them in contemporary terms. Restorationist theology is fundamentally conservative: it attempts to retrieve the tradition in question to demonstrate its efficacy in redeeming the utilitarianism, consumerism, alienation, and disorientation caused by the radical relativism of postmodern secularity.[11]

Gilkey's constructivist postmodern approach to theology evolves in its own unique way, by developing public claims to truth and an expanded account of experience—particularly through an analysis of the religious dimensions of common human experience. As a Christian theologian, Gilkey is committed to asserting the reality of certain foundations. The necessity of his assertions is not predetermined by a preestablished

---

[9]The importance of accepting the validity of such prelinguistic and preconceptual experience cannot be overemphasized: it allows for "*a dimension or element of perceptual experience that is not a product of culturally conditioned frameworks and is therefore common to us all*" (Griffin's emphasis); by means of appeal to such experience, it escapes the reductive elimination of all claims to know God that characterizes deconstructive postmodern theology (Griffin, *God and Religion in the Postmodern World*, 4).

[10]Griffin, *God and Religion in the Postmodern World*, 3-8.

[11]Griffin, "Introduction: Varieties of Postmodern Theology," 5-6.

faith, but rather by the compulsion to follow through on the postmodern commitment to question authorities in order to understand them better and work with them for the greater good. Gilkey's rejection of the fervent antifoundationalism of deconstructive postmodernism is born of other commitments that he shares with postmodernism, particularly both his emphasis upon experience as a definitive source for theology and his pursuit of a radically inclusive, egalitarian, and pluralistic democratic order.[12] His confidence in human rationality, however, is born not of the naïveté that deconstructive theologians scorn, but of experiences of the power of the divine to guide, heal, and liberate.

Gilkey will argue, against the deconstructionists, that these commitments to making experience rather than tradition authoritative, and to an inclusive, egalitarian, and democratic order require a move also scorned by many deconstructionists: he retains the typically modernist commitment to human autonomy and integrity. Precisely Gilkey's appeal to integrity guides his entire enterprise—both his public theological method and, in particular, the development in his later work of the concept of a "relative absolute." Gilkey's appeal to integrity informs his resistance to both premodern and deconstructive postmodern options, and ultimately serves as the fundamental criterion of public theology, the criterion from which all others are derived. Moreover, if he were more reflective and consistent about his own appeals to the relative absolute, he would evade the one typically postmodern criticism to which his vision falls prey: his constructivism sometimes reads like a restorationism that can turn oppressive when not properly qualified as only relatively valid. The extent to which his final vision and method do, in fact, fall prey to this typically modernist problem shall focus my final reflections.

---

[12]See, for instance, Jacques Derrida, "The Politics of Friendship," *Journal of Philosophy* 85 (November 1988): 632-44. For an analysis of the tendencies of postmodernism toward radical democracy, as opposed to the ruse of it currently operative in the West, see Stanley Aronowitz, "Postmodernism and Politics," *Social Text* 18: 99-115. John McGowan argues that, "whatever form it [postmodern politics] takes (whether aestheticist, textual, or tied to local, community action or to the new social movements), an underlying commitment to democracy reveals itself. Faith in traditional leftist visions of a revolutionary avant-garde, of a dictatorship of the proletariat, and of a scientifically managed technological Utopia has all but vanished, to be replaced by decentered, pluralistic visions of untroubled local diversity" (McGowan, *Postmodernism*, 28-29).

II. Origins of Gilkey's Emphasis on Integrity

To support these claims, I turn to the role of integrity in Gilkey's vision and method. Modernists typically understand selfhood as an integrated whole, the foremost virtue of which is to act autonomously and with integrity. For them, autonomy and integrity are inseparable: to act with integrity is to act in accordance with certain moral principles and rules, and that requires an integrated, unified self capable of resisting outside influences or secondary considerations, such as the possible outcome of one's actions.[13] The modernist embrace of autonomy reflects its obsession with purity, a concern to avoid being sullied by the pettiness, provincialism, self-interest, and brutality of contemporary capitalist, bourgeois existence.[14] The postmodern rejection of the ideal of the autonomous, integrated, unified self that is able to act with integrity comes from the conviction that such selves are particularly prone to asserting their wills upon others in oppressive, manipulative, and ultimately self-interested ways.[15] Throughout his work, Gilkey recognizes the tendency toward

---

[13]See, for instance, M. S. Halfon, *Integrity: A Philosophical Inquiry* (Philadelphia: Temple University Press, 1989); Lynn McFall, "Integrity," *Ethics* (October 1987): 5-20.

[14]McGowan, *Postmodernism*, 8-11. The full dynamics of the conflict between the modernist emphasis on autonomy and the postmodern attack on it focus much of McGowan's reflections in *Postmodernism*. McGowan argues that many postmodernists (particularly Derrida and the early Foucault) go to great lengths "both to deny the possibility of achieving autonomy and to indicate autonomy's pernicious consequences" (McGowan, *Postmodernism*, 4). "On the whole, modernists, whether avant-garde or not, work to ensure the primacy of the will, since they believe that only the integrity of the willful, autonomous self can afford them an escape from the general cultural condition that they abhor. Alone in the wasteland, threatened by the madness of being overwhelmed by society's decay and his own isolation, the poet can still assert that 'these fragments I have shored against my ruin.' This heroic maintenance of the self and its ability to create the artwork that represents and encapsulates its will stands as the quintessential modernist gesture when all hope of having any impact on the culture at large has been lost" (McGowan, *Postmodernism*, 11). In contrast, postmodernists have accepted the insight of Horkheimer and Adorno that an "inescapable compulsion to social domination of nature" (Max Horkheimer and Theodor W. Adorno, *Dialectics of Enlightenment*, trans. John Cumming [New York: Herder and Herder, 1972] 34) is intrinsic to Western reason, and becomes operative in the agent's single-mindedness by which s/he seeks control by repressing diversity and excluding any distracting, vitiating considerations (Horkheimer and Adorno, *Dialectics of Enlightenment*, 18-19).

[15]For a sensitive discussion of the poststructuralist philosophers' (Lyotard, Baudrillard, Derrida), Lacan's, and (to a lesser extent) the French feminists' (Kristeva, Irigaray) rejec-

nefarious self-interest, but still holds onto the necessity of acting with integrity—precisely to avoid such self-interest! Initially, he used the term "integrity" in a fairly casual, unreflective manner—a manner which belies its increasingly key role in his anthropology as well as in his theological vision and method—to indicate the ability to act with the courage of one's convictions, in accordance with accepted moral rules and principles. And yet, from the beginning, the net effect of Gilkey's thought is to expand this common understanding of integrity as a predominantly moral virtue characteristic of individuals to suggest both an understanding of (what I call) fully personal integrity and its communal counterpart, an expansion that has important consequences for his final position.

Gilkey did not begin with the intention of becoming a theologian. During his college years at Harvard University, Gilkey believed himself to be an "ethical humanist," who was skeptical of religion because he was convinced that humanity had moved beyond a need for it—until 1939.[16] Then the Nazi threat to overtake the free nations of Europe and annihilate its Jewish citizens highlighted the implicit contradiction between his commitment to pacifism, on the one hand, and his commitment to justice and freedom, on the other—a contradiction that compelled him (as it should any person of integrity) to seek an alternative solution. Just as his initially liberal, idealistic confidence in the progress of the world toward justice began to disintegrate, he discovered in the thought of Reinhold Niebuhr a way to reconcile his moral idealism with his growing sociopolitical realism. After his graduation in 1940, he embarked on what he later acknowledged to be "the most significant and formative period"

---

tion of autonomous, integrated selfhood, see James M. Glass, *Shattered Selves: Multiple Personality in a Postmodern World* (Ithaca NY and London: Cornell University Press, 1993) esp. 1-27. Consider also McGowan's comments. "The suppression of women and of minority groups within the society and of non-European races wherever they were encountered must be read as the outcome of the West's obsession with identity, singleness and purity, with its belief that only unified, homogeneous entities (be they selves or states) can act effectively. Postmodernism finds in the modernist drive for autonomy another version of Western reason's obsession with integrity and insists that this obsession has drastic political consequences, in both the oppression of women and minorities and in the establishment of hierarchical orders that must threaten the egalitarian distribution of power (as capacity to engage in and influence the social processes of decision making) espoused by democracy" (McGowan, *Postmodernism*, 21).

[16]Langdon Gilkey, "Introduction: A Retrospective Glance at My Work," in *The Whirlwind in Culture. Frontiers in Theology*, ed. Donald W. Musser and Joseph L. Price (Bloomington IN: Meyer-Stone Books, 1988) 5.

of his life: a stint teaching introductory English at Yenching University in Peking, China.[17] When the war began in 1941, the Japanese forcibly interned him, along with the other "enemy nationals," in what he described twenty years later in his book as the *Shantung Compound*.[18]

The Compound's internees were forced to develop their own systems of governance for ordering community life among the vastly diverse groups of people constituting them. During his four years in the compound, Gilkey repeatedly witnessed the manifold ways in which self-interest and pride could effectively foil God's creative purposes within their community life. This witness provoked him to reflect extensively upon the true dynamics and validity of the Christian faith in a moral and loving God—in particular, upon how the dynamics of fully personal integrity manifest true faithfulness. Strength of moral integrity was vastly important to preventing their fragile existence from descending into chaos; and yet, as Gilkey was shocked to observe, superficial commitments to Christian morality could also be used to excuse acts of blatant self-interest and to obstruct the achievement of justice and the common good. Thus, from the inception of Gilkey's career as a theologian, he was confronted with the difference between a self-righteous attempt to maintain "holiness" by adhering to certain narrowly defined rules of behavior (moral integrity narrowly conceived and divorced from its concern to build up the whole) and the integrity whose reigning principle is to promote the welfare of the whole and is willing to make personal sacrifices for it.[19] In retrospect, he realized that only by maintaining a commitment to something beyond one's own narrow self-interest, only by placing one's trust and center in God and not in oneself, is true integrity possible.[20]

Gilkey's personal experience in Shandong became the existential foundation of his theological anthropology and, through it, of his mature theological vision and method. Three convictions implicitly inform his early anthropology. First, true moral integrity both promotes fully personal integrity—that is, the wholeness which results from acting from a fully

---

[17]Gilkey, "Retrospective Glance at My Work," 9.

[18]Langdon Gilkey, *Shantung Compound: The Story of Men and Women under Pressure* (New York: Harper & Row, 1966); hereafter cited as *SC*. See also Gary Dorrien's study in this book.

[19]Gilkey, *SC*, 83-89, 148, 157, 168, 172-73, 182-85.

[20]Gilkey, *SC*, 230-35.

reflective consciousness of all that one is, knows, and feels, in light of certain principles and goals—and is itself a result of it. Chief among these principles and goals is the desire to "build up" the self and others, one interpretation of love (1 Cor. 8:1). Second, such fully personal integrity finds its correlate in the structure of the community that can only survive if it is sustained by its members acting with love to achieve justice; that is, community has a moral structure and, if this structure is ignored, community decays. Acting with fully personal integrity means that one acts to build up both oneself and the community; and, given the sinful tendency toward self-interest, such integrity often requires extraordinary courage. Retreat from such courageous action, however, not only reduces the self to self-serving rationalizations and hypocrisy, but, by repressing dimensions of the truth, breaks down the self and the fabric of communal life. Thus, truth, love, and justice are deeply intertwined; all are achieved by acting with fully personal integrity. Third, such fully personal integrity is the existential offspring of faith in the God of love and justice. Faith in the God of love and justice makes acting with integrity both possible and necessary: without such a God, integrity is not possible, and faith in such a God requires acting with integrity for it truly to be faith.

These convictions inform Gilkey's later theology, producing a holism that distinguishes it from the ultimately naïve and reductionistic idealism of nineteenth-century modern liberalism, on the one hand, and the conservative, ultimately dualistic mode of the early Barthian neoorthodoxy that reacted against liberalism, on the other. Gilkey personally witnessed how liberalism's naïve faith in moral and spiritual progress collapsed under the pressure of the onslaught of Nazism. Gilkey himself resisted returning, nevertheless, to the early Barth's repressive restorationism, which cast a great divide between religion and faith, reason and revelation. He has spent the succeeding decades formulating his creative alternative to them both. His alternative did not collapse the transcendent sacred into immanence, creating a bland monism, as modern liberal theology tended to do. Nor did Gilkey's alternative oppose the transcendent to the immanent or revelation to reason, creating a radical dualism, as did early Barthian neoorthodoxy's veer back toward premodern convictions about the Bible and revelation. Rather, he envisioned the sacred as transcendent to the world, but as working within it to be its healing, reconciling depth, so that together they form a differentiated unity, a unity encompassed by their irreducible difference.

Gilkey later acknowledged that he learned more about the importance of integrity and wholeness from his "spiritual father," Reinhold Niebuhr, and from Paul Tillich, during his graduate studies in theology at Union Theological Seminary in New York.[21] He began these studies when he returned from China to the United States in 1945 and, upon completing his doctorate, taught first at Vassar College from 1951 to 1954, and then at Vanderbilt University Divinity School from 1954 to 1963.

This was a period of tremendous theological ferment. During this period, Gilkey became increasingly convinced of the necessity for revelation and grace to return modern society—riven with sin and meaninglessness, and threatening to self-destruct because of it—to full expression of its true humanity. Still, as he struggled to discern the historical implications of the Christian faith, he found himself as much at odds with the literalism of the conservative evangelicals as with the ultimately irrelevant optimism of the old-style liberalism. His own recognition of the necessity for interpreting the Christian traditions from the perspective of issues arising within the contemporary existential and historical situation to keep faith relevant (not to mention, intellectually honest) distinguished him *as* liberal, precisely in the way postmodern theology retained the typically liberal, modernist emphasis upon the authority of experience. And yet his further recognition of the tragedy and sinfulness permeating the human situation and, as a result, of the need for the transcendent God to redeem humanity through the power of divine forgiveness and grace distinguished him *from* the old-style nineteenth-century liberalism that had flourished in the United States until the 1920s. These two realizations moved him decisively into the more liberal neo-orthodox camp dominated by Reinhold Niebuhr and Paul Tillich. This theological perspective marked his first three books: *Maker and Heaven and Earth* (1959), *How the Church Can Minister to the World without Losing Itself* (1964), and *Shantung Compound* (1966).

III. Integrity: The Key Criterion of Public Theology

In 1963, Gilkey left Vanderbilt to take up a new appointment in the University of Chicago Divinity School. He came accompanied by a new wife, Sonja (later, she took the name Ram Rattan), of Dutch descent and Sikh persuasion. To her influence, he credited his increasing originality

---

[21]Private conversation, July 1996.

in thought; and in personal appearance, his clean-shaven visage gave way to a beard and an earring in his left ear (as Dutch sailors wear them), his tweeds and flannels to tie-dyed shirts and corduroys. Shortly thereafter, from 1965 to 1966, a sabbatical year in Italy introduced him to the leading theologians behind Vatican II (Karl Rahner, Bernard Lonergan, Hans Küng, and Edward Schillebeeckx), deepened his appreciation for the resources within the Roman Catholic tradition for responding to the crises of postmodern secularity, and prepared him for the growing ecumenism among his students and colleagues. The impact of this expansion of his horizons comes to expression in *Catholicism Confronts Modernity* (1975).

In subsequent decades at the University of Chicago, Gilkey and another then-recent addition to the Chicago faculty, David Tracy, developed further what has become known as the "Chicago school of theology."[22] During the 1970s, the Chicago School became renowned for its insistence that theology should be genuinely "public"—that is, the grounds for the validity of any theological claim should be available and apparent to anyone genuinely aware, intelligent, reflective, and responsible, regardless of whether that person is a believer or not.[23] In opposition, the "Yale school of theology" led by George Lindbeck denied the possibility of public theology, and insisted upon the necessity for theology to be developed within a confessional context with its own unique norms for truth: theology is understood and developed only within a practicing community of faith. This controversy provoked heated debate among academic theologians during the 1970s, and focused the ways in which theologians contended methodologically with the growing secularism of twentieth-century life. To some extent, it reenacted the debates between liberalism and neoorthodoxy in new form: the "liberal" Chicago school emphasized the validity of natural powers of reason to adjudicate spiritual and theological truth by approaching it phenomenologically, from the perspective of an interpretation of human experience; the "conservative," more "orthodox," Yale school emphasized that such insights were gained only kerygmatically, through a life immersed in Scripture and ecclesial community, and empowered by grace. Unfortu-

---

[22]W. Creighton Peden and Jerome Arthur Stone, eds., *The Chicago School of Theology: Pioneers in Religious Inquiry*, 2 vols., Studies in American Religion 66 (Lewiston NY: Edwin Mellen Press, 1996).

[23]This is Tracy's preferred formulation, itself an appropriation of Bernard Lonergan's work: see Tracy, *Blessed Rage for Order*.

nately, supporters of the Yale school failed to grasp how Gilkey and Tracy had drawn from the best of liberalism and neoorthodoxy to formulate a new approach to the theological task. They accused Chicagoans of capitulating to secularity by denying the existence of the transcendent, and of reducing revelation to reason. The Yale school failed to see that the Chicago school only feared splitting revelation from reason so that revelation remained inexorably opposed to it, rather than its ultimate sustaining ground.[24] The Chicago approach remains fully open to the ways in which grace works upon those who reflect upon the Christian scriptures and traditions to guide and deepen rational insight. It merely demands that criteria be developed to help differentiate, for instance, true experiences of the sacred in paradox and mystery from false ones.

Gilkey developed his own distinctive approach to rendering theology public by making integrity its chief criterion during the late 1960s and early 1970s. This approach is operative in all of his work, although I have found only one place where he makes it explicit—in a chapter entitled "The Grammar of Assent" in *Catholicism Confronts Modernity*. There he argues that, in fully public theology, objectivity and rational argument interpenetrate existential involvement and participation in a dialectical search for truth. The truth sought is universally applicable and relevant, and itself seeks to elicit universal assent. Moreover, when we as rational beings seek the truth, we assume that the evidence and arguments we marshal will support the claims that we make—both in everyday and in religious or theological matters.[25] "Thus it is difficult, not to say contradictory, for us to claim at one moment that Christianity is the truth of all truths, and yet is totally unrelated to our ordinary ways of arriving at the truth, to our serious reflections in common sense, in the sciences and in philosophy."[26] The theological task is to interpret key symbols

---

[24]David Tracy, "Lindbeck's New Program for Theology: A Reflection," *The Thomist* 49 (July 1985): 460-72; Paul Lakeland, "Accommodation to Secularity: The Tracy-Dulles Controversy," *The Month* 11 (1978): 162-66. For a representative of the Yale School, see Peter L. Berger, "Secular Theology and the Rejection of the Supernatural: Reflections on Recent Trends," *Theological Studies* 38 (1977): 39-56. For responses by Gilkey, Schubert Ogden, and Tracy, see "Responses to Peter Berger," *Theological Studies* 19 (1978): 486-507. Also see Thomas B. Ommen, "Verification in Theology: A Tension in Revisionist Method," *The Thomist* 43 (July 1979): 357-89.

[25]Langdon Gilkey, *Catholicism Confronts Modernity: A Protestant View* (New York: Seabury, 1975) 156-57; hereafter cited as *CCM*.

[26]Gilkey, *CCM*, 158-59.

(scriptural and doctrinal symbols) in terms of common, ordinary, universal (as opposed to unique, extraordinary, or "supernatural") experience. Such interpretation is to render these symbols intelligible and meaningful to any person who is willing and able to follow the analyses and argumentation marshaled to support them, using whatever philosophical tools are deemed helpful in the task. To assent to religious truths must definitely not require sacrificing one's intellect in an act of submission to authorities; rather, such assent is guided by the correlation of religious symbols, whose meaning and validity has been elaborated by means of refined philosophical analysis, with the religious dimensions of common human experience. "Our modern understanding of intellectual autonomy and integrity forces us all to assert as true only what to us—to our minds, our understanding of existence, and our interpretation of our experience—is meaningful and true."[27]

In this way, Gilkey explicitly makes integrity the key criterion of public theological method: we cannot leave rationality behind when we move from assessing claims to truth in everyday matters to assessing theological claims to truth. There is a fundamental unity (though not strict identity) between the methods that we employ in knowing everyday realities and in knowing God. Consequently, we both can and must exercise our rational powers in eliciting and defending faith in theological reflection. In other words, we must exercise fully personal integrity in the performance of theology. The requirement of maintaining integrity in theological reflection is grounded in the belief in one universal God: "since truth is one, because God is one, our theological affirmations must be coherent with all else we believe to be true. And every theology must exhibit this coherence, in principle if not in fact."[28] Hence, integrity as the key criterion requires the criterion of intellectual coherence or consistency in developing one's theological vision. Likewise, integrity as key requires that one's interpretation of faith be both adequate to human experience and appropriate to Scripture.

Gilkey's approach dissolves the common distinction between apologetic or fundamental theology and confessional or dogmatic theology.[29]

---

[27]Gilkey, *CCM*, 161.

[28]Gilkey, *CCM*, 163.

[29]Gilkey's view of public theology distinguishes itself from David Tracy's perspective on this point. Tracy argues that different, though related, conceptions of publicness are operative in fundamental theology and in systematic theology: see *Blessed Rage for Order*

No theology should be presented to believers for assent unless the grounds for its meaning and validity have been rendered apparent in terms readily accessible to all rational persons. No theology should be presented for assent unless that particular, Christian interpretation of experience is the most relatively adequate one available. Moreover, the Christian interpretations offered must cohere with all else that we believe to be true on the basis of other disciplines, such as science and history.

This does not mean, however, that rational argument alone suffices to create and sustain faith. The theological analysis elaborating the religious dimensions of any symbol renders explicit not only its inner-worldly but its transcendent referent. Such analysis can adequately be performed only by a person whose mind is open to the symbol's essential reference to the transcendent, and such openness entails the participation in the transcendent made possible by faith. We are led toward faith by rational argument, but in the final analysis our assent is compelled by an experience of being grasped by the transcendent God "communicating himself to us in and through these symbols: we are grasped, we respond, and faith is born."[30] The power of symbols to order and illuminate our experience, and to make healing and hope possible, convinces us of their validity or truth. But such conviction is born of a prior participation in the divine: "reason can rise to ultimacy in the face of disorder, mystery, and ambiguity, only if ultimacy has first given itself to us for our participation, transformation, confidence and hope."[31]

Thus, Gilkey insists upon the Tillichian equivalent of grace for grasping the validity of religious (particularly Christian) symbols, even as he insists upon the essential role of autonomous human rationality in responding to and interpreting the authoritative Christian traditions. Nevertheless, Gilkey is far from blind to the implications of wedding rationality to gracious participation in performing the theological task: theological claims, as a function of rationality, now become relative, potentially pluralistic, hypothetical and fallible, like other arts and sciences. Insofar as a theologian interprets the tradition in light of an evolving understanding of anthropology and ontology, as well as emergent historical events, his or her perspective will be relative to his

---

and *The Analogical Imagination: Christian Theology and the Culture of Pluralism* (New York: Crossroad, 1981).
    [30]Gilkey, *CCM*, 167-68.
    [31]Gilkey, *CCM*, 168.

or her particular historical context. A theologian is forced to take risks in creatively reinterpreting the traditions in light of changing contexts and understandings. Although each theologian intends to express universal truth, none achieve more than one more, hopefully creative and new, but always partial expression of that truth. At times, the proposed understanding will, in fact, be wrong—not just partial and incomplete but distorted. The theologian will be emboldened by the faith that the Holy Spirit guides his reflections, and encouraged by that faith to believe that such guidance makes his claims more true than false. Far from being a situation to lament, the pluralism of theological perspectives bound to emerge from such a method expresses the true meaning of the catholicity of the Christian church, and with it, the ultimate mystery of God as it slowly unfolds to human minds and spirits. Diversity of opinion is to be welcomed and embraced, in the knowledge that God is at work and manifest within it.[32]

On one bright spring afternoon in 1973, at the close of my first year at the University of Chicago Divinity School, I visited Langdon Gilkey in his office, and he offered a compelling metaphor for his method. In response to my expression of frustration and confusion about how to decide among all of the theological visions being thrust before me, he leaned back in his chair, fixed me with those piercing eyes of his, and reflected on the perennial problem for theologians:

> Many theologians spend their careers standing frozen in the midst of the iceberg of someone else's system—Augustine's or Thomas's or Whitehead's or Tillich's—answering all questions that come at them in the terms of that system. Intellectually and theologically, they remain stuck, frozen stiff, never acknowledging how all of the questions challenging them are slowly melting the iceberg on which they stand—until they sink, into irrelevance and oblivion. To be a good theologian, you don't need to find some iceberg that never melts on which to stand. You just need to know when to get off that particular ice flow, onto another one, before it melts so much you sink.

This image of developing one's theological perspective by knowing when to move on, serves as an apt metaphor for both the method of developing warrants for one's theological vision in public theology, and Gilkey's own career as a postmodern theologian. It acknowledges that, as historical beings, we can achieve no absolute viewpoint that encompasses the whole

---

[32]Gilkey, *CCM*, 175-79.

with complete adequacy, but only changing viewpoints as we continually review and reformulate our theological perspectives in light of our developing experience and knowledge.

Despite Gilkey's insistence upon the limited, perspectival nature of all theological claims to truth, he still likewise insists, both in theoretical reflections and in practice, upon the need to strive for universal validity in developing one's claims to truth. These two dimensions of his method coexist in tension—perhaps even in conflict—with one another. Certainly, deconstructive theologians would argue that any claim to achieve universality is distorted, from the start, by self-interest. Many liberationist theologians would agree, and insist that, to be consistent, Gilkey should have limited his claims to truth by prefacing them with a qualifier: such as, these are the reflections of a twentieth-century white American male from a relatively privileged socioeconomic and educational background. Of course, the insistence upon such qualifications accounts for the current fragmenting of the theological landscape; such critics, however, would accept fragmentation as perhaps unfortunate but ultimately necessary to avoid oppressing others by pressing upon them a perspective inimical to their own experience.

Gilkey's defense is fundamentally twofold—one implicit, the other fully explicit. First, his arguments imply that his analyses of common human experience disclose religious dimensions that ground it everywhere; that, in effect, his analyses point toward the disclosure of conditions for the possibility of common human experience which elude the fragmenting empirical differences among individuals and groups as somehow prior to them. This defense is typical of constructive postmodern theologies.[33] Second, he explicitly resists the radical pluralism and relativism of deconstructive postmodernism by arguing that, to avoid succumbing to the worst forms of injustice, one must act with integrity and take a stand, and such resistance will require positing a "relative absolute." His first defense is manifest in his two most substantial books, *Naming the Whirlwind* (1969), and *Reaping the Whirlwind* (1976).

---

[33]Griffin, *God and Religion in the Postmodern World*, xi, xiv, 4-5. The work of process theologians such as John Cobb, Charles Hartshorne, and Harold H. Oliver, on the one hand, as well as that of transcendental Thomists such as Bernard Lonergan and Karl Rahner, on the other hand, exemplify two ways of understanding religious experience as preempirical.

Reaping the Whirlwind was developed in response to the challenge of world religions to Christianity's claims to universal truth.

IV. Performance of Public Theological Method

In *Naming the Whirlwind* (1969), Gilkey distinguished for the first time his own theological method and perspective from traditional liberal and neoorthodox positions, as well as from the atheistic theologies of the radical theologians, while exploring their adequacy in responding to the key issues of secularity. Throughout this work, his commitment to using integrity as the fundamental criterion of public theology guides his analyses.

In *Naming the Whirlwind*, Gilkey makes clear that he respects the fundamentally modernist liberals for their integrity—that is, for their commitment to integrating all of that which they knew and experienced into their final religious and theological visions. In particular, he commends their willingness to accept the validity of scientific and historical disciplines, and to integrate various facets of contemporary experience (rational and scientific inquiry, religious and/or moral experience) into the foundations of their visions, while jettisoning those claims of orthodoxy that contradict them. Rejecting two orthodox conceptions—the supernatural's total transcendence of humanity and humanity's complete dependence upon God's miraculous intervention for salvation—liberalism argued that the divine worked immanently within the evolutionary processes of the natural, cultural, and historical worlds to create increasingly advanced, adaptive, and complex modes of science, technology, morality, and justice. Gilkey particularly admired liberalism's recognition of the necessity to respond to secularity and its creative accommodations to it. Liberalism refused to sever reason and morality from belief in God and Christ. Yet, Gilkey also recognized the ways in which liberalism ran aground on the shoals of twentieth-century manifestations of barbarism during the world wars. These experiences of the radicality of human evil created growing skepticism both regarding the ability of metaphysical or speculative reason to discern an ultimate harmony and order within reality, and the validity of its claims that evolutionary progress in nature, history, and the morality of humankind manifested the creative, salvific, and providential purposes of the divine.[34]

---

[34]Gilkey, *Naming the Whirlwind: The Renewal of God-Language* (Indianapolis and

This skepticism, Gilkey argued, opened the way both for the radically antisecular perspective of the early neoorthodox theologians and for the growing secularity of twentieth-century Western consciousness.

In *Naming the Whirlwind*, Gilkey also characterized the dualism of neoorthodoxy and its pitfalls at length. Neoorthodox theologians argued that the grounds for human creativity must lie in the revelation of the Word of God found in the Bible, the Word which judged all human confidence in its own powers to be false pride and idolatry. Gilkey shared neoorthodoxy's conviction that biblical myths and symbols convey profound truths about humanity's lostness without the one sovereign and loving God, the brokenness of its existence, and about its need for faith in order to achieve truth and goodness. He was less impressed, however, with the ways in which neoorthodoxy conceived the roles of science and historiography in theology: science and history might inform one's understanding of those myths and symbols, but they offer scant foundation for the latters' claims to truth apart from the faith born of hard-won experiences of human brokenness and sin. In effect, Gilkey sharply criticized early neoorthodoxy in ways which implicitly recognized its fundamental lack of integrity. Neoorthodoxy created splits, first, in its epistemological claims: it was unable to specify the empirical or historical referents for its putatively historical claim that God acts in history to redeem. Second, neoorthodoxy promoted divisions between faith and both reason and human experience, by profoundly separating religious experience and human rationality from the revealed Word of God. The neoorthodox propensity to interpret Christianity's faith-claims in terms of the existential meaningfulness and transformative power of its symbols and myths was and remains a profoundly powerful and valid move. This very approach, however, needed constant renewal through constant reinterpretation. Unfortunately, neoorthodox theologians failed to do this: staying frozen on their seemingly impenetrable iceberg, they lost their hold upon the faithful and sank into irrelevance. Neoorthodoxy's power inevitably weakened in the 1950s and 1960s, when its own proponents reduced it to dry doctrinal formulas. In addition, secular confidence in human powers reemerged as the memory of the radicality of human evil faded.[35]

Finally, Gilkey criticized the radical theologians in *Naming the Whirlwind*, in effect charging that they were no better than the neoorthodox in

New York: Bobbs-Merrill, 1969) 73-80; hereafter cited as *NW*.
    [35]Gilkey, *NW*, 80-106.

meeting the demands of the criterion of integrity. From his perspective, the heart of postmodern secularity lies in its presumption that human experience possesses no relation beyond itself to any ground or order; on its terms, neither philosophy nor theology nor any other mode of rationality can achieve genuine knowledge of a transcendent ground or order.[36] The radical theologies of William Hamilton, Thomas Altizer, and Paul van Buren (which to some extent supplanted neoorthodoxy) appealed to this secular consciousness, on the one hand, by questioning the existence of God and the validity of language about God, the eschaton, and any other suprahistorical entity, and, on the other hand, by asserting humanity's self-sufficiency. Most did insist, however, that the historical Jesus remained Lord and that his life and teachings should serve to guide all ethical involvement in the personal, social, and political realms. Life in the here and now was of utmost significance; concern about an afterlife, mere escapism. Gilkey attacked the radical theologians for not living up to their own secular standards by not achieving the intellectual consistency and coherence demanded by secularity in developing their views. Their attempts to assert, on the one hand, the power and validity of human autonomy apart from a transcendent God and Jesus as Lord, on the other hand, were mutually contradictory.[37] These contradictions underlined, Gilkey argued, the need for a conception of a transcendent power that could effect the transformations which radical theologians seek to promote—the very transcendence that they are anxious to deny.

Gilkey's subsequent analyses in *Naming the Whirlwind* of the core experiences of secularity—contingency, temporality, relativity, and autonomy—manifest the profound influence of Tillich's theological method and metaphysical vision upon his thought, as well as the inclusivistic holism resulting from his emphasis upon integrity. Through a hermeneutical phenomenology which elaborated the manifest meanings of these core experiences, Gilkey sought to disclose within them a hidden dimension of ultimacy, an ultimate presupposition behind typical ways of coping with these experiences. This method disclosed not so much a new reality or presence—though Christians would surely interpret it as evidence for such—but a *final* or *ultimate* limit encountered through the threats and demands presented by the experiences of *being* limited. In

---

[36]Gilkey, *NW*, 188.

[37]For Gilkey's detailed analyses of the radical theologians' fundamental incoherence on this point, see Gilkey, *NW*, 151-66.

accordance with Tillich's method of critical correlation, Gilkey analyzed each of these dimensions of secular experience to demonstrate how it raises a question in the form of an experienced threat and, upon closer scrutiny, leads one to recognize at its limit intimations of an answer, an answer which is then thematized by religious faith in another dimension of reality. In this way, he elaborated the grounds for the validity of the transcendent referent of the God-language that radical theologies were intent to deny.[38]

One example of Gilkey's analyses of common human experiences to disclose an element of ultimacy will clarify his approach. The human experience of radical contingency discloses a sense that some infinite, inexorable power is also at work through the indeterminacies of history. This power, commonly known as fate, is often experienced as an unconditional, unbearable threat to our ability to control our own lives. Such secular experiences of radical insecurity raise the question of whether an unconditionally secure power might exist, a power that might rule over those fates that appear to threaten our lives with meaninglessness and insignificance. This question becomes a quest for God the Creator, as the ruler over all those fates that threaten us, and this quest becomes manifest in our individual struggles to create a unified, coherent, and meaningful whole of our lives. When we do actually become convinced that, in spite of the apparent insignificance of our lives, those same lives attain some lasting validity—not as achievements that we have created for ourselves but as inexplicable gifts—then we are drawn to some understanding of the Christian symbol of the providence of God.[39]

His further analyses of the hidden dimensions of ultimacy experienced in personal and moral freedom disclose the ontological bases for his convictions regarding the continuity between what human reason and morality can understand and require, on the one hand, and the meanings of the Christian symbols of sin, atonement, and forgiveness, on the other

---

[38]By these arguments Gilkey did not claim to offer proofs for the existence of God, only a defense of the meaningfulness of God-language, by grounding it in dimensions of human experience: for example, Gilkey, *NW*, 234-36, 243-60, 295-303.

[39]Gilkey, *NW*, 320-54. In his later work, *Reaping the Whirlwind*, Gilkey develops further his conception of fate, by drawing on Paul Tillich's notion of a polarity of destiny and freedom operative within every human life. Within this polarity, destiny becomes distorted through sin into fate: Langdon Gilkey, *Reaping the Whirlwind: A Christian Interpretation of History* (New York: Seabury, 1976) 54-56, 255-59, 278-85, 294, 315-16; hereafter cited as *RW*.

hand. He argued that freedom in itself presupposes certain norms by which to guide action and then developed his anthropology by highlighting the ultimate significance of integrity: integrity includes the freedom to act in accordance with chosen personal and moral ideals, but the tendency of autonomous freedom toward self-interest (as Reinhold Niebuhr argued) must be tempered by the ideals of self-sacrificial love and justice if the fabric of community is not to be destroyed. To respond to these ideals enables us to overcome any latent self-deception about our true motivations, and to achieve the fully personal integrity of true faithfulness. Our failures to achieve our goals lead us to experience the call to do so not as a void but as personal judgment. The quest to overcome our fragmentation, guilt, insecurity, and isolation leads us to search for ultimates—in effect, to the point where the Christian symbols of the sovereignty and forgiveness of God make sense.[40]

The development of theological anthropology in *Naming the Whirlwind* constitutes Gilkey's prolegomenon to a systematic theology. The full range and depth of Gilkey's theological vision comes most clearly to expression in his next major work, *Reaping the Whirlwind* (1976).[41] There he systematically responds to the problem that has haunted him from the inception of his theological career, the problem of developing a Christian interpretation of history for these "troubled times." His response constitutes a theological interpretation of history whose implications give fresh meaning to the traditional Christian symbols, particularly the Trinity, in order to clarify its relevance to and claims upon postmodern loyalties. Today, as never before, he argues, increasingly vast and rapid historical change confronts humanity with questions about the meaning and dynamics of history. The way in which humanity realizes itself is conditioned first and foremost by its temporality—its realization of itself in and through historical contingency and change. As temporal, humanity finds itself both threatened by the unknown and yet challenged by the possibility of creating something new. Humanity understands itself to be both determined by social, economic, and historical conditions far beyond its control and yet transcendent of such determinations, free to create its

---

[40]Gilkey, *RW*, 373-95.

[41]Hesitating to invest the time and energy necessary to construct a full systematic theology, Gilkey published a "minisystematic" in 1979, which he developed as an introduction to the Christian theological task and vision: Langdon Gilkey, *Message and Existence: An Introduction to Christian Theology* (New York: Seabury, 1979); hereafter cited as *ME*.

own destiny in spite of them. This polarity of destiny and freedom and the related polarity of actuality and possibility constitute the ontological structures of human temporality.

Gilkey worries that the postmodern loss of faith in progress characterizing the late twentieth-century milieu has led to a deadly fatalism in some and an equally deadly escapism in others. Still, he resists reverting to the naïve optimism of nineteenth-century liberalism and, instead, draws on classic Christian doctrines: the true foundation of hope lies not in humanity's innate goodness, but in the possibility of its discovering the way back to that goodness through the power of faith in a transcendent and beneficent deity. He elaborates a Christian interpretation of history that envisions God as a transcendent and unifying power reconciling the estranged and leading them to a deeper understanding of the meaning and ultimate validity of their historical lives. On his view, fate is not dumb and blind, but "the negative face of God, his left hand, his alien work."[42] The challenge of human existence is the task of transforming fate into freely chosen personal destiny, because the given that appears to determine us for ill has latent within it, through the creative and redemptive power of God, authentic possibilities for the good. The most adequate answers to the question, "What power ultimately rules history and gives it final validity?" lie in the Christian symbols regarding God's historical activity—providence and eschatology.

The most adequate interpretation of history will accept that history can never be rendered fully intelligible, that it will retain a complex dialectic between clarity and opacity, intelligibility and mystery. Actuality in history, Gilkey argues, is never fully reducible into meaning and order, for three reasons. First, the possibilities grounded in any particular actuality are never fully determined by or predictable because of it. Second, humanity, in actualizing its possibilities, also corrupts them. As a result, meaning fragments into meaninglessness, true norms become obscured by false ones, and real goals get sidetracked into spurious ones. As a result, the structure of history itself becomes warped. This explains why philosophical understandings of history based on its structure are never fully adequate. Only a theistic interpretation of history informed by the categories of sin and grace, estrangement and reconciliation—that is, an understanding developed within the context of the relationship of human-

---

[42]Gilkey, *RW*, 54.

ity to divinity—will be even relatively adequate to the task of expressing the problematics of self-actualization in history. This leads to the third reason for the irreducible mystery of history: Human freedom is enacted, whether consciously or not, within a relationship to the ultimate, transcendent ground of the whole which forever eludes full comprehension.[43]

In spite of the apparent dearth of meaning in our era, Gilkey finds three grounds for belief in the ultimate meaningfulness of history. First, what initially appears to be undesirable and destructive frequently proves to be the breeding ground for great creativity: Gilkey cites the experiences in the Shantung compound that led to his becoming a theologian as an example. Second, events that initially appear to be meaningless and destructive can prove to be quite intelligible when they are grasped in light of past injustices and the need for change: the dislocation of countless persons after World War II, when grasped in the light of past imperialism and greed, exemplify this. Finally, there are usually intimations—usually born out—that new creative possibilities will emerge out of revolutionary, even chaotic, events: witness the nationalist and socialist revolutions of the nineteenth and twentieth centuries, as well as potential in movements of women and other oppressed groups for equal rights today.[44]

The task of the theologian is to interpret theological symbols to disclose their many levels of meaning. The truth of symbols emerges out of their ability to bring order and coherence to a wide range of experiences and, in turn, to communicate a sense of the nature and dynamics of reality back to us. Again, such symbols not only order and communicate reality to us; they also convey a sense of the transcendent mystery from which the dynamics of reality emerge, most especially because they express the dynamics of our relationships to God. When a group of symbols is used to describe how God acts in history, they take on narrative or mythic form. Religious myths present this dialectic between meaning and mystery in narrative form. It is the task of the Christian theologian to render these narratives, their symbols and myths, relatively intelligible by explicating the multivalent meanings of the theological doctrines of creation, anthropology, providence, revelation, incarnation, redemption, and eschatology.[45]

---

[43]Gilkey, *RW*, 117-29.
[44]Gilkey, *RW*, 122-33.
[45]Gilkey, *RW*, 133-55.

Gilkey's rejection of the liberal, neoorthodox, and eschatological interpretations of history in terms of these symbols again reflects the inclusivistic holism of his thought in his concern to bring all of human historical experience to bear upon the concepts of providence and eschatology. Liberals such as Albrecht Ritschl and Friedrich Schleiermacher overemphasized the role of the divine in effecting progress toward realizing the Kingdom of God in history, but repressed the negative and cataclysmic reversals of such progress.[46] The dialectical or *krisis* theologies of early neoorthodoxy, such as the theologies of Karl Barth and Rudolph Bultmann, took such negations as their points of departure, but used the negations to support their denial that the Kingdom was relevant to the general course of history, thus separating secular from sacred history.[47] The eschatological theologies of Wolfhart Pannenberg, Jürgen Moltmann, Johannes Metz, Rubem Alvez, and Gustavo Gutierrez, which came to the fore in the 1960s, reasserted the conviction that the Kingdom would come in history, but that it would come solely as a result of God's future action in it. Unfortunately, while attempting to restore the significance of history, the eschatological theologies went only halfway: they detached contemporary human historical existence and action from the activity of God in space and time.[48] In contrast, Gilkey's view of divine providence evades the pitfalls of these views, while responding to the secular consciousness that our lives are not determined by any transcendent being but remain inexorably contingent, relative to a variety of factors, and transient, without any transcendental determinant. The divine mode of causality does not deny contingency, transience, and relativity, but sustains them; nor does it negate human freedom, but establishes and renders it creative and good.[49]

Gilkey argues that the pattern of God's intervention in history follows the pattern of Israelite history: God established the structures of Israel's communal life and then, through the prophets, called her people back to it again and again when they went astray.[50] He then reinterprets the classical doctrine of the Trinity—Father, Son, and Holy Spirit—in the traditional terms set up by Augustine—being, truth, and love—while

---

[46]Gilkey, *RW*, 210-16.
[47]Gilkey, *RW*, 216-26.
[48]Gilkey, *RW*, 226-36.
[49]Gilkey, *RW*, 306.
[50]Gilkey, *RW*, 262, 287.

leaving Augustine's neoplatonism far behind. Instead, Gilkey employs Tillichian and Whiteheadian process ontology to argue that three dimensions to the divine providential action in history correspond to the Trinity: the metaphor "father" indicates the divine action in preserving being through the transitions of each historical moment to the next, the ground of the preservation of the creature over time; "son," the divine action in creating new, unforeseen possibilities from given actuality—in effect, as the fount of human creativity; and "holy spirit," the divine action in loving the world by judging its sinful distortions of human possibility that it might be returned to God in the eschaton. In this, God discloses Godself as being, logos, and love: God establishes the structures of the world, sustains them through time, and restores them when they are broken. *God as being* mediates the transition of being from moment to moment, the movement from possibility to actuality. *God as logos* does not extrinsically determine all that happens, but instead serves as the condition and ground of its possibility, as the principle of order of the possibilities that we manage to bring into actuality, and as the ground of the meaning and creativity that we manage to express within it. The concept of *God as love* emerges when taking the tragedy—in theological perspective, the sinfulness—of history into account.[51] The divine providential work in love—in judgment and reconciliation—is most clearly manifest in the historical person of Jesus of Nazareth who proclaimed the coming Kingdom. The Kingdom symbolizes the ideal, a world in which all persons live out their own, authentic destinies, undistorted into fate by inordinate, concupiscent desire or demonically false claims of ultimacy. As such, the Kingdom symbolizes the ways in which God works providentially to bring about the good and the just in this world, and to command our commitment to it by working through our freedom. Thus, God as love "appears and acts in new and varied ways to reconcile, reunite and heal a world sundered in spirit from his creative providence."[52] In proclaiming the Kingdom, Jesus revealed both the alienation of the world from its true self and the possibility of returning the world to authentic relationship with God.

Unlike the early Greeks and certain Eastern religions, which see history as an inexorable cycle of progress and decline, Christians envision it as the emergence of new creative possibilities in spite of their distortion

---

[51]Gilkey, *RW*, 246-53, 297-99, 311-18.
[52]Gilkey, *RW*, 316.

by humanity. The distortions of possibility by concupiscent desire and the demonic receive the judgment of God—the hidden, alien work of God that destroys the destructive and works to bring new life by reconciling the broken and alienated to themselves, one another, and God. All of the divine providential activity is ultimately determined by this goal of reconciliation and return while creating the new and good. Christian faith in the providential action of God includes confidence in a future world in which no one will be determined by a harsh, unyielding fate, but rather by freely chosen creative possibilities. This confidence drives eschatology and finds symbolic expression in the doctrine of the Kingdom of God. Belief in the Kingdom of God is belief that each person's authentic possibilities will indeed be realized in history, in the eschaton toward which history, often in spite of appearances, is moving. Eschatology forms a lure, a vision of creative possibilities for the future. Thus, providence is the historical presupposition for eschatology, while eschatology is the defining and controlling symbol for providence.[53]

In *Reaping the Whirlwind*, Gilkey has developed a magisterial summation of his entire vision—his complex interpretation of the fatedness of our times by violence and oppression, industry, and technology, and his equally complex interpretation of the nuances of the Christian faith in God's action in history for offering hope in the midst of it. This vision is holistic: it envisions the Sacred as transcendent to the world, but as working within it to be its healing, reconciling depth, so that together they form a differentiated unity, a unity encompassed by their irreducible difference. And it is born of the methodological conviction that theologians must take into account all fields of knowledge and all dimensions of experience in their deliberations, but still not lose sight of their goal—elaborating the distinctive claims to meaning and validity of the Christian faith in promoting the Kingdom of God on earth. This holism, then, avoids the reductionistic tendencies of liberalism, the ultimately splitting reactivity of early neoorthodoxy, the equally self-defeating bifurcation between present and future of the eschatological theologians, and the inconsistencies of radical theologies to create a new synthesis responsive to our current scientific, technological, and pluralistic world.

In *Reaping the Whirlwind*, Gilkey vastly extended and complexified the analysis of postmodernity that he began in *Naming the Whirlwind*.

---

[53]Gilkey, *RW*, 271-88.

Whereas in *Naming the Whirlwind* he correlated his interpretations of human experience with attributes commonly ascribed to God in monotheistic religions (causality, eternity, and so on), his deeper analysis in *Reaping the Whirlwind* serves to render the traditional Christian trinitarian model of deity meaningful and coherent, and at least relatively adequate to human experience. Thus, his work both critically reconstructs and restores the tradition by rendering it fully public. There are moments, however, when his restorationism tends to be oppressive. For instance, few feminist or womanist theologians would be happy with his unqualified use of male language for the divine, no matter how much he reinterprets it in Tillichian terms of ultimacy and depth. Nor would they or other liberation theologians be pleased with his constant characterization of sin in terms of the self-interest that obstructs genuine faith and love. Self-interest is not always nefarious. Indeed, interpreting the Christian love that reverses such self-interest in terms of self-sacrifice and servanthood has served to discourage women and minorities from developing precisely the healthy senses of self-esteem and self-respect that might enable them to protect their own interests against exploitation by others.[54] Most liberation theologians today would insist that what might be quite true for him, as a white Western male of privilege, could be quite false for the disempowered. Gilkey exhibits no awareness of these possible restrictions to his claims apart from his general methodological insistence that his theological vision is constantly in process of refining itself in the attempt to become more relatively adequate to common human experience, as all others are. In his defense, it can be said that, if the analysis of experience

---

[54]For the classic statement of this objection, see Valerie Saiving Goldstein, "The Human Situation: A Feminine View," *Journal of Religion* 40 (April 1960): 100-12; reprinted in *Womanspirit Rising: A Feminist Reader in Religion*, ed. Carol P. Christ and Judith Plaskow (San Francisco: Harper & Row, 1979) 24-42. For an elaboration of the implications of Goldstein's critique in the theologies of Reinhold Niebuhr and Paul Tillich, see Judith Plaskow, *Sex, Sin, and Grace: Women's Experience and the Theologies of Reinhold Niebuhr and Paul Tillich* (Lanham MD: University Press of America, 1980). For a concise statement of feminist perspectives on this point, see Jennifer Rike, "The Lion and the Unicorn: Feminist Perspectives on Christian Love as Care," in *Christian Perspectives on Sexuality and Gender*, ed. Adrian Thatcher and Elizabeth Stuart (Grand Rapids MI: Eerdmans, 1996) 247-62. For a womanist critique of servanthood, see Jacqueline Grant, "The Sin of Servanthood: And the Deliverance of Discipleship," in *A Troubling in My Soul: Womanist Perspectives on Evil and Suffering*, ed. Emilie M. Townes (Maryknoll NY: Orbis Books, 1996) 199-218.

offered is not quite true to others, then he would be the first to encourage them to be true to their own experiences and interpretations, and to reason accordingly. In other words, it would seem that, to some limited extent, Gilkey's painstakingly careful elaboration of the grounds for asserting faith in such metaphysical foundations reflects the typically postmodern wariness of positing foundations, much less pressing them on others, and so he implicitly defends himself against such critiques. His best defense, however, follows from the full implications of his developing the concept of the "relative absolute."

Conclusion: The "Relative Absolute"

In the 1980's, in response to the growing awareness of the validity of religions other than Christianity, Gilkey joined other theologians in attempting to formulate a genuinely pluralist understanding of the relationship between Christianity and other religions.[55] A pluralist approach seeks to avoid the exclusivism which finds salvation only in Christ, as well as the inclusivism which finds salvation manifested elsewhere but understands these manifestations to be also, in some way, manifestations of Christ's redemptive work. Gilkey applauds the pluralist project for encouraging the love and understanding essential to ecumenical tolerance, and for its openness to genuine diversity. But he decries the radical relativity to which it leads religious claims to meaning and truth, when pluralism is understood as complete parity among different options. Such radical relativity offers grounds only for complete tolerance of every other option, not grounds for rejecting clearly demonic forms of religion, such as the absolutism of Khomeini and the Religious Right in America, that would deny others' claims to meaning and truth and so crush all pluralism. Paradoxically, for the sake of the toleration of pluralism, Gilkey argues, we must assert without reservation certain values which themselves disclose a particular worldview and its attendant absolute commitments. This worldview then becomes a center—a foundation, if you will—on which to base the praxis that resists demonic and destructive expressions of the religious. In other words, one must put limits on toleration in order to resist intolerance, and this requires positing a ground.[56]

---

[55]Langdon Gilkey, "Plurality and Its Theological Implications," in *The Myth of Christian Uniqueness: Toward a Pluralistic Theology of Religions*, ed. John Hick and Paul K Knitter (Maryknoll NY: Orbis, 1988) 37-50.

[56]Gilkey, "Plurality and Its Theological Implications," 42-47.

We need a ground for the apprehension and understanding of reality—a ground that undergirds our choices, our critiques of the status quo, our policies. We need a ground for the values and eros that fuel and drive toward justice, and for the confidence and hope necessary for consistent action. We need criteria for the judgments essential both for reflective construction and for liberative doing; and we need priorities in value if we would creatively and actively move into the future.[57]

Hence, the pragmatics of contending with intolerance and oppression, while affirming the validity of other faiths, demand a praxis of relative absoluteness. One absolutely affirms one's particular faith-stance to hold meaning and truth, and yet relativizes it by insisting that additional meaning and truth likewise remain with the other. Thus, "[w]hat to reflection is a contradiction, to praxis is a workable dialectic, a momentary but creative paradox."[58] What might be seen as a contradiction in theory becomes acceptable in praxis. Such a praxis is born of the integrity that is compelled to act to uphold justice, and that acts freely from a fully reflective consciousness of the relativity of our absolute commitments. It finds the courage to assert itself absolutely in spite of the recognition of the relativity of its perspective from the simultaneous consciousness of a dialectic between finite and infinite: that the Sacred and Absolute can nevertheless manifest itself in the profane and conditioned in unique and unpredictable ways. This praxis of relative absoluteness, Gilkey argues, must guide our responses to the radical pluralism of our time, if we are to live out of the whole that nourishes true life in us all.[59]

Had Langdon Gilkey integrated this concept of the relatively absolute character of all theological claims into his subsequent theological reflections, he would, I suspect, have stopped striving to formulate a theological vision that was universally valid, and prefaced his subsequent work with a disclaimer that notes the specific social and religious location and limited range of his claims.[60] Perhaps he even would have struggled with an issue thus far inadequately addressed by feminist and liberationist theologies: indeed, if we are all human beings, then perhaps some universal

---

[57]Gilkey, "Plurality and Its Theological Implications," 46.

[58]Gilkey, "Plurality and Its Theological Implications," 47.

[59]Gilkey, "Plurality and Its Theological Implications," 46-50.

[60]See, for instance, Langdon Gilkey, *Through the Tempest: Theological Voyages in a Pluralistic Culture*, ed. Jeff B. Pool (Minneapolis MN: Fortress, 1991).

claims about what transforms us in positive ways are warranted; and we would do well to focus our efforts, at least for awhile, on developing criteria for distinguishing universal claims grounded in our common humanity from those specific to gender, race, ethnic origin, and other distinguishing factors. Although many self-consciously postmodern theologians today fear specifying any notion of common humanity as "essentialist" and so potentially oppressive of diversity, even they cannot deny that they communicate to one another notions of what it means to be oppressed and liberated—notions that themselves suggest a sense of common humanity.[61] From this perspective, Gilkey's arguments in *Naming the Whirlwind*, which move from common human experiences to their implied presuppositions, might be worthy of reevaluation by women and a variety of racial and ethnic groups for the reach of their validity. Do not all human beings experience the threats of the contingency, transience, and relativity of life, and what might those threats compel us to conclude about the nature of ultimate reality? Working through such issues might go a long way to unite the currently fragmented theological scene in a mutually shared goal, such as saving us from the destructive trends of modernism.

We have seen that Gilkey's appeal to integrity as the key criterion of public theology, itself grounded in an emphasis on autonomous and integrated selfhood, has served to guide his reconstruction of the Christian faith. He has deployed this criterion to reject a panoply of theological options and, in particular, to resist the total relativism so characteristic of postmodernism. It has, however, also pushed toward unwarranted universalizing of his perspective—perhaps the original sin of all theological endeavor and, as such, most readily forgiven. To say this, however, is far from denying that his achievements have been awesome in the most profound (as opposed to popular) sense of the word. He has evolved, personally and theologically, in tandem with these troubled times, to formulate a fully public theological vision that shall guide and inspire for decades yet to come.

---

[61]For the implications of this issue for feminism today, see the following studies: Linda Alcoff, "Cultural Feminism Versus Post-Structuralism: The Identity Crisis in Feminist Theory," *Signs: Journal of Women in Culture and Society* 13 (3): 405-36; and Jennifer L. Rike, "The Cycle of Violence and Feminist Constructions of Selfhood," *Contagion: Journal of Violence, Mimesis, and Culture* 3 (Spring 1996): 21-42.

Chapter 15

Pedagogy and Theological Method:
The Praxis of Langdon Gilkey

Joseph L. Price

Prelude to Praxis

One of the signal contributions of late twentieth-century liberation theologies to the theological enterprise is the shift toward conceiving theological method as praxis, which emphasizes the interlocking interplay of experience, thought, and action, all of which mutually inform one another. While primary experience generates thinking, and thinking produces more than motive for acting (even acting itself), a self-reflecting oscillation takes place that generates and realizes praxis—a complex, interconnected, simultaneous power of experience, thought, action. A praxis theology, Ismael Garcia asserts, is the critical reflection and action, in the light of faith commitment, that grows from and seeks to contribute to the transformation of a social order, the creation of a new way of being the church, and the cultivation of a spirituality that is historically committed in the world.[1] In terms of method, praxis reduces the formal separation of ethics from theology, and as such praxis fosters a very practical or engaged dimension of theology. When characterized by praxis, theology cannot be esoteric; it must be active—personally, politically, persuasively, always proleptically pursuing the fullness of the kingdom of God.

In the several senses of Garcia's definition, the theology of Langdon Gilkey is characterized by, as Mark Kline Taylor has averred, a liberating praxis.[2] Gilkey's theology manifests the convergence of critical faith and concerted action. His theology seeks to transform the social order, by mapping a move toward the theonomous culture of the Kingdom of God, understands a new way of being the community of faithful as the *ecclesia*, and resounds with a continual wonder at the mysterious power of being that undergirds human interactions throughout history. Before the emergence of liberation theologies in the late 1960s with the powerful

---

[1]Ismael Garcia, "Praxis," in *A New Handbook of Christian Theology*, ed. Donald W. Musser and Joseph L. Price (Nashville: Abingdon Press, 1992) 377.
[2]Mark Kline Taylor, "Religion, Cultural Plurality, and Liberating Praxis: In Conversation with the Work of Langdon Gilkey," *Journal of Religion* 71 (April 1991): 145.

voices of Gustavo Gutierrez, James Cone, and Mary Daly,[3] Langdon
Gilkey was doing theology by means of praxis, for his thinking as a theologian constantly interacted with his experience, simultaneously emerging
from and shaping his life. In its association with liberation theologies,
praxis has been identified with the struggles of oppressed peoples—acting
on the basis of their commitment of faith—who have protested against
the structures generating their suffering, particularly the political, economic, and social (including domestic) structures of institutionalized violence.

   Resonating with the voices of and perspectives of liberation theologians, Gilkey never departed from the experiences that germinated his
contemplation and reflection. Yet, in contrast to the theologies of liberation, the praxis of Gilkey's theology is not so thoroughly identified with
structures of oppression, even though he had both endured internment in
a Japanese internment camp in China and actively participated in the
Civil Rights Movement of the 1960s. A distinct feature of Gilkey's praxis
is that his theological engagement emerged in the context of and vocational commitment to being a teacher. The argument of this essay, thus,
will proceed in two distinct phases. First, I will interpret Gilkey's
theological method of correlation in light of the method of praxis; and,
second, I will frame the praxis of his method within the context of his
vocation as a teaching theologian.

I. Correlational Method as Praxis

Discussion about theological method often resounds at a tertiary level of
religious experience and discourse, while the primary level focuses on the
spiritual experience itself and the secondary level identifies the theological constructs relevant to experience. In these discussions, the tertiary
level, then, devotes attention to hermeneutical, philosophical, and sociopolitical issues as well as the motives and means for interpreting experience from a theological mindset.[4] One of the most significant contribu-

---

[3]Gustavo Gutierrez, *Lineas pastorales de la Iglesia en American Latina: Analisis
teologico*, 7th ed. (Lima: Centro de Estudios y Publicaciones, 1983; [1]1968); James H.
Cone, *Black Theology and Black Power* (repr.: Maryknoll NY: Orbis Books, 1997;
original: New York: Seabury Press, 1969); and Mary Daly, *The Church and the Second
Sex, with the Feminist Post-Christian Introduction and New Archaic Afterwords by the
Author* (Boston: Beacon Press, 1985; 1st ed.: New York: Harper & Row, 1968).

[4]See Werner G. Jeanrond, "Theological Method," in *New Handbook of Christian
Theology*, ed. Musser and Price, 480-86; and John McCarthy, "Hermeneutics," in *New*

tions of liberation theologies has been to challenge the assumption that theological constructs, at a secondary level of reflection, pursue pure and permanent eternal truth that transcends the possibility of taint from experiences and imaginative projections of flawed humans. Liberation theologies have suggested that the self-inturning of praxis—the thoughtful character of experience itself—leads to reflection. This process generates a deeper, richer, or at least newer character of experience, and represents the most fertile way to conceive theological construction in its relation to experience. Reflection and experience are empirically inseparable, interdependent and simultaneous. Although experience and theological construction may oscillate in perceptibility and dominance, they cannot be divided into primary and secondary levels.

For Gilkey, theological method is not imposed as a set of extrinsic criteria upon experiences in faith, but instead arises from reflection in life lived in and for faith—a narrative coherence—which is understood in the Tillichian terms of ultimate concern, rather than dogmatic affirmations or transcendental spirituality. Although life itself may appear to have an unplanned character, the narrative about a person's experience reveals ongoing contemplation and insight about the experience of depth and the symbols of ultimacy therein engaged. Stories provide the context for experiencing, underlining, and elaborating theological points and possibilities. Previous commentators on Langdon Gilkey's method have identified his method as empirical.[5] According to Taylor, Gilkey's thought "meets us in many forms with creative theory and with liberating praxis demanded by the voices and actions of oppressed, exploited peoples."[6] None have made the clarifying connection, however, between Gilkey's self-designated label of "correlation" with praxis.

As one begins to read Gilkey's works, one might expect the reference notes to provide a record of the theological sources that have informed, engaged, and provoked Gilkey to develop his theological perspective. Certainly, this record is clear; Gilkey connects his ideas with the works of historical and contemporary theologians and philosophers of religion

---

Handbook of Christian Theology, ed. Musser and Price, 218-24.

[5]Cf. Thomas E. Hosinski, "Experience and the Sacred: A Retrospective Review of Langdon Gilkey's Theology," *Religious Studies Review* 11 (July 1985): 228-35; and Brian J. Walsh, *Langdon Gilkey: Theologian for a Culture in Decline* (Lanham MD: University Press of America, 1991) 27-32.

[6]Taylor, "Religion, Cultural Plurality, and Liberating Praxis," 145.

ranging from Augustine to Gerhard Ebeling, from Aristotle to Charles Hartshorne. Also, when the references appear at the bottom of the page as *foot*notes, for example, as they do in *How the Church Can Minister to the World without Losing Itself* and *Naming the Whirlwind*, they provide a visual metaphor for the way that Gilkey's personal experiences and collegial conversations undergird the narrative, often precipitating or clarifying his theological insights. Again, when Gilkey discusses churches' difficulties in maintaining their identities while participating in culture and ministering to the modern world, he uses his footnotes to express the extent to which the problem pervades everyday life. He mentions the confusion manifested by two "Dunker" couples whom he had seen eating hamburgers and drinking sodas at a roadside café in Indiana. The men donned "spare beards and homemade shirts, suits, and haircuts, and the women . . . [wore] white lace caps and black Mother Hubbards." The dissonance between their sectarian tradition and the contemporary world "reached a new pitch of confusion . . . when the four left their all-American meal and climbed into their new 1963 white Buick Le Sabre sedan." Gilkey relates this observation to another automotive/religious observation: While driving in New England, he had been passed by a priest in a black Buck Riviera with a vanity license plate, "X." Gilkey concludes, "[i]f General Motors' Buick Division represents the essence as well as the apex of what may be called 'American culture,' then the fact that the leading members of these historically widely divergent groups now tour the freeways in elegant Buicks has no small religious and social significance."[7]

Gilkey does not conceive his theological method of correlation as an abstract level of discourse in hermeneutical theory; instead, he regards the method as energized by and energizing discussion about the meaning of the mystery of human life in relation to human histories and the cosmic shaping of natural forces. In his analytical and assimilative celebration of Paul Tillich's theology, Gilkey offers a succinct description of the correlative method, which applies also to his own work: "Correlation is the *methodological expression* of fulfilled ontological reason, of theonomous reason, of thought and *eros*, rationality and faith, in short, of the *union*

---

[7]Langdon Gilkey, *How the Church Can Minister to the World without Losing Itself* (New York: Harper & Row, 1964) 17; also see 15-16, 45, 86, 89, 109, 111, 115; hereafter cited as *HCCM*.

of reason with its own creative depth and ground, of 'true philosophy.' "[8]
The "formal method" of correlation, Gilkey states elsewhere, "is a symptom and not a cause of a more basic pattern of thinking, namely to ponder the character of our existence, both personal and historical, before God in the light of the historical and social situation, the massive contours of events, in which we find ourselves."[9] For Gilkey, the personal, historical, and social contours of events shape the character of faith as it becomes understood and achieves theological conception and expression.

Although Gilkey himself has not aligned his own method with the praxis of liberation theologians, he does locate the formal theological method of correlation in the realm of human experience. In contrast to the liberation theologians who avoid detaching the conceptual dimensions of experience from the immediate physical and emotional dimensions of experience, however, Gilkey separates the immediacy of human experience from the more reflective mode of theological interpretation of that experience. He suggests that the distinction between immediate sensate impressions of experience and its reflective dimension parallels the distinction between religion as such and theology. "Religion consists negatively of *existential* anxieties, problems, and crises, and possibility of *existentially* received 'answers' or resolutions; it involves an experienced answer to an ultimate concern, but it does not *necessarily* involve a theoretical understanding of itself. To reflect on religion, however, *does* involve such theory, and this is theology."[10] According to Gilkey, as reflection on religious experience, theology is the process of reflecting on "the *meaning* of being."[11] One paradox of existence, which is the manifestation of being and becoming within finitude, is that experience both locates and obfuscates the human grounding in being itself. In itself, human experience is not necessarily "religious" experience, even though it manifests its rootedness in the creativity and power of being and becoming, thus in God. Specifically religious experience, Gilkey maintains, occurs if experience generates reflection on the depth of its meaning, on

---

[8]Langdon Gilkey, *Gilkey on Tillich* (New York: Crossroad, 1990) 71-72; hereafter cited as *GOT*.

[9]Langdon Gilkey, "A Retrospective Glance at My Work," in *The Whirlwind in Culture: Frontiers in Theology: Essays in Honor of Langdon Gilkey*, ed. Donald W. Musser and Joseph L. Price (Bloomington IN: Meyer-Stone Books, 1988) 1.

[10]Gilkey, *GOT*, 72.

[11]Gilkey, *GOT*, 177.

the connectedness of its immediacy with the power of Being and Becoming.[12]

Religious experience as meaningful already indicates the presence of cognitive processes at work in clarifying and classifying the kind of experience—in distinguishing religious experience from other sorts of experience, which might be functional, playful, pedantic, but perhaps not resounding with the significance that characterizes religious experience of being in touch with the power of Being and Becoming. That the hallmark of religious experience is its meaningfulness also suggests that various forms of experience—those perceived as touching upon or drawing from or resonating with the power of being—can be understood as religious. In this regard, even the functional experiences of eating, for instance, contain a religious dimension, when they reflect the overcoming of alienation with others, manifest sensitivity toward the spirit of life that generated the growth of the foods consumed, or re-create "charter" events imbued with symbolic significance, such as the Last Supper or the Paschal meal.[13]

If the categories that Gilkey applies to the work of Tillich are turned to Gilkey himself, theology of culture is perhaps the designation for this first theological impulse in assigning religious value to an experience. Other forms of theology, such as systematic theology, seek to reflect on narrated experiences, organizing them into a whole whereby the relation of one experience or idea to another can be conceived. The central theme of Tillich's theology of culture, and of Gilkey's, is "the interpenetration of religion and culture, the presence of a religious dimension or substance in each aspect of cultural life."[14]

---

[12]Drawing upon the works of Rudolf Otto and Mircea Eliade, Gilkey utilizes traditional theological language to remark about the connection between God as "a continuing source of being as it is actualized in time" and religious experience: "The mystery of God, or the holiness of God, for they are aspects of the same characteristic, is therefore initially an aspect of all religious experience" (Langdon Gilkey, *Message and Existence: An Introduction to Christian Theology* [New York: Seabury, 1979] 96, 97; hereafter cited as *ME*).

[13]See Edmund Leach, *Culture and Communication, the Logic by Which Symbols Are Connected: An Introduction to Use of Structural Analysis in Social Anthropology*, Themes in the Social Sciences (Cambridge: Cambridge University Press, 1976).

[14]Gilkey, *GOT*, 185.

For Tillich, whose understanding of the task and method of theology corresponds closely to Gilkey's,[15] correlation means "philosophical questions, theological answers." Like Tillich, Gilkey understood that theological answers are not confined to traditional theological statements and resources, because the deepest ground of all aspects of culture, including philosophy, is its "religious substance."[16] Consequently, theological responses or answers—relating the ground of being and the power of becoming—often are cast in the myths of common culture. The religious depth portended by all human experience demands that the theologian reflect on experience beyond the ecclesia and its creedal affirmations. Because of the fundamental concern that the theologian must express for ordinary experience, Gilkey emphasizes that theologians must explore the dimensions of ordinary experience, as well as the extraordinary experience of life in ecclesia, in order to explicate more thoroughly the insights and possibilities of Christian faith. "Both because it speaks, and must, of God as known in the experience of faith and because it sees the world in a new light because of that experience," Gilkey says the following in his introduction to theology:

> Christian theology is in important discontinuity with what is usually considered—on both a simple or a very sophisticated level—as our ordinary experience of the world and as the wisdom of the world. Yet because it seeks to be intelligible and meaningful in what it says both about God and about our human existence in history, Christian theology must also be in important continuity with our ordinary experience.[17]

The theologian should be "at home in culture with its religious substance and in *ecclesia* with its religious center."[18] In the case of a fully theonomous culture such as the kingdom of God, however, both theology of culture and systematic theology would constitute a single theological enterprise, because every act in a fully theonomous culture would express the depth of being to which Christians as the Church continue to aspire and bear witness. Yet, Gilkey concludes, "[i]n actuality, because of the alienation or estrangement *both* of the culture *and* of the church, no such

---

[15]Gilkey remarks that Tillich's understanding of "the role of the theologian in the contemporary situation . . . sail[s] pretty close to my own view of that role" (Gilkey, *GOT*, 177).

[16]Gilkey, *GOT*, 178.

[17]Gilkey, *ME*, 10-11.

[18]Gilkey, *GOT*, 179.

theonomy is ideally actual, nor is the Spiritual Presence anything but fragmentary, even in the church."[19]

Part of Gilkey's theological genius is that he separates neither the discussion of method nor its application from the praxis of the oscillating interplay between religious experience and theological construction. As such, theology's context and task reflect the *Geist* of the theologian's epoch or time in history.[20] Gilkey describes his own epoch as a "Time of Troubles." Regarding this "Time of Troubles," Arnold Toynbee's phrase, adopted to describe the *Geist* of the present age, Gilkey muses: "do I think this way *theologically* because of the actually perturbed history of the mid-twentieth century, or do I see that history in this particular way because I am a theologian?" Pondering this seemingly irresolvable question about the interplay between social history and personal experience, Gilkey is able to affirm that he "became a theologian because it *was* such a period," such a "Time of Troubles." In such a time of distress, disquietude, and discontent, he continues:

> it is intelligible that questions of personal existence, of the transcendence and the mystery of God, of the fall and sin of humans, of the direction of history, of the dominance and yet the ambiguity of a secular and scientific culture, and finally of the plurality of religions should arise and increasingly pose the kinds of theological problems I have found fascinating and the issues I have found most pressing. In such a turbulent period it is not only intelligible that one should become a believer and a theologian, but also that the resulting theology should be both *existential and historical-cultural* in its emphasis.[21]

Out of the existential character of his reflection on the sociocultural events in his life, Gilkey developed the praxis of thinking action and active thinking that has shaped his public theology.

Gilkey's awareness of the shaping force of culture on his thought began to emerge as he completed his undergraduate studies. As a collegian during the rise of the Nazi regime and the beginning of World War II, Gilkey and other liberal students at Harvard University found themselves engaged by two opposite, conflicting forces and courses of

---

[19]Gilkey, *GOT*, 190.

[20]See Langdon Gilkey, *Naming the Whirlwind: The Renewal of God-Language* (Indianapolis: Bobbs-Merrill, 1969) 190; hereafter cited as *NW*.

[21]Gilkey, "Retrospective Glance at My Work," 2.

action. According to Gilkey, "on the one hand, out of commitment to peace, we were determined to avoid war at all costs; on the other hand, out of commitment to justice, equality and freedom, we could not but loathe Nazism and be equally determined to resist it." Between these two absolutes of peace and justice, Gilkey felt "stretched" and, as he puts it, "quite unable to qualify or to relinquish either one." Faced with such a dilemma, he began to perceive the inadequacies of humanism; the only apparent alternative to relinquishing either of the moral imperatives of peace and justice would be to capitulate to cynicism.[22] With the intellectual foundation for his worldview so thoroughly challenged, he became ready for the kind of transformation and openness that a Christian worldview might provide—a worldview that became increasingly plausible to Gilkey as he read the work of Reinhold Niebuhr while traveling to China to begin his teaching career.

With his teaching disrupted by the beginning of war between Japan and the United States in 1943, Gilkey and almost two thousand other non-Chinese civilians were imprisoned in a compound in Shandong province by the Japanese forces occupying China. The camp was a confined community that provided a kind of laboratory for observing how people construct a society and live together. Unexpectedly, Gilkey discovered that most of the problems that he and the other international internees experienced were caused not by the Japanese soldiers but by their own behavior. The problems were not the consequences or responses to political policies and military maneuvers; instead, they were endemic to the human condition—attitudes such as greed and laziness.[23] Although the Japanese treatment of the prisoners was secondary to the problems of their own making, the extensive political, social, and personal oppression of the Chinese citizens by the Japanese convinced Gilkey, as he later reflected, "that historical evil could at times become so vast that resistance to that evil becomes inescapable." Like many liberation theologians, he realized that, if the need for violent response to oppression and aggression arose, he would take up arms. As he recalls, "I had for at least

---

[22]Gilkey, "Retrospective Glance at My Work," 6.

[23]Gilkey chronicled the devious attempts of internees to acquire more space than their allotted shares (Gilkey, *Shantung Compound: The Story of Men and Women under Pressure* [New York: Harper & Row Publishers, 1966] 75-96; hereafter cited as *SC*).

that period of my life ceased to be a pacifist in principle and so to abjure all resort under any circumstances to military violence."[24]

For Gilkey, Depression and wartime-era neoorthodox theology, which emphasized "transcendence, sin, revelation, and grace," precisely corresponded to his own experience:

> the pervasiveness of sin and meaninglessness continually threatening, even in the modern age, human history and personal existence; the ambiguous and ultimately self-destructive tendencies of a civilization built on secular grounds alone, even a scientific and technical civilization; the absolute necessity of revelation and grace for any help or renewal to appear in such a situation; and as a consequence the centrality and uniqueness of the appearance and presence of God in Jesus Christ and of the community that witnesses to that revelation.[25]

The correlation that Gilkey perceived between his own experience and these theological sinews served not only to validate the character of his own experience but also to enlighten and orient his subsequent action and thought. The age-old praxis of faith seeking understanding became manifest anew in Gilkey's life.

II. From Praxis to Pedagogy

Although Gilkey has not written extensively about the vocation of teaching or the purpose of education, as did theologian Martin Buber in *Between Man and Man*, philosopher Alfred North Whitehead in *Aims of Education*, and social theorist Paulo Friere in *The Pedagogy of the Oppressed*, Gilkey's theological projects and correlational method as praxis are conjoined to his vocation as teacher. Throughout his career, Gilkey returned persistently to vocational issues about teaching, pedagogical concerns about instruction, and political challenges prompted by student and faculty colleagues. Even before Gilkey became a theologian, his identity was shaped by teaching, both by the supportive, academically oriented household of his youth and by his initial vocational service as an instructor of English at Yenching University. Only subsequently, after becoming disenchanted with the study of international law, did he turn his formal study to theology. Even then, his pursuit was oriented toward an academic home rather than an ecclesiastical appointment. The following

---

[24]Gilkey, "Retrospective Glance at My Work," 10.
[25]Gilkey, "Retrospective Glance at My Work," 14, 13.

examples illustrate concerns that Gilkey has addressed in theological education.

Gilkey's first published theological work, an essay relating the question of academic freedom to his understanding of human nature, appeared shortly after he had assumed a teaching position at Vassar College.[26] Gilkey's insights in *Naming the Whirlwind* often owe their origin to the works by and discussions with his colleague, Mircea Eliade, a historian of religions who celebrated the phenomena of religions and the spiritual experiences of persons that occur beyond the frameworks of established religious traditions and systems.[27] Gilkey's experience of needing to select a text for beginning students in an introductory theology course, prompted Gilkey to write his short systematic theology, *Message and Existence*; consequently, the shape and style of the book address the particular audience of students that Gilkey engaged in the late 1970s.[28] In one of his most recent works, a celebration and analysis of the theology of his theological mentor, Paul Tillich, Gilkey not only pays tribute to his theological instructor, but also bemoans, in a focused critique of current educational styles, that technical and vocational rather than liberal or humanistic patterns of education rule more and more college and university curricula.[29] Engaged in and with each of these distinct instructional relationships and educational experiences, Gilkey reflected on their theological significance.

Gilkey's collegiate appointment occasioned his writing of the article, "Academic Freedom and the Christian Faith." In that study, Gilkey focused on inquiry, instruction, and academic freedom. He noted that the attitude of many Christians in the United States tended toward repression of academic freedom. Yet, Gilkey did not focus on the politics of academic freedom or the pedagogy of indoctrination as the supposed ideal spirit of religious education. Instead, he investigated the question of "whether religion is ultimately to gain or to lose by repressing or by aiding in the repression of these alternative points of view."[30] In this popular Christian concern about either the exposure of students to other

---

[26]Langdon Gilkey, "Academic Freedom and the Christian Faith," *Christianity and Crisis* 12 (22 November 1952): 171.

[27]Gilkey, *NW*, 38n.3.

[28]Gilkey, *ME*, 1.

[29]Gilkey, *GOT*, 183.

[30]Gilkey, "Academic Freedom and the Christian Faith," 171.

faiths or the criticism of their own traditions, Gilkey locates the central issues of human nature, the character of truth, the nature of salvation—all connected to the pedagogy of free inquiry.

For Gilkey, any attempt to align Christianity with a prescriptive mode of thinking and an intolerance for engaging other points of view fundamentally misrepresents the Christian faith. Following Tillich, who argued for the inclusion of doubt within faith, Gilkey observed a similarity between academic freedom and the risk of faith because, as Reinhold Niebuhr had argued, faith itself is at risk in the freedom of academic inquiry; faith cannot be gained or preserved, however, by refusing to acknowledge its fundamental freedom. Christian testimony about sin and salvation depends radically on the freedom of humans to err and to repent. "Christian salvation," Gilkey asserts, "is the achievement of a personal fellowship or communion with God . . . [that] cannot be forced; its very essence is its inwardness and therefore its freedom."[31]

The mind's free exploration and engagement form the foundation of academic inquiry. That exploration and engagement also provide an avenue for religious fulfillment.

> The power of the mind is only satisfied when the mind itself has understood and appropriated the truth. But the mind itself will appropriate and accept the truth as truth only when it has been given the full opportunity to weigh relevant evidence and to consider possible alternatives. The inward assent of the mind to truth involves, therefore, the freedom of the mind to inquire and to question.[32]

On this point, Gilkey concludes that both Christian faith and academic inquiry are grounded in the recognition that human fulfillment can only be attained through the freedom of the mind to question, to explore, to engage. In support of the metaphysical connection between truth and freedom, Gilkey appeals to the fourth evangelist, who writes that Jesus affirmed this fundamental connection for faithful followers: "If you continue in my word, you are truly my disciples, and you will know the truth, and the truth will make you free" (John 8:31-32).[33]

The connection between truth and freedom is so fundamental that Gilkey locates the identity of the Church itself in openness in its pursuit

---

[31]Gilkey, "Academic Freedom and the Christian Faith," 171.
[32]Gilkey, "Academic Freedom and the Christian Faith," 172.
[33]Gilkey, "Academic Freedom and the Christian Faith," 172.

of truth, that is, in its freedom: "If atheists and humanists and radicals are silenced, then the true Church will be silenced as well." For "to insist too strongly that *our* truth is *the* truth is to lose the truth because only truth can defend itself and because truth can only be defended in freedom."[34] As scripture says, " '[i]f we say that we have no sin, we deceive ourselves, and the truth is not in us' " (I John 1:8).[35] If we claim to possess the truth already, to be the truth's sole representatives, then we pretend that we have no sin; our pretentiousness, thus, belies the fact that we stand in the absence of truth rather than in its presence. Gilkey concludes his theological argument about academic freedom with the insight that, as Christians seek to serve and proclaim the God of truth who has created humans as free agents, it is both incoherent and unethical to consider that God would enjoin and enjoy the destruction of free inquiry.[36] With this final turn, then, Gilkey located both the source and goal of academic freedom in divine creativity and providence.

As central as it is to the vocation of teachers, the issue of academic freedom is not the only concern that Gilkey has addressed in theological education. He also has identified other components in the complex set of issues attending theological education: its place, purpose, and providers. In each instance, the issues can be related to the mission of the church, especially as local congregations endeavor to fulfill that mission. In *How the Church Can Minister to the World without Losing Itself* and in an essay on the authority of the Bible for the church, Gilkey addressed the crying need for *theological* education in the churches. Accordingly, he claims, "[t]oo long has religious education been the province of nursery school and child training experts"; Gilkey continues, "[f]or religious education is the fundamental need of the free churches if they are to recapture the authority of the Bible, an education . . . [the] main task [of which] is to mediate biblical revelation into the minds and hearts of today's Christians."[37]

In effect, the goal of this theological education, Gilkey maintains, is "to make the local church an extension of the intellectual activity of the

---

[34]Gilkey, "Academic Freedom and the Christian Faith," 172 (emphasis mine).

[35]Gilkey, "Academic Freedom and the Christian Faith," 173.

[36]Gilkey, "Academic Freedom and the Christian Faith," 173.

[37]Langdon Gilkey, "The Authority of the Bible: The Relation of the Bible to the Church," *Encounter* 27 (Spring 1966): 123.

seminary." Gilkey identified three emphases that might bring this expansive biblical and theological training to fruition.

First, *pastors* should be trained to be effective *instructors* of the Bible, rather than primarily as *preachers* or proclaimers of biblical texts. Pastors should operate as teaching-theologians who, rather than inculcating dogma or repeating biblical texts, inspire Christians to understand their faith, relate the witness of Scripture to the history and promise of their own experience, and cultivate the abilities of Christians to express their faith authentically and articulately.

Second, congregations need to become aware of their theological ignorance, in part by listening to the affirmations of creeds not as scientific formulae or historical treatises, but as symbolic, poetic testimonies of the kind of deep issues that orient belief. Frequently, the primary problem that Christians face is not that they believe incorrectly but that they do not know what to believe. Often, Gilkey insists, Christians suffer from "a vapid ignorance" of the depth and expanse of Christian thought about fundamental theological issues: the nature of human life, the character or God in relation to humankind, and the destiny of all persons.

Third, Gilkey focuses on the content of this theological education. He concludes with the following claims.

> What is necessary is that the Bible be *taught* in our churches as a credible, relevant document, mediating to us now where we are an intelligible faith that (a) is not contradictory to our scientific culture in which we live and believe, (b) that is the answer to our deepest personal, moral and spiritual needs, and (c) that requires of us actions of such a sort that they relieve and possibly reform the community's deepest need. Such an effort is, of course, the main function of theological education. . . . In seeking to relate biblical revelation to modern thought and modern obligations, theological education performs exactly that task of mediation.[38]

Accordingly, then, one of the goals of such churchwide biblical education is to train each member to become a novice theologian, one who is able to read the culturally conditioned and historically preserved texts of scripture with appreciation and new understanding.

Although Gilkey wrote about the importance of theological education for participants in local churches, and although he often spoke at denominational meetings and to church groups, his teaching found its home in

---

[38]Gilkey, "Authority of the Bible," 123.

the academy, particularly in divinity school settings where he could ride the cusp between mentoring theological instructors for the academy and the parish. A traditional lecturer in the Enlightenment tradition, relying on reason as the mode for reflection, Gilkey nonetheless manifested an uncanny ability to seize teachable moments, often turning to personal experience, in the feeling/experience tradition of Schleiermacher, as a means to underscore the vitality and validity of points that he would make. Always sensitive to his audience, he could grasp the expectations of his particular audience and challenge them in unexpected ways.

Perhaps there is no more dramatic example of this ability than an occasion outside the classroom—a courtroom where Gilkey was able to deliver a lecture, of sorts, on the character of religion, the theological significance of the Creation, and the Christian understanding of the nature of God. During the Arkansas creationist trial in 1981, Gilkey served as the expert theological witness to challenge the Arkansas law that required the inclusion of creation science in secondary school curriculum as a scientific theory—not as religious postulation. In an effort to coordinate specialist testimony and to make the strongest case, the lawyers for the American Civil Liberties Union (ACLU) had taken hours of depositions and had rehearsed repeatedly the questions and answers that were to be given in the trial. As the lead lawyer for the ACLU (Tony Siano) questioned, and as Gilkey provided testimony about the *"purely* religious idea" of creation science's presupposition of a Creator in the act of creating *ex nihilo*, Gilkey seized an unforeseen moment to baffle the defense and supporters of the law. The supporters of the law, in the back row of the courtroom, had gone to their knees in prayer as Gilkey had been sworn in as a witness. Gilkey proceeded to teach the audience in a moment of incredible pointedness and receptivity. Using language that would grab the attention of fundamentalists as well as officers of the court, Gilkey remarked that the idea of *creatio ex nihilo*, by presupposing a Creator, is necessarily more religious than Christmas! Gilkey reasoned that, for Christmas, the human Mary must somehow be involved; yet, for a creative act *ex nihilo*, only a creator God could be at work. Then, turning the tables and baffling those in prayer on the back row, Gilkey correlated the Arkansas law with early Christian history. With respect and verve, Gilkey testified:

> I do not wish to accuse the State of Arkansas, or its excellent lawyers, of anything culpable, and I am sure that they have done this innocently, not knowing what their words mean. But the *fact* is, . . . they have in their

presentation of the case come very close, yes, very close indeed, to the *first, and worst, Christian heresy!*

. . . I mean that to prove that the creator presupposed in the Act [590 of the Arkansas legislature]—and they admit this—is *not* religious, they try to separate him from God, from the personal God who reveals himself, who loves the world, who comes in the Covenant with Israel and later in Jesus Christ. Now this was precisely the early heresy of Marcion and the Gnostics (about 150 to 200 AD), who said that there were in fact two Gods, one a blind, cruel, but powerful God of creation (the God of the Old Testament), and the other a good, loving God of redemption (the God of the New Testament)—and thus that the creator God was *not* the same as the redeemer God. I don't think the creationists have this idea in mind, of course, but *if* they say the creator they presuppose is not *God*, nor is religious—they are willy-nilly saying precisely this.[39]

With acuity, wit, and compassion, Gilkey engaged the mixed courtroom audience of Arkansas preachers and laypersons, jurists and clerks, scientists and scholars, and taught them about theological reasoning and Christian history.

In less dramatic ways but with greater frequency, Gilkey seized moments in the classroom to reflect on personal experience and relationships in light of Christian scriptures and history. Most impressive were his recollections of family relationships (particularly those with his father and his sister) and his tales about his experience in China during the second world war. He told the stories of his family not because they provided a break from the subject of the lecture, but because they exemplified the topic. He conveyed a deep sense of spirituality about human experience in contact with the power of being and the possibilities and process of becoming. On such occasions, the emotion in the classroom would become palpable as his voice, with a rich baritone tempered by the winds of sea sailing, would crack as sharply as a sail being turned into the wind. Some might think that his emotional sensitivity merely reflected a sort of sentimentality, rather than a deep sense of the mystical spirit of connectedness with the power of being that emerges in intensely personal moments—negatively as anxiety, alienation, and ignorance; and,

---

[39]Langdon Gilkey, *Creationism on Trial: Evolution and God at Little Rock* (Minneapolis: Winston, 1985) 104; hereafter cited as *CT*. The summary rationale provides one of the most succinct statements of theological reasoning accessible to an audience of ordinary Christians, the theological audience that Gilkey promoted (Gilkey, *CT*, 106).

positively, as courage, love, and understanding. These represent the times when one experiences a foretaste of the triumph over alienation and estrangement, of separation's conquest through love, grace, and promise. So it is with praxis: Experience provokes understanding, which itself enriches and directs new experience and understanding.

Not only would Gilkey teach by means of drawing on personal experience; he was perceptive about the prospects for seeing the depth of another person's story, for understanding the course of faith and the presence of grace in encounters with colleagues, friends, and students. Their stories became part of the praxis of Gilkey's theology; for, in addition to compassion and understanding, the stories frequently prompted decisive action. Particularly, the stories of students effected personal and social response. Following a coffee-shop conversation with the student, John Andrati, who shared the story of his own struggle with cancer, Gilkey felt the impact of the hazards of smoking in a way that had previously eluded his intellectual understanding of statistics and medical experiments. While sitting with Andrati, Gilkey put out his cigarette—the last one that he smoked.[40]

Gilkey's social theological praxis was provoked, for example, by the story of James Lawson, a courageous student of Vanderbilt University Divinity School. As the civil rights movement was beginning to gain momentum in the early 1960s, Lawson had coached several students from Fisk University in nonviolent means of protest, as they prepared to "sit in" segregated Nashville restaurants. In response to the protest, the community called for sanctions against Lawson and the protesters, accusing him of being a communist agitator. In response to the community's uproar, the chancellor of the university expelled Lawson. Gilkey led the entire Divinity School faculty—except one—to revolt against the chancellor's decision. After three months of futile negotiations, the Divinity School's faculty readmitted Lawson without the approval of the university; furthermore, the faculty threatened to resign if Lawson were not allowed to reenter. At that point, the university refused to budge from its earlier position, and the faculty indeed resigned, an action that triggered several resignations by Medical School faculty. Thus challenged, the chancellor acquiesced, only to learn that the Board of the university refused to allow Lawson's readmission. With the entire university faculty

---

[40]Joseph L. Price, "The Ultimate and the Ordinary: A Profile of Langdon Gilkey," *Christian Century* (12 April 1989): 380.

now unified in response to the Board, the chancellor ignored the Board's injunction and readmitted Lawson. Incidentally, this incident contributed to the dissolution of Gilkey's first marriage. Although costly to Gilkey in personal terms, his decisive action generated a keener understanding of the promise of God's kingdom as portrayed in the teaching of Jesus, as well as a more comprehensive understanding of the culture of the university and the city.[41] So it is with praxis: Gilkey's engagement in intellectual issues prompts personal and social action that germinates increased understanding and compassion.

III. Prospectus on Praxis

Throughout Gilkey's career a recurrent issue—academic freedom—has stimulated his reflection and action, his praxis in pedagogy. The significance of academic freedom as a topic for Gilkey's theology and as the context for his career in higher education far exceeds the occasions when the issue of academic freedom prompted publication (as with his first essay, "Academic Freedom and the Christian Faith"), political action (as with his protest against the expulsion of James Lawson from Vanderbilt Divinity School), and public instruction (as with his concerns about the Arkansas "scientific creationism" model for public school curricula). The significance of academic freedom for Gilkey derives from other basic theological factors as well: its exemplification of the character of human beings as free agents created by God; its alignment with the understanding of salvation as freely given and received; and its representation of the liberating character of truth itself. In these sure senses, freedom—as manifest in the issue of academic freedom—begins to assume the importance of metaphysical concepts.

Because the pursuit of truth requires the process of free inquiry and because the exercise of human freedom facilitates an encounter with ultimacy, the issue of academic freedom lies at the heart of Gilkey's professional identity, and provides an important key to his theological life.[42] To a certain extent, Gilkey seems to have been born to teach because of the depth of his love for relating message to existence, his fondness for exploring the significance of human experiences and finding

---

[41]Gilkey, "Retrospective Glance at My Work," 16-19.

[42]See, for example, Langdon Gilkey, *Reaping the Whirlwind: A Christian Interpretation of History* (New York: Seabury, 1976) 379; hereafter cited as *RW*.

therein adumbrations of ultimacy. But his joy in understanding—and in the process of faith seeking understanding—becomes complete in the expressions of pleasure that he shares with others as teacher, as he leads them to new levels of understanding not only about the character of human experience, but about the particular significance of their own treks through times of trouble.

Indeed, Gilkey has been a good teacher, not only in the sense of enriching the lives of students and colleagues with informed action and an active mind. He has been a good teacher also in the sense described by his sometime colleague in the University of Chicago Divinity School, Wayne Booth. In an essay whose title—"What Little I Think I Know about Teaching"—reflects Gilkey's own wit and humility, Booth asserts that good teaching "leads students to want to continue to work in the given subject and to be able to, because they have the necessary intellectual equipment to continue work at a more advanced level."[43] Certainly, this description summarizes Gilkey's accomplishment and challenge: Whether in a university classroom, a Sunday School facility, a courtroom, or a coffee shop, Gilkey has inspired students and colleagues to seek further understanding of their faith. In so doing, he has modeled good teaching and prompted students to explore for themselves previously inaccessible avenues of understanding.

If praxis is a kind of oscillating interplay between experience and reflection, thought and action, then its termination cannot be conceived. In the ongoing process of praxis, thought and action intermingle constantly, informing and stimulating one another. And so it is with the pedagogy of Langdon Gilkey. Although his primary days of classroom and conversational instruction have now concluded, his instruction will continue through students who, inspired by his teaching and provoked by his works, continue the interactive process of praxis in their pedagogy.

---

[43]Wayne C. Booth, *The Vocation of a Teacher: Rhetorical Occasions 1967–1988* (Chicago: University of Chicago Press, 1988) 212.

Part 5

Reflections by Langdon Gilkey

Chapter 16

A Retrospective Glance at My Work

Langdon Gilkey

Introduction

When I look back on my life's work—on the major interests that have inspired it and the thoughts and writings that have resulted therefrom—I am impressed with its unplanned character. Seen by itself, it seems to meander from this to that with no apparent order or direction. There appears to me now, however, one thread that provides whatever consistency or intelligibility it may possess, and that is the changing shape of the historical context in which these thoughts, as essentially reactions, occurred. All this was quite unconscious; at no point did I deliberately decide to pattern my thought in relation to historical events, nor was I even particularly aware that this was happening. Consciousness does reflect being and, in this case, the being reflected was constituted by the historical events lying in the middle sixty years of the twentieth century. Quite unintentionally, therefore, my thought has reflected a "correlational" approach: as when a sailboat hugs a massive but variegated shoreline, its course has been determined by the twists and turns of twentieth-century events. As the little volume summing up my theology indicates, this life-work reflects a dialectic of message and existence.[1] In the end, to be sure, the explicit and therefore deliberate theological method which I use and defend has also been correlational. That formal method, however, is a symptom and not a cause of a more basic pattern of thinking, namely to ponder the character of our existence, both personal and historical, before God in the light of the historical and social situation, the massive contours of events, in which we find ourselves.

This lifework is that of a theologian. Thus, its elements represent a *theology*: an attempt to discern the truth about God and God's ways with us. But this is, as noted, a correlational or dialectical theology: these ways are experienced, uncovered, and articulated in relation—and only in relation—first to the changing character of personal existence in our age, including of course my own, and, second, in relation to the shifting forms

---

[1]Langdon Gilkey, *Message and Existence: An Introduction to Christian Theology* (New York: Seabury Press, 1979); hereafter cited as *ME*.

of social existence and the panorama of events that those personal existences inhabit. Thus, consciousness of both the career of individual personal existences and the contours of their historical environments in the mid-twentieth century is essential for any understanding of the grounds of the theology represented here. I became a theologian because of the historical context of my early adult life, and the subsequent characteristic of the theology that arose there and the issues over the decades with which it has been concerned have likewise reflected that changing historical context.

As will be evident from this unfolding story, the sequence of events from 1933 to 1999, through which as a person aware of his environment I lived, represents what I have frequently termed (following Toynbee) a "Time of Troubles," the apparent beginning of a process of social disintegration and historical decline, a *fin de siècle*. Consciousness of this has slowly developed in me, and most of my theological thoughts from their inception in the late 1930s to the present reflect this character. Obviously, the question is posed by this correlation of history and reflective thought: do I think this way *theologically* because of the actually perturbed history of the mid-twentieth century, or do I see that history in this particular way because I am a theologian? All I can say is that I became a theologian because it *was* such a period; and, subsequently, each time I have looked at it, I have been more convinced of the validity of that assessment. In any case, in such a Time of Troubles, it is intelligible that questions of personal existence, of the transcendence and the mystery of God, of the fall and sin of humans, of the direction of history, of the dominance and yet the ambiguity of a secular and scientific culture, and finally of the plurality of religions should arise and increasingly pose the kinds of theological problems I have found fascinating and the issues I have found most pressing. In such a turbulent period, it is not only intelligible that one should become a believer and a theologian, but also that the resulting theology should be both *existential and historical-cultural* in its emphasis.

Now I shall turn to the story itself, which will, I trust, add flesh and life to the bare bones of these generalizations. This is neither a personal autobiography nor an existential religious history of my life. Most of what has happened to me or how I felt about it will be omitted. The point of what follows is to give the existential, social, and historical background to my life's work—where the latter has "come from," insofar as it reflects the history in which it was thought out. I shall, therefore, mention only those situations and events in my life which provide the context for my theological work.

I. From Inherited Liberalism, through Naturalistic Humanism, to Niebuhrian Neoorthodoxy: 1919–1940

I appeared on earth in 1919, and I spent my boyhood in a liberal Protestant home in one of the most lively and progressive academic centers of American life, the University of Chicago. My father, Charles W. Gilkey, was the well-known and widely acclaimed minister of what was then in effect the "University Church," the Hyde Park Baptist Church; later (1928), he became the first dean of the University Chapel.[2] My mother was equally prominent and successful: an early feminist, a superb hostess for the university community, especially its students, and a leading YWCA officer (for one term in the late 1920s, she was the national president).[3] Together they created a potent, open, morally and socially concerned home (for years my father was head of the Chicago ACLU), filled every week with visiting preachers and church persons, students, professors, and prominent religious and secular reformers.

Above all, this environment was "liberal," theologically and politically. My father's personal religious lifestyle remained relatively

---

[2]*Editors' note.* Charles W. Gilkey's publications wonderfully illustrate Langdon Gilkey's story. See the following: *Jesus and Our Generation*, Barrows Lectures 1924–1925 (Chicago: University of Chicago Press, 1925); *Perspectives* (New York: Harper & Brothers, 1933); "The Distinctive Baptist Witness," *The Chronicle* 8 (July 1945): 97-106; "The Place of Religion in Higher Education," in *Religion and the Modern World: University of Pennsylvania Bicentennial Conference* (Port Washington NY: Kennikat Press, 1941) 73-87; "Present-Day Dilemmas in Religion," *Methodist Quarterly Review* 77 (April 1928): 297-98; "Present-Day Dilemmas in Religion," *Methodist Review* 111 (July 1928): 627-28; "Religion in Our College Generations," *Christianity and Crisis* 9 (1949): 147-50; and "Well-Proved Ministry," *Pastoral Psychology* 8 (February 1957): 9-12.

[3]*Editors' note.* In an address to the Mormon History Association in Independence, Missouri in 1985, Langdon Gilkey refers to his mother's background. She spent a large part of her childhood in Salt Lake City, where her father, Langdon's maternal grandfather, served as the minister of the Congregational Church from 1892 until 1902, at which time the family moved to San Diego, California (Langdon Gilkey, "Religion and Culture: A Persistent Problem," *Journal of Mormon History* 12 [1985]: 29). Langdon Gilkey published a short and anonymous reflection on the event of his mother's death: see Langdon Gilkey, "In Faith . . . Praise, Thanksgiving, and Joy," *Christianity and Crisis* 16 (10 December 1956): 168-69.

disciplined and Spartan (except for his sailboat); we had daily family prayers when my sister and I were children, and there was never any alcohol in our home. Nevertheless, as a family, we hardly represented a strict "evangelical" home, as had been the case with my father's family: guests smoked there; we were not sabbatarian; we played cards and enjoyed theater and movies—and we talked continually about current political events, moral causes, and social changes. In this home, to be "religious"—and so to be genuinely Christian—meant, as it did for so much of liberal Protestantism, the critical spirit and the social gospel: to be relatively relaxed with regard to both doctrines and rules, to be free of the obvious moral faults and the vices of tobacco and alcohol, to be vastly concerned about social and racial justice and peace—above all peace—and to be tolerant of the ideas, the habits, and mores of other groups. It was taken for granted in this atmosphere that any kind of racial or religious prejudice, any religious, racial, or patriotic fanaticism, any overt acts of materialistic or class self-interest, national aggression, or persecution were anathema to a genuine Christianity. It was also taken for granted that my parents' many Jewish and Negro (as they were then called) friends were normal visitors in this home. We were proud when father, along with many other liberals, appeared on the American Legion's "black list" of un-Americans, and when chapters of the Daughters of the American Revolution denounced both mother and father for their racial and social liberalism. Lifestyles—perhaps especially for theologians—have changed vastly since this culminating period of Protestant liberalism in the 1920s; yet, this inheritance—this "taking all this for granted"—made its permanent imprint on my conscience and has never ceased to provide the foundation for whatever has been good in my makeup. I grew up hating the anti-Semitism and the segregationist customs (not to mention the laws) still characteristic then of American society, scorning the "economic royalists" of the 1930s, and utterly devoted to the permanent establishment of peace. Thus, in the early 1930s, we all supported Roosevelt, were dismayed at the mounting aggression of the Japanese and of Mussolini, and came not only to be fearfully conscious of the dark cloud of Hitler, but to shudder at its evil portent for the world. My first original research paper during my freshman year in college in 1936 was a study of the early history and the rise to dominance (1924–1934) of the Nazi movement in the German Reich. That paper documented what was then public knowledge in Germany and elsewhere, namely, the mounting persecution of Jews and the determination to eradicate them from Germany's public life.

College (Harvard University) represented the continuation of all of this, except now on a more autonomous basis; for, in college, the same person lives on only now on his or her own. This meant certain real continuities: the same liberal, political, and social convictions (though the menace of social snobbishness in college life could hide behind and mock the most liberal convictions!), and the same intellectual, literary, and historical concerns. I majored in philosophy and, in that study, vastly preferred metaphysical, epistemological, and moral questions to logical subjects. In fact, I found in myself a marked prejudice for idealism over materialism, which I rightly ascribed to my father's influence. Still, to be autonomous also meant important changes: like so many in the 1930s, I smoked a pipe, drank an occasional beer or wine, and went on as many Wellesley dates and Smith weekends as I could. I found myself becoming more and more "Ivy League," in tweeds, flannels and button downs, a far cry from the less self-conscious Midwestern corduroys of my youth. Religion, or interest in it, played absolutely no part in my personal or my intellectual life. I knew nothing of and thought less about Christian doctrine and was not even aware of that lack in my philosophical repertoire. I went to chapel only occasionally to hear a friend of father preach and attended religious discussion groups for reasons that were vague and certainly obscure to me. It would not have occurred to me that there might be more to discuss in such religious groups than ethical and social issues. I wrote my senior honors thesis (Fall 1939) on George Santayana, praising his elegant, sensitive naturalism and agreeing thoroughly with his charming rejection of religious belief. I found myself tolerant of religious beliefs, but confident that civilization had progressed by the twentieth century beyond their mythical picture of reality. Why, I asked myself, do we need any more than ethical principles, a social conscience, and democracy to continue to progress? I was, I suppose, an ethical humanist, if I was anything—besides being a fairly serious student, an even more serious competitor in tennis, and a genial if circumspect *bon vivant*.

Twentieth-century history, however, was steadily encroaching on, surrounding, and threatening to engulf this easy, genteel, academic life. In 1938 at Munich, the worst nightmare of our collective youth, namely, the reappearance of war, of world war, which we had been brought up to hate, for a moment threatened to become reality—and then receded again.

In September of 1939, however, when the Harvard-Yale tennis team was touring in France, that dreaded war began in reality—and we barely got home, sickened, scared, and confused. We detested Hitler—but we (and here almost an entire generation spoke) detested war more. Thus, on my return in senior year, along with Avery Dulles, the lanky Presbyterian son of a liberal lawyer, I helped form the Keep America Out of the War Committee. I remained active in it, until Boston Irish tirades against the British empire ("the two empires, Hitler's and the British, are identical") drove Avery and me out. The war remained a ghastly specter during most of that winter: a dominant fact in the news, it yet seemed unreal, a possible portent of untold and meaningless horrors, but as yet only a threat and so now and again quite forgettable. Then, suddenly in the spring of a senior year replete with romantic weekends, tennis victories, scholastic honors, and all sorts of personal culminations, that spectral potency became an abysmally dark actuality: Hitler's armies quickly overran the smaller lands of western Europe, France fell, and apparently even England was about to be engulfed. I recall moving with genial unreality through the events of that senior spring, as confused inside as the world was outside. Since we were concerned and devoted liberals, we found ourselves in that year driven irresistibly along two quite contradictory courses: on the one hand, out of commitment to peace, we were determined to avoid war at all costs; on the other hand, out of commitment to justice, equality, and freedom, we could not but loathe Nazism and be equally determined to resist it. I was stretched between two moral absolutes, peace and justice, and quite unable to qualify or to relinquish either one. Further, I found that, for my humanism to survive, these must remain *absolute* requirements, else all descend into cynicism. In fact, I recall the cynical alternative becoming my increasingly frequent recourse. On one boat-race weekend, relaxed, sunny, and beery, I remember arguing, "after all, these moral ideals were irrelevant to history's course, that Europe did need at some point to be forcibly unified, and that such a process was (as liberal historians say about the past, but almost never about their own present) always a cruel matter, but one nevertheless justified by the necessities of history. Why shouldn't Hitler do it as well as anyone?—and so (I concluded) let us leave it to the march of history to work out Europe's unhappy destiny." Having intellectually won the argument, I hated myself for so thoroughly betraying myself and my world. Gone were the social ideals and the confidence in progress towards justice that heretofore—though I had not fully realized it—

buoyed up and guided my spiritual existence. I was left a clever cynic, directed only by the requirements of self-interest in a world going nowhere. The cold blast of historical reality had made my intellectual and moral humanism come apart at the seams; I realized that I detested myself and the world in which I lived.[4]

Into this state of slowly developing inner confusion and disillusionment—it was not quite yet clear—something unexpected entered, providing the new possibility of a realistic and not deluded spiritual existence and yet one replete with understanding and self-understanding, with moral direction and spiritual centeredness. On a Sunday in early April—when Hitler's armies were beginning to move and my spiritual world was, therefore, beginning to crumble—I went to the Harvard chapel to listen to an old friend of father. The latter had repeatedly said, "You ought to go hear Reinnie preach sometime." And, knowing nothing else but that, I wandered into the chapel. Suddenly, as the torrent of insight poured from the pulpit, my world in disarray spun completely around, steadied, and then settled into a new and quite firm and intelligible structure.

As I listened to Niebuhr's utterly sober and realistic analysis of the power struggles among the nations, I thought to myself: "Now I am in touch with *reality* and not with the illusions of humanistic idealism"; and then, as I listened to the strong moral judgments on that rebellious world that ushered forth from the same analysis, and the impassioned call—despite our failures—to be humble, to seek justice, and to show mercy, I realized that, in *this* framework (he called it, to my astonishment, "biblical"), one could be realistic and yet morally concerned; one could look the facts in the face and yet have confidence and hope. The dichotomy that had wrecked my humanism—*either* believe in moral ideals and the moral capacities of human groups at the price of ignoring the sordid realities of social life *or* be realistic about those realities and therefore cynical—had dissipated into a new understanding. We are

---

[4]*Editors' note.* Regarding this period of moral confusion and Gilkey's later insights about it, see his brief accounts of both his class's graduation from Harvard University in 1940 and of his eulogy for the dead members of that graduating class at the class's twenty-fifth reunion in 1965: Gilkey, *ME*, 255-56n.2; idem, "Dimensions of Basic Faith and the Special Traditions," *Second Opinion: Health, Faith, and Ethics* 2 (1986): 114-15; idem, "The Protestant View of Sin," in *The Human Condition in Jewish and Christian Traditions*, ed. Frederick E. Greenspahn (Hoboken NJ: KTAV, 1986) 152-53.

separated or estranged from the ideal, and thus is humanism impossible; but that does not mean the ideal has vanished from reality and only our alienated collective existence remains. For there is God, transcendent to the fallen, warring world and yet seeking to bring it back to its true self and all of us to our own true selves. The new "duality" of dubious, stricken world and transcendent God, of an estranged self and true self—and yet the continual relation between the two—made it possible for me to be again, to understand again, and to hope again. That personal and theological principle (theological and yet also ethical) of a divine transcendence and yet a continual relevance and relatedness Niebuhr gave to me at that chosen moment—and it has remained absolutely central to my life and my work ever since.

My conversion—and that is the right word—was quick and complete. I heard him, as did hundreds more, twice again that day, afternoon and evening; and I bought, read, and reread all his books then in print (up to *Beyond Tragedy*, 1936). At the end of two more weeks, I was a "Niebuhrian." In fact, during the next week, I quite rearranged the course that I was to teach the next year in Peking for the Yenching English Department on "Modern Western Thought." The new edition did not culminate, as I had first planned it, with the humanism of H. G. Wells, Bernard Shaw, George Santayana, and John Dewey, but with Niebuhr as the critique of that "now irrelevant" and evolutionary humanism and the appearance, or the reappearance, of a new religious understanding. As I slowly grew into this new viewpoint over the next two or three months, I was astounded with myself and with this "new world of the Bible," as Karl Barth had put it—though I had then never even heard of Barth. The notion that Christian faith could be "realistic" about human evil, rather than overlook it in favor of the "goodness of people," fascinated me. The concept that something could transcend and yet be related to nature, culture, and people was utterly new and intriguing; and, perhaps most significant, the idea that Christianity had something to declare about the nature of reality—a philosophy or a theology—and that it implied a new personal relation to reality, as well as a set of ethical rules, took me completely by surprise. Because it had been my "world," my understanding of human existence and of history, that had crumbled, not so much my ethical social norms, it was the *theological* message of Niebuhr that gripped me, and the theological teachings of the Christian tradition that captured my interest. Thus, my former undergraduate interest in metaphysical philosophy was transferred lock, stock, and barrel to a concern for theology, and by and large it has since remained there. Whereas, prior to that Sunday morning, naturalistic humanism appeared to me to represent hardheaded "reality" and religious doctrines a worthy but sentimental set of "illusions," now naturalistic humanism—despite its claim to scientific realism—seemed to me hopelessly mired in optimistic and naive illusions about progress and about human rational and moral goodness. On the other hand, Christian faith, initially irrational by the standards of the secular culture, now appeared in the end alone to make sense of our personal and social existence and so to be in touch with the only reality which we can directly encounter. I learned then to trust the requirements of *existence* and of normal *praxis*, rather than those of "objective inquiry," whenever ultimate questions about reality are at stake—although I had not, at that point, ever heard of Søren Kierkegaard. Meanwhile, I graduated in June. I was unsettled and confused, torn still between two worlds, on the boundary between my college humanism and the new intimations of divine reality that had so recently been opened up for me.

II. Neoorthodox Christian and the Global Crisis: 1940–1947

The summer of 1940, therefore, brought exciting new possibilities for my personal life, at the same time that it represented terrifying and tragic possibilities for the world. While Hitler's legions were poised on the Channel prepared to gobble up England, the one remaining center of resistance, I embarked in mid-August for Peking to teach the English language at Yenching University, an American-British university for Chinese students. As this brief history makes clear, I did not go as a missionary: uninterested, at that point, in further academic study and restless with all the seemingly boring alternatives open to a college graduate in the United States (business, preparatory school teaching, etc.). I had in midwinter signed up—thanks to a friend from China—with Yenching University for a two-year contract ($10 per month plus travel!) to teach introductory English classes (in English!). Since in early 1940 we were more than a year and a half away from the later actual war with Japan, this sojourn in Peking seemed to be sensible enough, and in August I sailed via Yokohama and Kobe to Peking. This experience in the Orient—I did not return home for five years—represented, without question, the most significant and formative period of my life. Whenever subsequently I have asked myself, "What is real and true in human experience? Where can I go to touch *reality*?" I find myself returning to that sequence of experiences.

When I arrived in 1940, China—and the entire Orient with it—reflected on every side the old colonial world. The British, Dutch, and French empires were still intact, and so European power dominated most of east Asia, as did British power in India, and British, French, and Belgian power in the Near East and Africa. Although China was technically a sovereign nation, it too had been completely dominated by the Western nations, especially by Great Britain. The treaty ports (Tien Tsin, Tsing Tao, and Shanghai) were British, and there British law ruled. Elsewhere, Westerners had all manner of extraterritorial rights, and without question any of them, rich or poor, powerful or powerless, prominent or insignificant, existed as members of a superior and so dominant race of beings amid, to them, the faceless sea of Chinese. One felt all this at once on arrival, this unaccustomed status of unquestioned superiority. I recall with some chagrin inwardly basking in its warmth, though I was also horrified at the gauche arrogance of many (though not all) of the British, French, and Americans whom I encountered in Peking. This aura of superiority was, moreover, total, covering every level of cultural life. It ranged from the levels of technology, industry, science, and medicine, to those of law and politics (democracy and individual rights), on up to attitudes of equality (for example, of the sexes) and of humanitarian concern for others, to issues of the purity and absoluteness of religion. All up and down the line, therefore, the West and Westerners assumed that their own civilization, and with it their religions (and themselves!), were innately and indubitably superior. What is worse, most outside the orbit of the West, who were thus looked down upon subconsciously if not consciously and certainly unwillingly, assented to that arrogant assessment of superiority. I remember being very conscious of this (while still enjoying its perquisites!) and saying to myself: "Seeing this dominance and superiority of the West, I can now understand why the Japanese are so irrationally angry, absurdly arrogant, and fanatically Shinto (as they were indeed), despite their advanced scientific, technical, and industrial culture." Then, I recall adding, "Wait until the even prouder Chinese (now our allies) are able to become conscious of and so to articulate fully these same hostile and explosive feelings." As *A Passage to India* documented this same social and spiritual situation of absolute Western dominance and superiority in the British Raj of the 1920s, so my brief experience in Peking in 1940–1941 was saturated with the identical delectable, but infinitely destructive, aura of our superiority, except that the twilight of that imperial supremacy had now deepened in 1940: I was there only moments before it was to be eclipsed forever.[5]

The other dominant political impression of that "free" year and a quarter (September 1940—December 1941) in Peking was of the ruthless brutality and the oppressive weight of the Japanese occupation of China, established in eastern China, and so in effect all around us roughly from 1936 until the end of the war. Since that time, a number of similarly brutal military occupations of civilian populations have horrified the world, with the result that few but the Chinese remember the outrageous character of this one. Still, contact with it convinced me that historical evil could at times become so vast that resistance to that evil becomes inescapable. I knew that, in a situation where my help was possible and relevant, I would take up arms against such oppression. I had, for at least that period of my life, ceased to be a pacifist in principle and so to abjure all resort under any circumstances to military violence. Meanwhile, the fascination of China grew apace; I was enthralled daily by what I saw all around me. Old China hands always told the newcomer: "Once here, you cannot return." I had laughed then—now I can hardly wait to get back again and again.

When the war began in December of 1941, we "enemy nationals" were rounded up at once and put under a sort of house arrest. During that time of forced inaction, I busied myself reading theology and teaching classes to missionaries on volume one of Niebuhr's *Nature and Destiny of Man*, which volume my father had sent to me in October of 1941, just before the war began (I had to wait until the end of the war to read

---

[5]*Editors' note*. In his descriptions of "warrants" in ordinary experience for "the search for a deeper meaning," or "clue[s]" or "intimations" of "an order transcendent to human intentions and surface conditions within the events we experience," Gilkey refers to his experiences of "a war internment camp and a divorce" as examples of experiences of "the creativity of the unwanted given in personal life and history" (Langdon Gilkey, *Reaping the Whirlwind: A Christian Interpretation of History* [New York: Seabury Press, 1976] 131-32; hereafter, cited as *RW*). See also Gilkey's similar comments in his reflection on the meaning of his experience in the Japanese internment camp: "One of the strangest lessons that our unstable life-passage teaches us is that the unwanted is often creative rather than destructive. . . . This is a common mystery of life, an aspect, if you will, of common grace: out of apparent evil new creativity can arise if the meanings and possibilities latent within the new situation are grasped with courage and with faith" (Langdon Gilkey, *Shantung Compound: The Story of Men and Women under Pressure* [New York: Harper & Row, 1966] 242).

volume two and so to hear from Niebuhr any hint of grace!). A year and a quarter later, in March 1943, we enemy nationals (mostly British and Americans) were sent to an internment camp in Shantung province, and there I remained until the war ended in August of 1945. Since the full story of that experience is contained in *Shantung Compound* (1966), I shall mention only briefly here its major impact on my convictions and my thinking.

The internment camp, populated by some 1,500 to 2,000 civilians including men, women, and children, represented a kind of laboratory experiment in social living. We had to organize ourselves politically, administer our common labor, do all our own cooking, baking, and stoking, repair our buildings and equipment, and discipline and entertain ourselves, in other words, construct and maintain a miniature civilization. Our task was limited radically by an absolute lack of machinery of any sort, a minimum of equipment, supplies, and conveniences, by an over-crowded and cramped space, and by continual and deep anxiety about the future. It was a life suffused with frustration, hunger, and insecurity, despite its many very real achievements and frequent joys, not least the personal relations—and the loving relations—that could characterize even such a comfortless and precarious life. For a young healthy person, the inconveniences and frustrations of that life were of minimal importance, being far less than soldiers suffered. And, for me, the fascination of our common enterprise of civilization building was endless.

More and more, I was impressed by the moral necessities of such communal living: without self-discipline and order, our civilization quickly disintegrated into anarchy; yet, without equal justice, it threatened to erupt into an equally destructive violence and discord. Moral decay—which made both order and justice impossible—was, thus, as dangerous to our life as was a stoppage of supplies or a bad epidemic. Yet, obviously, nothing was more difficult under these circumstances than to be self-disciplined enough to share space and supplies with others or to be self-disciplined enough not to steal common goods. However well we organized our labor corps and our production of goods, still such was our universal self-concern that we "fell" continually in the face of these spiritual requirements: we refused to cooperate or share; we hoarded goods to ourselves; we stole. As a consequence, our common life suffered recurrent and increasing crises. Communal life—civilization—requires moral strength: self-control, justice, equality, and autonomy, as much as it does knowledge, rationality, and technical expertise. And yet it was evident that nothing is more elusive in human existence than that same moral strength: we are apparently made for it, yet continually we reject and deny it. Again, therefore, these two and a half years of vivid experience had (for me) validated the Christian understanding of our situation as one lived in the presence of a moral and yet loving God, a life living out a predominant and very destructive self-concern, and yet one continually replete with new possibilities of repentance, trust, renewal, and self-giving. I was more convinced than ever of the relevance of the symbols of sin and estrangement, and the necessity of moral awareness and responsibility, of spiritual self-understanding and repentance, and most importantly, of a deep trust in God, if creative personal and communal life is to be possible. As I had not been able to understand the war-world of 1939 and 1940 without that theological framework, so now it was only on the same terms that I could deal with the long, arduous, but utterly fascinating, experience of an internment camp.

I was returned on a troopship to the United States in November of 1945, underweight, confused about myself and my future, and inwardly estranged from the new victorious, materialistic, militaristic, and above all self-righteous spirit now so pervasive in America. Noting the vast difference of all this from the less strident, certainly more pacifistic and humble America of the 1930s, I said to myself, "Nothing is so corrupting of a people as victory in a righteous war." Consequently, the parallels between our moral failures in the camp and the nationalism and self-concern of prosperous America soon struck me, and I began to speak to social clubs, schools, and churches about those parallels—the seed of the later volume of theological reflections on the camp experience. Meanwhile, after being bored to distraction in a course on international law in preparation for a possible career in diplomacy, I decided to begin formal study of theology, philosophy of religion, and ethics in preparation for teaching those subjects. There was no question of where I would go to study: only Union Theological Seminary in New York interested me, because it was there that my "spiritual father," Reinhold Niebuhr, taught. And so, a year later, I entered the Union-Columbia program and officially began my theological career. At twenty-seven, I felt infinitely old and thoroughly experienced (both quite in error!); but all that I was familiar with in theology was Niebuhr's work (which I knew line by line) and some of the early Brunner (whose books a missionary friend had loaned to me in Peking). As yet, I knew absolutely nothing else in theology,

biblical studies, historical theology, or the rest of religious studies. So
there was a lot to do.

III. From Eager Neoorthodoxy
to Renewed Liberalism: 1947–1963

I shall now turn to the next decade and a half: 1947 to 1963. It was full
of learning, personal relationships, and vivid, if often painful, experiences; and I shall mention only those matters or events that now seem to me
to have shaped the continuing development of my thought.

I came to Union Theological Seminary and to my first teaching jobs
(at Vassar, 1951–1954, and Vanderbilt University, 1954–1963) as a
committed, articulate, and enthusiastic—I am now tempted to say
"aggressive"—neoorthodox, at any rate, a Niebuhrian (I had still not read
a bit of Barth). This theological viewpoint seemed to me eminently true,
because it had been validated to me by twentieth-century events and by
my own experiences; and it was to me, after a few years of devoted
study, clearly also what the "tradition," biblical and historical, had said
all along—except, I told myself, where that tradition had been misunderstood (for example, by the early church, by the Catholics, by the
Protestant orthodox, and by the Protestant liberals!). This is still my
general orientation, to be sure; but I see it now *very* differently. I am
aware now of the essentially "liberal" elements within it as I was not
then, when in the 1940s and 1950s the main struggle was against an
expiring liberal establishment. After many more years of historical
reading, moreover, I see how varied the entire tradition actually was and
how fortunate that variety has been for its richness and its truth. Above
all, I now see (or think I do) the very significant weaknesses in that burst
of theological genius and vigor associated with the dialectical or crisis
theology that appeared after World War I in Europe and in America in
the 1930s and 1940s.

In any case, for me, the main elements, the sinews, of that theology—
one could call it a "doctrinal system" in spirit if not in actuality—had
been directly correlated with and validated by my personal (and historical) experience: the pervasiveness of sin and meaninglessness continually
threatening, even in the modern age, human history and personal
existence; the ambiguous and ultimately self-destructive tendencies of a
civilization built on secular grounds alone, even a scientific and technical
civilization; the absolute necessity of revelation and grace for any help or
renewal to appear in such a situation; and, as a consequence, the

centrality and uniqueness of the appearance and presence of God in Jesus Christ and of the community that witnesses to that revelation. The fact that this set of theological "symbols" was interpreted by all of us in a *liberal* and not an orthodox (literalistic) manner tended to escape our attention; and the fact that we all assumed, without question, the critical spirit and the concern for social justice that the liberals had established also went unnoticed. One might make the caustic comment that, as an erstwhile liberal, I was tolerant of every view except liberalism, and that I was orthodox about what was, in fact, a very unorthodox way of doing theology! My first three books illustrate well this firm "neoorthodox" (though quite non-Barthian) emphasis on transcendence, sin, revelation, and grace—and on correct theology: *Maker of Heaven and Earth* (1959); *How the Church Can Minister to the World Without Losing Itself* (1964); and *Shantung Compound* (1966). Fortunately, they also equally represent the strong correlation of theology with experience, and of the divine with personal existence and the social world, that I have already noted.

Two otherwise quite insignificant events illustrate this strange mixture of themes and attitudes within a fairly tightly woven theological viewpoint. Toward the end of my theological studies (1948), I was invited to be a Kent Fellow and so attended the famous Council on Religion and Higher Education's "Week of Work," held that year at a college campus in Maryland. One morning at breakfast, I found myself sitting across from perhaps the best—and deservedly so—liberal philosopher of religion in the older generation, Edgar Brightman. He was one of the men who, for that reason, was viewed by all of us as the leader of the "other side." He and I had a sprightly, not too hostile, conversation about theology, in which we quickly—in fact, before the shredded wheat was eaten—located our sharp points of disagreement. I had to admit that I found him, somewhat to my surprise, a very charming and intelligent man. I recall, we were both particularly delighted with the way we agreed about our disagreements: he said, "I believe in God *because* I believe that history represents a steady moral progress," to which I replied, "I believe in God because to me history precisely *does not* represent such a progress."

During the same week, the Council on Religion and Higher Education experienced a soul-revealing controversy; it was over a "liberal" social issue (racial justice), but it surely illustrated what the neoorthodox theologians were saying about human existence, even that of Kent Fellows! It was a terribly hot week, and we were meeting in segregated Maryland. The unexpected and shocking result was that the black members of our community were barred from the large public pool available to the rest of us. It seemed to me perfectly obvious that, under these conditions, *none* of our community should use the pool; and I said so at one of the early nightly meetings. Even more unexpectedly, a bitter, very existential debate followed, about half of our group finding (with the help of a newly appointed young professor of Christian ethics at Princeton!) exceedingly intellectual and intricate reasons why those families who could use the pool should do so, meanwhile feeling very sorry for and "spiritually identified with" those unfortunate families who could not! Our guest speaker, Professor Paul Weiss, said that he was "disgusted with this so-called Christian group" and would never return. I agreed and never have.

The second event illustrative of our complex, if not confused, theological situation happened about the same time (the late 1940s). There was a lively, interesting group of young "theologians" who were American (Northern) Baptists: Bob Handy, Bill Hamilton, Bob Spike, Howard Long, myself, and a young student of the history of religions, Chuck Long. We all came together for the first time at a conference of American Baptist clergy to discuss theology at Green Lake, Wisconsin. Since the denomination had long since been split asunder by a bitter conflict between conservative evangelicals and liberals, it was expected that this debate would continue. To everyone's surprise, however, the "young Turks," who seemed so much like the liberals, sided on the whole with the evangelicals, calling for a theology of revelation, sin, and grace and rejecting the older liberal progressivism. It was the first time either conservatives or older liberals had run into this new breed, and they were astounded. I remember in one session giving a short speech about history, in which I said that the traditional eschatological symbols, especially those of "divine judgment and the Second Coming," were essential for interpreting history in our age; Bob Handy rose to second my remarks. Afterwards, a kind, older evangelical came up to us and said very enthusiastically: "I can't tell you how wonderful it is to hear the younger men talking this way about the Second Coming! It's going to come soon, isn't it? And where do you think it will be? Just outside Jerusalem?" Bob and I looked at each other in astonishment. We hadn't meant *that*! As I admitted to Bob later, I was a bit ashamed that all I could think of was the incredibly crowed situation on Jerusalem's highways and in its motels when that event culminating world history took place! With this amusing encounter, I realized for the first time how "liberal," not to say "secular," at least how "unsupernaturalistic," we were about the objective course of history, and thus how very symbolic was our use of traditional theological concepts, such as judgment, last judgment, and Second Coming. The problem of what we *did* mean by these theological symbols, however intelligible they seemed to be in relation to all the evidence and in the encounter with Brightman, was beginning to appear on my horizon. To round out the confusion, that night, when all of us went off to find some beer to go with our theological discussions, I heard one of the liberals— another very kind middle-aged gentleman—remark: "Well, on these issues, those neoorthodox boys are too liberal for me!"

Two further events might be mentioned that had a much deeper effect on my developing existence and, therefore, ultimately on my professional career. Because during graduate school I found myself unable to carry through an engagement that I was sure I really wanted, I began to see a young analyst who worked near Union Seminary in New York. From the beginning, I realized that he was an even more gifted therapist than he was the outstanding theoretician for which he later became famous; his name was Rollo May. These biweekly sessions for more than three years did an incredible amount for me, though it is not easy to say just how. They showed me how vital feelings are, and being in touch with one's own feelings; they revealed how empty "attributes," even impressive ones, can be; how unreal and destructive is the intellect alone, its theories and arguments, if the self is unrelated to itself and therefore empty. In sum, they uncovered for me the heretofore buried *existential* level of self-feeling, of self-affirmation, of appropriating and being oneself, through which alone relations with others and creative action in the world become possible. From within, I discovered what Kierkegaard meant by "choosing" oneself, despite all that one was, and what Tillich was saying when he spoke of the "courage to be." If what I wrote after these sessions was outwardly little changed in its general theoretical shape, nevertheless, its meaning for me became entirely different. Through Rollo May, I discovered the *person* behind the words, the *self* behind the theories, *being* as the substratum of intellect and of consciousness—and I was given the chance to enjoy a healthy, if always stormy, personal and family life.

The other event came a decade or so later, when I was teaching at the Divinity School of Vanderbilt University in Nashville. By 1959, all seemed to be going exceedingly well for the young theologian: happily (so it seemed to me) married to a lovely and charming Virginia lady, a successful first book just out, and, above all, a wonderful adopted baby son. But other things were also brewing. Although there had been since

I came there in 1954 a few black students at Vanderbilt University Divinity School, still the university as a whole, the city of Nashville, and the entire region of the Middle South remained in 1959 and 1960 thoroughly segregated—hard as it is now to believe! During that year, black college students in North Carolina, in Knoxville, and at home in Nashville (from Fisk and Tennessee A & I) began the "sit-ins," in protest against the most blatant injustices of that culture, especially the law that black people could not eat in so-called white restaurants downtown—in the same areas in which they were also expected to shop! These students sat down at the lunch counters and refused to move, even though they were subjected not only to verbal and physical abuse but also to arrest. At the Divinity School, we had admired and supported their protests against what we all regarded without question as a set of unjust and oppressive laws that would have to change sooner or later (and that view was shared by ninety percent of the *Southern* students of the Divinity School). To us, it was obvious that nonviolent protest against such unjust laws was thoroughly justified morally and religiously, in fact incumbent on a responsible Christian. How else could creative change occur? How else could one be dedicated to the Kingdom? This was, however, by no means obvious to Nashville. Proud of its astounding level of church attendance, Nashville felt humiliated at this nationally publicized moral protest against its customs. Even more, it was scared, and rightly, that this situation could well result in a sea of blood flowing in the streets of downtown. That it was the white toughs who would initiate and largely commit the violence did not matter; it was the "uppity" blacks who were causing it all by breaking the law and by shattering the peace of "this lovely Christian city." It was like a chapter from Niebuhr's *Moral Man and Immoral Society* of 1933.

Suddenly, with the arrest of a number of Fisk students, it was discovered that one of *our* Vanderbilt students at the Divinity School, a very able and courageous man named James Lawson, had been "coaching" the protesters in nonviolence. We were proud of him, but the town was not. Instead of giving him its highest honors for saving the city from violence, as they should, they were shocked that a Vanderbilt student was, first, black and, second, involved in what was to them virtual insurrection. How could a Christian break the law in a Christian country and especially in a Christian city? He must be communist! The heretofore forward-looking and progressive chancellor of the university, wary of his conservative board and determined to follow his own schedule into liberalism, was furious and expelled Lawson forthwith. Knowing the convictions on such issues of the world Christian community (especially since Hitler's day), not to say of the liberal academic world, we on the faculty of the Divinity School were dumbfounded. We knew that our school would disappear without a trace, if it supported such an authoritarian defense of segregation as this; and, likewise, we knew that our own integrity as Christian teachers would be fatally compromised. How could we, Christian professors and students, support this act of expulsion, *our* version of the British Raj and the Amritsar massacre, *our* form of Hitler's persecution of the Jews? So the entire faculty (except one member) itself revolted, announced to the chancellor its refusal to approve his action of expulsion, and went on national radio and television as frequently as we could to make this position of faculty and students alike clear to the country. As the senior member of the theological department (age forty-two), and almost of that whole young faculty, I quite naturally became the spokesman for this public protest.

The chancellor never spoke to me again, and subsequently others, especially Lou Silberman, Bard Thompson, and Jim Sellers, had to carry on the long negotiations. For three months (March–June), we negotiated with the stubborn university, insisting (on I don't know how many grounds) that they allow Lawson to reenter the Divinity School. Finally, in June, *we* readmitted him and warned the university that a refusal to recognize that readmission would result in our mass resignations. They refused, so we resigned. Meanwhile, key members of the medical school (four full professors and the dean), from the beginning, had been urging us not to procrastinate further, but to resign at once. So, now that we had resigned, we told them to measure up themselves to their own words. This the five of them immediately did. The administration of the university was now itself dumbfounded: to lose a Divinity School is (in the South) possibly an irritation, but to lose a great medical school represents a major academic disaster! So, now the chancellor got on the phone, accepted our terms, and readmitted Lawson. To his amazement and ours, the genteel Southern board did not concur and adamantly refused to allow him to come back. With this, the rest of the faculty of the university, having been mainly against us from the beginning, swung violently in our favor: they could not bear being run by the board! So the chancellor overruled the board, readmitted Lawson, and we won our fight. Lawson, meanwhile, had been admitted to Boston University and decided to stay there. Though we hoped that he would come back, we could not really blame him for not doing so. It was a wild, chaotic sequence, and unbelievably lucky in its nonviolent outcome. Ironically, the town integrated its restaurants in May, a full month before the "liberal" university capitulated in June (1960)! Looking at the racially mixed character of present-day Southern (and Northern) life, at least on the surface, in universities, colleges, football teams, hotels, restaurants, and so on *ad infinitum*, this whole drama seems incredible, and to have occurred in some other epoch rather than a mere thirty-nine years ago!

Although objectively this struggle resulted in a significant victory, it was devastating—for the moment at least—to my personal existence. Slowly over the years, we as a couple, and especially my Virginia wife, had become part of the younger Nashville social scene. The Lawson event, however, horrified most of the community, and quite clearly our status among them was badly shaken. My doctor's wife remarked that I was the first communist whom she had ever met! Close personal friends remained utterly loyal and open, but things had really changed. This fact did not make any imprint on me—my wife had left in April to visit her family in Virginia—until summer, when it became clear to me that my family had by now thoroughly disintegrated, though certainly the Lawson case was by no means the sole cause. We spent an uneasy and alienated fall and winter on sabbatical leave in Munich; but that spring (1961) my wife left Munich to live alone with our son in New York. The following summer, on my return from Germany, she refused to accompany me back to Nashville, and so I agreed to seek a divorce. Ironically, I had gone to Germany to write a volume on the theological faith in providence; I returned with little faith in anything, certainly none in myself as a person or a theologian. It was not that I condemned divorce; nevertheless, it was one of those things that I had thought inconceivable for myself, and it was shattering to have to face it. I had also discovered how fallible I was: how much I had been myself at fault in this broken family, and how unable I was to handle with any grace such a personal crisis. All this seemed to represent the end: I had lost (I felt) my son, and with that all hope of creative family life; I had been a failure in the most important of life's endeavors; thus, I was void of any real sense of worth or even of cleanness. Because of all this, I felt that I could hardly function any longer as a theologian, as a witness to the power either of faith or of grace. Thus—so I told myself—when I recovered a bit, I would have to see what else at forty-two I might take up.[6]

The divine power does, however, work in our lives, and grace is very real and effective. There *are* new beginnings, and so things are never necessarily really at an end. This is not because of our own strength and virtue—important as they are—because these do arrive at an end, as mine clearly had done. The new beginnings come from a power not our own. A new loving relationship did appear, a much more creative one with a superbly attractive and talented Dutch woman. A year and a quarter later (1963) with remarriage, we started a new home, and I accepted a new position teaching theology at the University of Chicago Divinity School. And, in the years since, a new and wonderful family, the clear center of my own existence, has grown and prospered.

There was, however, a vast difference in my self-feeling about this new marriage, the family, and this new career: truly, they were of grace and not merit. I was now newly conscious of how precarious every aspect of good fortune is, how deeply confused and misguided we remain, and how uncertain is every step that we take. In 1960, for our twentieth class reunion at Harvard University, I had written smugly of my then obvious beginnings of success: a full professorship, a new book, a happy marriage, a new child. For the twenty-fifth class reunion in 1965, I wrote a very different summation of my existence to date: how easily, I said, even the most well-planned and well-established securities fall apart, how fragile our valued relations and accomplishments are, and how uncertain is every fortune—and how we must proceed by faith, if we are to proceed at all.

Because of this new and creative beginning, followed by the appearance of a marvelous new family in the form of two children, I was able to begin to ponder again, now from a quite existential standpoint, the symbol of providence.[7] The traditional and orthodox themes of sin and

---

[6]*Editors' Note.* Gilkey refers briefly to this series of events elsewhere: see Gilkey, *RW*, vii.

[7]*Editors' Note.* In Gilkey's discussion of "[t]he second intimation of meaning within the overwhelming contingency and destructiveness of events," or "the proximate intelligibility of much of the tragic," he notes that "in many cases destruction arises in our present because of the past injustices that same group has committed: of race against race, class against class, national group against national group." He then refers to his own experience during World War II in China, "in observing that the personal tragedies that overwhelmed the European communities of Asia, and sent them rootless wanderers around

grace, of human fall and providence, of crisis, disillusionment, and new beginnings, established as presuppositions in the last days of college and forged in the war experiences of the camp, continued as dominant in my experience as these decades unfolded. However, whereas at the beginning all of this existed as a set of concepts, one may say an almost *frozen theology*, now, through the painful ups and downs of social and personal life, they became less frozen as concepts and more ingredient in existence. And, consequently, as is appropriate, the theology itself, like the self thinking it, became progressively more tentative, more (ironically) "liberal," more open to the new.

IV. From Dialogue with Catholicism, through the Death of God, to Divine Providence: 1963–1981

Many changes occurred in this new world: a new and creative marriage, a new job in a new (but to me old) university and community, and a new family—and, after all, this was also the 1960s when all sorts of new attitudes, new costumes, and new mores appeared. During the next years, we enjoyed two long sessions in Europe, one for six months in Rome in 1965 and then one for fifteen months in Holland in 1970–1971.[8] At home, we gradually became acclimatized to the very different lifestyles of Hyde Park. By the end of the decade, not only was I surrounded by a charming, bilingual family, but also I was outwardly almost completely transformed: a knotted scarf instead of a tie, longish hair, a mustache or a beard, and an earring in my left ear. In 1970–1971, I had noticed an earring in the left ear of each massive sailor in North Holland and in Crete. As one Greek sailor explained, "Poseidon wears one, why

---

the globe after World War II, were not arbitrary," but rather resulted from "the past history of imperial arrogance and greed, not necessarily of themselves but of their communites." Again, more generally, he notes that "the experience of the meaningfulness or justice of the tragic because it arises as the result of the deep and immoral misuse of power is surely an ancient, and a contemporary, clue to a meaning that in some mysterious way coheres seemingly unrelated, arbitrary and so meaningless contingencies" (Gilkey, *RW*, 131).

[8]*Editors' Note.* Gilkey wrote a reflective, "personal statement" on his approach to producing Christian theology while he and his family were in Rome in 1965. See Langdon Gilkey, ""If There Is No God: The Problem of God and the Study of Theology," *Criterion* 6 (Spring 1967): 5-7. See also Gilkey's reference to his study leave in Holland: Gilkey, *RW*, vii.

shouldn't we?" As a consequence, since I sailed a small boat on the Maine coast, I decided to wear one, which I continued to do (except at the trial in Arkansas in 1981), until 1985.[9]

Most influential of all in this set of rather dramatic changes, outwardly visible in the shift from short to long hair but effective on much deeper levels as well, was certainly my wife. A very gifted sculptress and now an equally gifted therapist, she was even more a free spirit; she could exist creatively in all communities, but did not fit snugly into any one: suburban-business, academic-scholarly, church-theological. Every-

---

[9]*Editors' Note.* Gilkey's love for sailing appears in various ways through many of his publications. As I have noted previously, when *Shantung Compound* was published, the book was successful enough that he bought his first sailboat with royalties from that book; he christened that boat with the name *Kairos.* Also, "some of Gilkey's ancestors were shipbuilders in Maine; in honor of them, he named his second sailboat after a ship built by one of them: *Royal Welcome!*" (Jeff B. Pool, "Editor's Preface," in *Through the Tempest: Theological Voyages in a Pluralistic Culture,* ed. Jeff B. Pool [Minneapolis: Fortress Press, 1991] xii-xiii; hereafter cited as *TT*). Gilkey also employs nautical metaphors in many of his publications to illustrate a variety of experiences. See his use of such metaphors to describe human sin's obscuration of the essential structures of human finitude, to identify the exploratory theological efforts of others, to refer to theological discussion of "the relation of the many religions to truth and salvation" as embarking "across what is an almost uncharted sea," and even to describe the profession of theological education/religious studies as a sailing vessel with stowaways: Gilkey, *ME,* 104-105; idem, "A Theological Voyage with Wilfred Cantwell Smith: Early Opus and Recent Trilogy," a review of *Belief and History, The Meaning and End of Religion, Faith and Belief,* and *Towards a World Theology,* by Wilfred Cantwell Smith, in *Religious Studies Review* 7 (October 1981): 298, 306; idem, *Society and the Sacred: Toward a Theology of Culture in Decline* (New York: Crossroad, 1981) 157; hereafter cited as *SAS;* idem, "Theology for a Time of Troubles: How My Mind Has Changed," *Christian Century* 98 (29 April 1981): 479; reprinted under the same title in *Theologians in Transition: The Christian Century "How My Mind Has Changed" Series,* ed. James M. Wall (New York: Crossroad, 1981) 38; idem, "The AAR and the Anxiety of Non-Being," *Journal of the American Academy of Religion* 48 (March 1980): 17-18; idem, "Theological Frontiers: Implications for Bioethics," in *Theology and Bioethics: Exploring the Foundations and Frontiers,* ed. Earl E. Shelp (Dordrecht: D. Reidel Publishing Company, 1985) 131; idem, "A New Watershed in Theology," *Soundings* 64 (Summer 1981): 129-31; see revision as chap. 1, "The New Watershed in Theology," in *SAS,* 13-14. In the dedication of *Society and the Sacred* to his Dutch father-in-law, Wilhelm Hermann Weber, Gilkey describes him as a "skillful and indefatigable sailor" (Gilkey, *SAS,* xi). As I have recorded previously, many "former theology students from the Ph.D. program of the University of Chicago Divinity School will remember a set of guidelines for writing dissertations in theology, written by Professor Gilkey, in which his sailing metaphor tempered with humor the utter seriousness of those academic requirements" (Pool, "Editor's Preface," in *TT,* xiii.1). Langdon Gilkey's father had a fondness for the use of nautical metaphors in his writing as well. See the following examples: Charles Gilkey, *Jesus and Our Generation,* 13-14; idem, "The Place of Religion in Higher Education," 74-75.

thing that she touched bore its own stamp, represented an original creation, something developed from within rather than reflected from without. As a consequence, our home became under her hand, in its own modest way, unique: in decor, in its atmosphere and feel, and in the lifestyles that were present there. If I too became more myself or more original in appearance, dress, attitudes, and inner being, it was owed largely to her, who had been that way (as I had not) since she appeared on earth.

The first new personal, and as a consequence also professional, interest that appeared in this new Chicago existence came as a kind of accident. In 1964, we discovered that, after two years of teaching, my wife and I could in 1965 enjoy (if we could organize it) a quarter off somewhere abroad. Both of us wanted to live in and explore Italy—but, heretofore, Rome had hardly been a fruitful pasture in which Protestant theologians might graze! Then, all of a sudden, I awoke to the implications of Vatican II, whose astounding course I had been following since it had started in 1961. I recall saying to myself: "There *must* be some creative theology lying back of these massive changes—if there is *not*, then what we theologians do is vastly irrelevant."

Thus, as an act of faith, if I may put it that way, I applied for a grant "to study the new theological movements so evidently at work in the exciting new developments of reform in the Roman Catholic church." Since I was (apparently) about the first Protestant theologian to propose such a trek to Rome to study these new theological movements (many were already there, of course, as observers of the Council), I received a fellowship, and we embarked via Amsterdam for Rome in the summer of 1965. That fall and early winter, I read much of Karl Rahner and Bernard Lonergan, and all else I could on the "new theology" in Roman Catholic circles. Together, we went to seminars for the observers at the Council (and heard the young Hans Küng and Edward Schillebeeckx, among others) and to several Vatican II sessions—and we ate as only two enthusiasts can in Rome! All of this introduced me—though, to be sure, only in part—to the fascination and power of the Roman ecclesia: the reality and depth of its community, the seemingly (to a WASP) infinite class, ethnic, and cultural varieties of its manifestations, its real (and also its unreal) rationalism, its seemingly limitless intellectual and moral potentialities, and therefore the immensely creative moral and religious role it might play in the post-Christian *and* in the postmodern world.

I had barely returned to Chicago in early 1966, when Catholic students in increasing numbers began to apply to our graduate theological program. I felt (humorously) grateful that our yearnings for the aesthetic treasures of Italy, as a kind of "assist," had resulted in a provisional acquaintance with the intellectual power of present Catholic theology. Two years later, our first, and stunning, Catholic appointments were made in the theological area, and the new age of ecumenical learning and teaching theology, even more of deep ecumenical friendship, dawned. To my surprise and delight, soon I found myself lecturing and speaking as frequently at Catholic seminaries, colleges, and universities as at Protestant or secular ones.

As a result of all this, I became aware of the frequent feelings of ineptness and of self-doubt that plagued Catholics conscious of the inadequacies of their recent "orthodox" tradition, and their consequent lack of self-confidence that this tradition, even if "revised," could cope adequately with the modern situation. Increasingly, therefore, my addresses spoke of the difficulties—as a Protestant well knew—of any religious community in the secular modern age and, further, of what to me were the unique "gifts" that the Catholic tradition, as Catholic—if brought into focus with the cultural life it inhabited—could bring to the modern crisis. I came to feel that Protestantism would in the decades ahead need them as much, perhaps even more, than the reverse, and, thus, that it was important for the entire Christian enterprise that they be not only "brought up to date," but that they manage to do this in a genuinely Catholic form. Thus resulted in 1975 my book on Catholicism "from a Protestant perspective," one I entitled *Crisis and Promise*, but which the publishers labeled *Catholicism Confronts Modernity*.

Much else also was new in the theological world in the 1960s and early 1970s. This was the era when (as in the older liberal era a half-century earlier) the world was enthusiastically accepted, and so in new ways entered, served, and admired by the churches and so by the theological community: in dress and styles of life, in social causes and social action (especially, of course, vis-à-vis race and Vietnam), in many of its moral norms and attitudes, and now also in aspects of its "secularity," its fundamental attitudes about reality, and its standards of truth. Thus, the active social protests inherited from our common liberal background continually appeared and reappeared in this new era: almost the whole faculty at the Divinity School at the University of Chicago marched at Selma in 1965, and in 1972 David Tracy, Bernard McGinn, and I went twice to Washington to join the rallies against the war in Vietnam.

One important theological result of this new set of relations to the world was the "God is Dead" theology. By accident, and also by interest, I had a hand in the founding of that potent if brief movement. In the early fall of 1963, I finally read my old friend Bill Hamilton's earlier but relatively unnoticed book, *The New Essence of Christianity*. I was intrigued and yet horrified by his "abandonment of the word God" and the very cogent reasons that he gave for this new move in theology. Two weeks later, I met the vivacious and brilliant Tom Altizer at the Eliade's home, who at dinner also declared that God was now thoroughly dead. I told him to call Bill, of whom he had never heard, on the phone. The next week at an ecumenical conference in Swift Hall, I heard a very good paper by a young Episcopal theologian from Austin. When I told him afterwards how much I liked his paper, he introduced himself as Paul van Buren and told me that a new book would soon be out that I would like even better. It is called, he said, *The Secular Meaning of the Gospel*, and "it does theology without God." I gave him the telephone numbers of both Bill and Tom.

The movement utterly fascinated me. Declarations of the death of God from secular academics were part of the staple diet of my youth in Chicago, in college at Harvard, and certainly in the Columbia of the 1940s—but, coming from *theologians*, this had a different feel and a different relevance. Incidentally, none of these theologians meant what European theologians said that they meant by the death of God, namely, that the Christian God was hidden to the world's profane gaze and had revealed himself only in Christ's death.

I did not agree with this new secular theology at all; my cumulative experience of twenty-five years had assured me in countless ways of the reality, the power, and the grace of God. In addition, personal and social experience had also far too thoroughly convinced me of the relevance and validity of the classical symbols of theology for this. Nevertheless, I could feel in myself the powerful tug of their arguments. Secular attitudes and standards had also been part of my spiritual reality from the beginning, and certainly they had grown again in my consciousness since coming to Chicago. I knew that I needed to find some deeper theological grounding for my continuing allegiance to the Christian symbols than their (to me) obvious relevance in interpreting experience. How did I know, how could I know, in the secular world which we all inhabited, that the divine of which we spoke and to which we witnessed was *real*, as a part of our most fundamental experience? I could feel how powerful their arguments were—and see their effects on many of my friends (many of whom have later become "closet" God-is-dead theologians!). Could I also feel and then articulate an *answer* to these arguments, a defense of the religious discourse that they found now so meaningless?

Clearly, to appeal to *revelation*, as most European neoorthodox theologians did, was useless; this was one of the elements of God-language that was now being radically doubted in the name of secularity. Likewise, any argument *metaphysically* to the reality of God (as process theology suggested) was futile, since most current philosophy was doubting the possibility and legitimacy of metaphysical argument fully as radically as this theology was questioning the authority of divine revelation. So I turned to what we all had in common, to our fundamental experience, the experience of being and becoming ourselves in the world, in society, and in history, our "ontic" experience as *existing*, as searching for *meaning*, and so seeking to be and to achieve *value*. I was convinced that, at this existential level—whatever our intellectual or theoretical interpretation of reality may be—the modern age felt, acted, and trusted *religiously*, that is to say, in relation to what I called a dimension of ultimacy. Our fundamental anxieties reflected such a dimension, even in a secular world; and our "secular" answers to these anxieties, our ideologies, also reflected such a dimension. In a secular culture, our existence is in opposition to our understanding of it and certainly to our theories about that existence. For, in our actual existence, we *are* religious, whether we wish to be so or not. Thus, religious language—for example, the ideological language of politics—has "meaning," even secular meaning, because it was this sort of language alone that could articulate (thematize) this dimension of experience.

The results of this effort to answer the God-is-Dead theology were two books published in 1969 and 1970. The first book, *Naming the Whirlwind*, was certainly the better of the two. After a discussion of the sources of secular theology and a critique of its coherence, it represented an examination (phenomenological, I called it) of ordinary, common, and so secular experience of a mostly personal sort to uncover the religious dimension latent there—its dimension of ultimacy—and so to show the meaning and thus, in that sense, the use of religious discourse as language articulating that dimension of experience. The second book, *Religion and the Scientific Future*, was an inquiry into modern science, the heart of modern secular culture, to show the religious dimension latent there as well, first in the dimension of ultimacy present in all scientific knowing, and, second, in the inescapable use of "myth" whenever science sought to understand not only the natural order outside itself, but even more in its efforts to understand itself and its place in human life. Neither one of these volumes represented a systematic theology; for positive theology depends on a *particular* manifestation of the divine reality pervasive in our life, that is to say, on what Christians call revelation. This was an attempt to uncover, so to speak, the "shadow" of that divine presence in daily, secular experience as the possibility of and the basis for the meaning of the symbols that articulate our special relation to it in revelation and faith, namely theological symbols. I called this, therefore, a *prolegomenon* to theology proper, necessary to establish the grounds for the meaning of any set of theological symbols, but not sufficient for establishing either the validity or the particular meaning of a special religious faith. As is evident, I was seeking here to preserve what I regarded as the essential core of my earlier neoorthodoxy, while giving to that core a now much needed ground or base in common experience. There is little question that, in this analysis, Tillich had now joined Niebuhr as the central models for my theological efforts.

My next large theological effort, *Reaping the Whirlwind* (1976), represented in my mind an application to one major symbol in systematic theology (providence) of the method developed in *Naming the Whirlwind*. It also represented the culmination of many years of puzzlement and reflection on what I came to regard as the central existential and religious (if not philosophical) issue of the twentieth century, the question of the meaning of history. Thus, the book begins with an examination of ordinary experience to see how the questions of the meaning of time and of history inevitably arise there, and how with those questions a dimension of ultimacy, a religious dimension, illustrated by the ideological character of all politics, inescapably also arises. The volume concludes with an effort to rethink the traditional theological answers to this question.

Certainly, along with the issues of human nature and personal existence, that of history has been central for most of my theological thought since the 1930s, when the rise of Hitler and the fall of France had raised so sharply for my generation the question of where history was going. In this work, therefore, I was reflecting consciously on the issue that subconsciously has dominated my theological thinking from the beginning, namely, the question of the structure and career of history and its events. Central to this question in its contemporary form were three cultural/historical facts that I had come to take for granted: first, history was continually full of novelty; second, "learning," especially scientific knowledge and technological expertise, did cumulatively rise in history; nevertheless, third, despite this progress in knowledge, our mid-century had come to celebrate, not at all the death of God, but rather precisely the death of the belief in progress. Although the level of knowledge, theoretical and technical, may steadily rise, our ability to use it creatively does not, nor do self-concern and irrationality recede. Thus, civilization remains as ambiguous and precarious a venture as ever, as suffused with suffering and with tendencies toward self-destruction. I knew well, of course, that this belief in the progress of civilization was not yet dead in the scientific and academic worlds; still, it seemed obvious to me that the historical grounds for it certainly were. This merely shows that, with regard to ultimate issues of belief, falsification is as irrelevant with regard to "secular" as to "orthodox" faiths. Since belief in the progress of history represented, I felt, the "religious substance" or spiritual basis of modern culture, whether liberal capitalist or Marxist, this "death" heralded a major spiritual crisis, a crisis centering on the question: if history is *not* progressing, how are we to understand ourselves and our existence in time, and what *now* do we have in which to believe, on which to put our hope? In answer, I sought to spell out a new understanding of God and of God's providence, as providing a firmer and less precarious ground for a renewed confidence in history. Instead of the progress in which the modern West has believed, a "biblical" understanding of history, I argued, would understand history and the work of providence as characterized by covenant or creative beginning, betrayal, judgment, and crisis or breakdown, and creative new beginnings again.

This effort to articulate a theological interpretation, a "revised Christian theology," on the basis of the method of phenomenological prolegomenon and existential correlation—ordinary experience providing the ultimacy, the crisis of anxiety, and so the "question," and the reinterpreted theological symbol providing the answer—was continued (and concluded) in a short ("baby") systematic theology called *Message and Existence* (1979).

Two convictions basic to this theological viewpoint had grown in me during the decade of the 1970s, while this theological analysis of history and of personal existence had been under construction and, of course, while the historical career of our scientific and technological culture had been developing. The first conviction was that Western culture appeared to be more and more in a situation of crisis, a "Time of Troubles" as Toynbee had put it, when its own scientific, technical, and industrial achievements, not to mention its development of nationalism, were now increasing its dilemmas rather than resolving them. As a consequence, as in many other epochs of decline, fanaticism and irrationality could only be expected to grow rather than to diminish. The second conviction followed from the first: this was that, however secular it may still consider itself to be, modern culture continued to be "religious" in its essential existence, and that this religious character was growing in this period of recurrent crises, manifesting itself not only in the spread of new religious cults and in the expansion of older orthodoxies, but also in the increasingly religious character of its political myths: those of American capitalism, on the one hand, and those of Marxism, on the other. Like many another earlier epoch, our "secular" epoch was suffering from what were essentially *religious* conflicts, only now set within the terms of the awesome power of modern scientific and industrial culture. These thoughts, developed in addresses and papers in the later 1970s, were published in the series of essays entitled *Society and the Sacred: Towards a Theology of Culture in Decline* (1981).

V. From Debates with Creationism
to Interreligious Dialogue: 1981–Present

The next interest came as a complete surprise, and yet it continued—in fact added the stamp of specific empirical validation to—many of the reflections about religion and modern culture already set down in *Society and the Sacred*. In late summer of 1981, I was invited, after a rigorous testing process, to be a witness for the ACLU at the upcoming "Creationist Trial" at Little Rock in Arkansas. A state law mandating the teaching of "Creation Science" alongside "evolution science" had been passed, and most of the churches and synagogues of Little Rock, aided by the ACLU, were challenging that law. I, of course, accepted. I proceeded to study Creation Science as thoroughly as I could, and then I worked out slowly and carefully with Tony Siano, one of the lawyers on the case, my testimony as an "expert" theologian and philosopher of religion.

I found this participation in a significant legal process (provided one is innocent!) utterly fascinating, especially since it illuminated for me much of the obscurity of our complex scientific and technological culture and showed the unexpected ways in which religion and science join forces there. To the media and to most of the scientific observers of this controversy, the latter represented merely the latest skirmish in the "eternal warfare" of objective and mature science against fanatical and immature religion. In fact, as I discovered, it was anything but this.

In the first place, the creationist law was being challenged largely by religious forces: clergy, church groups, and Jewish congregations. Almost all the mainline Protestant, Catholic, and Jewish communities, and only one scientific group, were represented among the plaintiffs. Second, the major leaders—writers, debaters, theoreticians, and so forth—among the creationists were persons trained in science, possessing Ph.Ds. from reputable universities in one or another of the natural sciences. Thus, despite the fact that it was contrary both to the methods of science and to the content of modern science in all its branches, "Creation Science" could only be the strange, even deviant, product of scientists and of a wider scientific culture. That it was in fact contrary to science was obvious. Since it insisted that the universe was only ten to twenty thousand years old and that *none* of its essential forms (nebulae, stars, earth, mountains and valleys, forms of vegetable and animal life) had changed since the beginning, it was as destructive of the methods and conclusions of astrophysics, astronomy, and geology as it was those of biology. Nevertheless, it represents not so much a religious attack on science as such, as a new, and deviant, *amalgam* of modern fundamentalist religion and modern science, a "deviant union" of the two. In Creation Science, fundamentalists were not at all denying or rejecting Science as such, as they had done in the 1920s; rather, now fully participants in modern culture (for example, Sunday morning TV), they were absorbing science and, in so doing, reshaping it into their own quite different forms. As I now saw it, such an amalgamation appears in an advanced scientific culture when political, social, and historical anxieties mount and so where absolutistic certainty becomes necessary and fanaticism grows. In such situations, absolute types of religion unite with science—as they also do with technology—to create this sort of strange species.

When I saw this, I realized that Creation Science was no isolated instance of this process of amalgamation in our century; on the contrary, it had repeatedly been preceded by far more dangerous examples. Japan was perhaps the first. In the 1920s and 1930s, the rapidly developing science, technology, and industry of Japan shifted dramatically away from its liberal culture base (established at the end of the nineteenth century) to one founded upon a strident nationalism and a Shinto mythology. The same development appeared again in the 1930s in Germany, the most advanced scientific nation in the early twentieth century. There, at the advent of Nazi "religious" ideology, most of the scientific establishment—academic, medical, and industrial—capitulated lock, stock, and barrel and proceeded during the next decade to form "Nazi science." In slightly different form, Stalinist Russia created a rather rigid "Marxist science," and now, reworked and liberalized a bit, there is certainly still a Marxist science at Russian university centers. Had he lasted longer, Mao would have created in China a Maoist science—and probably, in the end, some form of Shi'ite science will appear in Iran. Both religion and science are here to stay. As these repeated cases in our century show, these two do not so much conflict (though particular forms of each will conflict with other particular forms) as they jostle with each other until they find ways of forming a viable union satisfactory to both—but frequently one as wildly deviant from liberal science as from liberal religion. And, when they form such a union, each of them (science and religion) reshapes the other, twentieth-century experience showing that it is more frequently the scientific side that is reshaped than it is the religious side. In a Time of Troubles, and so an age of uncertainty and anxiety, the religious element in society's life tends to expand, to become more fanatical, and in the end to dominate, refashion, and then direct the scientific and technical sides of the culture. Religion is, to be sure, permanent and significant—but it is also extremely dangerous.

One conclusion from all this is that the health of science and of technology depends not so much on the internal developments of science, as our culture has thought; much more does that health depend on the health and strength of the legal, political, moral, and especially the religious context of the culture within which science functions. A developed scientific establishment (universities, laboratories, advanced research, and so forth) lodged within an absolutistic ideology or religion remains powerful and important—but now infinitely dangerous. Thus, science needs the humanities, if it would preserve itself. All of this has been set down in my story of the Arkansas trial and reflections thereon: *Creationism on Trial: Evolution and God at Little Rock* (1985).

The most recent interest that has dominated my thoughts and my writings for the last several years has also represented a quite new departure. And, like the controversy with the creationists, it seems to represent a sharp turn toward the "liberal" side of my intellectual history, if not a step beyond even that. I refer to the interest in dialogue with other religions, especially Buddhism, and a corresponding theoretical concern for the theological challenge that is represented by this new sense of plurality in religion.

This interest really began with a trip by the entire family to Japan to teach for four months at Kyoto University in 1975. This was my first return to the Orient and my first touch again with Japan, since we had been at war thirty or more years before and I had been a prisoner. It reawakened all the slumbering fascination with the Orient that I had felt as a young man, and happily my wife and children now fully shared that fascination. Japan was, of course, transformed, infinitely more *modernized* than in 1940 when I had stopped there briefly on my way to Peking. As I now realized in living and working there, however, it was hardly more "Westernized," since all its social structures and fundamental ways of doing things, its customs and mores, remained thoroughly Japanese and so thoroughly different from our own. It had sufficiently and creatively absorbed modern culture, made it its own, and now it was proceeding to set all this into *Japanese* form. I realized with a start that the West was not spreading *its* culture around the globe, as it had told itself that it was in speaking over and over of "Westernization"; it had merely "passed on" to the Orient the modern culture that Europe and America had developed in their own forms. Thus, that culture *in these Western forms* was not becoming any more universal than it had been in the age of colonial empires; "modern culture" was now appearing and reappearing in countless novel and non-Western forms in a newly *plural* world. These last thoughts, moreover, received vivid confirmation later that summer when the whole family returned to Europe and Holland westward via the Trans-Siberian railway. In those nine days crossing the seemingly endless expanse of Russia, we witnessed still another very different, vastly poorer, and (to me) more depressive form of modern culture.

The colleague at Kyoto University who had issued the invitation to me, and with whom I taught a seminar on technology and religion, was the distinguished Buddhist philosopher, Takeuchi Yoshinori. Through my frequent talks with him about "doing theology" in the midst of a modern scientific culture, I found myself continually intrigued by our common set of problems and yet eager as well to explore our important differences. On that extraordinarily warm and fruitful personal level, therefore, my interest in interreligious dialogue began—and it has continued as the predominant concern of my thinking ever since.

Another factor, also very personal, has added to this growing interest. Anyone living through the later 1960s and especially the early 1970s in an urban and academic community could not help becoming aware of the many religious movements newly appearing in American life; in our case, this also meant participation in them. Over the next few years, our family, especially through my wife's increasing devotion to yoga, became involved with the Sikh movement in America; and, in 1974, she entered the Sikh Khalsa as one of its members. As a consequence, our family's lifestyle changed rather radically; I have, moreover, found myself since then doing yoga weekly in my wife's class and participating in tantric yoga on several weekends each year and for ten days at summer solstice in New Mexico. Thus, to the interchanges with Buddhism have been added this continual and intimate set of relations to modern Sikhism, frequent contacts with its extraordinary leader, Yogi Bhajan, and a growing understanding of—and admiration for—the community of Sikhs in the Western nations. There were several things here that were quite new to me: an Indian religion powerfully practiced (and so transformed) on Western soil by Europeans and Americans, incidentally former Protestants, Catholics, and Jews; a religion based on the practice of traditional techniques (especially yoga) and on strict personal discipline that clearly, despite its obviously "works" or "self-help" character, led to a deep and self-validating experience of the divine and to a transformation or renewal of personal existence; and, finally, a religion in which neither theological beliefs nor philosophical viewpoints played any noticeable role in conversion or loyalty, but rather followed entirely from, rather than leading to (as in my own case), an experience of a high consciousness and a renewed personal life. In all of this—as in my continual contacts with Buddhists—I realized, on a new and sharper level, the lacks and weaknesses, as well as the strengths, of my own tradition. For it was obvious on every hand that each member of the Khalsa had found in this very different stream of Indian tradition something significantly needed, and yet quite lacking, in their own experience of a Christian or a Jewish community. That these "nonbiblical" religious traditions possessed their own spiritual power (truth and grace, as we would say it in Christian terms) and had so much to teach us, as well as much to learn, was now too obvious even to wonder seriously about. The new task, therefore, was to understand this theologically: that is, to understand my own faith all over again in the new light of this incontestable "plurality." What I have later called the new experience in our time of "the rough parity" among religions came to me with unanswerable certainty in these experiences and has set for me the major theological task of the next years.

These were personal experiences with the wider religious culture beyond the West, with the Orient; as personal, they carried great weight in my thinking. They were to me, however, at the same time increasingly and vividly viewed (and understood) in relation to the most significant changes that had transpired in the wider historical background of our epoch. The deep dilemmas of modern Western culture, its potentialities for infinite evil, had been apparent since my youth in the 1930s. With the shattering experiences of the Bomb in the 1950s and later of the environmental crisis in the 1970s, this sense of the crisis of Western civilization deepened and the phrase, "time of troubles" for the West, became an important theme of my theological writing. Now, however, these renewed experiences with the Orient, beginning in 1973 to 1975, added a new dimension. For it became evident to me how dramatically the relations of the West with the Orient, in fact with the rest of the entire world, had changed during the course of my own lifetime. In 1940, when I went to China, the West was still dominant and so "superior" on almost every level. All of this was now quite gone: on every front, parity reigned. Western flaws, lacks, and sins have moved to the forefront of consciousness everywhere, much (let us recall) as the flaws in Oriental cultures were in the forefront of every Western consciousness in the nineteenth and early twentieth centuries. Correspondingly, a revitalization of non-Western traditions has accompanied that new consciousness. After 400 years of unquestioned Western dominance, a quite new set of relations between the national powers and the cultural traditions of our world has appeared.

My own life's experience, from the Japanese humiliation of the Westerners in East Asia in 1941 to these cumulative events of the immediate present, has witnessed and so validated this change. The era of Western military dominance and cultural superiority (and not just of *Europe's* empires) is over. A new parity of cultures and of powers is upon us. American as well as European power represents now only one among a number of power centers, and Western culture and its religions represent one among a number of equally vital cultural and religious possibilities. The rise of Islam as an economic, political, and religious reality is merely a more vivid illustration of this same theme. The deepest source, not so much for the parity of religions, but for our new ability to *recognize, appropriate, and possibly understand that parity* is this change in our world's historical and cultural context, apparent since mid-century, a context in which the dramatic loss of the dominance of the West, along with the excessive, even "demonic" power of science and technology, represents perhaps its major characteristic. Within this new age, we must now do theology, an age in which the plethora of national and ideological conflicts and crises—and the accompanying temptations to absolutism— may by no means be new, but in which the self-understanding of each tradition, in its relations to other traditions, is entirely new. For the first time, each tradition, like it or not, now finds itself one among many in a *plural* world, in a sort of "rough parity" with the others.

How does one do theology in this new context? Can one at the same time affirm and articulate a genuine and viable spiritual commitment, an existence centered on the relation to the divine beyond relativity, and yet also recognize, as now apparently we must, the "parity" of one's own stance with that of others and so the relativity in some sense of all our affirmations? Does not the relativity of religious viewpoints implied here swallow up all religious validity and so all existential or theoretical affir- mation or witness? How can a "relative" religious faith subsist, as it must, as an ultimate concern, an ultimate center of trust and confidence? Are we not then left with only relative religious viewpoints through none of which, therefore, we can receive any illumination or arrive at any certainty? To relativize all religious viewpoints, however, is necessarily to make some *other* viewpoint, probably that of a secular humanism based on science and democracy, ultimate. And our age has even more emphatically shown the relativism, in fact the parochialism as well as the barrenness, of that humanistic and scientific center of modern Western intellectual and spiritual life. Such a humanistic faith had seemed to be universal in the period of Western cultural dominance. Then the dream of a universal scientific and humanistic culture as the spiritual substance of future history more or less defined the notion of progress so important to "modern" culture. As we have noted, such a dream of a universal cul- ture—as an extension of *our* culture—still inspires most of academia. My point, however, is that in fact the possibility of the universality of *that* culture has vanished as thoroughly as has that of a universally triumphant Christianity. There is no aspiring center, be it traditionally religious, secular humanistic, or Marxist, that is not equally challenged by this new relativism and, as a consequence, that can avoid coming to terms with it.

On the other hand, if our history since the 1930s has shown anything, it is that one cannot live a human existence, especially in a stormy epoch, on relativism: uncommitted, undirected, empty of norms and of ultimate trust. The shock of Hitler had shown this point to us all: one must stand *somewhere*, if one is to resist such evil when it appears in power—and resist one must or lose one's soul completely. For to take no stand is not to be neutral, but to join with, to participate in, and so to acquiesce to an unacceptable evil. Such a stance is not to be applauded as "objective" and "neutral," but is to be condemned as cynical, loveless, and cowardly. Nothing since, whether it be the racial conflicts, the Vietnam debacle, or the new issues of liberation, has but validated this point. Humans in history, and especially in a time of troubles, must act and act creatively; to do this they inescapably relate themselves to something ultimate, and must do so in terms of commitment, self-surrender, and self-giving, if they are to live creatively. Our age has revealed both the necessity of a relation to the absolute—the *necessity*, if you will, of the religious; and, at the same time, it has revealed the relativity of all such relations—the *danger* of the religious. It has manifested the demonic character both of an unquestioned absolutism and of an uncommitted relativism. Theology is still utterly essential; but, in a new way and on a new level, it has now to be a relativized theology.

To interpret theologically the rough parity of the religions and so in that sense the relativity of each is, however, a puzzling and frustrating, as well as a new task. For all theology, as with the faith or the religious existence that theology expresses, seems to begin with some center, some absolute starting point that cannot itself be relativized, be it revelation, holy tradition, special religious experience, or even reason. In a situation of recognized parity, however, where each viewpoint shares truth and grace with others, the usual unconditional starting point for each tradition seems to have dissolved and constructive reflection of any sort appears to be frustrated. In an infinity of possible centers, where can one begin to build? One solution to this has been the effort to find a "post-Christian" starting point, one that lies beyond every particular religious tradition and, thus, seems (at first glance) to include them all. On this basis, the theology of the future can be built. So say many wise and influential voices today, each in different ways: Frithjof Schuon, Huston Smith, Wilfred Cantwell Smith, John Hick, Paul Knitter. I have found, however, that I cannot follow this route: such a reflected essence of religion, whatever it may be, is itself too parochial and relative; it represents—try as it may to avoid it—a particular way of being religious and so a particular interpretation of religion. Thus, it has to *misinterpret* every other tradition, in order to incorporate them into its own scheme of understanding. In the end, therefore, it represents in a new form the same religious colonialism that Christianity used to practice so effectively: the interpretation of an alien viewpoint in terms of one's own religious center and so an incorporation of that viewpoint into our own system of understanding, our own quite particular religious orientation.

A path that is sounder and more redolent with creative possibilities, it seems to me, is the enterprise of theological reinterpretation of one's own standpoint in the light of parity. One is, therefore, still "at home" with one's own symbols, sources, and authority—and, thus, in a continuity with the theological tradition one is now seeking in a new way to articulate. Yet, one is seeking to reinterpret that tradition in a new way, as in parity with others, as a valid but particular representation of the ultimate reality (or nonreality) that all are seeking to express. Can Christianity be legitimately understood in this "relative-absolute" way? That is the question with which now I am concerned, and only a bare beginning of thinking that question through has been accomplished. I am convinced that, within the Christian tradition itself, there are multiple symbols and themes, biblical and traditional, that support such an interpretation and will contribute to it; and it seems already apparent that many themes and symbols from other traditions—Buddhist, Sikh, Confucian, to name a few—are there that may aid in this effort. As is evident, this last volume is still only a dim shape on the distant horizon.

Conclusion

Far too long, this story has now come to a close. I have here only referred to and hinted at the theological content, the discussions of method, symbols, and norms for praxis, dominant at each of its stages. This is because that content, and not the personal history from which it arose, is itself the subject of the books and articles that I have written. I have here been concerned with the personal and historical context that helped give rise to those theological reflections. Looking back at this history of my history, I think that this narrative has shown unquestionably that, whatever else they may represent, these reflections appeared in the shape that they did because of the changing history, both personal and global, in which my life was set—which is, to me at least, to end squarely on the most emphatically "biblical" theme of all.

Bibliography

Works by Langdon Gilkey

Dissertation

"Maker of Heaven and Earth: A Thesis on the Relation between Metaphysics and Christian Theology with Special Reference to the Problem of Creation as that Problem Appears in the Philosophies of F. H. Bradley and A. N. Whitehead and in the Historic Leaders of Christian Thought." Ph.D. diss., Columbia University, 1954.

Books

Maker of Heaven and Earth: A Study of the Christian Doctrine of Creation. Garden City NY: Doubleday and Company, Inc., 1959. Paperback reprint: (expanded title on cover) *Maker of Heaven and Earth: The Christian Doctrine of Creation in the Light of Modern Knowledge.* Garden City NY: Anchor Books/Doubleday, 1965. Reprint: Lanham MD: University Press of America, 1985.

Der Himmel und Erde gemacht hat. Munich: Claudius Verlag, 1971. German edition of *Maker of Heaven and Earth.*

How the Church Can Minister to the World without Losing Itself. New York: Harper & Row Publishers, 1964.

Shantung Compound: The Story of Men and Women under Pressure. New York: Harper & Row Publishers, 1966.

Naming the Whirlwind: The Renewal of God-Language. Indianapolis and New York: The Bobbs-Merrill Company, 1969.

Religion and the Scientific Future: Reflections on Myth, Science, and Theology. New York: Harper & Row, Publishers, 1970. London: SCM Press, 1970. Reprint: ROSE 2 (Reprints of Scholarly Excellence). Macon GA: Mercer University Press, 1981.

Il Destino della Religione nell'era Technologica. Translated by P. Prini. Rome: Armando Armando Editore, 1972. Italian edition of *Religion and the Scientific Future.*

Catholicism Confronts Modernity: A Protestant View. New York: Seabury Press, 1975.

Reaping the Whirlwind: A Christian Interpretation of History. New York: Seabury Press, 1976.

Message and Existence: An Introduction to Christian Theology. New York: Seabury Press, 1979.
Society and the Sacred: Toward a Theology of Culture in Decline. New York: Crossroad Publishing Company, 1981.
Creationism on Trial: Evolution and God at Little Rock. San Francisco: Harper & Row Publishers, 1985.
Gilkey on Tillich. New York: Crossroad Publishing Company, 1990.
Through the Tempest: Theological Voyages in a Pluralistic Culture. Edited by Jeff B. Pool. Minneapolis: Fortress Press, 1991.
Nature, Reality, and the Sacred: The Nexus of Science and Religion. Theology and the Sciences series. Edited by Kevin J. Sharpe. Minneapolis: Fortress Press, 1993.

Contributions to Books, Encyclopedias, and Dictionaries
1950s

"Neo-Orthodoxy." In *A Handbook of Christian Theology*, ed. Marvin Halverson and Arthur Cohen, 256-61. New York: Meridian Books, 1958. Republished under the same title in *A New Handbook of Christian Theology*, ed. Donald W. Musser and Joseph L. Price, 334-37. Nashville: Abingdon Press, 1992.
"The Imperative for Unity—A Restatement." In *Issues in Unity*, 11-32. Indianapolis: Council on Christian Unity, 1958.

1960s

"A New Linguistic Madness." In *New Theology*, no. 2, ed. Martin Marty and Dean Peerman, 39-49. New York: Macmillan and Company, 1965. Previously published as a review of *The Secular Meaning of the Gospel*, by Paul M. Van Buren, in *Journal of Religion* 44 (July 1964): 238-43.
"Dissolution and Reconstruction in Theology." In *Frontline Theology*, ed. Dean Peerman, 29-38. Richmond: John Knox Press, 1966. Also translated and reprinted as "Abbau und Wiederaufbau in der Theologie" in *Theologie im Umbruch*, 32-41. Munich: Chr. Kaiser Verlag, 1968. Reprinted from an article by the same title in *Christian Century* 82 (3 February 1965): 135-39.
"Secularism's Impact on Contemporary Theology." In *Witness to a Generation*, ed. Wayne Cowan, 127-32. Indianapolis: Bobbs-Merrill, 1966. Reprinted in *Radical Theology: Phase Two*, ed. C. W. Christian and Glen R. Wittig, 17-23. Philadelphia and New York: J. B. Lippincott Company, 1967. Also reprinted in *The Theologian at Work*, ed. A. Roy Eckardt, 192-97. New York: Harper & Row Publishers, 1968. Reprinted originally, under the same title, from *Christianity and Crisis* 25 (5 April 1965): 64-67.

"Theology." In *The Great Ideas Today, 1967*, ed. R. M. Hutchins and M. Adler, 239-70. Chicago: Encyclopedia Britannica, Inc., 1967.

"Social and Intellectual Sources of Contemporary Protestant Theology in America." In *Religion in America*, ed. William McLaughlin and Robert Bellah, 137-66. Boston: Beacon Press, 1968. Reprinted under the same title from *Daedalus* 96 (Winter 1967): 69-98.

"The Contribution of Culture to the Reign of God." In *The Future as the Presence of Shared Hope*, ed. Maryellen Muckenhirn, 34-58. New York: Sheed and Ward, 1968.

"Modern Myth-Making and the Possibilities of Twentieth-Century Theology." In *Theology of Renewal*, vol. 1, ed. Lee K. Snook, 283-312. Montreal: Palm Publishers, 1968.

"Evolutionary Science and the Dilemma of Freedom and Determinism." In *Changing Man: The Threat and the Promise*, ed. Kyle Haselden and Philip Hefner, 63-76. Garden City NY: Doubleday and Company, 1968. Also in *Christian Century* 84 (15 March 1967): 339-43.

"Evolution and the Doctrine of Creation." In *Science and Religion: New Perspectives on the Dialogue*, ed. Ian G. Barbour, Harper Forum Books, ed. Martin E. Marty, 159-81. New York: Harper & Row Publishers, 1968. This chapter consists of two parts, a combined republication of two previous publications by Gilkey. (1) "Darwin and Christian Thought." *Christian Century* 77 (6 January 1960): 7-11. (2) "What the Idea of Creation Is About." Reprint of chapter 2 from *Maker of Heaven and Earth*, 15-40.

"New Modes of Empirical Theology." In *The Future of Empirical Theology*, ed. Bernard E. Meland, vol. 7, *Essays in Divinity*, ed. Jerald C. Brauer, 345-70. Chicago: University of Chicago Press, 1969. Later published, in a slightly different form, under the title "The Problem of God: A Programmatic Essay." In *Traces of God in a Secular Culture*, ed. George F. McClean, 3-23. Staten Island NY: Alba House, 1973.

"Trends in Protestant Apologetics." In *The Development of Fundamental Theology*, ed. J. B. Metz, 127-57. New York: Paulist Press, 1969. Also published under the same title in *Concilium* 6 (June 1969): 59-72.

"Unbelief and the Secular Spirit." In *The Presence and Absence of God*, ed. Christopher F. Mooney, 50-68. New York: Fordham University Press, 1969.

1970s

"The Universal and Immediate Presence of God." In *The Future of Hope*, ed. Frederick Herzog, 81-109. New York: Herder and Herder, 1970.

"Empirical Science and Theological Knowing." In *Foundations of Theology: Papers from the International Lonergan Conference*, ed. Philip McShane, 76-101. Dublin, Ireland: Gill and Macmillan, 1971.

"Biblical Symbols in a Scientific Culture." In *Science and Human Values in the 21st Century*, ed. Ralph Wendell Burhoe, 72-98. Philadelphia: Westminster Press, 1971.

"The Problem of God: A Programmatic Essay." In *Traces of God in a Secular Culture*, ed. George F. McClean, 3-23. Staten Island NY: Alba House, 1973. First published in a slightly different form, under the following title: "New Modes of Empirical Theology." In *The Future of Empirical Theology*, ed. Bernard E. Meland, vol. 7, *Essays in Divinity*, ed. Jerald C. Brauer, 345-70. Chicago: University of Chicago Press, 1969.

"Addressing God in Faith." In *Liturgical Experience of Faith*, ed. Herman Schmidt and David Power, *Concilium: Religion in the Seventies*, 62-76. New York: Herder and Herder, 1973. Later published under the same title as chapter 7 in *Catholicism Confronts Modernity*, 178-99.

"Idea of God Since 1800." In *Dictionary of the History of Ideas*, ed. Philip P. Wiener, vol. 2, 351-66. New York: Charles Scribner's Sons, 1973.

"The Spirit and the Discovery of Truth through Dialogue." In *Leven uit de Geest: Festschrift for Edward Schillebeeckx*, ed. Paul W. Brand. Hilversum, The Netherlands: Gooi en Sticht, 1974. Also published in French as "L'Esprit et la découverte de la vérité dans le dialogue." In *L'Expérience de L'Esprit: Melanges E. Schillebeeckx*, ed. Paul W. Brand, Le Point Theologique Series, vol. 18, 225-40. Paris: Beauchesne, 1976. Also published under the same title in *Experience of the Spirit*, ed. Peter Huizing and William Bassett, vol. 9, no. 10, *Spirituality, Concilium: New Series*, 58-68. New York: Seabury Press, A Crossroad Book, 1974.

"Reinhold Niebuhr's Theology of History." In *The Legacy of Reinhold Niebuhr*, ed. Nathan A. Scott, Jr., 36-62. Chicago: University of Chicago Press, 1975. Previously published under the same title in *Journal of Religion* 54 (October 1974): 360-86.

"Response to C. Meyer and Z. Hayes." *Catholic Theological Society of America: Proceedings of the 29th Annual Convention*, ed. L. Salm. New York: Catholic Theological Society of America, 1975.

"The Structure of Academic Revolutions." In *The Nature of Scientific Discovery*, ed. Owen Gingerich, 538-46. Washington DC: Smithsonian Institution Press, 1975.

"The Crisis of the Word 'God.' " In *The Contemporary Explosion of Theology: Ecumenical Studies in Theology*, ed. Michael D. Ryan, 20-26. Metuchen NJ: Scarecrow Press, 1975.

"The Crisis of 'God' Language." In *The Contemporary Explosion of Theology: Ecumenical Studies in Theology*, ed. Michael D. Ryan, 27-33. Metuchen NJ: Scarecrow Press, 1975.

"L'Esprit et la découverte de la vérité dans le dialog." In *L'Experience de l'Esprit: Melanges E. Schillebeeckx*, ed. Paul W. Brand, Le Point Theologique

Series, vol. 18, 225-40. Paris: Beauchesne, 1976. French translation of "The Spirit and the Discovery of Truth through Dialogue." In *Leven uit de Geest: Festschrift for Edward Schillebeeckx*, ed. Paul Brand. Hilversum, The Netherlands: Gooi en Sticht, 1974. Also published under the same title in *Experience of the Spirit*, ed. Peter Huizing and William Bassett, vol. 9, no. 10, *Spirituality, Concilium: New Series*, 58-68. New York: Seabury Press, A Crossroad Book, 1974.

"God: Eternal Source of Newness." In *Living with Change, Experience, Faith*, ed. Francis A. Eigo, 154-66. Villanova PA: Villanova University Press, 1976.

"The Future of Science." Address to Nobel Laureates at St. Olaf College, October 1975. Published as *The Future of Science: 1975 Nobel Conference*, ed. T. C. L. Robinson, 105-29. New York: John Wiley and Sons, 1977. Also published as chapter 6, "The Creativity and Ambiguity of Science," in *Society and the Sacred*, 75-89.

"Toward a Religious Criterion of Religions." In *Understanding the New Religions*, ed. Jacob Needleman and George Baker, 131-37. New York: Seabury Press, 1978.

"The Covenant with the Chinese." In *China and Christianity: Historical and Future Encounters*, ed. James D. Whitehead, Yu Ming Shaw, and N. J. Girardot, 118-32. Notre Dame IN: University of Notre Dame Press, The Center of Pastoral and Social Ministry, 1979. Previously published under the same title in *Dialog* 17 (Summer 1978): 181-87. Also published as chapter 10, "Revelation and an Ancient Civilization," in *Society and the Sacred*, 139-56.

"The Dialectic of Christian Belief: Rational, Incredible, and Credible." In *Rationality and Religious Belief*, ed. C. F. Delaney, no. 1, University of Notre Dame Studies in the Philosophy of Religion, 65-83. Notre Dame IN: University of Notre Dame Press, 1979. Also published as chapter 3, "The Dialectic of Christian Belief," in *Society and The Sacred*, 26-41.

"The Religious Dilemmas of a Scientific Culture: The Interface of Technology, History and Religion." In *Being Human in a Technological Age*, ed. Donald M. Borchert and David Stewart, 73-88. Athens, Ohio: Ohio University Press, 1979. Also published as chapter 7, "The Religious Dilemmas of a Scientific Culture," in *Society and the Sacred*, 90-103.

1980s

"Scripture, History, and the Quest for Meaning." In *Humanizing America's Iconic Book: Society of Biblical Literature Centennial Addresses 1980*, ed. by Gene M. Tucker and Douglas A. Knight, no. 6, Biblical Scholarship in North America, ed. by Kent Harold Richards, 25-38. Chico CA: Scholars Press, 1982. Republished in *History and Historical Understanding*, ed. C. T. McIntyre and Ronald A. Wells, 3-16. Grand Rapids MI: Wm. B. Eerdmans,

1984. Also published under the same title as chapter 5 in *Society and the Sacred*, 57-72.

"The Political Dimensions of Theology." In *The Challenge of Liberation Theology: A First World Response*, ed. Brian Mahan and L. Dale Richesen, 113-26. Maryknoll NY: Orbis Books, 1981. Reprint from *Journal of Religion* 59 (April 1979): 154-68. Also published under the same title as chapter 4 in *Society and the Sacred*, 42-56.

"Is Religious Faith Possible in an Age of Science." In *Unfinished . . . Essays in Honor of Ray L. Hart*, ed. Mark C. Taylor, *The American Academy of Religion, Thematic Studies*, 48 (1981): 31-44. Also published, under the same title, as a lecture at the University of Florida, The Department of Religion Lecture Series, 7 April 1981. Republished in *Religion, Science, and Public Policy*, ed. by Frank T. Birtel, Tulane Judeo-Christian Studies Series, 49-64. New York: Crossroad Publishing Company, 1987. Published under the same title as chapter 8, *Society and the Sacred*, 104-19.

"Theology for a Time of Troubles," in *Theologians in Transition: The Christian Century "How My Mind Has Changed" Series*, ed. James M. Wall, 29-40. New York: Crossroad Publishing Company, 1981. Reprinted from "Theology for a Time of Troubles: How My Mind Has Changed." *Christian Century* 98 (29 April 1981): 474-80.

"Secolarizzazione." In *Enciclopedia del Novecento*, vol. 6, 415-30. Istituto dell'Enciclopedia Italiana, 1982.

"Tillich: The Master of Mediation." In *The Theology of Paul Tillich*, 2d ed., ed. Charles W. Kegley, 26-59. New York: Pilgrim Press, 1982. Also published as chapter 4, "Master of Mediation: Theology of Culture and Correlation," in *Gilkey on Tillich*, 56-78.

"The Creationist Controversy: The Interrelation of Inquiry and Belief." In *Creationism, Science, and the Law: The Arkansas Case*, ed. Marcel C. La Follette, 129-37. Cambridge, Massachusettes: London, 1983. Previously published under the same title in *Science, Technology, & Human Values* 7 (Summer 1982): 67-71.

"The Creationist Issue: A Theologian's View." In *Cosmology and Theology, Concilium*, ed. David Tracy and Nicholas Lash, 55-69. Edinburgh: T & T Clark Ltd.; New York: Seabury Press, 1983.

"Creationism: The Roots of the Conflict." In *Is God a Creationist? The Religious Case Against Creation-Science*, ed. Ronald Mushat Frye, 56-67. New York: Charles Scribner's Sons, 1983. This chapter conflates two previously published articles on the same topic. "Creationism: The Roots of the Conflict." *Christianity and Crisis* 42 (26 April 1982): 108-15. "The Creationist Controversy: The Interrelation of Inquiry and Belief." *Science, Technology, & Human Values* 7 (Summer 1982): 67-71.

"On Thinking about the Unthinkable." Comments on Jonathan Schell's *Fate of the Earth*, with Stephen Toulmin, Paul Ricoeur, and David Tracy. *University of Chicago Magazine* (Fall 1983): 6-9, 28.

"Can Art Fill the Vacuum?" In *Art, Creativity, and the Sacred: An Anthology in Religion and Art*, ed. Diane Apostolos-Cappadona, 87-92. New York: Crossroad Publishing Company, 1984. Also published in *Criterion* 20 (Autumn 1981): 7-9.

"The Relevance of Luther Today." In *Protest and Vision: Martin Luther after 500 Years*, ed. Jim Bartruff, Barry Ferst, and William M. Thompson, 29-36. Carroll College, 1984.

"Theology of Culture and Christian Ethics." In *Annual of the Society of Christian Ethics*, ed. Larry L Rasmussen, 341-64. Vancouver: Society of Christian Ethics, 1984. Also published under the same title as chapter 9, in *Through the Tempest*, 143-55.

"God." In *Christian Theology: An Introduction to Its Traditions and Tasks*, rev. ed., ed. Peter C. Hodgson and Robert H. King, 88-113. Philadelphia: Fortress Press, 1985. Also published as chapter 5, "The Christian Understanding of God," in *Through the Tempest*, 69-88. Portions reprinted in *A New Handbook of Christian Theology*, ed. Donald W. Musser and Joseph L. Price, 198-208. Nashville: Abingdon Press, 1992.

"Theology as the Interpretation of Faith for Church and World." In *The Vocation of the Theologian*, ed. Theodore W. Jennings, Jr., 87-103. Philadelphia: Fortress Press, 1985. Also published as chapter 3, "Theology: Interpretation of Faith for Church and World," in *Through the Tempest*, 35-47.

"The New Being and Christology." In *The Thought of Paul Tillich*, ed. James Luther Adams, Wilhelm Pauck, and Roger Shinn, 307-29. New York: Harper & Row Publishers, 1985. Also published under the same title as chapter 8 in *Gilkey on Tillich*, 138-57.

"Theological Frontiers: Implications for Bioethics." In *Theology and Bioethics: Exploring the Foundations and Frontiers*, ed. Earl E. Shelp, 115-33. Dordrecht: D. Reidel Publishing Company, 1985.

"The Role of the Theologian in Contemporary Society." In *The Thought of Paul Tillich*, ed. James Luther Adams, 330-50. New York: Harper & Row Publishers, 1985. Also reprinted under the same title as chapter 10 in *Gilkey on Tillich*, 177-96.

"Religion and Science in an Advanced Scientific Culture." In *Knowing Religiously*, ed. Leroy S. Rouner, vol. 7, Boston University Studies in Philosophy and Religion, ed. Leroy S. Rouner, 166-76. Notre Dame IN: University of Notre Dame Press, 1985. Reprinted in *Zygon* 22 (June 1987): 165-78.

"An Appreciation of Karl Barth." In *How Karl Barth Changed My Mind*, ed. Donald K. McKim, 150-55. Grand Rapids MI: Wm. B. Eerdmans Publishing Company, 1986.

"The Creationism Issue: A Theologian's View." In *Science and Creation: Geological, Theological, and Educational Perspectives*, ed. by Robert W. Hanson, AAAS Issues in Science and Technology Series, 174-88. New York: Macmillan and Company, 1986.

"Religion and Public Policy." In *Religion and Public Life: The Role of Religious Bodies in Shaping Public Policy*, ed. Joseph A. Bracken, 29-42. Cincinnati, Ohio: Xavier University Press, 1986. Also published as chapter 11, "The Church and Public Policy," in *Through the Tempest*, 167-78.

"Culture and Religious Belief." In *The Life of Religion: A Marquett University Symposium on the Nature of Religious Belief*, ed. Stanley M. Harrison and Richard C. Taylor, 77-90. Lanham MD: University Press of America, 1986.

"Der Paradigmenwechsel in der Theologie." In *Das neue Paradigma von Theologie: Strukturen und Dimensionen*, ed. Hans Küng and David Tracy, 129-44. Zurich: Benziger; Gutersloher Verlagshaus G. Mohn, 1986.

"Plurality: Our New Situation." In *The Pastor as Servant*, ed. Earl E. Shelp and Ronald H. Sunderland, 102-22, 131. New York: Pilgrim Press, 1986. Also published as chapter 2, under the title, "Plurality: Christianity's New Situation," in *Through the Tempest*, 21-34.

"The Protestant View of Sin." In *The Human Condition in Jewish and Christian Traditions*, ed. Frederick E. Greenspahn, 147-68. Hoboken NJ: KTAV Publishing House, 1986.

"Reinhold Niebuhr as Political Theologian." In *Reinhold Niebuhr and the Issues of Our Time*, ed. Richard Harries, 157-82. Grand Rapids MI: Wm. B. Eerdmans Publishing Company, 1986.

"Baptists." In *Academic American Encyclopedia*, vol. 3, 73-74. Danbury CT: Grolier Incorporated, 1987.

"Events, Meanings and the Current Tasks of Theology." In *Trajectories in the Study of Religion: Addresses at the Seventy-Fifth Anniversary of the American Academy of Religion*, ed. Ray L. Hart, 175-92. Atlanta: Scholars Press, 1987. Previously published under the same title, in *Journal of the American Academy of Religion* 53 (1985): 717-34.

"Holy Spirit." In *Academic American Encyclopedia*, vol. 10, 211. Danbury CT: Grolier Incorporated, 1987.

"Niebuhr, Reinhold." In *Academic American Encyclopedia*, vol. 14, 184. Danbury CT: Grolier Incorporated, 1987.

"Theism." In *Academic American Encyclopedia*, vol. 19, 155. Danbury CT: Grolier Incorporated, 1987.

"Plurality and Its Theological Implications." In *The Myth of Christian Uniqueness: Toward a Pluralistic Theology of Religions*, ed. John Hick and Paul F. Knitter, 37-50. Maryknoll NY: Orbis Books, 1987.

"Tillich, Paul." In *Academic American Encyclopedia*, vol. 19, 199-200. Danbury CT: Grolier Incorporated, 1987.

"Trinity." In *Academic American Encyclopedia*, vol. 19, 300-301. Danbury CT: Grolier Incorporated, 1987.

"The Meaning of Jesus the Christ." In *The Christ and the Bodhisattva*, ed. Donald S. Lopez, Jr. and Steven C. Rockefeller, 193-207. SUNY Series in Buddhist Studies, ed. Kenneth K. Inada. Albany NY: State University of New York Press, 1987. Also published under the same title as chapter 7, in *Through the Tempest*, 101-13.

"Introduction: A Retrospective Glance at My Work." In *The Whirlwind in Culture: Frontiers in Theology—In Honor of Langdon Gilkey*, ed. Donald W. Musser and Joseph L. Price, 1-35. Bloomington IN: Meyer-Stone Books, 1988.

"The Paradigm Shift in Theology." In *Paradigm Change in Theology: A Symposium for the Future*, ed. Hans Küng and David Tracy, trans. Margaret Köhl, 367-83. New York: Crossroad Publishing Company, 1989.

1990s

"The Crisis of Christianity in North America: Its Implications for China." In *Morphologies of Faith: Essays in Religion and Culture in Honor of Nathan A. Scott, Jr.*, ed. Mary Gerhart and Anthony C. Yu, no. 59, American Academy of Religion Studies in Religion Series, ed. Lawrence S. Cunningham, 31-50. Atlanta: American Academy of Religion, 1990. Also published as chapter 1, "The Crisis of Christianity in North America," in *Through the Tempest*, 3-19.

"Creation, Being and Nonbeing." In *God and Creation: An Ecumenical Symposium*, ed. David B. Burrell and Bernard McGinn, 226-41. Notre Dame IN: University of Notre Dame Press, 1990. Also published as chapter 6, "Creation: Being and Nonbeing," in *Through the Tempest*, 89-100.

"Tanabe and the Philosophy of Religion." In *The Religious Philosophy of Tanabe Hajime: The Metanoetic Imperative*, ed. Taitetsu Unno and James W. Heisig, Nanzan Studies in Religion and Culture Series, 72-85. Berkeley CA: Asian Humanities Press, 1990.

"Whatever Happened to Immanuel Kant?" In *The Church and Contemporary Cosmology: Proceedings of a Consultation of the Presbyterian Church*, ed. James B. Miller and Kenneth E. McCall. Pittsburgh: Carnegie Mellon, 1990. Also published under the same title as chapter 4 in *Nature, Reality, and the Sacred*, 43-57.

"Forgotten Traditions in the Clergy's Self-Understanding." In *Clergy Ethics in a Changing Society: Mapping the Terrain*, ed. James P. Wind, 37-53. Louisville: Westminster John Knox Press, 1991.

"What Theology Can Learn from Science." In *Science, Technology, and the Christian Faith: An Account of Some Pilgrims in Search of Progress*, ed. Brent Waters and Vernon L. Barbour. Dallas: United Ministries in Higher Education, 1991. Also published as chapter 2, "Changes in Two Ways of Knowing," and chapter 11, "Human Viability in a Nature That Is Mortal," in *Nature, Reality, and the Sacred*, 17-33, 161-73.

"Creation." In *A New Handbook of Christian Theology*, ed. Donald W. Musser and Joseph L. Price, 107-13. Nashville: Abingdon Press, 1992.

"God." In *A New Handbook of Christian Theology*, ed. Donald W. Musser and Joseph L. Price, 198-208. Nashville: Abingdon Press, 1992. Previously published in *Christian Theology: An Introduction to Its Traditions and Tasks*, rev. ed., ed. Peter C. Hodgson and Robert H. King, 88-113. Philadelphia: Fortress Press, 1985. Also published as chapter 5, "The Christian Understanding of God," in *Through the Tempest*, 69-88.

"Neoorthodoxy." In *A New Handbook of Christian Theology*, ed. Donald W. Musser and Joseph L. Price, 334-37. Nashville: Abingdon Press, 1992. Previously published in *A Handbook of Christian Theology*, ed. Marvin Halverson and Arthur Cohen, 256-61. New York: World Publishing Company, Meridian Books, 1958.

"Power, Order, Justice, and Redemption: Theological Comments on Job." In *The Voice from the Whirlwind: Interpreting the Book of Job*, ed. Leo G. Perdue and W. Clark Gilpin, 159-71. Nashville: Abingdon Press, 1992.

"Tillich and the Kyoto School." In *Negation and Theology*, ed. Robert P. Scharlemann, Studies in Religion and Culture Series, ed. Robert P. Scharlemann 72-85. Charlottesville: University of Virginia, 1992.

"The Pluralism of Religions." In *God, Truth and Reality: Essays in Honor of John Hick*, ed. Arvind Sharma, 111-23. New York: St. Martin's Press, 1993.

"The Christian Congregation as a Religious Community." In *American Congregations*, vol. 2, *New Perspectives in the Study of Congregations*, ed. James P. Wind and James W. Lewis, 100-32. Chicago: University of Chicago Press, 1994.

"A Protestant Response" [reply to Catholic interpretations of Tillich's theology]. In *Paul Tillich: A New Catholic Assessment*, ed. Raymond F. Bulman and Frederick J. Parrella, 289-307. Collegeville MN: Liturgical Press, 1994.

"A Tribute." In *The Unrelieved Paradox: Studies in the Theology of Franz Bibfeldt*, ed. Martin Marty and Gerald Brauer, 216. Grand Rapids MI: Wm. B. Eerdmans Publishing Company, 1994.

"Biology and Theology on Human Nature." In *Biology, Ethics, and the Origins of Life*, ed. Holmes Rolston III, 163-90. Boston: Jones and Bartlett Publishers, 1995.

Articles in Journals and Periodicals

1950s

"Academic Freedom and the Christian Faith." *Christianity and Crisis* 12 (22 December 1952): 171-73.

"Morality and the Cross." *Christianity and Crisis* 14 (5 April 1954): 35-38.

"The Christian Response to the World Crisis." *Christianity and Crisis* 15 (8 August 1955): 107-11.

"In Faith . . . Praise, Thanksgiving and Joy." *Christianity and Crisis* 16 (10 December 1956): 168-69.

"Christ and the City." *Motive* 17 (April 1957): 2-3, 29.

1960s

"Darwin and Christian Thought." *Christian Century* 77 (6 January 1960): 7-11. Also reprinted as the first part of "Evolution and the Doctrine of Creation," chapter 8, in *Science and Religion: New Perspectives on the Dialogue*, ed. Ian Barbour, Harper Forum Books, ed. Martin Marty, 159-72. New York: Harper & Row Publishers, 1968.

"Calvin's Religious Thought." *Motive* 20 (February 1960): 5-6.

"Cosmology, Ontology, and the Travail of Biblical Language." *Journal of Religion* 41 (July 1961): 194-205. Reprinted under the same title in *Concordia Theological Monthly* 33 (March 1962): 143-54.

"The Concept of Providence in Contemporary Theology." *Journal of Religion* 43 (July 1963): 171-92.

"Stewards of the Mysteries of God." *Criterion* 3 (Winter 1964): 1-3.

"Is God Dead? An Examination of a Contemporary View." *The Voice: Bulletin of Crozier Theological Seminary* 57 (January 1965): 4-7.

"God Is *Not* Dead: The Meaning and Validity of Religious Language." *The Voice: Bulletin of Crozier Theological Seminary* 57 (January 1965): 8-11.

"Dissolution and Reconstruction in Theology." *Christian Century* 82 (3 February 1965): 135-39. Reprinted under the same title in *Frontline Theology*, ed. Dean Peerman, 29-38. Richmond: John Knox Press, 1966. Also translated and reprinted as "Abbau und Wiederaufbau in der Theologie" in *Theologie im Umbruch*, 32-41. Munich: Chr. Kaiser Verlag, 1968.

"Holy, Holy, Holy." *The Baptist Student* 44 (January 1965): 24-27.

"Secularism's Impact on Contemporary Theology." *Christianity and Crisis* 25 (5 April 1965): 64-67. Reprinted in *Witness to a Generation*, ed. Wayne Cowan,

127-32. Indianapolis: Bobbs-Merrill, 1966. Also reprinted in *Radical Theology: Phase Two*, ed. C. W. Christian and Glen R. Wittig, 17-23. Philadelphia and New York: J. B. Lippincott Company, 1967. Reprinted again in *The Theologian at Work*, ed. A. Roy Eckardt, 192-97. New York: Harper & Row Publishers, 1968.

"The Authority of the Bible: The Relation of the Bible to the Church." *Encounter* 27 (Spring 1966): 112-23.

"Evolutionary Science and the Dilemma of Freedom and Determinism." *Christian Century* 84 (15 March 1967): 339-43. Republished under the same title in *Changing Man: The Threat and the Promise*, ed. Kyle Haselden and Philip Hefner, 63-76. Garden City NY: Doubleday and Company, 1968.

"If There Is No God: The Problem of God and the Study of Theology." *Criterion* 6 (Spring 1967): 5-7.

"Social and Intellectual Sources of Contemporary Protestant Theology in America." *Daedalus* 96 (Winter 1967): 69-98. Reprinted under the same title in *Religion in America*, ed. William McLaughlin and Robert Bellah, 137-66. Boston: Beacon Press, 1968.

"American Policy and the Just War." *Criterion* 7 (Winter 1968): 9-16.

"Morality and the Law." Discussion with Francis L. Filas, Norval Morris, and Kenneth J. Northcott. *University of Chicago Round Table* No. 18 (1968): 3-18.

"Religious Dimensions of the Secular." *Barat Review* 3 (June-September 1968): 106-109.

"Religion and the Secular University." *Dialog* 8 (Spring 1969): 108-16. Reprinted in *Religious Education* 64 (November–December 1969): 458-66.

"Trends in Protestant Apologetics." *Concilium* 6 (June 1969): 59-72. Also published in *The Development of Fundamental Theology*, ed. J. B. Metz, 127-57. New York: Paulist Press, 1969.

Reply to "Why Evangelism?" by E. van den Haag with Discussion. *Midstream* 8 (Summer 1969): 72-83, 84-87.

1970s

"Religious Dimensions of Scientific Inquiry." *Journal of Religion* 50 (July 1970): 245-67. Also published simultaneously as chapter 2, "Religious Dimensions in Science," in *Religion and the Scientific Future*, 35-64.

"Theology in the Seventies." *Theology Today* 27 (October 1970): 292-301.

"Ervaring en Interpretatie van de Religieuze Dimensie: een Reaktie." *Tijdschrift voor Theologie* 11 (July/August/September): 292-302.

"Process Theology." *Vox Theologica* 34 (January 1973): 5-29.

"Reinhold Niebuhr's Theology of History." *Journal of Religion* 54 (October 1974): 360-86. Republished under the same title in *The Legacy of Reinhold*

Niebuhr, ed. Nathan A. Scott, Jr., 36-62. Chicago: University of Chicago Press, 1975.

"Christian Theology." *Criterion* 13 (Winter 1974): 10-13.

"Religion and the Technological Future." *Criterion* 13 (Spring 1974): 9-14.

"Symbols, Meaning, and the Divine Presence." *Theological Studies* 35 (June 1974): 249-67. Also published under the same title as chapter 4, in *Through the Tempest*, 49-65.

"Technology, History and Liberation." *Anticipation: Christian Social Thought in Future Perspective* No. 16 (March 1974): 14-19. Also published as the appendix, "The Technological Understanding of Humanity and Nature in a Technological Era," in *Reaping the Whirlwind*, 319-22.

"Robert S. Heilbroner's Vision of History." *Zygon* 10 (September 1975): 215-33.

"On Going to War over Oil." *Christian Century* 92 (12 March 1975): 259-60.

"Theology and the Future." *Andover Newton Quarterly* 17 (March 1977): 250-57.

"The Contribution of Theology to the Comprehension of History." *Perspectives in Religious Studies* 4 (Summer 1977): 200-208.

"Anathemas and Orthodoxy: A Reply to Avery Dulles." *Christian Century* 94 (9 November 1977): 1026-29.

"A Covenant with the Chinese." *Dialog* 17 (1978): 181-87. Previously published in *China and Christianity: Historical and Future Encounter*, ed. James D. Whitehead, Yu Ming Shaw, and N. J. Girardot, 118-32. Notre Dame IN: University of Notre Dame Press, 1979. Also published as chapter 10, "Revelation and an Ancient Civilization," in *Society and the Sacred*, 139-56.

"Mystery of Being and Nonbeing: An Experimental Project." *Journal of Religion* 58 (January 1978): 1-12.

"Namer and Tamer of the Whirlwind: Interview by Kendig Brubaker Cully." *New Review of Books and Religion* 2 (February 1978): 3.

"Responses to Peter Berger." *Theological Studies* 39 (September 1978): 486-507.

"Response to Lonergan." *Journal of Religion* 58 (Supplement 1978): 18-23.

"The Political Dimensions of Theology." *Journal of Religion* 59 (April 1979): 154-68.

"Proximate Ending for an Unfinished Man." *Journal of the American Academy of Religion* 47 (1979): 507-508.

1980s

"The AAR and the Anxiety of Non-being." *Journal of the American Academy of Religion* 48 (March 1980): 5-18.

"Meditation on Death and Its Relation to Life." *Archivio di Filosofia* 49 (1981): 19-32. Also published as chapter 15, "Death and Its Relation to Life," in *Through the Tempest*, 233-46.

"The Roles of the 'Descriptive' or 'Historical' and the 'Normative' in Our Work." *Criterion* 20 (Winter 1981): 10-17.

"Theology for a Time of Troubles: How My Mind Has Changed." *Christian Century* 98 (29 April 1981): 474-80. Reprinted as "Theology for a Time of Troubles," in *Theologians in Transition: The Christian Century "How My Mind Has Changed" Series*, ed. James M. Wall, 29-40. New York: Crossroad Publishing Company, 1981.

"A New Watershed in Theology." *Soundings* 64 (Summer 1981): 118-31. Revised version also published as chapter 1, "The New Watershed in Theology," *Society and the Sacred*, 3-14.

"Can Art Fill the Vacuum?" *Criterion* 20 (Autumn 1981): 7-9. Republished in *Art, Creativity, and the Sacred: An Anthology in Religion and Art*, ed. Diane Apostolos-Cappadona, 87-92. New York: Crossroad Publishing Company, 1984.

"Creationism: The Roots of the Conflict." *Christianity and Crisis* 42 (26 April 1982): 108-15. Portions of this article were later adapted for a chapter by the same title in *Is God a Creationist? The Religious Case Against Creation-Science*, ed. Ronald Mushat Frye, 56-67. New York: Charles Scribner's Sons, 1983. That chapter conflates the previously published article and a second article on the same topic: "The Creationist Controversy: The Interrelation of Inquiry and Belief." *Science, Technology, & Human Values* 7 (Summer 1982): 67-71.

"The Creationist Controversy: The Interrelation of Inquiry and Belief." *Science, Technology, & Human Values* 7 (Summer 1982): 67-71. Portions of this article later adapted for a chapter, under another title. "Creationism: The Roots of the Conflict." In *Is God a Creationist? The Religious Case Against Creation-Science*, ed. Ronald Mushat Frye, 56-67. New York: Charles Scribner's Sons, 1983.

"Some Words from the Faculty." *Criterion* 21 (Autumn 1982): 21-22.

"Responses to Ross Reat's Article, 'Insiders and Outsiders in the Study of Religion.' " *Journal of the American Academy of Religion* 51 (1983): 484-88.

"The Political Meaning of Silence." *Philosophy Today* 27 (Summer 1983): 128-32.

"The Christian Understanding of Suffering." *Buddhist-Christian Studies* 5 (1985): 49-65. Also published under the same title as chapter 14, in *Through the Tempest*, 215-31.

"Responses to Langdon Gilkey" (interactions with Masao Abe, following his response to Gilkey's "Christian Understanding of Suffering"). *Buddhist-Christian Studies* 5 (1985): 67-93.

"Events, Meanings and the Current Tasks of Theology." *Journal of the American Academy of Religion* 53 (1985): 717-34. Also reprinted under the same title, in *Trajectories in the Study of Religion: Addresses at the Seventy-Fifth*

Anniversary of the American Academy of Religion, ed. Ray L. Hart, 175-92. Atlanta: Scholars Press, 1987.

"Religion and Culture: A Persistent Problem." *Journal of Mormon History* 12 (1985): 29-41.

"Dimensions of Basic Faith and the Special Traditions." *Second Opinion: Health, Faith, and Ethics* 2 (1986): 107-19.

"The Symbol of God" [Paul Tillich]. *Soundings* 69 (Winter 1986): 384-400. Republished under the same title as chapter 6 in *Gilkey on Tillich*, 99-113.

"Religion and Science in an Advanced Scientific Culture." *Zygon* 22 (June 1987): 165-78. Previously published in *Knowing Religiously*, ed. Leroy S. Rouner, vol. 7, Boston University Studies in Philosophy and Religion, ed. Leroy S. Rouner, 166-76. Notre Dame IN: University of Notre Dame Press, 1985.

"Ordering The Soul: Augustine's Manifold Legacy." *Christian Century* 105 (27 April 1988): 426-30.

"Reply from the Author." *Biology and Philosophy* 3 (1988): 485-95. See Nils Chr. Stenseth, Audfinn Tjønneland, and Tore Lindholm, "Can Rationality and Irrationality Be Reconciled?" Review of *Creationism on Trial*. In *Biology and Philosophy*.

"Theodicy and Plurality." *Archivio di Filosofia* 56 (1988): 707-20. Also published under the same title as chapter 12, in *Through the Tempest*, 181-93.

"Nature, Reality, and the Sacred: A Meditation in Science and Religion." *Zygon* 24 (September 1989): 283-98. Published as chapter 1, "Issues of Language and Truth," and chapter 5, "Science, Philosophy, and Theology," in *Nature, Reality, and the Sacred*, 17-33, 59-76.

"Theology and Culture: Reflections on the Conference." *Criterion* 28 (Autumn 1989): 2-9.

"Ethics in Christianity and Buddhism." *Dialog* 28 (Winter 1989): 37-42. Also published under the same title as chapter 10, in *Through the Tempest*, 157-65.

1990s

"What of Value Does Religion Have to Say to Science?" *CTNS Bulletin* 10 (Autumn 1990): 6-9.

"Response to Stone's 'The Viability of Religious Naturalism.' " *American Journal of Theology and Philosophy* 14 (January 1993): 43-48.

"Nature as the Image of God: Signs of the Sacred." *Theology Today* 51 (April 1994): 127-41. Reprinted in *Zygon* 29 (December 1994): 489-505.

"From Shantung to Sarajevo: Reflections after 50 Years." *Christian Century* 112 (16-23 August 1995): 782-86.

"The Threshold of a New Common Freedom." *Criterion* 37 (Autumn 1998): 16, 18-19, 30.

Book Reviews by Gilkey

1950s

"Great Good Sense." Review of *Ultimate Questions*, by Nathaniel Micklem. In *Christian Century* 72 (3 August 1955): 896.

"Biblical Theology and Historical Reality." Review of *The Death of Christ*, by John Knox, and *Resurrection and Historical Reason*, by Richard R. Niebuhr. In *Encounter* 19 (Spring 1958): 214-18.

Review of *The Church Faces the Isms*, by Arnold B. Rhodes, ed. In *Religion in Life* 28 (Winter 1958–1959): 136-37.

1960s

"A History of Christian Ideas." Review of *Speculation in Pre-Christian Philosophy*, by Richard Kroner. In *Christian Scholar* 44 (Summer 1961): 169-72.

Review of *Love Almighty and Ills Unlimited: An Essay on Providence and Evil*, by Austin M. Farrer. In *Encounter* 24 (Spring 1963): 244-46.

Review of *Paul Tillich and the Christian Message*, by George H. Tavard. In *Union Seminary Quarterly Review* 18 (March 1963): 283-84.

Review of *The Secular Meaning of the Gospel*, by Paul M. van Buren. In *Journal of Religion* 44 (July 1964): 238-43. Reprinted as "A New Linguistic Madness," in *New Theology*, no. 2, ed. Martin Marty and Dean Peerman, 39-49. New York: Macmillan and Company, 1965.

"Is God Dead?" Review of *The Christian Belief in God*, by Daniel Jenkins. In *Christian Century* 82 (6 January 1965): 18-19.

Review of *Schleiermacher on Christ and Religion*, by Richard R. Niebuhr. In *Journal of Bible and Religion* 33 (April 1965): 182-86.

Review of *The Systematic Theology of Paul Tillich*, by Alexander J. McKelway. In *Foundations* 8 (July 1965): 18-19.

Review of *A Christian Natural Theology*, by John Cobb. In *Theology Today* 22 (January 1966): 530-45.

Review of *Is the Last Supper Finished? Secular Light on a Sacred Meal*, by Arthur A. Vogel. In *Theology Today* 22 (January 1966): 530-45.

"Seeds of Malaise." Review of *Nature, History and Existentialism*, by Karl Lowith. In *Christian Century* 83 (2 November 1966): 1341-42.

Review of *Paul Tillich's Philosophy of Culture, Science and Religion*, by James Luther Adams. In *Theology Today* 23 (January 1967): 565-69.

"The Integrity of History." Review of *Faith and the Vitalities of History*, by Philip Hefner. In *Una Sancta* 24 (Pentecost 1967): 67-71.

"A Theology in Process: Schubert Ogden's Developing Theology." Review of *The Reality of God and Other Essays*, by Schubert Ogden. In *Interpretation* 21 (October 1967): 447-59.

"Standing on the Promises." Review of *The Theology of Hope*, by Jürgen Moltmann. In *Christian Century* 84 (20 December 1967): 1630-32.

"A Paganized Judaism." Review of *After Auschwitz*, by Richard Rubenstein. In *Christian Century* 84 (10 May 1967): 627-28.

Review of *Faith and the Vitalities of History*, by Philip Hefner. In *Scottish Journal of Theology* 21 (September 1968): 336-39.

"Anatomy of Reconciliation." Review of *The Religious Dimension in Hegel's Thought*, by Emil L. Fackenheim. In *Christian Century* 86 (8 January 1969): 52-53.

1970s

Review of *Spirit in the World*, by Karl Rahner. In *Journal of Ecumenical Studies* 7 (Winter 1970): 138-44.

"That Mysterious Sleeping Dragon." Review of *Understanding Modern China*, ed. Joseph M. Kitagawa. In *Christian Century* 87 (26 August 1970): 1019-20.

"Comments on Emmanuel Levinas' *Totalité et Infini*." Review of *Totalité et Infini*, by Emmanuel Levinas. In *Algemeen Nederlands Tijdschrift voor Wijsbegeerte* 64 (1971): 26-38.

"The Dimensions of Dupre." Review of *The Other Dimension*, by Louis Dupre. In *Commonweal* 97 (20 October 1972): 63-66.

"Pannenberg's *Basic Questions in Theology*: A Review Article." Review of *Basic Questions in Theology*, vols. 1 and 2, by Wolfhart Pannenberg. In *Perspectives* 14 (Spring 1973): 34-55.

"Robert Heilbroner's Morality Play: Examining the Myths by Which We Might Have a Future." Review of *An Inguiry into the Human Prospect*, by Robert Heilbroner. In *Worldview* 17 (August 1974): 51-55.

"Robert L. Heilbroner's Vision of History." Review of *An Inquiry into the Human Prospect*, by Robert L. Heilbroner. In *Zygon* 10 (September 1975): 215-33.

1980s

"A Theological Voyage with Wilfred Cantwell Smith: Early Opus and Recent Trilogy." Review of *Belief and History, The Meaning and End of Religion, Faith and Belief*, and *Towards a World Theology*, by Wilfred Cantwell Smith. In *Religious Studies Review* 7 (October 1981): 298-306.

"On Thinking about the Unthinkable." Comments on Jonathan Schell's *Fate of the Earth*, with Stephen Toulmin, Paul Ricoeur, and David Tracy. *University of Chicago Magazine* 76 (Fall 1983): 6-9, 28.

"The Political Meaning of Silence." Review of *Silence: The Phenomenon and Its Ontological Significance*, by Bernard Dauenhauer. In *Philosophy Today* 27 (Summer 1983): 128-32.

Review of *The Limits of Science*, by P. B. Medawar. In *Bulletin of the Atomic Scientists* 41 (October 1985): 50-51.

"Abe Masao's *Zen and Western Thought*." Review of *Zen and Western Thought*, by Abe Masao. In *Eastern Buddhist*, New Series, 19 (Autumn 1986): 109-21.

Review of *Reinhold Niebuhr: A Biography*, by Richard Wrightman Fox. In *Journal of Religion* 68 (April 1988): 263-76.

"*Philosophy as Metanoetics*: A Review Article." Review of *Philosophy as Metanoetics*, by Hajime Tanabe. In *Journal of Religion* 68 (July 1988): 435-45.

"Nishitani Keiji's *Religion and Nothingness*." Review of *Religion and Nothingness*, by Keiji Nishitani. In *The Religious Philosophy of Nishitani Keiji: Encounter with Emptiness*, ed. Taitetsu Unno, Nanzan Studies in Religion and Culture Series, 49-69. Berkeley CA: Asian Humanities Press, 1989.

1990s

"Evolution, Culture, and Sin: Responding to Philip Hefner's Proposal." Review of *The Human Factor*, by Philip Hefner. In *Zygon* 30 (June 1995): 293-308.

Publications on Langdon Gilkey's Thought

Books

Dorrien, Gary. *The Word as True Myth: Interpreting Modern Theology*. Louisville: Westminster John Knox Press, 1997.

Musser, Donald W. and Price, Joseph L., eds. *The Whirlwind in Culture: Frontiers in Theology—Essays in Honor of Langdon Gilkey*. Bloomington IN: Meyer Stone Books, 1988.

Walsh, Brian J. *Langdon Gilkey: Theologian for a Culture in Decline*. Christian Studies Today Series. Lanham MD: University Press of America, 1991.

Chapters and Essays in Books

Alston, William P. "How to Think about Divine Action." In *Divine Action: Studies Inspired by the Philosophical Theology of Austin Farrer*, ed. Brian Hebblethwaite and Edward Henderson, 51-70. Edinburgh: T. & T. Clark, 1990.

Cathey, Robert A. "Three Christian Cosmologists: Karl Barth, Langdon Gilkey, and Kathryn Tanner." In *Festschrift in Honor of Charles Speel*, ed. Thomas J. Sienkewicz and James E. Betts, 59-70. Monmouth, Illinois: Monmouth College, 1996.

Cobb, John. "Response to Johann Baptist Metz and Langdon Gilkey" [response to Gilkey's "The Paradigm Shift in Theology"]. In *Paradigm Change in Theology: A Symposium for the Future*, ed. Hans Küng and David Tracy, trans. Margaret Köhl, 384-89. New York: Crossroad Publishing Company, 1989.

Farrelly, John. "Christian Interpretation of History: A Dialogue with Langdon Gilkey's *Reaping the Whirlwind*." In *Proceedings of the Catholic Theological Society of America*, 1978, ed. L. Salm, 182-91.

Geffré, Claude. "The Politcal Dimension of a New Theological Paradigm" [response to Gilkey's "The Paradigm Shift in Theology"]. In *Paradigm Change in Theology: A Symposium for the Future*, ed. Hans Küng and David Tracy, trans. Margaret Köhl, 390-94. New York: Crossroad Publishing Company, 1989.

Kannengiesser, Charles. "Response" [to Gilkey's "Creation, Being and Nonbeing"]. In *God and Creation: An Ecumenical Symposium*, ed. David B. Burrell and Bernard McGinn, 242-45. Notre Dame IN: University of Notre Dame Press, 1990.

Kliever, Lonnie D. "A New Style Natural Theology." In *Philosophy of Religion and Theology: 1971*, ed. David Ray Griffin, 82-103. Chambersburg, Pennsylvania: American Academy of Religion, 1971.

Marty, Martin E. "How Their Minds Have Changed." In *Theologians in Transition: The Christian Century "How My Mind has Changed" Series*, ed. James M. Wall, 1-18. New York: Crossroad Publishing Company, 1981.

Rike, Jennifer L. "Langdon Gilkey." In *A New Handbook of Christian Theologians*, ed. Donald W. Musser and Joseph L. Price, 158-70. Nashville: Abingdon Press, 1996.

Russell, Robert John. "Finite Creation without a Beginning: The Doctrine of Creation in Relation to Big Bang and Quantum Cosmologies." In *Quantum Cosmology and the Laws of Nature: Scientific Perspectives on Divine Action*, 2d ed., ed. Robert John Russell, 293-329. Vatican City State: Vatican Observatory; Berkeley California: Center for Theology and the Natural Sciences, 1996.

Sess, Dario. "Autocomprensione Secolare e Linguaggio Teologico: Il Contributo di Langdon Gilkey." In *Ecclesiae Sacramentum: Studi in Onore di Alfredo Marranzini*, ed. Giuseppe Lorizio and Vincenzo Scippa, vol. 2, Pontificia Facolta Teologica dell' Italia Meridionale Series, 363-92. Napoli: M. D'Auria, 1986.

Stone, Jerome. "What Religious Naturalism Can Learn from Langdon Gilkey: Uncovering the Dimension of Ultimacy." In *God, Values, and Empiricism: Issues in Philosophical Theology*, ed. W. Creighton Peden and Larry E. Axel, Highlands Institute Series 1, 209-19. Macon, Georgia: Mercer University Press, 1989.

Tracy, David. "The Question of Criteria for Inter-Religious Dialogue: A Tribute to Langdon Gilkey." In *The Whirlwind in Culture: Frontiers in Theology— Essays in Honor of Langdon Gilkey*, ed. Donald W. Musser and Joseph L. Price, 246-62. Bloomington IN: Meyer Stone Books, 1988.

Walsh, Brian J. "Langdon B. Gilkey." In *Dictionary of Christianity in America*, ed. D. G. Reid, R. D. Linder, B. L. Shelly, and H. S. Stout, 481-82. Downer's Grove, Illinois: InterVarsity Press, 1990.

Articles in Journals and Periodicals

Abe, Masao. "Responses to Langdon Gilkey" (to Gilkey's "Christian Understanding of Suffering"). *Buddhist-Christian Studies* 5 (1985): 67-93.

Becker, William H. "Creationism: New Dimensions of the Religion-Democracy Relation." *Journal of Church and State* 27 (Spring 1985): 315-33.

Benson, John E. "Two Types of Evangelicalism: The Inner Life as Mirror and as Lamp." *Dialog* 24 (Summer 1985): 193-96.

Berger, Peter L. "Secular Theology and the Rejection of the Supernatural: Reflections on Recent Trends." *Theological Studies* 38 (March 1977): 39-56.

Carr, Anne. "The God Who Is Involved." *Theology Today* 38 (October 1981): 314-28.

Clapp, Rodney. "Laboratories of the Soul: Testing God's New Creation in 2 Japanese Prison Camps." *Christianity Today* 30 (7 March 1986): 23-26.

Cook, Francis H. "Responses to Langdon Gilkey" (to Gilkey's "Christian Understanding of Suffering"). *Buddhist-Christian Studies* 5 (1985): 94-100.

Daly, Gabriel. "Catholicism and Modernity." *Journal of the American Academy of Religion* 53 (December 1985): 773-96.

Dean, William. "The Challenge of the New Historicism." *Journal of Religion* 66 (July 1986): 261-81.

Dillenberger, John. "Contemporary Theologians and the Visual Arts." *Journal of the American Academy of Religion* 53 (December 1985): 599-615.

Dulles, Avery. " 'Latent Heresy' and Orthodoxy." *Christian Century* 94 (16 November 1977): 1053-54.

Hosinski, Thomas E. "Experience and the Sacred: A Retrospective Review of Langdon Gilkey's Theology." *Religious Studies Review* 11 (July 1985): 228-35.

Inbody, Tyron. "Myth in Contemporary Theology: The Irreconcilable Issue." *Anglican Theological Review* 58 (April 1976): 139-57.

Jones, Justine, and Yeide, Harry, Jr. "Pluralism as a Perceptual Dimension: 'Now You See It, Now You Don't.' " *Religion and Intellectual Life* 1 (Fall 1983): 134-53.

Kane, Gordon Stanley. "God-Language and Secular Experience." *International Journal for Philosophy of Religion* 2 (Summer 1971): 78-95.

Long, Burke O. "Ambitions of Dissent: Biblical Theology in a Postmodern Future." *Journal of Religion* 76 (April 1996): 276-89.

Mason, David R. "Gilkey on 'God and the World': An Appraisal." *American Journal of Theology and Philosophy* 16 (September 1995): 315-34.

McClean, Mark D. "Toward a Pentecostal Hermeneutic." *Pneuma* 6 (Fall 1984): 35-56.

Mueller, David L. "Changing Conceptions of Christian Experience in Representative Contemporary Protestant Theologians." *Perspectives in Religious Studies* 1 (Fall 1974): 165-86.

Olsen, Arthur L. "Why the Church?" *Dialog* 12 (Summer 1973): 206-12.

Ommen, Thomas B. "Verification in Theology: A Tension in Revisionist Method." *The Thomist* 43 (July 1979): 357-84.

Otterstein, Paul. "Theological Pluralism in the Air Force Chaplaincy." *Military Chaplains' Review* 16 (Fall 1987): 89-121.

Pachence, Ronald A. "Sacramental Encounter among Religions." *Journal of Dharma* 6 (October–December 1981): 352-64.

Peters, Ted. "Langdon Gilkey: Theologian to the Modern Mind." *Dialog* 27 (Winter 1988): 55-62.

Peters, Ted. "Science and Religion: Toward a New Consonance." *Currents in Theology and Mission* 16 (December 1989): 417-24.

Peters, Ted. "The Whirlwind as Yet Unnamed." *Journal of the American Academy of Religion* 42 (December 1974): 699-709.

Price, Joseph L. "The Ultimate and the Ordinary: A Profile of Langdon Gilkey." *Christian Century* 106 (12 April 1989): 380-83.

Robbins, J. Wesley. "Religious Epistemology." *American Journal of Theology and Philosophy* 3 (September 1982): 80-89.

Schreurs, N. "Naar de basis van ons spreken over God: de weg van Langdon Gilkey." *Tijdschrift voor Theologie* 11 (1971): 274-92.

Seymour, Jack L. "The Future and the Past: History and Policy-Making in Religious Education." *Religious Education* 81 (Winter 1986): 113-33.

Smits, Kenneth. "Liturgical Reform in Cultural Perspective." *Worship* 50 (March 1976): 98-110.

Taylor, Mark Kline. "Religion, Cultural Plurality, and Liberating Praxis: In Conversation with the Work of Langdon Gilkey." *Journal of Religion* 71 (April 1991): 145-66.

Thomas, Owen C. "Theology and Experience." *Harvard Theological Review* 78 (January–April 1985): 179-201.

Thompson, William. "Theology's Method and Linguistic Analysis in the Thought of Langdon Gilkey." *The Thomist* 36 (July 1972): 363-94.

Thomsen, Mark. "The Lordship of Jesus and Secular Theology." *Religion in Life* 41 (Autumn 1972): 374-83.

Tracy, David. "Response to Gilkey." *University of Chicago Magazine* 76 (Fall 1983): 14.

Walsh, Brian J. "The Dimension of Ultimacy and Theology of Culture: A Critical Discussion of Langdon Gilkey." *Calvin Theological Journal* 24 (April 1989): 66-92.

Wiebe, Donald. "Is Science Really an Implicit Religion?" *Studies in Religion / Sciences Religieuses* 18 (1989): 171-83.

Reviews of Langdon Gilkey's Books

1. *Maker of Heaven and Earth*

Clark, Gordon H. Review of *Maker of Heaven and Earth*. In *Bulletin of the Evangelical Theological Society* 8 (1965): 121-23.

DeWolf, Harold L. "Creation, as Viewed by Science, Philosophy, and Theology." Review of *Maker of Heaven and Earth*. In *Religion in Life* 29 (Winter 1959–1960): 128-34.

Foreman, K. J. Review of *Maker of Heaven and Earth*. In *Interpretation* 14 (January 1960): 88-90.

Hamilton, William H. Review of *Maker of Heaven and Earth*. In *Foundations* 2 (October 1959): 370-73.

Klug, Eugene F. Review of *Maker of Heaven and Earth*. In *Springfielder* 30 (Spring 1966): 58-59.

Lazareth, W. H. Review of *Maker of Heaven and Earth*. In *Lutheran Quarterly* 11 (August 1959): 259-60.

Ogden, Schubert M. Review of *Maker of Heaven and Earth*. In *Perkins Journal* 13 (1960): 43.

Rust, Eric Charles. Review of *Maker of Heaven and Earth*. In *Review and Expositor* 57 (January 1960): 89-90.

Spalding, J. C. Review of *Maker of Heaven and Earth*. In *Union Seminary Quarterly Review* 16 (March 1961): 352-54.

2. *How the Church Can Minister to the World without Losing Itself*

Bennett, John C. "Guidance for Discerning the Remnant." Review of *How the Church Can Minister to the World without Losing Itself*. In *Christian Scholar* 48 (Summer 1965): 167-69.

Clark, Bayard Stockton. Review of *How the Church Can Minister to the World without Losing Itself*. In *Religion in Life* 34 (Spring 1965): 324.

Homrighausen, Elmer G. Review of *How the Church Can Minister to the World without Losing Itself*. In *Princeton Seminary Bulletin* 58 (October 1964): 70-71.

Stoughton, D. W. Review of *How the Church Can Minister to the World without Losing Itself*. In *Lutheran Quarterly* 17 (November 1965): 363.

Strong, R. Review of *How the Church Can Minister to the World without Losing Itself*. In *Westminster Theological Journal* 28 (May 1966): 225-26.

Van Dyck, David. Review of *How the Church Can Minister to the World without Losing Itself*. In *Japan Christian Quarterly* 31 (October 1965): 294-95.

West, Charles C. Review of *How the Church Can Minister to the World without Losing Itself*. In *Review of Religious Research* 7 (1966): 182-83.

3. Shantung Compound

Gordon, Ernest. Review of *Shantung Compound*. In *Christianity Today* 10 (16 September 1966): 39-40.

Latourette, Kenneth Scott. Review of *Shantung Compound*. In *Foundations* 10 (April–June 1967): 186-88.

Shinn, Roger L. Review of *Shantung Compound*. In *Religion in Life* 36 (Autumn 1967): 615-16.

Watkins, K. Review of *Shantung Compound*. In *Encounter* 28 (Spring 1967): 182.

Watts, Mac. Review of *Shantung Compound*. In *Touchstone* 9 (September 1991): 54-55.

4. Naming the Whirlwind

Barr, William R. "Meaning of 'God' in Secular Experience." Review of *Naming the Whirlwind*. In *Lexington Theological Quarterly* 5 (October 1970): 111-16.

Berkhof, Hendrikus. Review of *Naming the Whirlwind*. In *Nederlands Theologisch Tijdschrift* 24 (August 1970): 459-63.

Burrell, David. Review of *Naming the Whirlwind*. In *Theological Studies* 31 (September 1970): 560-61.

Caemmerer, Richard R., Sr. Review of *Naming the Whirlwind*. In *Concordia Theological Monthly* 41 (March 1970): 188.

Driver, Tom F. Review of *Naming the Whirlwind*. In *Union Seminary Quarterly Review* 25 (Spring 1970): 361-67.

Ferré, Frederick. "A Renewal of God-Language?" Review of *Naming the Whirlwind*. In *Journal of Religion* 52 (July 1972): 286-304.

Gibbs, John G. Review of *Naming the Whirlwind*. In *Journal of the American Academy of Religion* 39 (June 1971): 272-74.

Godsey, John D. Review of *Naming the Whirlwind*. In *Christian Century* 87 (10 June 1970): 729.

Heering, Herman J. Review of *Naming the Whirlwind*. In *Nederlands Theologisch Tijdschrift* 27 (April 1973): 195-96.

High, Dallas M. Review of *Naming the Whirlwind*. In *Journal for the Scientific Study of Religion* 9 (Winter 1970): 344-46.

Hunt, Boyd. Review of *Naming the Whirlwind*. In *Southwestern Journal of Theology* 12 (Spring 1970): 136-37.

Kerlin, Michael J. "Gilkey on God-Talk." Review of *Naming the Whirlwind*. In *Continuum* 7 (Autumn 1969): 504-506.

Noel, Daniel. "God-Language Grounded? A Review Article." Review of *Naming the Whirlwind*. In *Anglican Theological Review* 53 (January 1971): 57-70.

Peden, W. Creighton. "The Renewal of God-Language." Review of *Naming the Whirlwind*. In *Iliff Review* 28 (Spring 1971): 17-28.

Robbins, J. Wesley. "Professor Gilkey and Alternative Methods of Theological Construction." Review of *Naming the Whirlwind*. In *Journal of Religion* 52 (January 1972): 84-101.

Rust, Eric Charles. Review of *Naming the Whirlwind*. In *Review and Expositor* 68 (Spring 1971): 268-70.

Sheehan, Helena M. Review of *Naming the Whirlwind*. In *Journal of Ecumenical Studies* 7 (1970): 836-39.

van Buren, Paul M. Review of *Naming the Whirlwind*. In *Religion in Life* 39 (Summer 1970): 461-62.

_____. Review of *Naming the Whirlwind*. In *Theology Today* 27 (July 1970): 225-28.

Vick, Edward W. H. Review of *Naming the Whirlwind*. In *Andrews University Seminary Studies* 11 (July 1973): 199-200.

Vunderink, Ralph W. Review of *Naming the Whirlwind*. In *Westminster Theological Journal* 34 (May 1972): 201-205.

Williamson, Clark M. "The Divine Mortuary Was Premature: A Review Article." Review of *Naming the Whirlwind*. In *Encounter* 31 (Autumn 1970): 396-99.

Winquist, Charles E. Review of *Naming the Whirlwind*. In *Scottish Journal of Theology* 24 (November 1971): 489-90.

5. *Religion and the Scientific Future*

Cauthen, Kenneth. Review of *Religion and the Scientific Future*. In *Interpretation* 25 (October 1971): 520-21.

Chapman, W. E. Review of *Religion and the Scientific Future*. In *Review of Religious Research* 12 (Spring 1971): 195.

Dillistone, F. W. Review of *Religion and the Scientific Future*. In *Modern Churchman* 15 (1972): 263-64.

Engler, Barbara. Review of *Religion and the Scientific Future*. In *Drew Gateway* 41 (Winter 1971): 128-29.

Heering, Herman J. Review of *Religion and the Scientific Future.* In *Nederlands Theologisch Tijdschrift* 27 (April 1973): 195-96.

Lansing, J. W. Review of *Religion and the Scientific Future.* In *Theology Today* 27 (January 1971): 490-91.

Nelson, J. W. Review of *Religion and the Scientific Future.* In *Perspective* 12 (1971): 277-79.

Perry, Michael. Review of *Religion and the Scientific Future.* In *Church Quarterly* 3 (April 1971): 345-46.

Porteous, Alvin C. Review of *Religion and the Scientific Future.* In *Religion in Life* 39 (Winter 1970): 609-10.

Ramm, Bernard. Review of *Religion and the Scientific Future.* In *Christian Scholar's Review* 1 (1971): 241-42.

Schwarz, Hans. Review of *Religion and the Scientific Future.* In *Lutheran Quarterly* 23 (Fall 1971): 95-97.

Vick, Edward W. H. Review of *Religion and the Scientific Future.* In *Andrews University Seminary Studies* 12 (January 1974): 68-69.

Wing, Edward. Review of *Religion and the Scientific Future.* In *Christian Century* 97 (19 August 1970): 998.

Wright, J. H. Review of *Religion and the Scientific Future.* In *Theological Studies* 31 (December 1970): 745-47.

6. *Catholicism Confronts Modernity*

Atwood, Bertram. Review of *Catholicism Confronts Modernity.* In *Princeton Seminary Bulletin* 68 (Winter 1976): 121.

Carey, J. Review of *Catholicism Confronts Modernity.* In *Journal of Ecumenical Studies* 14 (Winter 1977): 121-22.

Coleman, John A. Review of *Catholicism Confronts Modernity.* In *Sociological Analysis* 38 (Summer 1977): 169-71.

Dulles, Avery. Review of *Catholicism Confronts Modernity.* In *Review of Books and Religion* 4 (1975): 1ff.

Fackre, Gabriel. Review of *Catholicism Confronts Modernity.* In *Christian Century* 92 (10 December 1975): 1138-39.

Hughes, John J. *Currents in Theology and Mission* 3 (April 1976): 122-23.

Klug, E. F. Review of *Catholicism Confronts Modernity.* In *Springfielder* 39 (March 1976): 244-46.

Mason, David R. Review of *Catholicism Confronts Modernity.* In *Anglican Theological Review* 60 (January 1978): 121-23.

O'Donnell, John. *Journal of Theological Studies* 36 (September 1975): 566.

Wangler, Thomas E. Review of *Catholicism Confronts Modernity.* In *Horizons* 3 (Spring 1976): 134-35.

7. *Reaping the Whirlwind*

Carmody, John. Review of *Reaping the Whirlwind*. In *Theological Studies* 39 (June 1978): 345-47.

Cooke, Bernard J. Review of *Reaping the Whirlwind*. In *Studies in Religion / Sciences Religieuses* 8 (1979): 104-105.

Farley, Edward. Review of *Reaping the Whirlwind*. In *Religious Studies Review* 4 (October 1978): 233-37.

Fiorenza, Francis S. Review of *Reaping the Whirlwind*. In *Religious Studies Review* 4 (October 1978): 237-40.

Franklin, Stephen. Review of *Reaping the Whirlwind*. In *Japan Christian Quarterly* 46 (Spring 1980): 117-19.

Heering, Herman J. Review of *Reaping the Whirlwind*. In *Nederlands Theologisch Tijdschrift* 33 (October 1979): 319-20.

Kaufman, Gordon D. "The Christian and History: Structure or Process?" Review of *Reaping the Whirlwind*. In *Interpretation* 32 (April 1978): 194-96.

McCann, Dennis P. "Dubious Enterprise." Review of *Reaping the Whirlwind*. In *Christian Century* 94 (2 November 1977): 1008.

McWilliams, Warren. Review of *Reaping the Whirlwind*. In *Review and Expositor* 74 (Fall 1977): 585-87.

O'Brien, W. J. Review of *Reaping the Whirlwind*. In *Horizons* 5 (Spring 1978): 114.

Shea, John. "Gilkey's New Whirlwind—Two Views." Review of *Reaping the Whirlwind*. In *New Review of Books and Religion* 1 (April 1977): 5.

Shelley, J. C. Review of *Reaping the Whirlwind*. In *Princeton Seminary Bulletin, New Series, 2* (1979): 173-75.

Shelley, J. Review of *Reaping the Whirlwind*. In *Princeton Seminary Bulletin* 2 (1978): 53-55.

Stinson, L. "Gilkey's Reaping the Whirlwind: A Review Article." Review of *Reaping the Whirlwind*. In *The Thomist* 42 (1978).

TeSelle, Eugene. "Being in History." Review of *Reaping the Whirlwind*. In *Journal of Religion* 58 (July 1978): 303-308.

van Buren, Paul M. Review of *Reaping the Whirlwind*. In *New Review of Books and Religion* 1 (April 1977): 4-5.

8. *Message and Existence*

Christiansen, Drew. Review of *Message and Existence*. In *Theological Studies* 41 (September 1980): 590-91.

Cobb, John B., Jr. Review of *Message and Existence*. In *Saint Luke's Journal of Theology* 24 (June 1981): 237-39.

Cole, Charles E. Review of *Message and Existence*. In *Quarterly Review* 6 (Winter 1986): 3-12.

Comstock, W. R. Review of *Message and Existence*. In *Journal of the American Academy of Religion* 49 (March 1981): 153-54.

Heering, Herman J. Review of *Message and Existence*. In *Nederlands Theologisch Tijdschrift* 35 (April 1981): 166-67.

MacCormac, E. R. Review of *Message and Existence*. In *Interpretation* 35 (April 1981): 212-14.

McBrien, R. P. Review of *Message and Existence*. In *Horizons* 7 (Fall 1980): 348-49.

Mesle, Robert. Review of *Message and Existence*. In *Process Studies* 11 (Fall 1981): 203-207.

Pinnock, Clark H. Review of *Message and Existence*. In *Christian Scholar's Review* 11 (1982): 159-60.

_____. Review of *Message and Existence*. In *Theological Students Fellowship Bulletin* 5 (January–February 1982): 20-21.

Reist, Benjamin A. Review of *Message and Existence*. In *Theology Today* 38 (April 1981): 100-102.

Schineller, Peter. Review of *Message and Existence*. In *Christian Century* 97 (3 December 1980): 1199-1200.

Sponheim, Paul. Review of *Message and Existence*. In *Word and World* 1 (Spring 1981): 198-200.

Stevenson, W. Taylor. Review of *Message and Existence*. In *Anglican Theological Review* 63 (January 1981): 98-99.

Taylor, Mark Kline. Review of *Message and Existence*. In *Princeton Seminary Bulletin*, n. s., 5 (1984): 72-74.

9. Society and the Sacred

Christiansen, Drew. Review of *Society and the Sacred*. In *Theological Studies* 43 (September 1982): 550-52.

Elshtain, Jean Bethke. Review of *Society and the Sacred*. In *Theology Today* 39 (January 1983): 428-34.

Nishi, Shunji F. Review of *Society and the Sacred*. In *Anglican Theological Review* 64 (October 1982): 602-603.

Outler, Albert C. Review of *Society and the Sacred*. In *Christian Century* 99 (21 April 1982): 489-90.

Rigali, N. J. Review of *Society and the Sacred*. In *Horizons* 10 (Spring 1983): 185-86.

Rowold, Henry. Review of *Society and the Sacred*. In *Currents in Theology and Mission* 10 (February 1983): 55.

Spalding, P. Review of *Society and the Sacred*. In *Journal of the American Academy of Religion* 51 (March 1983): 143-44.

Winter, Gibson. "The Meaninglessness of History." Review of *Society and the Sacred*. In *Journal of Religion* 64 (January 1984): 96-100.

10. *Creationism on Trial*

Bube, Richard H. Review of *Creationism on Trial*. In *Perspectives on Science and Christian Faith* 39 (March 1987): 50-51.

_____. Review of *Creationism on Trial*. In *Theological Students Fellowship Bulletin* 10 (January–February 1987): 37-38.

Garrett, Graeme. Review of *Creationism on Trial*. In *St. Mark's Review* no. 138 (Winter 1989): 33.

Geisler, Norman L. Review of *Creationism on Trial*. In *Bibliotheca Sacra* 144 (April–June 1987): 226-27.

Guinan, Michael D. Review of *Creationism on Trial*. In *Zygon* 23 (December 1988): 481-82.

Hefner, Philip. "The Significance of Creationism." Review of *Creationism on Trial*. In *Journal of Religion* 68 (January 1988): 72-77.

John, Erwin E. Review of *Creationism on Trial*. In *Book Newsletter of the Augsburg Publishing House* no. 521 (May–June 1986): 9.

Mazuk, Melody. Review of *Creationism on Trial*. In *Review and Expositor* 83 (Fall 1986): 640-42.

Musser, Donald W. Review of *Creationism on Trial*. In *Christian Century* 103 (16 April 1986): 395-96.

Noll, Mark A. Review of *Creationism on Trial*. In *Word and World* 6 (Fall 1986): 467-68.

Pierard, Richard V. Review of *Creationism on Trial*. In *Sociological Analysis* 50 (Spring 1989): 105-106.

Pinnock, Clark H. Review of *Creationism on Trial*. In *Theodolite* 7 (1986): 55-56.

Points, G. Phillip. Review of *Creationism on Trial*. In *Encounter* 48 (Spring 1987): 231-32.

Seeger, Raymond J. "What Is Science?" Review of *Creationism on Trial*. In *Perspectives on Science and Christian Faith* 40 (March 1988): 45-46.

Stenseth, Nils Chr; Tjønneland, Audfinn; and Lindholm, Tore. "Can Rationality and Irrationality Be Reconciled?" Review of *Creationism on Trial*. In *Biology and Philosophy* [see "Reply from the Author" (to a review of *Creationism on Trial*). *Biology and Philosophy* 3 (1988): 485-95.]

Wood, Charles M. Review of *Creationism on Trial*. In *Perkins Journal* 39 (October 1986): 4.

11. *Gilkey on Tillich*

Christopherson, John. Review of *Gilkey on Tillich*. In *Dialog* 30 (Winter 1991): 73-74.

Clifford, Anne M. Review of *Gilkey on Tillich*. In *Horizons* 19 (Spring 1992): 163-64.

Leupp, Roderick T. Review of *Gilkey on Tillich*. In *Journal of the Evangelical Theological Society* 36 (December 1993): 541-42.

Modras, Ronald. Review of *Gilkey on Tillich*. In *Theological Studies* 52 (June 1991): 370-71.

Otto, Randall E. Review of *Gilkey on Tillich*. In *Westminster Theological Journal* 54 (Fall 1992): 400-403.

Pasewark, Kyle A. Review of *Gilkey on Tillich*. In *Lutheran Quarterly*, n.s., 5 (Winter 1991): 545-46.

Scharlemann, Robert P. Review of *Gilkey on Tillich*. In *Journal of Religion* 72 (July 1992): 452-53.

Snook, Lee E. Review of *Gilkey on Tillich*. In *Word and World* 11 (Winter 1991): 92.

12. *Through the Tempest*

Burkhart, John E. Review of *Through the Tempest*. In *Journal of Religion* 74 (January 1994): 114-15.

Gounelle, André. Review of *Through the Tempest*. In *Etudes Théologiques et Religieuses* 68 (1993): 123-24.

Maddox, Randy L. Review of *Through the Tempest*. In *Critical Review of Books in Religion* 6 (1993): 508-509.

Roy, Louis. Review of *Through the Tempest*. In *The Thomist* 57 (October 1993): 717-20.

Stone, Jerome A. Review of *Through the Tempest*. In *American Journal of Theology and Philosophy* 14 (January 1993): 97-100.

Wilson, David Dunn. Review of *Through the Tempest*. In *Expository Times* 104 (December 1992): 95.

13. *Nature, Reality, and the Sacred*

Barad, Judy. Review of *Nature, Reality, and the Sacred*. In *Dialogue and Alliance* 9 (Spring–Summer 1995): 164-66.

Barnes, Michael H. Review of *Nature, Reality, and the Sacred*. In *Theological Studies* 55 (September 1994): 567-69.

Casey, Diane Dates. Review of *Nature, Reality, and the Sacred*. In *Trinity Seminary Review* 17 (Fall 1995): 82-83.

Hanna, Martin Frederick. Review of *Nature, Reality, and the Sacred*. In *Andrews University Seminary Studies* 33 (Autumn 1995): 300-302.

Lemke, Steve W. Review of *Nature, Reality, and the Sacred*. In *Southwestern Journal of Theology* 39 (Fall 1996): 75.

Murphy, George L. Review of *Nature, Reality, and the Sacred*. In *Dialog* 34 (Winter 1995): 71-72.

Piersma, Bernard J. Review of *Nature, Reality, and the Sacred*. In *Perspectives on Science and Christian Faith* 47 (June 1995): 138-39.

Podlich, Aub. Review of *Nature, Reality, and the Sacred*. In *Beacon Hill Books Reviewer* 1 (1995): 35-36.

Polkinghorne, John C. Review of *Nature, Reality, and the Sacred*. In *Theology* 97 (September–October 1994): 392-93.

Rottschaefer, William A. Review of *Nature, Reality, and the Sacred*. In *CTNS Bulletin* 15 (Fall 1995): 7-14.

Raymo, Chet. Review of *Nature, Reality, and the Sacred*. In *Commonweal* 121 (20 May 1994): 31-32.

Sturch, Richard. Review of *Nature, Reality, and the Sacred*. In *Themelios* 21 (October 1995): 25-26.

Reviews of Books on Langdon Gilkey's Thought

Roy, Louis. Review of *Langdon Gilkey: Theologian for a Culture in Decline*, by Brian Walsh. In *The Thomist* 57 (October 1993): 717-20.

Schwarz, Hans. Review of *Langdon Gilkey: Theologian for a Culture in Decline*, by Brian Walsh. In *CTNS Bulletin* 13 (Summer 1993): 31-32.

Spykman, Gordon J. Review of *Langdon Gilkey: Theologian for a Culture in Decline*, by Brian Walsh. In *Calvin Theological Journal* 28 (November 1993): 486-88.

Ucko, Hans. Review of *The Whirlwind in Culture*, ed. Donald W. Musser and Joseph L. Price. In *International Review of Theology and Mission* 79 (July 1990): 390-93.

Welch, Sharon. Review of *The Whirlwind in Culture*, ed. Donald W. Musser and Joseph L. Price. In *Journal of Religion* 70 (October 1990): 644-45.

Dissertations and Theses on Gilkey's Thought

1. Masters Theses

Abernathy, Anne B. "Langdon Gilkey's Understanding of God." M.A.Th. thesis, Aquinas Institute of Theology, 1980.

Bishop, Paul Estler. "Langdon Gilkey's Prolegomenon to Theology." M.A. thesis, American University, 1981.

Davis, George E. "Langdon Gilkey and Religious Language." M.C.S. thesis, Regent College (Canada), 1979.

Driscoll, Jeremy. "Prolegomenon in the Theological Method of Langdon Gilkey." M.A. thesis, Mount Angel Seminary, 1980.

Haddorff, David W. "Langdon Gilkey's Method of Correlation: Modern Historical Experience and a Theological Interpretation of History." M.A. thesis, Wheaton College, 1984.

Hinze, Bradford E. "The Notion of Symbol and Its Usage in the Writings of Langdon Gilkey from 1959 to 1977." M.A.Th. thesis, Catholic University of America, 1978.

Kapac, Jayne Laverne. "A Study of Sin as Self-Abnegation in Contemporary Theology with Special Reference to Liberation Theology, Langdon Gilkey, Karl Rahner, and John Cobb, Jr." M.A. thesis, University of Manitoba, 1984.

Marai, J. S. "The Problem of God-Language in the Theology of John Macquarrie and Langdon Gilkey." M.A. thesis, University of St. Michael's College (Toronto), 1975.

2. Doctoral Dissertations

Beaugh, Michael Bruce. "The Development of the Concept of Meaningful Existence in the Chicago Divinity School as Represented by Shailer Mathews, Henry Nelson Wieman, and Langdon Gilkey." Th.D. diss., Southwestern Baptist Theological Seminary, 1975.

Bessler-Northcutt, Joseph. "Shantung Trilogy: The Rhetorical Shaping of Langdon Gilkey's Theology of Culture and History." Ph.D. diss., University of Chicago, 1996.

Bihl, Hugh W. "Langdon Gilkey's Theology of Providence: An Interpretation for a Secular Culture." Ph.D. diss., Fordham University, 1987.

Clifford, Anne Marie. "The Relation of Science and Religion/Theology in the Thought of Langdon Gilkey." Ph.D. diss., Catholic University of America, 1988.

John, Emily Rebecca. "An Anthropology Revitalized: A Study of Langdon Gilkey." Ph.D. diss., University of St. Michael's College, 1991.

Littlejohn, Ronnie Lynn. "An Analysis of Langdon Gilkey's Phenomenology of Ultimacy and Its Implications for Theology and Ethics." Ph.D. diss., Baylor University, 1978.

McElwee, W. R. "An Analysis of the Relationship between Teleministry and the Church in the Light of Langdon Gilkey's Dialectic between Transcendence and Relevance." D.Min. diss., Princeton Theological Seminary, 1975.

Penick, Harold W. "The Interface of Creation and Providence in the Theology of Langdon Gilkey." Ph.D. diss., Southern Baptist Theological Seminary, 1993.

Sanders, Stephen A. "The Contribution of Phenomenology to Theology as Reflected in the Writings of Langdon Gilkey and Edward Farley." Th.D. diss., New Orleans Baptist Theological Seminary, 1986.

Shea, John. "Religious Language in a Secular Culture: A Study in the Theology of Langdon Gilkey." S.T.D. diss., University of St. Mary of the Lake, 1976.

Stiver, Danny Roy. "Converging Approaches to a Natural Awareness of God in Contemporary Natural Theology." Ph.D. diss., Southern Baptist Theological Seminary, 1983.

Tupper, Kerry M. "Courageous Consent: An Interpretation of Natural Evil Based on the Thought of Langdon Gilkey and James M. Gustafson." Ph.D. diss., University of Chicago, 1997.

Walsh, Brian J. "Theology and Modernity: A Study in the Thought of Langdon Gilkey." Ph.D. diss., McGill University, 1987.

News Articles about Langdon Gilkey

"Pathfinding Protestants." *Time*, 25 May 1962, 84, 86.

"Chicago at 100." *Time*, 25 March 1966, 74, 76.

"Toward a Hidden God." *Time*, 8 April 1966, 82-87.

"Langdon B. Gilkey." *Criterion* 2 (Winter 1963): insert.

Publications by Charles Whitney Gilkey, Father of Langdon Gilkey

Books

Jesus and Our Generation. The Barrows Lectures Series 1924–1925. Chicago: University of Chicago Press, 1925.

Perspectives. New York: Harper and Brothers Publishers, 1933.

Articles and Contributions to Books

"The Distinctive Baptist Witness." *The Chronicle* 8 (July 1945): 97-106.

"The Place of Religion in Higher Education." In *Religion and the Modern World: University of Pennsylvania Bicentennial Conference*, 73-87. Port Washington NY: Kennikat Press, Inc., 1941.

"Present Day Dilemmas in Religion." *Methodist Quarterly Review* 77 (April 1928): 297-98.

"Present Day Dilemmas in Religion." *Methodist Review* 111 (July 1928): 627-28.

"Religion in Our College Generations." *Christianity and Crisis* 9 (1949): 147-50.

"Well-Proved Ministry." *Pastoral Psychology* 8 (February 1957): 9-12.

Contributors

Joseph Bessler-Northcutt—Ph.D., University of Chicago Divinity School. Assistant professor of Theology and Rhetoric, Phillips Theological Seminary; Tulsa, Oklahoma.

Larry D. Bouchard—Ph.D., University of Chicago Divinity School. Associate professor of Religious Studies, Department of Religious Studies, University of Virginia; Charlottesville, Virginia. His publications include: *Tragic Method and Tragic Theology: Evil in Contemporary Drama and Religious Thought* (University Park: Pennsylvania State University Press, 1989); coeditor with L. Dale Richesin, *Interpreting Disciples: Practical Theology and the Christian Church (Disciples of Christ)* (Fort Worth TX: Texas Christian University Press, 1987).

Eric H. Crump—Ph.D., University of Chicago Divinity School. Associate professor of Systematic Theology, Lutheran Theological Seminary at Gettysburg; Gettysburg, Pennsylvania. "Between Critique and Conviction: Reflexive Philosophy, Testimony, and Pneumatology in the Thought of Paul Ricoeur," in *Ricoeur as Another: The Ethics of Subjectivity*, ed. James Marsh and Richard A. Cohen (forthcoming, Albany, New York: SUNY Press, 1999).

Gary J. Dorrien—Ph.D., Union Graduate School. Associate professor of Religion, chair of Humanities, and dean of Stetson Chapel, Kalamazoo College; Kalamazoo, Michigan. His publications include: *Soul in Society: The Making and Renewal of Social Christianity* (Minneapolis: Fortress Press, 1995); *The Neoconservative Mind: Politics, Culture, and the War of Ideology* (Philadelphia: Temple University Press, 1993); *The Word as True Myth: Interpreting Modern Theology* (Louisville, Kentucky: Westminster John Knox, 1997).

Langdon B. Gilkey—Ph.D., Columbia University. Emeritus professor of Theology, University of Chicago Divinity School. Charlottesville, Virginia.

Donald W. Musser—Ph.D., University of Chicago Divinity School. Sam R. Marks Professor of Religion, Department of Religion, Stetson University; Deland, Florida. His publications include: coeditor with Joseph L. Price, *The Whirlwind in Culture: Frontiers in Theology—In Honor of Langdon Gilkey* (Bloomington IN: Meyer-Stone Books, 1988); coeditor with Joseph L. Price, *A New Handbook of Christian Theology* (Nashville: Abingdon Press, 1992); coeditor with Joseph L. Price, *A New Handbook of Christian Theologians* (Nashville: Abingdon Press, 1996).

Kyle A. Pasewark—Ph.D., University of Chicago Divinity School. Currently pursuing studies at Yale Law School. His publications include: *A Theology of Power: Being beyond Domination* (Minneapolis: Fortress Press, 1993); coauthor with Garrett Paul, *The Emphatic Christian Center: Reforming American Political Practice* (Nashville: Abingdon Press, 1999); "The Body in Ecstasy: Love, Difference, and the Social Organism in Luther's Theory of the Lord's Supper," *Journal of Religion* 77 (October 1997): 511-40.

Jeff B. Pool—Ph.D. University of Chicago Divinity School. Director of Baptist Studies and lecturer in Theology, Brite Divinity School; Fort Worth, Texas. His publications include: editor, *Through the Tempest: Theological Voyages in a Pluralistic Culture*, by Langdon Gilkey (Minneapolis: Fortress Press, 1991); editor, *Sacred Mandates of Conscience: Interpretations of the Baptist Faith and Message* (Macon, Georgia: Smyth and Helwys Publishing, 1997); *Against Returning to Egypt: Exposing and Resisting Credalism in the Southern Baptist Convention* (Macon, Georgia: Mercer University Press, 1998).

Joseph L. Price—Ph.D., University of Chicago Divinity School. Professor of Theology, Department of Religious Studies, Whittier College; Whittier, California. His publications include: coeditor with Donald W. Musser, *The Whirlwind in Culture: Frontiers in Theology—In Honor of Langdon Gilkey* (Bloomington IN: Meyer-Stone Books, 1988); coeditor with Donald W. Musser, *A New Handbook of Christian Theology* (Nashville: Abingdon Press, 1992); coeditor with Donald W. Musser, *A New Handbook of Christian Theologians* (Nashville: Abingdon Press, 1996); "The Ultimate and the Ordinary: A Profile of Langdon Gilkey," *Christian Century* 106 (12 April 1989): 380-83.

H. Frederick Reisz, Jr.—Ph.D., University of Chicago Divinity School. President, Lutheran Theological Southern Seminary; Columbia, South Carolina. His publications include: "Cry Out Against the Deepening Night of Violence for the People of El Salvador," in *Peacework: 20 Years of Non-violent Social Change*, ed. Pat Farren (Cambridge: American Friends Service Committee, 1991); "The Demonic as a Principle in Tillich's Doctrine of God," in *Theonomy and Autonomy*, ed. John J. Carey (Macon, Georgia: Mercer University Press, 1984); "Liberation Theology of Culture: A Tillichian Perspective," in *Kairos and Logos*, ed. John J. Carey (Cambridge: North American Paul Tillich Society, 1978; new edition: Macon GA: Mercer University Press, 1984).

Jennifer L. Rike—Ph.D., University of Chicago Divinity School. Associate professor of Theology, University of Detroit, Mercy; Detroit, Michigan. Her publications include: coeditor with Werner Jeanrond, *Radical Pluralism and Truth: David Tracy and the Hermeneutics of Religion* (New York: Crossroad Publishing Company, 1991); "Faith under Trial: Ethical and Christian Duty in the Thought of Søren Kierkegaard," *Tijdschrift voor Filosofie* 44 (June 1982): 266-97.

Mary Ann Stenger—Ph.D., University of Iowa. Associate professor of Religious Studies, Department of Religious Studies, University of Louisville; Louisville, Kentucky. Her publications include: "A Critical Analysis of the Influence of Paul Tillich on Mary Daly's Feminist Theology," *Encounter* 43 (Summer 1982): 219-38; "Paul Tillich's Theory of Theological Norms and the Problems of Relativism and Subjectivism," *Journal of Religion* 62 (October 1982): 359-75; "The Significance of Paradox for Theological Verification: Difficulties and Possibilities," *International Journal for Philosophy of Religion* 14 (1983): 171-82.

Brian J. Walsh—Ph.D., McGill University. University chaplain, University of Toronto. His publications include: *Langdon Gilkey: Theologian for a Culture in Decline*, Christian Studies Today Series (Lanham, Maryland: University Press of America, 1991); coauthor with J. Richard Middleton, *The Transforming Vision: Shaping a Christian Worldview* (Downers Grove, Illinois: InterVarsity Press, 1984; "Langdon B. Gilkey," in *Dictionary of Christianity in America*, ed. D. G. Reid, R. D. Linder, B. L. Shelly, and H. S. Stout (Downer's Grove, Illinois: InterVarsity Press, 1990), 481-82.

Charles E. Winquist—Ph.D., University of Chicago Divinity School. Thomas J. Watson Professor of Religion, Department of Religion, Syracuse University; Syracuse, New York. His publications include: *Epiphanies of Darkness: Deconstruction in Theology* (Minneapolis: Fortress Press, 1986); *Desiring Theology* (Chicago: University of Chicago Press, 1995).

James O. Yerkes—Ph.D., University of Chicago Divinity School. Professor of Religion and Philosophy, Moravian College; Bethlehem, Pennsylvania. His publications include: *The Christology of Hegel*, SUNY Series in Hegelian Studies, ed. Quentin J. Lauer (Albany NY: State University of New York Press, 1982); " 'Glauben und Genuss': Hegel, Luther and the Holy Spirit," *Christian Scholar's Review* 12 (1983): 237-43.

The Theology of Langdon B. Gilkey. Systematic and Critical Studies.
edited by Kyle A. Pasewark and Jeff B. Pool.

Mercer University Press, Macon, Georgia 31210-3960.
Isbn 0-86554-643-6 H479 (casebound).
Isbn 0-86554-644-4 P191 (perfectbound).
Text and interior designs and composition by Edmon L. Rowell, Jr.
Cover and dust jacket designs by Jacqueline C. Rowell.
Jacket illustration: *Then the Lord Answered Job out of the Whirlwind*
   (ca. 1823) by William Blake.
Camera-ready pages (xvi+560) composed on a Gateway2000 386/33C
   and on an AOpen BG45-AP5VM via dos WordPerfect 5.1 and WordPerfect
     for Windows 5.1/5.2, and printed on a LaserMaster 1000.
Text fonts: TimesNewRomanPS (via Adobe Type Manager) 11/13.
Display fonts (headings): TimesNewRomanPS bf + Helvetica (via ATM).
Printed and bound by BookCrafters, Chelsea, Michigan 48118-0370,
   via offset lithography on 55# Booktext Natural Hi Bulk (360ppi).
Casebound: Smyth sewn and cased into Roxite B 51568 (brown) cloth with
   one-hit gold foil, with 80# matching endsheets, and with dust jackets
     printed black plus 1 PMS color (brown) on 80# Sterling Gloss Enamel.
Perfectbound: Trimmed and notchbound into 10-pt. c1s covers printed black
   plus 1 PMS color (brown).
Paper covers and dust jackets include layflat matte film lamination.
                 [November 1999 / 300 + 1M]

092499elr